Michael Nitsche

POLYGRAPH
WÖRTERBUCH
FÜR DIE
DRUCKINDUSTRIE
UND
KOMMUNIKATIONSTECHNIK

Deutsch–Englisch
Englisch–Deutsch

Michael Nitsche

POLYGRAPH
DICTIONARY
OF THE
GRAPHIC ARTS
AND
COMMUNICATIONS TECHNOLOGY

German–English
English–German

MICHAEL NITSCHE

POLYGRAPH WÖRTERBUCH FÜR DIE DRUCKINDUSTRIE UND KOMMUNIKATIONSTECHNIK

Deutsch–Englisch   Englisch–Deutsch

POLYGRAPH DICTIONARY OF THE GRAPHIC ARTS AND COMMUNICATIONS TECHNOLOGY

German–English   English–German

POLYGRAPH VERLAG · FRANKFURT AM MAIN

Printed in Germany
© by Polygraph Verlag GmbH, Frankfurt am Main

5. Auflage 1989
völlig überarbeitet und aktualisiert
von Wirt.-Ing. Michael Nitsche
auf der Grundlage der 1976 und davor erschienenen,
von Leonhard Trondt (†) bearbeiteten Ausgaben.

7. Auflage 1997

Nachdruck – auch auszugsweise – verboten

ISBN 3-87641-158-0

Besonderer Dank gilt den Mitarbeitern
Rolf Agte für zahlreiche terminologische
Anregungen und Ergänzungen sowie
Paul Callaghan für die gesamtheitliche
Prüfung des englischen Teils. Gedankt sei
auch anderen hier nicht namentlich
erwähnten Personen und Firmen für ihre
Unterstützung jedweder Art.

Printed in Germany
© by Polygraph Verlag GmbH, Frankfurt an Main

5th edition 1989
Based on the editions compiled
by Leonhard Trondt (†),
published in 1976 and before.
This edition completely revised and updated
by Wirt.-Ing. Michael Nitsche.

7th edition 1997

Reproduction – also of extracts – is prohibited

ISBN 3-87641-158-0

Special thanks to Rolf Agte for his many
terminological suggestions and
contributions as well as to Paul Callaghan
who verified the English-language entries.
Many thanks also to all contributing
persons and companies for their support
and assistance.

Inhalt

Vorwort zur 5. Auflage   VI
Übersicht über die berücksichtigten Fachbereiche   VIII
Benutzerhinweise für den deutsch-englischen
und englisch-deutschen Teil   X
Wörterbuch Deutsch-Englisch   1
Wörterbuch Englisch-Deutsch   161

Contents

Preface to the 5th edition   VII
An overview of the fields covered   IX
How to use the German-English
and the English-German section   XI
German-English dictionary   1
English-German dictionary   161

Vorwort zur 5. Auflage

Das Polygraph Wörterbuch für die Druckindustrie erscheint zwei Jahre nach dem Druck der 4., völlig überarbeiteten Auflage neu. In der Zwischenzeit konnte der Wortschatz der neueren Kommunikationstechniken so weit ergänzt und ausgebaut werden, daß es nunmehr berechtigt erscheint, den Titel des Werkes durch den Begriff ». . . und Kommunikationstechnik« zu ergänzen und so auf das erweiterte Fachwortangebot aufmerksam zu machen.

Generell zwingt die Formulierung von Buchtiteln immer zu äußerster Knappheit, weshalb an dieser Stelle präzisiert werden sollte, daß das vorliegende Werk die Terminologie der Kommunikationstechnik nicht global umfaßt, sondern nur den für die Druckindustrie beziehungsweise die grafische Kommunikation relevanten Teil.

Die 5. Auflage des Wörterbuchs umfaßt nun zirka 13 000 Stichwörter. Diesen sind 18 000 Übersetzungen zugeordnet. Die Gegenüberstellung dieser beiden Zahlen mag verdeutlichen, daß sehr viel Mühe darauf verwendet wurde, für das jeweilige Stichwort Alternativen je nach Sinnzusammenhang zu geben. Um dem (oft fachfremden) Übersetzer die Arbeit zu erleichtern, sind den meisten Stichwörtern in Klammern Geltungsbereiche hinzugefügt worden.

Die völlige Überarbeitung des Wörterbuchs für die 4. Auflage, die thematische Erweiterung mit der 5. Auflage und die stete Aktualisierung des Wortbestandes erfolgten und erfolgen weiterhin auf der Grundlage täglicher Redaktionsarbeit für die Fachzeitschriften »Der Polygraph« und »EPI Export Polygraph International«.

Autor und Verlag möchten alle »kritischen« Benutzer des vorliegenden Nachschlagewerkes dazu ermuntern, Hinweise auf Ergänzungen oder sprachliche Präzisierung zu geben, wo immer dies notwendig erscheint.

Michael Nitsche

Preface to the 5th edition

This latest edition of the Polygraph Dictionary of the Graphic Arts is published two years after the 4th and fully revised edition. In the interim, the vocabulary pertaining to the latest fields of communications technology has been supplemented and expanded to such a degree that we consider it appropriate to incorporate the term «. . . and Communications Technology» into the title in order to draw attention to the enhanced content of technical terms.

As a general rule, book titles must be formulated as concisely as possible. For this reason, we wish to point out that this work does not attempt to cover the terminology of communications technology in the universal sense, but only those fields that are of relevance to the printing industry, or «graphic communications technology« respectively.

The 5th edition of the dictionary now contains some 13,000 key words. These are matched by 18,000 translations, an indication that great efforts have been made to provide alternative translations to suit the context in which the individual key word appears. In order to facilitate the work of the translator (who in many cases may not be familiar with the industry), most key words are accompanied by an indication in parenthesis of the context concerned.

The complete revision of the dictionary for the 4th edition, the inclusion of additional fields for the 5th edition and the continuous updating of the vocabulary was and continues to be carried out on the basis of the daily editorial work for the trade magazines «Der Polygraph» and «EPI Export Polygraph International».

The author and the publisher wish to take this opportunity to encourage all «critical» users of this work of reference to communicate any suggestions or proposals for additional inclusions or linguistical refinements that they may consider appropriate.

Michael Nitsche

**Das Polygraph Wörterbuch
umfaßt die folgenden Fachbereiche:**

I in der Reihenfolge des grafischen Fertigungsablaufs:

Druckvorlagenherstellung, einschließlich CAD

Satzherstellung/Textverarbeitung (Texterfassung, -verarbeitung und -belichtung)

Reproduktionstechnik (Bilderfassung, -verarbeitung und -belichtung)

Typografie, Gestaltung, Design

Text-Bild-Integration

Druckformherstellung, einschließlich Montage und Kopie

Andruck, Proofing

Druckverfahren (Offset, Buchdruck, Flexodruck, Tiefdruck, Siebdruck und andere) und Druckmaschinentechnik, einschließlich Inline-Finishing

Buchbinderei und Druckverarbeitung, einschließlich Druckveredlung, Buch- und Faltschachtelherstellung

II nach Auftragsarten und Produktbereichen:

Akzidenz

Buch

Zeitung/Zeitschrift

Endlos/Formular

Verpackung

Inplant

III übergreifend und relevant:

Druck- und Verlagswesen

Medien und Kommunikation

Materialien (Druckfarbe, Bedruckstoff, Chemie)

Elektronische Datenverarbeitung, einschließlich Computer- und Bildschirmtechnik

Nachrichtentechnik, einschließlich Telekommunikation

Betriebstechnik, einschließlich Ver- und Entsorgung, Transport und Versand

The Polygraph Dictionary covers the following subject areas:

I In the sequence of the production process:

Printing copy production, including CAD

Typesetting/text processing (text recording, processing and exposure)

Reproduction technology (image recording, processing and exposure)

Typography, layout, design

Text-image integration

Printing forme production, including mounting and copying

Proofing

Printing processes (offset, letterpress, flexo, gravure, screen printing etc.) and press technology, including in-line finishing

Bookbinding and print finishing, including print converting, book and folding box production

II According to types of job and production:

Commercial

Book

Newspaper/Magazine

Continuous/Forms

Packaging

In-Plant

III Overlapping and related:

Printing and publishing

Media and communication

Materials (ink, substrate, chemistry)

Electronic data processing, including computer and VDU technology

Communication engineering, including telecommunication

Plant technology, including supply and waste removal, conveying and mailroom

Benutzerhinweise
für den deutsch-englischen und englisch-deutschen Teil

Die halbfett gedruckten Stichwörter stehen in alphabetischer Reihenfolge. Das Geschlecht der Hauptwörter im deutschen Text ist durch die in Kursiv gesetzten Buchstaben *m* (männlich), *f* (weiblich) und *n* (sächlich) bezeichnet. Die Abkürzung *pl* bezeichnet die Mehrzahlform. Wo ein Stichwort zum besseren Verständnis eine Zuordnung (Fachbereich) benötigte, ist diese kursiv in Klammern angegeben. Das Wiederholungszeichen (~) steht für das halbfett gesetzte Stichwort. Englische Verben sind nicht unter „to" eingereiht, sondern unter dem jeweils folgenden Wortteil. Zu ihrer Kenntlichmachung wurde ein kursives v nachgestellt.

Zur Raumersparnis wurden bei der Nennung der Fachbereiche die nachfolgenden Abkürzungen verwendet:

Bildverarb.	Bildverarbeitung (image processing)
Bogendruckm.	Bogendruckmaschine (sheet-fed press)
Buchherst.	Buchherstellung (book production)
Comp.	Computer (computer)
Druckverarb.	Druckverarbeitung (converting, finishing)
el.	elektrisch (electrical)
Faltschachtelherst.	Faltschachtelherstellung (folding box production)
Farbherst.	Farbherstellung (inkmaking)
Farbreprod.	Farbreproduktion (colour reproduction)
Formularherst.	Formularherstellung (forms production)
Fot.	Fotografie (photography)
Fotochem.	Fotochemie (photochemistry)
Inline-Fin.	Inline-Finishing (in-line finishing)
Lithogr.	Lithografie (lithography)
Masch.	Maschine (machine)
mech.	mechanisch (mechanical)
Papierherst.	Papierherstellung (paper making)
Reprod.	Reproduktion (reproduction)
Reprofotogr.	Reprofotografie (reprophotography)
Rollendruckm.	Rollendruckmaschine (web-fed press)
Schneidem.	Schneidemaschine (cutting machine)
Schriftklassif.	Schriftklassifizierung (type classification)
Telekomm.	Telekommunikation (telecommunication)
Texterf.	Texterfassung (text recording)
Textverarb.	Textverarbeitung (text processing)
Tiefdruckzyl.	Tiefdruckzylinder (gravure cylinder)
Typogr.	Typografie (typography)
Vorlagenherst.	Vorlagenherstellung (copy preparation)

How to use the German-English and English-German section

The key words printed in semi-bold are arranged in alphabetical order. The gender of the nouns in the German text is indicated by the characters set in italics, e. g. *m* (masculine), *f* (feminine), *n* (neuter). The abbreviation *pl* indicates the plural form. In cases where it has been deemed necessary to explain the context (subject field) of a key word, this is given in italics in parentheses. The repeat symbol (~) stands for the semi-bold key word. English verbs are not listed under "to" but according to the following part in the word. To identify them as such, they are accompanied by an italic v.

In order to save space, the following abbreviations were used to describe the subject fields:

book prod.	book production (Buchherstellung)
colour reprod.	colour reproduction (Farbreproduktion)
comp.	computer (Computer)
convert.	converting (Druckverarbeitung)
copy prep.	copy preparation (Vorlagenherstellung)
cutting m.	cutting machine (Schneidemaschine)
el.	electrical (elektrisch)
folding box prod.	folding box production (Faltschachtelherstellung)
forms prod.	forms production (Formularherstellung)
gravure cyl.	gravure cylinder (Tiefdruckzylinder)
image proc.	image processing (Bildverarbeitung)
in-line fin.	in-line finishing (Inline-Finishing)
lithogr.	lithography (Lithografie)
mach.	machine (Maschine)
mech.	mechanical (mechanisch)
papermak.	papermaking (Papierherstellung)
phot.	photography (Fotografie)
photochem.	photochemistry (Fotochemie)
photocomp.	photocomposition (Fotosatz)
reprod.	reproduction (Reproduktion)
reprophotogr.	reprophotography (Reprofotografie)
telecom.	telecommunication (Telekommunikation)
text proc.	text processing (Textverarbeitung)
text rec.	text recording (Texterfassung)
type classif.	type classification (Schriftklassifizierung)
typogr.	typography (Typografie)

WÖRTERBUCH DEUTSCH–ENGLISH
GERMAN–ENGLISH DICTIONARY

A

abätzen to etch away, to remove by etching
abbauen *(Masch.)* to disassemble, to dismantle
abbilden to illustrate, to picture
Abbildung *f* figure, illustration, picture, text figure
Abbildungen *f/pl (im Fotosatz auch)* art
Abbildungsbereich *m (Reprod.)* enlargement range, reproduction range
Abbildungsmaßstab *m (Reprod.)* reproduction ratio, reproduction scale; *im ~ 1:1* at a scale of 1:1
Abbildungsschärfe *f* definition of reproduction, reproduction sharpness
Abbindezeit *f (Leim)* drying time, setting time
abblättern *(Farbe, Lack)* to crack, to peel off
Abbreviatur *f (Satz)* abbreviation
abdämpfen *(Farbton)* to tone down
Abdeckasphalt *m* masking asphalt
Abdeckband *n (rotes Klebeband)* masking tape, red adhesive tape
Abdecken *n (Filmretusche)* film masking, film opaquing, masking, opaquing, retouching
Abdeckfarbe *f (Filmretusche)* film opaque, masking red
Abdecklack *m (Filmretusche)* masking lacquer, photoresist; *(Tiefdruckzyl.)* etching resist
Abdeckpapier *n* masking paper
Abdeckschablone *f* stencil mask
Abdeckstift *m (Filmretusche)* masking pen, opaquing pen, retouching pen
Abdecktusche *f (Filmretusche)* film opaque, masking red
Abdeckung *f (Maschine)* cover
Abdruck *m* off-print, print; *(Druckmaschinenvorgang)* impression; *(Exemplar)* copy; *(Fingerabdruck)* mark, print; *(Nachdruck)* reprint; *(Probedruck)* proof; *(Veröffentlichung)* printing, publication, reproduction
abdunkeln *(Farbton)* to darken, to deepen, to tone-down
Abendzeitung *f* evening paper
Aberration *f (Objektiv)* aberration
Abfälle *pl* waste
Abfallaufrollung *f (rotatives Stanzen)* waste re-reeling
Abfallausbrechen *n (nach Stanzen)* waste stripping
Abfallbehälter *m* waste container
Abfallentsorgung *f* waste disposal, waste removal
Abfallpapier *n* waste paper
Abfallrutsche *f* waste chute
Abfallstreifen *pl (Papier)* shavings *pl*, trimmings *pl*
abflachen *(Gradation)* to decrease contrast
abformen *(Mater)* to mould
abfräsen to rout off
Abführungszeichen *n (Satz)* close quote, end quotation mark
abgekürzt *(Satz) in ~ er Form* abridged
abgenutzte Schrift *f (Bleisatz)* battered type, worn type
abgequetschte Schrift *f (Bleisatz)* battered type
abgerundete Ecken *pl* rounded corners *pl*
abgestufte Tonwerte *pl* graduated tones *pl*
abgetönte Farbe *f* shaded colour
abgezeichneter Bogen *m (Druckfreigabe)* o.k. proof, o.k. sheet, passed proof, passed sheet
abgießen *(Mater)* to cast
Abgleich *m* adjustment; *(Meßgeräte)* calibration
abgleichen to adjust; *(Meßgeräte)* to calibrate, to match
abgraten to deburr
Abguß *m (Mater)* cast, casting
Abheftlochung *f* file hole punching, file holes *pl*
abkanten *(facettieren)* to bevel; *(Zeitungsoffsetplatte)* to edge-bend
abklappbares Aggregat *n* hinged unit, move-away unit, swing-away unit, swing-off unit, tilt-back unit
Abklatsch *m (Abzug)* proof; *(Druckform)* cast; *(Plagiat)* imitation
abkrätzen to skim
abkratzen to scrape off
Abkreiden *n (Farbe)* chalking
Abkürzungszeichen *n (Satz)* abbreviation sign
abkuppeln *(Aggregat)* to declutch, to disconnect, to disengage
Ablageregister *n* file index
Ablagerung *f (Galvanik)* deposit; *(Gummituch, Walzen usw.)* deposit
Ablaufsteuerung *f* sequence control
Ablegekasten *m (Handsatz)* distribution case
ablegen *(Daten)* to store; *(frische Druckfarbe)* to set off; *(Handsatz)* to distribute
Ableimmaschine *f* gluing machine
Ablieferung *f* delivery
abliegen *(frische Druckfarbe)* to set off
Abliegen *n (frische Druckfarbe)* offset(ting), set-off
ablösen *(z.B. Druckbogen vom Drucktuch)* to release

Abluft - Absorptionsspektrum

Abluft *f* exhaust air, waste air
Abluftgebläse *n* exhaust fan
Abluftgesetz *n* Clean Air Act
Abluftreinigung *f* exhaust air purification
Abmehlen *n (Farbe)* chalking
abmessen to measure
Abmessung *f (Maschine)* dimension
abmontieren *(Maschine)* to dismantle; *(Teile)* to remove
Abmusterung *f (Farbe)* colour match(ing), ink match(ing)
abnehmbares Aggregat *n* detachable unit, removable unit
Abonnement *n* subscription
Abonnement abbestellen to cancel a subscription
Abonnement der Zeitschrift XY subscription to the magazine XY
Abonnementpreis *m* subscription price
Abonnent *m* subscriber
Abonnent der Zeitschrift XY subscriber to the magazine XY
Abonnentenliste *f* list of subscribers
abonnieren to be subscribed to, to subscribe to
Abpalettierung *f* palletizing
abplatzen *(Farbe, Lack)* to crack, to peel off
Abpressen *n (Buchblock)* backing, nipping, pressing, smashing
Abpreßfalz *m (Buch)* backing joint
Abpreßmaschine *f (Buchherst.)* backing machine
abquetschen *(Bleisatzschrift)* to batter, to wear
Abquetschwalze *f* squeeze roller
Abrakeln *n (Feuchtwalzen)* squeezing
Abrakelung *f (Tiefdruck, Anilox)* doctoring
abreiben to rub off
Abreibeschrift *f (z.B. Letraset)* dry transfer letters *pl*, dry transfers *pl*, instant lettering *pl*, transfer characters *pl*
Abreißblock *m* tear-off pad
Abreißkalender *m* tear-off calendar
Abreißperforation *f (Packung)* tear-off perforation
Abrieb *m (Druck)* abrasion, rubbing
abriebfest *(Druck)* abrasion-proof, abrasion-resistant, rub-proof, rub-resistant
Abriebfestigkeit *f (Druck)* abrasion resistance, rub resistance, scuff resistance
Abriß *m (Buchauszug)* digest, summary
abrollen to unwind
Abroller *m (Rollendruckm.)* reelstand, unwinder, unwind unit
Abrollerbeschickung *f (Rollenwechsler)* loading of reelstand

Abrollung *f* unwinding; *(Vorrichtung)* unwinder, unwind unit
Abrollwelle *f* unwinding shaft
Abruf *m (Daten, Text)* call, recall, retrieval
Abrufauftrag *m* make-and-hold order
abrufen *(Daten, Text)* to call, to recall, to retrieve
abrunden to round off
Absatz *m (Typogr.)* break, break line, paragraph
Absatz/Einzug *m (Einzug der ersten Zeile eines Absatzes)* paragraph indent
absatzfreies Papierstapeln sheet piling without break lines
Absatz ohne Einzug flush paragraph
Absatzzeichen *n (Satz)* break mark
Absaugeinrichtung *f (Entsorgung)* exhauster, suction removal device
Absaughaube *f* exhaust hood, suction hood
Absaugung *f* extraction, suction removal
abschalten *(Aggregat, Maschine)* to cut off, to declutch, to disconnect, to disengage, to stop, to switch off, to turn off
Abschaltung *f* switch-off, throw-off, turn-off
Abschlagmesser *n (Rollenwechsler)* cut-off knife
abschleifen to grind off
abschmieren *(frischer Druck)* to set off
Abschmieren *n (frischer Druck)* smearing, smudging, offset(ting), set-off
Abschmutzbogen *m/pl* set-off sheets *pl*
abschmutzen *(frischer Druck)* to set off
Abschmutzen *n* smearing, smudging, offset(ting), set-off
Abschmutzmakulatur *f* set-off sheets *pl*
abschneiden to cut off, to trim off
Abschnitt *m (Buch)* chapter, section; *(Coupon, Formularsatz)* stub; *(Rollendruck)* cut-off
Abschnittlänge *f (Rollendruck)* cut-off
Abschnittregister *n (Rollendruck)* cut-off register
abschrägen *(facettieren)* to bevel
Abschrägung *f* bevel
abschreiben *ins Reine* ~ to make a clean copy
Abschreibung *f (Maschine)* depreciation
Abschreibungsperiode *f* write-off period
Abschrift *f* copy
abschwächen *(Film)* to etch, to reduce
Abschwächer *m (Film)* reducer
abschwenkbares Aggregat *n* hinged unit, move-away unit, swing-away unit, swing-off unit, tilt-back unit
absetzen *(Satz)* to set
absolute Adresse *f (Comp.)* absolute address
Absorptionsspektrum *n* absorption spectrum

Absparen/Überfüllen n *(Bildverarb.)* spread and choke
abspeichern *(Text, Daten)* to store
abstapeln to pile, to stack
Abstapeln n piling, stacking
Abstapler m down-stacker, stacker
Abstauben n *(Druckbögen)* dusting, dust removal, powder removal
abstellen *(Aggregat/Maschine)* to cut off, to declutch, to disconnect, to disengage, to stop, to switch off, to turn off
Abstellung f shut-down
Abstimmbogen m o.k. proof, o.k. sheet, passed proof, passed sheet
abstimmen *(Farbe)* to match
Abstimmtisch m *(Farbabst.)* colour matching desk
Abstimmung f *(Farbe)* colour match(ing), ink match(ing)
Abstreifer m stripper; *(Anlegersaugkopf auch)* sheet separator
Abstrich m *(beim Buchstaben)* stem; *(Farbprobe)* draw out
abstufen *(Tonwerte)* to graduate
Abstufung f *(Tonwerte)* gradation
Abtastauflösung f scanning resolution
Abtastbereich m scan(ning) area
Abtasteinheit f analyze unit, scanning unit
abtasten *(Scanner usw.)* to analyze, to read, to scan; *(Bahnsteuerung auch)* to sense
Abtastformat n scan(ning) area
Abtastgeschwindigkeit f scanning speed
Abtastkopf m scanning head; *(Bahnsteuerung auch)* sensor head
Abtastlichtquelle f *(Scanner)* scanning light source, analyze light source
Abtastoptik f scanning lens
Abtastscanner m scanner reader, scanner input unit
Abtaststrahl scanning beam
Abtasttrommel f scanning drum, analyze drum
Abtastung f scanning; *(Bahnsteuerung auch)* sensing
Abtastvorlage f *(Scanner)* input media, scanning copy, scanning media
Abtastvorrichtung f scanning device
Abtastwalze f analyze drum, scanning drum
Abtastzylinder m analyze drum, scanning drum
Abteilungsleiter m department head, department manager, divisional manager, supervisor
abtönen to shade, to tone-down
Abtrennkarte f *(Direktmail, Inline-Fin.)* detachable postcard

Ab- und Aufrollvorrichtung f unwind and rewind unit
abwaschen to wash off, to wash out
Abwasser n waste water
Abwassergesetz n Clean Water Act
Abweichung f *(Prozeß)* deviation
Abweichung vom Sollwert deviation from set value
abwickeln *(Rolle)* to unwind
Abwicklung f *(Rolle)* unwinding; *(Vorrichtung)* unwinder, unwind unit; *(Zylinder)* rolling
Abwicklungsverhältnisse pl *(Zylinder)* rolling conditions pl
abwischen to wipe off; *(mit dem Schwamm)* to sponge off
abzählen to count
abziehbare Maskierschicht f peelable masking layer
abziehbare Schicht f *(Maskierfilm)* peelable layer, strippable layer
Abziehbild n transfer picture, decalcomania (picture), decal
Abziehbilderdruck m transfer printing, decalcomania
Abziehbilderpapier n decalcomania paper
Abziehbilderverfahren n decalcomania process
abziehen *(Abliegen der druckfrischen Farbe)* to set off; *(Bleisatz)* to pull a proof; *(Schichten)* to peel off, to strip
abziehen in Fahnen to proof in galley
Abziehgelatine f stripping gelatine
Abziehlack m *(Retusche)* stripping varnish
Abziehpapier n proof paper
Abziehpresse f *(Buchdruck)* galley press, proofpress
Abziehschicht f *(Maskierfilm)* peelable layer, strippable layer
Abzug m *(Bleisatz)* pull
Abzug ohne Zurichtung flat pull
achromatisch achromatic
Achsel f *(beim Buchstaben)* shoulder
Achsenlager n *(Walze)* journal bearing
achsloses Wickeln n shaftless winding
Achszylinder m *(im Gs. zu Hohlzylinder)* shaft cylinder
Achtelgeviert n *(Typogr.)* hair space
Achterturm m *(Zeitungsoffsetrotation)* four-high unit
Achtseitenbogen m eight-page signature
Achtseitenprodukt n *(Rollendruck)* eight-page product
Achtseiten-Rollenoffsetmaschine f eight-page offset rotary, eight-page web offset press

Additiv - Algrafie

Additiv n *(Druckchemie)* additive
additive Farbmischung f additive colour synthesis
Adressat m *(Versandraum)* addressee
Adreßbuch n address book, directory
Adresse f *(auch Comp.)* address
Adressenformat n *(Comp.)* address format
Adressenregister n *(Comp.)* address register, index register
Adressenverzeichnis n *(Comp.)* address register, index register
Adressierkopf m addressing head, labelling head
Adressiermaschine f addressing machine, labelling machine
Adressierung f addressing, labelling
A/D-Wandler (Analog-Digital) m A/D converter (analogue-digital)
äquivalente Flächendeckung f equivalent dot area
Aerograf m aerograph, airbrush
Aerosol n aerosol
Ästhetik-Programm n *(Fotosatz)* aesthetic program
Ätzbad n etching bath
Ätzdauer f etching time
Ätze f acid, etching solution, mordant
Ätzen n *(Film)* dot etching, film etching, reducing; *(Klischee, Zylinder)* etching; *(Offsetplatte)* desensitizing
Ätzfarbe f etching ink
Ätzfilm m *(Tiefdruck)* etching film
Ätzkali n caustic potash
Ätzlauge f etching lye
Ätzlösung f etching solution
Ätzmaschine f etching machine
Ätznadel f engraving needle
Ätznatron n caustic soda
Ätzpulver n etching powder
Ätzreserve f *(Film)* etching capability
Ätzresist *(Tiefdruckzyl.)* etching resist
Ätztiefdruck m photogravure (process)
Ätztiefe f etching depth
Ätzung f *(Buchdruckklischee)* cut, engraving, etching
Ätzwasser n etching solution, mordant
äußere Form f *(Druckform)* outer forme
äußerer Papierrand m foredge margin, front(-edge) margin, outer margin
äußerer Seitenrand m foredge margin, front(-edge) margin, outer margin
Affiche f *(Plakat)* poster
Agentur f agency
Agenturbild n *(Nachrichtenagentur)* agency photo(graph), wire photo(graph)
Agenturmeldung f agency message, wire message

Aggregat n *(mech.)* aggregate, attachment, unit
Ahle f bodkin
Ahlenheft n bodkin handle
Ahlenspitze f bodkin tip
Akkoladen f/pl *(Nasenklammer)* braces pl
Akkumulator m accumulator
aktinische Dichte f actinic density
aktinisches Licht n actinic light
Aktivator m *(Fotochemie)* activator
Aktivkohlefilterung f activated carbon filtration
aktualisieren *(Daten, Text)* to up-date
Aktualität f *(redaktionell)* topicality
aktuelle Nachrichten pl late breaking news pl, topical news pl
aktuelle Satzparameter pl *(laufender Auftrag im System)* current typesetting parameters pl
aktuelle Technik f *(Stand der Technik)* state-of-the-art technology
Akustikkoppler m *(Telekomm.)* acoustic coupler
akustisches Warnsignal n acoustic warning signal
Akut m *(Akzent)* acute accent
Akzent m *(Satz)* accent
Akzentbuchstabe m accented letter
akzentuieren to accentuate
Akzentuierung f accentuation
Akzidenzarbeiten f/pl *(Bogen)* jobbing work; *(Rolle)* commercial (print)work
Akzidenzdruck m *(Bogen)* job printing; *(Rolle)* commercial printing
Akzidenzdrucker m *(Bogen)* job(bing) printer; *(Rolle)* commercial printer
Akzidenzdruckerei f *(Bogen)* job(bing) printer; *(Rolle)* commercial printer
Akzidenzen pl *(Bogen)* jobbing work; *(Rolle)* commercial (print)work
Akzidenzmaschine f *(Bogen)* jobbing press; *(Rolle)* commercial press
Akzidenzpresse f jobbing press
Akzidenzrollenoffsetmaschine f commercial web offset press
Akzidenzrollenrotation f commercial web press
Akzidenzsatz m job typesetting, jobbing work
Akzidenzschrift f typeface for jobbing work
Akzidenzsetzerei f job(bing) typesetter
Album n album
Albumin n albumen
Albuminkopie f albumen copy
Albuminpapier n albumen paper
Albuminverfahren n albumen process
algebraisches Zeichen n algebraical sign
Algen pl *(Feuchtwasser)* algae pl, mould
Algorithmus m *(Comp.)* algorithm
Algrafie f *(Aluminiumdruck)* algraphy

Alineazeichen *n* paragraph mark
Alkali *n* alkaline
alkalifestes Papier *n* alkali-proof paper
alkalischer Feuchtwasserzusatz *m* alkaline fountain additive
alkoholauswaschbare Fotopolymerplatte *f* alcohol-based photopolymer plate, alcohol-developed photopolymer plate, alcohol-washed photopolymer plate
Alkoholdosiergerät *n (Feuchtwasser)* alcohol metering device
alkoholentwickelbare Fotopolymerplatte *f* alcohol-based photopolymer plate, alcohol-developed photopolymer plate, alcohol-washed photopolymer plate
Alkoholfeuchtung *f* alcohol damp(en)ing
Alkoholfeuchtwerk *n* alcohol damp(en)ing system
Alkoholgehalt *m (Feuchtwasser)* alcohol concentration, alcohol content, alcohol percentage
Alkoholkonstanthalter *m (Feuchtwasser)* alcohol metering device
Alkoholregelung *f (Feuchtwasser)* alcohol control
alle Rechte vorbehalten all rights reserved
Allgemeinempfindlichkeit *f (Repromat.)* overall sensitivity
Allonge *f (angeklebtes Blatt)* fly-leaf
Allzweckschrift *f* all-purpose typeface
Almanach *m* almanac
Alphabet *n* alphabet
Alphabetblatt *n (Satz-, Schriftmuster)* alphabet sheet
Alphabetbreite *f (Satz)* alphabet width
alphabetische Reihenfolge *f* alphabetical order
alphabetisches Verzeichnis *n* alphabetical index
alphabetisch sortieren to sort in alphabetical order
Alphabetlänge *f (Satz)* alphabet length
alphanumerische Anzeige *f* alphanumeric display
alphanumerische Zeichen *pl* alphanumerical characters *pl*
Altarfalz *m* double gate fold
Altdeutsch *n (Schrift)* old German type
alte Ausgabe *f* back issue
Alterung *f* ageing
Alterungsbeständigkeit *f* non-ageing properties *pl*
Altpapier *n* old papers *pl*, waste paper
Alufolie *f* aluminium foil
alukaschiert aluminium coated, aluminium laminated
Aluminiumbedampfung *f* metallizing
Aluminiumpapier *n* aluminium paper
Aluminiumplatte *f* aluminium plate

Aluminiumverbundmaterial *n* aluminium compound
Amalgam *n* amalgam
Amalgamdruckverfahren *n* amalgam printing process
am Kopf geschlossen *(Falzbogen)* closed head
am Kopf offen *(Falzbogen)* open head
Ammoniakentwicklung *f* ammonia development
Amortisation *f* amortization
Amortisationszeit *f* amortization period, pay-back period
Ampère-Stunde *f (Galv.)* ampère hour
Amtsblatt *n* official gazette
An/Abstellen der Auftragswalzen throw on/off of forme rollers
An/Abstellen des Drucks throw on/off impression
anachromatisches Objektiv *n* anachromatic lens
anätzen *(Offsetplatte)* to desensitize, to etch
analoges Signal *n* analogue signal
Analogrechner *m (Comp.)* analogue computer
anamorphotisches Zerren *n* anamorphic distortion
anastatischer Druck *m* anastatic printing
anastigmatisches Objektiv *n* anastigmatic lens
Anbaumöbel *pl* add-on furniture
andere Seite *f* overleaf
an drei Seiten beschneiden to trim (on) three sides
Andruck *m* print proof, proof; *(im Gs. zum Fortdruck)* proof print, proof printing; *(im Gs. zum Proof)* press proof, press proofing
Andruckbogen *m* proof sheet
andrucken to pressproof, to proofprint
Andrucker *m* proofprinter
Andruckfarbe *f* proofing ink
Andruckmaschine *f* proofing press, proofpress
Andruckpapier *n* proof paper
Andruckplatte *f* proofing plate
Andruckpresse *f* proofing press, proofpress
Andruckskala *f (Farbskala)* progressive proofs *pl*, progs *pl*, set of progressives, set of progs
Andruckstudio *n* print proof studio, proofing studio, proof production studio
Andrückrollen *pl* rollers *pl*, trolleys *pl*
aneinanderstoßend *(Bilder, Bahnklebung)* butting
Anfahrmakulatur *f* start-up waste, white waste
Anfangsbuchstabe *m* head letter, initial character, initial (letter); **zweizeiliger** ~ two-line initial (letter)
Anfangsgeschwindigkeit *f (Druckm.)* initial speed
Anfangskolumne *f* opening column
Anfangspasser *m* start-up register

Anfangsseite - Anschlußleistung

Anfangsseite *f* opening page
Anfangszeile *f* first line, opening line
anfeuchten to damp(en), to moisten, to wet
anführen *(Satz)* to put in quotes, to quote
Anführung *f (im Gs. zur Abführung)* begin quote, commence quote; *(Zitat)* quotation
Anführung schließen *die* ~ to close with quotes
Anführungszeichen *pl (Satz)* quote marks *pl*, quotes *pl*
Angebot *n (Preis)* quotation
Angebotsmappe *f* quotation folder
angeschnitten bled-off, bleed
angeschnittener Druck *m* bleed printing
angeschnittenes Bild *n* bled-off illustration
Anhängeetikett *n* hang tag, string tag, tag, tie-on label
anhängen *(Satz)* to run on
Anhänger *m (Etikett)* hang tag, string tag, tag, tie-on label
Anhaltekopie *f (Mehrfarbmontage)* blue key (registration film), blue print, guide copy, montage colour key
Anhang *m (Buch)* addenda *pl*, appendix
Anilinblau *n* aniline blue
Anilindruck *m* aniline printing
Anilox-Druckwerk *n* anilox printing unit
Anilox-Farbwerk *n* anilox inking unit
Aniloxhochdruck *m* anilox letterpress
Aniloxoffset *m* anilox offset
Aniloxwalze *f* anilox roller
ankleben to glue on
Anlage *f (Anlagekante)* lay (edge); *(Anlegen)* feed(ing); *(Anleger)* feeder; *(Maschinenanlage)* set-up
Anlagekante *f (Bogen)* lay (edge)
Anlagetisch *m* feedboard, feeding table
Anlagewinkel *m (Seitenmarke-Vordermarke)* feed angle, lay angle
Anlauf *m (Maschine)* start-up
anlaufen (lassen) to start up
Anlaufmakulatur *f* start-up waste, white waste
Anlaufzeit *f* start-up time
Anlegeapparat *m* feeder
Anlegekante *f* lay (edge)
Anlegemarke *f* feed gauge, feed lay, lay gauge, lay mark
anlegen to feed
Anlegen *n* feed(ing)
Anleger *m* feeder
Anleger an/aus feeder on/off
Anlegerkopf *m* feeder head
Anlegermagazin *n (Druckverarb.)* feeder magazine, hopper loader
Anlegerstapel *m* feeder pile
Anlegertakt *m* feeder timing
Anlegertisch *m* feedboard, feeding table
Anlegevorrichtung *f* feeding device
anleimen to glue on
Anleimmaschine *f (Buchb.)* gluing machine
Anleimvorrichtung *f (Rollenwechsler)* paster
Anleitungshandbuch *n* instruction manual
anlernen to instruct
Anmachen der Farbe *n* ink mixing
Anmerkung *f (Text)* annotation, note, remark
Anmerkungszeichen *n (Hinweiszeichen)* dagger, reference mark
Annahmeschluß *m (Redaktion/Anzeigen)* closing date, deadline
Anode *f (Galv.)* anode
Anodenplatte *f* anode plate
anodisierte Aluminiumplatte *f* anodized aluminium plate
Anordnung *f* arrangement, configuration
anorganisch-mineralisches Druckbestäubungspuder *n* inorganic mineral spray powder
anpassen *(dem Schriftbild, dem Layout)* to adapt, to fit
Anpreßdruck *m (Beistelldruck)* impression pressure, printing impression, printing pressure
Anpreßstation *f (Buchherst.)* pressing station
Anpreßwalze *f* pressure roller
Anreiben *n (Farbe)* grinding, milling
Anreibeschrift *f (z. B. Letraset)* dry transfer letters *pl*, dry transfers *pl*, instant lettering *pl*, transfer characters *pl*
Anreibung *f (Farbherst.)* grinding, milling; *(Sonderanfertigung einer Farbe)* special production
Ansaugmattscheibe *f (Kamera)* combined ground glass/vacuum film back
Ansaugplatte *f (Kamera)* vacuum film back
Ansaugvorrichtung *f* suction device
Ansaugzeiten *pl* vacuum times
Anschaffungspreis *m* purchase price
Anschlag *m (Papierführung)* (aligning) stop
anschlagloser Drucker *m* non-impact printer
anschleiern *(Pigmentpapier)* to sensitize
anschließen *(Geräte, Aggregate, Peripherie)* to connect, to couple, to hook up, to interface, to link (up)
Anschluß *m (für Eingabe/Ausgabegeräte)* port; *(Geräte, Aggregate, Peripherie)* connection, link-up; *(Manuskript)* continuation
Anschlußleistung *f (el.)* power consumption

Anschlußstück - Anzeigenpreis

Anschlußstück n *(Ornamente im Bleisatz)* border piece, ornament piece, rule piece
Anschlußwert m *(el.)* power requirement
anschneiden *(Abbildung)* to bleed
Anschnitt m *(Abbildung)* bleed
Ansichtspostkarte f picture postcard
Ansichtssendung f *(Buchverkauf)* delivery on approval
anspruchsvoll demanding, exacting
anspruchsvoller Prospekt m high-quality brochure
anstellen *(Walzen, Zylinder, Rakel)* to bring into contact, to throw on; *(Aggregate, Maschine)* to clutch, to connect, to engage, to set in motion, to set on action, to start, to switch on, to turn on
Anstellwinkel m *(Tiefdruckrakel)* contact angle
Ansteuerung f control
anstreichen *(Korrekturlesen)* to mark(-up)
Anti-Haloschicht f *(Reprofilme)* anti-halation coating, anti-halo backing
Antihautmittel n anti-skinning agent
Antikeinband m *(Buch)* antique binding
Antikorrosionsschicht f *(Druckmaschinenzyl.)* anti-corrosion coating
Antimon n *(Bleisatz)* antimony
Anti-Newton-Beschichtung f *(Film, Glas)* anti-Newton coating
Antioxidationsmittel n anti-oxidant
Antiqua f *(Schrift)* old style, old face
Antiqua-Varianten pl *(Schriftklassif.)* Inciseds pl
Antiquaziffern pl *(im U. zu Mediävalziffern)* lining figures pl, modern figures pl
Antischaumzusatz m anti-foam additive, anti-foam agent, defoaming agent
Antistatikum n *(Film, Folie)* anti-static agent
antistatisch anti-static
Antitrockner m *(Druckfarbe)* anti-dryer, anti-drying agent, anti-oxidant
antreiben to drive
Antrieb m *(mech.)* drive
Antriebskraft f driving power
Antriebsmotor m drive motor
Antriebsräder pl drive gears pl
Antriebsriemen m driving belt
Antriebsseite *(im Gs. zur Bedienerseite)* drive side
Antriebswelle f drive shaft
Antrocknen n *(Druckfarbe)* piling
Antwortkarte f *(Direktmail, Inline-Fin.)* reply card, response card
Anwender m user
anwenderfreundlich user-friendly

Anwendersoftware f application software, user software
Anwendungsbereich m application area, application field
Anwendungsprogramm n application program
Anwendungstechnik f application engineering, application method
Anwendungstechniker m application engineer, operator instructor, professional demonstrator, technical instructor
Anzahl f *(Zeichen, Seiten usw.)* count
Anzahl Zeichen *(Umfangsberechnung)* character count
anzeichnen *(Korrekturlesen)* to mark(-up)
Anzeige f *(Anzeigenkarte)* announcement; *(optische)* display, read-out; *(Werbung)* ad(vertisement)
Anzeige mit Umrandung f boxed ad, framed ad
anzeigen *(optisch)* to display
Anzeigenabschluß m advertisement contract
Anzeigenabteilung f advertising department
Anzeigenagentur f advertising agency
Anzeigenakquisiteur m advertising representative, space salesman
Anzeigenakquisition f ad acquisition
Anzeigenannahme f *(Büro)* advertising office; *(Vorgang)* ad collection, adtaking
Anzeigenaufnahme f ad collection, adtaking
Anzeigenauftrag m advertising order, space order
Anzeigenbearbeitung f ad handling, ad processing
Anzeigenbeilage f advertising insert, advertising supplement
Anzeigenblatt n advertising journal
Anzeigenbüro n advertising agency, advertising office
Anzeigenchiffre f box number
Anzeigengestaltung f ad arrangement, ad design, ad display, ad layout
Anzeigengestaltungsterminal n display ad terminal
Anzeigenkarte f announcement
Anzeigenkorrekturbeleg m ad proof
Anzeigenkunde m advertising customer
Anzeigenlayout n ad arrangement, ad layout
Anzeigenleiter m ad(vertising) manager
Anzeigenmanuskript n ad(vertising) copy
Anzeigenmetteur m *(Bleisatz)* admaker, ad make-up man
Anzeigenplazierung f ad placement, ad position
Anzeigenpreis m ad(vertising) rate

Anzeigenprogramm - Assureelinie

Anzeigenprogramm n *(Textverarb.)* ad processing software
Anzeigensatz m ad composition, composition of advertising matter
Anzeigenschluß m ad collection deadline, advertising deadline
Anzeigenschrift f adface
Anzeigenserie f advertisement series
Anzeigensetzer m ad compositor
Anzeigensetzerei f *(Zeitungsdruckerei)* ad composing room
Anzeigenspiegel m *(Seitenspiegel)* advertising type area
Anzeigenstammkunde m regular advertising customer, regular ad subscriber
Anzeigentarif m adrates pl, ad tariff
Anzeigenteil m *(im U. zum red. Teil)* advertising section
Anzeigentext m ad copy, ad(vertising) copy, ad(vertising) text
Anzeigenumbruch m ad make-up, advertising make-up
Anzeigenunterlage f *(Vorlage)* ad(vertising) copy
Anzeigenverarbeitung f ad handling, ad processing
Anzeigenvertreter m advertising representative, space salesman
Anzeigenverwaltung f ad filing, ad management
Anzeigenvorlage f ad(vertising) copy; *(Grafik, Zeichnung)* advertising art
Anzeigenwerbung f advertising publicity
Anzeige schalten to advertise
aplanatisches Objektiv n aplanatic lens
apochromatisches Objektiv n apochromatic lens
Apostroph m *(Auslassungszeichen)* apostrophe
Appendix m *(Anhang)* appendix
Aquatinta f aquatint
Aquatone-Verfahren n aquatone process
Arabesken pl *(oriental. Ornamente)* arabesques pl
arabische Schrift f Arabic characters pl, Arabic type
arabische Ziffern pl Arabic figures pl, Arabic numerals pl
Aräometer n *(Dichtemesser für Flüssigkeiten)* areometer
Arbeit f job, work
arbeiten *(System, Maschine)* to operate, to run, to work
Arbeiten im Überformat n oversize work
Arbeiten nach dem Druck post-press operations pl

Arbeitsablauf m production cycle, production sequence, work flow, working procedures pl, working process, work routine
Arbeitsbedingungen pl working conditions pl
Arbeitsbelastung f workload
Arbeitsblende f *(Kamera)* basic lens aperture
Arbeitsbreite f working width
Arbeitsbuch n work book
Arbeitsfluß m work flow
Arbeitsgang m operation, pass; *in einem* ~ in one operation, in one pass, in one through
Arbeitsgeschwindigkeit f working speed
arbeitsintensiv labour intensive
Arbeitskleidung f working clothes pl
Arbeitskraft f operator, workman
Arbeitsleistung f efficiency, output, performance
Arbeitsmarkt m *(Anzeigenrubrik)* situations pl, vacancies pl
Arbeitsmuster n work sample
Arbeitsplan m work plan
Arbeitsplanung f work planning
Arbeitsplatz m work place; *(mit Bildschirm)* workstation
Arbeitsspeicher m *(Comp.)* working memory, working storage
Arbeitsstellung f *(Masch.)* operating position
Arbeitstasche f job docket
Arbeitstemperatur f *(Masch.)* working temperature
Arbeitsumfeld n working environment
Arbeitsvorbereitung f production planning, work planning, work preparation; *(Abteilung)* planning department
Arbeitszettel m job docket, job sheet, time sheet
Archiv n archive
Archivexemplar n file copy
Archivfestigkeit f *(Filmmaterial)* archival properties pl, filing properties pl, keeping properties pl
Archivierung f archiving, filing, long-term storage
Argon-Laser m *(Scanner)* argon laser
arithmetisches Zeichen n arithmetical sign
Arkansas-Ölstein m Arkansas oil stone
Arretierhebel m locking lever, stop lever
Artikel m *(Publikation)* article, feature
Artikelreihe f *(Publikation)* series of articles
Aschegehalt m ash content
Asphaltlack m *(Tiefdruckzyl.)* asphalt varnish
Asphalttinktur f *(Auswaschtinktur)* asphalt wash-out solution
Assureelinie f *(Satz)* cheques pl, combination rule

Astigmatismus m *(Objektiv)* astigmatism
Astralonfolie f astralon sheet
astronomisches Zeichen n astronomical sign
Atelier n studio
Atlas m atlas
Atlaspapier n map paper
auf Bänder genäht sewn on bands
Aufbau m *(Maschine)* installation
Aufbauen n *(Rückstände auf Gummituch, Walzen usw.)* build-up, piling(-up)
auf Bildschirm aufrufen to call on screen
aufbinden *(Buch)* to rebind
auf Block ausschließen to justify
auf Bünde genäht sewn on bands
auf das Format beschneiden to cut to size
auf dem Rücken stehend standing on the spine
Aufdruck m *(in Drucksache)* imprinting, overprinting
aufdrucken to imprint, to overprint
auf Druck gehen *(Walzen, Zylinder)* to go on impression
auf echte Bünde geheftet sewn on raised cords
Aufeinanderdruck m overprinting, superimposed printing
auf ein neues Format bringen *(Reprod.)* to re-scale, to re-size
auffächern *(Papierbogen)* to fan out
Auffangkorb m *(Filmentwicklungsm.)* collecting basket
auffrischen *(Farben)* to freshen up, to renew
Auffüllen mit Führungspunkten insert leaders, leadering
auf gleicher Schriftlinie with common baseline
Aufhänger m *(Wandkalender)* hanger
aufhellen *(Bildpartien, Farben)* to brighten, to lighten, to tone up
aufholzen *(Klischee)* to mount on wood
Aufholzen n *(Klischee)* blockmaking
aufkleben to glue on
Aufkleber m sticker
aufklotzen *(Klischee)* to mount on wood
Aufklotzen n *(Klischee)* blockmaking
Aufkupferung f *(Tiefdruckzyl.)* copper-plating
Aufkupferungsanlage f copper-plating installation
Auflage f *(Druck)* print run, run; *(Buch)* edition; *(Zeitung, Zeitschrift)* circulation
Auflagenangabe f *(Zeitung, Zeitschrift)* circulation statement
Auflagenbeständigkeit f *(Druckplatte)* length-of-run capacity, print run stability
Auflagendruck m *(Fortdruck)* final run, print run, production printing, production run
Auflagenfestigkeit f length-of-run capacity, print run stability
Auflagenhöhe f length of run, print volume; *(Zeitung, Zeitschrift)* circulation
Auflagenkontrolleinrichtung f *(IVW)* audit bureau of circulation
Auflagenzähler m *(Druckm.)* job counter
auflegen *(Bogen in Anlegermagazin)* to feed, to load; *(Buch)* to publish
Aufleger m *(Decker, Reprod.)* mask, overlay
aufleimen to glue on
Auflicht n on-light, reflected light
Auflichtdensitometer n reflection densitometer
Auflichtmessung f on-light measurement, reflected light measurement
auflockern *(Bogen)* to fan, to loosen up
Auflösung f *(optisch)* resolution
Auflösungsfeinheit f resolving power
Auflösungsvermögen n resolving power
Aufmachung f *(Zeitung)* make-up
aufnadeln to needle on, to pin on
Aufnahme f *(Kamera)* exposure, photo(graph), shot
Aufnahmeformat n exposure area
Aufnahmekassette f *(zur Aufnahme von Material)* take-up cassette
Aufnahmematerial n exposure material, exposure media, photographic material
Aufnahmeobjektiv n camera lens
aufnehmen *(Anzeige)* to accept; *(in der Kamera)* to expose, to make an exposure, to photograph
Aufquellen der Papierfasern fiber puffing
Aufrastern n screening
Aufrauhen m *(Buchrücken)* milling, roughening, routing; *(Platte, Stein)* graining
Aufreißlinie f *(Packung)* tear(-off) line
Aufreißstreifen m *(Packung)* tear-off tape
Aufriß m *(gestalterisch)* layout, outline, sketch
Aufrollung f winding-up, rewinding; *(Vorrichtung)* rewinder, rewind unit
Aufruf m *(Daten, Text)* call, recall, retrieval
aufrufen *(Daten, Text)* to call, to recall, to retrieve
Aufsatz m *(Publikation)* article
Aufschlag m *(Preis)* additional charge, extra charge, surcharge
Aufschrift f inscription, lettering
auf Schriftlinie stellen *(setzen)* to set to baseline
aufschuppen *(Bogen)* to shingle
Aufsichtsbeleuchtung f *(Kamera)* front lighting
Aufsichtsdensitometer n reflection densitometer

Aufsichtsvorlage - ausbinden

Aufsichtsvorlage *f* reflection artwork, reflection original, reflective copy
Aufspannen *n (Druckplatte, Drucktücher)* clamping, locking, mounting
Aufspindelung *f (Tiefdruckzyl.)* spindling
auf Stand *m* in position, in register
auf Stand bringen to position, to register
aufstechen *(Steindruck)* to needle on, to pin on
Aufstechnadel *f* fixing needle
aufsteilen *(Gradation)* to increase contrast
aufstellen *(Maschine)* to erect, to install, to mount, to set up; *(Faltschachtel)* to erect
Aufsteller *m (Werbung)* show card
Aufstellung *f (Maschine)* erection, installation, set-up
aufstoßen *(Papier)* to jog, to knock up
Aufstreichrakel *f (Papierherst.)* coating blade
Auftrag *m (Beschichtung)* application, coating; *(Job)* job, order; **kurzfristiger** ~ rush order, short-term order; **laufender** ~ current job
auftragender Falzrücken *m* bulky folding spine
auftragendes Papier *n* bulky paper
Auftraggeber *m* client, customer
Auftragsabwicklung *f* order handling
Auftragsannahme *f* order taking
Auftragsbearbeitung *f* order handling
Auftragsbegleitzettel *m* job docket
Auftragsdatei *f* job file
Auftragsdaten *pl* job data, job file
Auftragseingang *m* order entry, order intake
Auftragsformular *n* order form
Auftragskalkulation *f* job costing
Auftragsnummer *f* job number, order number
Auftragsstruktur *f* order structure
Auftragstasche *f* job docket
Auftragsvorbereitung *f* job planning, job preparation
Auftragswalze *f (auf Bedruckstoff)* application roller; *(auf Druckform)* forme roller
Auftragswechsel *m* job change(-over), order change
Auftragszettel *m* job docket, job sheet
Auftragung *f* application, coating
Auftragung der Farbe inking
auftupfen *(Farbe)* to tap out
auf volle Zeilenbreite ausschließen to justify to full measure
Aufwärmzeit *f (Maschinen)* warm-up time
aufwalzen *(Farbe)* to ink up
aufwickeln to wind up, to rewind
Aufwickelvorrichtung *f* rewinder, rewind unit
Aufwicklung *f* rewinding, winding-up; *(Vorrichtung)* rewinder, rewind unit

aufzeichnen to record, to expose, to plot, to scan
Aufzeichnung *f* recording, exposure, plotting, scanning
Aufzeichnungsart *f* recording mode
Aufzeichnungsauflösung *f* recording resolution, scanning resolution
Aufzeichnungsdichte *f* recording density, scanline density, scanning density
Aufzeichnungseinheit *f* recording unit, scanning unit
Aufzeichnungsfeinheit *f* recording resolution, scanning resolution
Aufzeichnungsformat *n* recording area, scan(ning) area
Aufzeichnungsgerät *n* recorder, scanner, plotter
Aufzeichnungsgeschwindigkeit *f* recording speed, scanning speed
Aufzeichnungskopf *m* recording head, scanning head
Aufzeichnungslichtquelle *f* expose light source
Aufzeichnungsmaterial *n* recording media
Aufzeichnungsscanner *m* scanner recorder, scanner output unit
auf Zeilenlänge ausschließen to justify
aufziehen *(Gummituch, Feuchtwalzenschläuche, Zylinderbogen usw.)* to mount
Aufziehkarton *m* mounting board
Aufzug *m (Lastenaufzug)* hoist, lift; *(Zylinderaufzug)* backing, dressing, packing, underpacking; **den** ~ **machen** to dress the cylinder, to pack the cylinder
Aufzugsblech *n* packing plate
Aufzugsbogen *m (Buchdruck)* packing sheet, tympan
Aufzugsspielraum *m* packing latitude
Aufzugsstärke *f* packing height, packing thickness
Aufzugsstärkemesser *m* packing gauge
Aufzugsstange *f (Buchdruckm.)* tympan clamp
Auge *n (Buchstabe)* face
Augenpulver *n (Kleingedrucktes)* very small print
Ausbau *m (modulares System)* expansion, extension, upgrade
ausbaufähiges System *n* expandable system, upgradable system
Ausbaustufe *f (modulares System)* extension phase, extension step
ausbelichten to burn out
Ausbelichtung *f (Reprod.)* burn-out
Ausbelichtungsmaske *f (Reprod.)* burn-out mask
Ausbilder *m* instructor
Ausbildung *f* training
ausbinden *(Bleisatz)* to tye up

Ausbleichen n (Farbe) bleeding, fading; (Fotochemie) bleaching
Ausbluten n (Farbe) bleeding, fading
Ausbrechen n (nach Stanzen) waste stripping
Ausbrechform f stripping die, stripping forme
Ausbrechstifte pl stripping pins pl
Ausbrechwerkzeug n stripping tool
Ausbrechzylinder m stripping cylinder
ausbringen (Satz) to drive out
Ausdecken n (Filmretusche) film masking, film opaquing, masking, opaquing, retouching
aus dem Register mis-registered, out of register
aus der Farbe f off-colour
Ausdruck m (Zeilendrucker) hardcopy, output, print-out
ausdrucken (Beleg, Protokoll) to hard-copy, to output, to print out; (fertigdrucken) to complete printing
Ausdrucken von Vollflächen n printing-out of solids
Auseinanderdriften n (Drucktücher auf doppelbestückten Gummituchzyl.) gapping
ausfächern (Bogen) to fan out
ausfahrbares Aggregat n move-away unit, removable unit
ausfallsicher (System) fail-safe
Ausfallzeiten pl down times pl
Ausflecken n (Filmretusche) film masking, film opaquing, opaquing, retouching, spotting-out
Ausführpunkte pl (Satz) dot leaders pl
Ausführungszeichen n (Satz) close quote, end quotation mark
ausfüttern (Umschläge, Beutel usw.) to line
Ausgabe f (Buch) edition; (von Material, Daten) output; (Zeitschrift) edition, issue, number
Ausgabe auf Film f output on film
Ausgabeeinheit f output unit
Ausgabeformat n output format
Ausgabegerät n output device
Ausgabelichtquelle f (Scanner) expose light source
Ausgabematerial n (Scanner) output media
Ausgabemöglichkeiten pl output options pl
Ausgang m (Rotationsmaschine) delivery
Ausgangskolumne f (Spitzkolumne) short page
Ausgangskontrolle f final quality control
Ausgangszeile f (Satz) break line, broken line, last line, widow line
ausgeben (Beleg, Material usw.) to output
ausgebildeter Bediener m qualified operator, skilled operator, trained operator
ausgeglichener Satz m equally spaced type matter, evenly spaced type matter

ausgelassener Buchstabe m omitted letter
ausgeschlossener Text m justified copy, justified text
ausgesparte Lackierung f cut-out varnishing, pattern coating, spot varnishing
Ausgewogenheit der Seite (Typogr.) page balance
ausgleichen (typogr.) to space equally, to space evenly
Ausgleichen n (im Fotosatz auch) kerning
Ausgleichsretusche f balanced retouching
Ausgleichswalze f (Rollendruckm.) compensating roller
Ausgleichszurichtung f equalization makeready
Aushängebogen m advance sheet, specimen sheet
Aushängeexemplar n advance copy, specimen copy
auskopieren to burn out
auskuppeln to declutch, to disconnect, to disengage
Auslage f (Druckm.) delivery
Auslagebänder pl delivery belts pl, delivery tapes pl
Auslagebeleuchtung f delivery lighting
Auslagebelüftung f delivery fans pl
Auslagegreifer pl delivery grippers pl
Auslagekette f delivery chain
Auslagerechen m delivery rake
Auslageschüttler m delivery jogger
Auslageschutz m (Unfallschutz) delivery guard
Auslagestapel m delivery pile
Auslagetisch m delivery table
Auslagetransportsystem n delivery conveyor system
Auslandsnachrichten pl foreign news
auslassen (Satz) to miss out, to omit
Auslassungszeichen n (Apostroph) apostrophe
Auslastung f (Maschine, System) utilization
Auslauf m (Aggregat) outlet
Auslaufband n outlet conveyor
Auslaufen n (Farbe) bleeding, fading
Auslaufviskosimeter n efflux viscosimeter
auslegen (Bogen) to deliver
Auslegen n delivery
Ausleger m delivery
Auslegerkette f delivery chain
Auslegerwagen m delivery carriage
auslesen (Zwiebelfische, Handsatz) to pick out
ausleuchten to illuminate
Ausleuchtung f (Reprod., Kopie) illumination, lighting
ausliefern to deliver
Auslieferung f delivery; (Zeitschriften, Zeitungen) distribution

Auslieferungsroute - Auszeichnungszeile

Auslieferungsroute f delivery route
Auslieferungstermin m delivery date, delivery deadline, delivery time
auslösen *(Funktion)* to release
Ausmalung f *(Buch)* illumination
Ausnahmelexikon n *(Textverarb.)* exception (word) dictionary
ausnutzen *(technisch, kapazitätsmäßig)* to fully utilize, to make full use of
Ausnutzung f *(Maschine, System)* utilization
Auspreßwalze f squeeze roller
Auspunkten n insert leaders, leadering
Ausrichtemarke f guide mark
ausrichten to align, to register
Ausrichtung f alignment, registration
Ausrichtung auf Schriftlinie base alignment
Ausrückkupplung f disconnecting clutch
Ausrückung f *(mech.)* throw-off
ausrüsten to equip, to fit, to outfit
Ausrüstung f equipment
Ausrufungszeichen n exclamation mark
ausschaben to scrape out
Ausschaber m scraper
ausschalten *(Maschine, Aggregat)* to cut off, to declutch, to disconnect, to disengage, to stop, to switch off, to turn off
Ausschießbogen m imposition sheet
ausschießen to impose
Ausschießen n imposition
Ausschießschema n imposition layout, imposition pattern, imposition scheme
Ausschlagtafel f *(Buch)* fold-out (plate)
Ausschleusweiche f *(Prod.linie)* divert gate, reject gate
Ausschließbereich m *(Satz)* justification range, justification zone
ausschließen *(Satz)* to justify, to quad, to space
Ausschließen n *(Satz)* justification, quadding, spacing
Ausschließkeil m *(Zeilengießm.)* spaceband
Ausschließprogramm n justification routine
Ausschluß m *(Ausschließen)* justification, quadding, spacing; *(Ausschließstücke)* blank spaces pl, spaces pl
Ausschlußart f *(Satz)* justification mode, quadding mode
Ausschnitt m *(Bild)* section; *(Zeitungsausschnitt)* clipping; *(Zurichtung)* overlay
Ausschnittretusche f spot retouching
ausschreiben *(Ziffern, Abkürzungen)* to spell out (in full)
ausschuppen *(Stapel)* to fan out

Ausschußbogen m/pl spoil sheets pl, waste sheets pl
Außenaufnahme f outside photo(graph)
Außenbüro n *(Zeitung)* remote bureau, remote office
Außendienstmitarbeiter m sales rep(resentative)
Außendruckort m *(Zeitung)* remote printing operation, remote printing site
Außenredaktion f *(Zeitung)* remote editorial department, remote editorial site
Außenstelle f *(Redaktion, Anzeigen)* remote location
Außenwerbung f outdoor advertising
aussetzen *(fertigsetzen)* to complete setting; *(nicht abkürzen)* to spell out (in full)
aussortieren to sort out
Aussparung f *(Umbruch, Druck, Lackierung)* areas left blank pl, cut-out, space left white, window
ausstanzen to punch
Ausstanzung f punching
ausstatten to equip, to fit, to outfit
ausstechen *(mit Stichel)* to cut away
ausstopfen *(auswattieren)* to pad
Ausstoß m output
ausstoßen to output
ausstreichen *(Farbe)* to distribute; *(Text)* to delete, to strike out
Ausstreichrad n *(Bogenanlage)* stroke wheel
austauschbares Aggregat n interchangeable unit
austragen *(Zeitungen)* to deliver
austreiben *(Satz)* to drive out, to space out
Auswaschemulsion f wash-out emulsion
auswaschen to rinse, to wash off, to wash out
Auswaschfilm m wash-off film
Auswaschtinktur f washing solution
auswattieren *(Buchdeckel)* to pad
auswechselbares Aggregat n interchangeable unit
auswerfen to eject
Auswerfer m ejector
Auswinkelung f *(Bildverarb.)* squaring
auswölben *(Schachteldeckel)* to dome
auszählen *(Manuskript)* to count
auszeichnen *(Schrift)* to accentuate, to display, to stress; *mit Halbfetter* ~ to accentuate with bold, to display in bold; *mit Kapitälchen* ~ to accentuate with small caps, to display in small caps; *mit Kursiv* ~ to accentuate with italic, to display in italic
Auszeichnung f *(typogr.)* stressing
Auszeichnungsschrift f display characters pl, display type
Auszeichnungszeile f display line

Ausziehtusche f drawing ink
auszubildender Buchbinder m apprentice bookbinder
auszubildender Drucker m apprentice printer
auszubildender Setzer m apprentice compositor
Auszug m *(eines Artikels)* abstract, summary; *(Farbauszug)* separation; *(Kamera)* extension
Auszugsfilm m *(Farbreprod.)* separation film
Auszugsfilter m separation filter
Auszugsnegativ n separation negative
Auszugspositiv n separation positive
Autobiographie f autobiography
Autografie f autography
Automationsgrad m degree of automation
automatische Programmierung f automatic programming
automatische Scharf(ein)stellung f *(Kamera)* automatic focusing, auto-focus(ing)
automatische Steuerung f automatic control
automatisieren to automate
Autopaster m *(Rollenwechsler)* (automatic) paster, (automatic) reel change, (automatic) reel splicer, (automatic) reelstand, autopaster, web splicing unit
Autor m author
Autorabzug m author's proof
Autorenexemplar n author's copy
Autorenrecht n copyright
Autorhonorar n author's royalties pl
Autorkorrektur f author's alterations pl, author's corrections pl
Autotypie f autotype, halftone engraving, halftone etching
Autotypieätzung f *(Klischee)* halftone engraving, halftone etching
Autotypieplatte f halftone plate
Autotypieraster m halftone screen
Autotypieverfahren n halftone process
autotypische Ätzung f *(Tiefdruckzyl.)* halftone etching
autotypische Farbmischung f autotypical colour synthesis
autotypischer Tiefdruck m halftone gravure (process), variable-area gravure (process)
AV f *(Arbeits-/Auftragsvorbereitung)* job planning, job preparation, production planning, work planning, work preparation
AV-System job preparation system
Azetat n acetate
Azetatfolie f acetate film
azetatkaschierter Karton m acetate laminated board
Azureelinie f *(Satz)* cheques pl, combination rule

B

Backe f *(techn.)* clamp, jaw
Back-up n *(Comp.)* back-up
Bad n bath
Badbewegung f bath agitation
Baderschöpfung f bath exhaustion
Badspannung f *(Galv.)* bath voltage
Badstabilität f bath stability
Badstrom m *(Galv.)* bath current
Badumwälzung f bath circulation
Badverschmutzung f bath contamination
Bänderauslauf m belt delivery, tape delivery
Bänderführung f tape guide
Bänderkitt m tape cement
Bändertisch m belt table
Bändertransporteur m belt conveyor, conveyor belt
Bahn f *(Papierbahn)* web
Bahn(ab)riß m web break
Bahnabtastung f *(Registersteuerung)* web scanning, web sensing
Bahnauslauf m *(aus Aggregat)* web outlet
Bahnbefeuchtung f web moistening
Bahnbeobachtungsgerät n optical web scanner, web inspection unit, web viewer
Bahnbetrachtungsgerät n optical web scanner, web inspection unit, web viewer
Bahnbreite f *(Rollenpapier)* web width
Bahnbruch m web break
Bahnbrucherkennung f web break recognition
Bahnbruchmelder m web break detector
Bahnbruchsicherung f web break detector
Bahndehnung f web elongation, web stretch
Bahndurchlauf m web path, web travel
Bahneinlauf m *(in Aggregat)* web inlet, web entry, web infeed
Bahneinzug m threading-in, webbing-up, web infeed
Bahneinzugswerk n webbing-up device, web infeed unit, web threading device
Bahnflattern n web fluttering
Bahnführung f web guide, web lead
Bahnkantenabtastung f web edge sensing
Bahnkantenregelung f web aligner; *(im U. zur Bahnmittenregelung)* web edge control
Bahnkantensteuerung f web aligner; *(im U. zur Bahnmittenregelung)* web edge control
Bahnkappvorrichtung f web severing device
Bahnklebung f *(Rollenwechsel)* web pasting, web splicing

Bahnkühlung - bedienerfreundlich

Bahnkühlung *f* web cooling
Bahnlängensteuerung *f* web length control
Bahnlauf *f* web travel
Bahnlaufregelung *f* (automatic) web guide, web guiding system
Bahnlaufregler *m* (automatic) web guide, web guiding system
Bahnlaufrichtung *f* direction of web travel, grain (direction), paper grain, running direction; *gegen die ~ /quer zur ~* across the grain, across the web, against the grain, cross grain, cross web; *in ~* along the web, in line, long grain
Bahnleitwalze *f* idler roller, web guide roller, web lead roller
Bahnmittenregelung *f* web aligner; *(im U. zur Bahnkantenregelung)* web center control
Bahnnachbefeuchtung *f* (*nach Trockner*) web remoistening
Bahnoberseite *f* upper side of web
Bahnreiniger *m* web cleaner
Bahnreserve *f* (*im Rollenspeicher*) web reserve
Bahnriß *m* web break
Bahnschneidegerät *n* (*Längsschnitt*) web slitter
Bahnspannung *f* web tension
Bahnspannungsregelung *f* web tension control
Bahnspannungsschwankungen *pl* web tension fluctuations *pl*
Bahnspeicher *m* (*Schlaufenspeicher*) festooning unit
Bahnspleißung *f* (*Rollenwechsel*) web splicing
Bahntemperaturregelung *f* web temperature control
Bahntrocknung *f* web drying
Bahnüberwachung *f* web inspection, web monitoring
Bahnumlenkung *f* web deviation; *~ um 90°* bump turn of web
Bahnunterseite *f* lower side of web
Bajonettverschluß *m* bayonet lock
Balgen *m* (*Kamera*) bellows *pl*
Balgenauszug *m* bellows extension
Balken *m* (*Typogr.*) bold rule, thick line
Balkendrucker *m* bar printer
Balkenkode *m* bar code
Balkenüberschrift *f* banner headline
Ballardhaut *f* (*Tiefdruckzyl.*) ballard skin
Ballardverfahren *n* (*Tiefdruck*) ballard process
Ballen *m* (*Papier*) bale; (*zum Farbauftragen*) ink ball, tampon
Ballenlänge *f* (*Tiefdruckzyl.*) face length
Ballenpresse *f* baling press

Ballon-Trichter *m* (*Rollendruckm.*) balloon former
Band *m* (*Buch*) volume
Band *n* (*techn.*) belt, tape
Bandauslage *f* belt delivery, tape delivery
Bandbreite *f* (*Telekomm.*) bandwidth
Banderole *f* (*Zeitung*) wrapper
Banderoleneinschlag *m* banderoling; (*Folienverp.*) sleeve-wrapping
Banderolieren *n* banderoling; (*Folienverp.*) sleeve-wrapping
Banderoliermaschine *f* banderoling machine, banding machine; (*Folienverp.*) sleeve wrapping machine, sleeving machine
Banderolierpackung *f* banderoled pack
Bandiermaschine *f* banding machine
Bandlaufwerk *n* (*Magnetband*) magnetic tape drive, tape streamer
Bandmaß *n* tape measure
Bandstahlform *f* steel rule die
Bandstahlschnitt *m* steel rule die-cutting
Banknoten *pl* banknotes *pl*
Banknotendruck *m* banknote printing, currency printing
Banknotenpapier *n* banknote paper
Bankpostpapier *n* bank paper
Barock-Antiqua *f* (*Schriftklassif.*) Transitionals *pl*
Barytpapier *n* baryta paper
Barytstrich *m* baryta coating
Barytweiß *n* baryta white
Basisbelichtung *f* (*Reprod.*) basic exposure
Basisgewicht *n* (*Papier*) basic weight
Basisprogramm *n* (*Comp.*) basic program, basic software
Bastardschrift *f* bastard type
Baujahr *n* year of construction
Baukastensystem *n* (*modulares System*) modular system
bauschiges Papier *n* bulky paper
Bauschigkeit *f* (*Papier*) bulk
Bauweise *f* construction, design
Bay-Window-Einrichtung *f* (*Rollendruckm.*) bay-window facility
Beanspruchung *f* (*mech.*) load, stress
Bearbeitung *f* handling, processing
Becken *n* (*zum Auswaschen*) sink
Bedarf *m* demand
bedienen (*Masch.*) to operate, to run
Bediener *m* operator, user
Bedienereingriff *m* operator intervention
bedienerfreundlich operator-friendly, user-friendly

Bedienerfreundlichkeit - belichten

Bedienerfreundlichkeit *f* operator convenience, ease of operation, operating comfort
Bedienerführung *f* operator guide, user guide
Bedienerkonsole *f* operator console
Bedieneroberfläche *f* operator surface, user surface
Bedienerschnittstelle *f* user interface
Bedienerseite *f (im Gs. zur Antriebsseite)* control side, operating side
Bedienung *f* operation
Bedienungsablauf *m* operating cycle, operation sequence
Bedienungsanleitung *f* operating instructions *pl*
Bedienungselemente *pl* operating elements *pl*
Bedienungsfehler *m* operating fault
bedienungsfreundlich operator-friendly, user-friendly
Bedienungsfreundlichkeit *f* siehe Bedienerfreundlichkeit
Bedienungshandbuch *n* operating manual
Bedienungshebel *m* operating lever
Bedienungshilfe *f* operating aid
Bedienungsknopf *m* control button
Bedienungskomfort *m* ease of operation, operating comfort, operator convenience
Bedienungsperson *f* operator
Bedienungspersonal *n* operating personnel, operating staff
Bedienungspult *n* control desk
Bedienungsseite *f* control side, operating side
Bedienungssicherheit *f* operational reliability, operational safety
Bedienungsstand *m* control console, operating console
Bedienungstafel *f* control panel, operating panel
bedruckbar printable
Bedruckbarkeit *f* printability
Bedruckbarkeitsprüfgerät *n* printability tester
bedrucken to print on
Bedruckstoff *m* print(ing) carrier, printing material, printing substrate, stock
bedruckter Stoff *m (Textil)* printed fabric
bedruckte Seite oben printed side up
bedrucktes Gewebe *n* printed fabric
beeinträchtigen *(Qualität, Leistung)* to affect adversely
Befehl *m (Comp.)* command, instruction
Befehlsadresse *f (Comp.)* instruction address
Befehlsdaten *pl (Comp.)* command data
Befehlskette *f (Comp.)* command chain, command string, instruction chain
Befehlskode *m (Comp.)* instruction code
Befehlssprache *f (Comp.)* command language

befeuchten to damp(en), to moisten, to wet
Beflocken *n (Textildruck)* flocking
Begazemaschine *f (Buchb.)* gauzing machine
Begazen *n (Buchblock)* gauzing
begrenzte Auflage *f* limited edition
Behördendruckerei *f* local authority printing plant
beidseitig both-sided, double-sided, twin-sided, two-sided
beidseitig bedruckt printed (on) both sides
Beihefter *m* bound-in insert, insert
Beilage *f (red. Beilage)* supplement; *(Werbebeilage)* flyer, insert, inset, loose insert
Beilageneinsteckmaschine *f* inserting machine
Beilagenfalzeinrichtung *f (Inline-Fin.)* insert folder
Beilagenwerbung *f* insert advertising
bei laufender Maschine *f* during machine run, during press run, on the fly, on the run
beilegen *(Vorprodukte in Zeitung)* to insert
bei stehender Bahn *f* with standing web
Beistelldruck *m (Druckspannung)* impression pressure, printing impression, printing pressure; *leichter* ~ kiss printing
Beistrich *m (Komma)* comma
Beitrag *m (Publikation)* article
Beklebepapier *n (Buchdecke)* covering paper; *(Kaschierung)* lining paper
Beklebung *f (Buchdecke)* covering; *(Kaschierung)* lining
Belag *m (Gummituch, Walzen)* deposit
Belastung *f (mech.)* load, stress
Beleg *m* hardcopy, print-out
Belegausdruck *m* hardcopy, print-out
Belegausgabe *f* hardcopy output, print-out
Belegdrucker *m* hardcopy printer
Beleg erstellen *(Protokoll)* to hardcopy, to output a hardcopy
Belegexemplar *n (Inserent)* checking copy, evidence copy, file copy, voucher copy
Belegleser *m (Maschine)* copy reader, document reader
Beleglesung *f (Texterf.)* document reading
beleimen to glue
Beleimung *f* glue application, gluing
beleuchten to illuminate
Beleuchtung *f* illumination, lighting
Beleuchtungsverhältnisse *pl* lighting conditions *pl*
Beleuchtungswinkel *m* illumination angle
belichten *(Fotosatz)* to image, to photoset, to typeset; *(Kamera, Kopie)* to expose; *(Text/Bildsysteme)* to image, to output, to photoplot, to plot, to record

Belichten - beschränkte Auflage

Belichten n *(Fotosatz)* imaging, photosetting, typesetting; *(Kamera, Kopie)* exposure; *(Text/Bildsysteme)* imaging, output, photoplotting, plotting, recording

Belichter m *(Fotosatz)* imagesetter, photosetter, phototypesetter, typesetter; *(Text/Bildsysteme)* imagesetter, output unit, photoplotter, plotter, recording unit, exposure unit, imager, imaging unit, photo unit

Belichterschnittstelle f typesetter interface

Belichtung f *(Fotosatz)* imaging, photosetting, phototypesetting, typesetting; *(im Fotosatz auch)* character flash; *(Kamera, Kopie)* exposure; *(Text/Bildsysteme)* imaging, output, photoplotting, plotting, recording

Belichtungs(ab)lauf m exposure cycle, exposure routine, exposure sequence

Belichtungscomputer m exposure calculator, exposure computer

Belichtungsdauer f exposure time

Belichtungseinheit f *(Fotosatz)* imagesetter, photosetter, phototypesetter, typesetter; *(Text/Bildsystem)* imagesetter, output unit, photoplotter, plotter, recording unit, exposure unit, imager, imaging unit, photo unit

Belichtungseinstellung f exposure setting

Belichtungsfächer m exposure fan, stepped exposures pl

Belichtungsgeschwindigkeit f exposure speed, output performance, recording speed; *(im Fotosatz auch)* character flash, lay-down speed

Belichtungslampe f exposure lamp, exposure light source

Belichtungsleistung f exposure speed, output performance, recording speed

Belichtungsmesser m *(Meßgerät)* exposure meter, light meter

Belichtungsprogramm n exposure programme, imaging software

Belichtungsquelle f exposure light source

Belichtungsschaltuhr f exposure clock

Belichtungsspielraum m exposure latitude

Belichtungssteuerung f exposure control

Belichtungstabelle f exposure table

Belichtungstakte pl exposure cycles pl

Belichtungszeit f exposure time

belüften to aerate, to fan, to ventilate

Belüftung f aeration, ventilation

Belüftungsanlage f ventilating system

Benetzung f wetting

Bengel m *(Handpresse)* bar

Benutzer m operator, user

benutzerdefinierbar user-definable

Benutzerfeld n *(Bildschirmmaske)* user field

benutzerfreundlich operator-friendly, user-friendly

Benutzerführung f operator guide, user guide

Benutzeroberfläche f operator surface, user surface

berechnen *(in Rechnung stellen)* charge; *(Kosten kalkulieren)* to calculate the costs, to estimate the costs; *(Manuskript-, Satzumfang)* to count characters, to estimate the volume

Bereitschaftsschaltung f *(Durchlaufgeräte)* stand-by control

Berichterstatter m *(Zeitung)* correspondent, reporter

Berührungsbildschirm m touch screen

berührungslose Auslage f contact-free delivery

berührungsloser Transport m contact-free transport

berührungsloses Druckverfahren n non-impact printing (process)

Berufsgenossenschaft Druck f Printing Trades Association

beschichten to coat

beschichtete Seite f coated side

Beschichtung f coating

Beschichtung mit lichtempfindlicher Emulsion f *(Platten, Filme)* sensitizing

beschicken to feed, to load

Beschickung f *(Maschinen, Aggregate)* feed(ing), loading

Beschickungsgerät n feeder, loader

Beschickungsvorrichtung f feeder, loader, loading facility

Beschlag m *(Buchecken)* metal corners pl

Beschneidelinie f cutting line, trimming line

Beschneidemarken f/pl *(Bildverarb.)* crop marks pl; *(Druckbogen)* cutting marks pl, trim marks pl

beschneiden *(Bild)* to crop; *(Papier)* to cut, to trim

Beschnitt m trim(ming), trim-off

Beschnittabfall m shavings pl, trimmings pl, trim waste

Beschnittabsaugung f trim removal, waste exhaustion

Beschnittbereich m trim area

beschnittenes Format n trim(med) size

Beschnittmarken f/pl *(Bildverarb.)* crop marks pl; *(Druckbogen)* cutting marks pl, trim marks pl

Beschnittrand m trim edge

beschränkte Auflage f limited edition

beschriften to letter
Beschriftung *f* inscription, lettering
Beschwerwalze *f* rider roller
besprechen *(Buch)* to review
Besprechung *f (Buch)* review
Besprechungsexemplar *n (Buch)* review copy
Bestäuber *m (Druckbestäubung)* powder sprayer, spray powder device
Bestäubung *f (Druckbestäubung)* dry spraying, powder application, powder spraying
Bestäubungsapparat *m* powder sprayer, spray powder device
Bestäubungsgerät *n* powder sprayer, spray powder device
Bestand gespeicherter Texte *(Textverarb.)* text pool stored
Bestellbuch *n* order book
Bestellcoupon *m (Direktmail, Inline-Fin.)* order coupon
Bestellformular *n* order form
Bestellnummer *f* order number
Bestellzettel *m* order sheet
Besuchskarte *f* calling card, visiting card
betätigen to activate, to actuate, to operate
Betonungszeichen *n* stress mark
Betrachtungsleuchte *f* viewing light
Betrachtungsnorm *f* viewing standard
Betrachtungswinkel *m* viewing angle
betreiben to operate
Betrieb *m (Maschine)* operation, running, working
betriebliche Ausbildung *f* in-house training
Betriebsanleitung *f (Buch)* instruction manual, operating manual
Betriebsart *f (Maschine)* operating mode
betriebsbereit ready to go
Betriebsdaten *pl* operating data, operational data
Betriebsdatenerfassung *f* operational data recording
Betriebsdatenprotokollierung *f* operating data logging
Betriebsführung *f* plant management, technical management, works management
Betriebsgeschwindigkeit *f* operating speed
Betriebskalkulation *f* operation costing
Betriebskosten *pl* operating costs *pl*
Betriebsleiter *m* plant manager, technical manager, works manager
Betriebsleitung *f* plant management, technical management, works management
Betriebsplanung *f* operation(al) planning
Betriebsprogramm *n (Comp.)* operating program, operating software

betriebssicher reliable
Betriebssicherheit *f* operational reliability, operational safety
Betriebsstruktur *f* operational structure
Betriebsstunden *pl* operating hours *pl*
Betriebsstundenzähler *m* running time totalizer
Betriebssystem *n (Comp.)* operating system
Betriebszustand *m* operating condition, operating status
Bett *n (Fundament)* bed
Beurteilung *f (fachmännisch)* assessment, evaluation
Beutel *m* bag
Beuteldruck *m* bag printing
bewegliche Lettern *pl* movable type
beweglicher Bildschirm *m* movable screen
Bewegungsrichtung *f* sense of motion
bewerben *(Produkt)* to advertise, to publicize
beziehen *(Abonnement)* to be subscribed to, to subscribe to; *(Buchdeckel)* to cover
Bezieherliste *f (Abonnements)* list of subscribers
bezogene Feuchtauftragswalze *f* cloth-covered plate damper, covered damper roller
Bezug *m (Abonnement)* subscription; *(Buchdeckel)* covering
Bezugsleinen *n (Buchdecke)* book cloth, covering cloth
Bezugspapier *n (Buchdecke)* covering paper
Bezugsquellenverzeichnis *n (Zeitschriftenrubrik)* directory of suppliers
Bezugsstoff *m (Buchdeckel)* book cloth, covering cloth
Bibeldruckpapier *n* Bible paper, India paper
Bibliografie *f* bibliography
Bibliothek *f* library
Bichromatlösung *f (Tiefdruck)* dichromate solution
Biegefestigkeit *f* bending strength
biegen to bend
Biegepresse *f (Buchherst.)* bending press
Biegepresseur *m (Tiefdruck)* elastic impression roller, self-compensating impression roller
biegesteif *(Zylinder, Maschinenteile)* distortion-free, of high flexural strength
Biege- und Formpresse *f (Buchherst.)* bending and forming press
Biege- und Richtpresse *f (Buchherst.)* bending and straightening press
Biegewulst *m* bending bulge
biegsame Bindung *f (flexible B.)* flexible binding
Bierdeckel *m* beer mat
Bieretikett *n* beer label

Bild - Bildschirmzeitung

Bild *n* image, graphics, illustration, picture; *(im Text)* figure, text figure
Bildabtastung *f (Scanner)* image scanning
Bildänderung *f* image modification
Bildagentur *f* photo agency, photo service house; *(Telekomm.)* wire photo agency, wire photo service house
Bildarchiv *n* photographic archive, picture archive, picture library
Bildaufbereitung *f* image preparation
Bildauflösung *f* image resolution
Bildaufruf *m (Comp.)* image retrieval
Bildaufzeichnung *f* image recording, imaging
Bildaufzeichnungsgerät *n* image recorder
Bildausschnitt *m* image section, picture detail
Bildausschnittsbestimmung *f* determination of image section
Bildbearbeitung *f* image processing, image handling, image manipulation, image editing, graphics processing
Bildbericht *m* photo report, picture report
Bildbreite *f* image width
Bilddetail *n* picture detail
Bilddrehen *n* image rotation
Bildeinstellung *f (Kamera)* focusing, focus setting
Bildelement *n* image element, picture element, pixel
Bildempfänger *m (Telekomm.)* image receiver
Bildentzerrung *f* image rectification
Bilderbeilage *f* picture supplement
Bilderbuch *n* picture book
Bilderdienst *m (Agentur)* photo agency, photo service house
Bilderdruck *m* art print, art printing, illustration printing
Bilderdruckpapier *n* art paper, illustration printing paper
Bilderschrift *f* hieroglyphics *pl*, pictography
Bilderseite *f* picture page
Bilderstreifen *pl (Comic Strips)* comics *pl*, comic strips *pl*, picture strips *pl*
Bilderteil *m (Buch)* picture section
Bildertext *m* caption
Bilder übereinanderlegen to superimpose images
Bildfehler *m* picture defect; *(Fot.)* aberration
Bildfläche *f* image area
Bildform *f (Druckform, im U. zur Textform)* picture forme
bildfreie Stellen *f/pl* non-image areas *pl*, non-printing areas *pl*
Bildfreistellung *f* image cut-out, image silhouette
Bildgenerator *m* image generator

Bildgröße *f* image size, picture size
Bild-in-Bild-Kombination *f* image-in-image combination
Bildinformation *f (auch digital)* image information
Bild kippen to tilt an illustration
Bildkombination *f* image combination
Bildkontrast *m* image contrast
Bildkoordinate *f* image coordinate
Bildlinie *f (Abtastung)* scanline
Bildmanipulation *f (elektronisch)* image manipulation
Bildmater *f (im U. zu Textmater)* picture matrix
Bildmischen *n* image merging
Bildplatte *f* videodisc
Bildpositionierung *f* image positioning
Bildpostkarte *f* picture postcard
Bildprägung *f* picture embossing
Bildpunkt *m (elektronischer Bildaufbau)* pixel; *(Rasterpunkt)* halftone dot
Bildqualität *f* image quality, picture quality
Bildrand *m* edge of picture, picture margin
Bildraster *m* halftone screen
Bildredakteur *m* picture editor
Bildrekorder *m* image recorder
Bildschärfe *f* image definition, image resolution
Bildschirm *m* screen, video screen, video display terminal, video display unit, VDT, VDU, viewing screen, monitor
Bildschirmanzeige *f* screen display, video display, monitor display
Bildschirmarbeitsplatz *m* VDT workstation, video workstation
Bildschirmerfassung *f* terminal input
Bildschirmfenster *n* screen window
Bildschirmfunktion *f* monitor function
Bildschirmgerät *n* VDT, VDU, video display terminal, video display unit
Bildschirmkode *m* screen code
Bildschirmkorrektur *f* on-screen editing, video editing
Bildschirmmaske *f* screen mask, video mask
Bildschirmschrift *f* generic characters *pl*, video characters *pl*, video type
Bildschirmspeicher *m* screen buffer, screen memory
Bildschirmteilung *f* screen splitting
Bildschirmterminal *m* VDT, video display terminal, video terminal
Bildschirmtext *m* videotext
Bildschirmzeile *f* screen line
Bildschirmzeitung *f* electronic newspaper, videotext

Bild schrägstellen - Blechemballage

Bild schrägstellen to tilt an illustration
Bildseite f picture page
Bildsender m *(Telekomm.)* image transmitter
Bildstellen pl *(im U. zu bildfreie Stellen)* image areas pl, printing areas pl
Bildstoß m image butting
Bildtafel f *(Buch)* plate
Bildteil m *(Buch)* picture section
Bildteilung f *(am Bildschirm)* image splitting
Bildtiefen f/pl image shadows pl
Bildträger m image carrier
Bildüberlappung f image overlap, image overlay
Bildüberschrift f caption
Bildübertragung f *(Kopie)* image transfer; *(Telekomm.)* image transmission
Bildumkehrung f *(Seitenverkehrung)* flip image, image reversal
Bild- und Textverarbeitung f image and text processing
Bildunterschrift f caption
Bildverarbeitung f image processing, image handling, image editing, image manipulation, graphics processing; *(EBV)* **elektronische ~** electronic image processing
Bildvergrößerung f image enlargement
Bildvorlage f picture copy
Bildwalze f *(Scanner)* image drum
Bildwiedergabe f image rendering, image reproduction
Bildzerlegung f *(Scanner)* image scanning
Bildzurichtung f *(Buchdruck)* makeready of illustrations
Billettdruckmaschine f ticket printing machine
Billettkarton m ticket board
Bimetallplatte f bimetal plate
Bimsstein m pumice stone
Bimssteinmehl n pumice powder
binärkodierte Dezimalzahlen (BCD) f/pl binary coded decimals (BCD)
Binärzahl f binary digit, bit
Binde f *(Buch)* band, belly band
Bindeart f binding method
Bindegerät n binding device
Bindegeräte n/pl binding equipment
Bindekosten pl binding costs pl
Bindemethode f binding method
Bindemittel n binder, binding agent, vehicle
binden to bind
Binden n binding
Bindequote f length of run, run
Bindestärke f binding thickness
Bindestrich m *(Satz)* dash, hyphen
Bindesystem n binding system

Bindeverfahren n binding method, binding process
Bindung f binding
biologisch abbaubar biodegradable
Bitdichte f bit density
Bitfolge f bit string
Bitmap f bitmap
Bitrate f bit rate
Bitslice n bit slice
Bits pro Sekunde bits per second
bitte umblättern please turn over
blanklaufende Walze f roller running blind, roller stripping
Blankobogen m blank sheet, white sheet
Blankoetiketten n/pl blank labels pl
Blankopapier n blank paper
Blankoseite f blank page, white page
Blankozeile f blank line, white line
blankschlagen *(Umbruch)* to blank, to leave blank
Blasdüse f air nozzle, blowing nozzle
Blase f *(Comic Strips)* balloon
Blasenbildung f *(Lack, Kaschierfolie, Heatsettrocknung usw.)* blistering
Blasluft f air blast, blast air
Blaslufttrommel f blast-air drum
Blasrechen m blast rake
Blas/Saugluft f *(Vorrichtung im Anleger)* suction/blower system
blasser Druck m pale impression
blaßgedruckte Stelle f *(Mönch)* imperfect ink coverage
Blatt n *(Papier)* sheet; *(Zeitung)* newspaper, paper
Blattfilm m *(im U. zu Rollfilm)* film cut to size, sheet film
Blattgolddruck m gold leaf printing
Blattleser m *(Texterf.)* page reader
Blattvergoldung f gold blocking
Blattzeichen n *(Buch)* bookmark
blauempfindlicher Film m blue-sensitive film
Blau-Gelb-Filterbelichtung f *(Reprod.)* blue-yellow filter exposure
Blaupause f blue print, diazo copy, diazo print, dyeline
Blechdose f can, tin
Blechdrucker m metal decorator, tin printer
Blechdruckmaschine f metal decorating machine, tin printing press
Blechdrucktuch n tin printing blanket
Blechemballage f metal container, metal packaging

Blechlackiermaschine - Bogenansaugung

Blechlackiermaschine *f* tinplate varnishing machine
Blechpackung *f* metal container, metal packaging
Blechschachtel *f* tin box
Blechtafel *f* sheet metal plate, tin plate
Blei *n* lead
Bleianode *f (Galv.)* lead anode
bleibt! *(Korrekturrücknahme)* stet
Bleibuchstaben *pl* lead characters *pl*, lead type
Bleichanlage *f (Papierherst.)* bleaching plant
Bleichbad *n* bleaching bath
Bleichen *n* bleaching
Bleichgold *n* pale gold
Bleikrätze *f* lead waste
Bleilegierung *f* lead alloy
Bleilinie *f* lead rule
Bleimater *f* lead matrix, lead mould
Bleimatrize *f* lead matrix, lead mould
Bleiprägung *f* lead mould
Bleisatz *m (Handsatz)* lead composition; *(Maschinensatz)* hot-metal composition
Bleisatzschrift *f* foundry type, hot-metal typeface, lead characters *pl*, lead type
Bleischnitt *m* lead cut, lead engraving
Bleistaub *m* lead dust
Bleistege *pl* lead furniture
Bleistereo *n* lead stereo
Bleistiftentwurf *m* pencil layout
Bleistiftzeichnung *f* pencil drawing
Bleiunterlage *f* lead base, lead mount
Blende *f* lens aperture, stop, diaphragm
Blendendurchmesser *m* stop diameter
Blendenebene *f* aperture plane, diaphragm plane
Blendeneinstellung *f* aperture adjustment, aperture setting
Blendenlamelle *f* diaphragm leaf
Blendenöffnung *f* lens aperture, stop
Blendenwert *m* lens aperture, stop
blendfreier Bildschirm *m* glare-free monitor
Blindband *m (Buch)* blank book, dummy, sample binding, sample volume
Blinddruck *m (Blindprägung)* blind embossing
Blindgußzeile *f* blank slug
Blindlaufen *n (Offsetplatte, Walze)* running blind
Blindmaterial *n (Bleisatz)* blank material, furniture, spacing material
Blindmuster *n (Musterband)* blank book, dummy, sample binding, sample volume
Blindpaginierung *f* blind folio, blind paging
Blindprägung *f* blind embossing
blindschlagen to blank, to leave blank
Blindsetzen *n* blind setting
Blindtastatur *f* blind keyboard
Blindtype *f (Handsatz)* spacer
Blindwerden *n (Schwinden der Zeichnung auf der Platte)* running blind
Blindzeichen *n* blank character
Blindzeile *f* blank line, white line
Blisterlack *m* blister varnish
Blisterpackung *f* blister box, blister packaging
Blitzlicht *n* flash, flashlight
Blitzlichtaufnahme *f (Fot.)* flash exposure, flash photo(graph)
Blitzlichtbelichtung *f* flash exposure
Block *m (Buchblock)* block; *(Satz)* block; *(zum Schreiben)* pad
Blockade *f (Bleisatz)* blacks *pl*, turned letter
Blockbuchstabe *m* block letter
Blockdiagramm *n* block diagram
Blocken *n (frischbedruckte Bogen)* blocking
Blockfertigung *f (Buchblock)* block production; *(Schreibblock)* padding
Blockfertigungsstraße *f (Buchblock)* block flow line
Blockfestigkeit *f (Druckfarbe)* blocking resistance
Blockheftmaschine *f (Buchblock)* block-stitching machine
Blockheftung *f (Buchblock)* block stitching; *(Schreibblock)* pad stapling
blockleimen to pad
Blockleimgerät *n* padding press
Blockleimung *f (Buchblock)* block binding; *(Schreibblock)* padding
Blockpressung *f (Buchblock)* block pressing
Blocksatz *m (Typogr.)* flush left and right, flush matter, flush setting, quad middle
Blockschrift *f* block capitals *pl*, block letters *pl*
Blockstärke *f (Buchblock)* block thickness
Blocktype *f (Handsatz)* block type
Blockverleimung *f (Buchblock)* block binding; *(Schreibblock)* padding
Bluten *n (Farbe)* bleeding
Blutlaugensalz *n gelbes* ~ potassium ferrocyanide; *rotes* ~ potassium ferricyanide
Bodenheftung *f (Faltschachtel)* bottom stitching
Bodenverschluß *m (Faltschachtel)* bottom locking
Bogen *m* sheet; *(Signatur)* signature
Bogenabschlagvorrichtung *f* sheet severer
Bogenabstreifer *m* sheet stripper
Bogenanklebemaschine *f* sheet gluing machine
Bogenanlage *f (Anlegen)* sheet feeding; *(Anleger)* sheet feeder
Bogenanleger *m* sheet feeder
Bogenansaugung *f* sheet suction

Bogenanschlag *m* sheet stop
Bogenauslage *f* sheet delivery
Bogenauslauf *m* *(aus Aggregat)* sheet outlet
Bogenausrichtung *f* sheet alignment, sheet registration
Bogenausschießen *n* signature imposition
Bogen beschleunigen to speed up sheets
Bogenbeschleunigung *f* sheet acceleration
Bogenbremse *f* sheet slow-down device
Bogendruckmaschine *f* sheet-fed (printing) press
Bogendurchgang *m* sheet pass, sheet travel
Bogendurchlauf *m* sheet pass, sheet travel; *in einem* ~ in one sheet pass
Bogendurchlaufkontrolle *f* sheet travel monitoring
Bogeneinlauf *m* *(in Aggregat)* sheet entry, sheet infeed
Bogeneinteilung *f* sheet division, sheet layout, sheet planning
Bogenende *n* rear edge of sheet, sheet tail
Bogenentnahme *f* *(Druckmaschinenauslage)* sheet pulling, sheet removal
Bogenentroller *m* edge-roll decurler, sheet decurler
Bogenerfassung *f* *(Greifer)* capture of sheet, seizure of sheet, sheet gripping
Bogenfänger *m* sheet catcher
Bogenfalzmaschine *f* sheet folder, sheet folding machine
Bogenformat *n* sheet format, sheet size
Bogenfreigabe *f* *(aus Greifern, Zylinderspalt)* sheet release
Bogenführung *f* sheet guide
Bogenführungselemente *pl* sheet guiding elements *pl*
Bogenführungsscheiben *pl* skeleton wheels *pl*
Bogengeradstoßer *m* sheet aligner, sheet jogger
Bogenglätter *m* edge-roll decurler, sheet decurler
Bogenglattstoßmaschine *f* sheet jogger
Bogengröße *f* sheet format, sheet size
Bogenhinterkante *f* rear edge of sheet, sheet tail
Bogenhochdruck *m* sheet-fed letterpress (printing)
Bogen im Doppelnutzen two-on signature
Bogenkante *f* sheet edge
Bogenkontrolle *f* sheet control
Bogenkorrektur *f* sheet correction, sheet revision
Bogenlampe *f* *(Reprod.)* arc lamp
Bogenlampenkohlen *f/pl* arc lamp carbons *pl*
Bogenlauf *m* sheet travel
Bogenliniermaschine *f* sheet ruling machine
Bogenlockerungsbläser *m/pl* *(Anlegersaugkopf)* sheet fanning blowers *pl*

Bogenmontage *f* sheet assembly
Bogenniederhalter *m* sheet hold-down device
Bogennorm *f* sheet title, signature title
Bogenöffnung *f* *(Falzbogen)* signature opening
Bogenoffset *m* sheet-fed offset
Bogenoffsetmaschine *f* sheet-fed offset press
Bogenpapier *n* paper cut to size, sheet paper
Bogenpreis *m* price per sheet
Bogen pro Stunde *(B/h)* sheets per hour
Bogenquerschneider *m* *(Rollendruckm.)* sheet cutter, sheeter
Bogenreiniger *m* sheet cleaner
Bogenrevision *f* sheet revision
Bogenrückseite *f* rear side of sheet, reverse side of sheet
Bogenschneider *m* sheet cutter, sheeter
Bogensignatur *f* sheet title, signature title
Bogenstapelung *f* sheet piling
Bogenstraffung *f* sheet straightening
Bogenteil *m* section, sheet section; *vierseitiger* ~ four-page section
Bogentiefdruck *m* sheet-fed gravure (printing)
Bogentiefdruckmaschine *f* sheet-fed gravure press
Bogentransport *m* sheet transport
Bogentrennung *f* sheet separation
Bogentrockner *m* sheet dryer
Bogenübergabe *f* sheet transfer
Bogenverlangsamung *f* sheet slow-down
Bogenvorausrichtung *f* sheet prealignment, sheet preregistration
Bogenvorderkante *f* front edge of sheet, lead edge of sheet
Bogenweiche *f* sheet deflector
Bogenwendetrommel *f* *(Schön- und Widerdruck)* sheet perfecting drum, sheet turning drum, sheet reversing drum
Bogenwendezylinder *m* *(Schön- und Widerdruck)* siehe Bogenwendetrommel
Bogenwendung *f* sheet turning, sheet reversing, sheet reversal
Bogenzähler *m* sheet counter
Bogenzählwerk *n* sheet counter
Bogenzahl *f* *(Druckverarb.)* number of signatures
Bogenzeichen *n* *(Signatur)* sheet signature
Bogenziffer *f* *(Signatur)* sheet signature
Bogenzuführung *f* sheet feeding
Bohren *n* *(Papierlochung)* drilling
Bohrmaschine *f* driller
Bohr- und Fräsmaschine *f* drilling and routing machine
Bologneser Kreide *f* Bologna chalk
Boltstichel *m* round chisel
Bolzen *m* *(Mechanik)* bolt

Bolzer *m (für Kupferstecher)* etching needle; *(Stichel)* scorper
Bordüre *f (Einfassung)* ornamental border
Bostonpresse *f* Boston press
Braunwerden *n (Fotos)* bronzing; *(Negative)* discoloration, staining
Breitbahn *f (Papier)* short grain
Breitbahnpapier *n* short grain paper
Breitband *n (Telekomm.)* broadband
Breitbandfilter *n (Densitometer)* wide-band filter
Breitbandkanal *m (Telekomm.)* broadband channel
Breiterdrucken *n (zum Bogenende hin)* fan-out
breite Schrift *f* expanded type
breitlaufende Schrift *f* expanded type
Bremswalze *f* braking roller
Brennebene *f (Optik)* focal plane
Brenner *m (Farbtrocknung)* burner
Brennpunkt *m (Optik)* focal point, focus
Brennweite *f (Optik)* focal length
Briefbogendruck *m* letterhead printing
Briefcouvert *n* envelope
Briefhülle *f* envelope
Briefkarte *f* letter-card
Briefkopf *m* letterhead
Briefmailer *m* lettermailer
Briefmarke *f* postage stamp
Briefmarkendruck *m* postage stamp printing
Briefpapier *n* letter paper, note-paper, stationery, writing paper; *(bedruckt)* letterhead paper
Briefumschlag *m* envelope
Briefumschlagfutterseide *f* envelope lining tissue
Briefumschlagmaschine *f* envelope-making machine
Briefumschlagpapier *n* envelope paper
Brillanz *f* brilliance
Bristolkarton *m* Bristol board
Bristolpapier *n* Bristol paper
Broadsheet-Format *f (Zeitung)* broadsheet size
Bromschleppe *f (Fotochemie, Entwicklungsmaschine)* bromide drag
Bronzedruck *m* bronze printing
Bronzedruckfarbe *f* bronze ink
Bronzedruckfirnis *m* bronze printing varnish
Bronzefarbe *f* bronze ink
Bronzepulver *n* bronze powder
Bronzeschrift *f* bronze letters *pl*, bronze type
Bronzestaub *m* bronze dust, bronze powder
Bronzeunterdruckfarbe *f* bronzing primer, bronzing size
Bronzierdruck *m* bronze printing, bronzing
bronzieren to bronze, to bronze-dust
Bronziermaschine *f* bronzing machine
Bronzierplüsch *m* bronzing plush
broschiert paperbound, stitched, wrappered
Broschüre *f* brochure, booklet, pamphlet, folder, leaflet
Broschürenbindung *f (im U. zur Hartdeckel-Buchbindung)* soft-cover binding
Broschürenheftung *f* booklet stitching, brochure stitching, pamphlet stitching
Broschürenherstellung *f* booklet production, brochure production, pamphlet production
Broschüreninhalt *m (ohne Umschlag)* brochure body, brochure content
Broschürenschnitt *m* flush cut
Broschürenumschlag *m* booklet cover, brochure cover, soft cover
Brotschrift *f* body type, bread-and-butter face
Bruchstrich *m (Satz)* fraction bar
Bruchziffern *pl* fractional numbers *pl; (Satz)* compound fractions *pl,* piece fractions *pl,* split fractions *pl*
Brückenbauweise *f (Rollendruckm.)* arch-type construction
Brückenkamera *f* bridge-type camera, gallery-type camera, overhead camera
BTX *n* videotext
Buch *n* book
Buchabpreßmaschine *f* book backing machine
Buchaushänger *m* drop-out, hang-out
Buchausstattung *f* book design, get-up of a book
Buchausstellung *f* Book Fair
Buchauszug *m* abstract, extract
Buchbeschlag *m* metal corners *pl*
Buchbesprechung *f* book review
Buchbinde *f* band, belly band
Buchbindekunst *f* art of bookbinding
Buchbinden *n* binding, bookbinding
Buchbinder *m* bookbinder
Buchbinderei *f (Handwerk)* bookbinding, binding, finishing; *(Unternehmen)* bookbinder; *(Abt. in Druckerei)* binding department, finishing department
Buchbindereimaschine *f* binding machine
Buchbindereimaschinen *pl* binding equipment, binding machinery
Buchbindereitermin *m* date of bookbinding
Buchbinderfarbe *f* bookbinder's ink
Buchbindergaze *f* binding gauze
Buchbinderhammer *m* bookbinder's hammer
buchbinderische Verarbeitung *f* finishing, paper processing, print converting, print finishing
Buchbinderleder *n* binding leather
Buchbinderleim *m* binding glue

Buchbinderleinen *n* binding cloth, bookbinder's calico
Buchbindermeister *m* master of bookbinding
Buchbindermesser *n* bookbinder's knife
Buchbindernadel *f* bookbinder's needle
Buchbinderpappe *f* bookbinder's board
Buchbinderpresse *f* binding press
Buchbinderschrift *f* bookbinder's type
Buchbinderstempel *m* bookbinder's brass
Buchbindetechnik *f* binding technique
Buchblock *m* book block
Buchblockanleger *m* book block feeder
Buchblockpresse *f* smashing machine
Buchdecke *f* book case, book cover
Buchdeckel *m* book cover, cover board
Buchdeckenautomat *m* automatic casemaker
Buchdeckenfertigung *f* casemaking
Buchdeckenmaschine *f* casemaker, casemaking machine
Buchdekoration *f* book decoration
Buchdreischneider *m* book trimmer
Buchdruck *m* letterpress (printing)
Buchdruckätzung *f (Klischee)* siehe Ätzung, Autotypieätzung, Klischee, Klischeeätzung
Buchdruckbogenrotation *f* sheet-fed letterpress rotary
Buchdruck-Eindruckwerk *n* letterpress imprinting unit
Buchdrucker *m* letterpress printer
Buchdruckerballen *m* leather ball, printer's ball, tampon
Buchdruckerei *f* letterpress printer, letterpress printshop
Buchdruckfarbe *f* letterpress ink
Buchdruckfarbwerk *n* letterpress inking unit
Buchdruckfirnis *m* letterpress varnish
Buchdruckgummituch *n* letterpress rubber blanket
Buchdruckhandpresse *f* hand-operated letter-press, hand press
Buchdruckklischee *n* siehe Ätzung, Autotypieätzung, Klischee, Klischeeätzung
Buchdruckmaschine *f* letterpress machine
Buchdruckpresse *f* letter-press
Buchdruckrollenrotation *f* letterpress rotary, web-fed letterpress machine
Buchdruckschwarz *n* letterpress black
Buchdruckwalze *f* letterpress roller
Buchdruck-Zylindereinschub *m* letterpress cartridge, slide-in letterpress unit
Buchecke *f* book corner
Bucheignerzeichen *n* exlibris
Bucheinband *m* bookbinding, book cover
Bucheinbandentwurf *m* book-cover design
Bucheinbandpapier *n* bookbinding paper, book cover paper
Bucheinhängemaschine *f* casing-in machine
Buchfertigung *f* book production
Buchfertigungsstraße *f* book flow line, book production line
Buchformat *n* book format, book size
Buchformen *n (Formpresse)* book forming
Buchformpresse *f* book forming and pressing machine
Buchgestalter *m* book designer
Buchgestaltung *f* book design
Buchhändler *m* bookseller
Buchhandel *m* book trade
Buchhandlung *f* bookshop, bookstore
Buchheftmaschine *f (Fadenheftung)* book-sewing machine
Buchherstellung *f* book production
Buchillustration *f* book illustration
Buchillustrator *m* book illustrator
Buchinhalt *m (ohne Einband/Umschlag)* body of book, book content
Buchklammer *f (Klebebinder)* book clamp
Buchkunst *f* art of the book
Buchladen *m* bookshop
Buchleinen *n* book linen, book calico, binding cloth, book cloth
Buchmalerei *f* book illumination
Buchmesse *f* Book Fair
Buch mit flachem Rücken flat-spine book, square-back book
Buch mit rundem Rücken round-back book, round-spine book
Buchrücken *m* backbone, back of book, book spine
Buchrückenbearbeitung *f* backbone preparation, book spine preparation
Buchrückenbeleimmaschine *f* book spine gluing machine
Buchrückenbeleimung *f* book spine gluing
Buchrückenform *f* book spine shape
Buchrundemaschine *f* book rounding machine
Buchrunden *n* book rounding
Buchrunde- und Abpreßmaschine *f* book rounding and backing machine
Buchschleife *f (Buchbinde)* band, belly band
Buchschmuck *m* book ornamentation, book decoration
Buchschnitt *m* book edge
Buchschrift *f* book face, book fount
Buchstabe *m* type, letter, character

Buchstabenabstand *m* character fit(ting), character spacing, interspacing, letterspacing, type fit
Buchstabenbreite *f* character set, character width, font width, set (size), width of letter
Buchstabendrehung *f* character rotation
Buchstabenfolge *f* character string
Buchstabenmatrize *f* type matrix
buchstabieren to spell
Buchstapler *m* book stacker
Buchtitel *m* book title
Buchumfang *m* book pagination, page count
Buchumschlag *m* book cover, book jacket, book wrapper
Buchverleger *m* book publisher(s *pl*)
Buchzeichen *n* *(Lesezeichen)* bookmark
Bücherdruck *m* book printing, bookwork
Bücherpapier *n* book paper
Bünde *pl* *(Buch)* bands *pl*, cords *pl*, ribs *pl*
Bündel *n* *(Paket, Versandraum)* batch, bundle
Bündelmaschine *f* bundling machine
Bündelpresse *f* *(Papierabfall)* baling press
bündig flush
bündiger Titel *m* flush head
bündig geschnitten *(Buch)* trimmed flush
bündig setzen *(Zeile ohne Einzug)* to set flush
Bündigstoßer *m* *(Bogenauslage)* side jogger
Büroautomation *f* office automation
Bürodokumentation *f* office documentation
Bürodruckmaschine *f* office duplicator
Büroformulare *pl* office forms *pl*
Bürokopierer *m* office copier
Bürosatz *m* *(Typogr.)* office typesetting
Bürovervielfältiger *m* office duplicator
Bürste *f* brush
bürsten to brush
Bürstenabzug *m* brush proof
Bürstenfeuchtwerk *n* *(Offset)* brush-type damping system
Bürstenrolle *f* *(Anlegertisch)* brush roll
Bürstenwalze *f* brush roller
Bütte *f* vat
Büttenkarton *m* hand-made board
Büttenpapier *n* hand-made paper
Büttenpresse *f* vat-press
Büttenrand *m* deckle edge
Büttenrandpapier *n* deckle-edged paper
Bund *m* back(-edge) margin, binding edge, binding margin, inner margin
Bundfalz *m* back fold
Bundsteg *m* gutter margin; *(Bleisatz)* gutterstick
bunt chromatic, coloured

Buntaufbau *m* *(Reprod.)* chromatic composition, chromatic construction
Buntdruck *m* colour printing, multi-colour printing
Buntdruckform *(im U. zur Schwarzform)* colour forme
bunte Farbe *f* *(Reprod.)* chromatic colour
buntes Papier *n* coloured paper, tinted paper
Buntfarbenaddition *f* *(Reprod.)* chromatic colour addition
Buntfarbendruck *m* colour printing, multi-colour printing
Buntpapier *n* coloured paper, tinted paper
Buntwert *m* chromatic value; *(im Gs. zum Grauwert)* non-neutral (tone)
Butzen *m/pl* hickies *pl*; *(Papierfusseln)* lint
Butzenfänger *m* hickey remover
Byte *n* byte

C

CAD (computergestützte Entwicklung) CAD (computer-aided design)
CAM (computergestützte Herstellung) CAM (computer-aided manufacturing)
Cartoon *m* cartoon
CCD-Kamera *f* CCD camera
CCD-Optik *f* CCD optics
CCD-Scanner *m* CCD scanner
Cedille *f* *(Satz)* cedilla
Cellophan *n* cellophane, celluloid film
Cellophanieren *n* *(Glanzfolienkasch.)* film laminating, acetate laminating, celloglazing
cellophanierter Karton *m* film-laminated board
Chagrinpapier *n* shagreen paper
Chalkografie *f* chalcography
Changierbewegung *f* *(Walzen)* oscillation
changierende Walze *f* oscillating roller, reciprocating roller
Chefredakteur *f* chief editor, editor-in-chief
Chemigraf *m* blockmaker, photo-engraver, process engraver
Chemigrafie *f* blockmaking, photo-engraving, process engraving
chemigrafische Anstalt *f* blockmakers *pl*, process engravers *pl*
Chemikalien *pl* chemicals *pl*

chemikalienbeständig chemical resistant
chemisches Symbol n *(Satz)* chemical sign
chemisches Zeichen n *(Satz)* chemical sign
Chiffreanzeige f box number advertisement
Chiffre-Nummer f *(Anzeige)* box number
Chinapapier n China paper, Chinese paper, India paper
chinesische Tusche f Indian ink
Chrom n chrome, chromium
chromatische Farbabweichung f *(Linse)* chromatic aberration
Chrombad n *(Tiefdruck)* chrome bath
Chromelektrolyt n *(Tiefdruck)* chrome-electrolyte
Chromgelatine f bichromated gelatine
Chromnickelstahl m chrome nickel steel
Chromoduplexkarton m chromo duplex board
Chromoersatzkarton m imitation chromo board
Chromokarton m chromo board
Chromolithograf m chromolithographer
Chromolithografie f chromo(lithography)
Chrompapier n chromo paper
Chrompolieren n *(Tiefdruckzyl)* chrome polishing
Chromrißdichte f *(Tiefdruckzyl.)* chrome fracturing density
Cicero n *(Typogr.)* cicero
Co-Autor m joint author
Coldset-Rollenoffset m *(ohne Trocknung)* cold-set web offset
Colordia n chrome, colour slide, colour transparency
Colorduplikat n colour duplicate
Colorduplikatherstellung f colour duplicating, duplication of colour transparency
Color-Hologramm n colour hologramme
Colorkey m *(syn. für Farbdurchsichtsproof)* acetate colour proof, colour key, overlay colour (film) proof
Comic Strips pl comics pl, comic strips pl
Compact Disc f compact disc
Compiler m *(Comp.; Übersetzungsprogramm)* compiler
Composersatz m *(z. B. IBM-Composer)* composer setting
Computer m computer
Computerformular n computer form
computergesteuert computer-controlled, computerized
computergestützt computer-aided
Computergrafik f computer graphics
Computerlauf m computer cycle, computer run
Computerperipherie f computer peripherals pl

Computerprogramm n computer program, computer software
Computersatz m *(Schriftsatz)* computer(ized) typesetting
Computerspeicher m computer memory
Computer-Tabellierpapier n listing paper
Computer-to-Plate-System n computer-to-plate system
COM (Rechnerausgabe auf Mikrofilm) COM (computer output on microfilm)
Containerpappe f container board
Copyright n copyright
Copyrightvermerk m copyright imprint
Corporate Publishing n corporate publishing
Crimplock-Einrichtung f *(Formularsatzherst.)* crimplock device
crimplockgehefteter Satz m *(Formularsatzherst.)* crimplock set
Crimplock-Heftung f *(Formularsatzherst.)* crimping, crimplocking, hooklocking
Cromalin n *(syn. für Farbaufsichtsproof)* cromalin, hardcopy colour proof
CRT-Belichter m *(Fotosatz)* CRT exposure unit, CRT photosetter, CRT photo unit
Cyan n *(Skalenfarbe)* cyan
Cyanauszug m *(Reprod.)* cyan separation
Cyanfilm m *(Auszugsfilm)* cyan film, cyan printer
Cyanform f cyan forme
Cyanplatte f cyan plate, cyan printer

D

Dachkantspiegel m *(Kamera)* double reversing mirror
Daguerreotypie f *(Verfahren und Bild)* Daguerreotype
Dampfentwicklung f *(Ammoniak)* vapour development
darstellen *(am Bildschirm)* to display, to represent
Darstellungsbildschirm m *(typogr./layoutgerechte Echtdarstellung im Fotosatz)* preview terminal, soft-copy monitor, soft typesetter
Darstellungsformat n *(Bildschirm)* display format

Data-Mailer - Defekte

Data-Mailer *(personalisierte Werbedrucksache)* data mailer
Datei *f* data file, file
Dateiverwaltungssystem *n* data management system, file manager (system)
Daten *pl* data; *(Datensatz)* data file, file
Daten (ab)speichern to save data, to store data
Datenaktualisierung *f* data update
Datenausgabe *f* data output
Datenaustausch *m* data exchange
Datenauswertung *f* data evaluation
Datenbank *f* data bank, database
Datenbasis *f* database
Datenbestand *m* database, data pool
Datendekomprimierung *f* data decompression
Dateneingabe *f* data entry, data input
Datenendgerät *n (Terminal)* data terminal
Datenerfassung *f* data collection, data recording
Datenfernübertragung *f (DFÜ)* data teletransmission
Datenfluß *m* data flow
Datenformat *n* data format
datengesteuert data-controlled
datengesteuerte Plattenbelichtung *f* computer-to-plate exposure
datengesteuertes Plattenkopiersystem *n* computer-to-plate system
Datenkanal *m* data channel
Datenkommunikation *f* data communication
Datenkompression *f* data compression
Datenkomprimierung *f* data compression
Datenkonverter *m* data converter
Datenkonvertierung *f* data conversion
Datenleitung *f* data line
Datenmenge *f* data set
Datennetz *n* data network
Datensatz *m* data file, data record, file, record
Datensicherung *f* back-up, data back-up, data securing
Datensichtgerät *n* data screen, data terminal
Datenspeicher(ung) *m/f* data storage, file storage
Datenträger *m* data carrier
Datenübermittlung *f* data transmission
Datenübernahme *f* data transfer
Datenübertragung *f* data transfer, data transmission
Datenübertragungskanal *m* data transmission channel
Datenübertragungsrate *f* data transmission rate
Datenverarbeitung *f* data processing, DP (data processing)
Datenverbindung *f* data link
Datenverbund *m* data network

Datenverwaltung *f* data management, file management
Datenverwaltungssystem *n* data management system, file manager (system)
Dauerbetrieb *m* continuous operation, permanent service
dauerhafte Bindung *f* durable binding
Dauerlast *f* continuous load
Dauerölschmierung *f* continuous oil lubrication
Daumenprobe *f (Papier)* thumb test
Daumenrad *n* thumb wheel
Daumenregister *n (Griffregister)* thumb index, thumb register
Daumenregisterausschnitt *m* thumb index cutting
D/A-Wandler (Digital-Analog) *m* D/A converter (digital-analogue)
DDCP (direkt-digitale Farbproofherstellung) DDCP (Direct Digital Colour Proofing)
DDES (Digitaldatenaustausch-Standard) DDES (Digital Data Exchange Standard)
Deckblatt *n (Bindung)* cover sheet; *(Versandraum)* top sheet; *(Zurichtung im Buchdruck)* drawsheet
Deckblattanleger *m (Versandraum)* top sheet feeder
Decke *f (Buchdecke)* book case, book cover
Deckelaufzug *m (Handpresse)* tympan packing
Deckelpappe *f (Buchb.)* binder's board, bookbinder's board, cover board
Deckenbiegeapparat *m (Buchherst.)* automatic casebender
deckend *(im Gs. zu lasierend)* opaque
deckende Retusche *f* opaque retouching
Deckenmachmaschine *f (Buchherst.)* casemaking machine
Deckenrückenformstation *f (Buchherst.)* case forming station
Decker *m (Reprod.)* mask, overlay
Deckerprioritätssteuerung *f (Bildverarb.)* overlay priority control
Deckertransparent *n (Vorlagenherst., Reprod.)* overlaid tracing
Deckfähigkeit *f (Farbe)* coverage properties *pl*, opaqueness
Deckfarbe *f* opaque ink
Deckkraft *f (Farbe)* coverage properties *pl*, opaqueness
Deckpapier *n* covering paper
Deckrechen *m (Falzm.)* buckle guide, overlay rake
Deckung *f (Farbe)* coverage; *(Film)* density
Deckweiß *n* opaque white, zinc white
Defekte *pl (Bleisatz)* sorts *pl*

Defekten *m/pl (fehlerhafte Bücher)* remainders *pl*
definieren *(Comp.)* to define
Definition *f (Comp.)* definition
Dehnfestigkeit *f (Gummituch, Gewebe)* stretch stability, tensile strength
Dehnung *f (Gummituch, Gewebe)* stretch
Dehnungsbeanspruchung *f (Gummituch, Gewebe)* tension stress
Deinking *n (Papier)* de-inking
Dekalkomanie *f* decalcomania
dekantieren to decant
Dekapierbad *n (Tiefdruckzyl.)* polishing bath
Dekoder *m* decoder
dekodieren to decode
Dekodierung *f* decoding
Dekorationsdruck *m* decoration printing, decorative printing
Dekorationspapier *n* decorative paper, fancy paper
Dekorschrift *f* decorative type, fancy type
Dekupiersäge *f* jig saw, scroll saw
Deleaturzeichen *n (Korrekturlesen)* delete mark
Deltafalz *m* delta fold, single gate fold
demografisches Splitting *n (Versandraum)* demographic splitting
demografisches Versandsystem *n* demographic mailroom system
demontieren *(Maschine)* to disassemble, to dismantle
Densitometer *n* densitometer
Densitometermeßwagen *m* densitometer carriage
Densitometrie *f* densitometry
densitometrische Abtasteinheit *f* densitometric scanning unit
densitometrische Messung *f* densitometric measurement
den Stand machen to bring into position, to bring into register, to position, to register
desensibilisieren to desensitize
Design *n* design
Designer *m* designer; *(Vorlagenherst.)* graphic designer
Desktop Publishing *n (DTP)* desktop publishing
Desktop-Satz *m* desktop composition, desktop type matter
Dessindruck *m* pattern printing
Dessinwalze *f* design roller, engraved roller, pattern roller
Detailkontraststeigerung *f (Scannerfunktion)* peaking, sharpness enhancement
Details *pl (Bild)* definition, details *pl*

Detailwiedergabe *f (Reprod.)* detail rendering, detail reproduction, detail separation
Dextrinleim *m* dextrine glue, dextrine gum
Dezimalpunkt *m* decimal point
Dezimalsystem *n* decimal system
Dezimalzahlen *pl* decimal figures *pl*
DFÜ-Einrichtung *f (Telekomm.)* telecommunication facilities *pl*
Dia *n* slide, transparency
Diabetrachter *m* slide viewer, transparency viewer
Diärese *f (Satz)* diaeresis
Diagonalausschluß *m (Bleisatz)* angular spaces and quads *pl*
diagonale Registerverstellung *f* cylinder cocking
Diagonalverstellung des Registers *(Druckm.)* cylinder cocking
Diagramm *n* diagram, graph
diakritische Zeichen *n/pl* cryptics *pl*
Dialeuchtplatte *f* slide viewing box, transparency viewing box
Dialeuchtwand *f* slide viewing wall, transparency viewing wall
dialogorientiert *(interaktiv)* interactive
Diapositiv *n* diapositive
Diarekorder *m* transparency recorder
Diaskop *n* diascope
Diazobeschichtung *f* diazo coating
Diazo-Entwicklungsmaschine *f (Reprod.)* diazo processor
Diazofarbstoff *m* diazo dye
Diazofilm *m* diazo film
Diazofolie *f* diazo film
Diazokopierschicht *f (Siebdruck)* diazo screen emulsion
Diazotypie *f* diazotype
Diazoverbindung *f* diazo compound
Dichromat-Gelatineschicht *f* dichromate gelatine coating
Dichte *f (opt.)* density
Dichteabweichung *f* density deviation
Dichtedifferenz *f* density difference
Dichtekontrollzeichen *n (Fotosatz)* density control mark, density control wedge
Dichtemesser *m* densitometer
Dichtemeßgerät *n* densitometer
Dichtemessung *f* densitometric measurement, densitometry, density measurement; *(Entwicklungsm.)* density scanning
Dichte Raster *(DR; Densitometrie)* halftone density, screen density
dichtes Negativ *n* dense negative
Dichteumfang *m* density range

Dichteumfangsverlängerung - Doppelbild

Dichteumfangsverlängerung f *(Reprod.)* density range extension

Dichte Vollton *(Dv; Densitometrie)* solid tone density

Dichtewert m density value; *(angezeigter)* density reading

Dickdruckpapier n bulky paper, thick printing paper

Dickenmesser m thickness gauge

dicker und dünner Rahmen ineinander heavy and thin boxes pl

dickflüssige Farbe f stiff ink, tacky ink, thick ink, viscous ink

Dickflüssigkeit f high viscosity

Dickte f *(Buchstabe)* character set, character width, font width, set (size), set width, width of letter

Dicktenkarte f *(Fotosatz)* width card

Dicktentabelle f *(Fotosatz)* width table

Didot-Punkt m *(Typogr.)* point Didot

Didotsches System n *(Typogr.)* Didot system

die Farbe liegt ab the ink sets off

die Farbe rupft the ink picks

die Farbe schlägt weg the ink penetrates, the ink strikes in

die Farbe setzt zu *(Rasterpartien)* the ink fills up

Dienstleistungsunternehmen n service house

Dienstprogramm n utility program

Diffusionslichthof m diffusion halo

Diffusionsübertragung f *(Reprod.)* diffusion transfer

Digitalanzeige f digital display, digital read-out

Digitalbelichter m *(Fotosatz)* digital typesetter, digital exposure unit, digital imager

Digitalbild n digital image

digitale Bildverarbeitung f digital image processing

digitale Plattenherstellung f computer-to-plate exposure

digitaler Farbproof m digital colour proof

digitaler Fotosatz m digital phototypesetting

digitale Textverarbeitung f digital text processing

digitalisieren to digitize

Digitalisiergerät n *(CAD)* digitizer

Digitalisiertablett n digitizing tablet

digitalisierte Schrift f digitized font, digitized typeface

Digitalisierung f digitization

Digitalproof m digital proof

Digitalrechner m digital computer

Digitalschrift f digitized font, digitized typeface

Digitalspeicher m digital storage

Digitaltechnik f digital technology

Digitalübertragung f digital transmission

Digitalzeichen n digital character

DiLitho dilitho, direct litho

Dimensionsstabilität f dimensional stability

(DIN) A4 hoch A4 portrait, A4 up(right)

(DIN) A4 quer A4 broadside, A4 landscape, A4 oblong

Diphthong m diphthong

Direktbeschichtung f *(Siebdruck)* direct coating

direkt-digitale Farbproofherstellung f direct digital colour proofing

Direktdruckplatte f *(Kleinoffset)* instant paper plate

direktes Drucken n direct printing

Direktfilm m *(Siebdruck)* direct film

Direktkopie f *(Tiefdruck)* direct copy

Direktmailings pl direct mailings pl

Direktpositiv n direct positive

Direktpositivfilm m direct-positive film

Direktrasterauszüge m/pl direct halftone separations pl

Direktrasterung f direct screening

Direktschablone f *(Siebdruck)* direct stencil

Direktumkehrfilm m direct-positive film

Direktwerbedrucksachen f/pl direct mailings pl

Direktwerbung f *(Direktmail)* direct mail advertising

Direktzugriff m direct access, random access

Direktzugriffsspeicher (RAM) m random access memory (RAM), direct access storage

Diskette f *(Comp.)* diskette

Diskettenformat n diskette format

Diskettenkonverter m diskette converter

Diskettenlaufwerk n diskette drive

Diskettenleser m diskette reader

Dispergiermaschine f *(Farbherst.)* dispersion machine

Dispersion f dispersion

Dispersionskleber m *(Klebebindung)* dispersion glue, water-based adhesive

Dispersionslack m *(Drucklackierung)* dispersion coating, dispersion varnish, water-based varnish

Display n display, read-out

Disponent m production planner

Dittozeichen n repeat mark

Divis n *(Bindestrich, Trennstrich)* hyphen

Dokumentation f documentation; *(EDV)* record-keeping

Dokumentenpapier n document paper

Dokumentenverarbeitung f document processing

Doppelbild n *(Druck)* ghost image

Doppelbogenanleger *m* dual sheet feeder, twin sheet feeder, two-up feeder
Doppelbogenauslage *f* dual sheet delivery, twin sheet delivery, two-up delivery
Doppelbogenkontrolle *f* double sheet control, double sheet detector, two-sheet detector
doppelbreite Rollendruckmaschine *f* double-width rotary press, double-width web press
Doppelbuchstabe *m* double letter, ligature
Doppeldruckwerk *n (Bogendruckm.)* double printing unit; *(Rollendruckm., Perfektor)* blanket-to-blanket print unit
doppelfeine Linie *f* double fine rule, double hairline
Doppelform *f (Doppelnutzen)* double forme, two-up forme
Doppelgeviert *n (Satz)* two-em quad
doppelgroßer Druckzylinder *m* double-size impression cylinder
Doppellaufwerk *n (Comp.)* dual drive
Doppellaut *m (Diphthong)* diphthong
Doppellinie *f* double line, double rule
Doppelnutzen *m im* ~ imposed two-up, in two-up production, two-up
Doppelnutzenverarbeitung *f* two-up processing
Doppelparallelfalz *m* double parallel fold
Doppelpunkt *m* colon
Doppelrahmen *m (Typogr.)* double box
Doppelrakel *f (Siebdruck)* double squeegee, dual squeegee
Doppelrollenständer *m (Rollendruckm.)* double reelstand, turnover reelstand, two-arm reelstand
Doppelseite *f (durchgehend, Panoramaseite)* center spread, double(-page) spread, two-page spread; *(nicht durchgehend, im Planbogen an unterschiedlichen Stellen, im U. zur Panoramaseite)* bastard double, crossover
doppelseitig bedruckt printed (on) both sides
doppelseitige Druckplatte *f* double-sided printing plate
Doppelsiebpapiermaschine *f* twin-wire paper machine
Doppelstromauslage *f (Rollendruckm.)* double-stream delivery, dual-stream delivery
doppelte Anführungszeichen *pl* double quotes *pl*
Doppeltondruck *m* duo-tone printing
Doppeltrichter *m (Rollendruckm.)* balloon former
Doppeltrichterfalzapparat *m (Rollendruckm.)* double former folder, two-former folder
Doppelumfangs-Rollenoffsetmaschine *f* double-circumference web offset press
Doppelumfangszylinder *m* double-circumference cylinder
Doppelvokal *m* diphthong
doppelwandiger Zylinder *m* double-walled cylinder
Doppelzeile *f* double line
Dosierpumpe *f* metering pump
Dosierrakel *f* metering blade
Dosierwalze *f* metering roller
Dosierzylinder *m* metering cylinder
Double-Loop-Bindung *f* double-loop binding
D$_R$ *(Densitometrie)* halftone density, screen density
Drachenblut *n* dragon's blood
Draht *m (zum Heften)* wire
Drahtabspulvorrichtung *f* wire dispenser
Drahtbürste *f* wire brush
Drahtgaze *f* wire gauze
drahtheften to wire-stitch
Drahtheftklammer *f* wire staple
Drahtheftmaschine *f* wire stitching machine, wire stitcher
Drahtheftung *f* wire-stitching
Drahtheftung durch den Rücken back stitching, saddle stitching
Drahtkammbindemaschine *f* wire comb binding machine
Drahtkammbindung *f* wire comb binding
Drahtklammer *f* wire staple
Drahtkopf *m* wire head
Drahtringbindung *f* wire ring binding
Drahtrolle *f (Drahtheftung)* wire spool
Drahtstärke *f* wire gauge
Drehbank *f (Tiefdruckzyl.)* lathe
Drehbewegung *f* rotary motion
Drehmomentschlüssel *m* torque wrench
Dreh-/Neigesattel *m (Schneidem.)* swivel/tilting backgauge
Drehraster *m (Kamera)* circular screen
Drehrichtung *f (Zyl.)* sense of rotation
Drehsauger *m (Anlegersaugkopf)* rotary sucker
Drehstapler *m* rotary stacker
Drehsternwickler *m* turret unwinder
Drehstrom *m* alternating current, A.C., three-phase current
Drehstromantrieb *m* A.C. drive
Drehstrommotor *m* A.C. motor
Drehtisch *m* turntable
Drehzahlregelung *f* speed control
Dreibruchfalz *m* three-directional fold
Dreibruch-Fensterfalz *m* three-directional gatefold

Dreibruch-Kreuzfalz - Druckerei

Dreibruch-Kreuzfalz *m* three-directional right-angle fold
3D-Hologramm *n* 3D hologram
3D-Objekt *n* 3D object
Dreifalz *m (Rollendruck)* quarter fold
Dreifarbendruck *m* three-colour printing
Dreimesserautomat *m* automatic three-knife trimmer
Dreipunktanlage *f (Bogenanlage)* three-point lay
Dreischichtbetrieb *m* three-shift operation
Dreischneider *m* three-knife trimmer
Dreiseitenbeschnitt *m* three-sided trimming
Dreiseitenschneider *m* three-knife trimmer
dreispaltige Seite *f* three-column page
Dreivierteltön *m (ca. 75% Flächendeckung)* three-quarter tone
Dreivierteltönrasterfeld *n (Druckkontrollstreifen)* three-quarter tone tint patch
Dreiwalzwerk *n (Farbherst.)* three-roll mill
Driografie *f* driography
Drittelgeviert *n (Satz)* three-to-em space
dritter Falz *m (Rollendruck)* quarter fold
dritte Umschlagseite *f* third cover
Driversoftware *f (Belichter)* driver software
Druck *m (Abdruck)* print; *(Druckarbeit)* printwork; *(mechanisch)* impression, pressure; *(Druckvorgang)* printing
Druckabnahme *f* acceptance of printwork
Druck abstellen to throw off impression
Druckabstellung *f* impression throw-off
Druckabwicklung *f* cylinder rolling
Druck an/ab impression on/off
Druckanfang *m (auf Bogen)* first line of print, lead edge of print, print start
Druckanlage *f (Druckmaschine)* printing plant; *(im U. zur Falzanlage)* printing lay, print lay mark
Druckanlauf *m* printing start-up
Druck anstellen to throw on impression
Druckanstellung *f* impression throw-on
Druckan- und -abstellung *f* throw-on/off impression
Druckarbeit *f* print(ing) job, printwork
Druckauflage *f* print run, production run
Druckauftrag *m* print(ing) job, print(ing) order
Druckausfall *m (Qualität)* print(ing) quality, print(ing) result
Druckausgabe *f* edition
Druckbedarfsartikel *pl* printer's supply, printing sundries *pl*
Druckbedarfsgeschäft *n* printer's supplier
Druckbedingungen *pl* printing conditions *pl*
Druckbeginn *m* print start

Druckbeistellung *f* printing impression, printing pressure, setting of printing pressure; *zu hohe* ~ cylinder squeeze
Druckbeistellung zwischen Gummi- und Druckzylinder blanket to impression cylinder pressure
Druckbeistellung zwischen Gummi- und Plattenzylinder blanket to plate cylinder pressure
Druckberater *m* graphic arts consultant
Druckberatung *f* graphic arts consultation
Druckbestäuber *m* powder sprayer, spray powder device
Druckbestäubung *f* dry spraying, powder application, powder spraying
Druckbestäubungspuder *n* anti set-off powder, offset spray (powder), spray powder
Druckbild *n* printed image, print(ing) image
Druckbild offenhalten to keep open the image
Druckbildträger *m* print image carrier
Druckbogen *m* printed sheet, print(ing) sheet, signature
Druckbogen abnehmen *(Kunde)* to pass a print sheet
Druckbogen abstimmen *(Kunde)* to pass a print sheet
Druckbreite *f* image width, print(ing) width; *(Zeilendrucker)* printing measure
Druckchemie *f* pressroom chemistry.
Druckchemikalien *pl* pressroom chemicals *pl*, printing chemicals *pl*
drucken to print, to process, to run
Drucken *n* printing
Druckende *n (auf Bogen)* tail edge of print
druckende Stellen *pl (im U. zu nichtdruckende Stellen)* image areas *pl*, printing areas *pl*
Drucken nach Bedarf *n (intelligente Drucker)* printing on demand
Drucke pro Stunde *m/pl* impressions per hour *pl*
Drucker *m (Beruf)* printer; *(Maschinenbediener)* pressman, press minder, press operator; *(Zeilendrucker)* printer
Druckeranschluß *m (Zeilendrucker)* printer connection, printer interface
Druckerballen *m* ink(ing) ball, printer's ball, tampon
Druckerei *f* printer, printing company, printing firm; *(größer)* printing house, printhouse; *(kleiner)* printing shop, printing office, printshop; *(Teil eines grafischen Betriebes)* pressroom; *(Betriebsanlage)* printing operation, printing plant, printing works

Druckereiausrüstung - Druckluftleitung

Druckereiausrüstung f printing equipment, pressroom equipment
Druckereibedarf m printer's supply; *(versch. kleine Bedarfsart.)* printing sundries pl
Druckereibetrieb m printing operation, printing plant, printing works
Druckereieinrichtung f pressroom equipment, printing equipment
Druckereifachgeschäft n printer's supplier
Druckereileiter m plant manager, pressroom manager, pressroom supervisor
Druckereiplanung f *(Betriebsplanung)* printing operation planning
Druckergebnis n print(ing) result
Druckerlaubnis f imprimatur, o.k. to print, permission to print
Druckerlehrgang m pressman's training course
Druckerlehrling m apprentice printer
Druckerschwärze f black ink, printer's ink
Druckerzeugnis n printed matter, print(ed) product, publication
Druckfachmann m print(ing) expert, printing specialist
Druckfachmesse f graphic arts exhibition
Druckfachzeitschrift f graphic arts magazine, print(ing) journal, print(ing) magazine
Druckfarbe f ink, printing ink
Druckfarbenfabrik f ink factory, inkmakers pl, ink manufacturers pl
Druckfarbentrocknung f ink drying
Druckfehler m misprint, printer's error
druckfertig press-ready
druckfertiges Manuskript fair copy
Druckfilz m felt blanket
Druckfirnis m print(ing) varnish
Druckfläche f image area, print(ing) area
Druckfolge f *(Farbfolge)* colour sequence, printing sequence
Druckfolie f *(Kleinoffsetplatte)* printing master
Druckform f forme, print(ing) forme
Druckformat n print(ing) format
Druckformhersteller m platemaker
Druckformherstellung f print(ing) forme production; *(Offset, Buchdruck, Flexo)* platemaking; *(Siebdruck)* screen preparation; *(Tiefdruck)* cylinder preparation
Druckformmontage f sheet assembly
druckfreier Kanalstreifen m *(Zylinderspalt)* non-printing gap
druckfreier Rand m *(Druckbogen)* image-free margin
Druckfreigabe f imprimatur, o.k. to print, permission to print
Druckfreigabebogen m o.k. proof, o.k. sheet, passed proof, passed sheet
druckfrisch freshly printed, hot off the press
Druckfundament n *(Flachdruckpresse)* forme bed, type bed
Druckgang *(Bogendruck)* **in einem** ~ in one sheet pass
Druckgenehmigung f imprimatur, o.k. to print, permission to print
Druckgeschwindigkeit f printing speed
Druckgradation f print(ing) gradation
Druckgrafik f print
Druckhaus n printhouse, printing company, printing firm, printing house
Druckhilfsmittel pl additives pl, printing aids pl
Druckindustrie f graphic arts industry, graphics industry, printing industry
Druckingenieur m engineer of printing, printing engineer
Druckinstrukteur m printing instructor
Druckkarren m *(Buchdruckm.)* bed, carriage
Druckkaschierung f *(i. U. zur Folienkaschierung)* print lamination
Druckkennlinie f characteristic curve of printing, press characteristics pl, printing characteristics pl
Druckknopf m push-button
Druckknopfsteuerung f push-button control
Druckkontrast m print(ing) contrast
Druckkontrolleiste f colour bar, colour control strip, print control bar, quality control strip
Druckkontrollstreifen m colour bar, colour control strip, print control bar, quality control strip
Druckkosten pl printing costs pl
Druckkraft f *(physik.)* impressional strength, impression pressure
Druckkunst f art of printing
Drucklack m overprint varnish, print varnish
Drucklackierung f overprint varnishing, print varnishing; *(inline in der Druckm.)* in-line coating, in-line varnishing
Drucklänge f image length, print(ing) length
Drucklegung f printing; **rechtzeitig für die** ~ in time for the press
Druckleistung f press output, press speed, printing capacity, printing performance
Druckletter f letter, print(ing) letter
Drucklinie f *(Druckmaschinenanlage)* press line; *(Druckzone)* contact area, printing zone
Druckluft f compressed air
druckluftbetrieben air-operated
Druckluftleitung f air ducts pl

Druckluftversorgung - Drucksachenmuster

Druckluftversorgung f compressed air supply
Druckmaschine f press, printing machine, printing press; *(Bürovervielfältiger)* duplicator; *(Gerät)* printer
Druckmaschine im Format VI format VI printing press, press of size VI
Druckmaschine in Reihenbauweise *(im U. zum Fünfzylindersystem; Bogenoffsetdruck)* unit type press
Druckmaschine mit gemeinsamem Gegendruckzylinder C. I. press, common impression cylinder press
Druckmaschinenanleger m press feeder
Druckmaschinenanordnung f press arrangement, press configuration
Druckmaschinenauslage f press delivery
Druckmaschinenausrüstung f press equipment
Druckmaschinenbau m press construction, press engineering, press manufacture
Druckmaschinenbedienung f press operation
Druckmaschinendemontage f press removal
Druckmaschineneinstellungen pl press adjustments pl, press settings pl
Druckmaschinenfabrik f pressmakers pl, press manufacturers pl, printing machine factory, printing press manufacturers pl
Druckmaschinenfalzwerk n *(Rollendruckm.)* press folder
Druckmaschinenfernsteuerung f off-press controls pl
Druckmaschinenführer m press minder, press supervisor
Druckmaschinenfundament n press foundation
Druckmaschinenfunktionen pl press functions pl
Druckmaschinengeschwindigkeit f press speed
Druckmaschinengestell n press frame
Druckmaschinenhersteller m pressmakers pl, press manufacturers pl, printing machine factory, printing press manufacturers pl
Druckmaschinenkapselung f press enclosure, press hooding
Druckmaschinenkenndaten pl press characteristics pl, press parameters pl
Druckmaschinenlauf m press run
Druckmaschinenleistung f press capacity, press output, press performance
Druckmaschinenpark m pressroom equipment
Druckmaschinenrahmen m press frame
Druck(maschinen)saal m pressroom, printshop
Druckmaschinenstart m press start-up
Druckmaschinensteuerpult n press control console
Druckmaschinensteuerung f press controls pl

Druckmaschinenstillstand m press downtime, press standstill, press stop(page)
Druckmaschinenstörung f *(Druckm.)* breakdown of press
Druckmaschinenüberwachung f press monitoring, press supervision
Druckmaschinenverschleiß m press wear
Druckmaschinenvoreinstellung f presetting of press
Druckmedien n/pl printed media, print media
Druckmeister m foreman, master of printing
Druck mit leichter Druckspannung kiss printing
Druck mit Sammelform combination run
Druckmotiv n print(ing) subject
Druckmuster n print(ing) specimen, print job sample
Drucköl n *(Farbzusatz)* print oil
Druckölumlaufschmierung f pressure oil lubrication
Druckpapier n printing paper, stock
Druckpaste f printing paste
Druckperforation f *(Perforation in der Druckm.)* in-line perforation, print perforation, rule perforation
Druckplatte f plate, pressplate, printing plate; *(Kleinoffset)* printing master
Druckplattenfördersystem n printing plate conveyor
Druckplattenhersteller m printing plate manufacturer
Druckpreis m printing price
Druckprobe f print(ing) specimen, print job sample
Druckprodukt n printed matter, print(ed) product, publication
Druckqualität f print(ing) quality
Druckregister n *(im U. zu Falz-, Schnitt-, Stanzregister usw.)* printing register, print-to-print register
druckreif can go over, o.k. to print, passed for press
Druckreiferklärung f imprimatur, o.k. to print, permission to print
Drucksaal m pressroom, printshop
Drucksache f printed matter, print(ed) product, publication
Drucksacheneinkäufer m print buyer
Drucksachengestalter m graphic designer
Druck(sachen)kalkulation f printing estimating
Drucksachenkalkulator m printing estimator
Drucksachenmarkt m print(ing) market, market for printed matter
Drucksachenmuster n print job sample

Drucksachenverbraucher *m* print consumer
Drucksachenwerbung *f* print advertising
Druckschlitzmaschine *f* printer-slotter
Druckschmierung *f* forced lubrication, pressure lubrication
Druckschrift *f* *(im U. zur Schreibschrift)* block letters *pl;* *(Drucktypen)* print(ing) type; *(Veröffentlichung)* publication
Druckschwierigkeiten *pl* printing difficulties *pl*
Druckslotter *m* printer-slotter
Druckspalt *m* nip, printing nip
Druckspannung *f* *(Beistelldruck)* impression pressure, printing impression, printing pressure
Druckstärkenregulierung *f* *(in Druckm.)* paper thickness adjustment
Druckstelle *f* *(Eindruckstelle)* indent
Druckstock *m* *(Buchdruck)* forme
Drucktaste *f* push-button
Drucktastensteuerung *f* push-button control
Drucktechnik *f* printing technology
Drucktechniken *pl* printing methods *pl,* printing techniques *pl*
Drucktermin *m* date of printing
Drucktest *m* print test
Drucktiegel *m* platen, platen press
Drucktuch *n* *(Gummidrucktuch)* blanket, printer's blanket, printing blanket
Drucktuch aufziehen to mount a blanket
Drucktype *f* print(ing) type, type
Druck- und Verlagsindustrie *f* printing and publishing industry
Druckunterbrechung *f* press stop(page)
Druckverarbeiter *m* converter
Druckverarbeitung *f* converting, finishing, paper converting, paper processing, print converting, print finishing
Druckveredlung *f* print finishing, surface finishing
Druckverfahren *n* printing method, printing process
Druckvermerk *m* *(Buch)* imprint
Druck von Albert Martin printed by Albert Martin
Druckvorbereitung *f* print(ing) preparation
Druckvorgang *m* press run, printing operation, printing process
Druckvorlage *f* printing copy
Druckvorlagenherstellung *f* artwork preparation, copy preparation, origination
Druckvorstufen *pl* pre-press stages *pl*
Druckvorstufenbereich *m im* ~ in the pre-press area

Druckvorstufensystem *n* pre-press system
Druckwalze *f* press roller
Druckweiterverarbeitung *f* converting, finishing, paper converting, paper processing, print converting, print finishing; *(einschl. Versand)* post-press processing
Druckwender *m* *(Siebdruck)* sheet turning device
Druckwerk *n* printing couple, printing group, printing unit, print unit
Druckwerksabkupplung *f* print unit disengagement
Druckwerksanordnung *f* arrangement of print units, print unit configuration
Druckwerkseinschub *m* *(Einschubwagen)* printing cartridge
Druckwerkskupplung *f* print unit clutch
Druckwerkssteuerung *f* print unit controls *pl*
Druckwiedergabe *f* printed reproduction
Druckzeile *f* printline
Druckzone *f* contact area, printing zone
Druckzylinder *m* *(Gegendruckzylinder)* impression cylinder
Druckzylindereinschub *m* *(Einschubwagen)* printing cartridge
DTP (Desktop-Publishing) DTP (Desktop Publishing)
DTP-Satz *m* DTP composition, DTP type matter
Dublieren *n* *(im Druck)* ghosting, slur
Dünndruckpapier *n* flimsy paper, Bible paper, India paper, light-weight paper, onion skin
dünne Spatien *pl* hairline spaces *pl*
dünnflüssige Farbe *f* low-viscosity ink
Dünnschliffrakel *f* *(Tiefdruck)* preground doctor blade
Düsenbeleimung *f* *(im U. zur Walzenbeleimung)* nozzle gluing
Düsenfeuchtwerk *n* jet spray damping system
Düsentrocknung *f* jet drying, nozzle drying
Duftdruckfarbe *f* scented ink
Duktorlineal *n* *(Farbmesser)* duct blade, ink duct blade
Duktorwalze *f* duct roller, fountain roller, pan roller
Dunkelkammer *f* darkroom
Dunkelkammerbeleuchtung *f* darkroom lighting
Dunkelkammerdrehtür *f* revolving darkroom door
Dunkelkammerlampe *f* darkroom safelight
Dunkelkammerschleuse *f* light lock for darkroom
dunkle Farbe *f* dark colour, shaded colour
dunklermachen *(Farben)* to darken, to deepen
Duplex-Betrieb *m* *(Telekomm.)* duplex mode

Duplexdruck *m* duo-tone printing, duplex printing
Duplexkarton *m* duplex board
Duplexpapier *n* duplex paper
Duplikat *n* *(Filmduplikat)* duplicate, dupe, duplicate print
Duplikatfilm *m* duplicating film
Duplikatherstellung *f* duplicating
durchbiegen *(Walzen, Zylinder)* to sag
Durchdrehen der Maschine von Hand hand cranking
Durchdruck *m* *(Siebdruck)* screen printing
Durchgang *m* *(durch Maschine)* pass; *in einem* ~ in one go, in one pass, in one through
durchgehende Doppelseite *f* *(Panoramaseite)* center spread, double(-page) spread, two-page spread
durchgehender Umschlag *m* *(Taschenbuch)* wrap-around cover
Durchhefter *m* *(Zeitschrift)* stabbed insert
Durchheftung *f* stabbing
Durchlauf *m* pass; *in einem* ~ in one go, in one pass, in one through
Durchlaufgeschwindigkeit *f* throughput speed
Durchlaufsystem *n* flowline system
Durchleuchtungseinrichtung *f* *(Kamera)* backlight facility, transparency facility
Durchlicht *n* through-light, transmitted light
Durchlichtdensitometer *n* transmission densitometer
Durchlichtmessung *f* through-light measurement, transmitted light measurement
durchlüften *(beim Stapeln)* to aerate, to fan, to ventilate
Durchsatz *m* *(verarbeitete Materialmenge)* throughput
durchsaugendes Papier *n* porous paper
Durchscheinen *n* *(Druck)* print-through, show-through
durchscheinendes Papier *n* translucent paper
durchschießen *(Auflage mit Abschmutzbogen)* to interleave; *(Satz)* to lead, to space
Durchschießen *n* *(Satz)* leading, line spacing, vertical spacing
Durchschlagdruck *m* *(Formularsatz)* crash printing
Durchschlagen *n* *(Farbe)* strike-through
Durchschlagnumerierung *f* *(Formularsatz)* crash numbering
Durchschlagperforierung *f* *(Formularsatz)* crash perforating

Durchschnittsleistung *f* average output, average production
durchschossene Auflage *f* interleaved print run
durchschossener Satz *m* leaded matter
Durchschreibeblock *m* duplicating pad
Durchschreibefarbe *f* carbon ink, copying ink
Durchschreibeformularsatz *m* *(karbonisiert)* carbonised forms set; *(mit Kohlepapier)* carbon copy forms set; *(ohne Kohlepapier, chem.)* carbonless forms set, NCR forms set
Durchschreibepapier *n* *(chem.)* auto-copying paper, carbonless copy paper, NCR paper, self-copying paper
Durchschuß *m* *(Satz)* leading, line spacing, vertical spacing
Durchschuß herausnehmen to reduce space between lines
Durchschuß hineinnehmen to insert space between lines
Durchschußlinie *f* *(Bleisatz)* space line
Durchschußpapier *n* interleaving paper, set-off paper
durchsichtiges Papier *n* transparent paper
Durchsichtsbeleuchtung *f* *(Kamera)* backlighting
Durchsichtsbild *n* transparent picture; *(Diapositiv)* transparency
Durchsichtsdensitometer *n* transmission densitometer
Durchsichtsoriginal *n* transparency
Durchsichtsvorlage *f* transparency, transparent copy
durchstreichen *(Textkorr.)* to cancel, to delete, to strike out, to strike through
durchtrocknen *(Farbe, Leim)* to dry thoroughly
Durchzeichnung *f* *(Pause)* tracing; *(Zeichnungsdetails)* details *pl*, image definition
Dvorak-Tastatur *f* *(fremder Tastaturplan)* Dvorak keyboard
dynamischer Speicher *m* *(Comp.)* cyclic storage, dynamic storage

E

EBV (Elektronische Bildverarbeitung) *f* EIP (Electronic Image Processing)

Echtdarstellung f *(layoutgerechte und/oder schriftgerechte Bildschirmdarstellung)* preview, softcopy, softproof
Echtgoldprägefolie f genuine gold blocking foil
Echtgrau n true grey
Echtheiten pl *(Druckfarbe)* fastness properties pl
Echtpergament n genuine parchment, vegetable parchment
Echtschrift f *(Bildschirm)* real type, true type; *in ~ darstellen* to display in true type
Echtschriftbildschirm m *(Fotosatz)* real type monitor, typeview monitor, WYSIWYG screen
Echtschriftdarstellung f *(Bildschirm)* real type display, true-typographic display, WYSIWYG display
Echtzeit f *(Comp.)* real time
Echtzeitausgabe f real time output
Echtzeitverarbeitung f *(Comp.)* real-time processing
Ecke f corner
Eckenabstoßgerät n corner cutter
Eckenausstanzmaschine f corner punching machine
Eckenheftklammern f/pl corner staples pl
Eckenheftmaschine f corner stapling machine
Eckenheftung f corner stapling
Eckenklebemaschine f corner gluing machine
Eckenleimmaschine f corner gluing machine
Eckenrunden n corner rounding
Eckenrundstoßmaschine f corner rounding machine, round-cornering machine
Eckenschneider m corner cutter
Eckenstanzmaschine f corner punching machine
Eckenverbindemaschine f *(Faltschachtelherst.)* corner staying machine
Eckenverzierung f corner ornament
Eckförderer m *(Versandraum)* right-angle conveyor
eckige Klammer f *(Satz)* bracket
eckiger Rahmen m square box
Eckstück n *(Bleisatz)* corner piece
Edelstahl m alloy steel
EDG-Scanner m *(mit elektron. Punktaufbau)* EDG scanner
Editierstation f *(Textverarb.)* editing terminal
EDV (elektronische Datenverarb.) EDP (electronic data processing)
EDV-Formular n computer form
EDV-gestützt computer-aided, computerized
EDV-Papier n listing paper, zoned paper
Effektkontaktraster m effect contact screen
egalisieren *(Walzen)* to equalize

Egalisierfräsen n *(Buchherst.)* levelling
Egoutteur m *(Papierherst.)* dandy roll
eichen *(elektronische Geräte)* to calibrate
Eichfeld n calibration patch
Eichplatte f calibration plate
Eichung f calibration
Einbad-Entwicklungsgerät n *(Reprod.)* one-bath processor
Einband m *(Buch)* binding, cover
Einbanddecke f book case, book cover
Einband mit gebrochenem Rücken binding with raised bands
Einband mit geradem Rücken flat binding, square (back) binding
Einband mit rundem Rücken round (back) binding
Einbandstoff m binding cloth, bookbinder's calico, book cloth
Einbau m *(Maschinenteil)* implementation, incorporation, installation
Einbausatz m *(für späteren Einbau)* retrofit kit
Einbelichtung f *(Reprod.)* overlay exposure
einbinden to bind; *(in Pappe)* to board, to put in boards
Einbinden n binding, bookbinding
Einbindenadel f bodkin, bookbinder's needle
Einblattformular n one-part form
Einbrennen n *(Offsetplatte)* baking, burning-in, heat-fusing
Einbrennmittel n *(Offsetplatte)* pre-baking solution
Einbrennofen m *(Offsetplatte)* baking oven, burning-in oven
einbringen *eine Zeile* ~ to get in a line, to take in a line
Einbruchfalz m one-directional fold
Einbuchstabenmatrize f *(Monotype)* single-type matrix
eindringen *(Farbe, Leim usw.)* to penetrate
Eindruck m *(in Drucksache)* imprinting, overprinting
eindrucken to imprint, to overprint
Eindruckform f overprint forme
Eindruckmaschine f imprinting machine, imprinter, overprinter
Eindruckstelle f *(Gummituch)* indent
Eindruck variabler Daten variable-data imprinting
Eindruckwerk n imprinting unit; *(Zeitungsdruckm.)* colour deck, deck, half-deck
eindrücken *(z.B. Gummituch)* to indent
einen Lehrling gautschen to initiate an apprentice

Einfachbogen - einklammern

Einfachbogen *m* plain sheet
einfachbreite Rollendruckmaschine *f* single-width web press
einfache Anführungszeichen *pl* single quotes *pl*
einfache Initiale *f* plain initial (letter)
einfache Linie *f (Satz)* plain rule
einfache Produktion *f (Rollendruck; im U. zu gesammelter Produktion)* non-collect run, straight-run production
einfacher Stich *m (Fadenheftung)* single stitch, standard stitch
Einfachnutzen *m im* ~ one-up
Einfärben *n (elektron. Bildverarb.)* colouring; *(Papier)* tinting; *(Walze, Farbwerk usw.)* inking-up
Einfärben der Druckform forme inking, inking-up of printing forme
Einfärbwalze *f (Tiefdruck)* inking roller
Einfärbwerk *n (Endlosformulardruckm.)* tinter, tinting unit; *(Tiefdruck)* inking unit
Einfallen *n (Gummituch)* sinking
einfalzen *(Klappe)* to fold in
Einfarbendruck *m* monocolour printing, single-colour printing
Einfarbendruckmaschine *f* monocolour (printing) press, single-colour (printing) press
Einfarben-Offsetmaschine *f* single-colour offset press
einfarbige Arbeiten *pl (Druck)* monocolour printwork, single-colour printwork; *(Reprod.)* monochrome work
einfarbiger Bildschirm *m* monochrome monitor
einfarbiger Schöndruck *m* 1/0 top, one colour front (side only)
einfarbiger Schön- und Widerdruck *m* one colour both sides, one colour front, one reverse
einfarbiger Widerdruck *m* 1/0 bottom, one colour reverse (side)
einfassen *(umrandern)* to border
Einfaß- und Fälzelmaschine *f (Buchb.)* bordering and backlining machine
Einfassung *f (Umrandung)* borders *pl*
Einfassungslinie *f* border rule
einfetten to grease
einfügen *(Text)* to insert
Einfügen von Text *n* drop-in of text, insertion of text
Einführband *n* infeed belt, inlet conveyor
Einführschlitz *m (Entwicklungsm.)* feed slot
Einführtisch *m (Entwicklungsm.)* feed tray
Einführwalze *f* infeed roller
Eingabe *f (Text, Daten)* entry, input
Eingabe/Ausgabe *f (Comp.)* input/output

Eingabebefehlssprache *f* input command language
Eingabedaten *pl* input data
Eingabefehler *m* input error
Eingabefehlerkontrolle *f* input error checking
Eingabegerät *n* input device, input unit, front-end unit
Eingabekanal *m* input channel
Eingabeplatz *m* input station, input terminal, front-end terminal
Eingabescanner *m* input scanner
Eingabestation *f* input station, input terminal, front-end terminal
Eingabetastatur *f* input keyboard
Eingabeterminal *m* input terminal, front-end terminal
Eingabetisch *m (Entwicklungsm.)* feed tray
Eingangssprache *f (Comp.)* input coding
eingebaut *(Maschinenteile)* built-in, incorporated, integral, integrated
eingeben *(Text/Daten)* to enter, to feed in, to input, to key in, to punch in
eingebrannte Druckplatte *f* baked printing plate, burned-in printing plate, heat-fused printing plate
Eingehen *n (Papier)* shrinkage
eingeklebte Beilage *f (Zeitschrift)* glued-in insert
eingeklebte Postkarte *f* glued-in postcard, tipped-in postcard
eingerahmter Titel *m* boxed head
eingeschlagene Klappe *f (Prospekt, Umschlag usw.)* folded-in flap, turned-in flap
eingeschlagener Umschlag *m (Zeitschrift)* covergate, folded-in cover, gatefolded cover
eingezogene Initiale *f* cut-in initial
eingezogene Marginalien *f/pl* cut-in marginal notes *pl*
eingezogener Titel *m* cut-in head
eingießen *(Stereot.)* to cast in
einhängen *(Buch)* to case in
Einhandbedienung *f* one-hand operation
Einhebelsteuerung *f* one-lever control
Einhebevorrichtung *f (Papierrolle)* lifting device
einheften to bind in, to sew in, to stitch in
Einhefter *m (Beihefter)* bound-in insert
einkapseln *(Schallschutz)* to enclose
Einkapselung *f (Schallschutz)* enclosure
Einkaufsabteilung *f* purchasing department
Einkaufsleiter *m* head of purchasing, purchasing manager
einkeilen *(Buchdruckform)* to quoin, to wedge
einklammern *(Satz)* to bracket, to put in parenthesis

einkleben *(Beilagen)* to glue in, to tip in
Einkomponentenkleber *m* one-component glue
einkopieren *(Film, Platte)* to burn into, to copy into, to expose into, to print into
Einkopierraster *m* film tint, mechanical tint
einkuppeln to clutch, to connect, to couple, to engage
Einladungskarte *f* invitation card
Einlagerung *f* storage
Einlauf *m* *(in Aggregat)* entry, infeed, inlet
Einlaufband *n* infeed belt, inlet conveyor
Einlaufbreite *f (Durchlaufsysteme)* feeding width
Einlegebreite *f (Schneidem.)* feeding width
Einlegehöhe *f (Schneidem.)* feeding height
Einlegekeil *m* inserting quoin
einlegen *(Material in Maschine)* to feed, to load; *(Vorprodukt in Zeitung)* to insert
Einleger *m (Beilage)* flyer, insert, loose insert
Einlegetiefe *f (Schneidem.)* feeding depth
Einleitung *f (Buch)* introduction
einlesen *(Daten, Text)* to enter, to input, to feed in, to read in
Einmalkohlepapier *n* one-time carbon (paper)
Einmalumreifung *f (Versandraumpakete)* single strapping
Einmetallplatte *f* monometal plate
einpassen *(Filmmontage)* to bring into position, to bring into register, to position, to register
Einpassen *n (Filmmontage)* positioning, registering, registration
einrahmen to border
Einreißfestigkeit *f* tear resistance
Einrichtemakulatur *f* makeready waste, start-up waste, white waste
einrichten *(Maschine für Auftrag vorbereiten)* to make ready, to prepare, to set up
Einrichten *n (der Maschine)* makeready, preparation, set up
Einrichteskala *f* set-up scale
Einrichtezeiten *f/pl* change-over times *pl*, makeready times *pl*, preparation times *pl*, set-up times *pl*
Einrichtung *f (der Maschine)* makeready, set up
einriesen *(Formatpapier)* to pack in reams
Einrollen der Bogen sheet curling
Einrollen der Bogenhinterkante back edge curl, curling of sheet tail
Ein-Rollenstand *m (Rollendruckm.)* single reelstand
einrücken *(Anzeige, Text)* to insert; *(Kupplung)* to engage; *(Zeile)* to indent
Einsatzhöhe *f (Schneidem.)* feeding height
einscannen to scan in

einschalten *(Aggregat, Maschine)* to start, to switch on, to turn on; *(Anzeige)* to insert
Einschalter *m* starting switch
Einschaltfolge *f **automatische** ~* automatic start-up sequence
Einschalthebel *m* starting lever
Einschaltung *f (Anzeige)* insertion
Einschieberahmen *m (für Stanzform)* frame drawer
Einschießbogen *pl* interleaves *pl*, set-off sheets *pl*, sheet interleavers *pl*, slip sheets *pl*
einschießen *(Makulaturbogen)* to interleave
Einschießpapier *n* interleaving paper, set-off paper
einschlagen *(den Stempel, zur Erzeugung der Matrize)* to impress; *(Falzklappe)* to fold in, to turn in; *(in Papier/Folie)* to wrap
Einschlagklappe *f (Buchumschlag)* flap
Einschlagpapier *n* wrapping paper
Einschneidesäge *f (Buchb.)* bookbinder's saw
Einschnitt *m* slot
einschnüren *(Buchb.)* to tie up
Einschnüren *(Auseinanderdriften von Gummitüchern auf doppelbreiten Rollenrotationen)* gapping
Einschubkassette *f (Wechseldruckwerk)* slide-in cassette
Einschubwagen *m (Wechseldruckwerk)* slide-in carriage
einschwärzen to ink up
Einschweißmaschine *f (Versandraum)* sealing machine, welding machine
1/1-farbig *(eine Farbe Schöndruck, eine Widerdruck)* one colour both sides, one colour front, one reverse
einseitig bedruckt printed one side (only)
einseitiger Druck *m* one-sided printing, single-sided printing
einseitig gestrichenes Papier *n* one-sided coated paper
Einsendeschluß *m* closing date, deadline
1/0 Schöndruck *m* 1/0 top, one colour front (side only)
1/0 Widerdruck *m* 1/0 bottom, one colour reverse (side)
einspaltige Überschrift *f* single-column headline
Einspannbacke *f* clamping jaw
Einspannen *n (Druckplatte, Drucktücher)* clamping, locking, mounting
Einspannvorrichtung *f* clamping device
einstampfen *(Papier, Bücher)* to pulp
einstechen *(Punkturen)* to puncture
Einsteckbeilage *f* flyer, loose insert

Einsteckbogen - Elektrolyse

Einsteckbogen *m* insert sheet, inset sheet
Einstecken *n (Beilagen in Zeitungen)* inserting; *(Falzbogen ineinander; im U. zum Zusammentragen)* insetting
Einsteckklappe *f (Faltschachtel)* flap
Einsteckmaschine *f (Beilagen)* inserting machine
Einsteckschlitz *m (Faltschachtel)* flap slot
Einstecktrommel *f* inserting drum
Einstelldaten *pl* set-up data
Einstellehre *f* setting gauge
einstellen *(Maschinen, Geräte)* to adjust, to set, to set up
Einstellhebel *m* adjusting lever
Einstellknopf *m* adjusting knob
Einstellskala *f* calibrated scale, graduated scale, positioning scale, setting scale
Einstellung *f (Maschine, System)* adjustment, setting
Einstellungen während des Laufs *(Maschine, System)* on the run adjustments *pl*
Einstellupe *f (Kamera)* focusing lens
Einstichtiefe *f (Zylinderunterschliff)* cylinder undercut
Einstiegsscanner *m* economy scanner, entry level scanner
Einstrippen von Text stripping-in of text
Einstrippen von Tonfläche tint laying
Einstufenätzung *f (Klischee)* powderless etching
eintasten *(Daten, Text)* to key in, to punch in
Eintauchtiefe *f (Tiefdruckzyl)* immersion depth
Eintauchung *f (Galv.)* dipping, immersion
Einteilungsbogen *m* layout sheet, planning sheet
Eintourenpresse *f* single-revolution press
eintragen *(Bildschirmmaske, Formular usw.)* to enter, to fill in
Eintrittskarte *f* admission ticket
Eintrocknen der Farbe ink dry-up
Ein- und Ausbau *m (z. B. Walzen)* installation and removal
Einwalzen *n (Druckfarbe in Buchdruckform)* inking-up
Einzeladressierung *f (Versandraum)* individual addressing
Einzelanleger *m (Druckverarb.)* hopper feeder
Einzelantrieb *m* individual drive
Einzelaufnahme *f (Reprod.)* individual exposure, individual shot
Einzelblatt *n* single sheet
Einzelblattverarbeitung *f* single-sheet processing
Einzelbogenanleger *m (im U. zu Schuppenanleger)* single-sheet feeder
Einzelbuchstabe *m* single letter, single type

Einzelbuchstabengießapparat *m (Monotype)* single-type caster
Einzelexemplar *n* single copy
Einzelfarbauszug *m* single-colour separation
Einzelfarbenpasser *m* colour register, colour-to-colour register
Einzelformularsätze *m/pl (im U. zu Endlosformularsätze)* unit forms sets *pl*
Einzelnummer *f (Zeitschrift)* single copy, single issue, single number
Einzelnutzen *m im ~* one-up
Einzelnutzen-Falzbogen *m* one-up folded sheet
Einzelnutzenverarbeitung *f* one-up production
Einzelplatzsystem *n* single-station system, stand-alone system
Einzelpreis *m (Zeitung, Zeitschrift)* copy price
Einzelschnitt *m (Schneidem.; im U. zu Repetierschnitt)* individual cut, single cut
Einzeltype *f (Handsatz, im U. zu Blocktype)* single type
Einzelverkauf *m (Zeitungen)* single copy sales *pl*
einziehen *(Papierbahn)* to draw in, to feed in, to thread in; *(Text, Absatz)* to indent
Einzug *m (Text, Absatz)* indent
Einzugsgebiet *n (Zeitung)* distribution area
Einzugswalze *f (Rollendruckm.)* infeed roller
Einzugswerk *n (Rollendruckm.)* infeed unit
Einzylinderdruckmaschine *f (mit gemeinsamem Gegendruckzylinder)* C. I. press, common impression cylinder press
Einzylinder-Flexodruckmaschine *f* common impression flexo press
Eisenchlorid *n (Galvanik)* ferric chloride
Eiweißkopie *f* albumen copy
Eiweißkopierverfahren *n* albumen copying process
Eiweißlösung *f* albumen solution
Eiweißplatte *f* albumen plate
Electronic Publishing *n* electronic publishing
Elefantenhaut *f (Buchdecke)* elephant skin
elektrische Ausrüstung *f* electrical equipment
elektrische Steuerung *f* electrical control
elektrochemisch gekörnte Platte *f* electrochemically grained plate
Elektrode *f (Galvanik)* electrode
Elektrodenspannung *f (Galv.)* electrode voltage
Elektrofotografie *f* electrophotography
elektrofotografische Druckplatte *f* electrophotographic printing plate
elektrofotografischer Drucker *m (Zeilendrucker)* electrophotographic printer
Elektrokorund *n* aluminium oxide
Elektrolyse *f (Galv.)* electrolysis

Elektrolyt n *(Galv.)* electrolyte
elektrolytisches Bad n electrolytical bath
elektrolytisches Entfetten n *(Tiefdruckzyl.)* electrolytical degreasing
elektromechanische Gravur f *(Tiefdruckzyl.)* electromechanical engraving
elektromotorisch electrically operated, motor driven, motorized
Elektronenstrahl m electron beam
Elektronenstrahlgravur f *(Tiefdruckzyl.)* electron beam engraving
Elektronenstrahltrocknung f *(Druckfarbe)* electron beam curing, EB curing
Elektronik f electronics
Elektronikschrank m electronic cabinet
elektronische Bildaufzeichnung f electronic image recording, electronic imaging
elektronische Bildverarbeitung f *(EBV)* electronic image processing
elektronische Datenverarbeitung f *(EDV)* electronic data processing
elektronische Gravur f *(Tiefdruck)* electronic engraving
elektronische Medien pl electronic media pl
elektronische Post f *(Telekomm.)* electronic mail
elektronische Rasterpunktbildung f *(Scanner)* electronic dot generation
elektronische Reproduktion f electronic reproduction
elektronische Retusche f electronic retouching
elektronischer Impuls m electronic pulse
elektronischer Rasterpunktaufbau m *(Scanner)* electronic dot generation
elektronischer Seitenumbruch m electronic page assembly, electronic page make-up
elektronische Schriftmodifikation f *(Fotosatz)* electronic type modification
elektronisches Dokumentationssystem n electronic documentation system
elektronisches Drucksystem n electronic printing system
elektronisches Druckvorstufensystem n electronic pre-press system
elektronische Seitenmontage f electronic page make-up, electronic page assembly
elektronisches Publizieren n electronic publishing
elektronische Steuerung f electronic control
elektronische Verzerrung f *(Fotosatz)* electronic distortion
elektronische Zeichengenerierung f *(Fotosatz)* electronic character generation
elektronisch kursiv *(Fotosatz)* pseudo-italic, slanted

elektronisch kursivstellen *(Fotosatz)* electronic slanting
Elektrostatik f electrostatics
elektrostatische Auflading f electrostatic charge
elektrostatische Bildübertragung f electrostatic image transfer
elektrostatische Druckbestäubung f electrostatic powder spraying
elektrostatische Druckfolie f *(Kleinoffset)* electrostatic printing master
elektrostatische Druckhilfe f *(Tiefdruck)* electrostatic print assist
elektrostatische Druckplatte f electrostatic printing plate
elektrostatische Folienkamera f *(Kleinoffset)* direct electrostatic platemaker
elektrostatische Plattenherstellung f electrostatic platemaking
elektrostatischer Drucker m electrostatic printer
elektrostatisches Farbprüfsystem n electrostatic colour proofing system
elektrostatisches Haften n electrostatic adherence, electrostatic clinging
Elfenbeinkarton m ivory board
Elfenbeinpapier n ivory paper
eloxierte Aluminiumplatte f anodized aluminium plate
Emailkarton m enamelled board
Emailkopierverfahren n *(Klischeeätzung)* cold-top process
Emballage f packaging
Empfängerpapier n *(chem. Durchschreibepapier)* receptor sheet of paper
Empfangsgerät n *(Telekomm.)* receiver, receiving device
Empfangsseite f *(Telekomm.)* receiving end, receiving site
Empfangsstation f *(Telekomm.)* receiving station
Empfehlungskarte f *(Geschäftskarte)* business card
Empfindlichkeit f *(Fot.)* sensitivity, speed
Emulator m emulator
Emulgiermittel n emulsifier
Emulgierverhalten n *(Offsetfarbe)* emulsifying properties pl
Emulsion f emulsion
Emulsionsleim m emulsion adhesive
Emulsionsschicht f emulsion layer
Endabschaltung f **automatische** ~ automatic stop
Endausgabe f final output
Endbehandlung f final treatment
Endbeschnitt m final cut, final trim
Enddichte f end density

Ende der Seite - Entwickler

Ende der Seite foot of page
Endfilm *m* final film, finished film
Endformat *n* final size; *(Papier)* trimmed size
Endgerät *n (Terminal)* terminal
Endgröße *f* final size
Endkontrolle *f* final check; *(Qualität)* final quality control
Endkosten *pl* final costs *pl*
Endlosdruck *m* continuous stationery printing
Endlosdruckmaschine *f* continuous stationery press
Endlosdrucksachen *m/pl* continuous stationery
Endloserfassung *f (Text)* idiot typing, non-counting text input
Endloserfassungsplatz *m (Text)* non-counting input station, non-counting keyboard, non-justifying input station
endlosfalzen *(spiralfalzen)* to fan-fold
Endlosflexodruckwalze *f* seamless flexo roller
Endlosformulardruck *m* continuous forms printing, continuous stationery printing
Endlosformulardruckmaschine *f* continuous forms press, continuous stationery press
Endlosformulare *pl* continuous forms *pl*, continuous stationery
Endlosformularsätze *m/pl* continuous forms sets *pl*
Endloslochstreifen *m* endless punched tape
Endlospapier *n* continuous paper, continuous stationery
Endlossatz *m (Text)* unjustified type matter, non-counted type matter, continuous type matter, unjustified setting
Endlosstapel *m* pack
Endlosstapeldruckmaschine *f* pack printer, pack-to-pack printer
Endlostext *m* unjustified text, non-counted text, continuous text, continuous copy
Endlostexterfassung *f* non-counting text input, non-counting text recording
Endpositiv *n* final positive
Endseite *f* final page
Endstück *n (typogr.)* tail-piece
Endtermin *m (Auftrag)* deadline, job completion date
Endtrocknung *f (am Ende der Maschine, im U. zur Zwischendruckwerkstrocknung)* end-of-press drying; *(Durchtrocknung)* final drying
Endzeile *f (Satz)* break, break line
eng ausgeschlossene Zeile *f* closely spaced line
eng ausschließen *(Satz)* to space closely

enger Ausschluß *m (Satz)* close spacing, tight justification
enger Satz *m* closely spaced matter, close setting
enge Zeile *f (Satz)* closely spaced line, tight line
eng halten *(Satz)* to space closely
englische Anführungszeichen *pl* inverted commas *pl*
Englische Schreibschrift *f* English Script
eng setzen *(Typogr.)* to space closely
Entchromen *n (Tiefdruckzyl.)* chrome removal, chrome stripping, dechroming
Entchromungssalz *n* dechroming salt
Ente *f (falsche Zeitungsnachricht)* canard, hoax
Entelektrisator *m* anti-static device, static eliminator, static neutralizer
Entfärben *n (Papier)* de-inking
Entfetten *n* degreasing
Entfettungsbad *n (Tiefdruckzyl.)* degreasing bath
entgraten to deburr
Entionisieren *n* de-ionization
Entionisierstab *m* de-ionizing rod
Entkupfern *n (Tiefdruckzyl.)* copper removal, copper stripping, decoppering
entkuppeln to declutch, to disconnect, to disengage
Entladegerät *n* unloader
Entladen *n* unloading
Entladerampe *f (Versand)* receiving ramp, unloading platform
Entnickeln *n (Tiefdruckzyl.)* nickel removal, nickel stripping
entoxidieren *(Tiefdruckzyl.)* to de-oxidize
Entrastern *n* descreening
entsäuern *(Offsetplatte)* to desensitize
Entschäumer *m* anti-foam agent
Entscheidungstabelle *f (Bildschirm)* prompt table
Entscheidungsträger *m (für Investitionen)* decision-maker
Entschichter *m (chem.)* de-coater
Entschichtung *f* coating removal, de-coating, stripping; *(Siebdruck)* stencil removal
Entschuppen *n (Auflösen des Schuppenstroms)* de-shingling
Entsorgung *f (Altstoffe)* disposal
Entsorgungssystem *n* disposal system
Entstäubung *f* dust removal, powder removal
Entstapeln *n* de-stacking
Entwässerung *f (Papierherst.)* dehydration
entwerfen to design, to draw, to outline
Entwerfer *m* designer, layout man
entwickeln *(Fot.)* to develop, to process; *von Hand* ~ to hand-develop
Entwickler *m (Fot.)* developer

Entwicklerbad *n* developer bath, developing bath
Entwicklerbecken *n* developing sink
Entwicklererschöpfung *f* developer exhaustion
Entwicklerlösung *f* developing solution
Entwickleroxidation *f* developer oxidation
Entwicklerschale *f* developing tray
Entwicklerschwankungen *pl* developer fluctuations *pl*
Entwicklerstreifen *m/pl (Film)* developer streaks
Entwicklersubstanzen *pl* developing agents *pl*
Entwicklertampon *m* developing pad
Entwicklung *f (Fot.)* developing, development, processing
Entwicklungsautomat *m* automatic film processor
Entwicklungschemikalien *pl* processing chemicals *pl*
Entwicklungsgerät *n* film processor
Entwicklungsmaschine *f* film processor
Entwicklungsschale *f* developing tray
Entwicklungsspielraum *m* developing latitude, processing latitude
Entwicklungstank *m* developing tank
Entwicklungstisch *m (Offset)* developing table
Entwicklungstrog *m* developing tray
Entwicklungstrommel *f* developing drum
Entwicklungszeit *f* developing time, processing time
Entwurf *m* draft, layout, outline, rough sketch, sketch
Entzerrung *f (Fot.)* rectification
Enzyklopädie *f* encyclopedia
Erdfarben *pl (z. B. Ocker, Umbra usw.)* mineral colours *pl*
erfahrener Fachmann *m* experienced specialist
erfassen *(Text, Daten)* to key, to key in, to record, to capture, to collect, to gather, to input, to keyboard, to punch in
Erfasser *m* keyboard operator, terminal operator
Erfassung *f (Text, Daten)* keyboard entry, collection, gathering, input, keyboarding, recording
Erfassungsaufwand *m* keyboarding time
Erfassungseinheit *f (Text, Daten)* recording unit
Erfassungsgeschwindigkeit *f* keyboard operating speed, recording speed
Erfassungsplatz *m (Text, Daten)* collecting terminal, input station, input terminal
Erfassungszeit *f* keyboarding time
Ergänzungen *f/pl (Werk)* addenda *pl*
Ergänzungsfarbe *f* complementary colour
Ergänzungsteil *m (Buch, Zeitung)* supplement
ergonomisches Design *n* ergonomic design
erhabene Bünde *m/pl (Buch)* raised bands *pl*

erhabenes Bild *n (Hochdruckmerkmal)* raised image
Ermüdung *f (mech.)* fatigue
Errata *pl (Buch)* errata *pl*
Ersatzmesser *n* spare knife
Ersatzteildienst *m* spare parts service
Ersatzteile *n/pl* spare parts *pl*, spares *pl*
Ersatzteilkatalog *m* spare parts manual, spares manual
Ersatzteillager *n* spares stock
Ersatzteilversorgung *f* spare parts supply
Ersatzwalze *f* spare roller
erscheinen *(Publikation)* to appear, to be issued, to be published, to come out
erscheint in Kürze to appear shortly, to be published soon, ready shortly
erscheint monatlich published monthly
erscheint nicht mehr discontinued
erscheint wöchentlich published weekly
erscheint zweimonatlich published bi-monthly
erscheint zweiwöchentlich published bi-monthly, published semi-monthly
Erscheinungsdatum *n (Publikation)* publication date
Erscheinungsjahr *n (Zeitung, Zeitschrift)* year of publication
Erscheinungstag *m* day of publication
Erschöpfungsregenerierung *f (Fotochemie)* exhaustion replenishment
Erstausgabe *f* first edition, original edition
erster druckfähiger Punkt *m* first printable dot
Erstlingsdrucke *m/pl* incunabula *pl*
erweitern *(System)* to expand, to extend, to upgrade; **schrittweise** ~ to expand in stages, to expand step by step
erweiterte Ausgabe *f* enlarged edition
erzeugen *(Bildverarb.)* to create, to generate
Eselsohr *n (umgeschlagene Ecke einer Seite)* dog's ear
Espartopapier *n* esparto paper
Essigsäure *f (Fotochemie)* acetic acid
Etagenmaschine *f (Rotation)* balcony-type press, gallery-type press
Etiketten *n/pl* labels *pl*
Etikettenanleimmaschine *f* label gluing machine
Etikettendruck *m* label printing
Etikettendrucker *m* label printer
Etikettendruckmaschine *f* label printing press
Etikettenfadenknotenmaschine *f (Anhängeetikett)* tag knotting machine
Etikettenknüpfmaschine *f* tag tying machine
Etikettenpapier *n* label paper
Etikettensammelbogen *m* multi-up label sheet

Etikettenschneider - Fahrkartendruck

Etikettenschneider *m* label cutter
Etikettenspender *m* label dispenser
Etikettenstanzmaschine *f* label punching machine
Etikettenträgerpapier *n* label carrier paper
etikettieren to label
Etikettiermaschine *f* labelling machine
Et-Zeichen *n (&)* ampersand
Euro(pa)skala *f (Druckfarbe)* European colour scale, Euroscale
Exemplar *n* copy
Exemplarauslage *f (Rollendruckm.)* copy delivery
Exemplarauslageband *n (Rollendruckm.)* copy delivery belt
Exemplarkontrolle *f (Rollendruckm.)* copy check(ing), copy monitoring
Exemplarschuppe *f* shingled copies *pl*
Exemplarstreuung *f (Densitometer)* inter-instrument agreement
Exemplartransporteur *m (Rotationsauslage, Versandraum)* copy conveyor
Exemplarzähler *m* copy counter
Exlibris *n* bookplate, exlibris
Expansionswickelwelle *f* air shaft, expanding shaft
explosionsgeschützt explosion-proof
Exponent *m (Satz)* exponent
externer Speicher *m (Comp.)* external storage
Extraarbeit *f* additional work
Exzenter *m* cam, eccentric
Exzenterantrieb *m* cam drive, eccentric drive
Exzenterbewegung *f* cam motion, eccentric motion
Exzenterkurve *f* cam
Exzenterrad *n* cam wheel
Exzenterscheibe *f* cam disc
Exzentersteuerung *f* cam control
Exzenterwelle *f* cam shaft, eccentric shaft

F

Fabelbuch *n* book of fables
Facette *f (Klischee)* bevel
Facettenhobel *m* beveller
facettenloses Klischee *n* straight-edge block
Facetten- und Kantenfräsmaschine *f (Klischeeherst.)* bevelling and cutting machine

facettieren *(abkanten)* to bevel
Facettiermaschine *f* bevelling machine
Facharbeiter *m* qualified worker, skilled worker
Fachausbildung *f* technical training
Fachausdruck *m* technical term
Fachbuch *n* technical book
Fachgeschäft für Druckereibedarf printer's supplier
Fachkräfte *pl* skilled personnel, skilled staff
Fachkraft *f* skilled operator, skilled worker, specialist
fachliche Schulung *f* technical training
Fachliteratur *f* technical literature
Fachmann *m* expert, specialist
Fachpresse *f* technical press, trade press
Fachredakteur *m* technical editor, trade editor
Fachredakteur für Druck graphic arts editor
Fachschule für Drucktechnik school of printing
fachsimpeln *(über Druck)* to talk print
Fachwissen *n* expertise, technical knowledge
Fachwörterbuch *n* technical dictionary
Fachzeitschrift *f* technical journal, technical magazin, trade journal, trade magazine, trade paper
Faden *m (Fadenheftung)* thread
Fadenbruchkontrolle *f (Fadenheftung)* thread break control, thread break detector
Fadenbuchheftung *f* book sewing
fadengeheftetes Buch *n* sewn book
fadenheften to sew, to thread-stitch
Fadenheftmaschine *f* thread-stitching machine, thread-stitcher, sewing machine
Fadenheftung *f* thread-stitching, sewing
Fadenkreuz *n* hairline cross
Fadensiegeln *n (Druckverarb.)* thread-sealing
Fadenzähler *m* linen tester, magnifier
fächeln *(zum Trocknen)* to fan
fächerartig auflockern *(Bogen)* to fan out
fächern *(Bogen)* to fan out
Fälschung *f* forgery
fälschungssicher forgery-proof
Fälzelmaschine *f (Buchherst.)* back-stripping machine, spine-taping machine
Fälzelstreifen *m* back strip, guard, lining strip, spine tape
Fälzelung *f* back-stripping, spine taping
Färbemittel *n* colorant, dye
Färbung *f* colouring, dying, tinting
Fahne *f (Satz)* galley
Fahnenabzug *m (Satz)* galley proof
fahrbares Aggregat *n* mobile unit, move-away unit, roll-away unit
Fahrkartendruck *m* ticket printing

Fahrkartendruckmaschine *f* ticket printing machine
Fahrkartenkarton *m* ticket board
Fahrplansatz *m* timetable setting
Faksimile *n* facsimile
Faksimiledruck *m* *(Bogen)* facsimile copy, facsimile print, facsimile reproduction; *(Vorgang)* facsimile printing
Faksimileleitung *f* *(Telekomm.)* facsimile link
Faksimile-Reproduktion *f* facsimile reproduction
Faksimile-Übertragung *f* *(Telekomm.)* facsimile transmission
Fallsauger *m* *(Anlegersaugkopf)* drop sucker
Fallverschluß *m* *(Kamera)* drop shutter
falschdrucken to misprint, to print waste
falsche Trennung *f* *(Satz)* bad break
falschlaufendes Material *n* *(statt Schmalbahn Breitbahn oder umgekehrt)* cross-grained material
Faltblatt *n* folder
Faltbodenschachtel *f* crash-lock bottom carton
Faltbroschüre *f* folded brochure, folder
Falte *f* *(Papier)* crease, wrinkle
faltenfreies Papier *n* crease-free paper, wrinkle-free paper
Falten glätten *(Papier)* to smooth creases
Faltprospekt *m* folded brochure, folder
Faltschachtel *f* collapsible carton, collapsible folding box, folding box, folding carton
Faltschachtelkarton *m* boxboard, cartonboard, folding boxboard
Faltschachtelklebemaschine *f* folder-gluer, folding box gluer
Faltschachtelklebung *f* folding box gluing
Faltschachtelzuschnitt *m* carton blank
Falz *m* *(Buch)* joint; *(Papier)* fold
Falzabpressung *f* *(Falzbogen)* fold pressing
Falzanlage *f* *(Bogenanlage, im U. zur Druckanlage)* folding lay, fold lay mark
Falzanleger *m* folder feeder
Falzapparat *m* *(Rollendruckm.)* folder, press folder
Falzapparatüberbau *m* *(Rollendruckm.)* folder super-structure
Falzaufbau *m* *(Rollendruckm.)* folder super-structure
Falzautomat *m* *(Bogenfalzm.)* automatic folding machine
Falzbefeuchtung *f* fold moistening, fold softening
Falzbein *n* bone folder, folding stick
Falzbogen *m* folded section, folded sheet, folded signature
Falzbruch *m* fold

Falzeinbrennen *n* *(Buchherst.)* burning-in of joint, joint forming
Falzeinbrennschiene *f* *(Buchherst.)* burning-in rail, heated joint iron, joint forming rail
Falzeinpressen *n* *(Buchherst.)* joint nipping, joint pressing
falzen to fold; **von Hand ~** to hand-fold
Falzgenauigkeit *f* fold(ing) accuracy
Falzheftung *f* *(Rückenheftung)* back stitching, saddle stitching
Falz hinten *(Druckverarb.)* fold trailing
Falzkassette *f* *(austauschbar)* folder cassette
Falzklappe *f* *(Falzapp.)* folding jaw
Falzklappenzylinder *m* *(Falzapp.)* jaw cylinder
Falzkleben *n* fold-gluing
Falzkontrolle *f* fold control, fold monitoring
Falzkreuz *n* *(Falzmarke)* fold(ing) mark
Falzlänge *f* *(Endlosformulardruck)* fold depth
Falzlage *f* quire, section
Falzlinie *f* *(Falzbruch)* fold
Falzmarke *f* fold(ing) mark
Falzmaschine *f* folding machine
Falzmesser *n* *(Falzapp.)* chopper (blade), tucker blade; *(Falzm.)* folding knife, folding blade
Falzmesserzylinder *m* *(Falzapp.)* tucker blade cylinder
Falzmuster *n* folding sample
Falzniederdruckpresse *f* *(Buchherst.)* joint nipping machine
Falzperforation *f* fold perforation
Falzpflug *m* *(Rollendruckm.)* folding plow
Falzprodukt *n* folded product
Falzregister *n* folding register, fold-to-print register
Falzrücken *m* folding spine
Falzschema *n* folding layout
Falzschwert *n* *(Falzapp.)* chopper (blade), tucker blade; *(Falzm.)* folding blade, folding knife
Falztasche *f* *(Falzm.)* buckle plate
Falztrichter *m* *(Falzapp.)* folder former, former, former plate
Falztrichtereinzugwalze *f* roller top of former
Falztrommel *f* folding cylinder
Falzung *f* folding
Falzvariationen *pl* fold variations *pl*
Falzverstärkung *f* fold tightening
Falz voraus, vorne *(Druckverarb.)* fold first, fold leading
Falzwalzen *pl* folding rollers *pl,* nip rollers *pl*
Falzwerk *n* folding unit
Falzwiderstand *m* folding resistance
Falzzylinder *m* folding cylinder
Fantasiepapier *n* fancy paper

Fantasieschrift - Farbe auf Ölbasis

Fantasieschrift *f* fancy type
Farbabbau *m (Zurückstellen der Dosierelemente im Farbkasten)* ink shut-off
Farbabfall *m (Druckbogen)* gradual fading
Farbabgabe *f* ink transfer
Farbabmusterung *f* colour match(ing), ink match(ing)
Farbabstimmleuchte mit Normlicht standard illumination lamp for colour control
Farbabstimmung *f* colour match(ing), ink match(ing)
farbabstoßend ink-repellent
Farbabstufung *f* colour gradation
Farbabweichung *f* chromatic aberration, colour deviation
farbabweisend ink-repellent
Farbabzug *m (Foto)* colour print
Farbätzer *m* colour process etcher
Farbätzung *f* colour process etching
Farbannahme *f* ink trapping, ink acceptance, trapping
Farbanteil *m (Bild)* colour component
Farbanzeige *f (Vierfarbanzeige)* full-colour ad(vertisement)
Farbaufbau *m (auf Walzen, Gummituch usw.)* ink build-up
Farbauflage *f (auf Druckbogen)* ink lay-down
Farbaufnahme *f (Papier, Feuchtwasser)* ink absorption
Farbaufnahmevermögen *n* ink absorptivity
Farbaufsichtsbild *n (Foto)* colour print
Farbaufsichtsproof *m (z. B. Cromalin)* cromalin, hardcopy colour proof
Farbaufsichtsvorlage *f* colour reflection original
Farbauftrag *m (auf Platte, Form usw.)* ink application, inking
Farbauftragswalze *f* ink forme roller; *(Offset)* plate inker, plate inking roller
Farbauftragswalzen an/ab *(Offset)* plate inkers on/off
Farbauszüge *m/pl* colour separations *pl*, separation films *pl*, separations *pl*
Farbauszugsdaten *pl (Scanner)* colour separation data
Farbauszugsfilm *m* colour separation film
Farbauszugsfilter *m* colour separation filter
Farbauszugsnegativ *n* colour separation negative
Farbauszugspositiv *n* colour separation positive
Farbbalance *f* colour balance
Farbbalancefeld *n (Druckkontrollstreifen)* colour balance patch
Farbballen *m* ink(ing) ball, printer's ball, tampon

Farbbehälter *m* ink container
Farbbeilage *f (Zeitung)* colour supplement
Farbbelegung *f (Zeitungsdruck)* colour combination pattern, colour imposition, colour placement
Farbbildmontage *f* colour image assembly
Farbbildrekorder *m* colour image recorder
Farbbildschirm *m* colour monitor
Farbbogen *m (im U. zu Text- oder Schwarzbogen)* colour signature
Farbbrillanz *f* ink brilliance
Farbbüchse *f* ink can, ink tin
Farbcontainer *m* ink container
Farbdeckung *f (auf Druckbogen)* ink coverage, ink lay-down
Farbdensitometer *n* colour densitometer
Farbdia *n* chrome, colour slide, colour transparency
Farbdichte *f* colour density, ink density
Farbdichtemeßanlage *f (Druckm.)* ink density measuring system
Farbdichtemeß- und -regelanlage *f (Druckm.)* ink density measuring and control system
Farbdichtemessung *f* colour densitometry, ink density measurement
Farbdichteregelung *f* ink density control
Farbdichtewert *m* ink density value
Farbdose *f* ink can, ink tin
Farbdosierhebel *m* ink metering lever
Farbdosierkasten *m* ink metering duct
Farbdosiersystem *n* ink metering system
Farbdosierung *f (Druckm.)* ink metering
Farbdosierzylinder *m* ink metering cylinder
Farbdruck *m (Bogen)* colour print, colour reproduction; *(Vorgang)* colour printing, multi-colour printing
Farbdruckwerk *n* colour unit; *(Zeitungsdruckm.)* colour deck, deck, half-deck
Farbduktor *m (Walze)* ink duct roller, ink fountain roller
Farbduplikat *n (Farbreprod.)* colour duplicate
Farbdurchsichtsproof *m (z. B. Color Key)* colour key, overlay colour (film) proof, acetate colour proof
Farbe *f (Druckf.)* ink, printing ink; *(Reprod.)* colour
Farbe abschwächen to reduce colour
Farbe anmachen *(Druckf.)* to mix ink
Farbe anreiben to grind the ink
Farbe auffrischen to freshen-up colour
Farbe aufhellen to brighten colour
Farbe auf Lösemittelbasis solvent-based ink
Farbe auf Ölbasis oil-based ink

Farbe auf wäßriger Basis water-based ink
Farbechtheit *f (Druckf.)* colour fastness
Farbe einlaufen lassen to prime the ink train, to run up the ink
Farbe geschmeidiger machen to soften the ink
farbehaltend keeping colour
Farbeindruckwerk *n* auxiliary colour unit; *(Zeitungsdruckm.)* colour deck, deck, half-deck
Farbeinstellung *f (Druck allgem.)* colour match(ing), ink match(ing); *(Druckm.)* ink (key) adjustment, ink (key) setting; *(Scanner)* colour adjustment, colour setting
Farbe kräftiger machen to intensify colour, to make colour stronger
Farbempfindlichkeit *f (Filmmaterial)* colour sensitivity
Farbemulsion *f (Offset)* ink emulsification
Farbendruck *m* siehe Farbdruck
Farb(en)form *f (im U. zur Text- oder Schwarzform)* colour forme
Farbenhersteller *m (Druckf.)* ink factory, inkmakers *pl*, ink manufacturers *pl*
Farbenherstellung *f (Druckf.)* inkmaking, ink manufacture, ink production
Farbenkarte *f* colour chart
Farbenlehre *f* colour theory
Farbenmischen *n* blending of colours, ink mixing
Farb(en)passer *m* colour register, colour-to-colour register
Farbenreibmaschine *f* ink mill
Farbentheorie *f* colour theory
Farbentwickler *m (Fot.)* colour developer
Farbe/Papierkombination *f* ink/paper combination
Farbe reiben to mill the ink
Farbe strenger machen to strengthen the ink
Farbe verdünnen to reduce the ink
Farbe verlängern to extend the ink
Farbe verreiben to distribute the ink
Farbe zugeben to feed ink; *(Druckm.)* to give more ink
Farbe zurücknehmen *(Bildverarb.)* to reduce colour; *(Druckm.)* to reduce ink
Farbfächer *m (z. B. Pantone, HKS)* colour gamut, colour guide, colour specimen book
Farbfernsteuerung *f (Druckm.)* remote control of ink keys, remote ink control, remote inking
Farbfernverstellung *f (Druckm.)* remote adjustment of ink keys, remote inking adjustment
Farbfilm *m (Druckf.)* ink film; *(Fot.)* colour film
Farbfilter *m* colour filter

Farbfläche *f* colour area, colour surface, colour solid; *(elektron. Bildverarb.)* tint block
Farbfluß *m (durch Farbwerk)* ink flow
Farbfördersystem *n* ink feed system
Farbfolge *f (Farbreihenfolge)* colour sequence, printing sequence
Farbfolienproof *m (z. B. Color Key)* acetate colour proof, colour key, overlay colour (film) proof
Farbfoto *n* colour photo(graph), colour print
Farbfotografie *f* colour photo(graph), colour photography
farbfreundlich *(Offset)* ink-receptive, oleophilic
farbführende Stellen *f/pl* ink-conducting areas *pl*
Farbführung *f* ink feed(ing), inking, ink supply
Farbgebung *f* ink feed(ing), inking, ink supply
Farbglätte *f (Walzen)* ink glaze
Farbglanz *m (Druckfarbe)* ink gloss
Farbglasur *f (Walzen)* ink glaze
Farbgleichgewicht *n* colour balance
Farbharmonie *f* colour harmony
Farbheber *m (Walze)* ink vibrator, vibrating ink roller
farbig chromatic, coloured, colourful
farbige Anzeige *f (vierfarbige)* full-colour ad(vertisement)
farbige Beilage *f (Zeitung)* colour supplement
farbige Prüfdarstellung am Bildschirm colour preview, soft-copy colour proof
farbiger Monitor *m* colour monitor
farbiger Steindruck *m* chromolithography
farbiges Papier *n* coloured paper, tinted paper
Farbinformation *f (auch digital)* colour information
Farbintensität *f* colour intensity, colour strength
Farbkanal *m (elektron. Reprod., Densitometer)* colour channel
Farbkarte *f* colour chart
Farbkasten *m (Farbwerk)* ink duct, ink fountain
Farbkastenschraube siehe Farbschraube
Farbkastenteiler *m* ink fountain separator
Farbkastenwalze *f* ink duct roller, ink fountain roller
Farbkissen *n (Stempel)* inking pad
Farbklischee *n* colour plate
Farbknoten *pl (Druckf.)* ink specks *pl*
Farbkörper *m* colour pigment
Farbkonsistenz *f (Druckf.)* ink consistency
Farbkontrolle *f* colour control, ink control
Farbkontrollfeld *n (Druckkontrollstreifen)* colour control patch
Farbkontrollstreifen *m* colour control bar, colour control strip, ink control bar, ink control strip

Farbkontrollterminal - Farbschicht

Farbkontrollterminal *m (Bildverarb.)* colour editing terminal
Farbkopie *f* colour copy, colour print
Farbkorrektur *f (Druckmaschine)* inking correction; *(elektron. Bildverarb.)* colour editing; *(Lithogr.)* colour correction, colour retouching
Farbkorrekturmaske *f (Reprod.)* colour correction mask
Farbkorrekturterminal *m (elektron. Bildverarb.)* colour editing terminal
Farbkraft *f* colour intensity, colour strength
Farbkreislauf *m (Tiefdruckm.)* inking circuit
Farblithograf *m* chromolithographer
Farblithografie *f* chromolithography
Farblöser *m (chem.)* ink solvent
farblos achromatic, colourless
Farbmesser *n (Farbfarbe)* ink duct blade, ink (duct) knife; *(Farbspachtel)* ink knife, spatula
Farbmesserspaltstellung *f* ink knife gap position
Farbmesserstellung *f* ink knife position, ink knife setting
Farbmeßstreifen *m* colour control bar, colour control strip, ink control bar, ink control strip
Farbmeßsystem *n* colour measuring system
Farbmessung *f* colorimetry, colour measurement
Farbmetrik *f* colourmetrics
Farbmischer *m (Druckfarbe)* ink mixer
Farbmischstein *m* ink stone, slab
Farbmischtafel *f* colour mixing chart
Farbmischung *f (Druckfarbe)* ink mixing; *(Farbentheorie)* colour synthesis
Farbmonitor *m* colour monitor
Farbmontage *f (Druckform)* colour image assembly, process colour stripping
Farbmühle *f (Druckfarbenherst.)* ink mill
Farbmuster *n* colour sample, colour specimen
Farbmusterkarte *f* colour specimen chart
Farbnachstellung *f (Farbherst.)* colour match(ing), ink match(ing)
Farbnäpfchen *n/pl (Tiefdruck)* ink cells *pl*
Farbnebel *m (schnellrotierende Farbwalzen)* ink mist
Farbnegativ *n* colour negative
Farbnegativpapier *n* colour negative paper
Farbniveau-Konstanthalter *m* ink leveller, ink level system
Farbniveauregelung *f* ink level control
Farbniveauregler *m* ink leveller, ink level system
Farbnorm *f* colour standard
Farbnuance *f* colour shade
Farbpasser *m* colour register, colour-to-colour register

Farbpigment *n* colour pigment
Farbplazierung *f (Zeitungsdruck)* colour combination pattern, colour imposition, colour placement
Farbpositivpapier *n* colour positive paper
Farbprägefolie *f (im U. zu Gold- bzw. Metallikprägefolie)* colour stamping foil
Farbproof *m* colour proof
Farbproofherstellung *f* colour proofing
Farbproofmaschine *f* colour proofer
Farbprüfdruck *m (Farbproof)* colour proof
Farbprüfleuchte *f* colour evaluation lamp; ~ *in Überkopfhöhe* colour evaluation overhead lamp
Farbprüfsystem *n (Farbproofherst.)* colour proofing system
Farbpumpe *f (Druckf.)* ink pump
Farbradierung *f* colour etching
Farbraum *m (Farbentheorie)* colour space
Farbreaktionspapier *n (chem. Durchschreibepapier)* autocopying paper, carbonless copy paper, NCR paper, self-copying paper
Farbrechner *m (Comp.)* colour computer
Farbregelanlage *f* colour control system, ink control system
Farbregelung *f* colour control, ink control, ink feed control, inking control, ink key control
Farbregister *n (Passer)* colour register
Farbregulierschraube *f (Farbkasten)* siehe Farbschraube
Farbreiber *m (Walze)* ink distributor (roller), oscillating ink roller
Farbreibzylinder *m* ink distributor (roller), oscillating ink roller
Farbreihenfolge *f (Mehrfarbendruck)* colour sequence, printing sequence
Farbreproduktion *f* colour process work, colour reproduction, process colour work
Farbretusche *f* colour retouching
Farbrezept *n (Druckfarbe)* ink formula, ink recipe
Farbrücknahme *f (Druckm.)* inking reduction; *(Reprod.)* colour reduction
Farbrückstände *pl* ink deposits *pl*, ink residues *pl*
Farbrührwerk *n* ink agitator
Farbsättigung *f (opt.)* colour saturation
Farbsatz *m (Farbauszugsfilme)* four-colour set
Farbscanner *m* colour scanner
Farbschattierung *f (Nuance)* colour shade
Farbschicht *f* ink film, ink layer

Farbschichtprofil n *(Farbwerk)* ink film profile, inking profile
Farbschieber m *(Dosierelement im Farbkasten)* ink slide
Farbschmitz m ink slur
Farbschnitt m *(Buch)* coloured edge
Farbschraube f *(Farbkasten)* ink key, duct screw, fountain key, fountain screw, ink screw, key
Farbschraubenstellmotor m ink key motor
Farbschwankungen pl *(Druckmasch.)* inking fluctuations pl; *(opt.)* colour fluctuations pl
Farbseite f *(Zeitung, Zeitschrift)* colour page; *(Anzeige)* full-colour full-page ad, full-page colour ad
Farbseitenübertragung f *(Telekomm.)* colour page transmission
Farbskala f colour scale; *(Andruckskala)* progressive proofs pl, progs pl, set of progressives, set of progs
Farbspachtel f ink slice, palette knife, spatula
Farbspalt m *(im Walzenzusammenlauf)* ink gap
Farbspaltung f ink splitting
Farbspatel m ink slice, palette knife, spatula
Farbspektrum n colour spectrum
Farbspritzen n *(in Druckm.)* ink splashing
Farbspritzgerät n *(Vorlagenherst.)* aerograph, airbrush
Farbsprühnebel m *(schnellrotierende Farbwalzen)* ink mist
Farbstabilität f *(im Farbwerk)* ink stability
Farbstärke f *(opt.)* colour intensity, colour strength
Farbsteindruck m chromolithography
Farbstellen n *(Druckmaschine)* ink (key) adjustment, ink (key) setting
Farbsteueranlage f colour control system, ink control system
Farbsteuerpult n colour control desk
Farbsteuerung f colour control, ink control, ink feed control, inking control, ink key control
Farbstich m colour cast
Farbstichrücknahme f *(Scanner)* colour cast removal
Farbstoff m colorant, dye
Farbstreifen m *(Farbheber)* ink stripe
Farbstreifenbreite f ink stripe width
Farbstricharbeiten f/pl colour linework
Farbtafel f colour chart; *(im Buch)* colour plate
Farbtank m ink container, ink tank
Farbteller m *(Tiegel)* ink disc
Farbtemperatur f *(Druckfarbe)* ink temperature; *(Lichtfarbe, in ° K)* colour temperature
Farbtestgerät n ink testing device

Farbtisch m ink stone, ink table, slab
Farbton m colour tone, hue; *(dunkler)* shade; *(heller)* tint
Farbtonabweichung f colour deviation
Farbtrennung f *(Strichreprod.)* colour separation
Farbtrocknen n ink drying; *(auf Walzen usw.)* ink dry-up
Farbüberstand m *(Farbreprod.)* colour lap
Farbübertragung f *(Druckf.)* ink transfer; *(Telekomm.)* colour transmission
Farbumkehrpapier n *(Farbreprod.)* colour reversal paper
Farbumschlag m *(Kopierschicht Offsetplatte)* colour change
Farbumwälzpumpe f ink circulating pump
Farbverbrauch m ink consumption
Farbverbrauchsberechnung f calculation of ink consumption
Farbverbrauchsmessung f measurement of ink consumption
Farbverdünner m ink reducer, ink thinner
Farbvergrößerer m *(Reprofotogr.)* colour enlarger
Farbverlängerer m *(Farbverdünner)* ink thinner
Farbverlagerung f *(opt.)* colour shift(ing)
Farbverlauf m *(opt.)* colour gradation; *(im Hintergrund)* vignetted colour background
Farbverreiber m *(Walze)* ink distributor (roller), oscillating ink roller
Farbverreibewalze f ink distributor (roller), oscillating ink roller
Farbverreibung f *(Druckf.)* ink distribution
Farbverreibwerk n ink distribution unit
Farbverrührer m ink agitator
Farbverschiebung f *(opt.)* colour shift(ing)
Farbversorgung f ink supply
Farbversorgungsanlage f ink supply system
Farbverstärkung f *(Reprod.)* colour boosting, colour intensification
Farbverteilung f *(Druckf.)* ink distribution
Farbviskosität f ink viscosity
Farbvoreinstellung f *(Druckm.)* ink key presetting
Farbvorlage f colour original
Farbwalze f inker, ink(ing) roller
Farbwalzenwascheinrichtung f ink roller wash-up device
Farbwanne f *(Druckm.)* ink trough
Farbwaschtrog m ink wash-up tray
Farb-Wasser-Emulsion f *(Offset)* ink-water emulsification
Farb-Wasser-Gleichgewicht n *(Offset)* ink-water balance
Farbwechsel m *(Druck)* ink change

Farbwechselkassette - Fensterfalz

Farbwechselkassette f *(Druckwerkseinschub)* interchangeable ink cassette
Farbwerk n *(Druckm.)* inking system, inking unit, ink train
Farbwerkseinstellung f siehe Farbeinstellung *(Druckm.)*
Farbwerkskühlung f ink unit cooling
Farbwerkssteuerung f ink unit control
Farbwerkstemperierung f ink unit temperature control
Farbwerkswascheinrichtung f ink unit wash-up device, press washer
Farbwert m chromatic value, colour value
Farbwertrichtigkeit f accuracy of colour value
Farbwiedergabe f colour rendering, colour rendition, colour reproduction
Farbzerlegung f colour break-up
Farbzone f ink zone; *(Farbschraube)* ink key
Farbzonenanzeige f ink zone display
Farbzoneneinstellung f ink key adjustment, ink key setting
Farbzonenfernsteuerung f remote control of ink keys, remote ink control
Farbzonenfernverstellung f remote adjustment of ink keys, remote inking adjustment
Farbzonenprofil n ink duct profile
Farbzonenschraube f siehe Farbschraube
Farbzonenstellung f ink key position
Farbzonenverstellung f ink key adjustment
Farbzügigkeitsmeßgerät n tackmeter
Farbzufuhr f ink feed(ing), ink supply
Farbzuordnung f *(elektron. Bildverarb.)* colour allocation
Farbzusatz m *(Druckfarbe)* ink additive
Farmer'scher Abschwächer m *(Lithogr.)* Farmer's reducer, Farmer's solution
Faserbindung f *(Papier)* fibre bonding
Faserbrei m *(Papierherst.)* pulp
Faserrichtung f grain (direction)
Faserriß m *(Papier)* fibre tear
Faserstoff m *(Papierherst.)* pulp
Faserstoffbleichung f pulp bleaching
Fassonbeleimung f pattern gluing
Fassonlackierung f pattern coating
Fassonperforierung f pattern perforation
fast holzfreies Papier n slightly mechanical paper
Fax n *(Telekomm.)* fax, facsimile
Feder f *(Zeichenfeder)* pen
Federstrich m pen stroke
Federzeichnung f pen drawing
Federzug m *(Zeichenfeder)* pen stroke
Fehlanlage f *(Bogenausrichtung)* misfeed

Fehlbedienung f operating error
Fehlbogen m *(Bogenanlage)* mis-fed sheet, missing sheet
Fehlbogenkontrolle f *(Bogenanlage)* mis-fed sheet detector, missing sheet detector, no-sheet detector
Fehldruck m imperfect impression, misprint
fehlende Rasterpunkte m/pl *(Tiefdruck)* missing dots pl
Fehlerdiagnose f *(Comp.)* fault diagnosis
Fehlererkennung f *(Comp.)* error identification
fehlerhafter Druckbogen m misprint(ed sheet)
fehlerhaftes Exemplar n defective copy, imperfect copy, incomplete copy
fehlerhaftes Register n imperfect register, mis-register
Fehlermeldung f *(Comp.)* error message
Fehlerrate f *(Telekomm.)* error rate
Fehlersuchsystem n *(Comp.)* fault-finding system
Fehlpasser m imperfect register, mis-register
Fehlschnitt m *(Schneidem.)* faulty cut, mis-cut
Fehlschnittüberwachung f *(Schneidem.)* mis-cut monitoring
Fehlwort n *(Satz)* missing word
Feinätzung f fine etching
feineinstellen to fine-adjust, to micro-adjust
Feineinstellschraube f micro-adjustment screw
Feineinstellskala f graduated scale
Feineinstellung f fine adjustment, micro adjustment
feine Linie f fine line, fine rule, hairline, thin line, thin rule
feiner Raster m fine screen
feinjustieren to fine-adjust, to micro-adjust
Feinkarton m fine board
Feinkörnigkeit f fineness of grain
Feinkorn n fine grain
Feinkornemulsion f *(Fot.)* fine grain emulsion
Feinkornentwicklung f *(Fot.)* fine grain development
Feinkornfilm m fine grain film
Feinpapier n fine paper
Feinpostpapier n bond paper
Feinstrichätzung f fine line engraving, fine line etching
Feldeintrag m *(Bildschirmmaske, Formular)* field entry
Fenster-Ausstanz- und -Einklebemaschine f *(Briefumschlagherst.)* window cutting and gluing machine
Fenstereinkleben n *(Briefumschlagherst.)* window gluing
Fensterfalz m double gatefold, gatefold

Fenstermaske f *(Bildschirm)* window mask
Fensterpackung f *(Packung mit Sichtfenster)* window packaging
Fensterstanzung f *(Briefumschlagherst.)* window cutting
Fenstertechnik f *(PC)* window technique
Fensterumschlag m window envelope
Fernbedienungspult m *(Leitstand)* remote control console
Fernbelegausgabe f remote proofing
Ferndiagnose f *(Comp.)* remote diagnosis
Ferndrucker m teleprinter
Fernkopierer m telecopier
Fernsehen n television
Fernsetzen n *(Maschinensatz)* teletypesetting
Fernsetzmaschine f *(TTS)* teletypesetter, TTS machine
Fernsteuerpult n remote control console
Fernsteuerung f remote control; *(Druckmasch. auch)* off-press controls pl
Fernübertragung f teletransmission
Fernverarbeitung f *(Telekomm.)* teleprocessing
Fernverstellung f remote adjustment
Ferritkernspeicher m *(Comp.)* core storage, ferrite core memory
Fertigbeschnitt m final trim, final cut
fertigdrucken to complete printing
fertigmontierte Seite f fully assembled page
Fertigprodukt n finished product; *(in Druckm. komplettiert)* press-finished product
fertigsetzen to complete setting
Fertigungseinrichtungen pl production facilities pl
Fertigungsingenieur m production engineer
Fertigungskontrolle f production control
Fertigungssteuerung f production control
Fertigungsstraße f production line
Festausschluß m *(Satz)* fixed space
festformatige Druckmaschine f *(im Gs. zu formatvariabler)* fixed-size printing press
Festkopfplatte f *(Comp.)* fixed head disk
Festkunde m *(im Gs. zu Gelegenheitskunde)* regular customer
festlegen *(Comp.)* to define, to specify
festmachen to fasten, to fix
Festplatte f *(Comp., im Gs. zu Wechselplatte)* fixed disk
Festplattenspeicher m fixed disk memory
Festpolymerplatte f solid polymer plate
Festspeicher m *(Comp.)* direct access memory, main memory
Feststellschraube f locking screw

Festwertspeicher (ROM) m read only memory (ROM)
festziehen to fasten, to tighten
Fett n *(zum Schmieren)* grease
fettdichtes Papier n grease-proof paper
fette Auszeichnungszeile f bold display line, line displayed in bold
fettecht grease-proof
Fettechtheit f grease-resistance
fette Linie f bold line, bold rule, heavy line, heavy rule
fetter Buchstabe m black letter, bold type
fetter mittestehender Punkt m *(Satz)* centered dot
fette Schrift f black face, bold face
Fettfarbe f *(Umdruck)* transfer ink
fettfeine Linie f shaded line, shaded rule
Fettkreide f litho(graphic) chalk, litho(graphic) crayon
Fettpapier n *(fettdichtes P.)* grease-proof paper
Fettpresse f grease gun
Fettschmierstelle f grease lubrication point, greasing point
Fettschmierung f grease lubrication
Fettzentralschmierung f central grease lubrication
Feuchtauftragswalze f *(Offset)* damper roller, damping forme roller, plate damper
Feuchtdehnung f *(Papier)* moisture expansion, wet expansion, wet-stretching
Feuchtduktor m *(Walze)* damping duct roller, water fountain roller
feuchten to damp(en), to moisten, to wet
Feuchtgehalt m *(Papier)* moisture content
Feuchtheber m *(Walze)* damping vibrator (roller), vibrating damping roller
Feuchtigkeit f humidity, moisture
Feuchtigkeitsaufnahme f *(Papier)* moisture pick-up
feuchtigkeitsempfindlich hygroscopic, moisture-sensitive
feuchtigkeitsfest moisture-proof
Feuchtigkeitsgehalt m *(Papier)* moisture content
Feuchtigkeitsmesser m *(Hygrometer)* hygrometer
Feuchtkasten m siehe Feuchtwasserkasten
Feuchtkastenwalze f damping duct roller, water fountain roller
Feuchtmengenregulierung f *(Feuchtwerk)* damping control
Feuchtmittel n damping solution, fountain solution
Feuchtmittelfilm m *(auf Offsetplatte)* fountain water film, damping film, moisture film
Feuchtmittelmeßgerät n damping measuring system, fountain solution measuring system

Feuchtmittelsteuerung - firmeneigene Drucksachenherstellung

Feuchtmittelsteuerung *f* damping control
Feuchttreiber *m (Walze)* damping distributor (roller), oscillating damping roller
Feuchttreibzylinder *m* damping distributor (roller), oscillating damping roller
Feuchtstabilität *f* hygrostability
Feuchtstreifenbreite *f (Feuchtheber)* damping stripe width
Feuchtübertragwalze *f* damping transfer roller
Feuchtung *f* damping, wetting
Feuchtwalze *f* damping roller
Feuchtwalzenbezug *m* damper cover
Feuchtwalzenschlauch *m* damper hose, damping roller sleeve
Feuchtwalzenstoff *m* moleskin, molleton
Feuchtwalzenwaschmaschine *f* damper washing machine, damping roller washing machine
Feuchtwasser *n* damping water, fountain water
Feucht(wasser)kasten *m* damping water fountain, water pan
Feuchtwasserkühlung *f* fountain solution cooling
Feuchtwassermischgerät *n* fountain solution mixer
Feuchtwasserumwälzanlage *f* fountain solution circulator
Feuchtwasserzusatz *m* fountain additive
Feuchtwerk *n* damping system, damping unit
Feuchtwerkssteuerung *f* damping unit control
Feuilleton *n (Zeitungsteil)* feuilleton
Film *m (Fot.)* film; *(Schicht)* film
Filmabstreifrakel *f* film squeegee
Filmabwicklung *f* film unwind
Filmaufwicklung *f* film rewind
Filmbühne *f (Kamera)* film holder
Filmchemie *f* film chemistry
Filmdecker *m* film overlay
Filmdicke *f* film gauge
Filmfarbwerk *n* continuous-feed inking system, continuous-type inking system
Filmfeuchtwerk *n* continuous-feed damping system, continuous-type damping system
Filmflecken *m/pl* film stains *pl*
Filmformat *n* film size
Filmkante *f* film edge, film edge marking
Filmklebeautomat *m* film adheser
Filmkleber *m* film glue
Filmkontakt *m* film contact
Filmkontaktraster *m* film contact screen
Filmkorb *m (Entwicklungsm.)* film basket
Filmkorn *n* film grain
Filmlithografie *f (im U. zur Steinlithografie)* film lithography
filmlose Plattenkopie *f* filmless platemaking

Filmmontage *f* film assembly, film flat, film montage, film stripping
Filmnutzen *m* film copy, film duplicate
Filmpackung *f* film pack
Filmrakel *f (Abstreifrakel)* film squeegee
Filmrand *m* film edge, film edge marking
Filmraster *m (im U. zu Glasraster)* film screen
Filmreiniger *m* film cleaner
Filmrekorder *m* film recorder
Filmrolle *f* film reel
Filmsatz *m (ein Satz Filme)* set of films; *(Fotosatz)* film setting
Filmsaugplatte *f (Kamera)* vacuum film holder
Filmsaugwand *f (Kamera)* vacuum film holder
Filmschablone *f* film stencil
Filmschneidegerät *n* film cutter
Filmschrank *m* film cabinet
Filmspule *f* film reel
Filmstanze *f (Registerlochung)* film punch, film register punch
Filmträger *m* film base
Filmtransport *m* film transport
Filmtrockenklammer *f* film drying clamp
Filmunterlage *f* film base
Filmverarbeitung *f* film handling, film processing
Filmverbrauch *m* film consumption
Filmvorschub *m (Fotosatz)* film advance, film feed
Filter *m* filter
Filterfaktor *m* filter factor
Filterhalter *m* filter holder
Filterrad *n* filter wheel
Filtersatz *m* set of filters
Filterung *f* filtration
Filterwahl *f* filter selection
Filtrieren *n* filtration
Filtrierleinen *n* filtering cloth
Filtrierpapier *n* filter paper
Filzaufzug *m (Zyl.)* felt dressing
Filzdecke *f (Kopierrahmen)* felt cover
Filzpappe *f* felt board
Filzseite *f (Papier)* felt side
Filztuch *n (Zyl.überzug)* felt blanket
Finalbuchstabe *m (Hebräisch, Schreibschriften usw.)* end letter, final letter
Fingerabdrücke *pl* finger marks *pl*, finger prints *pl*
Fingernagelprobe *f (Papierlaufrichtung)* fingernail test
Firmenbroschüre *f* company brochure, corporate brochure
firmeneigene Drucksachenherstellung *f* corporate publishing

Firmeneindruck *m* company name imprint
Firmensignet *n* company logo
Firmenzeichen *n* company logo
Firnis *m* varnish
Fisch *m (Handsatz)* wrong fount, wrong letter
Fischleim *m* fish glue
Fitzbund *m (Buchb.)* kettle stitch
Fixierbad *n* fixing bath
fixieren *(Fot.)* to fix
Fixierer *m (Fot.)* fixer, fixing agent
Fixiersalz *n* fixing salt
Fixkosten *pl* fix costs *pl*
Flachandruckpresse *f* flat-bed proofing press
Flachbettdruck *m* flat-bed printing
Flachbett-Druckmaschine *f* flat-bed printing press
Flachbett-Laserscanner *m* flat-bed laser scanner
Flachbett-Offsetandruckmaschine *f* flat-bed offset proofpress
Flachbett-Plotter *m (CAD)* flat-bed plotter
Flachbettscanner *m* flat-bed scanner
Flach(bett)stanze *f* flat-bed die-cutter
Flach(bett)stanzen *n* flat-bed die-cutting
Flachdraht *m (Drahtheftm.)* flat wire
Flachdruck *m (Flachbettdruck)* flat-bed printing; *(im U. zu Hoch- und Tiefdruck)* planographic printing
Flachdruckplatte *f* litho (offset) plate, offset (printing) plate
flache Gradation *f* flat gradation, soft gradation
flache Reproduktion *f* flat reproduction
flaches Negativ *n (flau)* flat negative
flache Tastatur *f* low-profile keyboard
flache Vorlage *f* flat copy, flat original
Flachform *f* flat forme
Flachformdruck *m* flat-bed printing
Flachformdruckmaschine *f* flat-bed printing press
flachliegen *(Papier)* to lay flat, to lie flat
Flachrücken *m (Buch)* flat spine, square back
Flachstapelanleger *m* vertical pile feeder
Flachstereo *n* flat stereo
Flachstichel *m* flat graver, flat scorper
Fläche *f* area, surface; *(Volltonfläche im Druck)* solid
Flächenausleuchtung *f (Reprod.)* area illumination
Flächenbelichtung *f (Zeitungssatz)* area composition
Flächendeckung *f (Rasterfläche)* area coverage, dot area
Flächendeckungsgrad *m* percent area coverage, percent dot area
Flächendruck *m* area printing, printing of solids
Flächengewicht *n (Papier)* grammage
Flächenmuster *n (Kartogr.)* area pattern; *(Untergrundmuster)* background pattern
Flächenton *m (Rasterfläche)* screen tint; *(Volltonfläche)* solid tint
flächenvariabler Tiefdruck *m* halftone gravure (process), variable-area gravure (process)
Flächenverlauf *m* graduated tint, vignetted tint
Flanke *f (Klischee)* side wall
Flankenschutzmittel *n (Klischeeherst.)* side protection resist
Flaschenetikett *n* bottle label
Flattermarken *f/pl (Buchb.)* collating marks *pl*, signature marks *pl*
Flattern *n (Papierbahn)* fluttering
Flattersatz *m* ragged composition, ragged setting, ragged type matter
Flattersatz linksbündig text ragged left
Flattersatz Mitte text ragged center
Flattersatz rechtsbündig text ragged right
flaue Flächen *pl (Druck)* faded solids *pl*
flaues Negativ *n* flat negative, weak negative
flaues Original *n* flat original
flaue Vorlage *f* flat copy, flat original
fleckig spotted, stained
fleckiger Druck *m* speckled impression, spotty impression
Fleisch *n (beim Buchstaben)* beard; *(Vor- und Nachbreite des Buchstabens)* side bearings
flexible Bindung *f* flexible binding
flexible Packstoffe *m/pl* flexible packaging
flexibler Einband *m (Buch)* flexible binding, flexible cover, soft-cover binding
flexibler Umschlag *m* flexible cover, soft cover
flexible Verpackung *f* flexible packaging
Flexodruck *m* flexographic printing, flexography, flexo printing
Flexodrucker *m* flexo printer
Flexodruckfarbe *f* flexographic ink, flexo ink, flexo printing ink
Flexodruckmaschine *f* flexographic press, flexo press, flexo printing press; *(klein)* flexo printer
Flexografie *f* flexography
Flexohülse *f* flexo sleeve
fliegende Akzente *m/pl* floating accents *pl*
fliegende Heftköpfe *pl (mitlaufend)* flying stitching heads *pl*
fliegender Eindruck *m* non-stop imprinting, on-the-fly imprinting, on-the-run imprinting
fliegender Rollenwechsel *m* flying reelchange, flying web-splice, reelchange on the run, web-splice on the run

fliegender Rollenwechsler - Formateinschub

fliegender Rollenwechsler *m* flying paster, flying splicer
fliegender Vorsatz *m (Buch)* fly-leaf
fliegendes Eindruckwerk *n (Rollendruckm.)* flying imprinting unit
fliegende Tabulatoren *pl (Fotosatz)* floating tabs *pl*
Fliegenkopf *m (Bleisatz)* turned letter
Fließbild *n* flow chart
Fließdreischneider *m* flowline (three-knife) trimmer
Fließfettschmierung *f* fluid grease lubrication
Fließsatz *m (Anzeigensatz)* classified ad matter, composition of classified ads
Fließsatzanzeige *f (Kleinanzeige)* classified ad
Fließsatzumbruch *m* classified pagination
Fließstrecke *f* flowline
Fließstreckenverarbeitung *f* flowline processing
flimmerfreier Bildschirm *m* flicker-free monitor
Flip-Top-Schachtel *f* flip-top box
Floppies *pl (Comp.)* floppies *pl*
Floppy-Disk *f* floppy disk
Floppy-Disk-Laufwerk *n (Comp.)* floppy disk drive
Florpostpapier *n* Bible paper, flimsy paper, India paper, light-weight paper, onion skin
flüchtiger Speicher *m (Comp.)* volatile memory, volatile store
flüssige Farbe *f (Tiefdruck)* ductile ink, liquid ink
Flüssigkristallanzeige *f (LCD)* liquid crystal display
Flüssigpackung *f* liquid carton
Flüssigpolymerplatte *f* liquid polymer plate
Flüssigtoner *m* liquid toner
Flugblatt *n* flyer, leaflet
Flugpostpapier *n* airmail paper
fluoreszierende Farbe *f* fluorescent ink
Flusen *pl (Papier)* fluff, fuzz, lint
flusenfreies Schneiden *n (Pappe)* fluff-free cutting
Flushen *n (Farbherst.)* flushing
Flußdiagramm *n* flow chart
Förderanlage *f* conveyor (line)
Förderband *n* conveyor belt
Förderkette *f* conveyor chain
Fördersystem *n* conveyor system
Fokus *m (Fot.)* focus
Fokussierlinsensystem *n (Kamera)* focusing lens system
Folgeschaltung *f (Maschine)* sequence control
Foliant *m* folio volume
Folie *f (Plastik)* film, film sheet, foil; *(Kleinoffsetplatte)* master; *(Metall)* foil

Folienabwicklung *f* film unwind, foil unwind
Folienaufwicklung *f* film rewind, foil rewind
Folienauswurf *m (Kleinoffsetm.)* master ejector
Folienbeschichtung *f (Kaschierung)* film laminating, foil laminating
Foliendicke *f* film gauge, film thickness
Foliendruck *m* film printing, foil printing
Folieneinschlag *m (Verpackung)* film wrapping
Folieneinzug *m (Kleinoffsetm.)* master pull unit
Folienextrusion *f* film extrusion
Folienkamera *f (Kleinoffset)* camera-platemaker, direct master camera
Folienkaschiermaschine *f* film laminating machine, foil laminating machine
folienkaschierter Karton *m* film-laminated board
Folienkaschierung *f* film laminating, film-to-print laminating, foil laminating
Folienpackmaschine *f (Versandraum)* film wrapping machine
Folienprägung *f* foil blocking, foil stamping
Folienreiniger *m* film cleaner
Folienstärke *f* film gauge, film thickness
Folienstanze *f* film punch, film register punch, foil punch
Folientasche *f (Heißversiegelung)* foil pouch
Folientastatur *f* membran switch
Folienverarbeitung *f* film processing, foil processing
Folienverpackung *f* film packaging, film wrapping
folieren to number, to page
Folioausgabe *f* folio edition
Folioformat *n* folio size
Fond *m (Hintergrundton im Druckmotiv)* background, background tint, tint, tinted background
Fond einziehen to lay a (background) tint
Font *m (Fotosatzschrift)* font
Fontanwahl *f (Fotosetzmasch.)* font selection
Form *f (Druckform)* forme, print(ing) forme; *(Gestalt, Umriß)* shape; *(Gießform)* cast
Format *n* dimensions *pl*, format, size
Formatänderung *f* format change, size change
Formatbegrenzung des Farbkastens narrowing of ink duct width
Formatberechnung *f* calculation of size, estimate of size
Formatbereich *m* format range, size range
Formatbogen *m* trimmed sheet
Formatbuch *n (Blindband)* blank book, dummy, sample binding, sample volume
Formateinschub *m (Kassettendruckwerk)* printing cartridge, slide-in carriage, slide-in cassette

Formateinstellung f *(Druckm.)* format adjustment, format setting, size adjustment, size setting; *(Reprod.)* copy scaling, scaling, sizing

formatierte Daten *pl* formatted data

formatierter Text *m* formatted text

Formatierung f *(Daten)* formatting

Format mit Beschnittzugabe *(Zeitschriftendruck)* bleed size

Formatpapier n *(im U. zu Rollenpapier)* paper cut to size, sheet paper

Formatskala f *(z. B. auf Filmsaugwand)* scale grid

Formatspeicher m *(Comp.)* format storage

Formatstege *pl (Bleisatz)* furniture

Formatumstellung f format change-over, size change-over

formatvariable Druckmaschine f *(im U. zu festformatiger)* variable-size printing press

Formatveränderung f format change, size change

Formatwechsel m format change, size change

Formbrett n *(Bleisatz)* type board

Formeinpassen n *(Druckform)* forme positioning

Formeinpaßvorrichtung f forme positioning device

Formel f formula

Formelsatz m formula setting, maths setting

Formenmontage f *(Druckform)* forme assembly

Formenregal n *(Bleisatz)* forme rack

Formenschlüssel m *(Buchdruck)* quoin key

Formentransportwagen m *(Buchdruck)* forme trolley

Formfundament n *(Buchdruckm.)* forme bed

formgestanzte Etiketten *n/pl* shaped labels *pl*

Formkarren m *(Buchdruckm.)* forme carriage

Formrahmen m *(Buchdruck)* chase, forme chase

Formsatz m *(Typogr.)* shape setting

Formschließen n *(Buchdruck)* chase locking, quoining

formschlüssiges Farbmesser n continuous ink duct blade

Formstanzen n *(im U. zu Lochstanzen)* die-cutting

Formular n blank (form), form

Formulardruck m forms printing, stationery printing

Formulardrucker m forms printer

Formulardruckmaschine f business forms press, forms press, stationery printing press

Formulargestaltung f form design

Formularheftung f forms binding, forms stitching

Formularherstellung f forms production, stationery production

Formularsatz m *(mehrere Einzelblätter zu einem Satz gebunden)* forms set; **Vierblatt ~** four-part forms set, four-ply forms set; *(Typogr.)* forms composition, forms setting

Formularsatzleimung f forms set gluing

Formularzusammentragmaschine f forms collator

Form- und Vulkanisierpresse f moulding and vulcanizing press

Formwalze f *(Auftragswalze)* forme roller

Form zum Umdrehen twist forme, work and twist forme

Form zum Umschlagen turn forme, work and turn forme

Form zum Umstülpen tumble forme, work and tumble forme

Formzylinder m forme cylinder

Fortbildung f advanced training

Fortdruck m *(im Gs. zum Andruck)* final run, production printing, production run

Fortdruckbogen m production printsheet

Fortdrucke *m/pl (Bogen)* run-ons *pl*

fortdruckgerechter Andruck m production-true print proof

Fortdruckleistung f production output

Fortdruckmakulatur f production run waste

Fortdruckmaschine f production press

Fortdruckplatte f production plate

fortlaufende Numerierung f consecutive numbering, sequential numbering, successive numbering

Fortsetzung folgt to be continued

Fortsetzungsroman m *(Zeitung)* serial story

Fortsetzung umseitig continued overleaf

Foto n photo(graph); *(Abzug)* print

Fotoabzug m photoprint, print

Fotoalbum n photo album

Fotochemie f photochemistry

Fotochemigraf m photo-engraver, process engraver

Fotochemigrafie f photo-engraving, process engraving

Fotochemikalien *pl* photochemicals *pl*

fotochemischer Prozeß m photo-chemical process

Fotocomposing n photocomposing

Fotodiode f photodiode

Fotodirektplatte f *(für Kameradirektbelichtung)* photo-direct plate

fotoelektronische Reproduktion f photo-electronic reproduction

Fotograf m photographer

Fotografie f *(Bild)* photo(graph); *(Vorgang)* photography

fotografieren to photograph

fotografische Gelatine - freistellen

fotografische Gelatine f photographic gelatine
fotografische Reproduktion f photographic reproduction
fotografische Verfremdung f photographic falsification
Fotogrammetrie f photogrammetry
Fotogravüre f heliogravure, intaglio engraving, intaglio photogravure
Fotohalbleiterschicht f photo semi-conductor coating
Fotohandsatz m photolettering
Fotokarton m photographic board
Fotokopie f photocopy, photostat
fotokopieren to photocopy
Fotokopiergerät n photocopier
Fotokorn n photographic grain
Fotolabor n photographic laboratory
Fotoleiter m photo-conductor
Fotolithograf m photo lithographer
Fotolithografie f photo lithography
Fotolithoretuscheur m photo-litho retoucher
Fotolyse f photolysis
Fotomaterial n photographic material, photographic media
fotomechanische Reproduktion f photomechanical reproduction
Fotometer n *(Lichtmeßgerät)* photometer
Fotomontage f photomontage
Fotomultiplier m *(Lichtverstärker)* photomultiplier
Fotopapier n photographic paper, photo paper
Fotoplotter m photoplotter
Fotopolymerplatte f photopolymer plate
Fotoreporter m photoreporter
Fotorestauration f photographic restoration
Fotosatz m photocomposition, photosetting, phototypesetting
Fotosatzbetrieb m phototypesetting house, phototypesetting studio
Fotosatzgerät n filmsetter, photosetter, phototypesetter
Fotosatzkompaktanlage f *(im U. zum modularen System)* direct-entry phototypesetter
Fotosatzmaschine f phototypesetting machine, photocomposition machine, filmsetter, photosetter, phototypesetter
Fotosatzschrift f font, photocomposition typeface, phototypesetting font
Fotosatzstudio n phototypesetting studio
Fotosatzsystem n photocomposition system, phototypesetting system
Fotoschablone f *(Siebdruck)* photo stencil
Fotoschablonenfilm m photo-stencil film

Fotosensor m *(Meßtechnik)* photo sensor
Fototypie f *(Lichtdruck)* collotype, phototype; *(Verfahren)* collotype printing, phototype printing
Fotozeichnung f photo drawing
Fotozelle f photocell
Fräsapparat m routing machine
Fräsen n *(Klebebindung)* routing
Fräskante f routing edge
Fräsklebebindung f *(im U. zu Perfoklebebindung)* routing adhesive binding
Fräskopf m routing head
Fräsmaschine f routing machine
Fräspantograf m pantographic routing machine
Fräsrand m routing margin
Fragezeichen n question mark
Fraktur f *(Schrift)* Black Letters and Broken, broken types *pl*, old black
Franzfilet n *(Buchb.)* floret
französische Anführungszeichen pl French quotes *pl*
Französische Renaissance-Antiqua f *(Schriftklassif.)* Garaldics *pl*
freibewegliche Tastatur f freely movable keyboard
frei definierbar *(Funktionen im System)* user-definable
freie Figuren f/pl *(CAD)* irregular shapes *pl*
Freiexemplar n complimentary copy, free copy
Freigabebogen m *(Druckreiferklärung)* o.k. proof, o.k. sheet, passed proof, passed sheet
freigeschlagener Raum m blank space, free space, space left white, window
freigestelltes Bild n cut-out figure, cut-out image, isolated figure, outlined figure, silhouette image
freilassen *(im Satz)* to leave blank, to leave white space
freilaufen *(Offsetplatte)* to run clean
frei pflegbares Programm *(Comp.)* user-updateable program
frei programmierbar *(Funktionen im System)* operator-programmable, user programmable
Freiraum m *(freigeschlagener Raum im Layout, Umbruch)* blank space, free space, space left white, window
freischlagen *(Räume in Layout, Umbruch usw.)* to blank, to leave blank, to leave white space
freistehendes Bild n cut-out figure, cut-out image, isolated figure, outlined figure, silhouette image
freistellen *(Bild)* to cut out, to isolate, to outline, to silhouette

Freisteller *m (Freistellmaske)* cut-out mask, outline mask, silhouette mask
Freistellmaske *f (Reprod.)* cut-out mask, outline mask, silhouette mask
Freistellung *f (Vorlagenherst.)* cut-out, silhouette
Freizeile *f (Satz)* blank line, white line
Fremddaten *pl (fremde Systeme)* external data, outside data
Fremddatenkonvertierung *f* external data conversion
Fremddatenübernahme *f* external data acceptance, external data transfer
fremder Tastaturplan *m (Texterf.)* Dvorak keyboard
Fremde Schriften *pl (Schriftklassif.)* Foreign Types *pl*
Fremdgerät *n (von anderem Hersteller)* device of a different make, external device
Fremdlicht *n* ambient light
Fremdspracheneindruck *m* foreign-language imprint
Fremdsprachensatz *m* composition of foreign language work, foreign language setting
Fremdsystem *n* external system, foreign system, system of a different make
Frequenzmodulierung *f (Comp.)* frequency modulation
Friktionsantrieb *m* friction drive
frisch bedruckt freshly printed, hot off the press
frischer Druck *m* freshly printed sheet, fresh print
Fröschchen *n (Anlegemarke)* gauge pin, lay mark
Frontanschlag *m* front stop
Frontausleger *m* front delivery
Frontbeschnitt *m* face cut, front trim(ming)
Frontdruck *m (Buchschnitt)* foredge printing, printing of front trim
Frontend-Geräte *n/pl* front-ends *pl*, front-end units *pl*
Frontend-System *n* front-end system
Frontend-Terminal *m* front-end terminal
Frontmesser *n* front knife
Frontschnitt *m* face cut, front trim(ming)
Frühausgabe *f (Zeitung)* early edition
Frühbogen *m (Anlage)* early sheet
Frühdrucke *m/pl (Wiegendruck)* incunabula *pl*
Fühler *m (Meßtechnik)* sensor
Fühlerlehre *f* feeler gauge
Führer *m (Leitfaden, Nachschlagebuch)* guide
Führungsblech *n* metal guide
Führungskanal *m (Sammelhefter, Zusammentragmaschine)* raceway
Führungskurve *f* guide cam

Führungsleiste *f* guide bar
Führungsmarke *f* guide mark
Führungspunkte *pl (Satz)* dot leaders *pl*, leaders *pl*
Führungsrandlochung *f (Endlosdruck)* line hole punching, line holes, sprocket hole punching, sprocket holes
Führungsschiene *f* guide rail
Führungsstift *m* guide pin
Führungsstriche *m/pl (Satz)* dash leaders *pl*
Führungswalze *f* guide roller
Füller *m (Zeitung)* filler
Füllstoffe *pl (Papierherst.)* fillers *pl*
Fütterung *f (Umschlag, Tüte)* lining
Fundament *n* base, bed, foundation
Funkbild *n* wire photo(graph)
Funktionsablauf *m* sequence of functions
Funktionskode *m* function code
Funktionssicherheit *f* functional reliability
Fuß *m (der Seite; des Buchstabens)* foot; *(Klischee)* base, mount
Fußantrieb *m* pedal operation, treadle operation
Fußbeschnitt *m* foot trim(ming), tail trim(ming)
Fusseln *pl (Papier)* fluff, fuzz, lint
Fußhebel *m* foot lever
Fußleiste *f (Verzierung)* tail-piece
Fußlinie *f (Satz)* bottom rule, foot rule
Fußnote *f (Satz)* bottom note, footnote
Fußnotenreferenz *f* footnote (callout) reference
Fußpresse *f* foot press
Fußsteg *m* foot stick
Fußtritt *m (zwischen Druckwerken)* footboard, platform
Fußzeile *f (Satz)* bottom line
Futter *n (Umschlag, Beutel)* lining
Futteral *n (Buch)* slip case
Futterpapier *n (Umschlag, Tüte)* lining paper
Futterseidenpapier *n (Umschlag, Tüte)* lining tissue

G

Gabelhubwagen *m* pallet truck
Gabelstapler *m* forklift truck
Gänsefüßchen *pl* German quote marks *pl*; *(Anführungszeichen)* quote marks *pl*, quotes *pl*

Galerie - gegenläufige Abrakelung

Galerie f *(Masch.)* balcony, gallery
Gallium-Jodid-Lampe f gallium iodide lamp
Gallytiegel m Gally platen press
galvanische Korrektur f electrolytical correction
galvanisches Bad n electrolytical bath
galvanisieren to electroplate, to electroplate
Galvanisierung f *(Buchdruck)* electrotyping; *(Tiefdruck)* electroplating
Galvano n electro(type)
Galvanoplastik f *(Buchdruck)* electro(type), electrotyping
galvanoplastische Prägepresse f moulding press for electrotypes
Gamma n *(Reprod.)* gamma
gammavariabler Film m variable-gamma film
Gammawert m gamma value
Gang m *(Masch.)* operation, running
Ganz(ein)band m *(Buch)* full binding
Ganzlederband m full leather binding
Ganzleinenband m full cloth binding
Ganzrücken m *(Buch)* full back
Ganzseitenausgabe f full-page output
Ganzseitenbelichtung f full-page exposure, full-page output, full-page recording
Ganzseitenfilm m full-page film
Ganzseitenmater f page matrix
Ganzseitenmontage f full-page make-up; *(geklebt)* full-page paste-up
Ganzseitenübertragung f *(Telekomm.)* full-page transmission
Ganzseitenumbruch m full-page make-up
ganzseitige Abbildung f full-page illustration
ganzseitige Anzeige f full-page ad(vertisement)
ganzseitiger Textkorrekturbeleg m full-page text proof
Gasbrenner m *(Farbtrocknung)* gas burner
Gasentladungslampe f gas discharge lamp
Gasflammentrockner m gas flame dryer
Gasofen m *(Farbtrocknung)* gas oven
Gastrockner m gas dryer
Gaufrieren n goffering
gautschen *(Papierherst.)* to couch
Gautschpresse f couch press
Gaze f *(Buchbind., Siebdruck)* gauze
Gazeaufspannvorrichtung f gauze stretching device
Gazeheftung f *(Buchb.)* book-sewing through gauze
Gazepapier n gauze paper
Gaze- und Fälzelstation f *(Buchherst.)* gauze and lining station
geätzte Platte f etched plate
geätzter Zylinder m *(Tiefdruck)* etched cylinder

Gebetbuch n prayer-book
Gebinde n *(Behälter)* container; *(Heftschnüre)* bands pl, cords pl
Gebläse n *(Gebläseluft)* blast; *(Masch.)* blowers pl
gebrauchsfertige Lösung f ready-to-use solution
Gebrauchsgrafik f advertising art(work), commercial art(work)
Gebrauchsgrafiker m advertising designer, commercial artist, commercial designer, industrial artist
Gebrauchtmaschine f second-hand machine
Gebrochene Schriften pl *(Schriftklassif.)* Black Letters and Broken, broken types pl
gebrochene Ziffern pl fractional numbers pl; *(Satz)* compound fractions pl, piece fractions pl, split fractions pl
gebürstete Aluminiumplatte f brushed aluminium plate
gebundenes Buch n bound book
Geburtsanzeige f birth announcement
gecrimpter Satz m *(Formularsatz)* crimplock set
gedämpfte Farbe f shaded colour
gedämpftes Licht n *(Reprod.)* subdued light
Gedankenstrich m dash
Gedichtsatz m poetry setting
gedruckt printed; *das Buch ist im Tiefdruck ~* the book is printed by gravure
gedruckte Medien pl printed media, print media
gedruckte Schaltung f printed circuit, printed circuit board
gedrucktes Manuskript n *(Drucksache als Satzvorlage)* printed copy, reprint copy
gedruckte Werbung f *(im U. zu Fernsehwerbung)* press and print advertising
gefährliche Abfallstoffe pl hazardous waste
gefälzelt *(Buch)* back-stripped, spine-taped
gefärbter Buchschnitt m coloured book edge
gefärbtes Papier n tinted paper
gefalzte Seite f *(im Gs. zur offenen)* folded edge
gefederter Stift m *(mech.)* spring-loaded pin
gefütterter Beutel m lined bag
gefütterter Papiersack m lined paper bag
gefütterte Schachtel f lined box
Gegendruck m *(Zylindersystem)* back pressure, impression pressure
Gegendruckzylinder m *(Druckzylinder)* impression cylinder
gegeneinanderlaufende Walzen pl counter-rotating rollers pl
gegenläufige Abrakelung f *(Tiefdruck)* negative doctoring, reverse (angle) doctoring

gegenläufige Rakel - Gesangbuch

gegenläufige Rakel f negative doctor blade, reverse angle doctor blade
Gegenmaske f counter mask
gegenprüfen to crosscheck
gegenüberliegende Seiten f/pl (Buch, Zeitschrift) opposite pages pl
gegenüber Redaktion (Anzeigenplaz.) opposite editorial
gegossene Schriftzeile f slug
gehämmertes Papier n hammer finished paper
Gehäuse n (Masch.) casing, housing; (Schachtel, Kassette) box
geheftet (Draht) stitched; (Faden) sewn
Gehrungslinien f/pl (Bleisatz) mitred rules pl
Gehrungsquadrat n (Bleisatz) mitred quad
Gehrungsschlitz m (Faltschachtel) stitch lap
Gehrungsschnitt m (Bleisatz) mitred cut
Geisterbild n (Druck) ghost image
gekapselt (Schallschutz) cased, enclosed
geklebter Karton m pasteboard
gekürzte Ausgabe f abridged edition
Gelatine f gelatine
Gelatinefilm m gelatine film
Gelatinefilter m gelatine filter
Gelatinelösung f gelatine solution
Gelatinepapier n gelatine paper
Gelatinepauspapier n gelatine tracing paper
Gelatinequellrelief n gelatine relief
Gelatineschicht f gelatine coating, gelatine film, gelatine layer
Gelatineschichtgerbung f gelatine hardening
Gelatinewalze f gelatine roller
Gelb n (Skalenfarbe) yellow
Gelbauszug m (Reprod.) yellow separation
Gelbfilm m (Auszugsfilm) yellow film, yellow printer
Gelbfilter m yellow filter
Gelbform f (Druckform) yellow forme
gelblich yellowish
Gelbplatte f yellow plate, yellow printer
Gelbstich m yellow cast
geleimte Pappe f pasteboard, sized board
geleimtes Papier n sized paper
Geleitwort n (Buch) foreword, introduction
gelernte Arbeitskraft f qualified operator, skilled operator, trained operator
gematerte Seite f page matrix
Gemeine pl (kleine Buchstaben) lower-case letters pl
Gemeinkosten pl overhead costs pl, overheads pl
gemischter Druck m (Sammelform) gang printing
gemischter Satz m mixed setting
genaue Abwicklung f (Zylinder) true rolling

genauer Passer m close register, hairline register
genaues Register n close register, hairline register
Generationskopie f (Zeichnung) generation copy
geometrische Figuren f/pl (CAD) regular shapes pl
geometrisches Zeichen n geometrical sign
geprägte Mater f moulded matrix
geprägte Schachtel f embossed box
geprägtes Papier n embossed paper
gepreßte Falzbogen m/pl compressed signatures pl
gepreßter Stapel m (Versandraum) compressed bundle
gerade Nummer f even number
geraderichten to straighten
gerader Rücken m flat spine, square back
gerade Seiten f/pl (Paginierung) even folios pl, even pages pl
gerad(e)stehende Schrift f roman type(face)
gerad(e)stoßen (Bogen) to jog, to knock up
geradlinige Gradation f (Reprod.) linear gradation
Geradstoßer m (Maschinenauslage) jogger, side jogger, vibrator
Geräteschrank m tool cabinet, tool cupboard
geräuschdämpfend noise-deadening
geräuschloser Lauf m (Maschine) silent operation
Geräuschminderung f noise reduction
gerasterte Ausgabe f (Belichter) screened output
gerasterte Farbauszüge m/pl halftone separations pl, screened separations pl
gerasterter Rahmen m screened box
gerasterter Vierfarbdruck m four-colour halftone print
gerasterter Vierfarbsatz m (Reprod.) four-colour halftone set
gerben (fot.) to tan
Gerbentwickler m tanning developer
Gerbsäure f tannic acid, tannin
Gerbung f tanning
geriffelte Walze f grooved roller, knurled roller
geringer Kontrast m low contrast
geripptes Papier n laid paper
geruchfreie Farbe f odourless ink, scentless ink
Geruchsabsaugung f (Trockner) odour extraction
gesammelte Produktion f (Rollendruckm.) collect-run production
Gesamtfertigungszeit f total production time
Gesamtkosten pl total costs pl
Gesamtseitenzahl f (Paginierung) total number of pages, total page count, total pagination
Gesangbuch n choir book

Geschäftsbericht - glänzend gestrichenes Papier

Geschäftsbericht *m* business report, company report, corporate report
Geschäftsbuch *n* ledger
Geschäftsdrucksachen *pl* business stationery, commercial stationery
Geschäftsformulare *n/pl* business forms *pl*, commercial forms *pl*
Geschäftskarte *f* business card
Geschenkpapier *n* gift-wrap
geschlängelte Linie *f* wavy line, wavy rule
geschlossene Kurvenführung *f* closed cam guide system
geschlossener Kopf *m (Falzbogen)* closed head
geschlossener Regelkreis *m* closed loop (circuit)
geschlossenes Regal *n* cabinet, cupboard
geschriebenes Manuskript *n* written copy, written manuscript
geschultes Auge *n* trained human eye
geschuppt shingled
geschweifte Klammern *f/pl (Satz)* braces *pl*
geschwindigkeitskompensierter Antrieb *m* speed-compensated drive
Geschwindigkeitsregler *m* speed regulator
gesetzt *(Schrift)* composed, set
Gesicht *n (Buchstabe)* face
gespeicherte Daten *pl* stored data
gespeicherter Text *m* stored text
gesprenkelt *(Buchschnitt, Vorsatz)* marbled, mottled
gestalten *(grafisch)* to create, to design
Gestalter *m (für Drucksachen)* graphic designer
gestaltete Anzeige *f (im U. zur Fließanzeige)* display ad
Gestaltung *f (grafisch)* graphic design, graphic display, layout design
Gestaltungsarbeitsplatz *m* graphic design workstation, graphic workstation, layout workstation
Gestaltungsbildschirm *m* graphic display screen
Gestaltungselement *n* design element, layout element
Gestaltungsredakteur *m* layout editor
Gestaltungsstudio *n* art studio, graphic design studio, graphics studio
Gestaltungsterminal *n* graphic display terminal, layout terminal
Gestehungskosten *pl* production costs *pl*
Gestell *n (Masch.)* frame
gestochene Platte *f* engraved plate
gestochen scharf crisp and clean, pinsharp, razor sharp
gestochen scharfer Rasterpunkt *m* pinsharp dot
gestrichenes Papier *n* coated paper, coated stock

gestürzter Buchstabe *m* rotated character, rotated type
gestürzte Seite *f* rotated page
gesundheitlich unbedenklich harmless to health, non-toxic
gesundheitsschädlich harmful to health, toxic
geteilter Bildschirm *m* split screen
Getrenntnutzenauslage *f (Stanzlinie)* separate blank delivery
Getrenntzähler *m (gute/unbrauchbare Exemplare)* good and bad copy counter
getreue Farbwiedergabe *f* colour fidelity
getreue Punkt-für-Punkt-Wiedergabe *f* dot fidelity
getreue Wiedergabe *f* faithful reproduction, reproduction fidelity
Getriebe *n* drive, gear
Getriebekasten *m* gearbox
Geviert *n (Satz)* em, em-quad, em space
Geviertstrich *m* em-dash
Gewebe *n (Siebdruck)* fabric, mesh, tissue
Gewebeaufrauhung *f* fabric roughening
Gewebebespanner *m* fabric stretcher
Gewebevorbehandlung *f (Siebdruck)* fabric preparation
Gewerkschaft Druck *f* Printers Union
gewöhnlicher Tastaturplan *m (Texterf.)* qwerty layout
gewöhnliche Schrift *f (geradstehend)* roman type(face)
gewölbter Karton *m* buckled board, warped board
gewölbter Deckel *m (Schachtel)* dome-shaped cover
gewölbter Rücken *m (Buch)* round(ed) back
gezeichnete Initiale *f* drawn initial (letter)
gezielte Retusche *f* pinpointed retouching
Gießapparat *m* caster, casting machine; *(Stereot.)* stereo caster
gießen *(Emulsionen)* to coat; *(Handsatzschrift)* to found; *(Maschinensatz/Stereo)* to cast
Gießform *f (Stereotypie)* casting mould
Gießmaschine *f* caster, casting machine
Gießmaschine für Zeilenguß slug caster
giftig toxic
Gigantografie *f (Großformatreprod.)* gigantography
Glacékarton *m* glazed board, glossy board
Glacépapier *n* glazed paper, glossy paper
glänzende Farbe *f* brilliant ink, glossy ink
glänzendes Papier *n* glazed paper, glossy paper
glänzend gestrichenes Papier *n* glossy coated paper

Glätte f *(Glanzglätte auf Walze, Gummituch usw.)* glaze; *(Papier)* glossiness, smoothness
Glätteprüfer m *(Papier)* smoothness tester
Glättpresse f *(Papierherst.)* glazing press
Glättwalze f *(Papierherst.)* glazing cylinder, glazing roller
Glättwerk n *(Papierherst.)* calender
Glättzylinder m *(Papierherst.)* glazing cylinder
Glanz m *(Farbe)* brilliance, gloss; *(Papier)* glaze, gloss
Glanzaufkupferung f *(Tiefdruck)* high-polish coppering
Glanzbad n *(Tiefdruck)* high-polish coppering bath
Glanzfarbe f *(Druckfarbe)* glossy ink
Glanzfirnis m glossy varnish
Glanzfolie f *(Kaschierung)* acetate film
Glanzfolienkaschierung f acetate laminating, celloglazing, film laminating
glanzgestrichenes Papier n glossy coated paper
Glanzglätte f *(auf Druckluch, Walzen)* glaze
Glanzkalander m calender
Glanzkarton m glazed board, glossy board
Glanzkaschierfolie f acetate film, laminating film
Glanzkupfer n *(Tiefdruck)* high-polish copper
Glanzkupferverfahren n *(Tiefdruck)* ballard process, high-polish coppering process
Glanzlack m *(Überdrucklack)* glossy varnish, high-gloss varnish
Glanzlicht n glare
glanzlos dull, matt
Glanzpapier n art paper, enamel paper, glazed paper, glossy paper
Glanzpappe f glazed board, glossy board
Glanzschwarz n *(Druckfarbe)* brilliant black
Glanzüberdrucklack m glossy overprint varnish
Glanzverschnitt m *(Tiefdruckfarbe)* glossy gravure varnish
Glanzzusatz m *(Farbe)* glossy additive
Glasabziehbild n transparent decal
Glasfaserkabel n fibre optic cable
Glasfasern f/pl optical fibres pl
Glasfasernetz n *(Telekomm.)* fibre optics network
Glasgravurraster m *(Kamera)* engraved glass screen
Glasgravur-Tiefdruckraster m engraved rotogravure screen
glasklare Folie f highly transparent film
Glasmärbeln pl *(Schleifkugeln)* glass graining marbles pl
Glasmaßstab m glass measure, glass scale
Glasmontage f glass mounting

Glasnegativ n glass negative
Glasperlentuch n *(farbabstoßend)* glass-bead blanket
Glasraster m *(im Gs. zu Filmraster)* glass screen
glatte Oberfläche f smooth surface
glatter Satz m *(im U. zu Layoutsatz)* body matter, straight matter, text matter
glattes Gummituch n *(Glanzglätte)* glazed blanket
glatte Volltonfläche f smooth solid
glatte Walze f *(Glanzglätte)* glazed roller
glattgeschnittene Etiketten n/pl straight-cut labels pl
glattklopfen *(Buchdruckform)* to knock flat, to plane down
glattstoßen *(Bogen)* to jog, to knock up
Glattstoßmaschine f *(Rüttler)* jogger
Gleichheitszeichen n *(Satz)* equal sign
Gleichlaufsteuerung zwischen den Druckwerken unit-to-unit phasing device
gleichmäßig ausschließen to space equally, to space evenly
gleichmäßige Farbführung f even inking, uniform inking
gleichmäßige Qualität f consistent quality
gleichmäßige Raumverteilung f even spacing
gleichmäßiger Lauf m smooth running
gleichmäßige Verteilung f even distribution
Gleichstrom m D.C., direct current
Gleichstrommotor m D.C. motor
Gleichung f *(Formelsatz)* equation
gleiten to slide
Gleitführung f slide guide
Gleitschiene f slide rail
Glossar n glossary
Glückwunschkarte f greetings card
Glühlampe f incandescent lamp
Glykol n glycol
Glyzerin n glycerine
GMCS *(Gelb Magenta Cyan Schwarz)* YMCB
Goldbronze f gold bronze
Golddruck m gold printing; *(Goldprägung)* gold blocking, gold stamping; *(Schnittvergoldung)* gilding
Golddruckfarbe f gold ink
Golddruckpresse f *(Prägepresse)* gold blocking press
Goldener Schnitt m *(Typogr.)* golden section
Goldfolie f gold foil
Goldfolienprägepresse f gold blocking press
Goldlinie f *(Buchb.)* gold rule
Goldpapier n gold paper
Goldprägepresse f gold blocking press

Goldprägung f gold blocking, gold stamping
Goldschnitt m *(Buch)* edge gilding, gilt edge
Goldschnittautomat m edge gilding machine
Goldschnittfolie f edge gilding foil
Goldunterdruckfarbe f *(Bronzieren)* gold bronzing primer
Gotisch f *(Schrift)* Black Letters and Broken, broken types *pl,* Gothic, Gothic face, old black
gotische Minuskel f Gothic minuscule
Grabstichel m chisel, graver
Gradation f gradation
Gradation in den Lichtern highlight gradation
Gradation in den Mitteltönen mid-tone gradation
Gradation in den Tiefen shadow gradation
Gradationskurve f gradation curve
Gradient m *(Reprod.)* gradient
Gradzeichen n *(°)* degree sign
Grafik f art(work), drawing, graph, graphics, print; *(Tafel)* chart
Grafikatelier n art studio, graphic design studio, graphics studio
Grafikbildschirm m graphic display screen
Grafik-Designer m graphic designer
Grafiker m commercial artist, graphic artist, graphic designer
Grafikscanner m graphic scanner
Grafikstudio n art studio, graphic design studio, graphics studio
Grafiktablett n *(elektron. Reprod.)* graphic tablet
Grafikterminal m graphic display terminal
Grafikverarbeitung f graphics handling, graphics processing
grafische Arbeitsstation f graphic design workstation, graphic workstation
grafische Darstellung f chart, diagram, graph
grafische Fachausstellung f graphic arts exhibition, graphic arts trade fair
grafische Fachzeitschrift f graphic arts magazine, print(ing) journal, print(ing) magazine
grafische Feinpapiere n/pl fine printing papers *pl*
grafische Industrie f graphic arts industry, graphics industry; *(Druckind.)* printing industry
grafische Kommunikation f graphic communications *pl*
grafische Künste *pl* graphic arts *pl*
grafischer Arbeitsplatz m graphic design workstation, graphic workstation
grafischer Betrieb m printing company, printing firm, printing house

grafischer Bildschirm m graphic display screen
grafischer Fachhändler m graphic arts dealer, graphic arts supplier, printer's supplier
grafischer Großbetrieb m industrial printer, industrial printhouse, large commercial printer, large printing concern
grafischer Zulieferer m graphic arts dealer, graphic arts supplier, printer's supplier
grafisches Atelier n art studio, graphic design studio, graphics studio
grafisches Gewerbe n graphic arts industry
grafisches Tablett n *(elektron. Reprod.)* graphic tablet
grafische Zulieferindustrie f graphics supply industry
Grafitierbürste f black leading brush
Grafitretusche f graphite retouching
Grat m *(Schnitt)* burr
gratfreies Schneiden n burr-free cutting
Gratulationskarte f greetings card
Grauaddition f *(Reprod.)* grey addition
Grauanteil m grey content
Graubalance f grey balance
Graufstufenkompression f grey scale compression
Grauguß m *(Maschinenteile)* cast iron
Graukarton m grey board
Graukeil m grey-wedge
Grauraster m *(im U. zu Magentaraster)* grey screen
Grauschleier m grey fog, grey veil
Grauskala f grey scale
Graustufe f grey level
Graustufenkeil m grey-scale wedge, grey step wedge
Grautöne *pl* grey tones *pl,* grey shades *pl,* grey tints *pl*
Grauwert m grey value; *(im Gs. zum Buntwert)* neutral tone
Graveur m engraver
gravieren to cut, to engrave
Gravierfilm m engraving film
Gravierinstrument n engraving tool
Graviermaschine f engraving machine
Graviernadel f engraving needle, engraving stylus
Gravierstichel m engraving stylus
gravierte Platte f engraved plate
gravierter Zylinder m engraved cylinder
Gravierwerkzeug n engraving tool; *(CAD)* scriber cutter, scribe tool
Gravis m *(è)* grave accent
Gravur f engraving
Gravurplatte f engraved plate

Gravurraster - Guillochenraster

Gravurraster *m* engraved screen
Gravurstichel *m* engraving stylus
Gravurwalze *f* engraved roller
Greifer *m* gripper
Greiferauflage *f* gripper pad
Greiferauslage *f* gripper delivery
Greiferbrücke *f* gripper bar
Greiferexzenter *m* gripper cam
Greiferkante *f (Bogen, Gummituch)* gripper edge
Greiferleiste *f* gripper bar
greiferloses Lackierwerk *n* gripper-free varnishing device
Greiferöffnung *f* gripper opening
Greiferöffnungskurve *f* gripper opening cam
Greiferrand *m (Bogen)* gripper margin
Greiferrandabfall *m (Bogen)* front waste
Greiferschluß *m (Greiferaktion)* grip, gripper bite, gripper closure
Greiferstange *f* gripper bar
Greifersteg *m (Rand)* gripper margin
Greifersystem *n* gripper system
Greiferüberführungssystem *n* gripper transfer system
Greiferwagen *m* gripper carriage
Greiffalz *m* gripper fold
griechische Schrift *f* Greek characters *pl*, Greek letters *pl*, Greek type
Griffel *m* stylus
griffiges Papier *n* paper of good feel
Griffregister *n* register tabs *pl*, tabs *pl*; *(Daumenregister)* thumb index, thumb register
Grobrasterätzung *f* coarse screen etching
Grobrasterautotypie *f* coarse screen halftone engraving
Grobraster/Feinrastermessung *f (Densitometrie)* coarse screen/fine screen measurement
Größe *f* format, size
Größeneinstellung *f (Druckm.)* format adjustment, format setting, size adjustment, size setting; *(Reprod.)* copy scaling, scaling, sizing
größtes Papierformat *n* maximum sheet size
Großauflage *f (Buch)* large edition; *(Druck)* large-volume printwork, long print run, long run (job), voluminous print run; *(Zeitschrift)* large circulation
Großbildplakat *n* large-size poster
Großbildreproduktion *f* large-scale reproduction, poster reproduction
Großbuchbinderei *f* industrial bookbinder, large commercial bookbinder
Großbuchstabe *m* capital (letter), uppercase letter
Großdruckerei *f* industrial printer, large commercial printer, large printing concern
große Auflage *f* siehe Großauflage
große Bindequote *f* large-volume bookbinding work
großer Anfangsbuchstabe *m* initial capital, large initial letter
großes R *(Satz)* uppercase R
große Zeitung *f (hohe Auflage)* large-circulation newspaper
Großfolio *n* large folio
Großformat *n* large format, large size; *(Zeitung)* broadsheet size
großformatige Druckmaschine *f* large-size (printing) press
großformatige Zeitung *f* broadsheet newspaper
Großkegel *m (Schrift)* large body size
Groß/Kleinschreibung *f (Satz)* capitals and lowercase
Großprojektion *f (Reprod.)* large-scale projection
Großrechner *m (System)* mainframe computer
Großschreibung *f* capitalization
Großstadtzeitung *f* metropolitan newspaper
Großvergrößerung *f* large-scale reproduction
Groteskschriften *pl* grotesque typefaces *pl*, sans serif typefaces *pl*
Grünfilter *m* green filter
grünlich greenish
Grundaufbau *m (System)* basic configuration
Grundausbildung *f* basic training
Grundeinstellung *f (Maschine)* basic setting, initial setting
Grundfarben *f/pl (Farbensystem)* basic colours *pl*
Grundgestell *n (Maschine)* basic frame
Grundierlack *m* varnishing primer
Grundierleim *m* gluing primer
Grundierung *f* primer coating
Grundkupfer *n (Tiefdruckzyl.)* base copper, copperplate base
Grundlinie *f (Schriftlinien)* baseline
Grundmontage *f (bei Mehrfarbenmontage)* guide assembly
Grundschleier *m (Reprofilm)* background fog, base fog, emulsion fog
Grundschrift *f (im U. zur Auszeichnungsschrift)* body type
Grundstrich *m (beim Buchstaben)* main stroke, stem
Grußkarte *f* greetings card
Guilloche *f (Schlangenlinienverzierung)* guilloche
Guillochenraster *m (Wertpapierdruck)* guilloche screen

guillochieren - haarfeine Serifen 62

guillochieren *(mit Schlangenlinienverzierung versehen)* to guilloche
Gummi *n* gum, rubber
Gummiätze *f* gum etch
Gummiarabicum *n (Plattenkonserv.)* gum arabic
Gummiaufzug *m (Zyl.)* rubber dressing, rubber packing
gummibezogene Walze *f* rubber-covered roller
Gummibuchstaben *m/pl* rubber type
Gummidecke *f (für Kopierrahmen)* rubber blanket
Gummideckplatte *f (vom Gummituch)* rubber face
Gummidessinwalze *f* rubber design roller
Gummidrucktuch *n* blanket, rubber printing blanket
gummieren to gum (up)
Gummierkalander *m* sizing calender
Gummierleim *m* gum
Gummiermaschine *f* gumming machine
gummierte Etiketten *pl* gummed labels *pl*
gummierter Briefumschlag *m* gummed envelope
gummiertes Papier *n* gummed paper
Gummierungsstation *f (Offsetplattenbearbeitungsstraße)* gumming station
Gummierwalze *f* gumming roller
Gummi/Gummi-Druckwerk *n (Rollenoffset, Perfektor)* blanket-to-blanket unit
Gummi/Gummi-Rollenoffsetmaschine *f* blanket-to-blanket web offset press
Gummihandschuhe *pl* rubber gloves *pl*
Gummiklischee *n (Flexo)* rubber plate
Gummiplatte *f (Flexo)* rubber plate
Gummipresseur *m (Tiefdruck)* rubber pressure roller
Gummiquetscher *m* rubber squeegee
Gummirakel *f* rubber doctor blade, rubber squeegee
Gummistempel *m* rubber stamp
Gummistereo *n* rubber stereo
Gummitonplatte *f* rubber tint plate
Gummituch *n* blanket, rubber blanket
Gummituchdehnung *f* blanket stretch
Gummituchdickenmesser *m* blanket thickness gauge
Gummituchglätte *f (Glanzglätte)* blanket glaze
Gummituchklemmleiste *f* blanket clamping bar
Gummituch mit vier Gewebelagen four-ply blanket
Gummituch-Regenerierungsmittel *n* blanket rejuvenator

Gummituchspaltversiegelung *f (Endlosformulardruck)* blanket gap filler, blanket gap sealer
Gummituchspannschiene *f* blanket clamping bar
Gummituchspannvorrichtung *f* blanket mounting device
Gummituchstärke *f* blanket gauge
Gummituchunterbau *m* blanket carcase
Gummituch-Unterlagebogen *m* blanket packing sheet
Gummituchwascheinrichtung *f (an Druckm.)* blanket washer, blanket wash-up device
Gummituchwaschen *n* blanket washing
Gummituchwaschintervall *n* blanket wash-up interval
Gummituchwaschmittel *n* blanket wash
Gummituchzylinder *m (Offsetdruckwerk)* blanket cylinder
Gummiverreibwalze *f* rubber distributor roller
Gummiwalze *f* rubber roller
Gummizylinder *(Offsetdruckwerk)* blanket cylinder
Gurt *m* belt
Gurtförderer *m* belt conveyor, conveyor belt
Guß *m (Stereotypie, Zeilenguß)* cast, casting; *(Handsatzschriften)* founding, fount
Gußeisen *n* cast iron
gußeisernes Maschinengestell *n* cast-iron frame
Gußform *f (Stereotypie)* casting mould
gußgestrichenes Papier *n* cast-coated paper
Gußlegierung *f* cast alloy
Gußunterbau *m* cast-iron substructure
Gußzeile *f (Bleisatz)* slug
Gutbogen *m* good sheet
Gutexemplarzähler *m* good and bad copy counter
gut gedeckte Vollfläche *f* well-covered solid
Guttapercha *f* gutta-percha
Gutzahl *f (verkaufbare Auflage)* acceptance number
gut zum Druck *n (druckreif)* can go over, o.k. to print, passed for press

H

haarfeiner Passer *m* hairline register
haarfeine Serifen *pl* hairline serifs *pl*

haargenauer Passer *m* hairline register
haargenaues Register *n* hairline register
Haarhygrometer *n* hair hygrometer
Haarlinie *f (Schrift)* hairline
Haarpinsel *m* hairbrush
Haarspatium *n (Bleisatz)* hair space
Haarstrich *m (Buchstabe)* hairline
Hadern *pl* rags *pl*
Hadernpapier *n* rag paper
Hadernpappe *f* rag board
Hadernstoff *m* rag fibres *pl*
Händeschutz *m* finger guard, hand guard
hängende Initiale *f* drop initial
hängender Einzug *m (Satz)* dropline indention, hanging indent
hängende Ziffern *f/pl* hanging figures *pl*
Hängeregistraturschrank *m (Archivierung von Druckunterlagen)* vertical filing cabinet
Härtebad *n* hardening bath
Härtefixierbad *n* hardening fixing bath
härten *(chemisch, Kopierschicht, Polymerschicht usw.)* to harden; *(Farbe durch Strahlung)* to cure
Härteprüfgerät *n* hardness meter
Härter *m (chem.)* hardener, hardening agent
Härtezusatz *m* hardening additive
Häubchen *n (Buchherst.)* headcap, tailcap
Haften *n (Farbe auf Papier, Folie auf Träger usw.)* adherence
Haftetikett *n (Selbstklebeetikett)* pressure-sensitive label, self-adhesive label
Haftfolie *f* adhesive film, adhesive foil
Haftwachs *n (Montagewachs)* adhesive wax, montage wax
Haftwachsgerät *n* waxer
halbautomatisch semi-automatic
halbautotypischer Tiefdruck *m* variable area/variable depth gravure (process)
Halbbogen *m* half sheet
halbbreite Rollendruckmaschine *f* half-size web press, half-width rotary press
halbdeckend semi-opaque, semi-transparent
Halb(ein)band *m (Buch)* half binding, quarter binding
halbe Seite über den Bund *(Anzeige)* half page spread
halbfette Schrift *f* semibold typeface
Halbgaze *f (Siebdruck)* thin linen
halbgeleimtes Papier *n* soft-sized paper
Halbgeviert *n (Satz)* en, en-quad, en space, half em-quad, half em space
Halbgeviertstrich *m* en-dash
halbglänzendes Papier *n* velvet finished paper

Halbkarton *m* thin (card)board
Halbleder(ein)band *m* half-leather binding, quarter-leather binding
Halbleinen *n* half-cloth, half-linen
Halbleinen(ein)band *m* half-cloth binding, half-linen binding, quarter-cloth binding
Halbleiter *m* semi-conductor
Halbsatellitendruckwerk *n (Rollenoffsetm.)* semi-satellite unit
halbseitige Anzeige *f* half-page ad(vertisement)
Halbton *m* continuous tone, con-tone
Halbtonätzung *f* continuous-tone engraving, continuous-tone etching
Halbtonaufnahme *f (Belichtung)* continuous-tone exposure; *(Foto)* continuous-tone photo(graph)
Halbtonbild *n* continuous-tone illustration, continuous-tone image, continuous-tone picture
Halbtondruck *m (Tiefdruck)* continuous-tone printing
Halbtonfarbauszüge *pl* continuous-tone (colour) separations *pl*
Halbtonfoto *n* continuous-tone photo(graph)
Halbtonkeil *m* continuous-tone wedge
Halbtonnegativ *n* continuous-tone negative
Halbtonpapier *n* continuous-tone paper
Halbtonpositiv *n* continuous-tone positive
Halbtonrasterfeld *n (Druckkontrollstreifen)* mid-tone tint patch
Halbtonreproduktion *f* continuous-tone reproduction
Halbtonskala *f* continuous-tone scale
Halbtonwiedergabe *f* continuous-tone reproduction, rendering of continuous tones
Halbunziale *f (Schrift)* half-uncial
Halbzylindersegment *n* half cylinder segment
Halogenlampe *f* halogen lamp
Halogen-Licht *n* halogen light, tungsten light
Halogensilber *n* halogen silver
Halogensilberschicht *f* halogen silver emulsion
Hals *m (Konus beim Buchst.)* bevel, shoulder
haltbare Bindung *f* durable binding
Haltbarkeit *f (Bindung)* durability; *(Lagerung von Farben, Chemikalien usw.)* shelf-life
Halteklammer *f* fastening clamp
Halterung *f (mech.)* bracket, support
Hammerschlaglackierung *f* hammertone finish
Handabweiser *m (Handschutz)* finger-guard, hand-guard
Handabzug *m* hand impression, hand pull
Handanlage *f* hand feed(ing), manual feed(ing)
Handantrieb *m* hand drive

Handauflage f *(Handanlage)* hand feed(ing)
Handauftragswalze f *(Einfärbung)* hand ink-feed roller, hand inking roller
Handauslösung f hand release
Handausschnitt m *(Kraftzurichtung)* hand-cut overlay
Handbetrieb m manual operation
Handbuch n handbook, manual
Handdensitometer n hand-held densitometer
Handdruck m block printing, hand impression
Handeinband m *(Buchb.)* hand binding
Handeinfärbung f manual ink-feed, manual inking-up
Handfalzmuster n hand-folded sample
handgebunden hand-bound
handgeschnitten hand-cut
handgeschöpftes Papier n hand-made paper, mould-made paper, vat paper
Handgriff m *(seitlicher Ausschnitt in Wellpappkisten)* handhole
Handhebel m hand lever
Handhebelpresse f hand lever press
Handhebelschneidemaschine f hand-operated guillotine
handkoloriert hand-coloured
Handkurbel f crank handle, hand crank
Handnumeriermaschine f hand-operated numbering machine
Handprägung f *(Handpressung)* hand blocking, hand stamping
Handpresse f hand press
Handpressendruck m hand press printing
Handpressung f *(Prägung)* hand blocking, hand stamping
Handrad n hand wheel
Handreichweite *in ~ des Bedieners* within operator's reach
Handreiniger m hand cleaner
Handsäge f handsaw
Handsatz m hand composition, manual typesetting
Handsatzschrift f foundry type
Handsatztype f foundry type
Handschnittplatte f hand-cut plate
Handschrift f handwriting
Handschriftliche Antiqua f *(Schriftklassif.)* Manuals *pl*
Handschutz(vorrichtung) m/f finger-guard, hand-guard
Handsetzer m hand compositor
Handsetzerei f *(Druckereiabt.)* hand composition department
Handvergoldung f hand gilding

Handwachsgerät n *(Klebemontage)* manual waxer
Handwalze f hand roller
handwerkliche Arbeit f craftman's work
Handwerksgewerbe n craftman's trade
Handwörterbuch n concise dictionary, pocket dictionary
Handzettel m *(Streuwerbung)* flyer, leaflet
Handzuführung f hand feed(ing), manual feed(ing)
Handzurichtung f manual makeready
Hanfpapier n hemp paper
Hardcopy f *(Beleg, Ausdruck)* hardcopy
Hardcover-Broschüre f hardcover brochure
Harddeckelbindung f hardcover binding
Hardproof m hard proof
Hardware f *(Comp.)* hardware
Hartdeckelbuch n hardcover book
harter Abzug m *(Foto)* hard print
harter Aufzug m *(Zylinder)* hard packing
hartes Negativ n hard negative
hartes Papier n hard paper
Hartfaserpappe f *(Buchb.)* hard fibreboard
hartgebundenes Buch n case-bound book, hardback, hard-bound book, hardcover book
Hartglanz m hard gloss
Hartgummi m hard rubber
Hartmetallmesser n *(Schneidem.)* carbid-tipped knife
hartnäckige Rückstände pl stubborn residues *pl*
Hartpappe f hardboard
Hartperforation f *(ohne Nut im Gegendruckzyl.)* hard perforation
Hartplatte f *(Comp.)* hard disk, rigid disk
Hartpostpapier n bank paper
hartverchromter Zylinder m hard-chromed cylinder
Harz n *(Druckfarbe)* resin
Harzleimung f *(Papier)* resin bonding, vegetable size
Haube f *(für Maschinen)* hood
Hauchlaut m *(Sprache)* aspirate
Hauerfalz m blade fold
Hauptantrieb m main drive
Hauptantriebswelle f main shaft
Hauptbedienungsstand m *(Druckm.)* main control console
Hauptbelichtung f *(Rasterfotogr.)* main exposure
Hauptlager n *(Zyl.)* main bearing
Hauptprodukt n *(Druckverarb.)* main section
Hauptrechner m *(Comp.)* central processing unit, host computer, mainframe computer, main processor

Hauptschalter m main switch
Hauptspeicher m *(Comp.)* cache memory, main memory, main storage
Hauptsystem n *(Comp.; im U. zum Subsystem)* central system, host system, main system
Haupttitel m main title; *(Buch; im Gs. zum Schmutztitel)* full title; *(Titelseite)* title page
Hauptwelle f main shaft
Hauptzeile f *(Überschrift)* catchline, headline
Hausbroschüre f company brochure, house brochure
Hausdruckerei f in-plant printer, in-plant printing department, in-plant printshop
hauseigene Herstellung von Drucksachen in-house publishing
hauseigener Standard m in-house standard
Hausfarbe f *(firmenspezifisch)* brand colour, house colour
hausinterne Druckproduktion f in-house publishing
Hauskorrektor m printer's reader, proofreader
Hauskorrektur f first proof, house corrections pl, proofreader's corrections pl, reader's proof
Hausstandard m in-house standard
Hauszeitschrift f house journal, house magazine, house organ, house paper
Hautaufkupferungsverfahren n *(Tiefdruck)* ballard process, skin coppering process
Hautbildung f *(Druckfarbe)* skin formation, skinning
Hautfarbe f *(Reprod.)* flesh colour
Hauttöne m/pl *(Reprod.)* flesh tones pl
Hautverhütungsmittel n *(Farbe)* anti-skinning agent
Heatset-Farbe f heat-set ink
Heatset-Rollenoffset m heat-set web offset
Hebebühne f hoist platform, lifting platform, platform elevator
Hebeeinrichtung f *(Papierrollen)* elevator, hoist, lifting device
Hebekran m *(Tiefdruck)* crane
Hebel m lever
Hebelanschlag m lever stop
Hebelpresse f lever-press
Hebelschalter m lever switch
Hebelschneidemaschine f lever-operated guillotine
Hebelstanze f lever punch
Hebelsteuerung f lever control
Hebelumschalter m lever switch
Hebelverschluß m lever fastener
Heben und Senken n lifting and lowering

Heber m *(Heberwalze)* ductor roller, vibrator, vibrator roller
Heberfarbwerk n ductor-type inking system, vibrator-type inking system
Heberfeuchtwerk n ductor-type damping system, vibrator-type damping system
heberloses Farbwerk n continuous-feed inking system, continuous-type inking system
heberloses Feuchtwerk n continuous-feed damping system, continuous-type damping system
Heberwalze f *(Farb-, Feuchtwerk)* ductor roller, vibrator, vibrator roller
Hebevorrichtung f elevator, hoist, lifting device
Hebräische Schrift f Hebrew characters pl, Hebrew type
Heft n *(geheftete Drucksache)* booklet, stitched booklet; *(Griff der Ahle, des Messers usw.)* handle; *(Schreibheft)* copy-book; *(Zeitschrift)* copy, issue, number
Heftaggregat n stitching unit
Heftapparat m stitching machine
Heftbünde pl bands pl, cords pl
Heftdraht m binding wire, stitching wire
heften to bind, to stitch; *(mit Draht)* to wire-stitch; *(mit Faden)* to thread-stitch; *(mit Klammern)* to staple
Heften mit unversetztem Stich *(Fadenheftung)* straight stitching
Heftfaden m binding thread, sewing thread
Heftgaze f sewing gauze
Heftklammer f staple
Heftkopf m stitching head
Heftlage f binding section, section for stitching
Heftlöcher pl *(Fadenheftung)* needle holes pl, stitching holes pl
Heftmaschine f stitcher, stitching machine
Heftnadel f bookbinder's needle, stitching needle
Heftrand m binding edge, binding margin, filing margin
Heftsattel m stitching saddle
Heftschnüre pl *(Gebinde)* bands pl, cords pl
Heftschnur f *(Buchb.)* bookbinder's cord
Heftstich m binding stitch
Heftumschlag m booklet cover
Heftung f binding, sewing, stitching
Heftzwirn m binding thread, sewing thread
Heiratsanzeige f *(Karte)* wedding announcement
Heißemailverfahren n hot enamel process
heißer Satz m *(metallischer Satz)* hot-metal composition, hot-metal type
Heißfolienprägung f hot foil stamping
heißkalandrieren to hot-calender

Heißkarbonisierung f hot (spot) carbonizing
heißkaschieren to heat-seal
Heißkaschiermaschine f heat-seal laminator
Heißkaschierung f heat-sealing
Heißklebefolie f *(für Heißkaschierung)* heat-sealing foil
Heißleim m hotmelt (adhesive)
Heißleimbindung f hotmelt gluing
Heißleimung f hotmelt gluing
Heißleimverbindung f hotmelt compound
Heißluftdüsentrockner m hot-air jet dryer
Heißluftschwebetrockner m hot-air floatation dryer
Heißlufttrockner m hot-air dryer
Heißlufttrocknung f hot-air drying
Heißprägefolie f hot stamping foil
Heißprägen n hot embossing, hot stamping
Heißprägepresse f hot stamping press
Heißprägeschriften f/pl hot embossing types pl
Heißprägung f hot embossing, hot stamping
Heißsiegelfolie f heat-sealing foil
heißsiegeln to heat-seal
Heißsiegeln n heat-sealing
Heißsiegelpapier n heat-sealing paper
heißtrocknende Farbe f heat-set ink
Heißversiegelung f heat-sealing
Heizsteg m *(Folienprägung)* heating bar
Hektograf m hectograph
Heliochrom n heliochrome
Heliografie f heliography
Heliogravüre f heliogravure
Helioklischograph m Helioklischograph
Helium-Neon-Laser m Helium-Neon laser
helldunkel chiaroscuro, clair-obscure
helle Farben pl bright colours pl, light colours pl
Helligkeit f brightness, lightness
Helligkeitsumfang m *(Bild)* brightness range
Hellraumfilm m bright room film
HeNe-Laser m *(Helium Neon)* HeNe laser
herausfahrbarer Druckwerkswagen m *(Kassettendruckwerk)* printing cartridge
herausgeben *(Publikation)* to bring out, to edit, to publish
Herausgeber m publisher
Herstellungskosten pl production costs pl
Herstellung von Firmenliteratur corporate publishing
hervorheben *(typogr.)* to accentuate, to display, to highlight
Hilfsantrieb m auxiliary drive
Hilfsbelichter m *(Fotosatz)* slave typesetter
Hilfsbelichtung f *(Rasterfotogr.)* supplementary exposure

Hilfseinrichtung f auxiliary equipment
Hilfsgerät n auxiliary device
Hilfskraft f *(Personal)* helper
Hilfsmaschine f auxiliary machine
Hilfsprogramm n utility program
Hilfsrechner m back-up computer
Hilfsstoffe pl *(Papierherst.)* additives pl
Hilfszeiten pl auxiliary times pl, servicing times pl
himmelblau azure, sky-blue
hinterer Anschlag m *(mech.)* backstop
hinterer Buchdeckel m back cover board
hintere Umschlaginnenseite f *(Zeitschrift, Buch)* inside back cover
Hintergießmetall n *(Galvano)* backing metal
Hintergrund m background
Hintergrundbetrieb m *(Comp.)* background mode
Hintergrundfläche f *(Bild)* background area, background tint
Hintergrundmuster n *(Bild)* background pattern
Hintergrundraster m background tint, screened background (tint)
Hintergrundverarbeitung f *(Comp.)* background processing, multitasking
Hintergrundverlauf m *(Bild)* graduated background, vignetted background
Hinterkante f back edge, rear edge, trailing edge
Hinterkasten m *(Kamera)* camera back
Hinterklebemaschine f *(Buchherst.)* backlining machine
Hinterklebepapier n *(Buch)* backliner, backlining paper, book backing paper
Hinterklebung f *(Buchherst.)* backlining, book backing
hinterlegter Raster m *(Reprod.)* background tint, laid tint
Hintertisch m *(Schneidem.)* rear table
Hinundherbewegung f oscillating movement, reciprocating movement
Hinundherbewegung der Walzen f roller reciprocation
Hinweiszeichen n *(Satz)* reference mark
hitzebeständig heat-resistant
HKS-Farbsystem n HKS matching system
Hobbock m *(Druckfarbe)* drum, pail
Hobel m plane(r)
hochätzen to etch in relief
Hochätzung f relief etching
Hochauflagenbereich m *im* ~ in the long run range
hochauflösender Bildschirm m high-resolution monitor
Hochdruck m *(Buchdruck)* letterpress (printing)

Hochdruckbogenrotation f sheet-fed letterpress rotary
Hochdruck(rollen)rotation f letterpress rotary, web-fed letterpress machine
Hochdruckwickelplatte f wrap-around letterpress plate
hochempfindlicher Film m high-sensitive film, high-speed film
Hochformat n portrait size, upright format
Hochformatseite f deep page, upright page
Hochfrequenztrocknung f radio-frequency drying
Hochgeschwindigkeitsdrucker m high-speed printer
Hochgeschwindigkeitsdruckmaschine f high-speed (printing) press
hochgestelltes Zeichen n *(Satz)* superior character, superscript
hochgestellte Ziffern pl superior figures pl
Hochglanz m high gloss
Hochglanzabzug m *(Fot.)* glossy print
Hochglanzfarbe f high-gloss ink
Hochglanzkaschierung f acetate laminating, high-gloss lamination
Hochglanzlack m high-gloss varnish
Hochglanzlackierung f high-gloss varnishing
Hochglanzpapier n art paper, enamelled paper
Hochglanzpolitur f *(Tiefdruckzyl.)* high polish
Hochglanzpresse f *(Papierherst.)* dryer glazer
Hochlauf m *(Masch.)* acceleration, run-up
Hochleistungs- heavy-duty, high-capacity, high-performance, high-speed
Hochlichtaufnahme f *(Reprod.)* highlight exposure
Hochlichter pl *(Rasterbild)* highlight dots pl, highlights pl
Hochlichtmaske f *(Reprod.)* highlight mask
Hochprägemaschine f high-relief embossing machine
Hochprägung f high-relief embossing
Hochregallager n high rack store
Hochreliefprägung f high-relief embossing
hochrüsten *(Systeme, Maschinen)* to upgrade
Hochrüstung f upgrade
hochsatiniertes Papier n high-glaze paper, super-calendered paper
Hochstapel m high pile
Hochstapelanleger m high-pile feeder
Hochstapelauslage f high-pile delivery
hochstellen *(Exponenten im Satz)* to shift upwards
hochwertiger Druck m high-quality printing
hochwertiges Produkt n high-grade product, top-grade product

Hochzeit f *(Bleisatz)* double
Hochzeitskarte f wedding announcement
Hochzoomen n *(Bildverarb.)* detail zooming, scaling up, zooming
Höchstgeschwindigkeit f top speed
Höchstleistung f maximum capacity, maximum output, maximum performance
Höheneinstellung f height adjustment, vertical adjustment
Höhenjustierung f height adjustment, vertical adjustment
Höhenmeßgerät n *(Zyl.aufzug)* height gauge
Höhenpunkte pl *(Kartogr.)* altitudes pl, heights pl
Höhenregister n *(Druckbeginn zu Kopfbeschnitt)* head register
höhenverstellbar *(Aggregat)* height adjustable
Höhenzurichtung f *(Buchdruck)* height justification
Hof m *(Fot.)* halo; *(Rasterpunktausfransung)* fringe
hohe Auflage f large circulation, large edition, large-volume printwork, long print run, long run (job), voluminous print run
hohe Druckqualität f top-grade print quality
Hohlkehle f channel, groove
Hohlkopie f *(Kontaktbelichtung)* miscontact, side lighting, undercutting
Hohlschnitt m *(der nach innen gerundete Vorderschnitt eines Buches)* cavity cut
Hohlzylinder m *(zum Aufschieben auf eine Achse)* hollow cylinder
Holländerbindung f yapp binding
Holländern n *(Fadenheftung)* French sewing
Holografie f holography
Hologramm n hologram
Hologrammprägung f hologram stamping
Holzbedruckmaschine f wood printing press
Holzbuchstaben pl wood letters pl, wood type
Holzdruckpresse f wooden toggle press
Holzfaserstoff m mechanical pulp, wood pulp
holzfreies Papier n wood-free paper
Holzfuß m *(Klischeeunterlage)* wood base, wood mount
holzhaltiges Papier n mechanical paper, woodpulp paper
Holzkohle f *(Schleifen von Platten)* charcoal
Holzschliff m *(Papier)* ground-wood pulp, mechanical pulp, wood pulp
Holzschneider m wood engraver, xylographer
Holzschnitt m woodcut, wood engraving, xylograph
Holzschrift f wood letters pl, wood type

Holzstich - indirekter Flachdruck

Holzstich *m* woodcut, wood engraving
Holzzellstoff *m* chemical woodpulp
Horizontalkamera *f* horizontal camera
Horizontalkopierrahmen *m* horizontal vacuum frame
Horizontalschleuder *f* horizontal whirler
Host-Computer *m* host computer
Hotmelt *m* hotmelt (adhesive)
Hotmelt-Auftragsgerät *n* hotmelt applicator
Hotmelt-Bindung *f* hotmelt binding
Hotmelt-Düsenbeleimung *f (im U. zur Walzenbeleimung)* hotmelt nozzle gluing
hotmeltgebunden hotmelt bound
Hub *m* stroke
Hubprägung *f (im Gs. zur Abrollprägung)* vertical stamping
Hubsauger *m (Anlegersaugkopf)* lifting sucker
Hubstanze *f (Flachbettstanze)* flat-bed die-cutter
Hubverstellung *f* stroke adjustment
Hubwagen *m* lift truck
Hülse *f (Flexodruckform)* sleeve; *(für Papierrolle)* tube
Hurenkind *n (Satz)* widow line
Hybridrechner *m (Comp.)* hybrid computer
Hydraulik *f* hydraulics, hydraulic system
hydraulisch hydraulic, hydraulically operated
hydraulische Pressung *f (Schneidemasch.)* hydraulic clamping
hydraulische Steuerung *f* hydraulic control
Hydrochinon-Entwickler *m (Fotochemie)* hydroquinone developer
Hydrocolor-System *n* combined inking and damping system, Hydrocolor system
Hydrogenkarbonat *n* hydrogen carbonate
Hydrolyse *f* hydrolysis
hydrophil *(wasserfreundlich)* hydrophilic
hydrophob *(wasserabstoßend)* hydrophobic
Hygrometer *n* hygrometer
hygroskopisch *(wasseranziehend)* hygroscopic

I

Illuminierung *f (Buch)* illumination
Illustration *f* illustration, picture; *(im Text auch)* figure, text figure
Illustrationsdruck *m (Rollendruck)* illustration printing, publication printing
Illustrationsdruckmaschine *f (Rollendruckm.)* heat-set commercial press, publication press
Illustrationsdruckpapier *n* illustration printing paper, imitation art paper
Illustrator *m (Bücher)* illustrator
illustrieren to illustrate
Illustrierte *f* magazine, review
im Beschnitt liegen to lie in the trim
im Bund in the back
im Druck in the press
im Falz mit Draht heften to saddle-stitch with wire
im Falz mit Faden heften to saddle-stitch with thread
im Format (DIN) A4 A4 sized, in A4 size
Imitationsprägedruck *m* imitation die-stamping
Imitationsreliefdruck *m* imitation die-stamping
im Lauf *m* on the fly, on the run
im Neigungswinkel verstellbarer Bildschirm tiltable monitor
Imposerkamera *f* imposer camera
imprägniertes Papier *n* impregnated paper, water-proof paper
Impressum *n* printer's imprint; *(Zeitung, Zeitschrift)* imprint, mast head
Imprimatur *n* imprimatur; *das ~ geben* to pass for press
Impulsgeber *m* impulse emitter
im Satz sein being set-up
im Stillstand *m* at standstill
im Strahlengang belichten *(Reprofotogr.)* to expose through the lens
im Takt *m* cycled, paced, timed
inaktinischer Filter *m* inactinic filter
in alphabetischer Reihenfolge *f* in alphabetical order
in Anführungszeichen setzen to put in quotes
in aufsteigender Reihenfolge *f* in ascending order
in beliebiger Reihenfolge *f* at random sequence
in bequemer Reichweite *f* within easy reach
Inbetriebnahme *f (Masch.)* putting into operation, start-up
Inbetriebsetzung *f (Masch.)* putting into operation, start-up
Inbus-Schlüssel *m* allen key
in der Größe 1:1 *(Reprod.)* in actual size
Indexbuchstabe *m* index letter
Indexorganisation *f (Comp.)* index management, index organisation
Indiapapier *n* India paper
indirekter Buchdruck *m* indirect letterpress (printing)
indirekter Flachdruck *m* offset printing

indirekter Tiefdruck *m* offset gravure
indirektes Druckverfahren *n* indirect printing process
Indirektfilm *m* *(Siebdruck)* indirect film
Indischrot *n* Indian red
in Druck gehen to go to press
Ineinanderfalzen *n* *(Ineinanderstecken von Falzbogen)* insetting
ineinandergesteckte Falzbogen *pl* wrapped-around signatures *pl*
Ineinanderstecken *n* *(von Falzbogen, im Gs. zum Zusammentragen)* insetting
Information *f* information
Informationsdienst *m* information service
Informationskanal *m* information channel
Informationsträger *m* data carrier, information carrier
Informationsübertragung *f* data transfer, data transmission, information transfer
Informationsverarbeitung *f* data processing, information processing
Infozeile *f* *(Fotosatzm.)* message line
Infrarot- siehe IR-
in Gänsefüßchen setzen to put in quotes
Ingangsetzen *n* putting into operation, start-up
Inhalt *m* *(Broschur/Buch ohne Umschlag)* body, content
Inhaltsverzeichnis *n* *(Comp.)* file directory, file index; *(Zeitschrift usw.)* table of contents
Inhaltsverzeichnis der gespeicherten Texte directory of stored copy
Initiale *f* head letter, initial character, initial (letter); *zweizeilige ~* two-line initial (letter)
Ink-Jet-Adressierung *f* ink jet addressing
Ink-Jet-Aufdruck *m* ink jet imprint
Ink-Jet-Beschriftung *f* ink jet addressing, ink jet lettering
Ink-Jet-Druck *m* ink jet printing
Inkjetdrucker *m* ink jet printer
in Klammern setzen to bracket, to put in brackets, to put in parenthesis
Inkunabeln *pl* incunabula *pl*
in kursiv setzen to set in italics
Inlandsnachrichten *pl* *(Zeitung)* domestic news
in Leder eingebunden leather-bound
in Leinen eingebunden cloth-bound
Inline-Betrieb *m* in-line operation
Inline-Finishing *n* in-line finishing, on-press web finishing
Inline-Lackierung *f* in-line coating, in-line varnishing
Inline-Verarbeitung *f* in-line finishing, in-line processing

in Linie bringen *(Satz)* to line up
in natürlicher Größe *(Reprod.)* in actual size
Innenblatt *n* *(im Gs. zum Umschlag)* inner sheet
Innenseite *f* inner page, inside page
Innentitel *m* inner title
innere Form *f* *(Druckform)* inner forme
innerer Papierrand *m* back(-edge) margin, inner margin
innerer Seitenrand *m* back(-edge) margin, inner margin
in Rechnung stellen to charge, to invoice
in Reichweite der Hand within operator's reach
Inserat *n* ad(vertisement)
Inserent *m* advertiser
inserieren to advertise
Insertion *f* *(Anzeigenschaltung)* insertion
Insertionsbedingungen *pl* advertising conditions *pl*
installieren to install
Instandhaltung *f* maintenance, servicing
Instandsetzung *f* reconditioning, repair(ing)
instruieren to instruct
Instruktionen *pl* instructions *pl*
Instruktor *m* instructor
integrale Dichte *f* integral density, integrated density
integrale Rasterdichte *f* integral screen density
Integralzeichen *n* *(math. Satz)* integral sign
integriert *(Maschinenteile)* built-in, incorporated, integral, integrated
integrierte Bild- und Textverarbeitung *f* combined image and text processing, image and text integration, integrated image and text processing
integrierte Schaltung *f* integrated circuit
intelligente Peripherie *f* intelligent peripherals *pl*
intelligenter Bildschirmarbeitsplatz *m* intelligent video terminal, intelligent video workstation
interaktive Arbeitsweise *f* interactive mode
interaktiver Bildschirm *m* interactive terminal
Interface *n* interface
Interferenzfilter *m* *(Fot.)* interference filter
intermittierende Leimung *f* *(im Gs. zu kontinuierlicher Leimung)* intermittent gluing
interner Speicher *m* *(Comp.)* internal memory, internal storage
Interpunktion *f* punctuation
Interpunktionszeichen *n/pl* punctuation marks *pl*
Investitionskosten *pl* investment costs *pl*
Ionenbläser *m* ion blower
Ionisationsstab *m* ionizer, ionizing rod
Ionisiereinrichtung *f* ionizer, ionizing unit
IR-empfindliches Papier *n* I.R. sensitive paper

Irisblende - Kaltkaschierung

Irisblende f *(Kamera)* iris diaphragm
Irisdruck m *(Regenbogeneffekt)* rainbow printing
IR-Strahler m I.R. emitter, I.R. radiator
IR-Strahlung f I.R. radiation
IR-Trockner m I.R. dryer
IR-Trocknung f I.R. drying
IR/UV-Kombinationstrockner m I.R./U.V. combination dryer
ISBN-Nummer f ISBN number
Isodensiten pl *(Reprod.)* isodensities pl
Isodensitenkurven pl isodensity curves pl
Isopropanol n isopropanol
Isopropanolersatz m isopropanol substitute
Isopropylalkohol m isopropylic alcohol
Ist-Höhe f *(Satz; im U. zur Sollhöhe)* actual depth
Ist-Wert m actual value
IVW f *(Auflagenkontrolleinrichtung)* audit bureau of circulation
IWT *(Fotosatz; „Immer Wiederkehrender Text")* UF
IWT-Aufruf m UF call
IWT-Definition f UF definiton
IWT-Verzeichnis n UF directory

J

Jahrbuch n almanac, annual, yearbook
Jahresabonnement n annual subscription
Jahresauslastung f annual capacity utilization
Jahresbericht m annual report
Jahrgang m *(Zeitschrift)* annual volume, year of publication
Japanpapier n Japanese vellum, Japan paper
(je) 1000 weitere *(Fortdruckangebot)* thousand run-ons pl
Job m job
Job-Nummer f job number
Jod-Quarz-Lampe f quartz-iodine lamp
Journal n journal, magazine
Jubiläumsschrift f jubilee publication
Jugendschriften pl publications for young people
Jugendstiltypografie f Art Nouveau typography
Justierung f adjustment, setting; *(Walzen)* justification

K

Kabelanschluß m cable connection
Kabelfernsehen n cable TV
Kabeltext m cable text
Kabelverbindung f cable connection, cable link
Kältemaschine f chilling machine, cooling machine, refrigerating machine
käseecht casein resistant
Kalander m *(Papierherst.)* calender, glazing machine
Kalanderlackierung f calender varnish glazing
Kalandern n calendering, glazing
Kalanderprägung f calender embossing, calender graining
Kalanderwalze f calender bowl, calender roller
kalandrieren to calender, to glaze
Kalandrierung f calendering, glazing
Kalbsleder(ein)band m calf binding
Kalender m calendar, diary
Kalenderaufhänger m calendar hanger
Kalenderbindung f calendar binding
Kalenderblock m calendar block, date block, diary pad
Kalenderfertigung f calendar production
Kalenderpapier n calendar paper
Kalenderrückwand f calendar back, calendar mount
kalibrieren *(elektron. Systeme, Meßgeräte)* to calibrate
kalibrierte Unterlagebogen m/pl calibrated underlay sheets pl, packing sheets of guaranteed gauge
Kalibrierung f calibration
Kaliko n *(Bucheinband)* bookbinder's calico, calico
Kalikopapier n calico paper
Kalken n *(Farbe)* chalking
Kalkschleier m chalky fog
Kalksteinpuder n *(Bestäubungspuder)* limestone powder
Kalkulation f calculation, estimate
Kalkulator m calculator, estimator
kalkulieren to calculate, to estimate
Kalligraf m calligrapher
Kalligrafie f calligraphy
Kaltemailverfahren n cold-top process
kalte Nadel f *(Radierung)* dry point
Kaltkaschiermaschine f cold laminator, cold sealing machine
Kaltkaschierung f cold lamination, cold sealing

Kaltleim *m (Klebebindung)* cold glue
kaltleimgebunden cold glue bound
Kaltleimverbindung *f* cold glue compound
Kaltlicht *n* fluorescent light
Kaltluftgebläse *n* cold air blast
Kaltnadelradierung *f* dry point engraving
Kaltprägung *f* cold blocking, cold embossing
Kaltsatz *m (nichtmetallischer S.)* cold composition, cold type
Kaltsiegelung *f* cold sealing
Kaltstereotypie *f* cold stereotyping
Kalziumkarbonat *n* calcium carbonate
Kamera *f* camera
Kameraarbeiten *pl* camera work
Kameraaufnahme *f* camera exposure
Kameraauszug *m (Farbauszug)* camera separation; *(Balgen)* bellows extension, camera bellows *pl*, camera extension
Kamerabalgen *m* bellows extension, camera bellows *pl*, camera extension
Kamerabelichtung *f* camera exposure
Kamerablende *f* diaphragm
Kameradensitometer *n* camera densitometer
Kameraeinstellung *f* camera adjustment, camera setting
Kamerahinterkasten *m* camera back
Kameralinse *f* camera lens
Kameraskala *f* camera scale
Kameraständer *m (Gestell, Rahmen)* camera frame
Kameravorderkasten *m* camera front box
Kamerawagen *m (Horizontalkamera)* camera trolley
Kammbindung *f* comb binding
Kammerrakel *f* chambered doctor blade
Kann-Feld *n (Bildschirmmaske, Formular; im U. zum Mußfeld)* optional field
Kante *f* edge
Kante anlegen to lay the edge
Kantenabschrägmaschine *f (Klischeebearb.)* edge-bevelling machine
Kantenanleimmaschine *f* edge-gluing machine
Kantenbeleimung *f* edge gluing
Kantenbeschnitt *m* edge trim(ming)
Kantenfräsen *n (Klebebindung)* edge milling, edge routing
kantengenau ausrichten to align accurately
kantengenaue Auslage *f* straight-edge delivery
kantengenauer Stapel *m* straight-edge pile
kantengenaues Ausrichten *n* straight-edge alignment
Kantenhobelmaschine *f (Klischeebearb.)* edge planing machine

Kantenschärfe *f* edge definition; *(Fotosatz)* character definition, contour definition, definition of outlines, image definition, image resolution
Kantenschutzmittel *n (Klischeeherst.)* edge resist
Kantenverleimautomat *m (Formularsatzherst.)* automatic edge-gluing machine
Kanvas *m (Leinen, Bucheinband)* canvas
Kaolin *n (Papierherst.)* caolin
Kapazitätsauslastung *f* capacity utilization
Kapillare *f* capillary tube
Kapillarfilm *m (Siebdruck)* capillary film
Kapitälchen *pl (Satz)* small caps *pl*; ~ **mit großen Anfangsbuchstaben** caps and small caps
Kapitalband *n (Buch)* headband
Kapitalen *n (Buchb.)* headbanding
Kapitalkosten *pl* capital costs *pl*
Kapitalmaschine *f (Buchb.)* headbanding machine
Kapitel *n (Buch)* chapter
Kapitelüberschrift *f* chapter heading
Kapuziner *m* gauge pin
Karbondruck *m* carbon printing
Karbondruckmaschine *f* carbonizing machine, carbon printing machine
Karbonfarbe *f* carbon black, carbon ink
Karbonisieren *n* carbonizing
Karbonisierpapier *n* carbonizing paper
karbonisierter Durchschreibeformularsatz *m* carbonized forms set
karbonisiertes Durchschreibepapier *n (Kohlepapier)* carbonized copy paper
Karbonpapier *n* carbon paper
Karborund *m* carborundum
Kardanwelle *f* cardan shaft, flexible drive shaft
kariertes Papier *n* cross-ruled paper, square ruled paper
Karolingische Minuskel *f (Schrift)* Caroline minuscule
Karren *m (Buchdruckm.)* bed, carriage
Karrenantrieb *m (Buchdruckm.)* bed drive, carriage drive
Karrenleisten *pl (Buchdruckm.)* bed rails *pl*, carriage rails *pl*
Karrenrücklauf *(Buchdruckm.)* carriage return
Karte *f* card; *(Landkarte)* map
Kartei *f* card index, index file
Karteikarte *f* file card, index card
Karteikartenstanzmaschine *f* index card punching machine
Karteikarton *m* index board
Kartendruck *m (Kartogr.)* map printing

Kartenkleber *m (Druckverarb.)* card gluer, card tipper
Kartenzeichner *m (Kartogr.)* cartographer, mapmaker
Kartograf *m* cartographer, mapmaker
Kartografie *f* cartography, mapmaking
Karton *m (im U. zu Papier)* board, cardboard, millboard, pasteboard; *(Schachtel)* cardboard box, carton
Kartonage *f* cardboard box, cardboard container, cardboard product, paperboards *pl*
Kartonageindustrie *f* board processing and converting industry
Kartonagendruck *m* boxboard printing, carton printing
Kartonagendruckerei *f* boxboard printer, carton printer
Kartonagenkarton *m* boxboard
Kartonagenpappe *f* boxboard
Kartonagenüberzugspapier *n* boxboard liner
Kartonagenzuschnitt *m* carton blank
Kartoneinlage *f* carton insert
Kartonfabrik *f* board mill
Kartonhülse *f* board tube
kartonieren *(Buch)* to bind in boards
kartoniertes Buch *n* book bound in boards
Kartonkaschiermaschine *f* board lining machine
Kartonkaschierung *f* board lining
Kartonkreisschere *f* circular board cutter
Kartonösenmaschine *f* board eyeletting machine
Kartonpapier *n* fine cardboard
Kartonpappe *f* boxboard
Kartonrolle *f* board reel
Kartonschere *f* board cutter
Kartonschneider *m* board cutter
Kartonstreifen *m* board strip
Kartonverarbeitung *f* board converting
Karussellbinder *m* rotary binder
Kaschierbogen *m* liner sheet, pre-print
kaschieren *(mit Folie)* to laminate; *(mit vorbedrucktem Papier)* to line
Kaschierfolie *f (Glanzkasch.)* acetate film, laminating film, laminating foil
Kaschierkalander *m* lining calender
Kaschierkarton *m* linerboard
Kaschierkleber *m* laminating adhesive, lining adhesive
Kaschiermaschine *f* laminating machine, lining machine
Kaschierpapier *n* lining paper
Kaschierpappe *f* linerboard
Kaschiertasche *f (für Rundumkunststoffversiegelung)* pouch pocket

kaschierter Karton *m* laminated board, lined board
kaschierte Wellpappe *f* lined corrugated (board)
Kaschierung *f (mit Folie)* laminating, lamination; *(mit Papier)* lining; *(zweiseitig mit fester Schutzfolie)* sealing
Kasein *n* casein
Kassette *f* cassette
Kassettendruckwerk *n (mit Formateinschüben)* cassette-type printing unit
Kassettenfalzapparat *m* cassette folder
Kassettenfarbwerk *n* cassette-type inking unit
Kastenauslage *f* box delivery
Kastenbauweise *f (Modulbauweise)* modular design
Kastenfach *(Setzkasten)* case box
Kastenregal *n (mit Setzpult)* frame rack; *(ohne Setzpult)* case rack
Kastenwalze *f (Feuchtwerk, Fabwerk, Lackwerk)* fountain roller, pan roller
Katalog *m* catalog(ue)
Katalogumschlag *m* catalogue cover
Kathode *f* cathode
Kathodenstrahlröhre *f (CRT, Fotosatz)* cathode ray tube
Kattundruck *m* calico printing
kaustische Sodalösung *f* caustic soda solution
Kegel *m (Schrift)* point size, body size
Kegelradgetriebe *n* bevel gear
Keil *m* wedge; *(Schließkeil)* quoin; *(Maschinensatz)* spaceband
keilen *(Buchdruckform)* to quoin
Keilleser *m (Reprod., Fotochemie)* wedge reader
Keilrahmen *m (Buchdruckform)* quoin chase
Keilriemen *m* V-belt
Keilriemenantrieb *m* V-belt drive
Keilschließzeug *n (Buchdruckform)* quoin
Keilschrift *f* cuneiform characters *pl*
Keilspatien *pl* quoin spaces *pl*
Kennlinie *f* characteristic curve
Kennung *f (Comp.)* file name
Kennziffernanzeige *f* box number advertisement
keramischer Druck *m* ceramic printing
keramisches Abziehbild *n* ceramic decal, ceramic transfer picture
keramisches Papier *n* ceramic paper
Kernspeicher *m (Comp.)* core memory
Kettenantrieb *m* chain drive
Kettenauslage *f* chain delivery
Kettendrucker *m* chain printer
Kettenförderer *m* chain conveyor
Kettengreifer *pl* chain grippers *pl*
Kettengreiferauslage *f* chain gripper delivery

Kettenmaß n *(Schneidem.)* incremental measurement
Kettenpunkt m *(Rasterpunktform)* chain dot, elliptical dot
Kettenrad n sprocket wheel
Kettentransporteur m chain conveyor
Kettenzug m *(Antrieb)* chain drive
Kinderbuch n children's book
Kinoplakat n cinema poster
Kiosk m *(Zeitungen, Zeitschriften)* bookstall, kiosk, newsstand
Kipphebel m rocking lever
kissenförmiger Rasterpunkt m cushion-shaped dot
Kistenpappe f container board
Klärbad n *(Fot.)* filter bath
Klammer f *(zum Heften)* staple
Klammer auf *(Satz)* open brackets
Klammerheftmaschine f wire-stapler
Klammerheftung f stapling, wire stapling
Klammer zu *(Satz)* close brackets
klappbare Schutze pl hinged guards pl
Klappdeckel m *(Maschine)* spring cover
Klappe f *(eingefalzt)* flap
Klappenfalz m jaw fold
Klappenfalzapparat m *(Rollendruckm.)* jaw folder
Klappenfalzwerk n jaw folder
Klappentext m *(Buch)* blurb
Klarschrift f clear type
Klarschriftanzeige f *(Display)* clear type display
Klarschriftleser m *(Texterf.)* optical character reader
Klarsichtdeckblatt n *(Bindung)* clear front cover
Klartextanzeige f clear text display
Klassizistische Antiqua f *(Schriftklassif.)* Didonics pl, Modern Face
Klatschspalten f/pl *(Zeitung)* gossip columns pl
Klaviatur f *(Tastatur)* keyboard
Klebeband n adhesive tape
Klebebandabroller m *(Tesaabroller)* tape dispenser
Klebebindemaschine f adhesive binder, perfect binder
Klebebinder m adhesive binder, perfect binder
Klebebindung f adhesive binding, perfect binding
Klebedispersion f glue dispersion
Klebefalzen n glue-folding
Klebefolie f adhesive film, adhesive foil
klebegebundenes Buch n perfect-bound book
Klebelasche f *(Faltschachtel)* glue flap
Klebelayout n *(Umbruchvorgabe)* mock-up, paste-up of layout

Klebemontage f paste-up
Kleben n gluing; *(druckfrische Bogen im Stapel)* blocking, sticking
Klebenaht f glue joint
Kleber m adhesive, glue, gum
Kleberänder pl *(Filmmontage)* tape prints pl
Kleberand m *(Klebebindung)* binding edge, binding margin, gluing edge
Klebestreifen m adhesive strip
Klebestreifenrückstände pl *(Filmmontage)* tape prints pl
Klebeumbruch m paste-up
Klebe- und Etikettiermaschine f gumming and labelling machine
Klebe- und Kaschiermaschine f gluing and lining machine
Klebevorrichtung f *(Rollenwechsler)* autopaster, paster
Klebewalze f *(Rollenwechsler)* paster roller
Klebezunge f *(Faltschachtel)* glue flap
Klebkraft f adhesive strength
klebrige Farbe f sticky ink, tacky ink
Klebstellenerkennung f *(Bahnbeobachtung)* splice recognition
Klebung f gluing, pasting; *(Bahnklebung)* splicing
klecksiger Druck m blotted impression, splotchy impression, spotted impression
Kleinanzeige f *(Verkaufsanzeige, Stellenanzeige usw.)* classified ad, small ad
Kleinanzeigenumbruch m classified pagination
Kleinauflage f low-volume printwork, short run (job); *(Buch)* small edition; *(Zeitung, Zeitschrift)* small circulation
Kleinbilddia n 35 mm slide
Kleinbildkamera f 35 mm camera
Kleinbuchstaben m/pl *(Gemeine, Minuskel)* lower-case letters pl, minuscules pl
Kleincomputer m microcomputer, minicomputer
Kleindrucksachen pl short-run and small-size printed products pl
kleine Ausgabe f *(Buch)* abridged edition
kleinerätzen *(Punkt)* to sharpen the dots
kleine Zeitung f *(kleine Auflage)* small-circulation newspaper
kleinformatige Druckmaschine f small-size (printing) press
Kleinformatzeitung f small-format newspaper
Kleinoffset m small offset
Kleinoffsetmaschine f small offset printer, small offset (printing) press
Kleinstapel m low pile
kleinstes Papierformat n minimum sheet size

Kleister - Kohlebogenlampe 74

Kleister *m (Buchb.)* adhesive, glue
Kleistermühle *f* glue mill
Kleistertopf *m* glue pot
Klemmbacke *f* clamping jaw
Klemme *f* clamp, fastening clamp
Klemmhebel *m* clamping lever
Klemmring *m* clamping ring
Klemmschiene *f* clamping bar
Klemmschienenbindung *f (Loseblattbindung)* slide binding
Klemmstange *f* clamping bar
Klemmvorrichtung *f* clamping device
Klimaanlage *f* air-conditioning system
Klimatisator *m* air conditioner
klimatisierter Raum *m* air-conditioned room
klimatisiertes Papier *n* air-conditioned paper
Klimatisierung *f* air conditioning
Klingelzeichen *n (Texterf.)* bell character
Klischee *n (druckfertig montiert auf Fuß)* block, printing block; *(nicht montiert, nur Ätzung)* cut, engraving, etching; *(aus Fotopolymer, Gummi usw.)* plate
Klischeeabzug *m* blockmaker's pull, block proof
Klischeeätzer *m* photo-engraver, process engraver
Klischeeätzung *f* photo-engraving, process engraving
Klischee-Andruckpresse *f* block proofing press
Klischeeanstalt *f* blockmakers *pl*, photo-engravers *pl*, process engravers *pl*
Klischeebearbeitung *f* block finishing
Klischeebiegeapparat *m* block bending device
Klischeebohrer *m* block drill
Klischeefuß *m* block base, block mount
Klischeegraviermaschine *f (Varioklischograph)* block engraving machine
Klischeegummi *n* stereo rubber
Klischeehersteller *m* blockmaker, photo-engraver, process engraver
Klischeeherstellung *f* blockmaking, photo-engraving, process engraving
Klischeehöhenmesser *n* block thickness gauge
Klischeeklebefolie *f* adhesive foil for blockmounting
Klischeemantel für Wickelplatten rotary shell for wrap-around plates
Klischeeplattenschere *f* block cutter
Klischeerandlinien *pl* block border rules *pl*
Klischeesperrholz *n* plywood for blockmounting
Klischeestärke *f* block gauge, block thickness
Klischeeträger *m* block holder
Klischeeunterlage *f* block base, block mount
Klischeezink *n* process zinc

Klischeezylinder *m (rotativer Hochdruck)* forme cylinder, plate cylinder
Klischeur *m* blockmaker, photo-engraver, process engraver
Klopfbrett *n (für Buchdruckform)* planer
klopfen *(Buchdruckform)* to knock down, to plane down
Klopfholz *n (für Buchdruckform)* planer
Klotz *m (Klischeefuß)* block base, block mount
Klumpenbildung *f (Bestäubungspuder)* lump formation
knapper Termin *m* tight deadline, tight schedule
knapper Zeitplan *m* tight schedule
Knautschbogen *m* crumpled sheet, jam sheet, wrinkled sheet
Knautscher *m* jam-up, paper jam; *(Gummituch)* smash
Kniegelenk *n (mech.)* knee-joint
Kniehebel *m* toggle lever
Kniehebelpresse *f* toggle press
Knitterprobe *f (Papier)* creasing test
Knochenleim *m* bone glue
knochentrockenes Papier *n* bone-dry paper
Knopfsteuerung *f* push-button control
Knotenfänger *m (Papierherst.)* knotter, pulp strainer
knotenfreies Papier *n* knot-free paper
Knotenheftmaschine *f* thread-stitching and knotting machine
Koaxialkabel *n* coaxial cable
Kobaltazetat *n* acetate of cobalt
kobaltblau cobalt blue
Kobalttrockner *m (Farbzusatz)* cobalt dryer
Kocher *m (Papierherst.)* digester
Kode *m* code, file name
Kodekonvertierung *f* code conversion
Kode-Leser *m* code reader, code scanner
Kodenumerierung *f* code numbering
Kodeumsetzung *f* code conversion
Kodeumwandler *m* code converter
Kodeumwandlung *f* code conversion
kodieren to code, to encode
Kodieren *n* coding, encoding
Kodierer *m* coder, encoder
Kodiergerät *n* encoder
Kodierung *f* coding, encoding
Kodierzeileneindruck *m (Wertpapierdruck)* code line imprint
körnen to grain
Körnigkeit *f (Film, Platte)* graininess
Körperfarbe *f* pigment colour, pigment dye
kohärentes Licht *n (Laser)* coherent light
Kohlebogenlampe *f (Reprod.)* carbon arc lamp

Kohledruck *m (Pigmentdruck)* carbon printing
Kohlefilter *m (Lösemittelrückgewinnung)* active carbon filter
Kohlepapier *n* carbon paper
Kohlepapierabrollung *f* carbon unwind (unit)
Kohlepapieranklebung *f* carbon gluing
Kohlepapieraufrollung *f* carbon rewind (unit)
Kohlepapierdurchschlag *m* carbon copy
Kohlepapierformularsatz *m* carbon copy forms set
Kohlestift *m (Bogenlampe)* carbon rod
Kohlezeichnung *f* charcoal drawing
Kolben *m (mech.)* piston
Kolbenstange *f* piston rod
Kollator *m (Formularherst.)* collator
Kollodium *n* collodion
Kollodiumwolle *f* collodion cotton
Kolon *n (Doppelpunkt)* colon
Kolonne *f (einzelne Spalte einer Tabelle)* column
Kolorieren *n* colouring
Kolorist *m* colourist
Kolumne *f* column
Kolumnenlänge *f* depth of column
Kolumnenschnur *f* page cord
Kolumnenziffer *f* folio, page number
Kolumnist *m* columnist
Kombi-Falzautomat *m (Schwertfalz + Taschenfalz)* combination folding machine
Kombifalzer *m (Rollendruckm.)* combination folder
kombiniertes Farb/Feuchtwerk *n* combined inking and damping system, Hydrocolor system
kombiniert versetzter Stich *m (Fadenheftung)* combined staggered stitch
Kombischablone *f (Siebdruck)* combined stencil
Komma *n* comma
Kommando *n (Comp.)* command, instruction
Kommunikation *f* communication
Kommunikationsindustrie *f* communications industry
Kommunikationsverbindung *f* communication link
Kompaktkamera *f* compact camera
kompatibel compatible
Kompatibilität *f* compatibility
Kompensationsfilter *m* compensating filter
Kompensativmaske *f (Reprod.)* compensating mask
Komplementärfarbe *f (Farbensystem)* complementary colour
Komplettdruck *m (komplett auf Rollendruckmasch. gefertigt)* press-finished product

komplettes System aus einer Hand *(Comp.)* turn-key installation
komplizierte Arbeit *f* complex work, tricky job
komplizierter Satz *m* complex matter
kompreß *(nicht durchschossen)* set solid, solid
kompresser Satz *m* close matter, solid matter, solid set type
Kompressibilität *f (Gummituch)* compressibility
kompressibles Gummituch *n (im U. zu konventionell)* compressible rubber blanket
Konkavlinse *f* concave lens
Konkordanz *f (Satz)* four-em quad
konservieren *(Offsetplatten)* to gum (up)
Konservierungsmittel *n (Offsetplatten)* gum
Konsole *f (Systemsteuerung)* console
Konsonant *m* consonant
Konsumentenzeitschrift *f* consumer magazine
Kontakt *m (Kontaktkopie)* contact
Kontaktabzug *m (Reprod.)* contact, contact copy, contact print
Kontaktarbeiten *pl (Reprod.)* contact work
Kontaktbeleimung *f (im U. zur Düsenbeleimung)* contact gluing
Kontaktbelichter *m* contact box, contact copier, contact printer
Kontaktbelichtung *f* contact exposure
kontakten to contact, to copy, to duplicate by contact
Kontakten *n (Reprod.)* contact copying, contacting, contact printing
Kontaktfilm *m* contact film
kontaktfreie Auslage *f* contact-free delivery
Kontaktkontrollstreifen *m* contact control strip
Kontaktkopie *f (Aktion)* contact copying, contact exposure, contact printing, film duplicating, printing-down; *(Produkt)* contact copy, contact print, film duplicate
Kontaktkopierer *m* contact box, contact copier, contact printer
Kontaktkopiergerät *n* contact box, contact copier, contact printer
Kontaktlinie *f (zwischen Zylindern)* contact line
Kontaktnegativ *n* contact negative
Kontaktpapier *n (Reprod.)* contact paper; *(zum Durchschreiben)* pressure-sensitive paper
Kontaktpositiv *n* contact positive
Kontaktraster *m* contact screen
Kontaktrasterscanner *m (im U. zum S. mit elektron. Rasterpunktbildung)* contact-screen scanner
Kontaktrasterung *f* contact screening
Kontaktzone *f (Druck)* area of contact
kontern *(Bild)* to reverse laterally, to turn

Kontern *n (Seitenumkehr im Bild)* lateral reversal
Konterumdruck *m* counter transfer
kontinuierliche Leimung *f* continuous gluing
Kontrast *m* contrast
Kontrastdämpfungsmaske *f* contrast reducing mask
Kontrastfilter *m* contrast filter
Kontrastkompression *f* contrast compression
kontrastloses Bild *n* flat image, low contrast image, soft image
Kontrast mindern to decrease contrast
Kontrastrand *m* contrast border
kontrastreiches Bild *n* high-contrast image
Kontrast steigern to increase contrast
Kontraststeigerung *f (Scannerfunktion)* contrast enhancement, detail enhancement
Kontraststeuerfolie *f* contrast control film
Kontrastumfang *m* contrast range
Kontrastverringerung *f* contrast compression
Kontrollampe *f* control light
Kontrollbildschirm *m* monitor
Kontrollbogen *m* checking sheet, control sheet, inspection sheet, proof sheet
Kontrolle *f* check(ing), control, inspection, monitoring, proofviewing, supervision, verification
Kontrollexemplar *n* checking copy, control copy, inspection copy
Kontrollfeld *n (Meßstreifen)* control patch, target
kontrollierte Verkaufsauflage *f (Zeitung)* certified sale
Kontrollkeil *m (Reprod., Formherst.)* control wedge
Kontrollkopie *f* control copy, proof copy
Kontrollprogramm *n* supervisor
Kontrollpult *n* control console, control desk
Kontrollstreifen *m* control bar, control strip
Kontrolltastatur *f* verifying keyboard
Kontrollzeichen *n* check mark
Kontur *f* contour, outlines *pl*
Konturenfilm *m* contour film
Konturensatz *m* outline setting
Konturenschärfe *f (Fotosatz)* character definition, contour definition, definition of outlines, image definition, image resolution
Konturform *f* outline form
konturieren to outline
Konturschrift *f* outline characters *pl*
Konturzeichnung *f* keyline drawing
konventionelle Ätzung *f (Tiefdruck)* conventional etching

konventioneller Tiefdruck *m* conventional gravure (process)
konventionelles Gummituch *n (im U. zu kompressibel)* conventional rubber blanket
Konversationslexikon *n* encyclopedia
Konverter *m* converter
konvertieren *(Daten, Text)* to convert
konvertierter Text *m* converted copy, converted text
Konvertierung *f (Daten, Text)* conversion, converting
Konvertierungstabelle *f* conversion table
Konvexlinse *f* convex lens
Konzentrat *n (Fotochemie, Druckchemie)* concentrate
koordinatengesteuerter Umbruch *m* coordinate-controlled page make-up
Koordinatenzeichentisch *m (CAD)* coordinate drawing table
Kopf *m* head; *(des Buchstaben)* neck; *(Zeitung, Zeitschrift)* title
Kopfabschlußlinie *f (Tabelle)* cross rule under heading
Kopf-an-Fuß-Belichtung *f (Repetierkopierm.)* head-to-foot exposure
Kopf-an-Kopf-Belichtung *f (Repetierkopierm.)* head-to-head exposure
Kopf auf Fuß gedruckt *(Nutzenanordnung)* printed head to foot
Kopf auf Kopf gedruckt *(Nutzenanordnung)* printed head to head
Kopfbeschnitt *m* head trim(ming)
Kopfgoldschnitt *m (Buch)* gilt top edge
Kopfleimung *f* top edge gluing
Kopfleiste *f (Verzierung)* head-piece
Kopflinie *f* head rule
Kopfsteg *m* head stick
Kopfzeile *f (Satz)* headline, page header
Kopie *f (Aktion)* contact copying, contact exposure, contact printing, copying, platemaking; *(fertiges Resultat)* contact copy, contact print, copy; *(Abteilung)* platemaking department, platemaking room
kopieren to contact, to copy, to print
Kopierer *m (Person)* plate frame operator, platemaker; *(Gerät)* copier
kopierfähig plate-ready, ready for contacting, ready for platemaking, ready for printing-down
kopierfähiger Film *m* plate-ready film, production film
kopierfertig siehe **kopierfähig**

Kopierfilm m *(Film zum Kopieren)* printing(-down) film
Kopierfolge f *(Repetierkopierm.)* exposure sequence
Kopiergerät n *(Büro)* copier
Kopierkontrollstreifen m exposure control strip
Kopierlack m photoresist
Kopierlampe f copying lamp, exposure lamp
Kopiermaschine f *(Repetierkopierm.)* step-and-repeat (copying) machine
Kopiermeßstreifen m exposure control strip, exposure measuring strip
Kopiermontage f automatic stripping
Kopiermontageautomat m stripper-stepper, stripping and stepping machine
Kopierpapier n copying paper
Kopierrahmen m copying frame, printing-down frame, vacuum frame
Kopierschicht f *(Film, Folie)* photo emulsion; *(Platte)* light-sensitive coating, photocoating; *(Siebdruck)* screen emulsion
Kopiertechnik f copying technique, platemaking technique
Kopiervorlage f film copy
kordeln *(Buch)* to cord
Korkaufzug m cork blanket
Korktuch n cork blanket
Korn m *(Fot.)* grain
Kornpapier n *(Abziehbilderdruck)* grained decalcomania paper, grained transfer paper
Kornraster m grain screen
Koronabehandlung f corona treatment
Koronastation f corona station
Korrektor m proofreader
Korrektorenzeichen n proofreader's mark
Korrektur f correction, editing; *(angezeichneter Fehler beim Satz)* mark, proofmark
Korrekturabziehpresse f galley press, proofpress
Korrekturabzug m galley proof, proof, proof sheet
Korrekturbelegausdruck m *(Fotosatz)* plain paper proof
Korrekturbildschirm m *(Texterf.)* video editing terminal
Korrekturbogen m proof sheet
Korrekturfahne f galley proof, slip proof
Korrekturfilter m correction filter
Korrekturfunktion f *(Texterf.)* editing function
Korrekturlesen n proofreading
Korrekturmittel n *(Platte)* deletion fluid
Korrekturprogramm n *(Texterf.)* editing program, editor

Korrekturstift m *(Platte, Film)* correction pen, deletion pen
Korrekturterminal m *(Texterf.)* video editing terminal
Korrekturzeichen n *(Satz)* mark, proofmark, proofreader's mark
Korrekturzeile f *(Zeilenguß)* corrected line
Korrespondent m correspondent
korrigieren to correct; *(korrekturlesen)* to mark(-up); *(Textverarb., Bildverarb.)* to edit
korrigierter Korrekturabzug m clean proof
korrigierter Text m clean copy
korrosionsbeständig corrosion-proof, corrosion-resistant
korrosionsfest corrosion-proof, corrosion-resistant
korrosionsgeschützt corrosion-proof, corrosion-resistant
Korrosionsschutz m *(Zylinder)* anti-corrosion coating
Kosmetikpackung f cosmetic box
Kostenberechnung f cost calculation, cost estimating, costing
Kostenkalkulation f cost calculation, cost estimating, costing
Kosten/Nutzen-Verhältnis n cost/benefit ratio
Kostenrechnung f cost accounting
Kostenstelle f *(Rechnungswesen)* cost center
Kostenvoranschlag m cost estimate
Kraftbedarf m power requirement
Kraftliner m kraftliner
Kraftpapier n kraft paper
Kraftübertragung f power transmission
Kraftzurichtung f mechanical makeready
Krananlage f *(Tiefdruckzyl.)* crane
Kratzer m scratch
Kratzfestigkeit f scratch resistance
Kratzprobe f scratch test
Kreativer m *(Vorlagenherst.)* creative designer
Kreide f chalk
Kreidefarbe f drawing chalk
Kreidelithografie f *(Kreidezeichnung)* chalk drawing, crayon drawing
Kreiden n chalking
Kreidereliefzurichtung f *(Buchdruck)* chalk relief makeready
Kreideretusche f *(Lithogr.)* crayoning
Kreidestift m chalk pencil, crayon
Kreidezeichnung f chalk drawing, crayon drawing
Kreiskartonschere f rotary board cutter
Kreismesser n circular cutter, circular knife
Kreissäge f circular saw

Kreisschere - Kupferhaut

Kreisschere f circular knife
Kreppapier n crepe paper
Kreuz(bruch)falz m cross fold, right-angle fold
Kreuzfadenstich m *(Fadenheftung)* thread cross-over
Kreuzfalz m siehe Kreuzbruchfalz
kreuzgelegter Stapel m compensated stack
Kreuzleger m *(Versandraum)* compensating stacker
Kreuzlinienraster m crossline screen
Kreuzschraffierung f cross hatching
Kreuzstapelauslage f compensated delivery, criss-cross delivery
Kreuzstapler m *(Versandraum)* compensating stacker
Kreuzumreifung f *(Versandraum)* cross-strapping, cross-tying
Kreuzverschnüren n *(Versandraum)* cross-strapping, cross-tying
kreuzweise criss-cross
kreuzweise Auslage f *(Druckm.)* compensated delivery, criss-cross delivery, crosswise delivery
kreuzweise stapeln to brickstack
Kreuzzählstapler m compensating counter stacker
Kreuz(zeichen) n dagger
Kronkorkendrucker m *(Blechdruck)* crown cork printer
Kühlaggregat n *(Rollendruckm.)* chilling unit, cooling device
Kühlmittel n coolant, cooling agent
Kühlschlange f cooling coil
Kühlwalze f *(Rollendruckm.)* chill roll
Kühlwalzenstand m chilling tower, chill roll assembly, chill roll frame, chill roll stand
Kühlwasserumlauf m *(Maschinentemperierung)* cooling water circulation
künstlerischer Leiter m art director, type director
Künstlerlithografie f lithograph drawn on plate (or stone)
Künstlerschrift f fancy type
Küvette f *(Film-, Plattenentwickl.)* dip tank
Kugeldüsen pl *(Lufttisch)* spherical nozzles pl
Kugellager n ball bearing
Kugelleiste f *(Bogenführung)* ball race
Kugelmühle f *(Farbherst.)* ball mill
Kunde m client, customer
Kundenauftrag m client's order, customer's order
Kundenbetreuung f after-sales service, customer service
Kundendienst m after-sales service, customer service

Kundenreklamation f customer complaint
Kundenstammdaten pl customer file data, customer record
Kundenstammsatz m *(EDV)* customer file data, customer record
Kundenwunsch m customer requirement
Kunstbild n art picture
Kunstblatt n art print
Kunstbuch n art book
Kunstbuchbinder m art bookbinder, craft bookbinder
Kunstdruck m art print, art printing
Kunstdruckerei f fine art printers pl
Kunstdruckkarton m art board
Kunstdruckpapier n art paper
Kunstfaserpapier n synthetic fibre paper
Kunstfirnis m synthetic varnish
Kunstkalender m art calendar
Kunstleder n artificial leather, imitation leather
Kunstledereinband m *(Buch)* artificial leather binding, imitation leather binding
Kunstleinen n *(Artlinnen)* imitation linen
Kunstlicht n artificial light
Kunstlichtfilm m *(Fot.)* tungsten film
Kunststoff m plastic material, synthetic material
Kunststoffbedruckung f plastics printing
kunststoffbeschichteter Tiefdruckzylinder m plastic-coated gravure cylinder
kunststoffbeschichtetes Papier n *(RC-Papier)* RC paper, resin-coated paper
Kunststoffdruckfolie f *(Kleinoffset)* plastic master, plastic (printing) plate
Kunststoffklischee n *(Fotopolymerplatte)* photopolymer plate
Kunststoffletter f *(Handsatz)* plastic letter
Kunststoffmater f synthetic matrix
Kunststoffwalze f plastic roller, synthetic roller
Kupfer abschälen to peel off copper, to strip copper
Kupferätzplatte f copperplate for photogravure
Kupferätzung f copper engraving, copper etching
Kupferanode f copper anode
Kupferautotypieätzung f halftone engraving on copper
Kupferbad n copper bath
Kupferbuchstaben pl *(Handsatz)* copper type
Kupferdruck m copperplate printing
Kupferdruckplatte f copperplate
Kupferdruckpresse f copperplate press
Kupfergehalt m copper content
Kupfergravüre f copper engraving
Kupferhärte f copper hardness
Kupferhaut f copper coating, copper skin

Kupferniederschlag *m* copper deposit
Kupferplatte *f* copperplate
Kupferrückgewinnung *f* copper recovery
Kupferschicht *f* copper coating
Kupferspäne *pl* copper chips *pl*
Kupferstecher *m* copperplate engraver
Kupferstereo *n* copper stereo
Kupferstich *m* copperplate engraving, copperplate print, intaglio
Kupferstichplatte *f* copperplate for engraving, engraved copperplate
Kupferstich-Tiefdruck *m* copperplate printing, intaglio printing
Kupfersulfat *n* copper sulfate
Kupfertiefdruck *m* gravure printing; *(im U. zum Tiefdruck mit kunstsoffbesch. Zyl.)* copper gravure process
Kupfertiefdruckzylinder *m* copper gravure cylinder
Kupondruck *m* coupon printing
kuppeln *(Wörter)* to hyphen(ate)
Kuppelwort *n* hyphened word
Kupplung *f (techn.)* clutch, coupling
Kupplungsbolzen *m* coupling bolt
Kurbel *f* crank
Kurbelbewegung *f* crank motion
Kurbelrad *n* crank wheel
Kurbelradantrieb *m* crank wheel drive
Kurbelwelle *f* crank shaft
Kursbuch *n (Fahrplanb.)* timetable
kursiv *(Satz)* italic, oblique; *(elektronisch schräggestellt)* pseudo-italic, slanted
Kursivgemeine *pl (Schrift)* italic lower-case
kursiv rechts oder links *(Fotosatz)* slanted left or right
Kursivschrift *f* italics *pl*, italic type
Kursivversalien *f/pl* italic capitals *pl*
Kursor *m (Bildschirm)* cursor
Kursorsteuerung *f* cursor control
Kurve *f (Maschinensteuerung)* cam
Kurvenband *n (Versandraum)* curved belt
Kurvenscheibe *f (Maschinensteuerung)* cam disc
Kurvensteuerung *f (Maschinensteuerung)* cam control
kurze Buchstaben *pl* short letters *pl*
kurze Farbe *f* short ink, viscous ink
kurze Meldung *f (Zeitung)* item
kurze Nachricht *f (Zeitung)* item
kurze Zeitungsmeldung *f* news item
Kurzfarbwerk *n (Anilox)* short inking unit, anilox inking unit, keyless inking system
kurzfaseriges Papier *n* short-fibred paper
Kurzgeschichte *f* short story

kurzlebiges Produkt *n* short-lived product
kurzwellige IR-Strahlung short-wave I.R. radiation
Kustoden *pl* catchword
Kuvert *n* envelope
Kuvertfutterseidenpapier *n* envelope tissue lining paper
Kyrillische Schrift *f* Cyrillic characters *pl*

L

Lack *m (Drucklack)* varnish
Lackieranstalt *f* varnishing house
Lackiereinheit *f* varnishing unit, coating unit
lackieren *(Druckveredlung)* to varnish, to coat
Lackiererei *f* varnishing department, varnishing house
Lackiermaschine *f* coating machine, varnishing machine
Lackiertuch *n (Gummituch für Lackauftrag im Offset)* varnishing blanket
Lackierung *f* varnishing, coating, varnish coating
Lackierwalze *f* varnishing roller, coating roller
Lackierwerk *n* varnishing unit, coating unit
Lackkasten *m (Lackierwerk)* varnish pan, varnish trough
Lackmuspapier *n (Chem.)* litmus paper
Lackschicht *f* coating film, coating layer, varnish coating, varnish film
Lacktauchwalze *f* varnish pan roller
Lacktuch *n (Wachsleinen)* oilcloth
Lacküberzug *m* varnish coating
Lackumlauf *m* varnish circulation
laden *(comp.)* to down-load, to load
Laderampe *f* loading platform
Längezeichen *n (über Buchstaben)* straight accent
Längsfalz *m* longitudinal fold, lineal fold, length fold; *(Rollendruck)* former fold
Längsheftung *f* longitudinal stitching
Längsleimung *f* longitudinal gluing, lineal gluing
Längsperforation *f* longitudinal perforation, lineal perforation
Längsregister *n* lineal register, longitudinal register
Längsrichtung *f* longitudinal direction
Längsrückentitel *m (Buch)* title along the spine
Längsschneidemesser *n* slitting knife

Längsschneider - laufende Arbeit

Längsschneider *m (Rollenverarb.)* reel slitter, slitter, slitter-rewinder, web slitter
Längsschnitt *m* slitting
Längs- und Querschnitt *m* slitting and sheeting
Längsverschiebung *f (Bahn, Rollendruck)* longitudinal shifting
Längswellenantrieb *m* longitudinal shaft drive
Lärmdämmhaube *f* noise reduction hood, sound insulating cover
Lärmdämpfung *f* noise reduction, sound absorption, sound dampening
Lärmkapselung *f* noise cover, sound enclosure
Lärmniveau *n* noise level
Lärmpegel *m* noise level
Lärmschutz *m* noise abatement, noise prevention
Lage *f* quire, section
Lagenfalzmaschine *f* quire folding machine
Lagenfalzung *f* quire folding
Lagenstapler *m* section stacker
Lager *n (Zylinderlager)* bearing
Lagerbolzen *m* bearing bolt
Lagerfähigkeit *f (Verbrauchsmaterialien)* shelf-life
Lagerfett *n* grease, lubricant
Lagerölung *f* bearing lubrication
Lagerschale *f* bearing bushing
Lagerschmierung *f* bearing lubrication
Lagerung *f (Zyl.)* bearing; *(Vorräte)* storage, warehousing
Lagerzapfen *m (Walze)* journal
Lamelle *f (Tiefdruckrakel)* tip
Laminat *n* compound, laminate
laminieren to laminate
Lampe *f* lamp
Lampengehäuse *n* lamp housing
Lampenwagen *m (Horizontalkamera)* lamp trolley
Landkarte *f* map
Landkarten aufziehen to mount maps
Landkartendruck *m* map printing
Landkartenpapier *n* map paper
Landleitung *f (Telekomm.)* land line, terrestrial connection
lange Farbe *f* long ink, low-viscosity ink, soft ink
langer Buchstabe *m (mit Ober- und Unterlänge)* tall letter
langfaseriges Papier *n* long-fibred paper
Langformat *n* landscape size, oblong format
langlebiges Produkt *n (Drucksache)* long-lived product
Langsiebpapiermaschine *f* fourdrinier machine

Langzeitarchivierung *f* long-term filing, permanent storage
Langzeitspeicherung *f* long-term filing, permanent storage
Lapidar *f (Steinschrift)* block letter
lappiges Papier *n* flabby paper
Lasche *f (Klappe)* flap
Laser *m* laser
Laseraufzeichnung *f* laser recording
Laseraufzeichnungsgerät *n* laser recorder
Laserausgabe *f* laser output
Laserausgabeeinheit *f* laser output unit
Laserbelichter *m* laser exposure unit, laser imager, laser imagesetter, laser output unit, laser plotter, laser recorder, laser setter, laser typesetter
Laserbelichtung *f* laser exposure, laser imaging, laser output, laser recording
Laserdiode *f* laser diode
Laserdiodenbelichter *m* laser diode imagesetter
Laserdrucker *m* laser printer
lasergraviert laser-engraved
Lasergravur *f (Tiefdruckzyl.)* laser engraving
Laserplattenherstellung *f (Offsetformherst.)* laser platemaking
Laserplotter *m* laser plotter
Laserpunktgenerator *m (Scanner)* laser dot generator
Lasersatz *m* lasersetting, laser typesetting
Laserscanner *m* laser scanner
Laserschrift *f* laser font
Laserstrahl *m* laser beam
Laserstrahlzählgerät *n (Exemplarzählung)* laser counter
Lasertechnik *f* laser technology
lasierende Farben *f/pl (Druckfarbe)* transparent inks *pl*
lasierende Retusche *f* transparent retouching
Lateinische Schrift *f* Latin characters *pl*, Latin type, Roman characters *pl*, Roman type
latentes Bild *n* latent image
latente Schwärzung *f* latent blackening
Lauf *m* operation, running
Laufblech *n (auf Maschinenanlagen)* footboard, runner board, runner board
Laufboden *m (Kamera)* footboard
Laufbrett *n (Masch.)* runner board
Laufeigenschaft *f (Papier)* runability, running properties *pl*
laufen *(Masch.)* to run
laufende Arbeit *f* current job, work in process, work in progress

laufende Produktion *f* current production, production in progress, running production
laufender Auftrag *m* current job, job in process, job in progress
laufender Text *m* body matter, running text, straight matter, text stream
Laufgeschwindigkeit *f* running speed
Laufleisten *f/pl (Flachdruckpresse)* bed bearers *pl*
Laufrichtung *f (Bahn)* direction of web travel, grain (direction), paper grain, running direction; *gegen die ~ /quer zur ~* across the grain, across the web, against the grain, cross grain, cross web; *in ~* along the web, in line, long grain
Laufring *m (Schmitzring)* bearer ring, cylinder bearer
Laufrollen *f/pl* rollers *pl*, trolleys *pl*
laufruhig *(Maschine)* smooth-running
Laufschiene *f* runner rail
Laufschrift *f* body type
Laufschriftanzeige *f (einzeiliges Display)* line display, moving display
Laufstege *m/pl (Buchdruckm.)* bed bearers *pl*
Laufstörung *f* malfunction
Laufweite *f (Schrift)* character fit(ting), character spacing, interspacing, kerning, letterspacing
Laufwerk *n (Comp.)* drive
Laufzettel *m (Arbeitszettel, Tageszettel)* time sheet
Lautschrift *f* phonetic lettering
Layout *n* layout
Layoutangaben *pl* layout instructions *pl*, layout specifications *pl*
Layouter *m* layout man
layoutgerechte Darstellung *f (Bildschirm)* layout-true display
Layoutgestaltung *f* layout design
Layoutsatz *m* display matter, display setting, layout matter, layout setting
Layoutsetzerei *f* layout typesetter
lebender Kolumnentitel *m* running head, tell-tale
lebender Kolumnentitel am Fuß *m* running feet, running foot
Lebensdauer *f (Maschine)* durability, service life
lebensmittelechte Farbe *f* non-toxic ink
Lebensmittelverpackung *f* food package
Leckwalze *f (Heber)* ductor roller, vibrator, vibrator roller
LED *(Leuchtdiode)* LED (light emitting diode)
LED-Anzeige *f* LED display
LED-Belichtung *f (Fotosatz)* LED exposure
Lederband *m (Buch)* leather-bound volume
Lederdecke *f (Buch)* leather case, leather cover
Ledereinband *m (Buch)* leather binding, leather case, leather cover
Lederimitation *f* artificial leather, imitation leather
Lederimitationspapier *n* imitation leather paper
Lederkarton *m* leather board
Lederpapier *n* leather paper
Lederpappe *f* leather board
Lederüberzug *m* leather covering
Lederwalze *f* leather(-covered) roller
LED-Zeile *f (Fotosatz)* LED array
Leerlauf *m* idle gear, idle running, idling
Leerschnitt *m (Schneidem.)* idle cut
Leerseite *f (Vakat)* blank page, white page
Leerzeile *f* blank line, white line
Legende *f (Bildunterschrift)* caption
Legierzinn *n* tin alloy
Lehrbuch *n* manual, school-book, textbook
Lehre *f (Fühlerlehre)* feeler gauge
leichter Bogen *m* light-weight sheet, light-weight signature
leichte Schrift *f* light typeface
leichtes Papier *n* low-grammage paper
leicht holzhaltiges Papier *n* slightly mechanical paper
Leichtpappe *f* light board
Leim *m (Druckverarb.)* adhesive, glue, gum; *(Papierherst.)* size
Leimauftrag *m* glue application
Leimauftragswalze *f (Klebebinder)* glue application roller
Leimbecken *n* glue pot
Leimdüse *f* glue nozzle
Leimen *n* gluing; *(Blockleimen)* padding; *(Papier)* sizing
Leimkopf *m (Leimwerk)* gluing head
Leimmaschine *f* gluing machine
Leimniveaukontrolle *f (Klebebinder)* glue level control
Leimpinsel *m* glue brush
Leimpresse *f (Papierherst.)* size press
Leimscheibe *f (Klebebinder)* glue applicator disc
Leimschicht *f* glue coating
Leimspur *f* glue line
Leimstreifen *m* glue strip
Leimtopf *m* glue pot
Leimung *f* gluing; *(Blockleimung)* padding; *(Papier)* sizing
Leimungsmittel *n (Papierherst.)* size, sizing agent
Leimwalze *f* gluing roller
Leimwerk *n* gluing unit
Leimwulstbildung *f* formation of glue beads

Leinen - Lichtgriffel

Leinen *n (Buchb.)* cloth, linen
Leinenband *m (Buch)* clothback, volume bound in cloth
Leinendecke *f (Buch)* cloth case, cloth cover
Leineneinband *m (Buch)* cloth binding, cloth case, cloth cover
Leinenkarton *m* linen board
leinenkaschiert cloth-lined
Leinenpapier *n* linen paper
Leinenpostpapier *n* linen embossed writing paper
Leinenstrukturraster *m (Reprod.)* linen grain screen
Leinöl *n* linseed oil
Leinölfirnis *m* linseed oil varnish
Leiste *f (Verzierung)* border, flourish, head-piece, printer's flower, tail-piece
Leistung *f (Masch.)* capacity, output, performance; *(Motor; el.)* power
Leistungsaufnahme *f (el.)* power consumption
Leistungsbedarf *m (el.)* power requirement
Leistungsbereich *m* performance range
Leistungsfähigkeit *f* capacity, efficiency, output, performance
Leistungsgrenze *f* performance limit
Leistungsvorgabe *f* performance targets *pl*
Leitartikel *m* leader, leading article
Leiterplatte *f* printed circuit board
Leitstand *m (Maschinenanlage)* central control console, remote control console
Leitungsnetz *n (Telekomm.)* line network
Leitwalze *f (Rollendruckm.)* idler roller, web guide roller, web lead roller
Leporellofalz *m* accordeon fold, concertina fold, harmonica fold, zigzag fold
Leporelloprospekt *m* zigzag-folded brochure
lesbar legible, readable
Lesbarkeit *f* legibility, readability
Leseanreiz *m* incentive to read
Lesegerät *n* reader, reading machine
Lesekopf *m* reading head
Lesemaschine *f* optical character reader, reading machine
Leser *m* reader
leserlich legible, readable
leserliche Schrift *f* clear type, readable type
leserliches Manuskript *n* clear copy
Lese/Schreibkopf *m (Comp.)* read/write head
Lesezeichen *n (Buch)* bookmark
Lesezeichenband *n (Buch)* bookmark
Letter *f* letter, type, printing character, printing letter
Letternmagazin *n* type magazine
Letternmetall *n* printer's metal, type metal

Letterset *m (Druckverfahren)* letterset
letzte Nachrichten *pl* late breaking news *pl*
Leuchtanzeige *f (LED)* LED display
Leuchtdiode *f (LED)* light emitting diode
Leuchtfläche *f (Leuchttisch)* illuminated area
Leuchtkasten *m* light box
Leuchtkraft *f* light intensity
Leuchtpult *m* light desk
Leuchttisch *m* light table
Lexikon *n* dictionary, encyclopedia
Libretto *n (Textbuch)* libretto
lichtbeständig *(Farbe)* siehe lichtecht
Lichtbeständigkeit *f (Farbe)* siehe Lichtechtheit
lichtdicht light-proof, light-tight
Lichtdosiergerät *n (Kopierrahmen)* light integrator
Lichtdosierung *f* light metering
Lichtdruck *m (Erzeugnis)* collotype, phototype; *(Verfahren)* collotype printing, phototype printing
Lichtdruckgelatine *f* collotype gelatine
Lichtdruckkarton *m* collotype board
Lichtdruckkorn *n* collotype grain
Lichtdruckpapier *n* collotype paper
Lichtdruckplatte *f* collotype plate
Lichtdruckwalze *f* collotype roller
lichtdurchlässig translucent, transparent
Lichtdurchlässigkeit *f* light transmission, transparency
lichtecht *(Druckfarbe)* bleach-resistant, colour-fast, light-fast, non-fading
Lichtechtheit *f (Druckfarbe)* bleach-resistance, colour-fastness, fade resistance, light-fastness
lichtempfindliche Platte *f* sensitized plate
lichtempfindliche Schicht *f* light-sensitive coating, photosensitive coating
Lichtempfindlichkeit *f* light sensitivity, speed
lichtempfindlich machen to sensitize
Lichter *pl (Hochlichter)* highlight dots *pl*, highlights *pl*
lichter Durchmesser *m* inner diameter
Lichtermaske *f (Reprod.)* highlight mask
Lichterpartie *f (Bild)* highlight areas *pl*
Lichterzeichnung *f (Bild)* highlight details *pl*, highlight separation, image definition in the highlights
lichte Schrift *f (Konturschrift)* outline characters *pl*
Lichtfang *m (unter Rasterpunkt)* light gathering, light trap
Lichtfarbe *f* light colour
Lichtfilter *m* light filter
Lichtgriffel *m* light pen

Lichthof m *(Fot.)* halo
Lichthofbildung f halation, halo-formation
Lichthofschutzschicht f anti-halation backing, anti-halation layer, anti-halo backing, anti-halo layer
Lichtintensität f light intensity
lichtleitend light-conducting, photoconductive
Lichtmeßgerät n light meter, photometer
Lichtmessung f exposure control, photometry
Lichtpause f blue print, diazo copy, diazo print, dyeline
Lichtpauskopie f blue printing, diazo printing
Lichtpausmaschine f blue-printing machine, diazo printing machine, dyeline machine
Lichtpauspapier n blue-printing paper, diazo paper, dyeline paper, ozalid paper
Lichtpausverfahren n blue-printing process, diazo process, dyeline process
Lichtpunkt m *(im Gs. zum Tiefenpunkt)* highlight dot
Lichtquelle f light source
Lichtsatz m *(Fotosatz)* photocomposition, photosetting, phototypesetting
Lichtschranke f light barrier
lichtschwach dim, faint
Lichtsignal n light signal
Lichtstärke f light intensity; *(Objektiv)* brightness
lichtstarkes Objektiv n fast lens, high-speed lens
Lichtstrahl m light ray
Lichtstrahlung f light emission
Lichttakte pl *(Kopie)* light cycles pl
lichtundurchlässig light-proof, opaque
Lichtverstärker m *(Fotomultipier)* photomultiplier
Lichtverteilung f light diffusion, light distribution
Lichtwert m light value
Liebhaberausgabe f collector's edition
Liefertermin m delivery date, delivery deadline
Liefertermin einhalten to meet delivery date
Liefertermin nicht einhalten to miss delivery date
Lieferung f consignment, delivery
Lieferungsbedingungen pl terms of delivery
liegendes Format n *(Rollendruck)* cross grain, short cut-off, short grain
Ligatur f *(Doppelbuchstabe)* diphthong, ligature
Lignin n *(Papierherst.)* lignin
Lindenholzkohle f limewood charcoal
Lineal n ruler
Linearität f *(Densitometrie)* linearity
Lineatur f *(Linierung)* ruling; *(Rasterfeinheit)* screen ruling

Line-Entwicklung f line development, line processing
Line-Entwicklungsmaschine f line processor
Line-Film m *(Reprod.)* line film
Linie f *(aus Metall; für Buchdruck, Stanzen, Perforieren usw.)* rule; *(gezogen auf Linierm./Fotosetzm.)* rule; *(typogr.)* line
Liniehalten n alignment
liniehaltende Ziffern pl *(Antiquaziffern)* lining figures pl, modern figures pl
Linienabstand m *(Tabellen)* ruling distance
Linienbiegemaschine f rule bending machine
Linienbreite f line width, rule width
Linien/cm *(Auflösung)* lines per cm
Liniendruck m ruling work
Linieneinfassung f *(Linienrand)* rule border
Liniengießmaschine f rule casting machine
Liniengitter n *(Tabellensatz)* rule grid
Linienhöhe f rule depth
Linienkasten m *(Bleisatz)* rule case
Linienornament n line ornament, rule ornament
Linienrahmen m boxed rules pl, rule box
Linienrahmen mit runden Ecken rule box with rounded corners
Linienrand m rule border
Linienraster m *(Reprod.)* line screen
Liniensatz m *(im U. zum Schriftsatz)* ruling work
Linienschneidemaschine f rule cutter
Linienstärke f line weight, rule weight
linieren to rule(-up)
Linieren n ruling-up
Linierfarbe f ruling ink
Liniermaschine f machine ruler, ruling machine
Liniermaschine mit Feder pen ruling machine
Liniermaschine mit Feder und Rolle pen and disc ruler
Liniermaschinenfaden m machine ruler thread
Liniersatz m *(im U. zu Schriftsatz)* ruling work
liniertes Papier n ruled paper
Liniertisch m rule-up table, ruling table
Linierung f ruling
Linierwalzen f/pl ruling rollers pl
linke Seiten pl left(-hand) pages pl
linksbündig *(Satz)* flush left, quad left
linksbündig setzen to adjust text to the left, to move matter to the left, to set flush left
Linoleumdruck m lino print, lino printing
Linolschnitt m lino cut
Linotype f *(Zeilengießmaschine)* linotype machine
Linotypesatz m *(Zeilenguß)* linotype composition
Linotypesetzer m linotype compositor, linotype operator

Linotypezeile - Lottoschein

Linotypezeile f *(Zeilenguß)* linotype slug
Linse f *(Fot.)* lens
Linsenanordnung f lens arrangement
Linsenfassung f lens mount
Linsenöffnung f lens aperture
Linsensystem n lens system
Linting n linting
Literaturangabe f bibliography
Literaturhinweis m bibliography
Literaturnachweis m bibliography
Literaturverzeichnis n bibliography
Litfaßsäule f advertising pillar, poster pillar
Lith-Entwicklung f *(Reprod.)* lith development, lith processing
Lith-Entwicklungsmaschine f lith processor
Lith-Film m *(Reprod.)* lith film
Litho n *(Offsetfilm)* film litho, litho, litho film, offset litho
Lithograf m lithographer, lithographic artist
Lithografenlack m lithographic varnish
Lithografenstift m lithographic pencil
Lithografie f *(gedrucktes Blatt)* lithograph, litho print; *(Technik)* litho etching, lithography; *(Offsetfilmbearbeitung)* film etching
Lithografieanstalt f lithographic printing house
Lithografiedruck m lithographic printing
Lithografiefeder f lithographic pen
Litho(grafie)kreide f litho(graphic) chalk, litho(graphic) crayon
Lithografiepresse f lithographic press
lithografieren to lithograph, to lithoprint
Lithografieschleifstein m lithographic graining stone
Lithografiestein m lithographic stone, litho stone
Lithografietusche f lithographic drawing ink
Lithomarker m *(für Filmmarkierung)* litho marker
Lithozeichnung f lithographic drawing
Lochband n punched tape
lochbandgesteuerte Setzmaschine f *(TTS)* teletypesetter
Lochbandleser m tape reader
Lochbandsteuerung f tape control
lochen to perforate, to punch
Lochkarte f punched card
Lochkartenleser m card reader
Lochkartenstanzer m card punch
Lochperforation f *(im U. zur Strichperforation)* hole perforation
Lochrand m *(Endlosformular)* file hole margin
Lochstanze f punch
Lochstreifen m punched tape
Lochstreifenleser m tape reader
Lochstreifenstanzer m tape punch
Loch- und Ösenmaschine f punching and eyeletting machine
Lochung f perforation, punching
Lockerungsbläser pl *(Bogenanleger)* fanning blowers pl
löschen *(Comp.)* to cancel, to clear, to delete, to erase
Löschen/Schreiben *(Comp.)* clear-write
Löschpapier n blotting paper
lösch- und programmierbarer Nur-Lese-Speicher (EPROM) m erasable and programmable read only memory (EPROM)
Lösemittel n solvent
Lösemittelabsaugung f solvent exhaust, solvent extraction
lösemittelbeständig solvent resistant
Lösemitteldämpfe pl solvent vapours pl
Lösemittelfarbe f *(Farbe auf Lösemittelbasis)* solvent-based ink
Lösemittelfestigkeit f solvent resistance
Lösemittelrückgewinnung f solvent reclamation, solvent recovery
lösliches Druckbestäubungspuder n vanishing spray powder
Lösung f *(chemische)* solution
Lösungsmittel n solvent
Logo n logo, logotype
Logoscanner m logo scanner
Logotype f logotype
Logotypenmatrize f *(Zeilenguß)* logotype matrix
Lohnbetrieb m commercial operation, trade house
Lohnbuchbinderei f trade binder, trade binding
Lohndruck m trade printing
Lohndruckerei f trade printer
Lohnkosten pl labour costs pl
Lohnsatz m trade setting
Lohnsetzerei f trade setter, trade typesetter
Lokalausgabe f *(Zeitung)* local edition
lokales Netzwerk n local area network, LAN
Lokalfernsehen n local TV
Lokalpresse f local press
Lokalradio n local radio
Lokalseiten pl *(Zeitung)* local pages
Lokalteil m local section
Lokalzeitung f local newspaper
Los n lottery ticket
Loseblattbindung f loose-leaf binding
lose Bogen pl *(ungebunden)* loose sections pl
lose gewickelte Rolle f slack reel
Lotterielos n lottery ticket
Lottoschein m Lotto form

Lückenbüßer m *(Zeitung)* gap filler
lüften *(Stapel)* to aerate, to fan, to ventilate
Lüftungsanlage f ventilation system
Luftaufnahme f *(Fotogr.)* aerial photo(graph)
Luftaufnahmefilm m film for aerial photography
Luftauspreßwalze f air squeezing roller
Luft ausstreichen *(Stapel)* to remove air, to smooth out
Luftbefeuchter m air humidifier
Luftbefeuchtung f air humidification
Luftbild n aerial photo(graph)
Luftblase f air bubble
Luftbremse f air brake
Luftbrettanlage f *(Bogenverarb.)* air pallet system
luftdicht air-tight
Luftdüse f air jet, air nozzle
Luftdusche f air blast
Lufteinschlüsse pl *(Hohlkopie)* air enclosures pl, air pockets pl
Lufteintritt m air intake
Luftfeuchtigkeit f humidity
Luftfilter m air filter
Luftfilterung f air filtration
luftgetrocknetes Papier n air-dried paper
Luftkissen n air cushion
Luftkissentrommel f *(Bogenoffsetm.)* air cushion drum
Luftkühlung f air cooling
Luftleitung f *(für Druckluftversorgung)* air ducts pl
Luftoxidation f *(Fotochemie)* aerial oxidation
Luftpinsel m *(Retusche)* aerograph, airbrush
Luftpolster n air cushion
Luftpolstertuch n *(kompr. Gummituch)* compressible rubber blanket
Luftpostpapier n airmail paper
Luftpostumschlag m airmail envelope
Luftpuffer m air cushion
Luftrakel f air knife
Luftreiniger m air cleaner
Luftspannwelle f *(Rollenfixierung)* expanding shaft, air shaft
Luftsteuerung f *(Druckluft)* air control
Lufttisch m air table
lufttrocken air-dry
luftumspülte Wendestangen f/pl air-cushioned turnbars pl, air-washed turnbars pl
Luftversorgung f air supply
Lumbecken n adhesive binding, padding
Lumineszenzdruckfarbe f luminescent ink
Lumpenpapier n rag paper
Lupe f magnifier, magnifying glass

Luxmeter n *(Lichtmessung)* luxmeter
Luxusausgabe f de luxe edition
Luxusdrucksachen f/pl de luxe printed material
Luxuseinband m de luxe binding
Luxuspackung f luxury package
Luxuspapier n de luxe paper
LWC-Papier n LWC paper

M

Mängel m/pl *(Qualität)* imperfections pl
mängelfrei faultless
Märbeln pl *(Schleifkugeln)* graining balls pl, graining marbles pl
Märchenbuch n book of fairy tales
Magazin n *(Zeitschrift)* journal, magazine, periodical; *(Vorratsbehälter in Anleger, Zeilengießmaschine usw.)* magazine
Magazinanleger m *(Druckverarb.linien)* hopper feeder
Magazinaufbau m *(Rollendruckm.)* magazine turner-bar superstructure
Magazinfalz m *(Rollendruckm.)* quarter fold
Magazinumschaltung f *(Zeilengießm.)* magazine shifting
Magazinwechsel m *(Zeilengießm.)* magazine change
Magazinwendestangen pl *(Rollendruckm.)* magazine turner bars pl
Magenta n *(Skalenfarbe)* magenta
Magentaauszug m *(Reprod.)* magenta separation
Magentadistanzraster m *(Kamera)* magenta glass screen
Magentafilm m *(Auszugsfilm)* magenta film, magenta printer
Magentaform f magenta forme
Magentakontaktraster m *(Reprod.)* magenta contact screen
Magentaplatte f magenta plate, magenta printer
magere Schrift f light typeface
Magnesiapulver n magnesia powder
Magnesiumätzung f magnesium etching
Magnesiumklischee n magnesium plate
Magnesiumplatte f magnesium plate
Magnetband n magnetic tape, magtape
Magnetbandkassette f magnetic cassette
Magnetbandleser m magnetic tape reader

Magnetbandspeicher - Maschinendemontage

Magnetbandspeicher *m* magnetic tape store
Magnetbandstation *f* magnetic tape station, tape streamer
Magnetblasenspeicher *m* (Comp.) bubble memory
Magnetfarbe *f* (Druckfarbe) magnetic ink
magnetische Beleglesung *f* magnetic document reading
magnetische Zeichenerkennung *f* (MICR) magnetic ink character recognition
Magnetkarte *f* magnetic card
Magnetografie *f* magnetography
Magnetplatte *f* magnetic disk
Magnetplattenspeicher *m* magnetic disk store
Magnetsattel *m* (für Klischeebefestigung) magnetic saddle
Magnetspeicher *m* magnetic memory, magnetic store
Magnettrommelspeicher *m* (Comp.) magnetic drum store
Magnetunterlage *f* (für Druckplatte) magnetic base
Magnetzeichennumerierung *f* MICR numbering
Magnetzylinder *m* (für Druckplatten) magnetic cylinder
Mailer *m* (Direktwerbung) mailer
Mailing *n* (Direktwerbung) mailing
Majuskel *f* (Großbuchstabe) capital letter, majuscule
Makro *n* (comp.) macro (command)
Makrobefehl *m* (comp.) macro (command)
Makroprogrammierung *f* macroprogramming
Makulatur *f* misprinted sheets *pl*, misprints *pl*, paper wastage, paper waste, reject sheets *pl*, sheet spoilage, spoilage, spoils *pl*, spoil sheets *pl*, waste, waste paper, waste sheets *pl*
Makulaturanfall *m* waste rate
Makulaturausschleusung *f* waste divert, waste ejection
Makulaturbogen *m/pl* misprinted sheets *pl*, misprints *pl*, reject sheets *pl*, spoils *pl*, spoil sheets *pl*, waste sheets *pl*
Makulaturerkennung *f* (Bahnbeobachtung, Rollendruck) waste recognition
Makulaturmarkierung *f* (Rollendruck) waste marking
Makulaturpapier *n* (zum Durchschießen) waste paper
Makulaturvorlauf *m* (zum Einrichten) waste run
Makulaturweiche *f* waste deflector, waste diverter, waste ejector, waste shunt
Malzeichen *n* (Multiplikationsz.) multiplication sign

Management-Informationssystem *n* management information system
Mangan *n* manganese
mangelhafte Qualität *f* imperfect quality
mangelhafter Druck *m* imperfect printing
Manilakarton *m* Manilla board
Manilapapier *n* Manilla paper
manipulieren (elektron. Bildverarb.) to manipulate
manuelle Retusche *f* manual retouching
Manuskript *n* copy, manuscript, text copy; *schreibmaschinegeschriebenes* ~ typewritten copy
Manuskriptaufbereitung *f* copy mark-up, copy preparation, mark-up
Manuskript auszählen to count characters
Manuskriptauszeichnung *f* copy mark-up, copy preparation, mark-up
Manuskriptbearbeitung *f* copy mark-up, copy preparation, mark-up
Manuskript berechnen to calculate the volume
Manuskriptberechnung *f* calculation of volume, cast-off, character count, copyfit calculation, copyfitting, estimate of volume
Manuskripthalter *m* copy holder
Manuskriptvorbereitung *f* copy mark-up, copy preparation, mark-up
Marginalie *f* marginal note, side note
Marginaltitel *m* marginal heading, side heading
Marginalziffer *f* marginal figure, side figure
markieren to identify, to mark
Markierungsleser *m* (Abtastung) mark reader
marmoriert (Buchschnitt, Vorsatz) marbled
marmoriertes Papier *n* marbled paper
Marmorierung *f* marbling
Marmorschnitt *m* (Buch) marbled edge
Maschenfüllung *f* (Siebdruck) mesh filling
Maschenöffnung *f* (Siebdruck) mesh opening
Maschenweite *f* (Siebdruck) mesh opening
Maschinenabzug *m* machine proof
Maschinenausrüstung *f* machinery equipment; (Comp.) hardware
Maschinenband *n* machine tape
Maschinenbau *m* machine construction, machine engineering
Maschinenbedienung *f* machine operation
Maschinenbetrieb *m* machine operation
Maschinenbogen *m* machine proof
Maschinenbütte *f* (Papierherst.) machine chest
Maschinenbüttenpapier *n* mould-made paper
Maschinendefekt *m* machinery failure, machinery trouble
Maschinendemontage *f* machine removal

Maschinenentwicklung f *(Fot., im U. zur Schalenentwicklung)* machine development, machine processing; *(Konstruktion)* machine design
Maschinenfabrik f engineering works, machine factory
Maschinenführer m machine minder, machine supervisor
Maschinenfundament n machine base, machine foundation
Maschinenfunktionen pl machine functions pl
maschinengeleimtes Papier n machine-sized paper
Maschinengeschwindigkeit f machine speed
maschinengesetzt *(Schrift)* machine-set
Maschinengestell n machine frame
maschinengestrichenes Papier n blade-coated paper, machine-coated paper
maschinenglattes Papier n machine-finished paper, mill-finished paper
Maschinengrundeinstellungen pl initial machine settings pl
Maschinenhersteller m machine maker, machine manufacturer
Maschinenkapazität f machine capacity
Maschinenkapselung f machine enclosure, machine hooding
Maschinenkode m machine code
Maschinenkonstruktion f machine design
Maschinenlauf m machine run
Maschinenleistung f machine capacity, machine output, machine performance
maschinenlesbares Dokument n machine-readable document
Maschinenmeister m machine minder
Maschinenpappe f mill board
Maschinenpark m machine equipment
Maschinenprogramm n machine program
Maschinenrahmen m machine frame
Maschinensaal m machine room
Maschinensatz m *(im U. zum Handsatz)* hot-metal composition, machine composition, mechanical typesetting, slug composition
Maschinenschema n machine diagram
Maschinensetzer m hot-metal compositor, machine compositor, machine typesetter
Maschinensetzerei f *(Abt.)* hot-metal composition department, machine composing room
Maschinensprache f *(Comp.)* computer language, machine language
Maschinenstart m machine start-up
Maschinensteuerpult n machine control console
Maschinensteuerung f machine controls pl

Maschinenstillstand m machine standstill, machine stop(page)
Maschinenstillstandszeiten pl idle machine times pl, machine down-times pl, unproductive machine times pl
Maschinenstörung f breakdown of machine, malfunction
Maschinenstopp m machine stop(page)
Maschinenüberwachung f machine monitoring, machine supervision
Maschinenverschleiß m machine wear
Maschinenvoreinstellung f presetting of machine
maserig *(Druck)* speckled
Maske f *(Reprod.; Bildschirm)* mask
Maskenaufbau m *(Bildschirm)* mask structure
Maskenbelichtung f mask exposure
Maskeneintrag m *(Bildschirm)* mask entry
Maskenerstellung f *(Bildschirm)* mask generation
Maskenfeld n *(Bildschirm)* mask field
Maskenfeldinhalt m *(Bildschirm)* mask field content
Maskenherstellung f mask production
Maskenschneidmesser n mask cutting knife
Maskenschneidsystem n *(CAD)* mask cutting system
Maskenverarbeitung f *(Bildschirm)* mask processing
maskieren to mask
Maskierfilm m masking film
Maskierfilm mit abziehbarer Maskierschicht peelable masking film
Maskierfolie f masking film, masking foil
Maskierung f masking
Maßanzeige f *(Schneidem.)* measurement display, measurement read-out
Maßband n measuring tape
Maßeingabe f *(Schneidem.)* measurement input
Maßeinstellung f *(Schneidem.)* measurement adjustment, measurement setting
Massenauflage f *(Publikation)* mass circulation, mass edition
Massendrucksache f bulk-printed matter, mass printed matter
Massenmedien pl mass media
Massenproduktion f mass production
Massenspeicher m *(Comp.)* bulk storage, mass storage
Massenzeitschrift f mass-circulation magazine, mass-produced magazine
maßgenau true to size
maßgeschneidert *(modulare Systeme)* customized, made to measure, tailor-made

Maßhaltigkeit - mehrfarbig

Maßhaltigkeit f *(Film, Folie)* dimensional stability
Maßskala f graduated scale
Maßstab m *(Reprod.)* scale
maßstabgerecht true to scale
Maßstabsbereich m *(Reprod.)* scale range
Maßstabseinstellung f *(Reprod.)* scale setting
maßstabsgetreue Reproduktion f true-to-scale reproduction
Maßstabsveränderung f *(Reprod.)* scale change, scale modification
Maßsystem n *(z. B. typografisches)* measurement system
Mater f mat, matrix, mould
Materialbedarf m material requirement
Materialfehler m faulty material
Materialfluß m material flow
Materialkasten m *(Handsatz)* lead and slug case
Materialkosten pl material costs pl
Materiallieferant m material supplier
Materialprüfung f materials testing
Materialrücktransport m *(Fotosetzm.)* reverse leading
matern to mould
Maternfeuchtkasten m wetting box for flongs
Maternjustiermaschine f matrix justifying machine
Maternkalander m matrix calender
Maternkarton m flong, matrix board
Maternpappe f flong, matrix board
Maternprägepresse f matrix moulding press
Maternprägung f matrix moulding
Maternpulver n matrix powder
Materntrockenpresse f matrix drying press
mathematischer Satz m mathematical matter, maths setting
mathematisches Zeichen n mathematical sign
Matrixdrucker m *(Belegdrucker)* matrix printer
Matrize f die, mat, matrix, mould; *(für Vervielfältigung)* stencil
Matrizenkreislauf m *(Setzmasch.)* matrix circulation
Matrizenpappe f flong, matrix board
Matrizenprägepresse f *(Mater)* matrix moulding press
Matrizenprägung f matrix moulding
Matrizensatz m set of matrices
matt dull, matt
mattes Papier n matt paper
Mattfarbe f matt ink
Mattfilm m matt film
mattgestrichenes Papier n dull-coated paper, matt-coated paper
Mattglanz m dull finish, matt finish
Mattlack m dull varnish, matt varnish
mattsatiniertes Papier n matt-calendered paper, velvet finished paper
Mattscheibe f *(Kamera)* focussing screen, ground glass screen
Mattstrich m *(Papier)* matt coating
Maus f *(Bildschirmsteuerung)* mouse, puck
Maximaldichte f *(D. max.)* maximum density
Maximalformat n maximum format, maximum size
Maximalgeschwindigkeit f maximum speed, top speed
mechanische Höchstgeschwindigkeit f mechanical top speed
mechanische Steuerung f mechanical control
mechanische Zurichtung f mechanical makeready
mechanisch gekörnte Aluminiumplatte f mechanically grained aluminium plate
Mediäval f *(Schrift)* old face, old style
Mediävalziffern pl non-lining figures pl, old style figures pl
Medien pl media
Medienverlag m media printhouse, media publishing house
Mehrarbeit f additional work, extra work
Mehrbadätzung f *(Tiefdruckzyl.)* multiple-bath etching
Mehrbahnbetrieb m *(Rollendruckm.)* multi-web operation
Mehrbahnen-Rotationsmaschine f multi-web rotary press
Mehrbenutzersystem n *(Comp.)* multi-user system
Mehrbuchstabenletter f *(Logotype)* logotype
Mehrbuchstabenmatrize f *(Zeilengießm.)* logotype matrix
Mehrfachanlage f *(Bogenanlage)* multiple-up feed(ing)
Mehrfachbelichtung f *(Fotosatz)* multiflash
Mehrfachformularsatz m multi-part forms set, multi-ply forms set
Mehrfarb(en)arbeiten pl colour work, multi-colour work
Mehrfarb(en)druck m colour printing, multi-colour printing
Mehrfarbendruckmaschine f multi-colour (printing) press
Mehrfarbenoffset m multi-colour offset
Mehrfarbenstrichätzung f *(Buchdruck)* multi-colour line engraving
Mehrfarbentiefdruck m multi-colour gravure (process)
mehrfarbig multi-colour(ed), polychromatic

mehrfarbige Arbeiten *pl* siehe Mehrfarbenarbeiten
Mehrkomponentenkleber *m* multi-component glue
mehrlagiger Karton *m* multi-ply board
Mehrlieferung *f* excess delivery
mehrmaliger Durchgang *m (durch Druckm.)* multiple run through press
mehrmaliger Durchlauf *m (durch Druckm.)* multiple run through press
Mehrmetallplatte *f (Offset)* multi-metal plate
Mehrnutzenarbeiten *pl* multi-up jobs *pl*, multi-up work
Mehrnutzenproduktion *f* multi-up production
Mehrnutzenverarbeitung *f* multi-up processing
Mehrplatzsystem *n (Comp.)* cluster system, multi-station system
Mehrrechnersystem *n (Comp.)* multi-computer system, multi-CPU system
Mehrschichtbetrieb *m* multi-shift operation
Mehrschichtenfilm *m* multi-layer film
mehrseitiger Katalog *m* multi-page catalogue
Mehrspaltensatz *m* multi-column composition, multi-column setting, multi-column work
mehrspaltiger Umbruch *m (Seitenumbruch)* multi-column page make-up
mehrspaltige Überschrift *f* straddle head
mehrstufige Herstellung *f (im graf. Betrieb: von der Vorlagenherst. bis zur Druckverarb.)* multi-stage production process
Mehrzweckmaschine *f* multi-purpose machine
Meldung *f (Comp.)* message
Mengensatz *m* mass composition
Mengentext *m* bulk copy
Menü *n (Comp.)* menu
Menüfeld *n (Bildschirm)* menu field
menügesteuert *(Comp.)* menu-controlled, menu-driven
Merkblatt *n* instruction leaflet
Meßbalken *m (Farbmeßpult)* measuring bar
Meßbecher *m* measuring cup
Meßbereich *m* measuring range
Meßblende *f* measurement aperture
Meßdaten *pl* measuring data
messen *pl* to measure
Messer *n* blade, knife
Messerabnutzung *f* knife wear
Messeranstellung *f* knife adjustment
Messerantrieb *m* knife drive
Messerblock *m* knife block
Messerfalztrommel *f (Falzapp.)* knife folding drum

Messerfarbkasten *m (Farbwerk)* blade fountain, blade-type ink fountain
Messerhalter *m* knife holder
Messerschleifmaschine *f* knife grinding machine
Messerstandzeit *f* edge life, knife life
Messerstellung *f* knife position
Messerstichel *m* scorper
Messerverschleiß *m* knife wear
Messerwechsel *m* knife change
Messerzylinder *m (Falzapp.)* cutting cylinder, knife cylinder
Meßfeld *n* measuring area, reading area; *(Druckkontrollstreifen)* measuring field, measuring target, patch, target
Meßfleck *m* measuring spot
Meßfühler *m* measuring sensor
Meßfunktion *f* measuring function
Meßgenauigkeit *f* measuring accuracy
Meßgeometrie *f* measuring geometry
Meßgerät *n* gauge, measuring instrument, meter
Messingätzung *f* brass engraving, brass etching
Messingdurchschuß *m* brass spaces *pl*
Messingecken *pl (Buch)* brass corners *pl*
Messingletter *f* brass letter
Messinglinie *f* brass rule
Messingmatrize *f* brass matrix
Messingplatte *f* brass plate
Messingprägeplatte *f* brass embossing plate
Messingschrift *f* brass type
Messingspatien *pl* brass spaces *pl*
Messingstempel *m* brass die
Messingtype *f* brass type
Meßinstrument *n* gauge, measuring instrument, meter
Meßkopf *m* measuring head, reading head
Meßlauf *m* measuring run
Meßlupe *f* measuring lens
Meßprinzip *n* measuring principle
Meßpult *n* measuring console
Meßpunkt *m* measuring point
Meßring *m (Schmitzing)* bearer ring
Meßschlitten *m* measuring carriage
Meßskala *f* measuring scale
Meßsonde *f* measuring probe, reading probe
Meßstreifen *m* measuring strip
Meßtechniken *pl* measurement techniques *pl*
meßtechnische Auswertung *f* evaluation of measurements
Meßuhr *f* dial indicator
Meßwalze *f* measuring roller
Meßwert *m* measured value, measurement reading
Meßwertanzeige *f* measurement reading

Meßzelle f probe
Metalldruckfarbe f metallic ink
Metalleinguß m pouring-in of metal
Metallfolie f metal foil
Metallfolienpapier n metal foil paper
Metallgewebe n *(Siebdruck)* metal gauze, metal mesh
Metall-Halogen-Lampe f *(Kopierrahmen)* metal halide lamp
Metallikbuntdruck m *(Metallikfarben in Vierfarbrasterdruck integriert)* process-integrated metallic printing
Metallikfarbe f metallic ink
metallisches Papier n metallic paper
metallisiertes Papier n metallized paper
Metallpapier n metal paper
Metallprägefolie f metallic stamping foil
Metallschablone f metal stencil
Metallschilderdruck m metal plate printing
Metallschmuckfarben f/pl metallic decorative colours pl, metallic decorative inks pl
Metallschnitt m *(Buch)* metallic edge
Metallspäne pl metal chips pl, metal cuttings pl
metamere Farben pl metameric colours pl
metereologisches Zeichen n metereological sign
Methanol n methanol
Methylalkohol m methyl alcohol
Metol-Hydrochinon n *(Fotochemie)* metol-hydroquinone
metrisches System n metric system
Mettage f *(Bleisatzumbruch)* make-up
Metteur m *(Bleisatzumbruch)* maker-up, make-up man
Mezzotinto n mezzotint
MICR (magnetische Zeichenerkennung) MICR (magnetic ink character recognition)
Mietleitung f *(Comp.)* leased line
Mikrocomputer m microcomputer
Mikrocomputersteuerung f microcomputer control
Mikrocomputertechnik f microcomputer(-based) technology
Mikroelektronik f microelectronics
Mikrofiche m microfiche
Mikrofilm m microfilm
Mikrofotografie f microphotography
mikrogekörnte Aluminiumplatte f micro-grained aluminium plate
Mikrolinie f microline
Mikrolinienfeld n *(Druckkontrollstreifen)* microline patch, microline target
Mikrometer n *(Meßgerät)* calliper, gauge, micrometer

Mikrometerschraube f micrometer screw
Mikroprogrammierung f microprogramming
Mikroprozessor m microprocessor
mikroprozessorgesteuert microprocessor-controlled
Mikroprozessortechnik f microprocessor(-based) technology
Mikrorastschraube f notched micrometer screw
Mikroverfilmung f microfilming
Mikrowellpappe f micro-corrugated board
Millimetereinteilung f millimeter division, millimeter grid
Millimeterpapier n graph paper, scale paper
Millimeterskala f millimeter scale
Millimeterzeile f *(Kleinanzeige)* millimeter line
Mindestformat n minimum format, minimum size
Mineralöl n *(Farbherst.)* mineral oil
Minicomputer m minicomputer
Minimaldichte f *(D. min.)* minimum density
Minuskel f *(Kleinbuchstabe)* minuscule
Minuskorrektur f *(Film)* dot reduction; *(Platte, Zylinder)* minus correction
Minuszeichen n minus sign
Mischfarben pl *(Farbensystem)* mixed colours pl
Mischsatz m *(Textsatz)* mixed setting
Mischweiß n *(Farbzusatz)* transparent white
Missing Dots pl *(Tiefdruck)* missing dots pl
mit Anschnitt m *(Druckarbeit)* bled-off
Mitautor m coauthor, joint author
mit dem Rücken hinten spine trailing
mit dem Rücken voran spine first, spine leading
mit der Seite ausgehen to end on the page
mitdrucken *(in derselben Form)* to print in the same forme
mit Faden auf Gaze geheftet sewn through gauze
mit Genehmigung des Verfassers by permission of the author
mit Goldschnitt m *(Buch)* gilt edged
mitlaufende Rakel f positive doctor blade
mit Linien einrahmen to border with rules, to box
mit marmoriertem Schnitt marble-edged
Mitnehmerfinger m *(Transportkette an Zusammentragm./Sammelhefter)* raceway (pusher) pin
mit Schlangenlinienverzierung versehen to guilloche
mit stehendem Sattel m without backgauge movement
Mitteilung f *(Comp.)* message
mittelfeines Papier n semi-fine paper

mittelformatige Druckmaschine f medium-size (printing) press
mittelgroßes Inserat n average-size advertisement
Mittellänge f *(Schrift)* x-height
Mittellängen pl *(kurze Buchstaben wie r, n, m)* short letters pl
Mittelschnitt m center cut; *(Papierbahn)* center slitting
Mitteltöne pl *(um 50 %)* middle tones pl, mid-tones pl
mittlere Auflage f medium-length run
mittlere Druckerei f medium-sized printhouse
mittlere Zeitung f *(Zeitung mit mittlerer Auflage)* medium-circulation newspaper
mm-Folie *(Montage)* millimeter grid
mm-System n *(Typogr.)* metric system
Modem n *(Telekomm.)* modem
moderne Schrift f modern typeface
moderne Technik f modern technology
Modezeitschrift f fashion magazine
Modul n module
Modularität f modularity
Modulation f modulation
Modulbauweise f modular design
modulieren to modulate
Modulsystem n modular system
Modus m *(Betriebsart)* mode
Mönch m *(nichtdruckende Stelle)* drop-out, friar, monk
Mönchsbogen m *(fälschlich unbedruckter Bogen)* blank sheet
Moiré n moiré (pattern), screen pattern
Moleskin m *(Feuchtwalzenstoff)* moleskin
Molettiermaschine f *(Tiefdruckzyl.)* die-transferring machine
Molton m *(Feuchtwalzenstoff)* molleton
Monatskalender m monthly calendar
Monatszeitschrift f monthly (journal), monthly (magazine)
Monitor m *(Kontrollbildschirm)* monitor
monofiles Polyester n *(Siebdruck)* monofilament polyester
Monogramm-Prägepresse f monogram stamping press
Monotype f *(Einzelbuchstaben-Gießmaschine)* monotype machine
Monotypesatz m *(Einzelbuchstabenguß)* monotype composition
Monotypesetzer m monotype compositor, monotype operator
Montage f *(Seite; Druckform)* assembly, assembly work, flat, make-up, montage, paste-up, stripping, stripping operation

Montageabdeckfolie f montage masking foil
Montageabteilung f make-up department, stripping department
Montageaufbewahrungsschrank m assembly storage cabinet
Montagebogen m assembly sheet, make-up sheet, montage sheet, mounting sheet, paste-up sheet
Montagefolie f montage film, mounting film
Montagekleber m montage glue, mounting glue
Montagekopiermaschine f assembly copying machine, step-and-repeat (copying) machine
Montagetisch m light table, make-up table, mounting table, stripping table
Montagewachs n adhesive wax, montage wax
Monteure pl *(für Wartung)* service engineers pl, servicing staff
montieren *(Seite; Druckform)* to assemble, to mount, to paste up, to strip
Montierer m *(Seiten-, Druckformmontage)* paste-up man, stripper, stripping man
Moosgummi n *(Ausbrechform)* sponge rubber
Morgenausgabe f morning edition
Morgenblatt n morning paper
Morgenzeitung f morning paper
Motiv n *(Sujet)* motif
Motorantrieb m motor drive
Motorwelle f motor shaft
Muldenauslage f *(Kleinoffsetm.)* chute delivery
multifiles Polyester n *(Siebdruck)* multifilament polyester
Multifunktionskabel n multi-function cable
Multifunktionstaste f *(Tastatur)* multi-function key
Multi-Kode m *(Comp.)* multi-code
Multiplex-Betrieb m *(Telekomm.)* multiplex mode
Multiplexer m *(Comp.)* multiplexer
Multiplikationszeichen n multiplication sign
Multiprozessor m multiprocessor
Musikaliendruck m music printing
Musiknote f music note; **ganze** ~ semibreve; **geschwänzte** ~ quaver; **halbe** ~ minim
Musiknotendruck m music printing
Musiknotenkasten m music typecase
Musiknotenlinien pl staff lines pl
Musiknotensatz m music type composition, music typesetting
Musikverlag m music publishers pl
Muß-Feld n *(Formular, Bildschirmmaske; im U. zu Kann-Feld)* obligatory field
Muster n dummy, sample, specimen; *(Schnittmuster)* pattern
Muster(be)leimung f pattern gluing

Musterblatt - Nähnadel

Musterblatt *n* sample sheet, specimen sheet
Musterbogen *m* sample sheet, specimen sheet
Musterbuch *n* sample book, specimen book
Muster(ein)band *m (Buchherst.)* blank book, dummy, sample binding, sample volume
Musterlackierung *f* pattern coating
Musterlackierwerk *n* pattern coater
Musterleimwerk *n* pattern gluer
Musterperforiereinrichtung *f* pattern perforator
Musterperforierung *f* pattern perforation
Musterzeile *f (Probezeile)* specimen line
Mutternegativ *n* master negative
Mutterraster *m* master screen

N

Nachätzung *f* final etching, fine etching, re-etching
Nachbehandlung *f* after-treatment, final treatment, post-treatment; *(Fotopolymerplatten)* anti-tacking, detacking
Nachbelichtung *f* post-exposure; *(Rasterfotogr.)* bump exposure, no-screen exposure
Nachdruck *m* off-print; *(nochmaliger D.)* reprint, reprinting; *(unberechtigter)* pirated edition, pirating
nachdrucken to reprint; *(unberechtigt)* to pirate
Nachdruck verboten all rights reserved
Nachdruckvermerk *m* copyright imprint
Nacheilung *f (Rollendruck)* lag
Nachfaßbrief *m (Werbung)* follow-up letter
nachfolgende Arbeiten *pl* downstream operations *pl*, subsequent operations *pl*
nachfolgendes Aggregat *n (Prod.linie)* subsequent unit
Nachführanzeige *f (Regeltechnik)* follow-up display
Nachführsteuerung *f (Regeltechnik)* follow-up control
nachfüllen to fill up, to refill
Nachhärtung *f* post-hardening
Nachjustierung *f* re-adjustment
Nachkalkulation *f (Kosten)* recalculation of job costs, statistical cost accounting
Nachkleben *n (Farbe)* blocking
Nachkontrolle *f* final check
Nachlaß *m* discount

Nachlegen *n (Anlegermagazin)* re-feeding, refilling, re-loading, replenishing
nach Manuskript *(Korrekturanweisung)* follow copy
nach Manuskript lesen to check proofs with copy, to read according to copy
nach Maß customized, made to measure, tailor-made
nach Plan arbeiten *(Terminüberw.)* to work to schedule
nach Postleitzahlen ordnen *(Versandraum)* to sort by zip code
Nachrichtenagentur *f* news agency, press agency
Nachrichtenbüro *n* news agency, press agency
Nachrichtendienst *m* information service, news service, wire service
Nachrichtenkanal *m* news channel
Nachrichtennetz *n* communications network
Nachrichtenseite *f* news page
Nachrichtentechnik *f* communication technology
Nachrichtenteil *m (Zeitung)* news section
Nachrichtenübertragung *f* news transmission; *(Telekomm.)* satellite communication
nachrüstbar retrofittable
Nachrüstpaket *n* retrofit package, upgrade kit, upgrade package
Nachrüstung *f (Systeme, Maschinen)* later installation, upgrade
Nachschlagewerk *n* reference book
nachschleifen to re-grind
Nachschneiden *n* final cutting, recutting
nachsehen *(Revision machen)* to check, to look over, to revise
Nachstapeln *n (Anlegermagazin)* re-feeding, refilling, re-loading, replenishing
nachstellbar adjustable
nachstellen *(Farbe)* to match
Nachtausgabe *f* late-night edition
nachträglich anbauen to retrofit
nachträglich ausrüsten to retrofit
Nachtrag *m (Anhang im Buch)* addendum, appendix
Nachtschicht *f* night shift
Nachübertragung *f (Tiefdruckzyl.)* re-transfer
Nachverbrennungsanlage *f* after-burner (system)
Nachwort *n (Buch)* epilog(ue)
Nadeldrucker *m (Belegdrucker)* needle printer
Nadellager *n (mech.)* needle bearing
Nadelperforation *f* needle perforation
Nadelstiche *pl* pinholes *pl*
nächste Seite *f* overleaf
Nähen *n (Heftung)* sewing
Nähnadel *f* sewing needle

Näpfchen *pl (Tiefdruck, Anilox)* cells *pl*
nagelfeste Farbe *f* scratch-proof ink
Nagelprobe *f* scratch test
Nahrungsmittelpackung *f* food package
Nahtleimauftragsgerät *n* seam gluer
narben *(Papier)* to grain
Nasenklammer *f (Akkolade)* braces *pl*
Naß-auf-Trocken-Druck *m* wet-on-dry printing
naßgebürstete Aluminiumplatte *f* wet-brushed aluminium plate
Naß-in-Naß-Druck *m* wet-on-wet printing
Naßklebeband *n* wet-adhesive tape
Naßklebeetiketten *pl* wet-adhesive labels *pl*
Naßoffset *m* wet offset
Naßpartie *f (Papiermasch.)* wet end
Naßprägung *f* wet stamping
Naßretusche *f (Film)* wet retouching
Naßrupfen *n* wet picking
Naßschleifen *n (abschleifen)* wet grinding; *(körnen)* wet graining
Naßtoner *m (Elektrofotogr.)* wet toner
Natriumdampflampe *f* sodium vapour lamp
Natronkraftpapier *n* sulphate kraft paper
Natronpackpapier *n* sulphate packing paper
Natronsackpapier *n* sulphate sack paper
Natronzellstoff *m (Papierherst.)* soda cellulose, sulphate pulp
Natronzellulose *f (Papierstoff)* sodium woodpulp
naturgetreue Wiedergabe *f* facsimile reproduction, faithful reproduction, reproduction fidelity
Naturkarton *m (ungebleicht)* unbleached cardboard
Naturkreide *f* Paris white
Naturpapier *n (ungestrichen)* uncoated paper
Naturseidengaze *f* raw silk gauze
Nebenantrieb *m (mot.)* auxiliary drive
nebeneinanderliegende Seiten *f/pl* adjacent pages *pl*
Nebenseite *f (Buch, Zeitschrift)* opposite page
Nebentitel *m* subtitle
nebenwirkungsfreie Farbdosierung *f (Farbkastentechnik)* side-effect free ink metering
Nebenzeiten *pl (im U. zu Produktionszeiten)* non-production times *pl*
Negativ *n* neg, negative
Negativaufbewahrung *f* negative storage
Negativbelichtung *f (Fotosatz)* reverse video setting; *(Reprod.)* negative exposure
Negativbühne *f (Kamera)* negative holder
negative Abrakelung *f (Tiefdruck)* negative doctoring, reverse (angle) doctoring

Negativhalter *m (Kamera)* negative holder
Negativkontaktraster *m (Reprod.)* negative contact screen
Negativkopie *f (Plattenkopie)* negative platemaking
Negativplatte *f* negative plate, negative working plate
Negativrasterung *f* negative screening
Negativretusche *f* negative retouching
Negativsatz *m (im Fotosatz)* reversed image
Negativschrift *f* reverse characters *pl*, reverse lettering, reverse type; *(am Bildschirm)* reverse video characters *pl*
Negativtext *m (am Bildschirm)* reverse text
Negativumkehrung *f* negative conversion
Nennwert *m* rating
Neodym-YAG-Laser *m* neodimium YAG laser
Nettoausstoß *m* net output
Nettoleistung *f (Maschine)* net output
Netz *n (Kommunikation)* network
Netzmittel *n (chem.)* wetting agent
Netzwerk *n (Kommunikation)* network
Netzwerkarchitektur *f* network architecture
Neuanfertigung *f* re-make
Neuauflage *f* new edition, re-edition, reprint, reprinting
Neuausgabe *f* new edition, re-edition, re-issue; *unveränderte* ~ reprint
neuausschießen to re-impose
neubinden to rebind
Neudruck *m* new edition, reprint, reprinting
neudrucken to reprint
neue Medien *pl* new media *pl*
neuer Absatz *m* new paragraph
Neuerfassung *f (Daten, Text)* re-keying, re-collection, re-entering
neu erschienen just published, recently published
neue Zeile *f* new line, new paragraph
Neuformatieren *n (Reprod.)* re-sizing
Neulauf *m (Comp.)* repeat run, re-run
Neurasterung *f* re-screening
Neusatz *m (Schrift)* re-setting
Neuscan *m* re-scan
neusetzen *(Schrift)* to re-set
Neutraldichtefilter *m (Reprod.)* neutral density filter
neutrale Farbe *f* achromatic colour, neutral colour
Neutralgrau *n* neutral grey
Neutralton *m* neutral tone
Neuumbruch *m* re-pagination
Newton-Ringe *pl* Newton rings *pl*

nichtdruckende Stellen — Notweiche

nichtdruckende Stellen *pl* non-image areas *pl*, non-printing areas *pl*
nichtdurchscheinendes Papier *n* opaque paper
nichtflüchtiger Speicher *m (Comp.)* non-volatile memory, non-volatile store
nichtgesammelte Produktion *f (Rollendruck)* non-collect run, straight-run production
nicht liniehaltend *(Satz)* out of alignment
nichtmetallischer Satz *m* cold composition, cold type
nicht passergenau mis-registered, out of register
nicht paßgenau mis-registered, out of register
nichtrechnender Erfassungsplatz *m (Texterf.)* non-counting input station, non-counting keyboard, non-justifying input station
nicht registergenau mis-registered, out of register
nicht registerhaltig mis-registered, out of register
nichtsaugendes Druckpapier *n* closed-surface substrate, non-absorbent printing stock
Nickelätzung *f* nickel etching
Nickelanode *f* nickel anode
Nickelbad *n* nickel(-plating) bath
Nickelelektrolyt *m* nickel electrolyte
Nickelgalvano *n* nickel electro(type)
Nickelstereo *n* nickel stereo(type)
Nickelüberzug *m* nickel coating
niederdrücken to press down
Niederhalterollen *pl* hold-down rollers *pl*
niederklopfen *(Buchdruckform)* to plane down
Niederlegvorrichtung *f (Druckverarb.)* laydown device
Niederschlag *m (Galv.)* deposit
niedrige Bauweise *f* low-profile design, low-silhouette design
Niedrigstapelauslage *f* low-pile delivery
Niete *f* rivet
nieten to rivet
Nietmaschine *f* riveting machine
Nietung *f* riveting
Nitrolack *m (Druckveredlung)* nitro(cellulose) varnish, NC varnish
Nitrolackierung *f* nitro varnishing
Nivellierkeil *m* levelling wedge
Nocken *m* cam
Nockenscheibe *f* cam disc
Nockensteuerung *f* cam control
Nockenwelle *f* camshaft
Nonstopp-Anleger *m* non-stop feeder
Nonstopp-Auslage *f* non-stop delivery
Nonstopp-Betrieb *m* non-stop operaton
Nonstopp-Eindruck *m* non-stop imprinting, on-the-fly imprinting, on-the-run imprinting
Nonstopp-Stapelwechsel *m* non-stop pile change

No-Pack-Gummituch *n (ohne Unterlage)* no-pack blanket
Norm *f* standard
Normalbetrieb *m (Masch.)* normal operation, normal mode
normaler Wortzwischenraum *m* normal word spacing
normale Schrift *f* standard type; *(geradestehend, keine Auszeichnung)* body type, roman type(face)
Normalfärbung *f (Druckm.)* normal inking
Normalformat *n* standard format, standard size
Normalhöhe *f (Buchdruck, Bleisatz)* standard height to paper
Normalpapier *n* plain paper
Normalpapierabzug *m (Fotosatz)* plain paper proof
Normalpapierkopierer *m* plain paper copier
Normbeleuchtung *f* standardized lighting
normen to standardize
Normlicht *n* standardized light
Normmaß *n* standard measure
Normung *f* standardization
Notauslage *f (Prod.linie)* emergency delivery, reject delivery
Notausschalter *m (Masch.)* emergency stop button, stop safe push button
Note *f (Anmerkung)* annotation, note; *(Musik)* music note
Notenblatt *n* music sheet
Notenbuch *n* music book
Notenbuchstabe *m* superior letter
Notendruck *m (Geld)* banknote printing, currency printing; *(Musik)* music printing
Notendruckpapier *n (Musik)* music printing paper
Notenheft *n* music notebook
Notenpapier *n* music-paper
Notensatz *m (Musik)* music type composition, music typesetting
Notenschreiber *m* music copyist
Notenstechen *n* music engraving
Notenstecher *m* music engraver
Notenstich *m* music engraving
Notenzeichen *n (Anmerkungsz.)* reference mark, reference number
Notizblock *m* memo pad, note block, note-pad
Notizbuch *n* notebook
Notizkalender *m* diary, notebook
Notizklotz *m* note-pad
Notstopp *m* emergency stop
Notweiche *f (Prod.linie)* emergency gate, escape gate, reject gate

Nuance *f* nuance, shade
Nullabgleich *m* *(Meßgeräte)* zero balance
Nullgeschwindigkeits-Rollenwechsler *m* zero-speed web splicer
Nullstellung *f* zero adjustment, zeroing, zero position
Nullunterdrückung *f* *(Comp.)* zero suppression
Numerierautomat *m* automatic numbering machine
numerieren to number
Numeriermaschine *f* numbering machine
Numerierung *f* numbering
Numerierwelle *f* numbering shaft
Numerierwerk *n* numbering box
numerisch numeric
Nummer *f* *(Zeitschrift)* number, issue
Nur-Lese-Speicher (ROM) *m* read only memory (ROM)
Nut *f* groove
nuten to groove
Nuten *n* grooving
Nutenfräser *m* groove router
Nuthobel *m* grooving plane
Nutkamm *m* grooving tool
Nutlinie *f* *(aus Stahl)* grooving rule
Nutmaschine *f* grooving machine
Nutung *f* grooving
Nutzen *m* *(Druck)* copy; *(Faltschachtelherst.)* blank; *(Nutzenfilm)* copy
Nutzen *m/pl* *(Druck)* multiple copies *pl*, multiple-ups *pl*; **zu vier** ~ four up
Nutzenauslage *f* *(Faltschachtelherst.)* delivery of blanks
Nutzenfilm *m* film copy, film duplicate
Nutzenkopie *f* *(Aktion)* repeat copying, step-and-repeat copying; *(Produkt)* film copy, film duplicate
Nutzenkopiermaschine *f* *(Repetierkopierm.)* step-and-repeat (copying) machine
Nutzenlackierung *f* *(ausgesparte Lackierung)* cut-out varnishing, pattern coating, spot varnishing
Nutzensammelfilm *m* cumulative film, gang film
Nutzenstanzung *f* *(Faltschachtelherst.)* blank cutting
Nutzentrennform *f* *(Faltschachtelherst.)* blank separating forme, blank stripping forme
Nutzentrennung *f* *(Faltschachtelherst.)* blank separation, blank stripping
Nutzenverarbeitung *f* multi-up processing
Nutzenverbindungsstege *pl* *(Nutzenstanzung)* blank attachment points *pl*

Nutzfläche *f* *(Arbeitsfläche)* useful size, working area, working surface
Nutzformat *n* *(Arbeitsformat)* useful size, working area, working surface
Nutzungsgrad *m* capacity utilization rate
Nutzylinder *m* grooving cylinder
Nylo *n* *(Fotopolymerplatte)* photopolymer plate
Nylongaze *f* nylon gauze
Nylongewebe *n* nylon cloth
Nylonklischee *n* *(Fotopolymerplatte)* photopolymer plate

O

obenliegendes Farbmesser *n* overshot ink duct blade
obenstehende Bruchziffern *pl* *(bei Brüchen)* superior fractional figures *pl*
Oberdeck *n* *(Zeitungsrotation)* upper deck
oberer Papierrand *m* head margin, upper margin
oberer Seitenrand *m* head margin, upper margin
Oberfläche *f* surface; *(Papier)* finish
oberflächenbehandelt surface-treated
Oberflächenbeschaffenheit *f* surface characteristics *pl*, surface properties *pl*
Oberflächenfestigkeit *f* *(Papier)* sizing strength, surface stability, surface strength
oberflächengeleimtes Papier *n* surface-sized paper, tub-sized paper
Oberflächengeschwindigkeit *f* surface speed
Oberflächenglätte *f* *(Papier)* surface smoothness
Oberflächenglanz *m* surface gloss, surface lustre
Oberflächenleimung *f* *(Papier)* surface sizing
Oberflächenspannung *f* surface tension
Oberflächentrocknung *f* surface drying
Oberflächenveredlung *f* surface finishing
Oberkante *f* top edge
Oberlänge *f* *(Buchstaben)* ascender
Oberlinie *f* *(Schriftlinien)* cap line
Obermesser *n* upper knife
Oberseite *f* top side, upper side
Oberseitendruck *m* *(Rollendruckm.)* upper side printing
Obersieb *n* *(Papiermasch.)* top wire, upper wire
Objektiv *n* lens
Objektivanwahl *f* lens selection
Objektiveinstellung *f* lens adjustment

Objektivfassung - Offset-Tiefdruck-Konversion

Objektivfassung *f* lens mount
Objektivfehler *m* lens defect
Objektiv mit großer Brennweite large focus lens
Objektivöffnung *f* lens aperture
Objektivrevolver *m* lens turret
Objektivsatz *m* set of lenses
Objektivschieber *m* lens carriage, lens slide
Objektivstandarte *f* lens holder
Objektivträger *m* lens holder
Objektivverschluß *m* lens shutter
Objektivverstellung *f* lens adjustment
Objektivwahl *f* lens selection
Ochsengalle *f* ox gall
OCR *(optische Zeichenerkennung)* OCR (Optical Character Recognition)
OCR-Formular *n* OCR form
OCR-Leser *m* OCR reader, optical character reader
OCR-Schrift *f* OCR characters *pl*
Öffentlichkeitsarbeit *f (PR)* public relations *pl*
Öffnungszeit *f (Leim)* open time
Ölauffangblech *n* drip pan, drip tray
Ölbad *n* oil bath
Ölbadschmierung *f* oil bath lubrication
Ölberieselung *f* drip lubrication, oil sprinkling, oil trickling
Ölbogen *m* tympan
Öldruck *m (Bild)* oleograph; *(Technik)* oleography
Öldrucklack *m* oilprint varnish
ölen to lubricate
Ölfarbe *f (Druckfarbe auf Ölbasis)* oil-based ink
Ölfirnis *m* oil varnish
Ölkanne *f* oil can
Ölpapier *n* oil paper
Ölpauspapier *n* oil tracing paper
Ölschmierstelle *f* oil lubrication point
Ölschmierung *f* oil lubrication
Ölstein *m* oilstone
Ölumlaufschmierung *f* oil circuit lubrication
OEM *(Originalgerätehersteller)* OEM (Original Equipment Manufacturer)
OEM-Produkt *n* OEM product
Öse *f* eyelet
ösen *(Ösen einsetzen)* to eyelet
Öseneinsetzmaschine *f* eyeletting machine
Ösenheftkopf *m* eyelet stitching head
Ösenheftung *f* eyelet stitching
Ösenmaschine *f* eyeletting machine
offener File *m (Comp)* open file
offener Kopf *m (Falzbogen)* open head
offene Schnittstelle *f (Interface)* open interface
offene Seite *f (Falzbogen)* cut edge, open side

offenes Format *n* open size
offenes System *n* open system
offenhalten *(Raster, Sieb)* to keep open
Offizin *f (Drucker)* office, printing office
Offline-Arbeitsplatz *m (Comp.)* independent workstation, offline workstation
Offline-Betrieb *m* off-line operation
Offset *m* litho offset, offset, offset lithography
Offsetandruckpresse *f* offset proofing press
Offsetbecken *n (Plattenentwicklung)* offset sink
Offsetdruck *m* litho (offset) printing, offset lithography, offset printing, process printing
Offsetdrucker *m* offset pressman, offset printer
Offsetdruckerei *f* offset company, offset printer, offset printhouse, offset printing operation, offset printshop
Offset(druck)farbe *f* litho (offset) ink, offset ink
Offset(druck)folie *f (Kleinoffset)* offset master
Offset(druck)form *f* offset printing forme
Offset(druck)maschine *f* litho (offset) press, offset (printing) press
Offset(druck)platte *f* litho (offset) plate, offset (printing) plate
Offset(druck)tuch *n* litho blanket, rubber offset blanket
Offset(druck)verfahren *n* litho offset (process), offset (printing) process
Offsetfarbe *f* siehe Offset(druck)farbe
Offsetkarton *m* litho board, offset board
Offsetkopie *f* offset platemaking
Offsetmaschine *f* siehe Offset(druck)maschine
Offsetmontage *f* litho stripping
Offsetmontierer *m* litho stripper
Offsetpapier *n* offset paper
Offsetperfektor *m* offset perfector
Offsetplatte *f* siehe Offset(druck)platte
Offsetplatten-Korrekturstift *m* offset plate correction pen; *(nur für Minuskorrektur)* offset plate deletion pen
Offsetplattenstraße *f* offset platemaking line, offset plate processing line
Offsetprozeß *m* litho offset (process), offset (printing) process
Offsetraster *m* litho (offset) screen
Offsetreproduktion *f* offset reproduction
Offset(rollen)rotation *f* offset rotary (press), rotary offset press, web offset press
Offsetrotation *f* siehe Offset(rollen)rotation
Offsettestkeil *m* offset control wedge
Offsettiefdruck *m* intaglio offset
Offset-Tiefdruck-Konversion *f (O-T-Konv.)* litho conversion (to gravure), offset-gravure conversion

Offsettuch *n* siehe Offset(druck)tuch
Offsetverfahren *n* siehe Offset(druck)verfahren
Offsetzeitungsrotation *f* newspaper offset rotary, web offset newspaper press
Offsetzink *n* offset zinc
Offsetzinkplatte *f* offset zinc plate
O.K.-Bogen *m* o.k. proof, o.k. sheet
o.k. zum Druck *n* can go over, passed for press, ready to print
oleophil *(öl/farbfreundlich)* oleophilic
oleophob *(öl/farbabweisend)* oleophobic
Online-Densitometer *n* on-line densitometer; *(Kamera)* camera densitometer
Online-Entwicklungsmaschine *f* on-line processor
Online-Prozessor *m (Fotosatz)* on-line processor
opak *(deckend)* opaque
Opakfilm *m* opaque film
Opal *n (Tiefdruck)* bromide
Opalglas *n* opal glass
Opallampe *f* opal lamp
Opalscheibe *f* opal glass plate
Opazität *f (Papier)* opacity
Optik *f* optics
Optikträger *m (Kamera)* lens holder
optisch ausgeglichen *(Satz)* optically spaced
optische Anzeige *f* display, read-out
optische Beleglesung *f* videoscan document reading
optische Dichte *f* optical density
optischer Leser *m* optical reader, optical scanner
optischer Markenleser *m* optical mark reader
optischer Plattenspeicher *m (Comp.)* optical disk
optische Speicherplatte *f (Comp.)* optical disk
optisches Plattenlaufwerk *n* optical disk drive
optische Verzeichnung *f* optical distortion
optische Zeichenerkennung *f (OCR)* optical character recognition
opto-elektronischer Sensor *m* opto-electronic sensor
opto-mechanischer Sensor *m* opto-mechanical sensor
organisch-pflanzliches Druckbestäubungspuder *n* organic vegetable spray powder
Original *n (Vorlage)* original, original art(work), original copy, master copy
Originalausgabe *f (Buch)* original edition
Originalbild *n* master image
Originaleinband *m* original binding
Originalgerätehersteller (OEM) *m* original equipment manufacturer (OEM)
originalgestrichenes Kunstdruckpapier *n* real art paper
originalgetreu true to original

originalgetreue Kopie *f* true copy
originalgetreue Wiedergabe *f* facsimile reproduction, faithful reproduction, reproduction fidelity
Originalgrafik *f (i. U. zur Druckgrafik)* original art(work)
Originalhalter *m* copy holder
Originalherstellung *f* art(work) preparation, copy preparation, origination
Originallitho *n* original litho
Originalretusche *f* retouching of original
Originalvorlage *f* original, original art(work), original copy, master copy
Ornament *n* ornament
orthochromatischer Film *m* orthochromatic film
Orthofilm *m (Reprod.)* orthochromatic film
Orthografie *f (Satz)* orthography, spelling
oszillierende Walze *f* oscillating roller, reciprocating roller
O-T-Konversion *f* litho conversion (to gravure), offset-gravure conversion
O-T-Konversionsraster *m* offset-gravure conversion screen
Overhead-Folie *f* overhead transparency
Oxid *n* oxide
Oxidation *f* oxidation
Oxidationsregenerierung *f (Fotochemie)* oxidation replenishment
Oxidationsschutzschicht *f* anti-oxidation coating
oxidative Trocknung *f (Farbe)* oxidative drying
oxidieren to oxidize
Ozalidkopie *f* blue print, diazo copy, diazo print, ozalid
Ozalidpapier *n* ozalid paper

P

Packmaterial *n* packing (material)
Packmittelkennzeichnung *f* packaging identification
Packpapier *n* packing paper, wrapping paper
Packung *f* pack, package, packaging
Pagina *f (Seitenzahl)* folio, page number
paginieren to number pages, to page
Paginierung *f* folios *pl*, page numbering, paging
Paket *n (Versandraum)* batch, bundle
Paketauslage *f* bundle delivery

Paketbildung - Papiergewicht

Paketbildung f bundle formation
Paketförderer m bundle conveyor
Paketiervorrichtung f bundler
Paketstapler m bundle stacker
Pakettransportsystem n bundle conveyor system
Paketverarbeitung f bundle processing
Palette f pallet
Palettenabtransport m pallet removal
Palettenanleger m pallet feeder
Palettenbeschickung f pallet loading
Palettenmagazin n pallet magazine
Palettenwagen m pallet trolley
Palettieranlage f palletizer
Palettierautomat m automatic palletizer
Palettieren n palletizing
panchromatischer Film m panchromatic film
Panfilm m panchromatic film
Panoramaseite f *(durchgehende Doppelseite)* center spread, double(-page) spread, two-page spread
Pantograf m pantograph
Pantone-Farbe f Pantone ink
Pantone-Mischsystem n *(Farbsystem)* Pantone matching system
Papier n paper; *120 g/m² ~* 120 gsm paper; *(Druckpapier auch)* stock
Papierabfall m waste paper
Papierabrollung f paper unwinding, paper unwind unit
Papierabschlagvorrichtung f *(Rollendruckm.)* web severing device
Papierabwicklung f paper unwinding, paper unwind unit
Papierabzug m *(Foto)* bromide, print
Papierakklimatisierung f paper conditioning
Papieraufhängevorrichtung f paper hanging device
Papierauflegen n *(Anlegermagazin)* paper refeeding, paper refilling, paper reloading, paper replenishing
Papieraufrollung f paper rewinding, paper rewind unit
Papieraufwicklung f paper rewinding, paper rewind unit
Papieraufzug m *(Zyl.)* paper dressing, paper packing
Papierbahn f paper web, web
Papierbahneinfärbung f *(Endlosdruck)* web tinting
Papierbahn einziehen to feed in the web, to introduce the web, to thread in the web, to web up
Papierballen m bale of paper

Papierband n paper tape
Papierbefeuchter m paper moistener, paper wetter
Papierbeleg m hardcopy, hard proof, paper copy, paper proof
Papierberechnung f *(Kalkulation)* estimate of paper quantity, paper quantity calculation
Papierbestand m paper inventory
Papierbeutel m paper bag
Papierbogen m paper sheet
Papierbohrer m paper drill
Papierbrei m pulp
Papierbreite f paper width
Papierdehnung f paper stretch
Papierdicke f paper thickness, paper gauge, paper calliper
Papierdruckplatte f *(Kleinoffset)* paper master, paper plate
Papiereinband m *(Taschenbuch)* paperback, paper binding
Papiereinlauf m paper in-feed
Papiereinstapeln n *(Anlegermagazin)* paper feeding, paper filling, paper loading
Papiereinziehvorrichtung f *(Rollendruckm.)* webbing-up device, web threading device
Papiereinzug m *(Rollendruckm.)* paper infeed, paper introduction, threading-in, webbing-up
Papiereinzugswalze f *(Rollendruckm.)* paper infeed roller
Papierfabrik f paper mill
Papierfalte f crease, wrinkle
Papierfangeinrichtung f *(Rollendruckm.)* web catcher
Papierfaser f paper fibre
Papierfaserstoff m pulp
Papierfeuchte f moisture content of paper
Papierfeuchtigkeitsmesser m paper hygrometer
Papierfilz m paper felt
Papierflusen pl fluff, fuzz
Papierfolie f *(Kleinoffsetdruckplatte)* paper master, paper plate
Papierformat n paper format, paper size, sheet size
Papierführung f paper guide, web quide
Papierführungselemente pl paper guiding elements pl
Papierfusseln m/pl fluff, fuzz, lint
Papiergeld n *(Banknoten)* banknotes pl
Papiergelddruck m banknote printing, currency printing
Papiergestell n *(für Formatpapier)* paper rack
Papiergewicht n *(Flächengewicht)* paper grammage

Papierglätte f paper glaze, paper smoothness
Papierglanz m paper glaze, paper gloss
Papiergröße f paper size, sheet size
Papiergroßhandlung f wholesale paper merchants pl
Papierhändler m paper merchants pl
Papierhandel m paper trade
Papierhersteller m papermaker
Papierherstellung f papermaking, paper production
Papierhülse f paper tube
Papierindustrie f paper industry
Papierkalander m *(Papierherst.)* paper calender
Papierkante f paper edge
Papierknäuel m *(in Druckm.)* jam-up, paper jam
Papierknautscher m jam-up, paper jam
Papierkonditionierung f paper conditioning
Papierlager n paper stock, paper store
Papierlagerung f paper stocking, paper storage
Papierlaufrichtung f direction of web travel, grain (direction), paper grain, running direction; **gegen die ~ /quer zur ~** across the grain, across the web, against the grain, cross grain, cross web; **in ~** along the web, in-line, long grain
Papierlehre f *(Stärkemessung)* paper thickness gauge
Papierleimung f paper sizing
Papierleitwalze f *(Rollendruckm.)* web guide roller, web lead roller
Papierlieferant m paper supplier
Papierlieferung f paper delivery
Papiermaché n papermaché
Papiermaschine f paper machine
Papiermaschinenglättwerk n paper machine glazer
Papiermaschinensieb n paper machine wire
Papiermasse f pulp
Papiermater f paper flong
Papiermatrize f paper mould
Papiermesser n paper knife
Papier mit Wasserlinien laid paper
Papiermontage f paper paste-up
Papiermühle f paper mill
Papiernachlegen n *(Anleger)* paper refeeding, paper refilling, paper reloading, paper replenishing
Papieroberfläche f paper surface
Papieroberflächenstruktur f paper surface structure, paper surface texture
Papierplatte f *(Kleinoffset)* paper master, paper plate
Papierpore f paper pore

Papierprüfung f paper testing
Papierqualität f paper quality; *(Sorte)* paper grade, stock type
Papierrand m *(Papierkante)* paper edge; *(Seitenrand)* margin
Papierrand des geschöpften Papiers deckle edge
Papierriß m *(Rollendruck)* web break
Papierrolle f mill roll, paper reel
Papiersack m paper bag
Papierschere f paper scissors pl
Papierschlupf m paper slipping
Papierschneidemaschine f guillotine, paper cutter, paper cutting machine
Papierschneidemesser n paper knife
Papierschneiden n paper cutting
Papierschneider m *(Maschine)* guillotine, paper cutter, paper cutting machine; *(Person)* cutter operator
Papierschnipsel pl paper shavings pl, paper shred, paper trimmings pl
Papierschnitzel pl paper shavings pl, paper shred, paper trimmings pl
Papierschrumpfung f paper shrinkage
Papierschuppe f *(Anlage, Auslage)* shingled sheets pl
Papiersorte f paper grade, stock type
Papierspäne pl paper shavings pl, paper shred, paper trimmings pl
Papierspeicher m *(Rollendruckm.)* festooning unit, paper storage
Papierstärke f paper calliper, paper gauge, paper thickness
Papierstärkemesser m paper thickness gauge
Papierstärkenregulierung f *(Druckm.)* paper thickness adjustment
Papierstapel m sheet pile, stack of paper
Papierstapeln n sheet piling
Papierstau m jam-up, paper jam
Papierstaub m fluff, fuzz, lint, paper dust
Papierstaubabsaugung f paper dust exhaust, paper dust extraction
Papierstoff m pulp
Papierstoß m sheet pile, stack of paper
Papierstrang m *(Rollendruck)* ribbon
Papierstreifen m paper strip
Papierstrich m *(Oberfläche)* paper coating
Papiertapete f wallpaper
Papiertransport m paper handling, paper transport
Papiertrockner m paper dryer
Papierunebenheiten pl paper unevenness
papierverarbeitende Industrie f paper converting industry

Papierverarbeitung *f* paper converting, paper finishing, paper processing; *(Papierfabrik)* mill converting
Papierverarbeitungsindustrie *f* paper converting industry
Papierverbrauch *m* paper consumption
Papierveredlung *f* paper finishing; *(Papierfabrik)* mill finishing
Papierverpackung *f (Verpackung in Papier)* paper packing, paper wrapping
Papierversorgung *f* paper supply
Papierverzug *m* paper distortion, paper shrinkage, paper stretch
Papiervolumen *n* bulk, paper volume
Papier vorklimatisieren to condition paper
Papierwaage *f* paper scales *pl*
Papierwalze *f (Papiermasch.)* paper bowl
Papierwaren *pl* stationery
Papierweg *m (Rollendruckm.)* web path
Papierweiß *n* paper white
Papierwolf *m* paper shredder
Papierwolle *f* paper shavings *pl*, paper shred, paper trimmings *pl*
Papierzähler *m* paper counter
Papierzerfaserer *m* paper shredder
Papierzufuhr *f* paper in-feed, paper supply
Papierzurichtung *f* paper makeready
Papierzuschuß *m (für Druck/Druckverarb.)* allowance
Pappband *m* paperback
Pappdeckel *m* board, cardboard
Pappe *f* board, cardboard, pasteboard
Pappebearbeitung *f* board converting
Pappeinband *m* paperback
Pappeinlage *f* board insert
Pappenbedruckmaschine *f* board printing machine
Pappenbiegemaschine *f* board bending machine
Pappenkreisschere *f* rotary board cutter
Pappenschlitzmaschine *f* board slotting machine
Papphülse *f* board tube
Pappkarton *m* board container, cardboard box, carton
Pappkiste *f* board container
Pappmaschine *f (Fabrik)* board machine
Pappmater *f* board matrix
Pappmatrize *f* board matrix
Pappmatrizenprägung *f* board matrix moulding
Papprolle *f* board reel
Pappschachtel *f* cardboard box, carton
Pappschere *f* board cutter
Paraffin *n* paraffin
paraffinieren to paraffin

Paraffiniermaschine *f* paraffining machine
Paraffinpapier *n* paraffin paper
Paragraphenzeichen *n (§)* section mark
Paragummi *n* para rubber
Parallaxe *f (Optik)* parallax
Parallelbruch *m (Falzen)* parallel fold
paralleles Licht *n* parallel light
Parallelfalz *m* parallel fold
Parallelverarbeitung *f (Comp.)* parallel processing
Parameterzeile *f (Fotosatzm.)* status line
Parenthese *f (runde Klammer)* parenthesis
parfümierte Druckfarbe *f* perfumed ink, scented ink
parfümiertes Papier *n* perfumed paper, scented paper
Parterredruckmaschine *f (Zeitungsrotation)* floor-type press
Partisanen *pl (Butzen)* hickies *pl*
Partisanenfänger *m (Offsetdruckm.)* hickey remover
Passagebestäubung *f (Druckm.)* line spraying
Passagepuderapparat *m* line powder spray device
Paßdifferenz *f* mis-register, register difference
passen *(Farbenregister)* to be in register
Passer *m (Farbregister)* colour register, register
Passerabweichung *f* register deviation
Passerdifferenz *f* mis-register, register difference
Passer einstellen to bring into register
passergenau in register, register-true, true to register
Passergenauigkeit *f* register accuracy, register precision
Passerhalten *n* register maintenance
passerhaltig in register, register-true, true to register
Passerkontrolle *f* register control, register monitoring
Passerkorrektur *f* register correction
Passermarke *f* register mark
Passermarkenerkennung *f* register mark recognition
Passerregelung *f (Druckm.)* register control
Passerschwankungen *pl* register fluctuations *pl*, register variations *pl*
Passertoleranz *f* register tolerance
Passerversatz *m* mis-register, register shifting
Paßform *f* key forme, register forme, skeleton forme
paßgenau in register, register-true, true to register
paßgenauer Stand *m* in register, registered position
Paßkreuz *n* crosshair mark, register cross

Paßlochstanze f register punch
Paßlochstanzung f register punching
Paßlochung f register holes pl, register punching
Paßmarke f register mark
Paßstifte pl register pins pl
Paßstiftleiste f register pin bar
Paßsystem n register system
Paßzeichen n register mark
Pastellton m pastel tone
Pastelltonkorrektur f (Scannerfunktion) pastel tone correction
pastöse Farbe f pasty ink, stiff ink, viscous ink
Patrize f (Prägen) counter die, embossing die; (Schrift) punch
Pause f (durchgepauste Zeichnung) tracing; (Lichtpause) blue-print
pausen to trace
Paushaut f tracing film
Pausleinen n tracing cloth
Pauspapier n tracing paper
PC m (Personal Computer) PC (personal computer)
PC-Diskette f PC diskette
PC-Satz m PC typesetting, PC composition; (DTP-Satz) desk-top composition, desk-top type matter, DTP type matter
PC-Satzsystem n PC(-based) typesetting system, PC composition system
PE-Folie f (Folienverpackung) PE film
Pelzen n (Druckfarbe) piling(-up)
Pendelwalze f (Rollendruckm.) dancer roller
Penplotter m pen plotter
Perfektor m (Schön- und Widerdruckm.) perfecting press, perfector
Perfoklebebindung f (im U. zur Fräsklebebindung) perforation adhesive binding
Perforation f perforation
Perforationsschnitt m perforating cut
Perforator m perforator
perforieren to perforate
Perforierkamm m perforating comb
Perforierleiste f perforating bar
Perforierlinie f perforating rule, perfo rule
Perforiermaschine f perforating machine, perforator
Perforiermesser n perforating knife
Perforierrädchen n/pl perforating wheels pl
Perforierscheibe f perforating disc
Perforierung f perforating
Perforiervorrichtung f perforating device
Perforierwerkzeug n perforating tool
Perforierzähnchen pl perforating teeth pl

Pergament n parchment
Pergament(ein)band m parchment binding
Pergamentersatz m imitation parchment
Pergamentkarton m parchment board
Pergamentpapier n parchment paper, vellum
Pergamin n (Pergamentimitation) imitation parchment
Pergaminfenster n (Briefumschlag) parchment window
Pergaminpapier n glassine paper
Periodika pl periodicals pl
Peripherie f (Comp.) peripherals pl, peripheral units pl, periphery; (Rollendruckm.) ancillary equipment
Peripheriegeräte pl (Comp.) peripheral units pl, peripherals pl
perlen (Farbe im Tiefdruck) to marble, to mottle
Permanentschablone f (Siebdruck) permanent stencil
Personal-Computer m (PC) personal computer
personalintensiv labour intensive
personalisierte Werbedrucksache f (Datamailer) data mailer, personalized mailer
Personalkosten pl personnel costs pl
Pflanzenöl n (Farbherst.) vegetable oil
Pflege (Maschinen) care, maintenance
Pflichtexemplar n (Buch bei Erscheinen) deposit copy
Pflugfalz m plow fold
Pflugfalzer m (Rollendruckm.) plow folder
Pfusch m botched job, botched piece of work
Phantombild n phantom image
phonetischer Satz m phonetic composition
phonetische Umschrift f phonetic transsscription
pH-Stabilisator m (Feuchtwasser) pH (value) stabilizer
pH-Wert m pH value
pH-Wert-Konstanthalter m (Feuchtwasser) pH (value) stabilizer
Pica (Typogr.) pica
Pica-Punkt m point pica
Pickel m (Folienkaschierung) speck
Pigment n pigment
Pigmentdiapositiv n (Tiefdruck) carbon diapositive
Pigmentdruck m (Kohledruck) carbon printing
Pigmentfarbe f carbon ink, pigment ink
Pigmentfilm m (Tiefdruck) carbon film, pigment film
pigmentiert pigmented
Pigmentierung f pigmentation
Pigmentkopie f (Tiefdruck) carbon film copy, pigment copy

Pigmentkopieranlage - Plattengröße

Pigmentkopieranlage f pigment copying machine
Pigmentpapier n *(Tiefdruck)* carbon tissue, pigment paper
Pigmentpapiersensibilisierung f carbon tissue sensitizing
Pigmentpapiertrockeneinrichtung f carbon tissue dryer, pigment paper dryer
Pigmentpapierübertragung f carbon tissue transfer, pigment paper transfer
Pigmentschicht f pigment layer
Piktogramm n ideogram, pictogram
Pilzbildung f *(Feuchtwasser)* formation of fungus, formation of mould, moulding
Pilztaste f *(Notausschalter)* emergency stop button, stop safe push button
Pinholes pl *(Nadellöcher)* pinholes pl
Pinolenlagerung f *(Tiefdruckzyl.)* center sleeve bearing
Pinsel m artist's brush, brush
Pinselätzung f brush etching
Pinselretusche f brush retouching
Pinselschrift f brush lettering, brush type
Pinselstrich m brush stroke
Pixel n *(Bildelement)* pixel
Pixelauflösung f pixelization
Pixelflächenrechner m *(RIP)* raster image processor
Pixelgrafik f pixel art(work), pixel graphics
Pixelkorrektur f pixel editing
Pixelretusche f pixel retouching
Plakat n poster; *mehrteiliges* ~ multi-part poster
Plakatbuchstaben pl *(Handsatz)* poster letters pl, poster type
Plakatdruck m poster printing, poster work
Plakatkarton m showcard board
Plakatpapier n poster paper
Plakatschrift f *(Handsatz)* poster type
Plakatversandhülse f poster mailing tube
Plakatwerbung f poster advertising
Plakatzeichner m poster artist, poster designer
Planfilm m *(Blattfilm)* sheet film
Planität f siehe Planlage
Planlage f flatness, flat position
planliegen to lay flat, to lie flat
planliegend flat
plano *(ungefalzt)* flat
Planoauslage f *(Rollendruckm.)* open sheet delivery, sheeter
Planoausleger m *(Rollendruckm.)* open sheet delivery, sheeter
Planobogen m broadsheet, flat sheet, open sheet
Planobogenausgang m *(Rollendruckm.)* open sheet delivery, sheeter

Planoformat n open sheet size
Planschneider m cutting machine, guillotine, paper cutter, paper cutting machine
Planspiegel m *(Kamera)* plane mirror
Planung f planning
Planungsfilm m planning film
Planungstafel f *(Disposition)* planning board
Plastikbinderücken m plastic comb
Plastikbindung f plastic binding
Plastikkammbindung f plastic comb binding
Platine f *(gedruckte Schaltung)* printed circuit board
Platte f *(Comp.)* disk; *(Druckplatte)* plate
Platte einspannen to clamp a plate, to mount a plate
Platte farbfreundlich machen to make the plate ink-receptive
Platte mit beweglichem Kopf moving head disk
Plattenabkantautomat m automatic plate bender
Plattenabnutzung f plate wear
Plattenantrieb m *(Comp.)* disk drive
Plattenaufrauhung f plate graining
Plattenaufspannen n plate clamping, plate mounting, plating-up
Plattenaufspannvorrichtung f plate clamping device, plate mounting device
Plattenautomat m *(Kleinoffsetplattenherst.)* camera-platemaker
Plattenbearbeitung f plate handling, plate processing
Plattenbearbeitungslinie f platemaking line, plate processing line
Plattenbelichtung f plate exposure
Plattenbeschichtung f plate coating
Plattenbeschichtungsmaschine f plate coater
Plattenbett n *(Flachformdruckm.)* plate bed
Plattenbiegegerät n plate bender
Plattenbruch m plate crack
Plattencrash m *(Comp.)* disk crash
Platteneinbrennen n plate baking
Platteneinspannen n plate clamping, plate mounting, plating-up
Plattenempfindlichkeit f plate sensitivity
Plattenentwicklung f plate development, plate processing
Plattenentwicklungsmaschine f plate processor
Platte neumachen to remake a plate
plattenfertiger Film m plate-ready film
Plattenfeuchtung f plate damp(en)ing
Plattenfixierung f plate fixing
Plattenformat n plate format, plate size
Plattenfundament n *(Flachbettdruckm.)* plate bed
Plattengröße f plate format, plate size

Plattengummi *m* plate gum
Plattengummierung *f* plate gum, plate gumming
Plattengummierungsmittel *n* plate gum
Plattenherstellung *f (Druckformherst.)* platemaking; *(Plattenfabrik)* plate manufacture, plate production
Plattenhinterkante *f* rear edge of plate, tail edge of plate
Plattenhöhe *f (auf Zylinder)* plate height
Plattenjustierung *f (in Druckm.)* plate adjustment
Plattenkamera *f (Kleinoffset)* camera-platemaker
Plattenkeil *m (Kopie)* plate control wedge
Plattenklemme *f (Einspannen)* plate clamp
Plattenklemmvorrichtung *f* plate clamping device, plate lock-up system
Plattenkörnung *f* plate graining
Plattenkopie *f* plate exposure, platemaking
Plattenkopie direkt aus Datenbestand computer-to-plate exposure
Plattenkopiekontrollfeld *n (Meßstreifen)* plate exposure control patch
Plattenkopiersystem *n* platemaking system
Plattenkorn *n* plate grain
Plattenkorrektur *f* plate correction
Plattenkorrekturstift *m* plate correction pen; *(nur für Minuskorrektur)* plate deletion pen
Plattenlaufwerk *n (Comp.)* disk drive
Plattenleser *m (für Farbvoreinstellung)* plate reader
Plattenmagazin *n (Kleinoffset)* plate dispenser
Plattenoberfläche *f* plate surface
Plattenregister *n* plate register
Plattenreiniger *m (chem.)* plate cleaner
Plattensattel *m (Rollendruckm.)* plate saddle
Plattensatz *m (Druckplatten)* set of plates
Plattenscanner *m (für Farbvoreinstellung)* plate scanner
Plattenschere *f* plate cutter
Plattenschleuder *f (Selbstbeschichtung)* plate whirler
Plattenschneider *m* plate cutter
Plattenschnellspanneinrichtung *f (Druckm.)* fast-acting plate clamps *pl*, quick locking plate clamps *pl*
Plattenschrank *m* plate cabinet
Plattenspannklemme *f (Druckm.)* plate clamp
Plattenspannschiene *f (Druckm.)* plate clamping bar, plate locking bar
Plattenspannsystem *n* plate clamping system, plate lock-up system
Plattenspeicher *m (Comp.)* disk storage
Plattenständer *m* plate rack

Plattenstärke *f* plate thickness
Plattenstanze *f (Registerstanze)* plate punch
Plattenstapel *m (Comp.)* disk pack
Plattenstapler *m* plate stacker
Plattenstraße *f (vollautomatische Plattenverarbeitungslinie)* platemaking line, plate processing line
Plattenunterlage *f* plate mount; *(Zylinderaufzug)* plate dressing, plate packing
Plattenverarbeitung *f* plate processing
Plattenverarbeitungslinie *f* platemaking line, plate processing line
Plattenvorderkante *f* front edge of plate, lead edge of plate
Plattenwechsel *m* plate change
Plattenzurichtung *f* plate makeready
Plattenzylinder *m* plate cylinder
Platte unterlegen to dress a plate, to pack a plate
Platte wasserfreundlich machen to make the plate water-receptive
Platzbedarf *m* space requirements *pl*
Platzkosten *pl (Betriebskostenrechnung)* departmental running costs *pl*, department's costs *pl*, production department costs *pl*
Plazierung *f (Anzeige)* position; *(Bildelemente in der Montage)* positioning
Pleuelstange *f* connecting rod, piston rod
Plotter *m* plotter
plüschbezogene Feuchtwalze *f* plush-covered damper roller
Plüschbezug *m (Feuchtwalze)* plush cover
Plüschtampon *m* plush tampon
Pluskorrektur *f* plus correction
Pluszeichen *n* plus sign
PLZ (Postleitzahl) *f* postal code, zip code
pneumatischer Kopierrahmen *m* vacuum frame
pneumatische Steuerung *f* pneumatic control
Polarisationsfilter *m (Densitometrie)* polarizing filter
Polarisator *m (Densitometrie)* polarizing filter
polarisieren to polarize
polarisiertes Licht *n* polarized light
Polfilter *m* polarizing filter
polieren *(Tiefdruckzyl.)* to polish, to burnish
Polierfilz *m* polishing felt
Poliergummi *m* polishing rubber
Polierkopf *m* polishing head
Poliermaschine *f* polishing machine
Polierscheibe *f* polishing disc
Polyäthylen *n (PE)* polyethylene
polyäthylenbeschichtetes Papier *n* polyethylene coated paper

Polyäthylenfolie - Prägepresse

Polyäthylenfolie f *(PE-Folie, Folienverpackung)* polyethylene film
Polyamid n polyamide
Polyester n polyester
Polyesterfilm m polyester film
Polyesterfolie f polyester film
Polygonspiegel m polygon mirror
Polymerisation f polymerization
Polymerplatte f polymer plate
Polypropylen n *(PP)* polypropylene
Polystyrol n polystyrene
Polyurethan n polyurethane
Polyvinylalkohol m *(PVA)* polyvinyl alcohol
Polyvinylchlorid n *(PVC)* polyvinyl chloride
Pony-Wendestange f *(Falzapp. Rollendruckm.)* pony turner-bar
Popel pl *(Butzen, Partisanen)* hickies pl
porenfrei pore-free
poröses Papier n porous paper
Porzellandruck m porcelain printing
Porzellanmärbeln pl porcelain marbles
Positionierautomatik f *(Schneidem.)* automatic positioning
positionieren to position
Positioniergenauigkeit f positioning accuracy
Positionierung f positioning
Positionsanzeige f *(Bildschirm)* cursor
Positiv n positive
positive Abrakelung f *(Tiefdruck)* conventional doctoring, positive doctoring
Positivkontaktraster m *(Reprod.)* positive contact screen
Positivkopie f *(Plattenkopie)* positive platemaking
Positiv/Negativ-Darstellung f *(Bildschirm)* positive/negative display
Positiv/Negativumwandlung f *(Reprod.)* flip image, positive/negative transposition
Positivpause f *(Lichtpause)* positive blue-print, positive dyeline
Positivplatte f positive plate, positive working plate
Positivrasterung f positive screening
Positivretusche f positive retouching
Positivretuscheur m positive retoucher
postalische Sortierung f *(Versandraum)* postal sorting
Postauflage f *(einer Zeitung, Zeitschrift)* mail circulation
Poster n poster
Posteraufhänger m poster hanger
Postgebühren f/pl *(Zeitungsversand)* postage rates pl

Postkarte f postcard
Postkartendoppeln n postcard doubling
Postkartenformat n postcard size
Postkartenkarton m postcard board
Postleitzahl f *(PLZ)* postal code, zip code
Postleitzahlenleser m *(Versandraum)* zip code reader
Postleitzahlensortierung f *(Versandraum)* zip code sorting
PostScript-fähig PostScript compatible
Postversand m *(Zeitung, Zeitschrift)* postal distribution
Postvordrucke pl postal forms pl
Postvorschriften pl postal regulations pl, postal requirements pl
Postwertzeichen n postage stamp
Postzeitungsdienst m postal newspaper distribution
potentieller Kunde m prospective customer
Potentiometer n potentiometer
Pottasche f potash
Prachtausgabe f de luxe edition
Prägeautomat m *(Folienprägung)* automatic blocking press, automatic stamping press; *(Maternprägung)* automatic moulding press; *(Reliefprägung)* automatic embossing press
Prägedruck m *(Folienprägung)* blocking, stamping; *(Reliefprägung)* embossing; *(Stahlstich)* die-stamping
Prägefilz m embossing felt
Prägefolie f stamping foil
Prägeform f embossing forme, stamping forme
Prägegravur f engraved embossing plate
Prägegummituch n rubber embossing blanket
Prägehologramm n stamped hologram
Prägekalander m embossing calender
Prägeklischee n *(Folienprägung)* blocking plate, stamping plate; *(Reliefprägung)* embossing plate
Prägemaschine f siehe Prägepresse
Prägemater f *(Stereotypie)* matrix
Prägematrize f *(Relief)* female die, female embossing
Prägen n *(Folienprägen)* blocking, stamping; *(Maternprägen)* moulding; *(Reliefprägen)* embossing
Prägepappe f *(Stereotypie)* moulding board
Prägepatrize f *(Relief)* male die, male embossing
Prägeplatte f die-plate, embossing plate
Prägeplatte aus Stahl steel die
Prägepresse f *(Folienprägung)* blocking press, stamping press; *(Maternprägung)* moulding press; *(Reliefprägung)* embossing press

Prägepulver n embossing powder
Prägeregister n print-to-embossing register
Prägeschrift f bookbinder's type, embossing type
Prägeschrift für Goldprägung gold-blocking type
Prägestempel m *(für Folienprägung)* stamping die; *(für Reliefprägung)* embossing die
Prägetiegel m *(Folienprägung)* blocking press, stamping press; *(Relief)* embossing press
Präge- und Vergoldepresse f embossing and gold blocking press
Prägung f *(Folienprägung)* blocking, stamping; *(Maternprägung)* moulding; *(Reliefprägung)* embossing; *(Stahlstich)* die-stamping
Präzisionsmaschinenbau m precision engineering
Präzisionstechnik f precision engineering
Praxisbedingungen pl field conditions pl
praxiserprobt field-tested, proven, time-proven
praxisgerecht practice-oriented
praxisorientiert practice-oriented
Preisberechnung f price calculation, price estimating, pricing
Preiseindruck m price imprint
Preiskalkulation f price calculation, price estimating, pricing
Preis/Leistungsverhältnis n price/performance ratio
Preisnachlaß m *(bei Mängelrügen)* allowance
Preßbacke f backing jaw
Preßbalken m *(Schneidem.)* clamp, clamping bar
Preßbengel m *(Handpresse)* press jack, press stick
Preßdeckel m tympan
Preßdruck m *(Druckkraft)* impression pressure; *(Schneidem.)* clamping pressure
Presse f *(Journalisten)* press
Presseabteilung f press department
Pressen n compressing, pressing
Pressendruck m *(Handpresse)* hand press printing
Pressenpartie f *(Papiermaschine)* press section
Pressenrahmen m press frame
Presserfarbe f *(Buchb.)* bookbinder's blocking ink
Presseur m *(Tiefdruck)* impression roller, pressure roller
Preßleiste f *(Preßbalken; Schneidem.)* clamping bar
Preßluft f compressed air
Preßpappe f pressboard
Preßrolle f nip roller, pressing roller
Preßschwengel m *(Handpresse)* press jack, press stick
Preßspan m pressboard

Preßstempel m *(Dreischneider)* clamping block, pressing block
Pressung f pressing
Preßvergoldung f gold blocking, machine gilding, press-gilding
Preßvorrichtung f pressing device
Preßwalze f nip roller, pressing roller, squeeze roller
Preview-Betriebsfunktion f *(Echtdarstellungsmöglichkeit am Erfassungsbildschirm)* preview mode
Preview-Darstellung f *(layoutgerechte und/oder schriftgerechte Echtdarstellung am Bildschirm)* preview
Preview-Terminal m *(vom Erfassungsbildschirm separater Bildschirm für Echtdarstellung)* preview terminal, soft-copy monitor, soft typesetter
Primärfarben pl *(Farbsystem)* primary colours pl
Printing on Demand n *(Drucken nach Bedarf)* printing on demand
Printmedien pl printed media, print media
Printplatte f *(gedruckte Schaltung)* printed circuit board
Prisma n *(Umkehrprisma am Objektiv)* prism
privater Rundfunk m private radio
privates Fernsehen n private television
Probeabonnement n trial subscription
Probeabzug m proof, proof sheet, pull, test pull
Probeband m *(Musterbuch)* blank book, dummy, sample binding, specimen volume
Probebelichtung f text exposure
Probebogen m checking sheet, control sheet, inspection sheet, proof sheet, sample sheet, specimen sheet
Probedruck m *(Musterdruck)* specimen print, specimen sheet
Probeexemplar n checking copy, control copy, inspection copy, sample copy, specimen copy
Probeheft n *(Zeitschrift)* specimen copy
Probelauf m test run, trial run
Probenummer f *(Zeitschrift)* specimen copy
Probeseite f specimen page
Probezeile f *(Satz)* specimen line
Producer m producer
Produktaufnahme f *(Fot.)* product exposure
Produktdicke f copy thickness, product thickness
Produktioner m productioneer
Produktion Rolle/Bogen f reel-to-sheet production
Produktion Rolle/Falz f reel-to-fold production
Produktion Rolle/Rolle f reel-to-reel-production

Produktion Rolle/Stapel *f* reel-to-pack production
Produktionsablauf *m* production cycle, production sequence
Produktionsanlage *f* production plant
Produktionsbetrieb *m* production operation, production plant
Produktionsfluß *m* production flow
Produktionsgeschwindigkeit *f* production output, production performance, production rate, production speed
Produktionskapazität *f* production capacity
Produktionskosten *pl* production costs *pl*
Produktionsleiter *m* production manager
Produktionsleitung *f* production management
Produktionsplanung *f* production planning
Produktionsprogramm *n (Software)* production program, production software; *(Sortiment)* product line, product range
Produktionsprozeß *m* production cycle, production process
Produktionssicherheit *f* production reliability
Produktionsstätte *f* production site
Produktionsstatistik *f* production statistics
Produktion Stapel/Stapel *f (Zick-Zackfalzung)* pack-to-pack production
Produktionsüberwachung *f* production monitoring, production supervision
Produktionsüberwachungssystem *n* production monitoring system
Produktionszählsystem *n* production totalizing system
Produktionszeiten *pl* production times *pl*
Produktivitätssteuerung *f* productivity control
Produktstrom *m* copy stream, shingle stream
Produktüberlappung *f (Schuppe)* shingled copies *pl*
Produktverbesserung *f* product enhancement
Programm *n (für Computer)* program, software
Programmablauf *m* program cycle, program sequence
Programmdaten *pl* program data
Programmeingabe *f* program loading
Programmfolge *f* program sequence
programmgesteuert software-controlled, software-driven
Programmierautomatik *f* automatic programming
programmierbar programmable
programmierbarer Nur-Lese-Speicher (PROM) *m* programmable read only memory (PROM)
programmierbare Tasten *f/pl* programmable keys *pl*, soft keys *pl*
programmieren to program

Programmierer *m* programmer
Programmiergerät *n* programmer, programming unit
Programmierschritt *m* program step
Programmiersprache *f* programming language
programmierte Belichtung *f* computer exposure
programmierte Folgeeinschaltung *f (Druckm.)* programmed in-sequence throw-on
programmierter Maschinenanlauf *m* programmed start-up of machine
programmiertes Drucken *n* programmed printing
Programmierung *f* programming
Programmodul *n* software module
Programmpaket *n* software package
Programmschneider *m (Schnellschneider)* computerized guillotine, programmatic guillotine
Programmschnitt *m (Schneidem.)* programmed cutting
Programmspeicher *m* program memory, program storage
Programm speichern to load the program
Programmsteuerung *f* program control
Programmwahl *f* program selection
progressiver Einzug *m (Satz)* skewed indent
Projektion *f* projection
Projektionsbelichtung *f (Plattenkopie)* projection platemaking; *(Reprofotogr.)* projection exposure
Projektionsebene *f* projection plane
Projektionsfotografie *f* projection photography
Projektionskamera *f* projection camera
Projektionskopie *f (Plattenkopie)* projection platemaking
Projektionsvergrößerung *f (Reprofotogr.)* blow-up, giant reproduction
Proof *m (meist Farbproof)* proof, off-press proof, pre-press proof, pre-scan proof
Proofherstellung *f (meist Farbproof)* proofing, off-press proofing
Proofmaschine *f* proofer
Propellergreifer *m (Heidelberger Tiegel)* propeller-type gripper
proportionaler Abschwächer *m* proportional reducer
Prospekt *m* brochure, folder, leaflet, pamphlet, prospectus
Protokoll *n (Belegausdruck)* hardcopy, log, print-out, protocol, record strip
Protokolldrucker *m* hardcopy printer
prozentuale Flächendeckung *f* percent area coverage, percent dot area
Prozentwert *m* percentage

Prozentzeichen n *(%)* percent sign
Prozeßrechner m process computer
Prozeßschwankungen pl process fluctuations pl, process variations pl
Prozeßstabilität f process stability
Prozeßsteuerung f process control
Prüfbeleg m hardcopy proof
Prüfbit n check bit, parity bit
Prüfdarstellung am Bildschirm f softcopy, softcopy (colour) proof, soft proof, soft proofing, preview
Prüfdruck m siehe Proof
prüfen to check, to control, to examine, to test, to verify
Prüfgerät n test device, testing instrument
Prüfkeil m *(Reprod.)* test wedge
Prüfverfahren n testing method
Prüfzeichen n *(Kontrollzeichen)* check mark
Prüfziffer f *(Comp.)* check digit
Publikation f publication
Puderabsaugung f dust removal, powder removal
Puderautomat m *(Druckbestäubung)* automatic spray powder device, powder sprayer
Puderbehälter m *(Druckbestäubung)* powder container
Puderbestäuber m powder sprayer, spray powder device
Puderdosierung f powder metering
Puderklumpen pl powder lumps pl
pudern to spray
Puderverbrauch m powder consumption
pünktliche Lieferung f on-time delivery
Puffer m buffer
Pufferspule f *(Versandraum)* buffer reel
Puffersubstanzen pl *(Feuchtwasser)* buffer agents pl
Pulper m *(Papierherst.)* pulper
Punkt m *(Interpunktionsz.)* full point, full stop; *(Rasterp.)* dot; *(typogr.)* point
Punktätzung f *(Film)* dot etching
Punktaufbau m *(Film)* dot structure
Punktbildung f *(Rasterpunkt)* dot formation
punktgenaue Wiedergabe f dot fidelity, dot-for-dot reproduction
Punkthof m *(Rasterpunkt)* dot halo
punktieren to dot, to puncture; *(lithogr.)* to stipple
Punktiernadel f stippler
Punktierrädchen n dotting wheel
Punktierstichel m stipple-graver
punktierte Linie f dotted line, dotted rule
Punktleimeinrichtung f spot gluer
Punktleimung f spot gluing

Punktlicht n point light
Punktlichtlampe f point light lamp, point light source
Punktlinie f dotted line, dotted rule
Punktmatrix f *(elektron. Rasterpunkterzeugung)* dot matrix
Punktquetschen n *(Rasterpunkt)* dot squeeze
Punktraster m *(Reprod.)* dot screen
Punktschärfe f *(Rasterpunkt)* dot definition, dot sharpness
punktscharfer Druck m dot-sharp printing
Punktsystem n *(Typogr.)* point system
Punkturen f/pl impaling pins pl, pins pl
Punkturfalzwerk n *(Rollendruckm.)* pin folder
Punkturlöcher n/pl pin holes pl
Punkturnadeln f/pl pins pl
Punkturrand m *(Rollendruck)* pin edge
Punkturzylinder m *(Rollendruckm.)* pin cylinder
Punktverbreiterung f dot enlargement, dot spread
Punktvergrößerung f dot enlargement, dot spread
Punktverkleinerung f dot reduction
Punktzunahme f dot gain
Punktzuwachs m dot gain
Punze f *(lichter Raum zw. den Grundstrichen der Buchstaben)* eye (of type)
Putzbürste f cleaning brush, polishing brush
Putzlappen m cleaning cloth, cleaning rag
Putzwolle f cleaning wool
PVA-Bichromat-Schicht f dichromate polyvinyl alcohol coating
PVA-Bindung f *(Klebebindung)* PVA binding
PVC *(Polyvinylchlorid)* PVC
PVC-Bucheinband m PVC book case
PVC-Etikett n PVC label
PVC-Folie f PVC film
PVC-kaschiert PVC coated, PVC laminated

Q

QR-Effekt m *(Gummituch)* QR effect
Quadrätchen n *(Bleisatz)* em-quad
quadräteln *(Bleisatz)* to quad
Quadrat n *(Ausschluß, Bleisatz)* quad, quadrat; *(geom. Zeichen)* square
Quadratenkasten m *(Bleisatz)* quad case
Quadratenzeile f *(Bleisatz)* white line
quadratieren *(Bleisatz)* to square up

quadratischer Rasterpunkt - Rakelwechsel

quadratischer Rasterpunkt *m* square dot
Quadratmetergewicht *n (Papier)* grammage, grams per sqm, gsm; *Papier mit einem ~ von 120 g* 120 gsm paper
Qualitätsanspruch *m* quality requirement
Qualitätsbeurteilung *f* quality assessment, quality evaluation
Qualitätsdruck *m* high-quality printing
Qualitätskontrolle *f* quality control
Qualitätsmaßstab *m* quality standard
Qualitätsminderung *f* detereoration in quality, quality impairment
Qualitätsniveau *n* quality standard
Qualitätspapier *n* high-quality paper, top-grade paper
Qualitätsprodukt *n* high-quality product, top-grade product
Qualitätsschwankungen *pl* quality fluctuations *pl*, quality variations *pl*
Qualitätsstandard *m* quality standard
Qualitätsüberwachung *f* quality control, quality monitoring, quality supervision
Quecksilberdampflampe *f* mercury vapour lamp
Quellbeständigkeit *f (Gummituch, Walze)* swell resistance
Quellenprogramm *n (Comp.)* source program
Quellensprache *f (Comp.)* source language
Quellfestigkeit *f (Gummituch, Walze)* swell resistance
Quellung *f* swelling
Querfalz *m* cross fold
Querformat *n* landscape size, oblong format
Querformatseite *f* broadside page, oblong page
querheften to stab
Querheftung *f* stabbing
Querleimeinrichtung *f* cross gluing device
Querleimwerk *n* cross gluing unit
Querlinie *f* cross line, cross rule; *(Tabellensatz)* space rule
Querperforierung *f* cross perforation
Querrichtung *f* cross direction; *(Papier) in ~* across the grain, across the web, against the grain, cross grain, cross web
Querschneider *m* cross cutter, sheeter
Querschnitt *m* cross cut
Querstapelauslage *f (Kreuzstapelauslage)* compensated delivery, criss cross delivery
Querstrich *m (bei E, F usw.)* arm; *(Bindestrich)* hyphen; *(Bruchziffer)* stroke
Querverweis *m (im Text)* cross reference
quetschen *(Druck)* to squeeze
Quetschfalte *f (Papier)* crease, wrinkle
Quetschrand *m* dot fringe

Quetschwalze *f* squeeze roller
Quicksetfarbe *f* quick-set ink

R

radieren *(auf Papier)* to erase, to rub out; *(in Kupfer und dergl.)* to engrave, to etch
Radierer *m (Person)* engraver, etcher
Radiermesser *n* erasing knife
Radiernadel *f* dry needle, etching needle
Radierung *f* dry point engraving, engraving, etching
Räderantrieb *m* gear drive
Räderzug *m (Antrieb)* gear train
Rahmen *m (Maschinenrahmen)* frame; *(Schließrahmen)* chase; *(Typogr.)* box, frame
Rahmenkopie *f* frame exposure
Rahmenlinie *f (typogr.)* box rule, frame border
Rahmen mit runden Ecken box with rounded corners
Rahmenprägung *f (Folie)* frame stamping; *(Relief)* frame embossing
Rahmenweite *f (Schließrahmen)* chase width
Rakel *f (Siebdruck)* blade, squeegee; *(Tiefdruck/Anilox)* blade, doctor blade
Rakelanstellung *f (Tiefdruck)* blade setting
Rakelanstellwinkel *m* blade setting angle
Rakeldruck *m (Siebdruck)* screen printing
Rakeleinstellung *f* blade setting
Rakelfarbwerk *n (Anilox)* anilox inking unit
Rakelfase *f* blade tip
Rakelhalter *m* blade holder
Rakellamelle *f* blade tip
Rakelmesser *n* doctor blade
Rakelprofil *n* blade profile
Rakelschlag *m* blade stroke
Rakelschleifen *n* blade grinding
Rakelschleifgerät *n (Siebdruck)* squeegee grinder
Rakelschleifmaschine *f (Tiefdruck)* blade grinder
Rakelstellung *f* blade position
Rakelstreichverfahren *n (Papier)* blade coating process
Rakelstreifen *f* blade streaks *pl*
Rakeltiefdruck *m* gravure (printing), gravure process, photogravure (process), rotogravure
Rakelung *f* doctoring
Rakelwechsel *m* blade change

Rakelwinkel *m* blade angle
RAM-Speicher *m (Comp.)* RAM memory, Random Access Memory
Rand *m (Einfassung)* border; *(Rasterpunkt)* fringe; *(Seitenrand)* margin
randabfallend *(Bilder, Anzeige)* bled-off, bleed
Randanschnitt *m (Bilder, Anzeige)* bleed
Randausgleich *m (Satz)* justification
Randbemerkung *f (Satz, Manuskript)* marginal note, side note
Randbeschnitt *m* edges trimmed, edge trim(ming); **ohne** ~ edges untrimmed
Randbreite *f* margin width
Randgummierung *f (Briefumschläge)* edge gumming
Randheftung *f* flat stitching, side stitching
Randlinie *f* border rule
Randlochung *f (Endlosformulardruck)* line hole punching, line holes *pl*, sprocket hole punching, sprocket holes *pl*
randlos *(Druck, Foto)* bled-off
Randnote *f (Satz)* marginal note, side note
Randschärfe *f* edge definition; *(Fotosatz)* character definition, contour definition, definition of outlines, image definition, image resolution
randscharf with perfect edge definition
Randschleier *m* edge fog
Randstreifenabfall *m (Rollenbeschnitt)* waste edge cuttings *pl*
Randverzierung *f* marginal decoration
Randwelligkeit *f (Papier)* waviness
Randzeichen *n* marginal mark
Randziffer *f* marginal figure
Rapid-Access-Entwickler *m (Reprod.)* rapid access developer
Rapid-Access-Entwicklungsmaschine *f* rapid access processor
Rapid-Access-Film *m* rapid access film
Rapport *m (Musterwdh. im Rollendruck)* repeat, repeat length
Raster *m* halftone screen, screen; *48er* ~ 48 l/cm screen; *(Einkopierraster)* film tint
Rasterabstand *m (Glasraster, Kamera)* screen distance
Rasterätzung *f (Klischee)* halftone engraving, halftone etching
Rasteraufnahme *f* halftone exposure, halftone reproduction, screen exposure
Rasterausgabeeinheit *f (Text/Bildverarb.)* raster image recorder, raster output unit
Rasterauszug *m (gerasterter Farbauszug)* halftone separation, screened separation

Rasterauszugsnegativ *n* halftone separation negative, screened separation negative
Rasterauszugspositiv *n* halftone separation positive, screened separation positive
Rasterbelichtung *f* halftone exposure, screen exposure
Rasterbild *n* halftone image, halftone reproduction, screened image
Rasterbildprozessor *m (RIP)* raster image processor
Rasterdichte *f* screen density
Rasterdrehung *f (Kamera)* screen rotation
Rasterdruck *m* autotype, halftone print, halftone printing
Rastereinstellung *f (Kamera)* screen adjustment
Rastereinziehen *n (Einkopierraster)* tint laying
Rasterfarbauszug *m* halftone colour separation, screened colour separation
Rasterfeinheit *f* screen count, screen definition, screen resolution, screen ruling
Rasterfeld *n (Druckkontrollstreifen)* halftone patch, screen patch, tint patch
Rasterfenster *n (Raum zw. Rasterpunkten)* screen aperture, screen window
Rasterfilm *m (Kontaktraster)* contact screen, screen film; *(Produkt der Aufrasterung)* halftone film, screened film; *(techn. Raster)* film tint, mechanical tint
Rasterfläche *f* screen tint
Rasterfond *m* background tint, screen tint, tint, tinted background
Rasterfotografie *f* camera screening, halftone photography
Rastergenerator *m* siehe Rasterpunktgenerator
Rasterhalter *m (Kamera)* screen holder
Rasterhinterlegen *n (techn. Raster)* tint laying
Raster-Image-Prozessor *m (RIP)* raster image processor
Rasterkassette *f (Kamera)* screen cassette
Rasterkeil *m* halftone wedge
Rasterklischee *n* halftone engraving, halftone etching
Rasterkopie *f (Tiefdruck)* screen copying
Rasterkopierrahmen *m (Tiefdruck)* screen copying frame
Rasterlinienzähler *m* screen counter, screen indicator
rastern to screen
Rasternäpfchen *pl (Tiefdruck)* cells *pl*
Rasternegativ *n* halftone negative, screened negative
Rasteröffnung *f* screen aperture, screen window

Rasterpartien - Redakteursterminal

Rasterpartien *f/pl* halftone areas *pl*, screened areas *pl*
Rasterpositiv *n* halftone positive, screened positive
Rasterprojektion *f* blown-up halftone, screen projection
Rasterprozentwert *m* dot percentage, percent area coverage, percent dot area, screen percentage
Rasterpunkt *m* dot; *(im Rasterbild)* halftone dot; *(in Filmraster, Rasterfonds, Rasterfeldern)* screen dot
Rasterpunktbildung *f* dot formation, dot generation
Rasterpunkte pro Zoll dots per inch *pl*, d.p.i. *pl*
Rasterpunktform *f* dot form, dot shape
Raster(punkt)generator *m (Scanner)* electronic dot generator
Rasterpunktgröße *f* dot size
Rasterpunktschärfe *f* dot definition
Rasterpunktverformung *f* dot distortion
Rasterpunktwiedergabe *f* dot reproduction, rendering of halftone dots
Rasterreproduktion *f* halftone reproduction, screened reproduction
Rasterscandaten *pl* rasterized data
Rastersteg *m (Tiefdruck)* cell wall
Rasterstellung *f (Kamera)* screen position
Rastertiefdruck *m* halftone gravure (process)
Rasterton *m (Rasterfläche)* screen tint
Raster(ton)wert *m* dot percentage, halftone value, screen percentage, screen value, tint level
Rasterumfang *m* halftone range, screen range
Rasterung *f* screening
Rasterunterlegen *n (techn. Raster)* tint laying
Rasterverfahren *n* halftone process
Rastervergrößerung *f* blown-up halftone, halftone enlargement
Rasterverlauf *m* vignetted halftone (screen), vignetted screen tint
Rasterwalze *f* anilox roller, screen roller
Rasterweite *f* screen count, screen definition, screen resolution, screen ruling; ~ **von 48 L/cm** 48 line/cm screen ruling
Rasterwert *m* siehe Raster(ton)wert
Rasterwiedergabe *f* halftone reproduction, rendering of halftone dots
Rasterwinkelmesser *m* screen angle indicator
Rasterwinkelung *f* screen angle
Rasterzähler *m* screen counter, screen indicator
Rastral *n (Instrument zum Ziehen von Notenlinien)* music pen

rauhe Oberfläche *f* rough surface
Rauhheitsprofil *n (Tiefdruckzyl.)* roughness profile
Raumbedarf *m* space requirements *pl*
Raumlicht *n* room light
Raumlichtfilm *m* room light film
Raumlichtkontaktkopiergerät *n* room light vacuum printer
Raumlufttrocknung *f* ambient curing
Raumtemperatur *f* ambient temperature
Raumverteilung *f (Satz)* spacing
Raum zwischen den Spalten *(Zwischenschlag)* column gutter
Rautenraster *m (Reprod.)* rhomb shaped screen
RC-Papier *n (kunststoffbeschichtet)* RC paper, resin-coated paper
Reagenzpapier *n (chem.)* litmus paper
Reaktionszeit *f (Comp.)* response time
Rechenauslage *f (Druckm.)* flyer delivery, rake delivery
Rechenscheibe *f* calculation disc
rechnender Erfassungsplatz *m (Texterf.)* counting input station, counting keyboard, justifying input station
Rechner *m (Comp.)* calculator, computer, controller
rechnergesteuert computer-controlled, computerized
rechnergestützt computer-aided
Rechnerlauf *m (Comp.)* computer cycle, computer run
Rechnerprogramm *n* computer program, computer software
Rechnersatzprogramm *n* computer composition program
Rechnungsformular *n* invoice form
Rechnungskopf *m* bill head, invoice head
rechteckig rectangular
rechte Seiten *f/pl* right(-hand) pages *pl*
rechtsbündig *(Satz)* flush right, quad right
rechtsbündig setzen to adjust text to the right, to set flush right, to move matter to the right
Rechtschreibfehler *m* spelling mistake
Rechtschreibprüfung *f (Texterf.)* spell check, spelling checking
Rechtschreibung *f* orthography, spelling
rechtwinkliger Papiereinlauf *m* right-angle paper in-feed
rechtwinkliger Schnitt *m* right-angle cut, square cut
Rechtwinkligkeit *f* squareness
Redakteur *m* editor
Redakteursterminal *m* journalist workstation

Redaktion f *(Personen)* editorial staff, editors *pl; (Raum)* editorial department, editorial office, newsroom; *(Tätigkeit)* editing, editorial work
redaktionelle Berücksichtigung f editorial coverage
redaktionelle Meldung f *(Agentur)* editorial bulletin
redaktioneller Beitrag m editorial
redaktioneller Bericht m editorial
redaktioneller Teil m *(im Gs. zum Anzeigenteil)* editorial section
Redaktionsabteilung f editorial department
Redaktionsarbeit f editorial work, copy-desk work
Redaktionsbüro n editorial office
Redaktionsprogramm n *(Software)* editorial software; *(Zusammenstellung von Themen)* editorial features *pl*, editorial programme
Redaktionsraum m editorial office, newsroom
Redaktionsschluß m copy deadline, editorial deadline, news deadline
Redaktionssystem n editorial system
Redaktionsthemen *pl* editorial features *pl*
Redaktionszentrale f *(bei Verlagshäusern mit Außenstellen)* central editorial site
redigieren to edit
Redundanz f *(Comp.)* redundancy
Referenzart f *(Marginalie, Fußnote usw.)* reference type
Referenzaufruf m *(Textverarb.)* reference call
Referenzierung f *(Textverarb.)* referencing
Refiner m *(Papier)* refiner
Reflektor m *(Lampe)* lamp housing, reflector
Reflexkopf m *(Lichtschranke)* light beam receiver
Reflexkopie f reflex copy
Regal n *(für Stehsatz, Formen, Satzkästen usw.)* rack
Regal mit Setzpult frame rack
Regal ohne Setzpult case rack
regelbar adjustable
Regelbereich m control range
Regelelektronik f electronic control
Regelgenauigkeit f control accuracy
Regelgetriebe n variable(-speed) gear
Regelkreis m control circuit
regeln to adjust, to control, to govern, to regulate
Regelung f *(techn.)* adjustment, control, regulation
Regelungstechnik f control engineering, control technology

Regenerat n *(Fotochemie)* replenisher; *(für Walze, Gummituch)* rejuvenator
Regenerationsmittel n *(Fotochemie)* replenisher; *(Walze, Gummituch)* rejuvenator
Regeneriereinheit f *(Fotochemie)* replenishing unit
Regenerierung f *(Fotochemie)* replenishment; *(Walze, Gummituch)* rejuvenation
Regenerierung gegen Erschöpfung *(Fotochemie)* replenishment against exhaustion
Regenerierung gegen Oxidation *(Fotochemie)* replenishment against oxidation
Regionalausgabe f *(Zeitung)* regional edition
Regionalbeilage f *(Zeitung)* regional supplement
Regionalmarkt m regional market
Regionalnetz n *(Telekomm.)* regional area network
Regionalteil m *(Zeitung)* regional section
Regionalzeitung f regional newspaper
Register n *(Druck)* register; *(Buch)* index
Registerabweichung f register deviation
Registeranlegetrommel f *(Druckm.)* register feed drum
Registerbeobachtungsgerät n siehe Bahnbeobachtungsgerät
Registerdiagonalverstellung f cylinder cocking, diagonal register adjustment
Registerdifferenz f mis-register, register difference
Registereinschnitte *m/pl (Griffreg.)* index tabs *pl*, register tabs *pl*
Register einstellen to bring into register, register
Registereinstellung f *(Druckm.)* register adjustment, registering, register setting, registration
Registerfernsteuerung f *(Druckm.)* remote register control
Registerfernverstellung f *(Druckm.)* remote register adjustment
registergenau in register, register-true, true to register
Registergenauigkeit f register accuracy, register precision
Registerhalten n register maintenance
registerhaltig in register, register-true, true to register
Register in engen Grenzen halten to maintain register within narrow limits
Registerkontrolle f register control, register monitoring
Registerkorrektur f register correction
Registerlochung f register holes *pl*, register punching

Register machen - Repetiermontage

Register machen to bring into register, register
Registermachen *n* register adjustment, registering, register setting, registration
Registermarke *f* register mark
Registerperforation *f (Griffreg.)* index perforation
Registerregelung *f (Druckm.)* register control
Registerschneidemaschine *f (Griffreg.)* index cutting machine
Registerschneide- und -druckmaschine *f (Griffreg.)* index cutting and printing machine
Registerschnitt *m (Griffreg.)* index cutting, index tab cut
Registerschwankungen *pl (Druck)* register fluctuations *pl*, register variations *pl*
Registerstanze *f* register punch
Registerstanzung *f (Griffreg.)* index cutting; *(Paßlöcher)* register holes *pl*, register punching
Registerstellen *n (Druckm.)* register adjustment, registering, register setting, registration
Registersteuerung *f* register control
Registerstifte *pl (Paßstifte)* register pins *pl*
Registersystem *n (Paßsystem)* register system
Registertoleranz *f* register tolerance
Registerverstellung *f (Druckm.)* register (re-)adjustment
Registerwalze *f (Rollendruckm.)* compensator roller, register roller
Registraturschrank *m* filing cabinet
Reglette *f (Bleisatz)* reglet
Reglettenkasten *m* reglet case
regulierbar adjustable
Reguliergetriebe *n* variable(-speed) gear
Regulierschraube *f* adjusting screw
Regulierung *f* adjustment, control, regulation
Reiber *m (Reibwalze)* distributor roller, oscillating roller
Reiberleder *n* ink roller leather
Reibfarbwerk *n* ink distribution unit
Reibungskupplung *f* friction clutch
Reibwalze *f* distributor roller, oscillating roller
Reibzylinder *m* distributor drum, oscillator drum
Reichbleichgold *n* rich pale gold
Reichgold *n* rich gold
Reihenbauweise *f (Druckmaschinenbau)* unit construction (principle)
Reihenfolge *f* order, sequence
Reihenornament *n* border ornament
Reinätzung *f (Nachätzung)* final etching, fine etching, re-etching
Reinigung *f (Druckm.)* clean-up, wash-up

Reinigungsintervalle *pl (Druckm.)* wash-up intervals *pl*
Reinigungsmittel *n (Platte, Gummituch)* cleaner, wash
Reinigungsrakel *f (Farbwerk)* cleaning blade
Reinigungsvorgang *m (Druckm.)* clean-up, wash-up
Reinigungszeit *f (Druckm.)* clean-up time, wash-up time
Reinschrift *f* fair copy
Reinzeichnung *f* final draft, final drawing, finished artwork
Reisebuch *n (Reiseführer)* travel guide
Reisekarte *f* touring map
Reispapier *n* rice paper
reißen to tear; *(Rollenpapier)* to break
Reißfeder *f* drawing pen
Reißfestigkeit *f* tear resistance, tear strength, tensile strength
Reißlänge *f (Papier)* tear length
Reißprobe *f (Papier)* tearing test
Reißschiene *f* T-square
Reiterwalze *f (Beschwerwalze)* rider roller
Rekorder *m* recorder
relative Luftfeuchtigkeit *f* relative humidity
Reliefätzung *f* relief etching
Reliefbild *n* relief picture
Reliefdruck *m* relief printing; *(Stahlstich)* die-stamping; *(Thermografie)* thermographic printing
Reliefkarte *f (Landkarte)* relief map
Reliefplatte *f (Hochdruck, Polymerplatte)* photopolymer plate, relief printing plate; *(Prägeplatte)* die-plate, embossing plate
Reliefprägemaschine *f* relief embossing machine
Reliefprägung *f* relief embossing; *(blind)* blind embossing; *(mit Folie)* embossed stamping
Reliefschrift *f* relief type
Reliefzurichtung *f* relief makeready
Remalinerlochung *f (Endlosformularherst.)* line hole punching, line holes *pl*, sprocket hole punching, sprocket holes *pl*
Remission *f (Licht)* remission
Remittenden *pl (Buch)* returns *pl*
Renaissance-Antiqua *f (Schrift)* old face, old style
Rentabilität *f* profitability
Reorganisationslauf *m (Comp.)* purge and consolidate run
Reparatur *f* repair
Repetierkopiermaschine *f* step-and-repeat (copying) machine
Repetiermontage *f* step-and-repeat assembly

Repetierschnitt m *(Schneidem., im Gs. zu Einzelschnitt)* repeat cut
Reportage f report(age)
Reporter m reporter
Reproabteilung f process department, repro department
Reproanstalt f photo-engravers pl, process engravers pl, repro house, repro shop, repro studio
Reproanweisung f process instructions pl, process specifications pl
Reproaufnahme f *(Kamera)* reproduction photograph
Reproduktion f *(Bildverarb.)* processing, reproduction; *(Bildwiedergabe)* rendering, reproduction
Reproduktion im Maßstab 1:1 reproduction in actual size, same-size reproduction
Reproduktionsabteilung f siehe Reproabteilung
Reproduktionsanstalt f siehe Reproanstalt
Reproduktionsaufnahme f siehe Reproaufnahme
Reproduktionsautomat m automatic process camera
Reproduktionsfilm m graphic arts film, process film, repro film
Reproduktionsfotograf m siehe Reprofotograf
Reproduktionsfotografie f siehe Reprofotografie
Reproduktionsgeräte pl siehe Reprogeräte
Reproduktionskamera f siehe Reprokamera
Reproduktionsmaßstab m reproduction ratio, reduction scale
Reproduktionsobjektiv n siehe Reproobjektiv
Reproduktionsqualität f siehe Reproqualität
Reproduktionstechnik f *(im U. zur Drucktechnik, Satztechnik usw.)* reproduction technology
Reproduktionstechniken pl *(z. B. Unbunt, UCR usw.)* processing techniques pl, reproduction methods pl, reproduction techniques pl
Reproduktionsverfahren n reproduction process
reproduzierbare Ergebnisse pl repeatable results pl, reproducible results pl
Reproduzierbarkeit f repeatability, reproducibility
reproduzieren to process, to reproduce
reprofähig reproducible, camera-ready, scanner-ready, ready for reproduction
Reprofilm m graphic arts film, process film, repro film
Reprofotograf m camera operator, process cameraman, process photographer, reproduction photographer

Reprofotografie f graphic arts photography, process photography, reproduction photography
Reprogeräte pl reproduction equipment
Reprografie f reprography
Reprokamera f graphic arts camera, process camera, repro camera
Reprokennlinie f process characteristics pl, reproduction characteristics pl
Reproobjektiv n process lens, reproduction lens
Reproqualität f reproduction quality
reproreif camera-ready, ready for reproduction, scanner-ready
Reprotechnik f siehe Reproduktionstechnik(en)
Reprotechniker m process operator, process technician
Reprovorlage f repro artwork, repro copy, repro original
Reprozeichnen n repro-drafting, repro draughting
Reserverechner m back-up computer
Reservewalze f spare roller
Restgitter n *(Nutzenstanzen)* waste skeleton
Restrolle f *(Rollenwechsel)* reel stub, rest roll
Retusche f retouching
Retusche(abzieh)lack m stripping varnish
Retuscheur m retoucher
Retuschierapparat m *(Luftpinsel)* aerograph, airbrush
Retuschierbesteck n retouching tools pl
retuschieren to retouch
Retuschierfarbe f retouching paint
Retuschierfeder f retouching pen
Retuschiermesser n retouching knife
Retuschierpinsel m retouching brush
Retuschierpult m retouching desk
revidieren to revise
revidierte Ausgabe f revised edition
Revision f final proof, revision
Revision lesen to read for press, to revise
Revisionsabzug m final proof, press-proof
Revisionsbogen m clean proof, final proof, press proof, revised proof sheet
Revisor m press revisor
Revolverblende f revolving diaphragm
Rezensent m critic, reviewer
rezensieren to review
Rezension f review
Rezensionsexemplar n review copy
RGB *(Rot Grün Blau)* RGB
Rheologie f *(Druckfarbe)* rheology
rheologische Eigenschaften pl *(Druckfarbe)* rheological properties pl
Riemen m belt

Riemenanleger - Rollenoffset

Riemenanleger *m* belt feeder
Riemenantrieb *m* belt drive
Riemenförderer *m* belt conveyor
Riementransporteur *m* belt conveyor
Ries *n (Papier)* ream
rieselfähiges Druckbestäubungspuder *n* flowing spray powder
Riesenplakat *n* giant poster
Riffelwalze *f* knurled roller
Rille *f* crease
rillen to crease
Rill-Linie *f (Stahllinie zum Rillen)* creasing rule
Rillmaschine *f* creasing machine
Rillmatrize *f* channel matrix, creasing matrix
Rillmesser *n* creasing knife
Rillrad *n* creasing wheel
Rill- und Ritzmaschine *f* creasing and scoring machine
Rillung *f* creasing
Rillwalze *f* creasing roller
rilsanbeschichteter Zylinder *m* rilsan-covered cylinder
Ringbeschichtung *f (Tiefdruck)* ring coating
Ringbindung *f* ring binding
Ringbuch *n* ring binder
Ringheftung *f* ring binding
Ringleitung *f (Comp.)* ring network connection
Ringoptik *f (Densitometer)* ring lens system
Ringordner *m* ring binder
Rippenplatte *f* ribbed plate
RIP (Raster-Image-Prozessor) *m* RIP (Raster Image Prozessor)
Riß *m* tear; *(Rollenpapier)* break
ritzen to score
Ritzen *n* scoring
Ritzlinie *f* score, scoring rule
Ritzmaschine *f* scoring machine
Ritzmesser *n* scoring knife
Ritz- und Rillmaschine *f* scoring and creasing machine
robust *(Maschine)* robust, sturdy
römische Antiqua *f* Roman, Roman face
römische Kapitalschrift *f* Roman capitals *pl*
römische Ziffern *f/pl* Roman figures *pl*, Roman numerals *pl*
Rötel *m (Abdeckfarbe)* red chalk, reddle, red opaque
Rohbogen *m (unbeschnitten)* untrimmed sheet
Rohdaten *pl* raw data
Rohentwurf *m* rough sketch
Rohling *m (Tiefdruckzyl.)* cylinder base
Rohpapier *n* base paper
Rohzylinder *m (Tiefdruck)* cylinder base

Rolle *f (Papier)* reel
Rolle/Bogen-Anleger *m* reel-to-sheet feeder
Rolle/Bogen-Verarbeitung *f* reel-to-sheet processing
Rolle/Falz-Verarbeitung *f* reel-to-fold processing
Rollenabwicklung *f* reel unwinding; *(Vorrichtung)* unwinder, unwind unit
Rollenandruckmaschine *f* proof printing rotary, web-fed proofing press
Rollenantrieb *m (Papierrolle)* reel drive
Rollenaufwicklung *f* reel rewinding, winding-up; *(Vorrichtung)* rewinder, rewind unit
Rollenauslage *f (Auslage auf Rollen)* roller delivery
Rollenbeschickung *f* reel loading
Rollenbeschleuniger *m* reel accelerator
Rollenbreite *f* reel width
Rollenbremse *f* reel brake
Rollenbuchdruck *m* rotary letterpress printing, web-fed letterpress printing
Rollenbuchdruckmaschine *f* letterpress rotary, web-fed letterpress machine
Rollendrehstern *m* reel star, reel turret
Rollendruck *m* rotary printing, web printing
Rollendruckmaschine *f* rotary press, web press
Rolleneinheben *n* reel lifting
Rolleneinhebevorrichtung *f* reel hoist, reel lifting device
Rollenflachformdruckmaschine *f* web-fed flat-bed (printing) press
Rollenförderanlage *f (Papierrollen)* reel conveying system
Rollenförderer *m (Versandraum)* roller conveyor
Rollenfördersystem *n (Papierrollen)* reel conveying system
Rollenhochdruck *m* rotary letterpress printing, web-fed letterpress printing
Rollenhochdruckmaschine *f* letterpress rotary, web-fed letterpress machine
Rollenhülse *f (Papphülse)* reel core
Rollenkaschiermaschine *f* web-to-web laminating machine
Rollenkaschierung *f (im U. zur Taschenkaschierung)* roll(-to-roll) laminating, web-to-web laminating
Rollenkern *m (Rollenhülse)* reel core
Rollenkollator *m (Endlosformularherst.)* roll collator
Rollenkonus *m* reel chuck, reel cone
Rollenlager *n (Papier)* reel storage, reel store; *(Zyl.lager usw.)* roller bearing
Rollenoffset *m* rotary offset, web offset

Rollenoffsetmaschine f offset rotary (press), rotary offset press, web offset press
Rollenpapier n reel paper
Rollenrotation f rotary press, web press
Rollenrotationsdruck m rotary printing, web printing
Rollenrotationsdruckerei f web printer
Rollenrotationsmaschine f rotary press, web press
Rollenrutsche f *(Produktauslage)* roller slide
Rollenschneidemaschine f *(Längsschneider)* reel slitter, slitter-rewinder
Rollenschneider m reel slitter, slitter-rewinder
Rollensiebdruckmaschine f rotary screen printing press
Rollenständer m reelstand
Rollenstand m reelstand; *dreiarmiger ~* three-arm reelstand
Rollenstand mit Drehstern m star-type reelstand
Rollenstern m reel star
Rollentiefdruck m rotogravure
Rollentiefdruckanlage f rotogravure press, web-fed gravure press
Rollentiefdruckmaschine f rotogravure press, web-fed gravure press
Rollentisch m *(Versandraumlinie)* roller table
Rollentransportsystem n *(Papierrollen)* reel handling system
Rollenverarbeitung f reel converting, reel processing
Rollenwagen m *(Papier)* reel truck
Rollenwechsel m reelchange
Rollenwechsler m *(autom.)* automatic paster, automatic reelchange, automatic reel splicer, autopaster, web splicing unit
Rollenzuführung f reel supply
Rolle/Rolle-Verarbeitung f reel-to-reel processing
Rolle/Stapel-Verarbeitung f reel-to-pack processing
Rollfilm m roll film
Rollfilmkamera f roll film camera
Rollfilmkassette f roll film cassette
Rollfilmschneider m roll film cutter
Rollfilmspender m roll film dispenser
Rollneigung des Bogens sheet curling
Rolltuch n *(Schlitzverschluß)* roll shutter
Rollwagen m trolley
Roman m novel; *(Gattung; im U. zu Sachbuch)* fiction
Ronde f *(Schreibschrift)* Ronde
Rostschutz m rust-proofing
Rotation f *(Druckm.)* rotary press, web press
Rotationer m *(Rotationsdrucker)* rotary press minder, rotary printer

Rotationsanleger m rotary feeder
Rotationsausgang m press delivery, web press delivery
Rotationsausstoß m press output, web press output
Rotationsdreischneider m rotary three-knife trimmer
Rotationsdruck m rotary printing, web printing
Rotationsdrucker m rotary press minder, rotary printer, web printer
Rotationsdruckmaschine f rotary press, web press
Rotationsgeschwindigkeit f rotary press speed
Rotationsheftmaschine f rotary stitching machine
Rotationshochdruck m rotary letterpress printing, web-fed letterpress printing
Rotationsleimwerk n rotary gluer
Rotationsmaschine f *(Druckm.)* rotary press, web press
Rotationsmaschinenauslage f press delivery, web press delivery
Rotationsnumeriergerät n rotary numbering box
Rotationsprägewerk n rotary embossing unit
Rotationsschneider m rotary cutter, rotary sheeter, rotary trimmer
Rotationsstanzen n rotary die-cutting
Rotationsstanzform f rotary cutting die
Rotationsstanzmaschine f rotary die-cutter
Rotationsstanzwerkzeug n rotary cutting tool
Rotationstiefdruck m rotogravure
Rotationstiefdruckmaschine f rotogravure press
Rotationszusammentragmaschine f rotary gatherer
rotativer Siebdruck m rotary screen printing
rotativer Zeitungsdruck m rotary newspaper printing
rotempfindlicher Film m red-sensitive film
Rotfilter m red filter
Route f *(Versand)* route
Routenpaketauslage f *(Versandraum)* bundle delivery by route
Routenverteilsystem n *(Versandraum)* route distribution system
Routine f *(Textverarb.)* routine, utility
Rubbelfarbe f rub-off ink
Rubbellos n rub-off lottery ticket
Rubrik f *(Zeitung, Zeitschrift)* column, heading, section
Rubrikkopf m column heading; *mehrspaltiger ~* straddle
Rubriktitel m column heading; *mehrspaltiger ~* straddle
ruckfreier Maschinenanlauf m machine start-up without jerking, machine start-up without jolting

Rückantwort-Briefumschlag *m (Direktmail)* return envelope
Rücken *m* back, backbone, spine
Rücken an Rücken back to back
Rückenbearbeitung *f* back preparation, spine preparation
Rückenbeleimung *f* back gluing, spine gluing
Rückenfalz *m* back fold, spine fold
Rückenfeld *n* panel
Rückenformgebung *f* back shaping, spine shaping
Rückenfräsen *n* back routing, spine routing
Rückenfräser *m* back router, spine router
Rücken/Front back to front
Rückenhöhe *f (Rückenstärke)* spine thickness
Rückenlänge *f* spine length
Rückenleimung *f* back gluing, spine gluing
Rückenpresse *f (zum Runden der Einbände)* backing press
Rückenrundemaschine *f* back rounding machine, spine rounding machine
Rückenrunden *n* back rounding, spine rounding
Rückensäge *f* pad-saw
Rückenschrenz *m* back strip, spine strip
Rückenstichheftung *f* wire-stitching through the back
Rückentitel *m* back title, spine lettering
Rückfederung *f (Gummituch)* recovery
Rückgewinnungsanlage *f* reclamation system, recovery system
Rücklauf *m (mech.)* return movement
Rückmeldung *f (Comp.)* status message
Rückprallelastizität *f (Gummituch)* rebound capacity
Rückschicht *f (Film)* back coating
Rückseite *f* back page, back side, reverse page, reverse side, verso page, verso side
Rückseite beschichtet *(chem. Durchschreibepapier)* coated back (CB)
Rückseitendruck *m* backing-up, back(-side) printing, reverse (side) printing, verso printing
Rückseitenregister *n* back-up register, fit
Rückseitenschwärzung *f (im Druck)* print-through
Rückseite unbedruckt verso blank
Rückstichbroschüre *f* back-stitched brochure, saddle-stitched booklet
Rückstichheftmaschine *f* back-stitcher, saddle-stitcher
Rückstichheftung *f* back-stitching, saddle stitching
Rücktransport *m (Belichter)* reverse leading
Rückvergrößerung *f (Reprofotogr.)* blowback, re-enlargement

rückwärtszählende Numerierung *f* backward numbering
Rückwand *f (Kalender)* back, mount
Rührbütte *f (Papierherst.)* pulp box
Rüstzeiten *f/pl* change-over times *pl*, makeready times *pl*, preparation times *pl*, set-up times *pl*
Rüttelmaschine *f* jogger
Rütteltisch *m* jogger, jogging table
Rüttler *m* jogger
Ruhelage *f* rest position
Ruhestellung *f* rest position
ruhiger Maschinenlauf *m (Druckm.)* smooth running of press
Rundbelichtung *f* siehe Rundumbelichtung
Rundbiegemaschine *f* round bending machine
Rundblende *f* round diaphragm
Runddraht *m* round wire
Runddruckform *f* rotary printing forme
Rundecken *pl* round(ed) corners *pl*
Rundeckenschneider *m* round corner cutter
runde Klammer *f (Satz)* parenthesis
runder Rücken *m* round(ed) back
Rundguß *m (Stereo)* curved stereo casting
Rundlauf *m (Zylinder)* concentric running
Rundschau *f (Titel oder Rubrik)* review
Rundschreiben *n (Kleinstdrucksache)* circular letter
Rundstapelanleger *m* rotary pile feeder
Rundstereo *n* curved stereo, round stereo
Rund(um)belichtung *f* all-round exposure, circular exposure
Rundumbeschnitt *m (an allen vier Seiten)* all-around square trim, four-sided trimming
Runzel *f (im Papier)* crease, wrinkle
Runzelkorn *n* collotype grain, reticulated grain
rupfempfindlich susceptible to picking
Rupfen *n* picking
Rupffestigkeit *f* picking resistance, sizing strength
Rutschauslage *f* chute delivery, slide delivery

S

Sachregister *n (Buch)* subject index
Sack *m* bag, sack
Sägezahneffekt *m (Schrift)* saw-tooth effect, serrated effect

Sägezahnschnitt - Satzprogramm

Sägezahnschnitt *m* serrated cut
Säule f *(Abstrich beim Buchstaben)* stem
Säulenpresse f *(Druckpresse)* column press
Säurebad *n* acid bath
Säureentwicklung f acid development
säurefestes Papier *n* acid-proof paper
säurefreies Papier *n* acid-free paper
Saffianeinband *m* morocco(-leather) binding, saffian(-leather) binding
Sammelauszüge *m/pl (Farbauszüge)* ganged separations *pl*
Sammelbogen *m (Mehrnutzenverarb.)* combination sheet, gang sheet, mixed sheet
Sammelform f *(verschiedene Aufträge in einer Form)* combined forme, gang forme, mixed forme
Sammelhefter *m (Druckverarb.)* gang-stitcher, gatherer-stitcher
Sammelheftung f gang stitching, gathering-stitching
Sammelkanal *m (Transportkette in Sammelheftern, Zusammentragm.)* raceway
Sammelleitung f *(Datenkomm.)* bus
Sammellinse f convex lens
Sammelproduktion f *(Rollendruck)* collect-run production
Sammeltrommel f collecting cylinder, collector drum, gathering drum
Sammelzylinder *m* collecting cylinder, collector drum, gathering drum
Sammler *m (Zeilengießm.)* assembler
Samtpapier *n* velvet paper
Sandwich-Montage f multi-layer montage
sanfter Maschinenanlauf *m* smooth machine start-up
Satellitendruckwerk *n (Rollenoffsetm.)* satellite printing unit
Satellitenfernsehen *n* satellite television
Satellitenübertragung f *(Telekomm.)* satellite transmission
Satellitenverbindung f satellite link
Satinage f *(Papier)* calendering, glazing
Satinfarbe f satin ink
satinieren to calender, to glaze
Satinierkalander *m (Papierherstl.)* glazing calender, glazing machine, super calender
satiniertes Papier *n* calendered paper, glazed paper
Satinierwalze f glazing roller
satte Farbgebung f *(Druckm.)* deep inking
Sattel *m (Drahtheftm.)* saddle; *(für Druckplattenbefestigung)* saddle; *(Schneidem.)* backgauge

Sattelantrieb *m (Schneidem.)* backgauge drive
Sattelhefter *m* saddle-stitcher
Sattelheftung f saddle stitching
Sattelposition f *(Schneidem.)* backgauge position
Sattelrechen *m (Schneidem.)* backgauge rake
Sattelspindel f *(Schneidem.)* backgauge screw
Sattelstand *m (Schneidem.)* backgauge position
Sattelvorschub *m (Schneidem.)* backgauge advance
satter Auftrag *m* rich application
satte Vollfläche f dense solid, high-density solid
Satz *m (Schriftsatz)* composition, composition work, setting, type matter, typeset matter, typesetting, typesetting work, matter
Satzabzug *m (Fahne)* galley proof, text proof
Satzanordnung f typographical arrangement
Satzanweisung f typographical instruction, typographical specification
Satzarbeit f composition work, typesetting job
Satz auf Mitte stellen to center type
Satzbefehl *m (Fotosatzm.)* typesetting code, typesetting command, typesetting instruction
Satzberechnung f *(Umfang)* calculation of volume, cast-off, character count, copyfitting, estimate of volume
Satzbetrieb *m* typesetting operation
Satzbreite f line length, line measure, measure, setting width
Satzbrett *n (Bleisatz)* type board
Satzfehler *m* compositor's error, keyboarding error, typing error
Satzfläche f type area
Satzform f *(Form des Satzes)* shape of type matter; *(im U. zur Bilderform)* type forme
Satzformatierung f composition formatting
Satzgestaltung f typographical arrangement, typography
Satzherstellung f typesetting production
Satzhöhe f page depth
Satzkante f *(Satzrand)* margin
Satzkapazität f typesetting capacity
Satzkode *m* typesetting code
Satzkommando *n* typesetting command
Satzkorrektur f editing, typesetting correction; *(angezeichnete)* mark-up
Satzkosten *pl* typesetting costs *pl*
Satzmontage f text assembly
Satzmuster *n* type specimen
Satzparameter *m* typesetting parameter
Satzpreis *m (für Herst. des Satzes)* typesetting price
Satzprogramm *n (Fotosatz)* composition program, typesetting program

Satzrand - Schalenätzung

Satzrand *m* margin
Satzrechner *m* typesetting computer
Satzregeln *pl* typesetting rules *pl*
satzreif ready for typesetting
Satzsoftware *f* composition software, typesetting software
Satzspiegel *m* image area, type area
Satzspiegelbreite *f* image width
Satzspiegelhöhe *f* image depth
Satzsystem *n* composition system, typesetting system
Satztermin *m* typesetting deadline
Satzvorbereitung *f* copy mark-up, copy preparation, mark-up
Satzvorlage *f* copy, manuscript, setting copy, text copy
Satzvorverarbeitung *f* text pre-processing
Satzzeichen *n* punctuation mark
sauberer Abzug *m* clean proof
Sauganleger *m* suction feeder
Saugbändertisch *m* (Anleger) suction tape feed table
Saug/Blasluft *f* (Bogentrennung) suction and air blast
Saugbürste *f* (Anleger) suction brush
Saugdüse *f* suction nozzle
Saugerkippung *f* (Anlegersaugkopf) sucker tilting
saugfähiges Papier *n* absorbent paper
Saugfähigkeit *f* (Papier) absorption capacity
Saugkopf *m* (Anleger) suction head
Saugluft *f* suction air
Saugpapier *n* absorbent paper; (Löschpapier) blotting paper
Saugplatte *f* (Kamera) suction plate
Saugstange *f* suction bar
Saugstapelanleger *m* suction pile feeder
Saugvermögen *n* (Papier) absorption capacity
Saugwalze *f* suction roller
Saugwand *f* (Kamera) suction board, suction plate
Scan *m* scan
Scan-Densitometer *m* scan(ning) densitometer
Scanformat *n* (Abtastformat) scan area, scan format, scanning size
Scanlinie *f* scanline
Scanliniensignal *n* scanline signal
Scanlinienstrahl *m* scanline beam
scannen to scan
Scannen *n* scanning
Scanner *m* scanner
Scannerausgabegerät *n* scanner recorder, scanner output unit

Scannerauszug *m* (Farbauszug) scanner separation
Scannereichung *f* scanner calibration
Scannereingabegerät *n* scanner reader, scanner input unit
Scannereinstellgerät *n* scanner set-up device
Scannereinstellung *f* scanner setting, scanner set-up
scannerfähig scanner-ready
Scannerkalibrierung *f* scanner calibration
Scanner-Kontaktraster *m* scanner contact screen
Scanner mit Rasterpunktgenerator *m* EDG scanner, electronic dot generator scanner
Scanner-Operator *m* scanner operator
Scannerrekorder *m* scanner recorder
Scannervorbereitung *f* scanner preparation, scanner set-up
Scannervoreinstellgerät *n* pre-scanning device
Scanraster *m* scanning raster
Scanvorlage *f* scanning copy
Schaben *n* (Film/Klischee) scraping
Schaber *m* scraper
Schabernadel *f* scraper
Schabkunst *f* mezzotint (engraving)
Schablone *f* (Siebdruck) stencil
Schablonendruck *m* (Siebdruck) screen printing
Schablonenfilm *m* stencil film
Schablonengewebe *n* stencil fabrics *pl*
Schablonenherstellung *f* stencil making
Schablonenöffnung *f* stencil opening
Schablonenpapier *n* stencil paper
Schablonenschrift *f* stencil lettering
Schablonieren *n* (Druckproblem) ghosting
Schabmesser *n* scraper, scraping knife
Schachbrettpunkt *m* (Rasterreprod.) square dot
Schachtel *f* box, carton
Schachtelaufrichter *m* (Faltschachtelherst.) box erector
Schachtelbeklebemaschine *f* box covering machine, box lining machine
Schachteldeckel *m* box cap, box cover, box lid
Schachteleckenverbindemaschine *f* box corner staying machine
Schachtelgeradrichter *m* (Faltschachtelherst.) box aligner
Schachtelüberziehmaschine *f* box covering machine, box lining machine
Schärfe *f* acutance; (Fot.) definition, sharpness
Schärfentiefe *f* (Fot.) depth of focus
schätzen (Satzumfang u. ä.) to calculate, to estimate
Schaft *m* (des Buchstabens) shank
Schalenätzung *f* tray etching

Schalenentwicklung f *(Reprod.)* tray development, tray processing
schalldämmende Verkapselung f noise-abating enclosure, sound-absorbing covering, sound-deadening casing
Schallisolierung f sound insulation
Schallplattenalbum n record album
Schallplattenetikett n record lable
Schallplattenhülle f record cover, record sleeve
Schallschutz m noise abatement
Schallschutzabdeckung f noise reduction hood, sound insulating cover
Schallschutzverkleidung f sound-proof enclosure
Schaltbild n wiring diagram
Schaltbrett n control panel, switchboard
Schalter m switch
Schaltgetriebe n switch gear
Schalthebel m control lever
Schaltkasten m *(Steuerung)* control box, switchbox
Schaltknopf m switch button
Schaltkreis m switch circuit
Schaltpult n control console, control desk
Schaltschrank m control box, switchbox, switch cabinet
Schalttafel f console, control panel, switchboard
Schaltungsdruck m *(elektron. Schaltungen)* circuitry printing
Scharfätzung f final etching, fine etching, re-etching
scharfe Kante f sharp edge, sharply defined edge
scharfer Druck m sharp impression, sharp print
scharfer Wettbewerb m tough competition
scharfes Bild n sharp image
scharf(kantig)er Falz m sharp-edged fold, tight fold
scharfstellen *(Kamera)* to focus
Scharfstellung f *(Kamera)* focusing, focus setting
Scharte f *(Rakel)* notch
Schattenmaske f *(Reprod.)* shadow mask
Schattenpartien f/pl *(Bild)* shadow areas pl
Schattenrahmen m *(Typogr.)* shaded box
Schattenstellen f/pl *(im Bild)* shadow areas pl
Schattenstich m *(Farbstich in Schattenpartien)* shadow cast
schattierte Schrift f shaded type
Schaubild n chart, diagram, graph
Schaufelradauslage f *(Rollendruckm.)* fan delivery, paddle wheel delivery, spider wheel delivery
Schaufensterdisplay n shop-window display
Schaumbildung f foam formation
Schaupackung f display package

Scheckdruckmaschine f cheque printing machine
Scheckfarbe f cheque ink
Scheckformular n cheque form
Scheckheft n cheque book
Schecknumerierung f cheque numbering
Scheckpapier n cheque paper
Scheckvordruck m cheque form
Scheibenanleger m disc feeder
Scherengittertisch m lattice feed table
Scherschnitt m shear cut
scheuerfest abrasion-proof, abrasion-resistant, rub-proof, scuff-resistant
Scheuerfestigkeit f abrasion resistance, rub resistance, scuff resistance
Schicht f film, layer; *(Filmschicht)* emulsion; *(Plattenschicht)* coating
Schicht auf Schicht *(Filmkopie)* emulsion against emulsion
Schichtdicke f coating thickness, layer thickness
Schichtempfindlichkeit f *(Film)* emulsion sensitivity, emulsion speed; *(Platte)* coating sensitivity
Schichtgravur f *(Kartogr.)* coating engraving
Schichtseite f *(Film)* emulsion side
Schichtseite oben *(Film)* emulsion (side) up
Schichtseite unten *(Film)* emulsion (side) down
Schichtwechsel m *(Arbeitsschicht)* shift change
Schichtzeichnen n *(Vorlagenherst.)* overlay drafting, overlay draughting
Schiebe/Dublierfeld n *(Druckkontrollstreifen)* slur/doubling patch
Schiebekopie f fanned exposures pl, multiple plate exposures pl, step exposures pl
Schiebemarke f *(Bogenausrichtung)* push guide, push sidelay
Schiebemontage f montage for step exposures
Schieben n *(Druckproblem)* slur
Schieber m *(Winkelhaken)* sliding bar
Schieberanleger m shuttle feeder
Schieberblende f sliding diaphragm
Schieblehre f sliding calliper
schiefer Bogen m cocked sheet, out-of-square sheet
Schieferpapier n slate paper
schieferschwarz slate black
schiefstehender Satz m *(Bleisatz)* fallen type, hanging type
schiefwinklige Anlage f out-of-square feed(ing)
schiefwinklige Falzung f cocked folding, out-of square folding
Schiff n *(Setzschiff)* galley
Schilfpapier n reed paper
Schimmelbogen m blind print, blind sheet

Schirting m *(Drucktuch)* shirting
Schlaglicht n *(Bild)* strong light
Schlagpresse f *(Maternprägung)* moulding press
Schlagschatten m *(Typogr.)* drop shadow
Schlagtaster m *(Notausschalter)* emergency stop button, stop safe push button
Schlagzeile f catchline, headline, news headline
Schlangenlinie f wavy line, wavy rule
Schlangenlinienverzierung f guilloche
Schlauchverbindung f hose connection
Schlaufenheftung f loop stitching
Schlaufenspeicher m *(Rollendruckm.)* festooning unit
schlecht ausgerichtet out of alignment
schlechte Buchstaben pl *(Bleisatz)* battered type
schlechte Raumverteilung f uneven spacing
schlechter Bogen m bad sheet
schlechter Druck m bad printing, poor printing
schlechter Passer m imperfect register
schlechtes Manuskript n bad copy
schlechtes Papier n low-grade paper, low-quality paper
schlechtsaugendes Papier n poorly absorbent paper
Schleichgang m *(Maschine)* crawl speed, slow gear, worm drive
Schleierbildung f *(Film)* fogging; *(Lichthof)* halation, halo formation; *(Siebdruck)* scumming
Schleierfreiheit f *(Film)* absence of fog, anti-halation
Schleifbild n *(Tiefdruckzyl.)* polishing structure
schleifen *(Messer)* to grind, to sharpen; *(Platte)* to grain; *(Stein, Zylinder)* to polish
Schleifkohle f grinding charcoal
Schleifkopf m *(Tiefdruckzyl.)* polishing head
Schleifkugeln pl *(Plattenkörnung)* graining balls pl, graining marbles pl
Schleifmaschine f grinding machine; *(Tiefdruckzyl.)* polishing machine
Schleifmittel n abrasive
Schleifsand m *(Lithostein)* graining sand
Schleifscheibe f grinding disc
Schleifstein m grinding stone
Schleif- und Körnmaschine f grinding and graining machine
Schleif- und Poliermaschine f *(Tiefdruck)* grinding and polishing machine
Schleppe f *(Siebdruck)* squeegee
Schleppsauger m *(Saugkopfanleger)* forwarding sucker, pull sucker
Schleuder f *(Plattenselbstbeschichtung)* whirler

Schleuderfeuchtwerk n centrifugal damping system
Schlieren pl streaks pl
Schließe f *(beim Buch)* clasp
schließen *(Buchdruckform)* to lock up, to quoin
Schließgeviert n *(Bleisatz)* M quad
Schließkeil m *(Bleisatz)* quoin
Schließplatte f *(Bleisatz)* imposing stone, imposing table
Schließquadrat n *(Bleisatz)* M quad
Schließrahmen m *(Bleisatz)* chase, lock-up frame
Schließrahmenhalter m *(Tiegel)* chase holder
Schließstege pl *(Bleisatz)* furniture
Schließtisch m *(Bleisatz)* imposing table
Schließvorrichtung f *(Bleisatz)* lock-up device
Schließzeug n *(Bleisatz)* quoin
Schlitten m slide; *(Kamera)* carriage
Schlittenführung f slide rails pl
Schlittenkamera f carriage-type camera
Schlitz m slot
Schlitzblende f slit diaphragm
Schlitzen n slotting
Schlitzloch n slot
Schlitzlochung f slot perforation
Schlitzmaschine f slotting machine
Schloß n *(Buch)* clasp
Schlüsselschalter m lock switch
Schlupf m slippage, slip(ping)
schlupffrei slip-free, slippage-free
Schlußpunkt m *(Interpunktion)* full stop
Schluß-s n *(ß)* German final s
Schlußtermin m *(Redaktion, Anzeigen)* closing date, deadline
Schlußzeile f *(auf einer Seite)* bottom line
Schmalbahn f *(Papier)* long grain
Schmalbahnpapier n long grain paper
Schmalbandfilter m *(Densitometer)* narrow-band filter
schmale Antiqua f condensed Roman
schmale Grotesk f condensed Grotesque
schmale Schrift f condensed typeface
schmales Format n narrow size
schmalfette Schrift f bold condensed typeface
schmallaufende Schrift f condensed typeface
Schmelzbecken n melting pot
Schmelzhaftkleber m permanent contact hotmelt
Schmelzkessel m melting pot
Schmelzkleber m hotmelt (adhesive)
Schmelzmetall n melting material
Schmelzofen m melting furnace
Schmelztiegel m melting pot
Schmiedestahl m forged steel
Schmierbüchse f grease cup

schmieren to grease, to lubricate
Schmieren *n (Druckproblem)* smearing, smudging
Schmierfett *n* lubricating grease
schmierfreie Auslage *f* smear-free delivery, smudge-proof delivery
Schmiermittel *n* lubricant
Schmiernippel *m* grease nipple, lubricating nipple
Schmieröl *n* lubricating oil
Schmierstelle *f* greasing point, lubrication point
Schmierstellen *pl (auf Druckbogen)* markings *pl*
Schmitz *m* mackle, slur
schmitzen to mackle, to slur
Schmitzleisten *f/pl (Flachdruckpresse)* bed bearers *pl*
Schmitzring *m* bearer ring, cylinder bearer
Schmitzringabstreifer *m* bearer ring wiper
Schmitzringhöhe *f* bearer height, cylinder undercut
Schmitzringläufer *m (Druckmaschinentyp)* bearer-to-bearer printing press
Schmitzringpressung *f* bearer-to-bearer pressure
Schmuckfarbe *f* decorative colour; *(zweite Farbe neben Schwarz)* spot colour
Schmuckrahmen *m (Typogr.)* ornamental box
Schmuckschrift *f* decorative type, fancy type, ornamented type
Schmutzbogen *m/pl (Abschmutzbogen)* set-off sheets *pl*
Schmutzfleck *m* smudge
Schmutzpartikel *pl* dirt particles *pl*
Schmutztitel *m* bastard title, fly-title, half title, mock title
Schnappschuß *m* snapshot
Schneckenantrieb *m* worm drive
Schneckengetriebe *n* worm gear
Schneidabfall *m* cutting waste, shavings *pl*, trimmings *pl*, trim waste
Schneidabfallabsaugung *f* trim exhaust, trim waste extraction
Schneidabfallbeseitigung *f* trim removal system
Schneidbefehl *m (Fotosetzm.)* cut command
Schneidefilm *m* cutting film
Schneid(e)linien *f/pl* cutting rules *pl*
Schneid(e)marken *f/pl (Bildverarb.)* crop marks *pl*; *(Druckbogen)* cutting marks *pl*, trim marks *pl*
Schneid(e)maschine *f* cutter, cutting machine, guillotine
schneiden to cut, to trim
Schneid(e)rädchen *pl (Längsschneiden)* slitting wheels *pl*

Schneid(e)stapel *m* cutting pile
Schneidgut *n* cutting material
Schneidleiste *f (Schneidem.)* cutting bar, cutting stick
Schneidmaschinenmesser *n* cutting blade, cutting knife
Schneidmesser *n* cutting blade, cutting knife
Schneidrollen *pl (Längsschneiden)* slitting wheels *pl*
Schneidwalze *f* cutting roller, slitting roller
Schneidzylinder *m (Rollendruckm.)* cut-off cylinder, cutting cylinder, knife cylinder
Schnelläufer *m (Druckm.)* high-speed press
Schnelldrucker *m (Sofortdruckerei)* instant printer, instant printshop, minute printer, quick-print shop; *(Gerät)* high-speed printer
schnelle Bogenfreigabe *f* quick (sheet) release; *(Gummitucheigenschaft)* QR effect
schnelles Zum-Druck-Kommen *n* quick getting to print
Schnellpaßsystem *n* instant register system, quick register system
Schnellpresse *f (Buchdruckpresse)* automatic cylinder press
Schnellschneider *m* high-speed cutter
Schnellschußauftrag *m* rush order
Schnellspannschiene *f (Druckplatte)* quick-action clamping bar
Schnelltrennperforation *f (Formularherst.)* snap-out perforation
Schnelltrennsatz *m (Formularsatz)* snap-apart set, snap-out set
schnelltrocknende Farbe *f* fast-drying ink, quick-drying ink, quick-set ink
Schnitt *m* cut, trim(ming)
Schnittandeuter *m (Schneidem.)* cutting line indicator
Schnittanzahl *f* number of cuts
Schnittauslösung *f (Schneidem.)* cut release
Schnittbedruckautomat *m (Buchherst.)* edge printer
Schnittbogen *m (Schnittmuster)* pattern
Schnittbreite *f* cutting width
Schnittfärbemaschine *f (Buchherst.)* edge colouring machine
Schnittfolge *f (Schneidem.)* cutting sequence
Schnittgenauigkeit *f* cutting accuracy, trim accuracy
Schnittgeschwindigkeit *f* cutting speed
Schnittgrat *m* cutting burr
Schnittkanten *pl* cut edges *pl*, cutting edges *pl*, trim(med) edges *pl*; *(Filmkanten)* film edge markings *pl*, film edges *pl*

Schnittkraft f cutting pressure
Schnittlänge f (Schneidem.) cutting width
Schnittmarken f/pl (Bildverarb.) crop marks pl; (Druckbogen) cutting marks pl, trim marks pl
Schnittmaß n (Schneidem.) cutting measurement
Schnittmuster n (Zeichnung) pattern
Schnittmusterbeilage f (Zeitschrift) pattern supplement
Schnittmusterbogen m pattern
Schnittposition f (Schneidem.) cut position
Schnittregister n (Druck) cut-off register, cutting register, print-to-cut register; (im Mehrstrang-Rollendruck) web-to-web register
Schnittregistersteuerung f (Rollendruckm.) cut-off register control
Schnittreihenfolge f siehe Schnittfolge
Schnittschablone f (Siebdruck) cut film stencil
Schnittstelle f (Interface) interface
Schnittvergolder m (Buch) edge gilder
Schnittvergoldung f (Buch) edge gilding
Schnittwerkzeug n cutting tool
Schnittwerkzeug zum Vergolden gilding tool
Schnittzähler m (Schneidem.) cut counter
Schnittzeichen f/pl siehe Schnittmarken
Schnitzel pl (Abfall) scrap, shavings pl, shred, trimmings pl
Schnüre pl (Heftschnüre) bands pl, cords pl
Schnürloch n (Öse) eyelet
Schöndruck m face printing, first-run printing, front-side printing, one-sided printing, single-sided printing; (im U. zu Schön- und Widerdruck) straight colour printing
Schöndruckform f first forme
Schöndruckmaschine f straight printing (only) press
Schöndruckseite f (Druckbogen) front side, recto side, top side
Schöndruckwerk n front-side printing unit
Schön- und Widerdruck m face and back printing, perfecting, printing and perfecting, printing both sides, recto/verso printing; (im U. zu Umschlagen, Umstülpen usw.) work and back
Schön- und Widerdruckform f work and back forme
Schön- und Widerdruckmaschine f perfecting press, perfector
Schön- und Widerdruck-Offsetmaschine f offset perfector
Schön- und Widerdruckseite f (Papier) front and back side, recto and verso side, top and under side
Schön- und Widerdruckwerk n perfector unit, printing and perfecting unit
Schöpfwalze f dip roller, pan roller
Schokoladeneinwickler m chocolate wrapper
Schrägbogen m (Anlage) cocked sheet, misaligned sheet, out-of-square sheet
Schrägbogenkontrolle f misaligned sheet detector
schräge Ecke f cut-off corner
schräggestellt (Fotosatz) pseudo-italic, slanted
Schrägrollenauslage f angled-roller delivery
Schrägschneider m (Kuvertherst.) angle cutter, diagonal cutter
Schrägschnitt m (Buch) oblique edge
Schrägstellung f (elektronisch im Fotosatz) backslanting
Schrägstrich m (Satz) diagonal stroke, oblique stroke, shilling stroke, slash, solidus
schrägverzahnt helically toothed
schrägverzahnte Antriebsräder pl helical (drive) gears pl
Schraffe f (Landkarte) hatching
Schraffierapparat m hatching apparatus
schraffieren to hatch
Schraffierlineal n hatching ruler
schraffierte Schrift f hatched type
Schraffierung f hatching
Schraffur f hatching
schraubenloses Farbwerk n keyless inking system
Schraubenpresse f screw press
Schraubenrahmen m (Schließrahmen) screw chase
Schraubenschlüssel m spanner, wrench
Schreibblock m writing pad
Schreibdichte f (Scanner) recording density, scanline density, scanning density
schreiben (aufzeichnen) expose, to plot, to record, to scan
Schreibfeder f lettering pen
Schreibfehler m (Rechtschreibfehler) spelling mistake
Schreibheft n copy book, exercise book
Schreibheftumschlag m copy book cover
Schreibkopf m (Scanner) recording head, scanning head
Schreibkunst f calligraphy
Schreib/Lesekopf m (Comp.) write/read head
Schreib-Lese-Speicher (RAM) m random access memory (RAM)
Schreibmaschinenmanuskript n typescript, typewritten copy
Schreibmaschinenschrift f typewriter face
Schreibpapier n writing paper

Schreibsatz m *(z. B. IBM-Composer)* composer setting, typewriter composition
Schreibschriften pl *(Schriftklassif.)* Scripts pl, script types pl
Schreibsetzmaschine f typewriter composing machine
Schreibtischkalender m diary
Schreibung f *(Rechtschreibung)* spelling
Schreibweise f *(Rechtschreibung)* spelling
Schrift f type, characters pl, face, typeface, typestyle, font, fount
Schriftabnutzung f *(Bleisatz)* type wear
Schriftart f typestyle, face, typeface
Schriftbild n type design, typeface, typestyle
Schriftdecker m *(Reprod.)* lettering overlay
Schriftdicke f character width, font width, set width, width of letter
Schriftenbibliothek f font library, type library
Schriftenfertigung f typeface production
Schriften im direkten Zugriff *(Fotosatz)* directly accessible fonts, fonts in direct access, online fonts, online typefaces
Schriften mit Einheitsabstand unit count fonts pl
Schriften mit Proportionalabstand unitized fonts pl
Schriftenprogramm n library routine
Schriftenspeicher m *(Fotosatz)* font memory, font storage
Schriftentwicklung f typeface development
Schriftfamilie f type family
Schriftform f *(im U. zur Bilderform)* type forme
Schriftfundament n *(Buchdruck)* type bed
Schriftgattung f type group
schriftgerechte Darstellung f *(Bildschirm)* true-typographic display, real type display, WYSIWYG display
Schriftgießer m *(Fabrik)* type founder
Schriftgießerei f *(Fabrik)* type foundry
Schriftgießmaschine f *(Zeilengießmaschine)* type casting machine
Schriftgrad m body size, character size, point size, type size
Schriftgradbereich m point size range
Schriftgröße f body size, character size, point size, type size
Schriftgrößenabstufung f *(Fotosatzm.)* character sizing increments
Schriftgrößenbereich m point size range
Schriftgrößeneinstellung f *(Fotosatzm.)* character sizing
Schriftguß m cast type, foundry type, type casting, type founding
Schrifthobel m *(Bleisatz)* type planer

schrifthoch type-high
Schrifthöhe f character height, type height; *(Bleisatz)* height to paper
Schrift in negativ lettering reversed white on black, type reversed white on black
Schriftkasten m letter case, type case
Schriftkastenregal n type cabinet, type rack
Schriftkegel m body size, type body
Schriftkontur f character outlines pl
Schriftkünstler m type designer
Schriftkunst f typography
Schriftlegierung f type alloy
Schriftleiter m *(Redaktion)* editor
Schriftlinie f baseline, type line
Schriftlinienhaltung f *(Fotosatz)* baseline alignment
Schriftlinienverschiebung f baseline shifting
Schriftmater f type matrix
Schriftmaterial n type material
Schriftmetall n printer's metal, type metal
Schriftminimum n *(Bleisatz)* minimum weight fount
Schriftmischen n mixing of typefaces
Schriftmodifikation f type modification
Schriftmuster n type specimen
Schriftmusterblatt n type specimen sheet
Schriftmusterbuch n type specimen book, type specimen collection
Schriftmustersammlung f type specimen collection
Schriftname m typeface name
Schriftornament n printer's flower, type ornament
Schriftprägung f type embossing
Schriftprobe f type specimen
Schriftqualität f type quality
Schriftrasterung f screening of type
Schriftregal n *(Bleisatz)* type cabinet
Schriftsatz m lettering, type matter, typeset matter, typesetting
Schriftscheibe f *(optomechanische Belichter)* font disc, grid
Schriftschneiden n punch cutting, type cutting
Schriftschnitt m type design, typeface, typestyle
Schriftsetzer m compositor, typesetter
Schriftstärke f weight
Schriftsteller m author, writer
Schriftstempel m punch
Schriftträger m font, type carrier
Schrifttype f type
Schriftweite f character set, character width, set (size), set width, width of letter

Schriftwiedergabe f rendering of type, type reproduction
Schriftzeichen n character, letter
Schriftzeichner m type designer
Schriftzeichnung f type design, typeface drawing
Schriftzeile f type line
Schriftzeug n printer's metal, type metal
Schriftzug m lettering
Schrittmotor m servo motor, stepping motor
schrittweiser Ausbau m *(modulares System)* step by step expansion
Schrumpfbanderolierung f *(Versandraum)* shrink sleeving
Schrumpffolie f *(Folienverp.)* shrink film
Schrumpffolienverpackung f *(Versandraum)* shrink (film) wrapping
Schrumpfobjektiv n *(Reprod.)* anamorphic lens
Schrumpfpackanlage f *(Versandraum)* shrink-wrap installation
Schrumpftunnel m *(Folienverp.)* shrink tunnel
Schrumpfung f *(Papier)* shrinkage
Schuber m *(Buch)* slip carton, slip case
Schublehre f sliding calliper
Schüttelauslage f jogging delivery
Schüttelmaschine f jogger
Schulbuch n school book
Schulheft n exercise book
Schulheftmaschine f exercise book making machine
Schulter f *(Buchstabe)* shoulder
Schulwörterbuch n school dictionary
Schummern n *(Kartogr.)* ground hatching
Schuppe f *(Schuppenstrom)* shingle
Schuppenabstand m *(Schuppenstrom)* copy-to-copy distance, shingle spacing
Schuppenanlage f overlap feeding, stream feeding
Schuppenanleger m stream feeder
Schuppenauslage f shingle delivery, stream delivery
Schuppenband n shingling belt, stream conveyor
Schuppeneinlauf m stream in-feed
Schuppenlücke f stream gap
Schuppenstrom m copy stream, shingle stream
Schuppenstromadressierung f shingle-stream addressing
Schuppentrennung f shingle separator, stream separator
Schusterjunge m *(Satz)* orphan
Schutzabdeckung f guard cover, protective cover
Schutzblech n guard plate
Schutze pl *(Unfallverhütung an Maschinen)* guards pl, safeguards pl, safety guards pl

Schutzfarbe f *(Offsetplattenlagerung)* storage ink
Schutzgitter n guard grid, protective grid
Schutzhaube f guard hood, protection hood
Schutzkarton m *(Buchschuber)* slip carton, slip case
Schutzlackierung f *(Druck)* protective coating, protective varnishing
Schutzschicht f photoresist, protective coating, protective layer, resist
Schutzumschlag m *(Buch)* book jacket, book wrapper, dust cover, dust jacket, jacket, wrapper
Schutzumschlagklappe f *(Buch)* jacket flap
Schutzumschlagmaschine f *(Buchherst.)* book jacketing machine
Schutzumschlagumlegen n jacket wrapping
Schutzvorrichtung f safety guard
Schwabacher f *(Schrift)* Black Letters and Broken, broken types pl, old black
schwacher Druck m faint impression
Schwärze f *(Farbe)* black ink
Schwärzung f *(Fot.)* blackening, density
Schwärzungskurve f *(Reprod.)* density curve
Schwärzungsüberschuß m *(Reprod.)* excess density
Schwankungen pl *(Prozeß)* fluctuations pl, variations pl
Schwarz n black
Schwarzauszug m *(Reprod.)* black separation
Schwarzdruckwerk n *(Zeitungsrotation)* mono(-colour) unit
schwarze Farbe f black ink
Schwarzfilm m *(Auszugsfilm)* black film, black key, black printer, black skeleton
Schwarzform f black forme
Schwarzplatte f black key, black plate, black printer, black skeleton
Schwarzschildeffekt m *(Fot.)* reprocity effect
schwarzweiß black and white; *(einfarbig)* monochrome, monocolour
Schwarzweißabbildung f black and white illustration
Schwarzweißaufnahme f black and white exposure, black and white photo(graph)
Schwarzweißbild n black and white picture
Schwarzweißdensitometer n black and white densitometer
Schwarzweißdia n black and white transparency, monochrome transparency
Schwarzweißfoto n black and white photo(graph)
Schwarzweißoriginal n black and white original
Schwarzweißscanner m black and white scanner, monochrome scanner

Schwarzweißvorlage f black and white original, black and white artwork, monochrome original

Schwebetrockner m *(Rollendruckm.)* floatation dryer

schwefelsaures Elektrolyt n *(Galv.)* sulphuric electrolyte

Schweinsleder(ein)band m *(Einband)* pigskin binding

Schweißstation f *(Folienverp.)* sealing station, welding station

Schweizer Broschur f Swiss brochure

Schweizerdegen m compositor-pressman

Schwellenwert m *(Meßtechnik)* threshold value

schwenkbarer Kopierrahmen m flip-top vacuum frame

schwere Fläche f heavy solid

schwere Form f heavy forme

schweres Papier n high-grammage paper

Schwertfalz m *(Bogenfalzung)* knife-fold; *(Rollendruck)* chopper fold

Schwertfalzmaschine f knife folder, knife folding machine

Schwertöffnung f *(Falzbogenanlage)* sword opening

Schwingfundament n *(Maschine)* swinging foundation

Schwinggreifer m swing gripper

Schwingschnitt m *(Schneidem.)* swinging shear cut

Schwingspiegel m *(Optik)* oscillating mirror

Schwingung f *(Maschine)* vibration

schwingungsarmer Lauf m *(Maschine)* low-vibration running

schwingungsdämpfend vibration absorbent

schwingungsfreier Maschinenlauf m vibration-free machine run

Schwungrad n fly-wheel

Scrollen n *(Bildschirmfunktion)* scrolling

Sechzehnseitenprodukt n *(Rollendruck)* sixteen-page product

Sechzehnseiten-Rollenrotation f sixteen page rotary press

segmentierte Platte f *(Comp.)* segmented disk

segmentiertes Farbmesser n segmented ink duct blade

Seidendruck m silk printing

Seidengewebe n *(Siebdruck)* silk fabrics

seidenmatter Glanz m matt satin finish

Seidenpapier n tissue paper

Seite f *(Buch, Zeitschrift usw.)* page;
vierspaltige ~ four-column page

Seite im Hochformat deep page, upright page

Seite im Querformat broadside page, oblong page

Seitenabzug m *(Text)* page proof

Seitenanlegemarke f *(Bogenanlage)* side guide, side lay

Seitenanordnung f page layout

Seitenanschlag m *(Bogenführung)* side guide aligner, side lay, side stop

Seitenanzahl f number of pages, page count, pagination

Seitenaufbau m *(typogr.)* page composition, page layout

Seitenaufbereitung f *(typogr.)* page planning

Seitenaufriß m page dummy, page layout

Seitenbelegung f *(Zeitungsrotation)* page combination pattern, page imposition, page placement

Seitenbeleimung f side gluing

Seitenbeleimungsgerät n side gluer

Seitenbeschreibungssprache f page description language

Seitenbreite f *(Typogr.)* page width

Seitendrucker m page printer

Seitenendfilm m final page film

Seitenentwurf m *(Typogr.)* page dummy, page layout

Seitenformat n page format, page size

Seitenführung f *(mech.)* side guide

Seitengestell n *(Masch.)* side frame

seitenglatter Film m final page film, full-page film, one-piece page film

Seitengröße f page format, page size

Seitenheftung f *(seitliche Heftung; im U. zur Rückstichheftung)* flat stitching, side stitching

Seitenhöhe f page depth

Seitenkoordinaten pl *(elektron. Seitenumbruch)* page coordinates pl

Seitenlage f *(hoch/quer)* page orientation

Seitenlayout n page layout

Seitenleimung f *(seitliche L.)* side gluing

Seitenmarke f *(Bogenanlage)* side guide, side lay

Seitenmontage f page make-up, page assembly, page composition, pagination

Seitenmontagesystem n page make-up system, page assembly system, pagination system

Seitennumerierung f *(Paginierung)* folios pl, page numbering, paging

Seitenpaar n center spread, double(-page) spread, two-page spread

Seitenplanung f *(Typogr.)* page planning

Seitenrahmen m *(Druckm.)* side frame

Seitenrand m margin

Seitenraster - Setzer

Seitenraster *m (Typogr.)* layout pattern, page grid, page layout
Seitenregister *n (im U. zu Umfangsreg.)* lateral register, side(lay) register
seitenrichtig right-reading; *(Film)* emulsion (side) up
Seitenschweißgerät *n (Folienverp.)* side sealing device, side welding unit
Seitensteg *m* side stick
Seitentitel *m (Typogr.)* header
Seitenumbruch *m* page make-up, page assembly, page composition, pagination
Seitenumbruchsystem *n* page make-up system, page assembly system, pagination system
Seitenumfang *m (Druckprodukt)* number of pages, page content, page count, pagination
Seitenumkehr *f (Reprod.)* lateral reversal
seitenverkehrt wrong-reading, laterally reversed, mirror image, right-left reversed; *(Film)* emulsion (side) down
Seitenwand *f (Druckm.)* side frame
Seitenzahl *f (Anzahl)* number of pages, page content, page count, pagination; *(Nummer)* folio, page number
Seitenzahl am Fuß drop folio
seitliche Ausrichtung *f* lateral alignment
seitliche Heftung *f (im U. zur Rückenstichheftung)* flat stitching, side stitching
seitliches Wandern der Bahn *(Rollendruck)* lateral shifting of web
seitliche Verreibung *f (Farbe)* lateral distribution
seitlich verstellbar laterally adjustable
Seitwärtsbewegung *f* lateral movement
Sekundärfarben *pl (Farbsystem)* secondary colours *pl*
selbstanpressender Presseur *m* elastic impression roller, self-compensating impression roller
selbstbeschichtete Druckplatte *f* in-house sensitized printing plate
Selbstbeschichtung *f (Platte)* in-house coating, in-house sensitizing
Selbstdurchschreibepapier *n (chem.)* autocopying paper, carbonless copy paper, NCR paper, self-copying paper
Selbstdurchschreibesatz *m (Formularsatz)* carbonless forms set, NCR forms set
Selbstklebe(druck)tuch *n (Endlosformularm.)* self-adhesive blanket, sticky-back blanket
Selbstklebeetikett *n (Haftetikett)* pressure-sensitive label, self-adhesive label, self-sticking label
Selbstklebeumschlag *m* self-sealing envelope

selbstschmierende Lager *pl* self-lubricating bearings *pl*
selbsttrennende Formularsatzleimung *f* self-separating forms set gluing
Selbstverleger *m* author-publisher
selektive Farbkorrektur *f* selective colour correction
selektives Einstecken *n (Zeitung)* selective inserting
Selfmailer *m* selfmailer
Semiduplex-Betrieb *m (Telekomm.)* semi-duplex mode
Semikolon *n* semicolon
Sender *m (Telekomm.)* sender, transmitter
Senderseite *f (Telekomm.)* transmission site
Sendestation *f (Telekomm.)* transmitting station
Senken und Heben *n (Schneidgut)* lowering and lifting
Senkrechtstapelauslage *f (Buchherst.)* vertical stack delivery
Sensibilisator *m (Fotochemie)* sensitizer
sensibilisieren to sensitize
Sensibilisierung *f* sensitizing
Sensitometrie *f* sensitometry
Sensor *m* sensor
Sensortaste *f* sensor key
separat angetriebenes Aggregat *n* independently driven unit, individually driven unit
Separierwerkzeug *n (Nutzentrennung nach Stanzen)* blanking tool, separating tool, stripping tool
Sepia *f* sepia
sepiabraun sepia brown
Sepiapause *f* sepia dye
sequentieller Zugriff *m (Comp.)* sequential access
Sequenz *f (Zeichenfolge)* string
Serie *f (Zeitung)* running story
serienmäßig standard
serienmäßige Ausstattung *f* standard equipment
Serif *m* serif
Serifenbetonte Linear-Antiqua *f (Schriftklassif.)* Slab Serif, Mechanistics *pl*
serifenbetonte Schrift *f* serif typeface
Serifenlose Linear-Antiqua *f (Schriftklassif.)* San Serif, Lineals *pl*
serifenlose Schriften *pl* sans-serif typefaces *pl*
Serifenschrift *f* serif typeface
Servicefreundlichkeit *f (Masch.)* ease of servicing
Servicenetz *n* service network
setzen *(Schrift)* to compose, to set, to typeset
Setzer *m (Schriftsetzer)* compositor, typesetter

Setzerei f composition room, composition shop, typesetting department, typesetting house, typeshop
Setzerlehrling m apprentice typesetter
Setzfehler m compositor's error, keyboarding error, literal error, spelling mistake, typing error
Setzkasten m letter case, type case
Setzkasteneinteilung f case lay
Setzlinie f composing rule, setting rule
Setzmaschine f typesetter, typesetting machine
Setzmaschinenzeile f slug
Setzmaterial n *(Bleisatz)* typesetting material
Setzpult n *(Bleisatz)* composing frame, compositor's desk
Setzregal n *(Kastenregal)* case rack, composing rack
Setzregeln pl typesetting rules pl
Setzschiff n *(Bleisatz)* galley
Setz- und Gießmaschine f typesetting and casting machine
Shore-Härte f *(Gummituch)* shore hardness
Sicherheitsfarbe f safety ink
Sicherheitsfilm m safety film
Sicherheitspapier n *(Wertpapierdruck)* security paper
Sicherheitsstopptaste f emergency stop button, stop safe push button
Sicherheitsverriegelung f *(Abdeckung, Maschinenteil)* safety lock
Sicherheitsvorschriften pl safety regulations pl
sichern *(Comp.)* to back up, to secure
Sicherung f *(Comp.)* back-up
Sicherungsdaten pl *(Comp.)* back-up files pl
Sichtkontrolle f *(Bildschirm)* visual check(ing), visual control, visual monitoring
Siderografie f *(Ätzung in Stahl)* siderography
Sieb n *(Siebdruck)* screen, mesh
Siebdruck m screen printing, silk-screen printing
Siebdrucker m screen printer
Siebdruckerei f screen printer, screen printshop
Siebdruckfarbe f screen printing ink
Siebdruckform f screen (process) printing forme, screen stencil
Siebdruckformherstellung f stencil making
Siebdruckfotoschablone f screen process photo-stencil
Siebdruckgaze f screen gauze
Siebdruckgewebe n screen fabrics
Siebdruck-Kopierrahmen m screen printing frame
Siebdruckmaschine f screen printing machine; *(klein)* screen printer
Siebdruckrahmen m screen frame

Siebdruckschablone f screen stencil
Siebdruckschablonenfilm m screen stencil film
Siebentfetter m screen degreaser
Siebentschichter m stencil remover
Siebfüller m screen filler
Siebpartie f *(Papiermaschine)* wire section
Siebseite f *(Papier)* wire side
Siebwaschgerät n screen washer
Siegelfalzautomat m folding and sealing machine
Siegelmarke f sealing label
siehe Manuskript see copy
Signatur f *(Bogen)* signature; *(Buchstabenmatrize)* nick
Signet n *(Typogr.)* logo
Signieren n *(Versandraum)* marking
Sikkativ n *(Trocknerzusatz)* siccative
Silbe f syllable
Silbentrennprogramm n *(Textverarb.)* hyphenation program, hyphenation software
Silbentrennung f *(Textverarb.)* hyphenation; **automatische** ~ hyphenation routine
Silbentrennung und Ausschließen *(Unterprogramm)* H&J, hyphenation and justification
Silbentype f *(Handsatz)* logotype
Silberbad n *(Fot.)* silver bath
Silberbromid n silver bromide
Silberbronze f silver bronze
Silberdiffusionsverfahren n *(Reprod.)* diffusion transfer process
Silberdruckfarbe f silver printing ink
Silberfilm m *(Fotogr.)* silver film
Silberhalogenid n *(Silberfilm)* silver halide
Silbermaske f *(Farbreprod.)* silver mask
Silberrückgewinnungsanlage f silver recovery unit
Silbersalz n *(Silberfilm)* silver salt
Silbersalz-Diffusions-Verfahren n *(Reprod.)* diffusion transfer process
Silhouette f silhouette
Silikonauftragsgerät n *(Rollendruckm.)* silicone applicator
Silikonbeschichtung f silicone application, silicone coating
Silikon-Elastomer n *(Gummituchspaltversiegelung)* silicone-elastomer
Silikonspray n silicone spray
Silikonsprüheinrichtung f *(Rollendruckm.)* silicone spray device
Silikonstempel m *(Prägen)* silicone rubber die
Simplex-Betrieb m *(Telekomm.)* simplex mode

Simultanbetrieb - Spannkanal

Simultanbetrieb m *(Comp.)* simultaneous operation
Simultanmeßkopf m *(Scan-Densitometer)* simultaneous measuring head
Skala f scale
Skalenblau n *(Cyan)* process blue
Skalendrucke pl *(Andruck)* progressive proofs pl, progs pl
Skalenfarben pl *(für autotyp. Vierfarbdruck)* process colours pl, process inks pl
Skalengelb n process yellow
Skalen-Handrad n dial handwheel
Skalenrot n *(Magenta)* process red
Skelettschwarz n *(Auszugsfilm)* ghost key, skeleton black
Skizze f dummy, layout, outline, rough sketch, sketch
SM-Papier n *(Schreibmaschinenpapier)* typing paper
soeben erschienen just published, hot off the press
Sofortbild n *(Polaroid usw.)* instant picture
Sofortbildsystem n instant picture system
Sofortdruck m *(Service)* instant printing, express printing
Sofortdrucker m instant printer, instant printshop, minute printer, quick-print shop
Sofortzugriff m *(Daten, Schriften usw.)* instant access
Softcopy f *(Prüfdarstellung am Bildschirm)* softcopy
Softcoverbindung f *(Broschürenbindung)* soft-cover binding
Softproof m *(Prüfdarstellung am Bildschirm)* soft proof
Software f software
Software-Befehlskette f routine
softwaregestützt software-based
Softwarepaket n software package
Softwarepflege f software update
Solarisation f solarization
Solarisationseffekt m *(Fotogr.)* solarization effect
Soll-Höhe f *(Satz)* nominal depth
Soll/Ist-Vergleich m nominal and actual value comparison
Sollwert m nominal value, reference value, target value
Solo-Maschine f *(im U. zum Inline-Aggregat)* off-line machine, stand-alone machine
Sonderausgabe f special edition, special issue
Sonderbeilage f *(redaktionell)* special supplement
Sonderdruck m offprint, reprint, special print

Sonderfarbe f *(Druckfarbe außerhalb der Skalenfarben)* special colour
Sonderheft n *(Zeitschrift)* special edition, special issue
Sondernummer f *(Zeitschrift)* special edition, special issue
Sonderzeichen n *(Satz)* pi-character, special character
Sonderzeichen n/pl peculiars pl
Sonderzeichenfont m *(Fotosatz)* pi-font
Sonderzubehör n *(Masch.)* optional accessories pl
Sonnen pl *(Reprod.)* sun spots pl
Sonntagsausgabe f Sunday issue
Sonntagsblatt n Sunday paper
Sonntagszeitung f Sunday paper
Sorter m *(Kleinoffset)* sorter
Sortieranlage f *(Versandraum)* sorter
sortieren to sort
Sortierkennung f *(Comp.)* sort(ing) code
Sortierlauf m *(Comp.)* sort(ing) run
Sortiermaschine f sorting machine
Sortierprogramm n *(Comp.)* sort(ing) program
Sortierquerschneider m *(Papierherst.)* cutter-sorter, single-roll cutter-sorter
Sortierschlüssel m *(Comp.)* sort(ing) key
Sortierung f sorting
Sortimentsbuchhändler m retail bookseller
Späne pl *(Buchherst.)* chips pl, shavings pl, trimmings pl
Späneabsaugung f shavings extraction
Spätausgabe f late issue
späterer Einbau m later installation
Spalte f *(in Zeitung, Zeitschrift)* column
Spaltenabziehpresse f galley proof press
Spaltenabzug m galley proof, slip proof
Spaltenausgabe f *(Fotosatz)* galley output
Spaltenbelichtung f *(Fotosatz)* galley exposure
Spaltenbreite f *(Satz)* column measure, column width
Spaltenhöhe f *(Satz)* column depth
Spaltenkopf m column heading
Spaltenlinie f column rule
Spaltensatz m column composition, column matter, column setting
Spaltenschiff n *(Bleisatz)* column galley
Spaltenschneider m *(Montage)* column cutter
spaltenweise in columns
spaltenweise setzen to set in columns
Spaltschutz m *(Zylindereinlauf)* nip guard
Spaltverschluß m gap sealing
Spanndorn m **pneumatischer** ~ air jack
Spannkanal m *(Druckmaschinenzyl.)* cylinder gap, lock-up gap

Spannkopf m *(Rollenständer)* core chuck
Spannleiste f *(Druckmaschinenzyl.)* clamping bar, locking bar
Spannrahmen m *(Siebdruck)* stretching frame
Spannschiene f *(Druckmaschinenzyl.)* clamping bar, locking bar
Spannsystem n *(Druckmaschinenzyl.)* lock-up system
Spatien pl *(Bleisatz)* spaces pl
Spatienkeil m *(Zeilengießmaschine)* spaceband
spationieren to space
Spationieren n character spacing, letterspacing, text spacing
Spatium n *(Bleisatz)* space
Speckstein m soap stone
Speicher m *(Comp.)* buffer, memory, storage
Speichergröße f *(Comp.)* core size, memory size, storage capacity
Speicherkapazität f storage capacity
Speichermedium n storage medium
speichern *(Comp.)* to store
Speicherrollenwechsler m *(Rollendruckm.)* zero-speed web splicer
Speicherung f storage
Speicherzugriffszeit f *(Comp.)* memory access time
Spektralanalyse f *(Farbmessung)* spectral analysis
Spektralbereich m spectral range
spektrale Empfindlichkeit f *(Kopierschicht, Fotoemulsion)* spectral sensitivity
spektrale Farbdichte f spectral colour density, spectral ink density
spektrale Farbdichtemessung f *(Druck)* ink density measurement
spektrale Lichtverteilung f *(Lichtquelle)* spectral light distribution
Spektralfarbe f spectral colour
Spektralfotometer n *(Farbmessung)* spectrophotometer
spektralfotometrische Messung f *(Farbmessung)* spectrophotometric measurement
Spenderkassette f *(Fotomaterial)* supply cassette
sperren to space
Sperren n *(Satz)* character spacing, letterspacing, text spacing
Spezialeffektraster m special effect screen
Spezialfarbe f *(Druckfarbe)* special ink
Spezialrechner m dedicated computer
Spezialsystem n *(Comp.)* dedicated system
spezifisches Volumen n *(Papier)* bulk(ing) index

Sphäroguß m *(Maschinenrahmen)* alloy cast iron, nodular cast iron, spherical cast iron, spheroid casting alloy
Spiegelschrift f mirror type
spielfrei *(Getriebe)* without backlash
Spielkarten pl playing cards pl
Spielkartenkarton m playing cardboard
Spieße pl *(Bleisatz)* blacks pl, fall-out, pull-out, rising spaces pl
Spießen n rising of spaces
Spindelantrieb m *(Schneidem.)* screw drive
Spindelpresse f screw press
Spiralbindemaschine f *(Buchb.)* spiral binding machine
Spiralbindung f spiral binding
Spiralbürstenfeuchtwerk n *(Offset)* spiral brush damping system
Spiraldraht m spiral wire
Spiraldrahtbindung f spiral wire binding
Spiralfalz m fan fold, spiral fold
Spiralfalzer m fan folder, spiral folder
spiralgebundene Broschüre f spiral-bound brochure
Spiralheftung f spiral binding
spiralisierte Broschüre f spiral-bound brochure
spitze Kopie f pinsharp copy
Spitzenbelastung f peak load
Spitzengeschwindigkeit f top speed
Spitzenleistung f peak performance
spitzerätzen *(Rasterpunkt)* to sharpen the dots
spitzermachen *(Rasterpunkte)* to sharpen the dots
spitzer Punkt m *(Raster)* highlight screen dot
Spitzkolumne f *(Ausgangskolumne)* short page
Spitzlichter pl *(Rasterbild)* highlight dots pl, highlights pl
Spitzpunktfeld n *(Druckkontrollstreifen)* highlight patch, small dot patch
splendider Satz m loosely spaced matter, open matter, widely-spaced matter
Splitfilterbelichtung f *(Reprod.)* split filter exposure
Spotfarbe f *(Zusatzfarbe)* spot colour
Spotretusche f *(im Gs. zur Vollretusche)* localized retouching, spot retouching
Sprachaufschlag m *(Fremdsprachensatz)* extra charge for foreign language setting
Springsauger m *(Saugkopfanleger)* spring sucker
Spritzapparat m *(Retusche)* aerograph, airbrush, spray gun
Spritzpistole f *(elektron. Bildverarb.)* airbrush; *(manuelle Vorlagenherst.)* spray gun
Spritzretusche f airbrushing, airbrush retouching
Spritzschablone f airbrush stencil

Spritztechnik - Stanzformenmacher

Spritztechnik f airbrushing
spröde *(getrocknete Farbe)* brittle
Sprühbeleimung f *(im Gs. zur Walzenbeleimung)* spray gluing
Sprühfeuchtwerk n *(Offset)* spray damping system
Spülbecken n *(Plattenentwicklung)* sink, wash basin
spülen to rinse, to wash
Spültrog m *(Plattenentwicklung)* sink, wash basin
Spule f *(Draht)* spool; *(zur Zwischenlagerung von Vorprodukten)* reel
Staatsanzeiger m official gazette
Staatsdruckerei f government printer
Stabhygrometer n *(Stapelfeuchte)* sword-type hygrometer
Stabilisationsfilm m *(Reprod.)* stabilization film
Stabilisationspapier n stabilization paper
Stabilisator m *(Fotochemie)* stabilizer
Stabthermometer n *(Stapelwärme)* sword-type thermometer
Stacker m *(Stapler)* stacker
Stärkekleister m starch glue
Stärkemesser m *(Meßgerät)* thickness gauge
Stärkemischleim m mixed starch glue
Stärkepuder m *(Druckbestäubung)* starch powder
Stärketoleranz f *(Gummitücher)* piece-to-piece gauge tolerance
Stärkeverlust m *(Gummituch)* gauge loss, thickness loss
Stahlätzung f steel engraving
Stahlbandmaß n steel tape measure
Stahldrahtbürste f steel wire brush
Stahlgalvano n steel-plated electrotype
Stahlguß m steel casting
Stahllinie f steel rule
Stahlreiber m *(Walze, Zylinder)* steel distributor
Stahlstecher m die stamper, steel(-plate) engraver
Stahlstempel m steel die, steel punch
Stahlstich m die-stamping, steel(-plate) engraving
Stahlstichbronze f die-stamping bronze
Stahlstichdruck m die-stamping
Stahlstichdruckfarbe f die-stamping ink
Stahlstichgravur f steel(-plate) engraving
Stahlstichhandpresse f die-stamping hand press
Stahlstichimitation f imitation die-stamping
Stahlstichprägepresse f die-stamping press
Stahlstichpresse f die-stamping press
Stahlstützpresseur m *(Tiefdruck)* steel back-up roller
Stahlunterbau m steel base

Stahlwalze f steel roller
Stammbaum m *(Satzart)* family tree
Stammblende f *(Reprofotogr.)* basic lens aperture
Stammdaten pl *(Comp.)* master file data
Stammdatensatz m *(Comp.)* master file, master record
Stammdatenverwaltung f master file management
Stammkunde m regular customer
Stand m position, register
Standard m standard
Standardformat n standard format, standard size
standardisieren to standardize
standardisierter Mehrfarbenoffsetdruck m standardized process-colour offset printing
Standardisierung f standardization
Standardprogramm n *(Comp.)* standard software
Standbogen m *(Montage)* imposition sheet, line-up sheet, planning and assembling grid, sheet layout, planning sheet
Stand der Technik state of the art
Standentwicklung f tank development
Standfilm m *(Montage)* film grid, imposition film, layout film, planning film
Standfläche f *(Maschine)* floor space
Standgenauigkeit f *(Register, Druckbild)* positioning accuracy, register accuracy
Standmachen n positioning, registering
Standmachen der Platte n plate positioning, plate registering
Standskizze f imposition layout
Stangenanleger m *(Druckverarb.)* bundle feeder
Stangenauflösung f *(Druckverarb.)* break-up of bundles
Stangenbeschickung f *(Druckverarb.)* bundle loading
Stangenbildung f *(Druckverarb.)* bundle formation
Stangenbündler m *(Druckverarb.)* stacker-bundler
Stangenpresse f *(Druckpresse)* lever-press
Stangenverarbeitung f *(Druckverarb.)* bundle processing
Stannioldruckmaschine f tin-foil printing press
Stanze f *(Registerlochung)* punch
Stanzen n *(Lochstanzen)* punching; *(Nutzenstanzen/Formstanzen)* die-cutting
Stanzfalz m perforation fold
Stanzform f *(Nutzenstanzen/Formstanzen)* cutting die, cutting forme, die-board, die-cutting forme, die-plate, steel rule die
Stanzformenbau m die-making
Stanzformenmacher m die-maker

Stanzform-Laserschneider *m* laser die-board cutter
Stanzgegenzurichtung *f (Nutzenst.)* counter die, counter plate
Stanzhub *m* cutting stroke, punching stroke
Stanzlinien *pl (aus Stahl)* cutting rules *pl*, steel rules *pl*
Stanzmaschine *f (Lochstanzen)* punching machine; *(Nutzenstanzen/Formstanzen)* die-cutter, die-cutting machine
Stanzmesser *n* cutting die
Stanznutzen *m* blank
Stanzperforation *f* punch perforation
Stanzplatte *f* cutting die, die-plate
Stanzpresse *f* cutter-creaser, die-cutting platen press
Stanzregister *n* punching register, die-cutting register, print-to-cut register
Stanzstempel *m (Lochst.)* punch, punching tool
Stanztiegel *m* cutter-creaser, die-cutting platen press
Stanztype *f* punching letter, punching type
Stanzwerkzeug *n* punching tool
Stanzzurichtung *f (Nutzenstanzung)* makeready of cutting-die
Stapel *m (Comp.)* batch; *(Endlosstapel)* pack; *(Papierbogen)* pile, stack
Stapelanleger *m* pile feeder
Stapelauslage *f* pile delivery
Stapelausleger *m* pile delivery
Stapelbestäubung *f* pile spraying
Stapelbetrieb *m (Comp.)* batch mode
Stapelbildung *f* pile formation
Stapelbrett *n* pile board
Stapelbrettpuffer *m* pile board buffer
Stapelbrettregal *n* pile board shelf
Stapelendplatte *f* pile end board
Stapelfeuchte *f* pile humidity
Stapelheber *m* pile elevator
Stapel hochfahren to raise the pile
Stapelhöhe *f* pile height
Stapelkollator *m (Endlosformularherst.)* pack collator
Stapelkreuzleger *m (Versandraum)* compensating stacker
Stapellift *m* pile hoist, stacklift
Stapelmagazin *n (Druckverarbeitungsmaschinen)* pile magazine
Stapelmarkierung *f* pile marking
stapeln to pile (up), to stack
Stapeloberkante *f* top edge of pile
Stapelplatte *f* pile board
Stapelrechen *m (Ausleger)* stacking rake

Stapel senken to lower the pile
Stapelsenkung *f* pile descent, pile drop, pile lowering
Stapel/Stapel-Eindruckmaschine *f* pack-to-pack imprinter
Stapeltemperatur *f* pile temperature
Stapeltisch *m* pile board; *absenkbarer ~* descending pile board
Stapelverarbeitung *f (Comp.)* batch processing
Stapelverhalten *n (Druckfarbe)* piling properties *pl*
Stapelvibrator *m* pile vibrator
Stapelwärme *f* pile temperature
Stapelwechsel *m* pile change
Stapelwender *m* pile reverser, pile turner
Stapelzähler *m* batch counter
Stapler *m (Stacker)* stacker
starker Kontrast *m* high contrast
starkes Papier *n* strong paper
Startknopf *m* start button
statische Aufladung *f* static charge, static loading
statische Elektrizität *f* static electricity
statischer Speicher *m (Comp.)* static memory
statistische Qualitätskontrolle *f* statistical quality control
Staubänder *pl (Versandraum)* buffer belts *pl*
staubdicht dust-tight
Stauben *n (Papier)* dusting, linting
staubfrei dust-free
staubig dusty
Stauchbiegen *n (Pappe)* rough bending
stauchen *(Falzung)* to buckle
Stauchfalz *m* buckle fold
Stauchfalzung *f* buckle folding
Staustrecke *f (Versandraum)* buffer section
Stautaktförderer *m (Versandraum)* accumulation conveyor, roller accumulating conveyor
Stearin *n* stearin
Steatitkugeln *pl* steatite marbles *pl*
stechen *(Kupferstich usw.)* to engrave
Stechhygrometer *n (Stapelfeuchte)* sword-type hygrometer
Steckblende *f* sliding diaphragm
Steckkarte *f (Comp.)* plug-in circuit board
Steckkontakt *m (Comp.)* plug-in connection
Steckmodul *n (Comp.)* plug-in module
Steckschriftkasten *m* display type case
Steckverbindung *f (Comp.)* plug-in connection
Steg *m (Blei)* furniture, stick; *(Tiefdruckrastersteg)* cell wall; *(Typogr., z. B. Bundsteg)* gutter, margin
Stegregal *n (Bleisatz)* furniture cabinet

Stehendbogenauslage f *(Druckverarb.)* upright sheet delivery
stehende Bahn f *(Rollendruck)* standing web
stehender Sattel m *(Schneidem.)* stationary backgauge
stehender Stapel m vertical pile
stehendes Bild n *(Bahnbeobachtung)* stationary image
stehendes Format n *(Rollendruck)* long cut-off, long grain
Stehform f standing forme
Stehmanuskript n canned copy
Stehmontage f assembly for reuse, standing forme
Stehsatz m live matter, standing matter; *(Fotosatz)* long-term data, long-term storage
Stehsatzkonvertierung f conversion of standing matter
Steifbroschur f stiff paper binding
steifes Material n rigid material, stiff material
steifes Papier n stiff paper
Steigung f *(Densitometer)* slope
steile Gradation f steep gradation
Steilheit f *(Densitometer)* slope
Steindruck m lithograph, lithographic printing, lithography, stone printing
Steindruckfarbe f lithographic printing ink
Steindruckgummiwalze f lithographic rubber roller
Steindruckhandpresse f lithographic hand press
Steindruckklederwalze f lithographic leather roller
Steindruckpapier n lithographic printing paper
Steindruckpresse f lithographic press
Steinglättung f *(Tiefdruckzyl.)* agate smoothing
Steingravur f stone engraving
Steingrund m stone surface
Steinkarren m stone carriage
Steinkopie f stone transfer
Steinkopierrahmen m stone copying frame
Steinlithografie f stone lithography
Steinradierung f stone engraving
Steinschleifen n stone graining, stone polishing
Steinzeichnung f lithographic drawing
Stellenanzeigen pl *(Rubrik)* situations pl, vacancies pl
Stellglied n *(Farbzonenfernverstellung)* actuator, motorized adjusting element, servo-component
Stellmotor m servomotor
Stellrad n adjusting wheel
Stellschraube f adjusting screw
Stellung f *(Bild, Text)* position

Stempel m *(Prägestempel)* die, punching die; *(Stanzstempel)* punch; *(zum Stempeln)* stamp
Stempelfarbe f stamp ink
Stempelgummi m stamp rubber
Stempelpresse f *(Handpresse)* hand press
Stempelschneiden n *(Schriftstempel)* punch cutting
Stereo n stereo(type)
Stereofotografie f stereoscopic photograph
Stereokamera f stereo camera
Stereomater f stereotype mat(rix)
Stereoskop n stereoscope
Stereotype f stereotype
Stereotypeur m stereotyper
Stereotypie f stereotype making, stereotyping
Stereotypiemaschine f stereotyping machine
Stereotypiepappe f flong
Stereo(typie)platte f stereo(type) plate
stereotypieren to stereotype
Stereounterlage f stereo mount
Sternanleger m star feeder
Sternblende f star-shaped diaphragm
Sternchen n *(*)* asterisk
Steuereinheit f control unit
Steuerelektronik f electronic control
Steuergerät n control device, controller
Steuerkasten m control box
Steuerkurve f cam
steuern to control, to drive, to govern
Steuersignal n control signal
Steuerstand m *(Maschinenanlage)* control console
Steuerung f control
Steuer(ungs)automatik f automatic control
Steuer(ungs)elektrik f electrical control
Steuer(ungs)elektronik f electronic control
Steuer(ungs)genauigkeit f control accuracy
Steuer(ungs)hydraulik f hydraulic control
Steuer(ungs)mechanik f mechanical control
Steuer(ungs)pneumatik f pneumatic control
Steuerzeichen n *(Fotosatz)* control character
Stich m *(Ätzung)* engraving; *(Farbstich)* cast; *(Heftung)* stitch
Stichel m burin, chisel, engraver's tool, graver, scorper; *(Tiefdruckzyl.-Gravur)* stylus
Stichprobe f *(Qualitätskontr.)* random sample, random test
Stichprobenentnahme f random sampling
Stichprobenmessung f *(Qualitätskontrolle)* random sample reading
Stichtiefdruck m intaglio (printing)
Stichwort n catchword, keyword
Stichwortregister n keyword index

Stichwortverzeichnis n keyword index
stillegen *(Aggregat)* to put out of operation, to shut down
Stillstand m standstill, stop
Stillstandsrollenwechsler m zero-speed web splicer
Stirnseite f front side
Stockfleck m *(Papier)* dampstain, mould stain
Stockpresse f screw press
Störmeldung f *(Comp.)* error message
Störung f *(techn.)* breakdown, fault, malfunction
Störungsbehebung f fault clearance, trouble-shooting
störungsfrei faultless, trouble-free
Störungsüberwachung f malfunction monitoring
Stoff m *(Papierherst.)* pulp, stock
Stoffaufbereitung f *(Papierherst.)* pulp preparation, stock preparation
Stoffauflauf(kasten) m *(Papierherst.)* headbox
Stoffauflöser m *(Papierherst.)* pulper
stoffbezogene Walze f cloth-covered roller
Stoffdruck m cloth printing, textile printing
Stoffmahlung f *(Papierherst.)* pulp refining
Stoffüberzug m *(Bucheinband, Schachtel)* cloth lining
Stopfer m *(Knautscher, Wickler)* jam-up, paper jam
Stoppbad n *(Fotochemie)* stop bath
Stoppblende f *(Kamera)* simple stops
Stopper m *(Druckm.)* press stop(page); *(wegen Fehlbogen)* fail-sheet stoppage
Stoppschalter m stop switch
Stoppstelle f *(Texterf.)* break point
Stopptrommel f *(Druckm.)* stop drum
Stoppzylinderpresse f stop-cylinder press
Storchschnabel m pantograph
Stoß m *(Erschütterung)* chock; *(Fuge)* butt joint, joint; *(Stapel)* pile
Stoß-an-Stoß-Bahnklebung f *(Rollenwechsel)* butt splicing, web-butt splicing
Stoßmarke f *(Bogenausrichtung)* push guide
straff tight
Straffen m *(Buchdruckzyl.)* drawsheet, top sheet, tympan
Straffpackung f stretch package
straff spannen to tighten
Strang m *(Rollendruck)* ribbon
Strangheftapparat m ribbon stitcher
Strangregister n *(Rollendruck)* ribbon register
Strangzusammenführung f *(Rollendruck)* ribbon gathering, ribbon interleaving
strapazierfähige Bindung f durable binding

Straße f *(Übereinanderstehen der Zwischenräume beim Satz)* gutter
Streckwerk n *(Rollendruckm.)* stretching unit
Streichanlage f *(Papierherst.)* coating plant
streichen *(Papier)* to coat; *(Text)* to cancel, to delete
Streichmaschine f *(Papierherst.)* coating machine
Streichradanleger m *(Falzm.)* friction feeder
Streichsatz m *(Satz zum Löschen)* deleted matter
Streifband n postal wrapper
Streifbandumlegemaschine für Zeitungen newspaper wrapping machine
Streifbandzeitung f newspaper posted in wrapper
Streifen pl *(auf Platte usw.)* streaks pl
Streifenauftrag m *(Lack, Kleber, Wachs usw.)* strip coating
Streifenausschnitt m *(Mehrnutzenverarb.)* strip trimming
Streifen(be)leimung f strip gluing
Streifenbildung f *(Druck)* streaking
Streifeneinschießer m *(Bogenzählung)* tape inserter
streifenfrei *(Druck)* streak-free
Streifenprobe f *(Papier)* strip test
strenge Farbe f stiff ink, strong ink, tacky ink
Streufolie f dispersion sheet
Streufolienbelichtung f dispersion sheet exposure
Streugebiet n *(Werbung)* distribution area
Streulicht n scattered light, stray light
Streuverlust m *(Werbung)* distribution loss
Strich m *(Papier)* coating; *(Typogr.)* dash, line
Strichabbildung f line illustration
Strichätzung f line engraving, line etching
Stricharbeiten pl *(Reprod.)* line work
Strichaufnahme f *(Reprod.)* line exposure
Strichfilm m *(Reprod.)* line film
Strichgrafik f lineart
Strichklischee n line engraving, line etching
Strichkode m bar code
Strichkodeleser m bar code reader, optical bar reader
Strichmaske f *(Reprod.)* line mask
Strichnegativ n *(Reprod.)* line negative
Strichperforation f *(im U. zur Lochperforation)* line perforation, slot perforation
Strichpositiv n *(Reprod.)* line positive
Strichpunkt m *(Semikolon)* semicolon
Strichreproduktion f line reproduction
Strichschärfe f line definition, line sharpness
Strichstärke f line weight, rule weight; *(Schrift)* weight
Strichumsetzung f *(Reprod.)* conversion to lineart, line conversion

Strichvorlage f lineart
Strichzeichnung f line drawing
Stripfilm m strip(ping) film
Stripmesser n *(für Stripfilm)* stripping knife
strippen to strip
Stromdichte f *(Galv.)* current density
Stromstärke f *(Galv.)* amperage, current intensity
Studio n studio
Stückdurchschuß m *(Bleisatz)* cut and leads *pl,* short leads *pl*
Stückkosten *pl* unit cost
Stülpdeckelschachtel f double wall carton
Stülpschachtel f turnbox
Stützrakel f *(Tiefdruck)* backing blade, blade support
Stützwalze f backing roller, support roller
Stufenbelichtung f exposure fan, fanned exposures *pl,* step exposures *pl*
Stufenkeil m *(Reprod., Kopie)* step wedge
stufenlose Drehzahlregelung f infinitely variable speed control
stufenloses Regelgetriebe n infinitely variable(-speed) gear
stufenlos verstellbar infinitely adjustable, infinitely variable
stumpf anfangen *(Zeile ohne Einzug)* to begin even, to set without indent
stumpf ausgehen lassen *(Satz)* to end a full line, to end even
stumpfes Messer n blunt knife
stumpfe Walze f roller out of condition
stumpffeine Linie f medium-face line, medium-face rule
Stundenbuch n book of hours
Stundenleistung f hourly output
Stundensatz m *(Maschine)* hourly cost rate, hourly machine rate
Subskription f subscription
Substrat n *(Bedruckstoff)* substrate, substratum
subtraktive Farbmischung f subtractive colour synthesis
Suchanzeige f *(im U. zur Verkaufsanzeige)* want ad
Suchbegriff m *(Comp.)* search term
Suche-Ersetze-Automatik f *(Textverarb.)* search and replace routine
Suchkennung f *(Comp.)* search code
Suchlauf m *(Comp.)* search run
Suchroutine f *(Comp.)* search string
Suchschlüssel m *(Comp.)* search code, search key
Suchverzeichnis n *(Comp.)* search directory
Suchwort n catchword, keyword
Sujet n *(Druckmotiv)* subject

Sulfatelektrolyt n *(Tiefdruckzyl.)* sulphuric electrolyte
Suspension f *(Papierherst.)* suspension
sw (schwarzweiß) b + w
Symbol n symbol
Synchronbetrieb m synchronous mode
synchronisiert *(Fertigungslinie)* synchronized
synthetisches Papier n synthetic paper
System n system
Systemanweisung f system instruction
Systemanwender m system operator, system user
Systemaufbau m system configuration, system design
Systembediener m system operator
Systembefehl m system command, system instruction
Systembetrieb m system operation
Systemdrucker m *(Belegdrucker)* system printer
Systemgerätegruppe f cluster (configuration)
Systemkommando n system command
Systemkonfiguration f system configuration
systemneutral system-independent
Systemprogramm n system program, system software
Systemrechner m system computer, system processor
Systemsicherung f system back-up
Systemsteuerung f system control
Systemüberwachung f system monitoring
systemunabhängig system-independent
Systemverbund m system network

T

tabellarischer Satz m tabular matter
Tabelle f table
Tabellendefinition f *(Tabellensatz)* table definition
Tabellenfeld n tabular field
Tabellenform f tabular form; *in* ~ tabulated
Tabellenfuß m bottom of table
Tabellenkopf m head of table, table head; **mehrspaltiger** ~ straddle
Tabellensatz m tabbing, tabular composition, tabular matter, tabular work
Tabellensatz mit Querlinien tabular matter with vertical rules

Tabellensatzprogramm *n (Fotosatz)* tabular composition software
Tabellenspalte *f* tabular column
Tabellenzeile *f* table line, table row
Tabelliermaschine *f* tabulating machine
Tabellierpapier *n* listing paper, zoned paper
Tableau *n (Reprod.)* gang
Tabloidbogen *m* tabloid signature
Tabloidfalz *m* tabloid fold
Tabloidformat *n* tabloid format, tabloid size
Tabloid-Zeitungsseite *f* tabloid newspaper page
Tabulator *m (Tabellensatz)* tab stop, tab(ulator)
Tabulieren *n* tabbing
Tachometer *n* speedometer
Tack *m (Druckfarbe)* tack
Tänzerwalze *f* dancer roller
Tafel *f (ganzseitige Abb. im Buch)* plate; *(grafische Darstellung)* chart, diagram, table
Tageskapazität *f* capacity per day
Tagesleistung *f (Masch.)* capacity per day, daily output
Tagesleuchtfarbe *f* fluorescent (printing) ink
Tageslichtfilm *m* daylight film, brightlight film
Tageslichtkamera *f* daylight camera
Tageslichtkassette *f* daylight cassette
Tageslichtkopierrahmen *m* daylight printing frame, daylight copying box
Tageslichtprojektion *f* overhead projection
Tageslichtverarbeitung *f (Reprod.)* daylight processing
Tagespresse *f* daily press
Tageszeitung *f* daily, daily (news)paper; *(Verlag)* newspaper publisher
Tageszettel *m (Arbeitszettel)* daily docket, time sheet
Takt *m (Prod.-Linie)* cycle
Taktanlage *f (Anleger)* paced feeding, timed feeding
Taktauslage *f* paced delivery
Takte/min *m/pl* cycles/min
taktfrei independent of operating cycle, irrespective of machine cycle, non-cyclical
taktgebunden cycled, paced, timed
taktgenau synchronized
taktgesteuert cycled, paced, timed
taktkonform synchronized
Taktradauslage *f (Rollendruckm.)* stepping wheel delivery, timed fan delivery
Taktschalter *m* timing switch
Taktsteuerung *f* cycle control, timed control
Takttransportband *n (Versandraum)* paced conveyor

taktunabhängig independent of operating cycle, irrespective of machine cycle, non-cyclical
taktungebunden independent of operating cycle, irrespective of machine cycle, non-cyclical
Taktweiche *f* cycled separator
Taktzahl *f* cycle time
Talkum *n* talcum
Tampon *m (Druckerballen)* ink(ing) ball, tampon
Tampondruckmaschine *f* pad printer, pad transfer machine
Tamponieren *n* dabbing
Tapete *f (Druckprodukt)* wallpaper; *(Zusammenst. der Bogenteile in der Zeitschriftenprod.)* list of signatures
Tapetendruckmaschine *f* wallpaper printing machine
Tapetenprägemaschine *f* wallpaper embossing press
Taschenatlas *m* pocket atlas
Taschenausgabe *f* pocket edition
Taschenbuch *n* paperback, pocketbook
Taschenbuchausgabe *f* paperback edition
Taschenfalz *m (Stauchfalz)* buckle fold
Taschenfalzmaschine *f* buckle folder, buckle-plate folding machine
Taschenkalender *m* pocket diary
Taschenkaschierung *f (im U. zur Rollenkaschierung)* pocket laminating, pouch laminating
Taschenwörterbuch *n* pocket dictionary
Tastatur *f* keyboard; *(klein, z. B. Zehnertastatur)* keypad
Tastaturplan *m* keyboard layout
Tastbetrieb *(langsames Vor und Zurück der Maschine)* **im ~ fahren** inching
Taste *f* key
tasten *(Daten, Text)* to key
Tastenanschlag *m* keystroke
Tastenfeld *n* keypad
Tastenfolge *f* key sequence
Taster *m (Erfassen)* keyboard operator
Tastfehler *m* keyboarding error
Tastgeschwindigkeit *f* keyboard operating speed
Tauchfärbemaschine *f (Papier)* immersion colouring machine
Tauchfarbwerk *n (Tiefdruck)* immersion-type inking unit
Tauchwalze *f* dip roller, pan roller
Tauenpapier *n* Manilla (paper)
Tausend *n (Auflage)* thousand; *16. bis 20. ~* 16th to 20th thousand
1000 Fortdrucke *pl* 1000 run-ons *pl*
Tausendbogenpreis *m* thousand-sheet price

Tausendbuchstabenpreis *m (Satz)* price per 1,000 ens
tausend weitere Druck thousand run-ons *pl*
Techniker *m* technician
technische Dokumentation *f* technical documentation
technischer Leiter *m* plant manager, technical manager, works manager
technischer Raster *m (Einkopierraster)* film tint, mechanical tint
technisches Personal *n* technical staff
Teilauflage *f* offprint, part edition, partial run
Teilbelegung *f (Aggregate in einer Verarbeitungslinie)* partial occupation
Teilbelichtung *f (Reprod.)* partial exposure, sectional exposure
Teilfarbe *f (Auszug)* separated colour
Teilfarbennegativ *n* separation negative
Teilfarbenpositiv *n* separation positive
teilgebundenes Buch *n* part-bound book
Teilprodukt *n (Druckverarb.)* section
Teilzeit *f (Comp.)* time sharing
Telebrief *m* teleletter
Telefax *n (Telekomm.)* telefax, facsimile, fax
Telefaxgerät *n* facsimile machine, faxcopier
Telefax-Mitteilung *f* telefax message, fax message
Telefonbuchdruck *m* phone book printing
telefonische Anzeigenannahme *f* telephone adtaking
Telefonleitung *f (Telekomm.)* dialling line, telephone line
Telefonnetz *n (Telekomm.)* dial-up network, telephone network
Telefoto *n* telephoto(graph)
Telekommunikation *f* telecommunication
Telekopie *f* telecopy
Teleskopsauger *m (Anlegersaugkopf)* telescopic sucker
Teletext *m* teletext
Tellerbildung *f (Papier)* cockling
Tellerfarbwerk *n (Tiegel)* disc inking unit
Temperaturbeständigkeit *f* temperature resistance
Temperaturregelung *f* temperature control
Temperaturregler *m* thermostat
Temperiermittel *n* temperature control fluid
Termin *m* date, deadline
Terminal *n* terminal
Termindruck *m* deadline pressure
termingerechte Lieferung *f* on-time delivery
Terminkontrolle *f* delivery date control, progress chasing
Terminplanung *f* production schedule

Terminüberschreitung *f* delay
Terminüberwachung *f* progress chasing
Testbelichtung *f* test exposure
Testkeil *m (Plattenkopie)* control wedge
Testlauf *m* test run
Testtafel *f (Reprod., Druck)* test chart
Text *m* copy, text, text copy
Textabbildung *f (Abb. im Text)* text figure
Textabrufsystem *n* text retrieval system
Textabzug *m* text proof
Textanfang *m* beginning of text
Text anhängen to run on copy
Text auf Mitte stellen to center copy
Text aufrufen to recall copy, to retrieve copy
Textausdruck *m (Drucker)* text print-out
Textausgabe *f* copy output, text output; *(Buch)* text edition (only)
Textbaustein *m* text module
Text bearbeiten to edit copy
Textbearbeitung *f* text editing
Textberechnung *f* calculation of volume, copyfit calculation, estimate of volume
Textberechnungsprogramm *n (Textverarb.)* copyfit software, text counting software
Text/Bildintegration *f* text-image integration
Text/Bild-Verschmelzung *f* text-image integration, text-image merging
Textbuch *n* text book
Textdaten *pl* text data, text file
Textdrucker *m* text printer
Texteinätzung *f (Tiefdruck)* drop-in etching of text
Texteindruck *m* text imprint
Text einer Figur anpassen to fit copy into a figure
Text einfügen to insert copy
Texteingabe *f* copy input, text entry, text input
Text eingeben to enter copy
Text einpassen to fit copy to layout, make copy fit into
Texteinpassen *n (Text in vorhandenen Raum)* copy fitting
Text einziehen to indent copy
Texte kollationieren to collate
Texterfasser *m* galley typist, keyboard operator
Texterfassung *f* text entry, text recording, text keyboarding, collection of text copy, text input
Texterfassungsterminal *n* text input terminal, text recording terminal
Textfilm *m* text film
Textfolge *f* text string

Textform *f (Form des gesetzten Textes)* shape of text matter; *(im U. zur Bilderform)* type forme
Textformatierung *f* text formatting
Text gestalten to arrange copy
Texthöhe *f* depth of text
Textildruck *m* cloth printing, textile printing
Textildruckmaschine *f* textile printing machine
Textkonverter *m* text converter
Textkorrektur *f* text correction, text editing
Text löschen to cancel copy, to delete copy
Textmaske *f* lettering overlay
Text mischen to merge copy
Textmontage *f* text assembly, text stripping
Textpositionierung *f* text positioning
Textprüfung *f* copy checking
Text rücken to move copy
Textsatz *m (im U. zu Layoutsatz)* body matter, straight matter, text matter
Textschrift *f* body type, bread-and-butter face, text face
Textseite *f* text page
Text speichern to store copy
Textspeicherung *f* text storage
Textsystem *n* text system
Textteil *m (Buch, im U. zum Bilderteil)* text section; *(Passage)* text passage
Text überarbeiten to edit copy, to revise copy
Textüberlauf *m* text overrun
Text überschreiben to overstrike copy
Textübertragung *f* text transmission
Text umstellen to move copy
Text und Bilder auf Stand *m* text and graphics in position
Text unterbringen to accomodate copy
Textverarbeitung *f* text processing, word processing, text handling
Textverarbeitungsanlage *f* text processing system, word processor
Textvorlage *f* text copy
Textzeile *f* text line
thermische Nachverbrennung *f* thermal after-burning, thermal incineration
thermische Nachverbrennungsanlage *f* thermic after-burner (system)
Thermoband *n (Fälzeln)* thermotape
Thermobindegerät *n* thermal binder
Thermobindung *f* thermal binding
Thermodruck *m* thermographic printing
Thermodrucker *m* thermal printer
Thermografie *f* thermographic printing, thermography

thermografischer Druck *m* thermographic printing, thermography
Thermopapier *n* thermal paper
thermoplastische Bindung *f* thermoplastic binding
thixotropische Farbe *f* thixotropic ink
thyristorgesteuert thyristor-controlled
tiefätzen to deep-etch
Tiefätzfarbe *f* deep-etch ink
Tiefätzlack *m* deep-etch lacquer
Tiefätzung *f* deep-etching, intaglio
Tiefdruck *m* gravure (printing), gravure (process), photogravure, rotogravure; *(Stichtiefdruck)* intaglio (printing)
Tiefdruckätzung *f* gravure etching
Tiefdruckbogenrotation *f* sheet-fed gravure press
Tiefdrucker *m* gravure printer
Tiefdruckfarbe *f* gravure ink, rotogravure ink
Tiefdruckfirnis *m* gravure varnish
Tiefdruckformherstellung *f* cylinder preparation, gravure cylinder production
Tiefdruck-Glasgravurraster *m* engraved glass gravure screen
Tiefdruck-Kopierraster *m* film copy gravure screen
Tiefdruckmaschine *f* gravure machine, gravure (printing) press, rotogravure press
Tiefdruckpapier *n* gravure paper, rotogravure paper
Tiefdruckraster *m* gravure screen
Tiefdruckretuscheur *m* gravure retoucher
Tiefdruckrollenrotation *f* rotogravure press, web-fed gravure press
Tiefdruckrotation(smaschine) *f* rotogravure press, web-fed gravure press
Tiefdruckübertragungsmaschine *f* gravure transfer machine
Tiefdruckwerk *n* gravure (printing) unit
Tiefdruckwickelplatte *f* wrap-around gravure plate
Tiefdruckzylinder *m* gravure cylinder
Tiefdruckzylinderherstellung *f* gravure cylinder production
Tiefe *f (Schwarzauszug)* black
Tiefen *pl (Bild)* shadow areas *pl*, shadows *pl*
Tiefenmaske *f (Reprod.)* shadow mask
Tiefenmaß *n* depth gauge
Tiefenmesser *n* depth gauge
Tiefenpunkt *m (Rasterbild)* shadow dot
Tiefenschärfe *f (Fot.)* depth of focus
tiefenvariabler Tiefdruck *m* variable-depth gravure (process)

Tiefenzeichnung - Trägermaterial

Tiefenzeichnung *f (Bild)* image definition in the shadows, shadow details *pl*, shadow separation
tiefgeätzte Platte *f* deep-etched plate
tiefgestelltes Zeichen *n (Satz)* inferior character, subscript
tiefgestellte Ziffern *f/pl* inferior figures *pl*
Tiefkühlbeständigkeit *f (Druckfarbe)* deep freeze resistance
Tiefprägung *f* deep embossing
Tiefstapel *m* low pile
Tiefstapelauslage *f* low-pile delivery
tiefstellen *(Indices im Satz)* to shift downwards
Tieftankentwicklungsmaschine *f* deep tank processor
Tiegel *m* platen; *(Druckm.)* platen press
Tiegelaufzug *m* packing of platen
Tiegeldruckautomat *m* automatic platen press
Tiegeldruckform *f* platen forme
Tiegeldruckpresse *f* platen press
Tiegelstanzautomat *m* automatic cutter-creaser, platen cutter-creaser
Tiegelstanzen *n (im Gs. zu Flachbett- bzw. Rotationsstanzen)* platen press die-cutting
tierischer Leim *m* animal glue, animal size
Tilde *f* swung dash, tilde
Timesharing *n (Comp.)* time sharing
Tintenfestigkeit *f (Papier)* ink resistance
Tintenstrahldruck *m* ink jet printing
Tintenstrahldrucker *m* ink jet printer
Tippfehler *m* typing error
Tischdrucker *m* table-top printer
Tischfarbwerk *n* table inking unit
Tischkalender *m* desk calendar, desk diary
Tischmodell *n* bench-top model, desk-top model, table-top model
Tischterminal *n* desk-top terminal
Titananode *f (Galv.)* titanium anode
Titel *m* heading, title
Titelbild *n (Zeitschrift)* cover picture; *(Buch)* frontispiece
Titelblatt *n* front cover, front page, title page
Titelbogen *m (Buchprod.)* preliminary pages *pl*
Titelei *f (Buch)* preliminary matter, prelims *pl*
Titelkopf *m* heading, title
Titelprägung *f* title embossing
Titelsatz *m* composition of titles, headline setting, photolettering
Titelsatzgerät *n (Fotosatz)* photoheadliner
Titelschrift *f* headline display type, headline typeface
Titelseite *f* front cover, front page, title page
Titelstory *f (Zeitung)* cover story

Titelzeile *f* heading, headline
Titelzeile in negativ headline reversed white on black
Todesanzeigen *pl (Rubrik)* deaths columns *pl*
Toleranz *f (techn.)* allowance, tolerance
Toluol *n (Tiefdruckfarbe)* toluene
Toluol-Rückgewinnungsanlage *f* toluene recovery unit
Ton *m (Farbton allgemein)* tone; *(dunklerer Ton)* shade; *(leichter, heller Ton)* tint
Tonabstufung *f* tonal gradation
Tonätzung *f* tint engraving
Tonen *n (Offset)* scumming
Toner *m (Elektrofotogr.)* toner
Tonfläche *f (leichter, heller Ton; meist aufgerastert)* tint area, tint block; *(Volltonfläche)* solid, solid area
Ton-Index-Methode *f (Reprod.)* tone-index method
Tonpapier *n* tinted paper
Tonplatte *f (Buchdruck)* solid plate, tint plate
Tonskala *f* tone scale
Tontrennung *f* tone separation
Tonumkehrung *f (Reprod.)* tonal inversion
Tonverlauf *m* graduated tint, tonal gradation, vignetted tint
Tonverlust *m (Reprod.)* loss of tone
Tonwert *m* tonal value, tone value; *(digital)* tone data
Tonwertabstufung *f* tonal gradation
Tonwertatlas *m* tone value atlas
Tonwertbalance *f* tone balance
Tonwertkompression *f* tone compression
Tonwertkorrektur *f* tonal correction, tone correction
tonwertrichtig with correct tonal value
Tonwertskala *f* tone scale
Tonwertübertragung *f (Kopie)* tonal transfer
Tonwertumfang *m* tonal range, tone range
Tonwertveränderung *f* tonal change, tone change
Tonwertverlauf *m* tonal gradation
Tonwertverschiebung *f* tonal shift
Tonwertwiedergabe *f* tonal reproduction, tone rendition, tone reproduction
Tonwertzunahme *f (Punktzunahme)* dot gain
topaktuell *(Zeitungsmeldung)* up to the minute
topografische Karte *f* topographical map
Totalisator *m (Zählwerk)* totalizer
toter Kolumnentitel *m* folio, page number
Tourenzähler *m* speed indicator
Tourenzahl *f* number of revolutions
Trägerbandformularsatz *m* snap-band forms set
Trägermaterial *n (Foto, Film usw.)* base, carrier

Trägerpapier *n* base paper
Tragbeutel *m* carrier bag
Transferdruck *m* transfer printing
Transferfarbe *f* transfer ink
Transparentfolie *f* transparent film
Transparenthaut *f* transparent film
Transparentpapier *n* *(für Zeichnungen, Decker usw.)* tracing paper
Transparentumleger *m* *(Buchumschlag)* acetate overlay
Transparentweiß *n* *(Farbzusatz)* transparent white
Transparentzeichenpapier *n* tracing paper
Transparenz *f* translucency, transparency
Transportband *n* conveyor belt
Transporteur *m* *(Versandraum)* conveyor
Transportgerät *n* *(kleines)* trolley
Transportkanal *m* *(Sammelhefter, Zusammentragmaschine)* raceway
Transportkette *f* conveyor chain
Transportklammer *f* conveyor clamp
Transportlochung *f* *(Endlosformularherst.)* feed holes, line hole punching, line holes *pl,* sprocket hole punching, sprocket holes *pl*
Transportsauger *m* *(Anlegersaugkopf)* transport sucker
Transportsystem *n* conveyor system
Transportwalze *f* transport roller
Transportzange *f* conveyor clamp
Trapping *n* *(Farbannahme)* trapping
Traverse *f* *(mech.)* cross bar
traversierende Walze *f* oscillating roller, reciprocating roller
Treiberprogramm *n* *(Belichter)* driver software
Treibersoftware *f* *(Belichter)* driver software
Treibrad *n* driving wheel
Treibriemen *m* drive belt
Trema *n* *(ë)* diaeresis
Trennbläser *pl* *(Anleger)* fanning blowers *pl*
Trennblatt *n* *(Bindung)* divider sheet
trennen *(Bogen)* to separate; *(gestanzte Nutzen)* to strip; *(Sandwichmaterial)* to peel apart; *(Wörter)* to divide
Trennfuge *f* *(Textverarb.)* discretionary hyphen
Trennlinie *f* dividing rule
Trennsauger *m* *(Anlegersaugkopf)* pick-up sucker, separator sucker
Trennschnitt *m* trim cut
Trennung *f* *(Wörter)* division
Trennungsstrich *m* hyphen
Trennverbot *n* *(Textverarb.)* forbid hyphenation
Trennwerkzeug *n* *(Nutzentrennung)* blanking tool, stripping tool
Tretpresse *f* treadle press

Triazetatfilm *m* triacetate film
Trichter *m* *(Falzer)* former
Trichtereinlaufwalze *f* *(Falztrichter)* roller top of former
Trichterfalz *m* *(Rollendruck)* former fold
Trichterfalzapparat *m* former folder
Trichternase *f* *(Falztrichter)* former nose
Trichterüberbau *m* *(Rollendruckm.)* former superstructure
Trichterwalze *f* *(Rollendruckm.)* former roller
Trimetallplatte *f* trimetallic plate
Triplexkarton *m* triplex board
Trittbrett *n* footboard, running board
Tritthebel *m* treadle
Tritthebelpresse *f* treadle press
Trockenätzung *f* *(Reprod.)* dry dot etching
Trockenaggregat *n* drying unit
Trockenbestäubung *f* dry spraying, powder spraying
Trockendruck *m* *(Folienprägung)* dry printing
Trockendruckgerät *n* *(Folienprägung)* dry printer
Trockenfähigkeit *f* drying capacity
Trockenfirnis *m* drying varnish, siccative varnish
trockengebürstete Aluminiumplatte *f* dry-brushed aluminium plate
Trockengestell *n* drying rack
Trockenkaschierung *f* dry lamination
Trockenklammer *f* drying clamp
Trockenlithografie *f* *(Trockenätzung)* dry dot etching
Trockenmater *f* dry flong, dry mat
Trockenmittel *n* *(Farbzusatz)* siehe Trockenstoff
Trockenofen *m* drying oven
Trockenoffset *m* dry offset
Trockenpartie *f* *(Papiermasch.)* dryer section, dry(ing) end
Trockenpaste *f* *(Farbzusatz)* paste dryer
Trockenrahmen *m* drying frame
Trockenraum *m* drying room
Trockenregal *n* drying rack
Trockenretusche *f* *(Reprod.)* dry dot etching
Trockenschrank *m* *(Filmtrocknung)* drying cabinet
Trockenstereotypie *f* dry stereotyping process
Trockenstoff *m* *(Farbzusatz)* drying agent, siccative
Trockentoner *m* *(Elektrofotogr.)* dry toner
Trockentrommel *f* drying cylinder, drying drum
Trockentunnel *m* tunnel dryer
Trockenzeit *f* drying time
Trocken-zu-Trocken-Entwicklung *f* *(Entwicklungsm.)* dry-to-dry processing
trocknen to dry; *(durch Strahlung auch)* to cure

Trockner m *(Additiv)* drying agent, siccative; *(Gerät)* dryer
Trocknerabluft f dryer exhaust
Trocknerband n dryer conveyor
Trocknerhaube f drying hood
Trocknungseigenschaft f *(Farbe)* drying properties pl
Trocknungsofen m drying oven
Trommelanleger m drum feeder, rotary feeder
Trommelfalzwerk n *(Rollendruckm.)* drum folder
Trommelscanner m *(im U. zum Flachbettscanner)* drum scanner
Tuchstange f *(Buchdruckm.)* blanket bar
Tüte f bag
Tütenkleben n bag gluing
Tupfballen m dabber
tupfen to dab
Tusche f *(Zeichentusche)* drawing ink
Tuschezeichnung f ink drawing
Tympan m tympan
Type f *(Schrifttype)* letter, printing letter, type
Typengießmaschine f type casting machine
Typenraddrucker m type wheel printer
Typenträger m *(Fotosatz)* font, type carrier
Typogestaltung f typo design, typographical arrangement, typography
Typograf m typographer
Typografie f typography
typografische Einheit f typographic unit
typografische Gestaltung f typo design, typographical arrangement, typography
typografischer Aufbau m typographic layout, typo layout
typografischer Punkt m typographical point
typografischer Zeilenmesser m type gauge
typografisches Layout n typographic layout, typo layout
typografisches Maß n typographical measurement
typografisches Maßsystem n *(Typogr.)* typographic scale system
typografisches Muster n typographical pattern
Typogravüre f typogravure
Typolayout n typo layout
Typometer n type gauge

U

UCR (Unterfarbenreduktion) UCR (Under Colour Reduction/Removal)
überalterte Emulsion f *(Film)* out-of-date emulsion
überarbeiten *(Foto und dergl.)* to retouch; *(Text)* to revise
Überbau m *(Rollendruckm.)* superstructure
überbelichten to overexpose
Überbelichtung f overexposure
überdeckte Anlage f overlap feeding
Überdehnen n *(Gummituch)* overstretching
Überdruck m *(Druckbeistellung)* cylinder squeeze, overpack; *(Eindruck in Drucksache)* imprinting, overprinting
überdrucken to imprint, to overprint
Überdrucklack m overprint varnish
Übereinanderbelichtung f *(Fotosatz)* overlay exposure, overlay setting
Übereinanderdruck m overprinting, superimposed printing
übereinanderdrucken to overprint
Übereinanderdruckfeld n *(Druckkontrollstreifen)* solid colour overprint patch, solids superimposition patch
übereinandergelegte Bilder pl superimposed images pl
Überentwicklung f overdevelopment
Überfärbung f *(Druck)* overinking
Überfalz m gripper fold, overfold
Überfeuchtung f *(Offset)* overdamping
Überformat n oversize
Überführung f transfer
Überführungsband n transfer conveyor
Überführungssystem n transfer system
Überführungstrommel f transfer cylinder
Überführungswalze f transfer roller
Überfüllen n *(Reprod.)* spread exposure, spreading
Übergabezylinder m transfer cylinder
überhängender Buchdeckel m overhang cover board
überhängender Buchstabe m kerned letter
Überhang m *(Buchstabe)* kern; *(Übersatz beim Textumbruch)* break over, over
überholt *(Masch.)* overhauled, re-built, reconditioned
Überholung f *(Masch.)* overhaul, reconditioning
Überkopfkamera f overhead camera, suspension-type camera

überlappende Anlage f overlap feed(ing), stream feed(ing)
überlappende Bahnklebung f overlap (web) splicing
Überlastsicherung f overload protection
Überlastung f overload
Überlauf m *(Textumbruch)* break over, over
Überlaufen des Stapels n overpiling
Überlaufweiche f overflow diverter
Überlieferung f *(mehr Exemplare als bestellt)* excess delivery, overdelivery, overrun
übermäßiger Aufzug m *(Zyl.)* overpacking
übermitteln *(Daten, Text)* to transfer, to transmit
Übernähstich m *(Fadenheftung)* kettle stitch
Überproduktion f *(im Druck)* overproduction, overrun
überprüfen siehe kontrollieren
überregionale Zeitung f national newspaper, supra-regional newspaper
Übersatz m *(zuviel Satz)* break over, over, overmatter, oversetting
Überschießbogen m *(Bogenanleger)* early sheet
Überschießkontrolle f *(Stapel)* overpiling control
Überschlag m *(Bleisatz)* head white
überschlagen *(kalkulieren)* to calculate roughly, to estimate roughly
überschreiben *(Texterf.)* overstrike
Überschrift f heading, headline
Überschrift über volle Seitenbreite f banner, full title, streamer
Überschuß m *(Druckprod.)* excess sheets pl, oversheets pl
überspringende Numerierung f skip numbering
überstehender Buchdeckel m extended cover
Überstrahlung f *(Kopie)* spread exposure
übertippen *(Texterf.)* overstrike
übertragen to transfer; *(Telekomm.)* to transmit
Übertragung f transfer; *(Telekomm.)* transmission
Übertragungsgeschwindigkeit f *(Telekomm.)* bit rate, transmission rate, transmission speed
Übertragungsnetz n *(Telekomm.)* communications network, transmission network
Übertragungszeit f transmission time
Übertragung von Druckvorlagen *(Telekomm.)* copy transmission
Übertragung von Zeitungsseiten *(Telekomm.)* transmission of newspaper pages
Übertragwalze f transfer roller
Überwachung f *(Prozeß)* monitoring, supervision
überziehen *(Buchdeckel, Schachtel usw.)* to cover, to line

überzogene Schachtel f covered box
Überzug m *(Buchdeckel, Schachtel usw.)* covering, lining
Überzugspapier n covering paper, lining paper
üblicher Tastaturplan m qwerty layout
UEF (Benutzeraustauschformat) UEF (User Exchange Format)
Ultraviolett- siehe UV-
umbrechen *(Seite)* to make up, to assemble, to paginate, to compose
Umbrechschiff n *(Bleisatz)* make-up galley
umbrochener Seitenjob m *(Fotosatz)* paginated job
Umbruch m make-up, pagination
Umbruchabteilung f *(Mettage)* make-up department
Umbruchgestaltung f pagination layout
Umbruchlayout n pagination layout
Umbruchlinien pl make-up rules pl
Umbruchredakteur m make-up editor
Umbruchterminal n page make-up terminal
Umbruchtisch m make-up table
Umdrehen n *(im U. zu Umschlagen, Umstülpen)* work and twist
umdrehter Bogen m twisted sheet
Umdrehungen pro Stunde *(U/h)* revolutions per hour
Umdrehungszahl f number of revolutions
Umdruck m transfer printing
Umdruckabzug m transfer proof
umdrucken to transfer
Umdruckfarbe f transfer ink
Umdruckmaschine f transfer printing machine
Umdruckpapier n transfer paper
Umdruckpresse f transfer press
Umfang m *(Dichte, Raster usw.)* range; *(Körper)* circumference; *(Seitenzahl)* total number of pages, total page count, total pagination
Umfangsberechnung f *(Satz)* calculation of volume, cast-off, copyfit calculation, copyfitting, estimate of volume
Umfangsgeschwindigkeit f circumferential speed
Umfangsregister n *(Rollendruck)* circumferential register, length register
Umfeldblende f *(Scannerfunktion)* sharpness enhancement
Umgebungsdichte f *(Reprod.)* ambient density, surround density
Umgebungslicht n *(Fremdlicht)* ambient light
Umgebungstemperatur f ambient temperature
umgekehrtes Bild n reversed image
umgeknickte Ecke f dog ear, dog-eared corner
Umkehrbad n *(Fot.)* reversal bath

Umkehrbild *n* reversed image
Umkehrentwicklung *f (Reprod.)* reversal processing
Umkehrfilm *m* reversal film
Umkehrkopie *f* reversal exposure
Umkehrmaterial *n* reversal material
Umkehrpapier *n (Fotopapier)* reversal photo paper
Umkehrplatte *f (Konversion)* conversion plate
Umkehrprozeß *m* reversal process
Umkehrspiegel *m (Kamera)* reversing mirror
Umkehrung *f (Fot.)* reversal
umknicken to fold over
umkopieren to contact, to copy, to duplicate by contact
umlaufender Text *m (um Figur)* runaround; *(von einer Seite auf die andere)* turnover
Umlaufkopiermaschine *f (Tiefdruck)* all-around copying machine, rotating copying machine
Umlautzeichen *n (Satz)* German accent, umlaut accent
Umlegevorrichtung *f (Buchherst.)* laydown device
Umlenkspiegel *m* deflecting mirror
Umlenkstation *f* deviation station
Umlenkwalze *f (Rollendruckm.)* idler roller
Umrahmung *f (Typogr.)* border, box
Umrandung *f (Typogr.)* border, box
Umrechnen von Daten data conversion, data transformation
Umreifen *n (Versandraum)* strapping, tying
Umreifungsband *n* strap
Umreifungsmaschine *f* strapping machine
Umroller *m* re-reeler
Umrollmaschine *f* re-reeling machine
Umrollung *f* re-reeling
Umrüstung *f (Einrichten auf neuen Auftrag)* change-over; *(technisch, neue Maschinen)* conversion
Umrüstzeiten *pl* change-over times *pl*
umschaltbar convertible, reversible
Umschalter *m* switch
umschießen *(neu ausschießen)* to re-impose
Umschlag *m* cover; *(Briefumschlag)* envelope; *(Schutzumschlag)* jacket, wrapper
Umschlaganleger *m* cover feeder
Umschlaganleimung *f* cover gluing
Umschlaganpreßstation *f* cover nipping station
Umschlagbild *n* cover picture
Umschlagen *n (im U. zu Umstülpen, Umdrehen usw.)* work and turn
umschlagener Bogen *m* turned sheet
Umschlagfoto *n* cover photo(graph)

Umschlaggreifer *m/pl (Schön- und Widerdruck)* turning grippers *pl*
Umschlagkarton *m* cover board
Umschlagklappe *f (Briefumschlag)* envelope flap; *(Zeitschrift, Buch)* cover flap, cover gate
Umschlag mit Klappe cover with flap
Umschlagpapier *n* cover paper
Umschlagregister *n* cover register
Umschlagseite *f* cover page
Umschlagtitel *m* cover title
Umschlingungswinkel *m (Zylinder)* angle of wrap, wrap (angle)
umschmelzen to re-cast
Umschmelzofen *m* remelting furnace
Umschnüren *n (Versandraum)* strapping, tying
umsetzen *(neu setzen)* to re-set
Umspulentwicklung *f (Reprod.)* rewind development
Umstapeln *n* re-piling
umstellbar convertible
umstellbar auf Schön- und Widerdruck convertible to perfecting
umstellbare Schön- und Widerdruckmaschine *f* convertible perfector
umstellbare Vierfarben-Bogenoffsetmaschine *f* convertible four-colour sheet-fed offset press
umstellen to convert
Umstellen von Text re-arrangement of text
Umstellung *f (technisch)* change-over, conversion
Umstellungszeiten *pl (für neuen Auftrag)* change-over times *pl*
umsteuerbar convertible, reversible
umsteuerbares Satellitendruckwerk *n (Rollendruckmasch.)* reversible satellite printing unit
Umstülpen *n (im U. zu Umschlagen)* work and tumble
umstülpter Bogen *m* tumbled sheet
Umwälzpumpe *f* circulation pump
Umwälzsystem *n* circulation system
umwandeln *(Daten, Signale)* to convert
Umwandlung *f (Daten, Signale)* conversion
umweltfreundlich environment-friendly, non-polluting
umweltschädlich polluting
Umweltschutz *m* environmental control, environment protection, pollution control
Umweltverschmutzung *f* environment pollution
unabhängige Einheit *f (im Gs. zum Inline-Aggregat)* off-line unit, stand-alone unit
unaufgeschnittene Bogen *pl* closed sections *pl*, closed signatures *pl*
unausgeschlossener Satz *m* unjustified setting

unbedruckt blank, plain, unprinted, vacat
unbedruckte Etiketten *n/pl* blank labels *pl*
unbedruckte Seite *f* blank page
unbelichtet unexposed
unbeschichtet uncoated, unsensitized
unbeschnittenes Format *n* bleed size, untrimmed size
unbezogene Feuchtwalze *f* bareback damping roller
Unbuntaufbau *m (Reprod.)* achromatic composition, achromatic construction, grey component replacement
unbunte Farbe *f* achromatic colour
Unbuntfarbsatz *m* achromatic colour separations *pl*
Unbuntreproduktion *f* achromatic reproduction
undurchschossen *(kompreß)* set solid, solid
Undurchsichtigkeit *f (Opazität)* opacity, opaqueness
Und-Zeichen *n (&)* ampersand
unechter Stahlstich *m* imitation die-stamping, thermographic printing
unechtes Pergament *n* imitation parchment
Unechtgrau *n* imitation grey
Unendlichkeitszeichen *n* infinity sign
Unfallschutz *m* accident prevention
Unfallverhütungsvorschriften *pl* accident prevention regulations *pl*
unformatierte Daten *pl* unformatted data
ungebundene Bogen *pl* flat sections *pl*, loose sections *pl*, unbound sections *pl*
ungebundenes Buch *n* book in sheets, unbound copy of book
ungedruckt unprinted; *(Werk und dergl.)* unpublished
ungefalzt unfolded
ungefalzter Bogen *m* open sheet
ungekürzt *(Text)* unabridged
ungeleimtes Papier *n* unsized paper
ungelernte Kraft *f* unqualified workman, unskilled operator, untrained operator
ungerade Seiten *f/pl* odd folios *pl*, uneven pages *pl*
ungesammelte Produktion *f (Rollendruckm.)* non-collect run, straight-run production
ungesperrt *(Satz)* set solid
ungestrichenes Papier *n* uncoated paper, uncoated stock
ungiftige Druckchemikalien *pl* non-toxic pressroom chemicals *pl*
unkorrigiert uncorrected

unkorrigierter Korrekturabzug *m* dirty copy, foul proof, rough proof, uncorrected proof, unread proof
unleserlich illegible
unleserliches Manuskript *n* bad copy
unruhiger Druck *m* mottled impression
unsatiniert unglazed
Unschärfe *f (Reprod.)* lack of definiton
Unscharfeinkopieren *n (Reprod.)* unsharp printing-in
unscharfer Druck *m* unsharp print
unscharfer Punkt *m* soft dot, unsharp dot
Unscharfkontur *f (elektron. Bildverarb.)* softened outline, unsharp contours *pl*
Unscharfmaskierung *f (Scannerfunktion)* unsharp masking
unsensibilisiertes Pigmentpapier *n (Tiefdruck)* unsensitized carbon tissue
untenliegendes Farbmesser *n* undershot ink duct blade
Unterätzung *f (Tiefdruckzyl.)* underetching
Unterbau *m* substructure
unterbelichtet underexposed
Unterbelichtung *f* underexposure
Unterbogenanleger *m* bottom sheet feeder
Unterbrecher *m (Texterf.)* break point
Unterdruckfarbe *f* inking primer
unterentwickelt under-developed
Unterentwicklung *f* underdevelopment
unterer Papierrand *m* bottom margin, foot margin, lower margin, tail margin
unterer Seitenrand *m* bottom margin, foot margin, lower margin, tail margin
Unterfärbung *f (Druck)* underinking
Unterfarbenbeseitigung *f (UCR)* Under Colour Removal
Unterfarbenreduktion *f (UCR)* Under Colour Reduction
Unterführungszeichen *n (Dittozeichen)* repeat mark
Unterhalt *m (Masch.)* maintenance
Unterlänge *f (Buchstaben)* descender
Unterlage *f (Klischee usw.)* base, mount; *(Zylinderaufzug)* packing
Unterlageblech *n (Druckm.)* metal underlay, oil drip pan
Unterlagebogen *m (Druckmaschinenzyl.)* packing sheet, underlay sheet
Unterlagefolie *f (Druckmaschinenzyl.)* packing foil, underlay foil
Unterlagetuch *n (Gummizyl.)* under(lay) blanket
Unterlappung *f (Schuppe)* underlapping

Unterlegfolie f *(Druckmaschinenzyl.)* packing foil, underlay foil
Unterlicht n *(Kamera)* backlight
Unterlieferung f *(weniger Exemplare als geordert)* underdelivery, underrun
Untermesser n bottom knife, lower knife
Unternehmensverband Druck m Printing Management Association
Unterprogramm n *(Comp.)* routine, software routine, sub-routine
Unterrubrik f sub-heading
Unterschlag m *(Bleisatzumbruch)* foot white
Unterschneidemesser n *(Schriftguß)* kerning knife
Unterschneiden n *(Zeichen im Satz)* kerning, pair kerning
Unterschnitt m *(Buch)* tail edge
unterschnittener Buchstabe m kerned letter
Unterseite f bottom side, lower side
Unterseitendruck m *(Rollendruckm.)* lower side printing
Untersieb n *(Papierherst.)* bottom wire, lower wire
Unterstrahlung f *(Kopie)* side lighting, undercutting
Unterstreichung f *(Satz)* underlining, underscoring
Untertitel m sub-heading, subtitle
untrennbare Zeile f indivisible line
unverkaufte Exemplare n/pl dead stock; *(Remittenden)* returns pl
unverschränkte Stapel pl uncompensated stacks pl
unvollständiges Exemplar n incomplete copy
Unzialbuchstabe m uncial letter
Unziale f uncial, uncial letter
Unzialschrift f uncial
Urheberrecht n copyright
Urkundenpapier n document paper
Urschrift f original (text)
UV-Druckfarbe f U.V. printing ink
UV-empfindlich U.V. sensitive
UV-Filter m U.V. filter
UV-Härtung f *(Farbe, Lack)* U.V. curing
UV-Lack m U.V. coating, U.V. varnish
UV-Lampe f U.V. lamp
UV-Strahler m U.V. emitter, U.V. radiator
UV-Strahlung f U.V. radiation
UV-Trockner m U.V. dryer
UV-Trocknung f U.V. curing, U.V. drying

V

vakat blank
Vakatseite f blank page, white page
Vakuum n vacuum
Vakuumaufbau m *(Kopierrahmen)* vacuum build-up
Vakuumdose f *(Farbe)* vacuum-sealed can
Vakuumfilmhalter m *(Kamera)* vacuum film holder
Vakuumkopierrahmen m vacuum frame
Vakuummeter n vacuum meter
Vakuumpumpe f vacuum pump
Vakuumsauger pl suckers pl, suction cups pl
Vakuumzeiten pl *(Kontaktkopierer, Kopierrahmen)* suction times pl, vacuum times pl
Vektorgrafik f clock diagram, vector chart, vector graph
Vektortechnik f *(Bildverarb.)* vector technique
Velinpapier n vellum (paper)
Velourspapier n velvet paper
Venezianische Renaissance-Antiqua f *(Schriftklassif.)* Humanistics pl
veränderliches Format n variable size
verätzt over-etched
verantwortlicher Schriftleiter m editor-in-chief
Verarbeitbarkeit f *(Material)* workability
Verarbeitung f handling, processing
Verarbeitungsangaben pl processing instructions pl
Verarbeitungsbetrieb m *(Druckverarbeitung)* converter, converting operation
Verarbeitungslinie f converting line, finishing line
Verarbeitungspräparate pl *(chem)* processing chemicals pl
verbesserte Auflage f revised edition
verbesserte Ausgabe f corrected edition, revised edition
verbinden *(techn.)* to connect, to couple, to interface, to link (up), to network
Verbindungsstege pl *(gestanzte Bogen)* connecting points pl
Verblassen n *(Farbe)* discoloration, fading
Verblocken n *(Kleben im Stapel)* blocking
Verbraucherzeitschrift f consumer magazine
Verbrauchsprodukte pl consumables pl
Verbreitung f *(Zeitung)* circulation
Verbrennungsluft f *(Gastrockner)* combustion air
Verbundfolie f compound foil, sandwich foil

Verbundmaterialien *pl* compounds *pl*
Verbundsystem *n (Comp.)* network system
verchromter Zylinder *m* chrome-plated cylinder
Verchromung *f (Tiefdruck)* chrome-facing, chrome-plating
Verchromungsanlage *f* chrome-plating installation
Verdickungsmittel *n (Druckfarbe)* thickener
verdruckbar workable
Verdruckbarkeit *f* runability, workability
verdrucken *(falsch drucken)* to misprint, to print waste
Verdünner *m (Farbe)* reducer, thinner
Verdünnungsmittel *n* reducer, thinner
Veredler *m (graf. Betrieb)* converter
Veredlung *f (Druck)* converting, finishing, surface finishing
vereinzeln *(Bogen in Anlage)* to separate
Verfärben *n* discoloration, fading
verfahrensbedingt process-inherent
Verfahrenstechnik *f* process engineering, process technology
Verfahrenstechniker *m* process engineer
Verfasser *m* author
verflachen *(Gradation)* to become flat, to become soft
vergilben to turn yellow
vergilbte Vorlage *f* yellowed copy
Vergilbung *f* yellow discoloration, yellowing
Vergleichsmuster *n* reference sample
Vergoldefarbe *f* gold-blocking ink
Vergoldepresse *f* gilding press, gold blocking press
Vergoldeschrift *f* gold-blocking type
Vergolde- und Prägepresse *f* gold blocking and embossing press
Vergoldung *f (Buchschnitt)* gilding; *(Prägung)* gold blocking, gold stamping
vergriffen *(Buch)* out of print, out of stock, sold out
Vergrößerer *m (Reprod.)* enlarger
Vergrößern *n (Reprod.)* enlarging, magnifying, scaling up; *(auf Postergröße)* posterizing
vergrößerter Maßstab *m* enlarged scale
Vergrößerung *f (Reprod.)* enlargement, exposure in enlarged scale, magnification, reproduction in enlarged scale
Vergrößerungsbereich *m* enlargement range
Vergrößerungsglas *n* magnifier, magnifying glass
Vergrößerungskamera *f (Reprod.)* process enlarger
Vergrößerungsmaßstab *m* enlargement ratio, enlargement scale

Vergrößerungsstufen *pl* enlargement increments *pl*
Verharzung *f (Farbe)* resinification
Verkäufe/Gesuche *pl (Anzeigenrubrik)* sales and wants *pl*
verkanten *(Bogen)* to cock
verkaufbare Exemplare *pl* saleable copies *pl*
Verkaufsanzeige *f* sales ad
Verkaufsgebiet *n* sales territory
Verkaufspersonal *n* sales people, sales staff
Verkaufsprospekte *pl* sales folders, sales literature
Verkeilung *f (Schließform)* quoining
Verkleben *n (frisch bedruckte Bogen)* blocking
Verkleinern *(Reprod.)* reducing, scaling down
verkleinerter Maßstab *m* reduced scale
Verkleinerung *f (Reprod.)* reduction, exposure in reduced scale, reproduction in reduced scale
verkupferter Draht *m* coppered wire
verkupfertes Stereo *n* copper-faced stereo
Verkupferung *f* copper-facing, copper-plating
Verkupferungsanlage *f* copper-plating installation
Verladerampe *f* loading platform
Verlag *m* publishers *pl,* publishing house
Verlagsbuchhändler *m* publisher and bookseller
Verlagsdruckerei *f* publishing and printing house
Verlagshaus *n* publishing house
Verlagslektor *m* publisher's reader
Verlagsrecht *n* copyright, right of publication
Verlagsvertrag *m* author-publisher agreement
Verlauf *m (Ton-, Hintergrund-, Rasterverlauf)* gradation, vignette, vignetting
Verlaufätzung *f* gradation etching
verlaufende Rasterfläche *f* vignetted halftone (screen), vignetted screen tint
Verlaufsraster *m (zum Aufrastern)* gradation screen
verlegen *(Buch, Zeitschrift)* to publish
Verleger *m* publisher
Verleimen *n* gluing(-up)
Vermaßen *n (Vorlagen)* scaling
vernickeltes Stereo *n* nickel-faced stereo
Vernickelung *f* nickel-facing, nickel-plating
Vernickelungsanlage *f* nickel-plating installation
veröffentlichen to publish
Veröffentlichung *f* publication
Verpacken *n* packing; *(besonders maschinell auch)* packaging; *(in Folie/Papier einschlagen)* wrapping
Verpackung *f* package, packaging, packing
Verpackungsdruck *m* package printing
Verpackungsdrucker *m* packaging printer
Verpackungsentwurf *m* packaging design

Verpackungsgestaltung f packaging design
Verpackungshersteller m packaging manufacturer
Verpackungsindustrie f packaging industry
Verpackungslinie f *(Versandraum)* packaging line
Verpackungsmaschine f *(Versand)* packaging machine; *(Folien-/Papiereinschlag)* wrapping machine
Verpackungspapier n wrapping paper
Verpackungstiefdruck m gravure package printing
Verpuderung f *(Druckm.)* powder contamination
Verreibewalze f distributor roller, oscillating roller
Verreibung f *(Farbe)* distribution
Versalbuchstabe m capital letter, uppercase letter
Versalhöhe f cap height
Versalien f/pl capital letters *pl*, capitals *pl*, caps *pl*, uppercase letters *pl*; **fette** ~ bold face capitals *pl*; **große** ~ full caps *pl*
Versaliensatz m all-caps setting
Versalschrift f *(Schrift ohne Kleinbuchstaben)* titling face
Versand m *(Zeitung, Zeitschrift)* distribution
Versandabteilung f distribution department, mailroom
Versandadresse f mailing address
Versandanlage f mailing line
Versandhauskatalog m mail-order catalogue
Versandraum m mailroom
Versandraumanlage f mailroom system
Versandraumausrüstung f mailroom equipment
Versandraumeinrichtung f mailroom equipment
Verschalung f *(Maschinen)* enclosure
Verschießen n *(Farbe)* discoloration, fading
Verschleißteil n wearing part
verschlüsseln to code, to encode
Verschluß m *(Kamera)* light chopper, shutter
Verschlußgeschwindigkeit f *(Kamera)* shutter speed
Verschlußklappe f *(Briefumschlag)* sealing flap
Verschlußklebung f seal gluing, sealing
Verschmieren n *(Druckproblem)* smearing, smudging
verschmierter Bogen m smeared sheet, smudged sheet
verschneiden *(Tiefdruckfarbe)* to extend, to thin
Verschnitt m *(Tiefdruckfarbe)* extender, gravure varnish, thinner; *(Papier)* cutting waste, trim waste
Verschnüren n *(Versandraum)* strapping, tying
Verschnürmaschine f strapping machine, tying machine

Verschränktauslage f compensated delivery, criss-cross delivery
verschränkter Stapel m compensated stack
verschrammtes Negativ n scratched negative
Verschwärzlichung f *(Farbe)* greyness
Verschweißen n *(Folienverpackung)* thermosealing
verschwommener Druck m blurred impression
versenkbare Paßstifte m/pl retractable register pins
versenkbare Tastatur f retractable keyboard
versetzte Auslage f staggered delivery
versetzter Stich m *(Fadenheftung)* staggered stitch
Verssatz m poetry setting
verstählen *(Stereoplatten)* to steel-face, to steel-plate
Verstählungsanlage f *(Stereotypie)* steel-facing installation, steel-plating installation
verstärkter Einband m reinforced binding
verstellbar adjustable
verstellen to adjust
Verstellung f adjustment
Versuchsdruckerei f experimental pressroom, experimental printshop
Verteiler m *(Versandraum)* diverter
verteilte Intelligenz f *(Comp.)* shared logic
Verteilung f *(Farbe)* distribution
vertiefter Druck m *(Tiefdruck)* recessed printing
vertieftes Bild n *(Tiefdruckcharakteristik)* recessed image
vertikaler Ausschluß m *(Satz)* vertical justification, vertical spacing
Vertikalkamera f vertical camera
Vertikallinie f *(Tabellensatz)* verticale rule
Vertikalschraffierung f vertical hatching
Vertriebsnetz n distribution network
Vervielfältigung f duplicating
Vervielfältigungsauftrag m duplicating job
Vervielfältigungsmaschine f duplicator
Vervielfältigungsrecht n copyright, right of reproduction
Verweis m *(Hinweis)* reference
Verweißlichung f *(Farbe)* desaturation
Verweisungszeichen n *(Satz)* reference mark
verwindungssteif *(Maschinenrahmen)* torsion-free, torsion-resistant
verwischter Druck m blurred impression
Verzeichnis der Druckfehler n errata, list of misprints
Verzeichnis der Inserenten n index to advertisers
Verzeichnung f *(Optik)* distortion
Verzeichnungsfehler m *(Objektiv)* aberration

Verzerrung f *(Fot.)* distortion
verzerrungsfreier Bildschirm m distortion-free monitor
Verziehen n *(Film, Gummituch, Druckbogen usw.)* distortion
verzierte Initiale f decorative initial, ornamented initial
verzierte Linie f fancy line, fancy rule, ornamented line, ornamented rule
verzierter Buchstabe m fancy letter, ornamented letter
Verzierung f *(Ornament)* floral ornament, floret, ornament, printer's flower, vignette
verzinnter Draht m tinned wire
vibrationsarmer Betrieb m low-vibration operation
Videoaufnahme f video recording
Videobilderfassung f video grabbing
Videobildschirmgerät n VDT, VDU, video display terminal, video display unit
Videorekorder m video recorder
Videostandbild n video still
Videotext m videotext
Vierbad-Entwicklungsgerät n *(Reprod.)* four-bath processor
Vierbruchfalz m four-directional fold, quadruple fold
4/1-farbig *(4 Farben Schöndruck, 1 Farbe Widerdruck)* four colour front, one reverse
Vierfarbanzeige f full-colour ad(vertisement), four-colour ad(vertisement)
Vierfarbarbeiten f/pl four-colour work, process-colour work
Vierfarbdruck m colour process printing, colour process work, four-colour print, four-colour printwork, four-colour process, full-colour process printing, process-colour work, process printing
Vierfarben-Andruckmaschine f four-colour proofpress
Vierfarben-Bogenoffsetmaschine f four-colour sheet-fed offset press
Vierfarbendruck m siehe Vierfarbdruck
Vierfarb(en)druckmaschine f four-colour (printing) press
Vierfarben-Naß-in-Naß-Druck m four colour wet-on-wet printing
vierfarbige Arbeiten pl siehe Vierfarbarbeiten
vierfarbiger Schöndruck m *(4/0 farbig)* four colour front, none reverse
vierfarbiger Schön- und Widerdruck m *(4/4 farbig)* four colour both sides, four colour front, four reverse

Vierfarbmaschine f four-colour (printing) press
Vierfarbmontage f process-colour stripping
Vierfarbreproduktion f four-colour process, four-colour reproduction
Vierfarbsatz m *(Auszugsfilme)* four-colour set, full-colour set
Vierfarbsujet n four-colour subject
Vierkantstichel m square scorper
4/0 farbig four colour front, none reverse
vierspaltige Seite f four-column page
Viertelbogen m quarter sheet
Viertelcicero f four-to-pica
Viertelfalz m quarter fold
Viertelgeviert n *(Satz)* four-to-em space, quarter em space, thin space
Vierteljahrsschrift f quarterly publication
Vierteltonraster m quarter tone
Vierteltonrasterfeld n *(Druckkontrollstreifen)* quarter tone tint patch
vierte Umschlagseite f fourth cover
4/4 farbig four colour both sides, four colour front, four reverse
vierzehntäglich erscheinende Zeitschrift f bi-monthly (publication), fortnightly (publication), semi-monthly (publication)
Vignette f *(Ornament)* ornament, vignette
Visitenkarte f calling card, visiting card
Viskoseschwamm m viscose sponge
Viskosimeter n visco(si)meter
Viskosität f viscosity
Viskositätsregler m *(Druckfarbe)* viscosity controller
visuelle Beurteilung f visual assessment, visual evaluation, visual judgement
visuelle Kommunikation f visual communication
visuelle Kontrolle f visual check(ing), visual control
Vokal m vowel
Volksausgabe f popular edition
voll ausnutzen *(technisch, kapazitätsmäßig)* to use to full potential, to utilize to capacity, to utilize to full advantage
vollautomatisch fully automatic
volle Kopie f *(im U. zur spitzen K.)* too dark copy
Vollerwerden n *(Punktzuwachs im Druck)* dot gain
vollfette Linie f full face line, full face rule
Vollfläche f *(im Druck)* flat tint, solid, solid area
Vollflächenauftrag m *(im U. zu Streifen-, Musterauftrag)* full-surface application
vollflächige Lackierung f full-surface coating, full-surface varnishing

Vollkapselung f *(Maschine)* full enclosure, total enclosure
Vollkarton m solid board
Vollkupferverfahren n *(Tiefdruck)* full-copper process
Vollpappe f *(im Gs. zur Wellpappe)* solid board
Vollretusche f *(im Gs. zu Spot-, Ausschnittretusche)* global retouching, overall retouching, thorough retouching
Vollton m full tone, solid, solid tint, solid tone
Volltondichte f density in the solids, full-tone density, solid (ink) density, solid (tone) density
Volltonfeld n *(Druckkontrollstreifen)* full-tone patch, solid ink patch
Volltonfläche f flat tint, solid, solid area
Vollton-Übereinanderdruckfeld n *(Druckkontrollstreifen)* solid colour overprint patch, solids superimposition patch
Vollverschalung f full enclosure, total enclosure
Vollzylinder m *(im U. zum Hohlzylinder)* solid cylinder
Volumen n *(Papier)* bulk (factor)
voluminöses Papier n bulky paper, voluminous paper
Vorätzung f first etching
Vorarbeiten pl preparatory work
Vorausexemplar n advance copy
Vorausrichtung f *(Bogenanlage)* pre-alignment, preregistration
Vorbehandlung f pre-treatment
Vorbelichtung f *(Rasterfotogr.)* flash exposure
Vorbelichtungslampe f *(Rasterfotografie)* flash lamp
vorbeschichtete Druckplatte f presensitized printing plate
Vorbrechvorrichtung f *(Faltschachtelherst.)* pre-breaker
vordefinierte Fläche f *(Bildschirmumbruch)* pre-defined area
Vorderanschlag m *(Bogenausrichtung)* front stop
Vorderbeschnitt m face cut, face trim(ming), front trim(ming)
Vorderdeckel m *(Buch)* front cover board
vorderer Buchdeckel m front cover board
vorderer Papierrand m foredge margin, front(-edge) margin, outer margin
vordere Umschlaginnenseite f inside front cover
Vordergrund m foreground
Vordergrund und Hintergrundbetrieb m *(Comp.)* foreground and background operation
Vordergrund- und Hintergrundzuweisung f *(Comp.)* foreground and background assignment
Vordergrundverarbeitung f *(Comp.)* foreground processing
Vorderkante f foredge, front edge, lead(ing) edge
Vordermarke f *(Bogenanleger)* front guide, front lay
Vorderschnitt m *(Buch)* foredge
Vorderseite f front page, recto page; **an der ~ beschneiden** to face-trim
Vorderseite beschichtet *(chemisch behandeltes Selbstdurchschreibepapier)* coated front (CF)
Vorder- und Rückseite f *(Papierbogen)* front and back, recto and verso
Vordruck m *(Formular)* blank, form
Vordrucken n *(mit Vordruckfarbe, z. B. Golddruck)* primer printing, priming
Vordruckfarbe f *(z. B. für Golddruck)* primer ink
Voreilung f *(Rollendruck)* advance, lead
Voreinrichten n *(Druckm.)* pre-makeready
Voreinstellsystem n presetting system
Voreinstellung f pre-adjustment, presetting
Voreinstellwert m presetting value
Vorfalz m *(Überfalz)* gripper fold, overfold
Vorfalzer m *(Rollendruckm.)* pre-folder
Vorfräsen n *(Tiefdruckzyl.)* rough milling
Vorführdruckerei f demonstration pressroom, demonstration printshop
vorgedruckte Bogen pl preprinted sections pl, preprinted signatures pl, preprints pl
vorgerastert pre-screened
vorgerüttelter Stapel m prejogged stack
vorgeschaltetes Aggregat n previous unit
vorgesehener Termin m scheduled deadline
vorgewinkelte Rasterfilmsätze pl pre-angled sets of screen films
Vorgreifer m pre-gripper
vorhergehende Zeile f preceding line
vorhersagbare Ergebnisse pl predictable results pl
Vorkalkulation f preliminary calculation
Vorlackierung f primer varnish coating
Vorlage f copy; *(für Reprod. auch)* art(work); *(für Scanner auch)* media
Vorlagenformat n copy size; *(für Scanner auch)* media format
Vorlagengestaltung f art design, copy design, copy display
Vorlagenhalter m copy board, copy holder
Vorlagenherstellung f art(work) preparation, copy preparation, origination
Vorlagenmaterial n *(Scanner)* scanning media
Vorlagenstudio n art studio

Vorlagenverarbeitung f copy processing
Vorlaufbogen pl *(Einrichten der Maschine)* advance sheets pl
Vorleim m primer glue
vorlockern to separate
Vorprodukte n/pl *(bedruckt)* preprinted products pl, preprinted sections pl, preprints pl
Vorprodukteanleger m preprint(ed section) feeder
Vorratskassette f *(Fotomaterial)* supply cassette
Vorregistersystem n preregister system
vorrillen to prescore
Vorrücken n *(der Maschine im Tastbetrieb)* inching
Vorsatz m *(Buchherst.)* endleaf, endpaper, endsheet
Vorsatzblätter n/pl endleaves pl
Vorsatzblatt n endleaf, endpaper, endsheet, fly-leaf
Vorsatzklebemaschine f *(Buchherst.)* endpapering machine, endsheet gluing machine
Vorsatzklebung f endpapering, endsheet gluing
Vorsatzpapier n endleaf, endpaper, endsheet
Vorschlag m *(Bleisatzumbruch)* head white
Vorschmelzgerät n *(Hotmelt)* premelter
Vorschub m *(Fotosatz; vertikal)* feeding, leading; *(Fotosatz; horizontal)* escapement
Vorschub Null m *(Fotosatz)* linefeed inhibit, zero leading
Vorschubsattel m *(Schneidem.)* backgauge
Vorspann m *(Satz)* header
Vorstapeleinrichtung f *(Druckm.)* preloading device, prepiling device, prestacker
Vortippen n *(Druckm.)* inching
Vortitel m *(Schmutztitel)* half title
Vor- und Zurücktippen n *(Druckm.)* inching
Vorwärts/Rückwärtstippen n *(Druckm.)* inching
vorwärtszählende Numerierung f consecutive numbering, sequential numbering, successive numbering
Vorwahlzähler m preselection counter
Vorwort n *(Buch)* foreword, introduction, preface
Vorzurichtung f pre-makeready
Vulkanisation f vulcanization
vulkanisieren to vulcanize
Vulkanisierpresse f vulcanizing press

W

wabenförmiger Rasterpunkt m hexagonal dot
Wabenfundament n honeycomb mount
Wabenlochplatte f *(Prägestempel)* honeycomb plate
Wachs n wax
Wachsabdruck m wax moulding
Wachsauftragsgerät n *(Klebemontage)* waxer
Wachsbeschichtungsgerät n *(Klebemontage)* waxer
Wachsleim m *(Papier)* wax size
Wachsleinen n oilcloth
Wachsleinwand f oilcloth
Wachsmatrize f wax matrix
Wachspapier n wax paper
Wachsprägung f *(Galvanopl.)* wax moulding
Wachsradierung f cerotype, wax engraving
Wählleitung f *(Telekom.)* dialling line, telephone line
während des Drucks during press operation, during press run
während des Laufs during machine run
Wälzlager n rolling bearing
Wärmeabfuhr f *(Gastrockner)* evacuation of heat
wärmebeständig heat-resistant
Wärmerückgewinnung f *(Druckm.)* heat recovery
Wässerung f *(Platten, Filme usw.)* rinsing, washing
Wässerungsbecken n rinsing sink, wash sink
wäßrig *(auf Wasserbasis)* aqueous, water-based
wäßriger Entwickler m aqueous developer
Wagen m *(techn.)* carriage, trolley
Wagenauslage f carriage delivery
Wagenrücklauf m *(Buchdruckm.)* carriage return
Wahlschalter m selector switch
Walze f roller
Walze ausbauen to remove roller
Walze einbauen to install roller
Walzen an/abstellen *(Druckm.)* to throw rollers on/off (impression)
Walzenauffrischung f roller reconditioning
Walzenaustausch m roller change
Walzenbeschichtung f roller coating
Walzenbezieher m *(Feuchtwalzen)* roller covering device
Walzenbezug m roller covering
Walzen einstellen to adjust rollers, to set rollers
Walzeneinstellung f roller adjustment, roller setting

Walzenfarbwerk n *(Tiefdruck)* roller-type inking unit
Walzengestell n roller frame
Walzenglätte f *(Glanzglätte)* roller glaze
Walzenjustierung f roller adjustment
Walzenkern m roller core
Walzenkühlung f roller chilling, roller cooling
Walzenlager n roller bearing
Walzenlaufschiene f roller rail
Walzenmasse f roller composition
Walzennachstellung f roller re-adjustment
Walzenpaar n roller pair
Walzenquellen n roller swelling
Walzenreinigungsgerät n roller cleaning device
Walzenschlauch m siehe Feuchtwalzenschlauch
Walzenschloß n roller lock
Walzenschlupf m roller slippage
Walzenschmitz m roller slur
Walzenschrank m roller cabinet
Walzenschuhe pl *(Handgriffe)* roller handles pl
Walzensektion f *(Entwicklungsm.)* rack
Walzenspalt m roller nip
Walzenspindel f roller core
Walzenständer m roller rack
Walzenstandprüfer m roller gauge
Walzensteller m roller gauge
Walzenstreifen m/pl *(Offset)* roller marks pl
Walzenstuhl m *(Farbherst.)* roller mill; *(Masch.)* roller frame
Walzentransportwagen m roller trolley
Walzenwagen m *(Tiegeldr.)* roller carriage
Walzenwascheinrichtung f *(Farbwerk)* roller wash-up device
Walzenwaschen n roller washing
Walzenwaschmaschine f roller washing machine
Walzenwaschmittel n roller wash
Walzenzapfen m roller journal
Wandern des Gummituchs blanket creep
Wandern des Zylinderaufzugs packing creep
Wandkalender m wall calendar
Wandkarte f wall chart, wall map
Wappenbuch n book of heraldry
Wappengraveur m heraldic engraver
Warenmuster n *(als Beilage)* sample
Warenprobe f *(als Beilage)* sample
Warenzeichen n trade mark
Warnsignal n buzzer
Warteschlangenverarbeitung f *(Comp.)* queue processing
Wartung f *(techn.)* maintenance, servicing
Wartungsbedarf m *(Maschine)* maintenance requirements pl
wartungsfrei maintenance-free

wartungsfreundlich service-friendly
Wartungspersonal n service engineers pl, service staff
Waschalkohol m alcohol wash
Waschbenzin n spirit wash
Waschbürste f cleaning brush, scrubbing brush
waschen *(Formen usw.)* to wash
Waschmarken pl *(Offset)* water marks pl
Waschmittel n wash, washing solution
Waschtrog m washing trough
Waschzettel m *(Buchhandel)* blurb
wasserabstoßend *(Offset)* hydrophobic, water-repellent
wasseranziehend hygroscopic
Wasseraufnahme f *(Offsetfarbe, Papier)* water absorption
Wasseraufnahmevermögen n water-ábsorbing capacity
wasserauswaschbare Fotopolymerplatte f water-based photopolymer plate, water-washed photopolymer plate
Wasserechtheit f *(Offsetfarbe)* water fastness
wasserentwickelbare Fotopolymerplatte f water-based photopolymer plate, water-developed photopolymer plate
Wasserentzug m dehydration
Wasserfarbe f *(Druckfarbe auf wäßriger Basis)* water-based ink
wasserfestes Papier n water-proof paper
wasserfreundlich *(Offset)* hydrophilic, water-receptive
wasserführende Stellen pl *(Offsetplatte)* water-conducting areas pl
Wasserführung f *(Offset)* damping, water distribution, water supply
wassergekühlt water-cooled
Wasserhärte f water hardness
Wasserkasten m *(Offsetdruckm.)* damping water fountain, water pan
Wasserkastenlack m *(Offset)* water-pan varnish
Wasserkastenwalze f damping duct roller, water fountain roller
Wasserkühlung f water-cooling
Wasserlinien pl *(Briefpapier)* laid lines pl, watermark lines pl, wire marks pl
wasserlose Offsetplatte f waterless offset plate
wasserloser Offsetdruck m waterless offset printing
Wassermarken pl *(Offset)* water marks pl
Wasserverschmutzung f water pollution
Wasserzeichen n *(Papier)* watermark
Wasserzeichenpapier n watermark(ed) paper
Wasserzeichenwalze f dandy roll

Wasserzufuhr f *(für Offsetfeuchtung)* water supply
Wattebausch m cotton(-wool) wad
wattierte Buchdecke f padded book case
Wechselfarbwerk n interchangeable inking unit
Wechselkassette f interchangeable cassette
Wechselplatte f *(comp.)* removable hard disk
Wechselreiber m distributor roller, oscillating roller
Wechselstich m *(Fadenheftung)* off-and-on stitch
Wechselstrom m A.C., alternating current
Wechselstrommotor m A.C. motor
wedeln to fan
wegbelichten n *(Schnittkanten)* to burn out
Wegbelichten von Schnittkanten pl burning-out of cutting edges, elimination of cutting edges
wegbrechen to break off
wegkratzen to scratch off
weglassen *(Satz)* to leave out, to miss out, to omit
wegschaben to scrape off
Wegschlagen n *(Farbe)* absorption, penetration, setting, striking-in
Wegschlagen der Farbe n ink absorption, ink setting
wegwischen to wipe off
Weiche f *(Prod.-Linie)* diverter, gate, switch
weiche Kombinationsnaht f *(elektron. Bildverarb.)* soft transition outline
weicher Aufzug m soft packing
weicher Punkt m soft dot
weicher Umschlag m flexible cover, soft cover
weiches Negativ n flat negative, soft negative
weiches Papier n soft paper
weichkantiger Punktaufbau m soft-edged dot structure
weichkantiger Rasterpunkt m soft-edged dot
Weichpackung f flexible packaging, soft pack
Weich-PVC n flexible PVC, soft PVC
weichverlaufende Freistellung f *(elektron. Bildverarb.)* soft outline vignetting
weichzeichnen *(fotogr.)* to soften
Weichzeichner m *(Objektiv)* soft focus lens
Weihnachtskarte f Christmas card
Weinetikett n wine label
Weißabgleich m *(Densitometer)* white alignment
Weißbelichtung f *(Rasterfotogr.)* white light exposure
Weißdruck m *(Blinddruck, Prägedruck ohne Farbe)* blind embossing
Weiße f *(Papier)* whiteness
Weißgrad m whiteness
Weißmacher m *(Papier)* whitener

weit ausschließen to space widely
weiter auf der nächsten Seite continued overleaf
weiter Satz m widely spaced matter, wide setting
Weiterverarbeitung f *(Druckverarbeitung)* converting, finishing, paper converting, paper processing, print converting, print finishing
weit setzen to space widely
Weitwinkelobjektiv n wide angle lens
Welle f *(Antrieb)* shaft
Wellenantrieb m shaft drive
Wellenlager n shaft bearing
Wellenlinie f waved rule, wavy line
Wellenlinienraster n wavyline screen
Wellenschnitt m wavy cut
wellige Kanten f/pl slack edges pl
welliges Papier n buckled paper, warped paper
Welligwerden n *(Papier)* buckling, cockling, warping
Wellpappe f corrugated; *E-* ~ E-flute corrugated
Wellpappenherstellung f corrugated production
Wellpappenindustrie f corrugated industry
Wellpappkarton m corrugated box, corrugated case
Wellpappkiste f corrugated container
Wendekopierrahmen m flip-top frame
Wendekreuz n *(Rollendruckm.)* turncross
Wendestangen f/pl *(Rollendruckm.)* angle bars pl, turnbars pl, turner bars pl; **luftumspülte** ~ air bars pl
Wendestangenüberbau m angle-bar superstructure
Wendetrommel f *(Schön- und Widerdruckm.)* perfecting drum, reversing drum, turning drum
Werbeabteilung f advertising department
Werbeagentur f advertising agency
Werbeaufsteller m advertising display, window card
Werbebeilage f advertising insert, advertising supplement
Werbeblätter pl *(Direktwerbung)* mailings pl
Werbebroschüre f advertising brochure, advertising folder, advertising leaflet
Werbebroschüren f/pl advertising literature
Werbedruck m advertising printing, publicity printing
Werbedrucksache f advertising matter, mailer, mailing, publicity matter
Werbegrafiker m advertising artist, advertising designer
Werbekampagne f advertising campaign
Werbeleiter m advertising manager
Werbematerial n advertising material
Werbemedium n advertising medium

Werbemittel n *(Medium)* advertising medium
werben to advertise
Werbeprospekt m advertising brochure, advertising folder, advertising leaflet
Werbetext m advertising copy, advertising text
Werbetexter m ad writer, copy writer
Werbeträger m advertising carrier, advertising medium
Werbetreibende m advertiser
werbetreibende Industrie f advertising industry
Werbezeichner m siehe Werbegrafiker
Werbung f advertising, promotion, publicity
Werkdruck m book printing, bookwork
Werkdruckerei f book printer
Werkdruckfarbe f book ink
Werkdruckmaschine f book press, book printing press
Werkdruckpapier n book paper
Werksatz m bookwork, bookwork composition
Werksatzschrift f book face, book fount, book type
Werksatzumbruch m book pagination
Werkszeitung f works paper
Werkzeugschrank m tool cabinet
Wertpapier n security paper
Wertpapierdruck m security printing
Wertpapierdruckerei f security printer
wetterfeste Druckfarbe f weather-proof ink
wetterfestes Plakat n weather-proof poster
Wetterfestigkeit f *(Druckfarbe)* weatherability, weather resistance
Wettscheine pl betting slips pl
Wickelfalz m letterfold, parallel fold
Wickelplatte f wrap-around plate
Wickelwelle f winding shaft
Wickler m *(Rollendruck)* jam-up, paper jam, wrap-around, wrapper, wrap-up
Wicklung f *(Papier)* reeling, winding
Widerdruck m backing-up, back(-side) printing, perfecting, reverse (side) printing, second side printing, verso (side) printing
Widerdruckform f backing forme, perfecting forme, second forme
Widerdruckregister n back-up register, fit, perfecting register
Widerdruckseite f *(Druckbogen)* back side, perfecting side, reverse side, verso side; *(Rollenpapier)* under side
Widerdruckseiten pl *(im Buch, in Zeitschriften)* verso pages pl
Widerdruckwerk n perfecting unit, perfector unit
Widerstandskraft gegen Knautscher smash-resistance

Widmung f *(Buch)* dedication
Wiederabdruck m *(Aufsatz)* reprint
wiederabdrucken to reprint
Wiederanfahren n *(Maschine)* re-start
wiederanfeuchtbarer Leim m *(Briefumschläge, Briefmarken)* remoistenable glue
Wiederanfeuchtgummierung f remoistenable glue
Wiederanlauf m *(Maschine)* re-start
Wiederauflegen n *(Anleger, Magazin)* re-feeding, refilling, re-loading, replenishing
Wiederaufrufen n *(Daten, Text)* recall, retrieval
Wiederaufwicklung f re-reeling, rewinding
Wiederbefeuchtung f *(Papierbahn)* remoistening
Wiedereingabeschlitz m *(Entwicklungsm.)* re-feed slot
Wiedergabe f *(Reprod./Druck)* rendering, reproduction
Wiedergabe im Offset offset reproduction
Wiedergabequalität f reproduction fidelity, reproduction quality; *(Fotosatz)* character definition
Wiedergabetreue f reproduction fidelity
wiedergeben to reproduce
Wiedergewinnungsanlage f reclamation system, recovery system
Wiederholbarkeit f repeatability, reproducibility
Wiederholgenauigkeit f repeat accuracy
Wiederholnumerierung f *(Numerierapparat)* skip numbering
Wiederholungsanzeige f *(in Publikation)* repeat ad(vertisement)
Wiederholungsauftrag m repeat job, repeat order, re-run
Wiederholungslauf m *(Comp.)* repeat run, re-run
Wiederholungszeichen n repeat mark
Wiegendruck m *(Inkunabeln)* incunabula pl
Winchester-Platte f Winchester disk
Window-Technik f *(PC)* window technique
winkelgenaues Falzen n rectangular folding
Winkelhaken m *(zum Setzen)* composing stick, setting stick
Winkelhaken mit Hebelverschluß lever stick
Winkelhaken mit Keilverschluß lever stick
Winkelhaken mit Schraubenverschluß screw composing stick
Winkelmaßhaltigkeit f squareness
Winkelschnitt m square cut, square trim, true rectangular cut
Winkelspatium n *(Bleisatz)* angle space
Winkelstellung f *(Raster)* angular position
Winkeltransportband n *(Versandraum)* angled conveyor
Wipe-on-Platte f wipe-on plate

wird fortgesetzt to be continued
Wirtschaftlichkeit *f* cost-effectiveness, cost-efficiency, profitability
Wirtschaftlichkeit in der Produktion production efficiency
wischfest rub-proof, smudge-proof
Wischtuch *n* wiping cloth
Wischwalze *f* damping roller
Wischwasser *n* damping solution, damping water, fountain solution, fountain water
Wochenendausgabe *f (Zeitung)* weekend issue
Wochenendbeilage *f (Zeitung)* weekend supplement
Wochenkalender *m* weekly calendar
Wochenzeitschrift *f* weekly (magazine)
Wochenzeitung *f* weekly (newspaper), weekly paper
wölben *sich* ~ to buckle
Wörterbuch *n* dictionary
Wolfram-Halogenlampe *f* tungsten-halogen lamp
Wolkenbildung *f (im Druck)* cloud formation
wolkiger Druck *m* mottled impression
Workstation *f (Comp.)* workstation
Workstation-Publishing *n (i. U. zu Desktop-Publishing)* workstation publishing
Wortabstand *m* interword spacing, wordspace
Wortanzahl *f (Texterf.)* word count
Wortkupplung *f* coupling of words
Wortregister *n (eines Werks)* index of terms
Worttrennung *f* word division
Wortzwischenraum *m* word space
Wrattenfilter *n* Wratten filter
Wulst *m (Biegewulst)* bulge
Wurzelzeichen *n* radical sign
WYSIWYG-Bildschirm *m (Fotosatz)* typeview monitor, WYSIWYG screen
WYSIWYG-Display *n (Echtschriftdarstellung)* WYSIWYG display

X

Xenonblitz *m* xenon flash
Xenon-Impuls-Lampe *f* pulsed xenon lamp
Xenonlampe *f* xenon lamp
Xerografie *f* xerography
Xylografie *f (Holzschneidekunst)* wood engraving, xylography

Y

Y-Druckwerk *n (Zeitungsoffsetrotation)* Y-type printing unit

Z

Zackenschnitt *m* serrated cut
zähe Farbe *f* sticky ink, tacky ink, viscous ink
Zähigkeit *f (Farbe)* stickiness, tackiness
Zähler *m* counter
Zählgenauigkeit *f* count accuracy
Zählstapler *m* counter-stacker
Zählung *f* count
Zählwerk *n* counter
Zahlbuchstabe *m (a), b) usw.)* numerical letter
Zahlenbruch *m (Satz)* fractional number
Zahl in Ziffern setzen to set in figures
Zahnlinie *f* serrated line, serrated rule
Zahnrad *n* cogwheel, gear wheel, tooth wheel
Zahnradantrieb *m* gear drive
Zahnradeingriff *m (Getriebe)* gear meshing
Zahnradgetriebe *n* toothed gear(ing)
Zahnriemen *m* toothed belt
Zahnspiel *n (Antrieb)* backlash
Zahnstreifen *m (Schmitzstreifen)* gear mark
Zange *f (Klebebinder)* clamp
Zangengreifer *pl* pincer grippers *pl*
Zaponlack *m* cellulose lacquer
Zeichenabstand *m* character fit(ting), character spacing, interspacing, letterspacing
Zeichenband *n (Lesezeichen)* bookmark
Zeichenbandeinlegemaschine *f (Buchherst.)* bookmark inserting machine
Zeichenbreite *f* character set, character width, set (size)
Zeichenbrett *n* drawing board
Zeichendarstellung *f (Bildschirm)* character display
Zeichenerkennung *f (Abtastung)* character recognition
Zeichenerklärung *f (auf Tafeln, Karten usw.)* legend
Zeichenfeder *f* drawing pen
Zeichenfolge *f* character string

Zeichenfolie f drafting film
Zeichengenerierung f character generation
Zeichenkarton m drawing board
Zeichenkohle f drawing charcoal
Zeichenkreide f drawing chalk
Zeichen löschen to delete character
Zeichenpaar n (Satz) character pair
Zeichenpapier n drafting paper
Zeichenpinsel m drawing brush
Zeichen pro Sekunde (Z/s, Fotosatz) characters per second
Zeichensatz m (Fotosatzm.) character set, repertoire (of characters)
Zeichensetzung f punctuation
Zeichenspeicher m (Texterf.) character memory
Zeichentisch m drawing table
Zeichentusche f drawing ink; **chinesische ~** India ink
Zeichenunterschneidung f (Satz) character kerning, kerning, pair kerning
Zeichenvorlage f drawing copy
Zeichenvorrat m (Fotosatz) character pool, character set
Zeichenwerkzeug n (CAD) drawing tool
zeichnen to draw
Zeichner m draftsman, draughtsman
Zeichnung f drawing; (Durchzeichnung im Bild) details pl, image definition
Zeigerskala f dial indicator
Zeile f line
Zeile auf Zeile setzen to set line by line
Zeile für Zeile line by line
Zeile halten to keep baseline
Zeilenabstand m line spacing, white space between lines
Zeilenabtastung f line scanning
Zeilenausgang m line ending
zeilenausschließende Schreibmaschine f justifying typewriter
Zeilenausschluß m (Satz) horizontal justification, line justification
Zeilenbreite f line measure, line width, measure
Zeilendrucker m (Belegdrucker) line printer
Zeilendurchschuß m leading, line spacing, vertical spacing, white space between lines
Zeilenende n end of line, line ending
Zeilenendkommando n (Fotosatz) end-of-line instruction
Zeilenfall m (Satz) copy flow, line fall
Zeilenfüller m line filler
Zeilengießmaschine f line caster, line casting machine, slug casting machine

Zeilenguß m line casting, slug casting; (gegossene Zeile) slug
Zeilenlänge f line length, line measure
Zeilenmaß n type gauge
Zeilenrestlänge f (Fotosatz) line length remainder
Zeilensäge f (Bleisatz) slug saw
Zeilensatz m line composition, slug composition
Zeilenschiff n (Bleisatz) galley
Zeilenschneider m (Bleisatz) slug cutter
Zeilensetz- und -gießmaschine f line composing and casting machine
Zeilenspaltung f line splitting
Zeilenstart m line start
Zeilenvorschub m (Fotosatzm.) advance, advance leading, leading, linefeed
Zeilenzahl f line count
Zeilen zur Mitte stellen to center lines
Zeitgeber m timer
Zeitschalter m timing switch
Zeitschrift f journal, magazine, periodical, review
Zeitschriftendruck m magazine printing, periodical printing, publication printing
Zeitschriftendruckerei und -verlag magazine printer and publisher, magazine printing and publishing house
Zeitschriftenkopf m magazine title
Zeitschriftentiefdruck m gravure publication printing
Zeitschriftenwerbung f magazine advertising
Zeitung f newspaper, paper
Zeitungsabonnement n newspaper subscription
Zeitungsagentur f news agency
Zeitungsanzeige f newspaper ad(vertisement)
Zeitungsarchiv n newspaper archive
Zeitungsausschnitt m (Beleg) newspaper clipping, newspaper cutting, press cutting
Zeitungsausträger m newspaper carrier
Zeitungsbeilage f (Redaktionsb.) newspaper supplement; (Werbebeil.) newspaper insert
Zeitungsbetrieb m newspaper operation, newspaper printing plant
Zeitungsbild n newspaper illustration
Zeitungsbündelpresse f newspaper bundling press
Zeitungsdruck m news(paper) printing
Zeitungsdrucker m newspaper printer
Zeitungsdruckerei f newspaper printer, newspaper printhouse, newspaper printing plant
Zeitungsdruckerei und -verlag newspaper printer and publisher, newspaper printing and publishing house

Zeitungs(druck)farbe f news ink
Zeitungs(druck)maschine f newspaper (printing) press, newspaper rotary (press)
Zeitungs(druck)papier n newsprint
Zeitungseinsteckmaschine f newspaper inserting machine
Zeitungsexemplar n newspaper copy
Zeitungsfalz m newspaper fold
Zeitungsfarbe f siehe Zeitungsdruckfarbe
Zeitungsflexodruck m newspaper flexo(graphic) printing, newspaper flexography
Zeitungsflexoplatte f newspaper flexo plate
Zeitungsformat n newspaper format, newspaper size
Zeitungsherstellung f newspaper production
Zeitungshochdruck m newspaper letterpress (printing)
Zeitungsimpressum n newspaper imprint
Zeitungsindustrie f newspaper industry
Zeitungskolumne f newspaper column
Zeitungskopf m newspaper title
Zeitungsleser m newspaper reader
Zeitungslinie f *(Verarbeitungslinie)* newspaper (processing) line
Zeitungsmetteur m *(Bleisatzumbruch)* newspaper maker-up
Zeitungsnachricht f news
Zeitungsnotiz f press item
Zeitungspaket n newspaper bundle
Zeitungspapier n newsprint
Zeitungsrotation f siehe Zeitungsrotationsmaschine
Zeitungsrotationsdruck m newspaper rotary printing
Zeitungsrotation(smaschine) f newspaper rotary (press)
Zeitungssatz m newspaper composition, news setting, newswork
Zeitungsschlagzeile f news headline
Zeitungsschrift f newspaper typeface, news type
Zeitungsseite f news page
Zeitungssetzer m news compositor
Zeitungsstereotypie f newspaper stereotyping
Zeitungsstreifband n newspaper wrapper
Zeitungssystem n *(elektron. Druckvorstufe)* news publishing system
Zeitungstechnik f newspaper technology
Zeitungsträger m newspaper carrier
Zeitungsumbruch m newspaper page make-up, newspaper pagination
Zeitungsverlag m newspaper publisher, newspaper publishing house
Zeitungsverleger m newspaper publisher

Zeitungswerbung f newspaper advertising
Zellglas n *(Cellophan)* cellophane
Zellglasfenster n cellophane window
Zellstoff m *(Papierherst.)* chemical pulp
Zellstoffabrik f pulp mill
Zellstoffauflöser m *(Papierherst.)* chemical pulp digester
Zellstoffherstellung f chemical pulping
Zellulose f cellulose
Zelluloseazetat n cellulose acetate
Zelluloselack m cellulose lacquer
Zentraldruckschmierung f central pressure lubrication
zentrale Steuerung f centralized control
Zentralrechner m *(CPU)* central processing unit, central processor, CPU
Zentralschmierung f central lubrication
Zentralspeicher m central storage
Zentralverschluß m *(Kamera)* central shutter
Zentralversorgungssystem n central supply system
zentral verstellbar centrally adjustable
zentrieren to center
Zentriervorrichtung f centring device
Zerfaserer m *(Papierfabrik)* pulper, shredder
zerknittert *(Papier)* creased, crumpled
zerknüllt *(Bogen)* crumpled
Zerstäuber m *(Puderbestäuber)* powder sprayer, spray powder device
Zerstäuberdüse f spraying nozzle
Zerstreuungslinse f dispersing lens
Zeug n *(Schriftmetall)* type metal
Zickzackfalz m accordeon fold, computer fold, concertina fold, fan fold, harmonica fold, z-fold, zigzag fold
Zickzackfalzapparat m fan folder, zigzag folder
zickzack-gefalzter Stapel m fan-folded pack, zigzag folded pack
Zickzacklinie f zigzag line, zigzag rule
Zickzackperforierung f zigzag perforating
Ziehfeder f ruling pen, straight-line pen
Ziehmarke f *(Bogenanleger)* pull lay
Ziehpappe f moulded board
Ziehpresse f drawing press
zielgruppenorientierte Werbung f advertising in selected target groups
Zierbuchstabe m fancy letter, ornamented letter, swash letter
Zierleiste f *(typogr.)* border, floral ornament, floret, head-piece, tail-piece
Zierlinie f ornamented rule
Zierrand m ornamented border
Zierschnur f fancy cord

Zierschrift - Zuschweißen

Zierschrift f fancy type, ornamented type, swash type
Zierstück n flourish, ornament, vignette
Ziffer f *(Zahlzeichen)* figure, numeral
Ziffernkasten m *(Handsatz)* figure case
Ziffern mit Unterlängen *(Mediäval)* old-style figures pl
Ziffernsatz m setting of numerals
Zigarettenausstellkarton m cigarette outer
Zigarettenpackung f cigarette pack
Zigarettenschachtel f cigarette box
Zinkätzplatte f zinc-etch plate
Zinkätzung f zinc engraving, zinc etching
Zinkdruckplatte f zinc printing plate
Zinkklischee n zinc engraving, zinc etching
Zinkoffsetplatte f lithographic zinc plate, zinc offset plate
Zinkoxydpapier n zinc oxide paper
Zinkplatte f zinc plate
Zinkweiß n zinc white
Zirkellinienraster m *(Reprod.)* concentric line screen
Zirkumflexakzent m *(Satz)* circumflex accent
ziselieren to engrave with a chisel
Zitat n quotation
zitieren to quote
zonale Farbdosierung f zonal ink metering
Zonenschraube f *(Farbkasten)* ink key, duct screw, fountain key, fountain screw, ink screw, key
Zoomen n *(Reprod.)* zooming
Zoomobjektiv n zoom lens
zügige Farbe f sticky ink, tacky ink, viscous ink
Zügigkeit f *(Druckfarbe)* stickiness, tackiness
Zuführgreifer m feed grippers pl
Zuführung f *(Material)* feed(ing), supply
Zuführwalze f feed roller
Zugabe f *(Papier)* allowance
Zugänglichkeit f *(Aggregate)* accessibility
Zugang m *(Aggregate)* access
Zugbeanspruchung f *(Papier)* tensile strain
Zugbogen m *(Straffen)* drawsheet, top sheet, tympan
Zugehen n *(Raster)* filling-in
zugeschnitten *(Systeme, Maschinenkonfigurationen)* customized, made to measure, tailor-made
Zugfestigkeit f tensile strength
Zugkraft f *(Walzen)* pull strength
Zugriff m *(Daten, Texte)* access
Zugriffszeit f *(Comp.)* access time
Zugrollen f/pl nip pulleys pl

Zugwalze f *(Rollendruckm.)* draw roller, pull roller
Zulaufen n filling-in
zulaufender Raster m *(Druck)* filled-in halftones pl
Zulieferfirma für die Druckindustrie graphic arts dealer, graphic arts supplier, printer's supplier
Zupfbogen m pull sheet
Zurichtebogen m *(Buchdruck)* makeready sheet, overlay sheet
Zurichtemesser n makeready knife
zurichten to make ready
Zurichtepapier n makeready paper
Zurichtepappe f overlay board
Zurichtung f makeready
Zurichtungsabzug m makeready proof
Zurückfedern n *(Bogen)* bounce-back
zusätzlich lieferbar available on option
Zusammendruck m combination printing, combined printing
Zusammendruckfeld n *(Druckkontrollstreifen)* solid colour overprint patch, solids superimposition patch
Zusammendrückbarkeit f compressibility
zusammenfassender Text m *(am Anfang eines Zeitungsartikels)* capsule
Zusammenfassung f summary
zusammengestoßene Linien pl *(Handsatz)* butted rules pl
zusammenklappbar collapsible
Zusammenkleben n *(frischbedruckte Bogen)* blocking
Zusammenkopieren n combined exposure
zusammenrücken *(Zwischenraum herausnehmen)* to close up
zusammentragen *(Bogen)* to collect, to gather; *(Einzelblätter)* to collate
Zusammentragmaschine f *(Bogen)* gatherer, gathering machine; *(Einzelblätter)* collator
Zusammentrag- und Heftmaschine f siehe Sammelhefter
Zusatzausrüstung f optional equipment
Zusatzfarbe f *(Schmuckfarbe)* spot colour
Zusatzfarbwerk n *(Kleinoffset)* imprinting unit; *(Zeitungsrotation)* colour deck, deck, half-deck, spot-colour printing unit
zuschalten to clutch, to connect, to engage
Zuschmieren n *(Raster)* filling-in
Zuschnitte pl *(Kartonagen)* blanks pl
Zuschuß(bogen) m/pl *(Papier zur Auflage)* allowance, oversheets pl, plus sheets pl
Zuschweißen n *(Folienverpackung)* sealing, welding

Zusetzen *n (Raster)* filling-in
Zuweisung *f (Comp.)* allocation
Zweibadentwicklung *f* two-bath processing
Zwei-Bahn-Betrieb *m (Rollendruck)* two-web operation
Zweibruch-Fensterfalz *m* two-directional gatefold
Zweibruchkreuzfalz *m* two-directional right angle fold
Zweibuchstabenmatrize *f* two-letter matrix
2/1-farbig *(2 Farben Schöndruck, 1 Farbe Widerdruck)* two colour front, one reverse
Zweifarbenauszug *m* two-colour separation
Zweifarben-Bogenoffsetmaschine *f* two-colour sheet-fed offset press
Zweifarbendruck *m* two-colour printing
Zweifarben(druck)maschine *f* two-colour (printing) press
Zweifarbenoffsetmaschine *f* two-colour offset press
Zweifarben-Schön- und Widerdruckmaschine *f* two-colour perfecting press
Zweifarbenübereinanderdruck *m (Druckkontrollstreifen)* two-colour overprint
zweifarbiger Schöndruck *m (2/0 farbig)* two colour front, none reverse
zweifarbiger Schön- und Widerdruck *m (2/2 farbig)* two colour front, two reverse, two colours both sides
Zwei-Filter-Kontraststeuerung *f (Reprod.)* two-filter contrast control
zweimonatlich erscheinende Zeitschrift *f* bi-monthly (publication)
2/0-farbig *(2 Farben Schöndruck, kein Widerdruck)* two colour front, none reverse
Zweiraumkamera *f* darkroom camera, two-room camera
Zweischichtbetrieb *m* two-shift operation
Zweischichtenfilm *m* two-layer film
zweiseitig double-sided, two-sided
zweiseitig bedruckt printed (on) both sides
zweiseitig bedruckter Bogen *m* two-sided printed sheet
zweiseitiger Druck *m* two-sided printing
zweiseitig gestrichenes Papier *n* two-sided coated paper
zweiseitig kalandriert two-sided calendered
Zweiseitigkeit *f (Papier)* two-sidedness
zweiseitig lackieren to varnish both sides
zweiseitig satiniert two-sided calendered
zweiseitig vorbeschichtete Druckplatte *f* two-sided sensitized printing plate
zweispaltige Anzeige *f* two-column advertisement
zweispaltige Seite *f* two-column page

zweiter Längsfalz *m (Rollendruck)* quarter fold
zweite Umschlagseite *f* second cover
Zweitoriginal *n* second(-generation) original
Zweitourenpresse *f* two-revolution press
Zweitvorlage *f (Reprod.)* second(-generation) original
zweiwöchentlich erscheinende Zeitschrift *f* siehe vierzehntäglich erscheinende Zeitschrift
zweizeilige Initiale *f* two-line initial
zweizeiliger Anfangsbuchstabe *f* two-line initial
2/2 farbig two colour front, two reverse, two colours both sides
Zwiebelfische *pl (in Unordnung geratener Satz)* pie
Zwielaut *m* diphthong
Zwischenätzung *f* intermediate etching
Zwischenbogeneinlage *f (Bogendurchschuß)* binder sheet insetting
Zwischendeckausführung *f (Rollendruckm.)* intermediate floor design
Zwischendruckwerkstrocknung *f (zwischen den Druckwerken)* inter-unit drying
Zwischenfilm *m (Reprod.)* intermediate film
Zwischenkopie *f* intermediate copy
Zwischenlagerung *f* buffer storage, intermediate storage, short-term storage, temporary storage
Zwischennegativ *n (Reprod.)* inter(mediate) negative
Zwischenraum *m (typogr.)* character fit, space, type fit
Zwischenraum erweitern to insert space, space out, to space wider
Zwischenraum herausnehmen to close up, to space closer
Zwischenschlag *m (Raum zwischen den Spalten)* column gutter
Zwischenschnitt *m (Schneidem.)* intermediate cut
Zwischenspeicher *m (Comp.)* buffer memory, buffer storage, intermediate storage
Zwischenstapeln *n* intermediate piling
Zwischensteg *m (Bleisatz)* gutter stick
Zwischentitel *m* chapter heading, subtitle
Zwischentöne *pl (Bild)* intermediate tones *pl*
Zwischenwalze *f* intermediate roller
Zwischenzeile *f (Leerzeile)* blank line, space line, white line
zyklischer Speicher *m* cyclic storage
Zylinder *m* cylinder; *(Buchdruckm.)* cylinder flat-bed press, cylinder (printing) press
Zylinderabstellung *f* cylinder throw-off
Zylinderabziehpresse *f* cylinder proof press
Zylinderandruckpresse *f* cylinder proof press

Zylinderanordnung - Zylinderzurichtung

Zylinderanordnung *f* cylinder arrangement, cylinder configuration
Zylinderauflager *n (Tiefdruckzyl.)* cylinder support
Zylinderaufzug *m* cylinder dressing, cylinder packing
Zylinderballen *m* cylinder body, cylinder face
Zylinderbearbeitung *f (Tiefdruck)* cylindering, cylinder machining
Zylinderbüchse *f (Tiefdruck)* cylinder bushing
Zylinderdreh- und Poliermaschine *(Tiefdruck)* cylinder turning and polishing machine
Zylinderdruckautomat *m* automatic cylinder press
Zylinderdruckpresse *f* cylinder (printing) press
Zylindereinschub *m (Kassettendruckwerk)* printing cartridge, slide-in carriage
Zylindereinstich *m (Unterschliff)* cylinder undercut
Zylindereintauchung *f (Tiefdruck)* cylinder immersion
Zylinderfalz *m* chopper fold, cylinder fold
Zylinderflachformpresse *f* cylinder flat-bed press
Zylindergalvanik *f (Tiefdruck)* cylinder plating
Zylindergreifer *pl* cylinder grippers *pl*
Zylinderherstellung *f (Tiefdruck)* cylinder preparation
Zylinderhinterschliff *m* cylinder undercut
Zylinderkanal *m (Offset)* cylinder gap, non-printing gap
Zylinderkern *m* cylinder core
Zylinderkorrektur *f (Tiefdruck)* cylinder correction
Zylinderlager *n (Aufbewahrung)* cylinder storage; *(Lagerung)* cylinder bearing
Zylinderlagerbüchse *f* cylinder bearing bush
Zylinderlagergestell *n (Tiefdruck)* cylinder storage rack
Zylinderlagerung *f* cylinder bearing
Zylinderlaufring *m (Schmitzring)* cylinder bearer
Zylindermantel *m* cylinder jacket
Zylindermarke *f* cylinder gauge, cylinder lay
Zylinderpoliermaschine *f* cylinder polishing machine
Zylinderpressung *f (Beistelldruck)* impression pressure
Zylinderpunktur *f* cylinder pins *pl*
Zylinderreinigungsanlage *f (Tiefdruck)* cylinder washing machine
Zylinderreparatur *f (Tiefdruck)* cylinder repair
Zylinderretusche *f (Tiefdruck)* cylinder retouching

Zylinderschleifmaschine *f (Tiefdruck)* cylinder grinding machine
Zylinderspalt *m (Einlaufspalt zwischen zwei Zyl.)* cylinder nip
Zylinderspaltschutz *m* cylinder nip guard
Zylinderüberzug *m* siehe Zylinderaufzug
Zylinderumdrehung *f* cylinder revolution
Zylinderumdruckpresse *f* cylinder transfer press
Zylinderumfang *m* cylinder circumference
Zylinderunterschliff *m* cylinder undercut
Zylinderzapfen *m* cylinder journal
Zylinderzurichtung *f* cylinder makeready

Persönliche Ergänzungen

Persönlicher Ergänzungen

WÖRTERBUCH ENGLISH – DEUTSCH
ENGLISH – GERMAN DICTIONARY

A

abbreviation *(typesetting)* Abbreviatur *f*
abbreviation sign *(typesetting)* Abkürzungszeichen *n*
aberration *(lens)* Aberration *f*, Bildfehler *m*, Verzeichnungsfehler *m*
abrasion Abrieb *m*
abrasion-proof abriebfest, scheuerfest
abrasion resistance Abriebfestigkeit *f*, Scheuerfestigkeit *f*
abrasion-resistant abriebfest, scheuerfest
abrasive Schleifmittel *n*
abridged *(typesetting)* in abgekürzter Form
abridged edition *(book)* gekürzte Ausgabe *f*, kleine Ausgabe *f*
absence of fog *(film)* Schleierfreiheit *f*
absolute address *(comp.)* absolute Adresse *f*
absorbent paper saugfähiges Papier *n*, Saugpapier *n*
absorption *(ink)* Wegschlagen *n*
absorption capacity *(paper)* Saugfähigkeit *f*, Saugvermögen *n*
absorption spectrum *(light)* Absorptionsspektrum *n*
abstract *(book)* Buchauszug *m*; *(of an article)* Auszug *m*
A.C. Drehstrom *m*, Wechselstrom *m*
acceleration *(mach.)* Beschleunigung *f*, Hochlauf *m*
accent *(typesetting)* Akzent *m*
accented letter Akzentbuchstabe *m*
accentuate *v* akzentuieren; *(typogr.)* auszeichnen, hervorheben; ~ **with bold** mit Halbfetter auszeichnen; ~ **with italic** mit Kursiv auszeichnen; ~ **with small caps** mit Kapitälchen auszeichnen
accentuation Akzentuierung *f*
accept *v* *(advertisement)* aufnehmen
acceptance number *(of copies)* Gutzahl *f*
acceptance of printwork Druckabnahme *f*
access *(data, text)* Zugriff *m*; *(machine parts)* Zugang *m*
accessibility *(machine parts)* Zugänglichkeit *f*
access time *(comp.)* Zugriffszeit *f*
accident prevention Unfallschutz *m*
accident prevention regulations *pl* Unfallverhütungsvorschriften *pl*
accomodate copy *v* *(text)* Text unterbringen
accordeon fold Leporellofalz *m*, Zickzackfalz *m*

accumulation conveyor *(mailroom)* Stautaktförderer *m*
accumulator Akkumulator *m*
accuracy of colour value Farbwertrichtigkeit *f*
A.C. drive Drehstromantrieb *m*
acetate Azetat *n*
acetate colour proof *(colour key)* Colorkey *m*, Farbdurchsichtsproof *m*, Farbfolienproof *m*
acetate film Azetatfolie *f*; *(film laminating)* Glanzfolie *f*, Glanzkaschierfolie *f*, Kaschierfolie *f*
acetate laminated board azetatkaschierter Karton *m*
acetate laminating *(film laminating)* Cellophanierung *f*, Glanzfolienkaschierung *f*, Hochglanzkaschierung *f*
acetate of cobalt Kobaltazetat *n*
acetate overlay *(book wrapper)* Transparentumleger *m*
acetic acid *(photochem.)* Essigsäure *f*
achromatic achromatisch, farblos
achromatic colour neutrale Farbe *f*, unbunte Farbe *f*
achromatic colour separations *pl* Unbuntfarbauszüge *m/pl*, Unbuntfarbsatz *m*
achromatic composition *(reprod.)* Unbuntaufbau *m*
achromatic construction *(reprod.)* Unbuntaufbau *m*
achromatic reproduction Unbuntreproduktion *f*
acid Ätze *f*, Säure *f*
acid bath Säurebad *n*
acid development Säureentwicklung *f*
acid-free paper säurefreies Papier *n*
acid-proof paper säurefestes Papier *n*
A.C. motor Drehstrommotor *m*, Wechselstrommotor *m*
acoustic coupler *(telecom.)* Akustikkoppler *m*
acoustic warning signal akustisches Warnsignal *n*
across the grain *(paper)* gegen die ~/quer zur Bahnlaufrichtung *f*, gegen die ~/quer zur Laufrichtung *f*, gegen die ~/quer zur Papierlaufrichtung *f*, in Querrichtung *f*
across the web gegen die ~/quer zur Bahnlaufrichtung *f*, gegen die ~/quer zur Laufrichtung *f*, gegen die ~/quer zur Papierlaufrichtung *f*, in Querrichtung *f*
actinic density aktinische Dichte *f*
actinic light aktinisches Licht *n*
activate *v* aktivieren, betätigen
activated carbon filtration *(solvent recovery)* Aktivkohlefilterung *f*
activator *(photochem.)* Aktivator *m*

actual depth *(typesetting; as opp. to nominal depth)* Ist-Höhe *f*
actual size *(reprod.)* **in** ~ in der Größe 1:1, in natürlicher Größe
actual value Ist-Wert *m*
actuate *v* betätigen
actuator *(remote control)* Stellglied *n*
acutance Schärfe *f*
acute accent *(typesetting)* Akut *m*
ad see ad(vertisement)
ad acquisition Anzeigenakquisition *f*
adapt *v (typogr.)* anpassen
ad arrangement Anzeigengestaltung *f*, Anzeigenlayout *n*
ad campaign see advertising campaign
ad collection Anzeigenannahme *f*, Anzeigenaufnahme *f*
ad collection deadline Anzeigenschluß *m*
ad composing room Anzeigensetzerei *f*
ad composition Anzeigensatz *m*
ad compositor Anzeigensetzer *m*
A/D converter (analogue-digital) A/D-Wandler (Analog-Digital) *m*
ad copy Anzeigentext *m*
addenda *pl (book)* Anhang *m*, Ergänzungen *f/pl*, Nachträge *m/pl*
ad department see advertising department
ad design Anzeigengestaltung *f*
ad display Anzeigengestaltung *f*
additional charge Aufschlag *m*
additional work Extraarbeit *f*, Mehrarbeit *f*
additive colour synthesis additive Farbmischung *f*
additives *pl (papermaking)* Hilfsstoffe *pl*; *(pressroom chem.)* Additive *n/pl*, Druckhilfsmittel *pl*
add-on furniture Anbaumöbel *pl*
address *(also comp.)* Adresse *f*
address book Adreßbuch *n*
addressee *(mailroom)* Adressat *m*
address format *(comp.)* Adressenformat *n*
addressing Adressierung *f*
addressing head Adressierkopf *m*
addressing machine Adressiermaschine *f*
address register *(comp.)* Adressenregister *n*, Adressenverzeichnis *n*
adface *(type)* Anzeigenschrift *f*
ad filing Anzeigenverwaltung *f*
ad handling Anzeigenbearbeitung *f*, Anzeigenverarbeitung *f*
adherence *(ink, glue etc.)* Haften *n*
adhesive Kleber *m*, Leim *m*, Kleister *m*
adhesive binder Klebebindemaschine *f*, Klebebinder *m*

adhesive binding Klebebindung *f*, Lumbecken *n*
adhesive film Klebefolie *f*, Haftfolie *f*
adhesive foil Klebefolie *f*, Haftfolie *f*
adhesive foil for blockmounting Klischeeklebefolie *f*
adhesive strength Klebkraft *f*
adhesive strip Klebestreifen *m*
adhesive tape Klebeband *n*
adhesive wax *(paste-up)* Haftwachs *n*, Montagewachs *n*
adjacent pages *pl* nebeneinanderliegende Seiten *f/pl*
adjust *v* abgleichen, einstellen, regeln, verstellen
adjustable nachstellbar, regelbar, regulierbar, verstellbar
adjusting knob Einstellknopf *m*
adjusting lever Einstellhebel *m*
adjusting screw Regulierschraube *f*, Stellschraube *f*
adjusting wheel Stellrad *n*
adjustment Abgleich *m*, Einstellung *f*, Justierung *f*, Regelung *f*, Regulierung *f*, Verstellung *f*
adjust rollers *v (press)* Walzen einstellen
adjust text to the left *v* linksbündig setzen
adjust text to the right *v* rechtsbündig setzen
ad layout Anzeigengestaltung *f*, Anzeigenlayout *n*
admaker *(lead comp.)* Anzeigenmetteur *m*
ad make-up Anzeigenumbruch *m*
ad make-up man *(lead comp.)* Anzeigenmetteur *m*
ad management Anzeigenverwaltung *f*
admission ticket Eintrittskarte *f*
ad placement Anzeigenplazierung *f*
ad position Anzeigenplazierung *f*
ad processing Anzeigenbearbeitung *f*, Anzeigenverarbeitung *f*
ad processing software Anzeigenprogramm *n*
ad proof Anzeigenkorrekturbeleg *m*
adrates *pl* Anzeigentarif *m*
ad subscriber *(regular)* Anzeigenstammkunde *m*
adtaking Anzeigenannahme *f*, Anzeigenaufnahme *f*
ad tariff Anzeigentarif *m*
advance *(of the web)* Voreilung *f*; *(photocomp.)* Zeilenvorschub *m*
advance copy Aushängeexemplar *n*, Vorausexemplar *n*
advanced training Fortbildung *f*
advance leading *(photocomp.)* Zeilenvorschub *m*
advance sheet Aushängebogen *m*
advance sheets *pl (for adjusting the press)* Vorlaufbogen *pl*

advertise v Anzeige schalten, bewerben, inserieren, werben
ad(vertisement) Anzeige f, Inserat n
advertisement contract Anzeigenabschluß m
advertisement series Anzeigenserie f
advertiser Inserent m, Werbetreibende m
advertising Werbung f
advertising agency Anzeigenagentur f, Anzeigenbüro n, Werbeagentur f
advertising artist Werbegrafiker m
advertising art(work) Anzeigenvorlage f, Gebrauchsgrafik f
advertising brochure Werbebroschüre f, Werbeprospekt m
advertising campaign Werbekampagne f
advertising carrier Werbeträger m
advertising conditions pl Insertionsbedingungen pl
advertising copy *(artwork)* Anzeigenunterlage f, Anzeigenvorlage f; *(text copy)* Anzeigenmanuskript n, Anzeigentext m, Werbetext m
advertising customer Anzeigenkunde m;
 regular ~ Anzeigenstammkunde m
advertising deadline Anzeigenschluß m
advertising department Anzeigenabteilung f, Werbeabteilung f
advertising designer Gebrauchsgrafiker m, Werbegrafiker m
advertising display *(for shop windows etc.)* Werbeaufsteller m
advertising folder Werbebroschüre f, Werbeprospekt m
advertising industry werbetreibende Industrie f
advertising in selected target groups zielgruppenorientierte Werbung f
advertising insert Anzeigenbeilage f, Werbebeilage f
advertising journal Anzeigenblatt n
advertising leaflet Werbebroschüre f, Werbeprospekt m
advertising literature Werbebroschüren f/pl
advertising make-up Anzeigenumbruch m
advertising manager Anzeigenleiter m, Werbeleiter m
advertising material Anzeigenmaterial n, Werbematerial n
advertising matter Werbedrucksache f
advertising medium Werbemedium n, Werbemittel n, Werbeträger m
advertising office Anzeigenannahme f, Anzeigenbüro n
advertising order Anzeigenauftrag m

advertising pillar Litfaßsäule f
advertising printing Werbedruck m
advertising publicity Anzeigenwerbung f
advertising rate Anzeigenpreis m
advertising representative Anzeigenakquisiteur m, Anzeigenvertreter m
advertising section *(as opp. to editorial section)* Anzeigenteil m
advertising supplement Anzeigenbeilage f, Werbebeilage f
advertising text Anzeigentext m, Werbetext m
advertising type area Anzeigenspiegel m
ad writer Werbetexter m
aerate v *(sheets)* durchlüften, belüften, lüften
aeration Belüftung f
aerial oxidation *(photochem.)* Luftoxidation f
aerial photo(graph) Luftaufnahme f, Luftbild n
aerograph Aerograf m, Farbspritzgerät n, Luftpinsel m, Retuschierapparat m, Spritzapparat m
aerosol Aerosol n
aesthetic program *(photocomp.)* Ästhetik-Programm n
affect adversely v *(quality, performance)* beeinträchtigen
A4 broadside (DIN) A4 quer
A4 landscape (DIN) A4 quer
A4 oblong (DIN) A4 quer
A4 portrait (DIN) A4 hoch
A4 sized im Format (DIN) A4
A4 up(right) (DIN) A4 hoch
after-burner (system) Nachverbrennungsanlage f
after-sales service Kundenbetreuung f, Kundendienst m
after-treatment Nachbehandlung f
against the grain *(paper)* gegen die ~/quer zur Bahnlaufrichtung f, gegen die ~/quer zur Laufrichtung f, gegen die ~/quer zur Papierlaufrichtung f, in Querrichtung f
agate smoothing *(gravure cyl.)* Steinglättung f
ageing Alterung f
agency Agentur f
agency message Agenturmeldung f
agency photo(graph) Agenturbild n
aggregate *(mech.)* Aggregat n
air bars pl Luftwendestangen f/pl
air blast Blasluft f, Luftdusche f
air brake Luftbremse f
airbrush Farbspritzgerät n, Retuschierapparat m, Spritzapparat m, Luftpinsel m; *(electronic image proc.)* Spritzpistole f
airbrushing Spritzretusche f, Spritztechnik f
airbrush retouching Spritzretusche f

airbrush stencil Spritzschablone f
air bubble Luftblase f
air cleaner Luftreiniger m
air-conditioned paper klimatisiertes Papier n
air-conditioned room klimatisierter Raum m
air conditioner Klimatisator m
air conditioning Klimatisierung f
air-conditioning system Klimaanlage f
air control *(compressed air)* Luftsteuerung f
air cooling Luftkühlung f
air cushion Luftkissen n, Luftpolster n, Luftpuffer m
air cushion drum *(sheet-fed offset press)* Luftkissentrommel f
air-cushioned turnbars pl Luftwendestangen f/pl
air-dried paper luftgetrocknetes Papier n
air-dry lufttrocken
air ducts pl *(for compressed air supply)* Druckluftleitung f
air enclosures pl *(contact printing)* Lufteinschlüsse pl
air filter Luftfilter m
air filtration Luftfilterung f
air humidification Luftbefeuchtung f
air humidifier Luftbefeuchter m
air intake Lufteintritt m
air jack pneumatischer Spanndorn m
air jet Luftdüse f
air knife Luftrakel f
airmail envelope Luftpostumschlag m
airmail paper Luftpostpapier n, Flugpostpapier n
air nozzle Blasdüse f, Luftdüse f
air-operated druckluftbetrieben
air pallet system *(sheet processing)* Luftbrettanlage f
air pipes pl see air ducts
air pockets pl *(contact printing)* Lufteinschlüsse pl
air shaft *(reel fixing)* Luftspannwelle f, Expansionswickelwelle f
air squeezing roller Luftauspreßwalze f
air supply Luftversorgung f
air table Lufttisch m
air-tight luftdicht
air-washed turnbars pl Luftwendestangen f/pl
album Album n
albumen Albumin n
albumen copy Albuminkopie f, Eiweißkopie f
albumen copying process Eiweißkopierverfahren n
albumen paper Albuminpapier n
albumen plate Eiweißplatte f
albumen process Albuminverfahren n
albumen solution Eiweißlösung f
alcohol-based photopolymer plate alkoholauswaschbare Fotopolymerplatte f, alkoholentwickelbare Fotopolymerplatte f
alcohol concentration *(fountain solution)* Alkoholgehalt m
alcohol content *(fountain solution)* Alkoholgehalt m
alcohol control *(fountain solution)* Alkoholregelung f
alcohol damp(en)ing Alkoholfeuchtung f
alcohol damp(en)ing system Alkoholfeuchtwerk n
alcohol-developed photopolymer plate alkoholauswaschbare Fotopolymerplatte f, alkoholentwickelbare Fotopolymerplatte f
alcohol metering device *(fountain solution)* Alkoholdosiergerät n, Alkoholkonstanthalter m
alcohol percentage *(fountain solution)* Alkoholgehalt m
alcohol wash Waschalkohol m
alcohol-washed photopolymer plate alkoholauswaschbare Fotopolymerplatte f, alkoholentwickelbare Fotopolymerplatte f
algae pl *(fountain solution)* Algen pl
algebraical sign algebraisches Zeichen n
algorithm *(comp.)* Algorithmus m
algraphy *(aluminium printing)* Algrafie f
align v ausrichten
(aligning) stop *(paper transport)* Anschlag m
alignment Ausrichtung f; *(type)* Linienhalten n
alkaline Alkali n
alkaline fountain additive alkalischer Feuchtwasserzusatz m
alkali-proof paper alkalifestes Papier n
all-around copying machine *(gravure)* Umlaufkopiermaschine f
all-around exposure Rund(um)belichtung f
all-around square trim Rundumbeschnitt m
all-caps setting *(typesetting)* Versaliensatz m
allen key Inbus-Schlüssel m
allocation *(comp.)* Zuweisung f
allowance *(for spoils)* Zugabe f, Zuschuß(bogen) m/pl, Papierzuschuß m; *(reduction of price)* Preisnachlaß m; *(tolerance)* Toleranz f
alloy cast iron *(machine frame)* Sphäroguß m
alloy steel Edelstahl m
all-purpose typeface Allzweckschrift f
all rights reserved alle Rechte vorbehalten, Nachdruck verboten
almanac Almanach m, Jahrbuch n
along the web in Bahnlaufrichtung f, in Laufrichtung f, in Papierlaufrichtung f

alphabet Alphabet n
alphabetical index alphabetisches Verzeichnis n
alphabetical order alphabetische Reihenfolge f
alphabet length *(typesetting)* Alphabetlänge f
alphabet sheet *(type specimen)* Alphabetblatt n
alphabet width *(typesetting)* Alphabetbreite f
alphanumerical characters pl alphanumerische Zeichen pl
alphanumeric display alphanumerische Anzeige f
alternating current Drehstrom m, Wechselstrom m
altitudes pl *(mapmaking)* Höhenpunkte pl
aluminium coated alukaschiert
aluminium compound Aluminiumverbundmaterial n
aluminium foil Alufolie f
aluminium laminated alukaschiert
aluminium oxide Elektrokorund n
aluminium paper Aluminiumpapier n
aluminium plate Aluminiumplatte f
amalgam Amalgam n
amalgam printing process Amalgamdruckverfahren n
ambient curing Raumlufttrocknung f
ambient density *(reprod.)* Umgebungsdichte f
ambient light Fremdlicht n, Umgebungslicht n
ambient temperature Raumtemperatur f, Umgebungstemperatur f
ammonia development Ammoniakentwicklung f
amortization Amortisation f
amortization period Amortisationszeit f
amperage *(electropl.)* Stromstärke f
ampère hour *(electropl.)* Ampère-Stunde f
ampersand *(&)* Et-Zeichen n, Und-Zeichen n
anachromatic lens *(camera)* anachromatisches Objektiv n
analogue computer Analogrechner m
analogue signal analoges Signal n
analyze v *(scanner)* abtasten
analyze drum *(scanner)* Abtasttrommel f, Abtastwalze f, Abtastzylinder m
analyze light source *(scanner)* Abtastlichtquelle f
analyze unit *(scanner)* Abtasteinheit f
anamorphic distortion anamorphotisches Zerren n
anamorphic lens *(camera)* Schrumpfobjektiv n
anastatic printing anastatischer Druck m
anastigmatic lens *(camera)* anastigmatisches Objektiv n
ancillary equipment *(web press)* Peripherie f
angle bars pl *(web press)* Wendestangen f/pl
angle-bar superstructure Wendestangenüberbau m

angle cutter *(envelope prod.)* Schrägschneider m
angled conveyor *(mailroom)* Winkeltransportband n
angled-roller delivery Schrägrollenauslage f
angle of wrap *(cylinder)* Umschlingungswinkel m
angle space *(lead comp.)* Winkelspatium n
angular position *(screen)* Winkelstellung f
angular spaces and quads pl *(lead comp.)* Diagonalausschluß m
aniline blue Anilinblau n
aniline printing Anilindruck m
anilox inking unit Anilox-Farbwerk n, Kurzfarbwerk n, Rakelfarbwerk n
anilox letterpress Anilox-Hochdruck m
anilox offset Anilox-Offset m
anilox printing unit Anilox-Druckwerk n
anilox roller Aniloxwalze f, Rasterwalze f
animal glue tierischer Leim m
animal size tierischer Leim m
annotation Anmerkung f, Note f
announcement *(wedding, birth etc.)* Anzeige f, Anzeigenkarte f
annual *(book)* Jahrbuch n
annual capacity utilization Jahresauslastung f
annual report Jahresbericht m
annual subscription Jahresabonnement n
annual volume *(publication)* Jahrgang m
anode *(electropl.)* Anode f
anode plate Anodenplatte f
anodized aluminium plate anodisierte Aluminiumplatte f, eloxierte Aluminiumplatte f
anti-corrosion coating *(press cyl.)* Antikorrosionsschicht f, Korrosionsschutzschicht f
anti-dryer *(ink)* Antitrockner m
anti-drying agent *(ink)* Antitrockner m
anti-foam additive Antischaumzusatz m
anti-foam agent Antischaumzusatz m, Entschäumer m
anti-halation *(phot.)* Schleierfreiheit f
anti-halation backing *(graphic arts films)* Anti-Haloschicht f, Lichthofschutzschicht f
anti-halo backing *(graphic arts films)* Anti-Haloschicht f, Lichthofschutzschicht f
antimony *(lead type)* Antimon n
anti-Newton coating *(graphic arts films, glass)* Anti-Newton-Beschichtung f
anti-oxidant Antioxidationsmittel n, Antitrockner m
anti-oxidation coating Oxidationsschutzschicht f
antique binding *(book)* Antikeinband m
anti set-off powder Druckbestäubungspuder n

anti-skinning agent (ink) Antihautmittel n, Hautverhütungsmittel n
anti-static antistatisch
anti-static agent (film, foil) Antistatikum n
anti-static device Entelektrisator m
anti-tacking (photopolymer plates) Nachbehandlung f
aperture adjustment (camera lens) Blendeneinstellung f
aperture plane (camera lens) Blendenebene f
aperture setting (camera lens) Blendeneinstellung f
aplanatic lens (camera) aplanatisches Objektiv n
apochromatic lens (camera) apochromatisches Objektiv n
apostrophe Apostroph m, Auslassungszeichen n
appear v (publication) erscheinen
appear shortly v (publication) erscheint in Kürze
appendix (book) Anhang m, Appendix m, Nachtrag m
application (coating) Auftrag m, Auftragung f
application area Anwendungsbereich m
application engineer Anwendungstechniker m
application engineering Anwendungstechnik f
application field Anwendungsbereich m
application method Anwendungstechnik f
application program Anwendungsprogramm n
application roller Auftragswalze f
application software Anwendersoftware f
apprentice bookbinder auszubildender Buchbinder m
apprentice compositor auszubildender Setzer m, Setzerlehrling m
apprentice printer auszubildender Drucker m, Druckerlehrling m
aquatint Aquatinta f
aquatone process Aquatone-Verfahren n
aqueous wäßrig, auf Wasserbasis
aqueous developer wäßriger Entwickler m
arabesques pl (oriental ornaments) Arabesken pl
Arabic characters pl arabische Schrift f
Arabic figures pl arabische Ziffern pl
Arabic numerals pl arabische Ziffern pl
Arabic type arabische Schrift f
archival properties pl Archivfestigkeit f
archive Archiv n
archiving Archivierung f
arch-type construction (web press) Brückenbauweise f
arc lamp (reprod.) Bogenlampe f
arc lamp carbons pl Bogenlampenkohlen pl
area Fläche f

area composition (news composition) Flächenbelichtung f
area coverage (halftones) Flächendeckung f
area illumination (reprod., copying) Flächenausleuchtung f
area of contact (printing) Kontaktzone f
area pattern (mapmaking) Flächenmuster n
area printing Flächendruck m
areas left blank pl (page make-up, printing, varnishing) Aussparung f
areometer Aräometer n
argon laser (scanner) Argon-Laser m
arithmetical sign arithmetisches Zeichen n
Arkansas oil stone Arkansas-Ölstein m
arm (part of the letter) Querstrich m
arrange copy v (text) Text gestalten
arrangement Anordnung f
arrangement of print units Druckwerksanordnung f
art see art(work)
art board Kunstdruckkarton m
art book Kunstbuch n
art bookbinder Kunstbuchbinder m
art calendar Kunstkalender m
art design Vorlagengestaltung f
art director künstlerischer Leiter m
article (publication) Artikel m, Aufsatz m, Beitrag m
artificial leather Kunstleder n, Lederimitation f
artificial leather binding (book) Kunstledereinband m
artificial light Kunstlicht n
artist's brush Pinsel m
Art Nouveau typography Jugendstiltypografie f
art of bookbinding Buchbindekunst f
art of printing Druckkunst f
art of the book Buchkunst f
art paper Bilderdruckpapier n, Glanzpapier n, Hochglanzpapier n, Kunstdruckpapier n
art picture Kunstbild n
art print Kunstdruck m, Kunstblatt n, Bilderdruck m
art printing Kunstdruck m, Bilderdruck m
art studio Gestaltungsstudio n, Grafikatelier n, Grafikstudio n, grafisches Atelier n, Vorlagenstudio n
art(work) Grafik f, Reinzeichnung f, Vorlage f; (photocomp.) Abbildungen f/pl
artwork preparation Druckvorlagenherstellung f, Originalherstellung f, Vorlagenherstellung f
ascender (part of the letter) Oberlänge f
ash content Aschegehalt m
asphalt varnish (gravure cyl.) Asphaltlack m

asphalt wash-out solution Asphalttinktur *f*
aspirate Hauchlaut *m*
assemble *v (page assembly)* montieren, umbrechen
assembler *(line caster)* Sammler *m*
assembly *(page assembly)* Montage *f*
assembly copying machine Montagekopiermaschine *f*
assembly for reuse Stehmontage *f*
assembly sheet Montagebogen *m*
assembly storage cabinet Montageaufbewahrungsschrank *m*
assembly work *(page assembly)* Montage *f*
assessment Beurteilung *f*
asterisk *(*)* Sternchen *n*
astigmatism *(lens)* Astigmatismus *m*
astralon sheet Astralonfolie *f*
astronomical sign astronomisches Zeichen *n*
at a scale of 1:1 *(reprod.)* im Abbildungsmaßstab *m* 1:1
atlas Atlas *m*
at random sequence in beliebiger Reihenfolge *f*
at standstill im Stillstand *m*
attachment *(unit)* Aggregat *n*
audit bureau of circulation Auflagenkontrolleinrichtung *f*, IVW *f*
author Autor *m*, Schriftsteller *m*, Verfasser *m*
author-publisher Selbstverleger *m*
author-publisher agreement Verlagsvertrag *m*
author's alterations *pl* Autorkorrektur *f*
author's copy Autorenexemplar *n*
author's corrections *pl* Autorkorrektur *f*
author's proof Autorabzug *m*
author's royalties *pl* Autorhonorar *n*
autobiography Autobiografie *f*
autocopying paper Selbstdurchschreibepapier *n*, Durchschreibepapier *n*, Farbreaktionspapier *n*
auto-focus(ing) *(camera)* automatische Scharf(ein)stellung *f*
autography Autografie *f*
automate *v* automatisieren
automatic casemaker *(book prod.)* Buchdeckenautomat *m*
automatic control automatische Steuerung *f*, Steuer(ungs)automatik *f*
automatic cylinder press *(letterpress)* Schnellpresse *f*
automatic focusing *(camera)* automatische Scharf(ein)stellung *f*
automatic positioning *(cutting m.)* Positionierautomatik *f*
automatic programming automatische Programmierung *f*, Programmierautomatik *f*

automatic stop *(end of operation)* automatische Endabschaltung *f*
autopaster Autopaster *m*, Klebevorrichtung *f*, Rollenwechsler *m*
autotype *(halftone engraving)* Autotypie *f*; *(halftone print)* Rasterdruck *m*
autotypical colour synthesis autotypische Farbmischung *f*
auxiliary colour unit *(press unit)* Farbeindruckwerk *n*
auxiliary device Hilfsgerät *n*
auxiliary drive Hilfsantrieb *m*, Nebenantrieb *m*
auxiliary equipment Hilfseinrichtung *f*
auxiliary machine Hilfsmaschine *f*
auxiliary times *pl* Hilfszeiten *pl*
available on option zusätzlich lieferbar
average output Durchschnittsleistung *f*
average production Durchschnittsleistung *f*
average-size advertisement mittelgroßes Inserat *n*
azure himmelblau

B

back *(book, journal)* Rücken *m*; *(calendar)* Rückwand *f*
backbone *(book)* Buchrücken *m*, Rücken *m*
backbone preparation *(book)* Buchrückenbearbeitung *f*
back coating *(film)* Rückschicht *f*
back cover board *(book)* hinterer Buchdeckel *m*
back edge Hinterkante *f*
back edge curl *(sheet)* Einrollen der Bogenhinterkante
back(-edge) margin Bund *m*, innerer Papierrand *m*, innerer Seitenrand *m*
back fold Bundfalz *m*, Rückenfalz *m*
backgauge *(cutting m.)* Sattel *m*, Vorschubsattel *m*
backgauge advance Sattelvorschub *m*
backgauge drive Sattelantrieb *m*
backgauge position Sattelposition *f*, Sattelstand *m*
backgauge rake Sattelrechen *m*
backgauge screw Sattelspindel *f*
back gluing Rückenbeleimung *f*, Rückenleimung *f*
background Fond *m*, Hintergrund *m*

background area - banderoling

background area Hintergrundfläche f
background fog *(film)* Grundschleier m
background mode *(comp.)* Hintergrundbetrieb m
background pattern Flächenmuster n, Hintergrundmuster n
background processing *(comp.)* Hintergrundverarbeitung f
background tint Fond m, Hintergrundfläche f, Rasterfond m; *(screened background)* Hintergrundraster m, hinterlegter Raster m
backing *(book block)* Abpressen n; *(press cyl.)* Aufzug m; *(printing)* see backing-up, back(-side) printing
backing blade *(doctor blade)* Stützrakel f
backing forme *(perfecting forme)* Widerdruckform f
backing jaw Preßbacke f
backing joint *(book)* Abpreßfalz m
backing machine *(book prod.)* Abpreßmaschine f
backing metal *(electrotyping)* Hintergießmetall n
backing press *(book prod.)* Rückenpresse f
backing roller Stützwalze f
backing-up *(backside printing)* Rückseitendruck m, Widerdruck m
back issue *(publication)* alte Ausgabe f
backlash Zahnspiel n
backlight *(camera)* Unterlicht n
backlight facility *(camera)* Durchleuchtungseinrichtung f
backlighting *(camera)* Durchsichtsbeleuchtung f
backliner *(book)* Hinterklebepapier n
backlining *(book prod.)* Hinterklebung f
backlining machine *(book prod.)* Hinterklebemaschine f
backlining paper *(book)* Hinterklebepapier n
back of book Buchrücken m
back page Rückseite f
back preparation Rückenbearbeitung f
back pressure *(impression pressure)* Gegendruck m
back rounding *(book prod.)* Rückenrunden n
back rounding machine Rückenrundemaschine f
back router Rückenfräser m
back routing *(book prod.)* Rückenfräsen n
back shaping *(book prod.)* Rückenformgebung f
back side Rückseite f; *(of printed sheet)* Widerdruckseite f
back(-side) printing Rückseitendruck m, Widerdruck m
backslanting *(photocomp.)* Schrägstellung f
back-stitched brochure Rückstichbroschüre f
back-stitcher Rückstichheftmaschine f

back stitching Drahtheftung durch den Rücken, Falzheftung f, Rückstichheftung f
backstop hinterer Anschlag m
back strip *(book)* Fälzelstreifen m, Rückenschrenz m
back-stripped gefälzelt
back-stripping Fälzelung f
back-stripping machine Fälzelmaschine f
back title Rückentitel m
back to back *(book prod.)* Rücken an Rücken
back to front Rücken/Front
back-up *(comp.)* Back-up n, Datensicherung f, Sicherung f
back up v *(comp.)* sichern
back-up computer Hilfsrechner m, Reserverechner m
back-up files pl *(comp.)* Sicherungsdaten pl
back-up register *(printing)* Rückseitenregister n, Widerdruckregister n
backward numbering rückwärtszählende Numerierung f
bad break *(typesetting)* falsche Trennung f
bad copy *(text copy)* schlechtes Manuskript n, unleserliches Manuskript n
bad printing schlechter Druck m
bad sheet schlechter Bogen m
bag Beutel m, Sack m, Tüte f
bag gluing Tütenkleben n
bag printing Beuteldruck m
baked printing plate eingebrannte Druckplatte f
baking *(offset plate)* Einbrennen n
baking oven *(offset plate)* Einbrennofen m
balanced retouching Ausgleichsretusche f
balcony *(web press)* Galerie f
balcony-type press *(web press)* Etagenmaschine f
bale *(paper)* Ballen m
bale of paper Papierballen m
baling press *(waste paper)* Ballenpresse f, Bündelpresse f
ballard process *(gravure)* Ballardverfahren n, Glanzkupferverfahren n, Hautaufkupferungsverfahren n
ballard skin *(gravure cyl.)* Ballardhaut f
ball bearing Kugellager n
ball mill *(ink prod.)* Kugelmühle f
balloon *(comics)* Blase f
balloon former *(press folder)* Ballon-Trichter m, Doppeltrichter m
ball race *(sheet guidance)* Kugelleiste f
band *(book)* Binde f, Buchbinde f, Buchschleife f
banderoled pack Banderolierpackung f
banderoling Banderoleneinschlag m, Banderolieren n

banderoling machine Banderoliermaschine *f*
banding machine Banderoliermaschine *f*, Bandiermaschine *f*
bands *pl (book)* Bünde *pl*, Gebinde *n*, Heftbünde *pl*, Heftschnüre *pl*, Schnüre *pl*
b + w *(black and white)* sw (schwarzweiß)
bandwidth *(telecom.)* Bandbreite *f*
banknote paper Banknotenpapier *n*
banknote printing Banknotendruck *m*, Notendruck *m*, Papiergelddruck *m*
banknotes *pl* Banknoten *pl*, Papiergeld *n*
bank paper Bankpostpapier *n*, Hartpostpapier *n*
banner (headline) Balkenüberschrift *f*, Überschrift *f* (über volle Seitenbreite)
bar *(hand press)* Bengel *m*
bar code Balkenkode *m*, Strichkode *m*
bar code reader Strichkodeleser *m*
bareback damping roller unbezogene Feuchtwalze *f*
bar printer Balkendrucker *m*
baryta coating Barytstrich *m*
baryta paper Barytpapier *n*
baryta white Barytweiß *n*
base Fundament *n*; *(blockmaking)* Fuß *m*, Unterlage *f*; *(photo, film etc.)* Trägermaterial *n*
base copper *(gravure cyl.)* Grundkupfer *n*
base fog *(film)* Grundschleier *m*
baseline *(typelines)* Grundlinie *f*, Schriftlinie *f*
baseline alignment *(typesetting)* Ausrichtung auf Schriftlinie, Schriftlinienhaltung *f*
baseline shifting *(photocomp.)* Schriftlinienverschiebung *f*
base paper Rohpapier *n*, Trägerpapier *n*
basic colours *pl (colour system)* Grundfarben *f/pl*
basic configuration *(system)* Grundaufbau *m*
basic exposure *(reprod.)* Basisbelichtung *f*
basic frame *(mach.)* Grundgestell *n*
basic lens aperture *(camera)* Stammblende *f*, Arbeitsblende *f*
basic program *(comp.)* Basisprogramm *n*
basic setting *(mach.)* Grundeinstellung *f*
basic software Basissoftware *f*
basic training Grundausbildung *f*
basic weight *(paper)* Basisgewicht *n*
bastard double Doppelseite *f*
bastard title Schmutztitel *m*
bastard type Bastardschrift *f*
batch *(comp.)* Stapel *m*; *(mailroom)* Bündel *n*, Paket *n*
batch counter Stapelzähler *m*
batch mode *(comp.)* Stapelbetrieb *m*

batch processing *(comp.)* Stapelverarbeitung *f*
bath Bad *n*
bath agitation Badbewegung *f*
bath circulation Badumwälzung *f*
bath contamination Badverschmutzung *f*
bath current *(electropl.)* Badstrom *m*
bath exhaustion Baderschöpfung *f*
bath stability Badstabilität *f*
bath voltage *(electropl.)* Badspannung *f*
batter *v (lead type)* abquetschen
battered letters *pl (lead comp.)* see battered type
battered type *(lead comp.)* abgenutzte Schrift *f*, abgequetschte Schrift *f*, schlechte Buchstaben *pl*
bayonet lock Bajonettverschluß *m*
bay-window facility *(web press)* Bay-Window-Einrichtung *f*
beard *(part of the letter)* Fleisch *n*
bearer see cylinder bearer, bed bearers
bearer height *(press)* Schmitzringhöhe *f*
bearer ring *(press)* Schmitzring *m*, Laufring *m*, Meßring *m*
bearer ring wiper Schmitzringabstreifer *m*
bearer-to-bearer pressure *(press)* Schmitzringpressung *f*
bearer-to-bearer printing press Schmitzringläufer *m*
bearing *(mech.)* Lagerung *f*, Lager *n*
bearing bolt Lagerbolzen *m*
bearing bushing Lagerschale *f*
bearing lubrication Lagerölung *f*, Lagerschmierung *f*
become flat *v (gradation)* verflachen
become soft *v (gradation)* verflachen
be continued *v* Fortsetzung folgt, wird fortgesetzt
bed Bett *n*, Fundament *n*; *(letterpress m.)* Druckkarren *m*, Karren *m*
bed bearers *pl (flat-bed press)* Laufleisten *f/pl*, Laufstege *m/pl*, Schmitzleisten *f/pl*
bed drive *(letterpress m.)* Karrenantrieb *m*
bed rails *pl (letterpress m.)* Karrenleisten *pl*
beer label Bieretikett *n*
beer mat Bierdeckel *m*
begin even *v (typesetting; no indenting)* stumpf anfangen
beginning of text Textanfang *m*
begin quote Anführung *f*
being set-up im Satz sein
be in register *v (colour register)* passen
be issued *v (publication)* erscheinen
bell character *(text rec.)* Klingelzeichen *n*
bellows *pl (camera)* Balgen *m*

bellows extension *(camera)* Balgenauszug *m*, Kameraauszug *m*, Kamerabalgen *m*
belly band *(book)* Binde *f*, Buchbinde *f*, Buchschleife *f*
belt Band *n*, Gurt *m*, Riemen *m*
belt conveyor Bändertransporteur *m*, Gurtförderer *m*, Riemenförderer *m*, Riementransporteur *m*
belt delivery Bänderauslauf *m*, Bandauslage *f*
belt drive Riemenantrieb *m*
belt feeder Riemenanleger *m*
belt table Bändertisch *m*
bench-top model Tischmodell *n*
bend *v* biegen
bending and forming press *(book prod.)* Biege- und Formpresse *f*
bending and straightening press *(book prod.)* Biege- und Richtpresse *f*
bending bulge Biegewulst *m*
bending press *(bookb.)* Biegepresse *f*
bending strength Biegefestigkeit *f*
be published *v* erscheinen
be published soon *v* erscheint in Kürze
be subscribed to *v* beziehen
betting slips *pl* Wettscheine *pl*
bevel *(block)* Abschrägung *f*, Facette *f*; *(part of the letter)* Hals *m*
bevel *v (block)* abkanten, abschrägen, facettieren
bevel gear Kegelradgetriebe *n*
beveller *(blockmaking)* Facettenhobel *m*
bevelling and cutting machine *(blockmaking)* Facetten- und Kantenfräsmaschine *f*
bevelling machine *(blockmaking)* Facettiermaschine *f*
Bible paper Bibeldruckpapier *n*, Dünndruckpapier *n*, Florpostpapier *n*
bibliography Bibliografie *f*, Literaturangabe *f*, Literaturhinweis *m*, Literaturnachweis *m*, Literaturverzeichnis *n*
bichromated gelatine Chromgelatine *f*
bill head Rechnungskopf *m*
bimetal plate Bimetallplatte *f*
bi-monthly (publication) zweimonatlich erscheinende Zeitschrift *f*, zweimal monatlich erscheinende Zeitschrift *f*
binary coded decimals (BCD) binärkodierte Dezimalzahlen (BCD) *f/pl*
binary digit *(comp.)* Binärzahl *f*
bind *v* binden, heften; *(book)* einbinden
binder *(binding agent)* Bindemittel *n*; *(bookb.)* see bookbinder
binder's board Deckelpappe *f*
binder sheet insetting Zwischenbogeneinlage *f*

bind in *v* einheften
bind in boards *v* kartonieren
binding Binden *n*, Bindung *f*, Buchbinden *n*, Buchbinderei *f*, Einband *m*, Einbinden *n*, Heftung *f*
binding agent Bindemittel *n*
binding cloth Buchbinderleinen *n*, Buchleinen *n*, Einbandstoff *m*
binding costs *pl* Bindekosten *pl*
binding department Buchbinderei *f*
binding device Bindegerät *n*
binding edge Bund *m*, Heftrand *m*; *(adhesive binding)* Kleberand *m*
binding equipment Bindegeräte *n/pl*, Buchbindereimaschinen *pl*
binding gauze Buchbindergaze *f*
binding glue Buchbinderleim *m*
binding leather Buchbinderleder *n*
binding machine Buchbindereimaschine *f*
binding machinery Buchbindereimaschinen *pl*
binding margin Bund *m*, Heftrand *m*; *(adhesive binding)* Kleberand *m*
binding method Bindeart *f*, Bindemethode *f*, Bindeverfahren *n*
binding press Buchbinderpresse *f*
binding process Bindeverfahren *n*
binding section Heftlage *f*
binding stitch Heftstich *m*
binding system Bindesystem *n*
binding technique Buchbindetechnik *f*
binding thickness Bindestärke *f*, Heftstärke *f*
binding thread Heftfaden *m*, Heftzwirn *m*
binding wire Heftdraht *m*
binding with raised bands Einband mit gebrochenem Rücken
biodegradable biologisch abbaubar
birth announcement Geburtsanzeige *f*
bit *(comp.)* Binärzahl *f*, Bit *n*
bit density Bitdichte *f*
bitmap Bitmap *f*
bit rate *(telecom.)* Bitrate *f*, Übertragungsgeschwindigkeit *f*
bit slice Bitslice *n*
bits per second Bits pro Sekunde
bit string Bitfolge *f*
black Schwarz *n*, Tiefe *f*
black and white schwarzweiß
black and white artwork Schwarzweißvorlage *f*
black and white densitometer Schwarzweißdensitometer *n*
black and white exposure Schwarzweißaufnahme *f*

black and white illustration
Schwarzweißabbildung *f*

black and white original Schwarzweißoriginal *n*, Schwarzweißvorlage *f*

black and white photo(graph)
Schwarzweißaufnahme *f*, Schwarzweißfoto *n*

black and white picture Schwarzweißbild *n*

black and white scanner Schwarzweißscanner *m*

black and white transparency Schwarzweißdia *n*

blackening *(phot.)* Schwärzung *f*

black face *(type)* fette Schrift *f*

black film *(separation film)* Schwarzfilm *m*

black forme Schwarzform *f*

black ink schwarze Farbe *f*, Druckerschwärze *f*, Schwärze *f*

black key *(black plate)* Schwarzplatte *f*; *(black sep. film)* Schwarzfilm *m*

black leading brush Grafitierbürste *f*

black letter fetter Buchstabe *m*

Black Letters and Broken *(type classif.)*
Gebrochene Schriften *pl*

black plate Schwarzplatte *f*

black printer *(black plate)* Schwarzplatte *f*; *(black sep. film)* Schwarzfilm *m*

blacks *pl (lead comp.)* Blockade *f*, Spieße *pl*

black separation *(reprod.)* Schwarzauszug *m*

black skeleton *(black plate)* Schwarzplatte *f*; *(black sep. film)* Schwarzfilm *m*

blade Messer *n*; *(doctor blade)* Rakel *f*; *(squeegee; screen printing)* Rakel *f*

blade angle *(doctor blade)* Rakelwinkel *m*

blade change *(doctor blade)* Rakelwechsel *m*

blade-coated paper maschinengestrichenes Papier *n*

blade coating process *(paper)*
Rakelstreichverfahren *n*

blade fold Messerfalz *m*, Schwertfalz *m*

blade fountain *(inking unit)* Messerfarbkasten *m*

blade grinder *(doctor blade)*
Rakelschleifmaschine *f*

blade grinding *(doctor blade)* Rakelschleifen *n*

blade holder *(doctor blade)* Rakelhalter *m*

blade position *(doctor blade)* Rakelstellung *f*

blade profile *(doctor blade)* Rakelprofil *n*

blade setting *(doctor blade)* Rakelanstellung *f*, Rakeleinstellung *f*

blade setting angle *(doctor blade)*
Rakelanstellwinkel *m*

blade streaks *pl (doctor blade)* Rakelstreifen *m/pl*

blade stroke *(doctor blade)* Rakelschlag *m*

blade support *(doctor blade)* Stützrakel *f*

blade tip *(doctor blade)* Rakelfase *f*, Rakellamelle *f*

blade-type ink fountain Messerfarbkasten *m*

blank *(folding box prod.)* Stanznutzen *m*, Nutzen *m*; *(printed form)* Formular *n*, Vordruck *m*; *(unprinted)* unbedruckt, vakat

blank *v (layout, page make-up)* blankschlagen, blindschlagen, freischlagen

blank attachment points *pl (die-cutting)*
Nutzenverbindungsstege *pl*

blank book Blindband *m*, Blindmuster *n*, Formatbuch *n*, Muster(ein)band *m*, Probeband *m*

blank character Blindzeichen *n*

blank cutting *(folding box prod.)*
Nutzenstanzung *f*

blanket *(printing blanket)* Drucktuch *n*, Gummidrucktuch *n*, Gummituch *n*;
four-ply ~ Gummituch mit vier Gewebelagen

blanket bar *(letterpress m.)* Tuchstange *f*

blanket carcase Gummituchunterbau *m*

blanket clamping bar Gummituchklemmleiste *f*, Gummituchspannschiene *f*

blanket creep Wandern des Gummituchs

blanket cylinder *(offset printing unit)*
Gummituchzylinder *m*, Gummizylinder *m*

blanket gap filler *(continuous forms press)*
Gummituchspaltversiegelung *f*

blanket gap sealer *(continuous forms press)*
Gummituchspaltversiegelung *f*

blanket gauge Gummituchstärke *f*

blanket glaze Gummituchglätte *f*

blanket mounting device
Gummituchspannvorrichtung *f*

blanket packing sheet
Gummituch-Unterlagebogen *m*

blanket rejuvenator *(chemical)*
Gummituch-Regenerierungsmittel *n*

blanket stretch Gummituchdehnung *f*

blanket thickness gauge Gummituchdickenmesser *m*

blanket-to-blanket print unit *(web press, perfector)* Doppeldruckwerk *n*, Gummi/Gummi-Druckwerk *n*

blanket-to-blanket web offset press
Gummi/Gummi-Rollenoffsetmaschine *f*

blanket to impression cylinder pressure
Druckbeistellung zwischen Gummi- und Druckzylinder

blanket to plate cylinder pressure
Druckbeistellung zwischen Gummi- und Plattenzylinder

blanket wash - block letters

blanket wash *(chemical)* Gummituchwaschmittel *n*
blanket washer *(on press)* Gummituchwascheinrichtung *f*
blanket washing Gummituchwaschen *n*
blanket wash-up device *(on press)* Gummituchwascheinrichtung *f*
blanket wash-up interval Gummituchwaschintervall *n*
blank (form) Formular *n*
blanking tool *(waste-stripping)* Trennwerkzeug *n*, Separierwerkzeug *n*
blank labels *pl* Blankoetiketten *n/pl*, unbedruckte Etiketten *n/pl*
blank line *(typesetting)* Zwischenzeile *f*, Blankozeile *f*, Blindzeile *f*, Freizeile *f*, Leerzeile *f*
blank material *(lead comp.)* Blindmaterial *n*
blank page Blankoseite *f*, Leerseite *f*, unbedruckte Seite *f*, Vakatseite *f*
blank paper Blankopapier *n*
blanks *pl* *(carton)* Zuschnitte *pl*
blank separating forme *(folding box prod.)* Nutzentrennform *f*
blank separation *(folding box prod.)* Nutzentrennung *f*
blank sheet Blankobogen *m*; *(unintentionally not printed)* Mönchsbogen *m*
blank slug *(hot-metal comp.)* Blindgußzeile *f*
blank space *(layout, page make-up etc.)* freigeschlagener Raum *m*, Freiraum *m*
blank spaces *pl* *(lead comp.)* Ausschluß *m*
blank stripping *(folding box prod.)* Nutzentrennung *f*
blank stripping forme *(folding box prod.)* Nutzentrennform *f*
blast Gebläse *n*
blast air Blasluft *f*
blast-air drum Baslufttrommel *f*
blast rake Blasrechen *m*
bleaching Bleichen *n*; *(photochem.)* Ausbleichen *n*
bleaching bath Bleichbad *n*
bleaching plant *(papermak.)* Bleichanlage *f*
bleach-resistance *(ink)* Lichtechtheit *f*
bleach-resistant *(ink)* lichtecht
bled-off *(illustration, ad)* randabfallend, angeschnitten, mit Anschnitt *m*; *(photo, print)* randlos
bled-off illustration angeschnittenes Bild *n*
bleed *(illustration, ad)* Randanschnitt *m*, Anschnitt *m*
bleed *v (illustration, ad)* anschneiden

bleeding *(colour)* Auslaufen *n*, Bluten *n*, Ausbleichen *n*, Ausbluten *n*
bleed printing angeschnittener Druck *m*
bleed size unbeschnittenes Format *n*; *(magazine printing)* Format mit Beschnittzugabe
blending of colours Farbenmischen *n*
blind blocking see blind embossing
blind embossing Blinddruck *m*, Blindprägung *f*, Reliefprägung *f*, Weißdruck *m*
blind folio Blindpaginierung *f*
blind keyboard Blindtastatur *f*
blind paging Blindpaginierung *f*
blind print Schimmelbogen *m*
blind setting *(type)* Blindsetzen *n*
blind sheet *(printing)* Schimmelbogen *m*
blister box Blisterpackung *f*
blistering *(problem with varnishing, laminating, heatset printing etc.)* Blasenbildung *f*
blister packaging Blisterpackung *f*
blister varnish Blisterlack *m*
block *(book)* Block *m*; *(printing block)* Klischee *n*; *(typesetting)* Block *m*
block base *(letterpress)* Klischeefuß *m*, Klischeeunterlage *f*, Klotz *m*
block bending device *(letterpress)* Klischeebiegeapparat *m*
block binding *(book prod.)* Blockleimung *f*, Blockverleimung *f*
block border rules *pl* Klischeerandlinien *pl*
block capitals *pl* *(typesetting)* Blockschrift *f*
block cutter *(letterpress)* Klischeeplattenschere *f*
block diagram Blockdiagramm *n*
block drill *(letterpress)* Klischeebohrer *m*
block engraving machine *(Varioklischograph)* Klischeegraviermaschine *f*
block finishing *(letterpress)* Klischeebearbeitung *f*
block flow line *(book prod.)* Blockfertigungsstraße *f*
block gauge *(letterpress)* Klischeestärke *f*
block holder *(letterpress)* Klischeeträger *m*
blocking *(foil blocking)* Prägung *f*, Prägedruck *m*, Prägen *n*; *(freshly printed sheets sticking together)* Zusammenkleben *n*, Verblocken *n*, Nachkleben *n*, Blocken *n*, Kleben *n*, Verkleben *n*
blocking plate Prägeklischee *n*
blocking press Prägepresse *f*, Prägetiegel *m*; **automatic** ~ Prägeautomat *m*
blocking resistance *(ink)* Blockfestigkeit *f*
block letter Blockbuchstabe *m*, Lapidar *f*
block letters *pl* Blockschrift *f*, Druckschrift *f*

blockmaker Klischeur *m*, Chemigraf *m*, Klischeehersteller *m*
blockmakers *pl* chemigrafische Anstalt *f*, Klischeeanstalt *f*
blockmaker's pull Klischeeabzug *m*
blockmaking Klischeeherstellung *f*, Aufholzen *n*, Aufklotzen *n*, Chemigrafie *f*
block mount *(letterpress)* Klotz *m*, Klischeefuß *m*, Klischeeunterlage *f*
block pressing *(book block)* Blockpressung *f*
block printing Handdruck *m*
block production *(book block)* Blockfertigung *f*
block proof *(letterpress)* Klischeeabzug *m*
block proofing press Klischee-Andruckpresse *f*
block stitching *(book block)* Blockheftung *f*
block-stitching machine Blockheftmaschine *f*
block thickness *(book block)* Blockstärke *f*; *(letterpress)* Klischeestärke *f*
block thickness gauge *(letterpress)* Klischeehöhenmesser *n*
block type *(hand comp.)* Blocktype *f*
blotted impression klecksiger Druck *m*
blotting paper Löschpapier *n*, Saugpapier *n*
blowback *(reprophotogr.)* Rückvergrößerung *f*
blowers *pl* Gebläse *n*
blowing nozzle Blasdüse *f*
blown-up halftone Rasterprojektion *f*, Rastervergrößerung *f*
blow-up *(reprophotogr.)* Projektionsvergrößerung *f*
blue key *(registration film) (film guide)* Anhaltekopie *f*
blue print *(diazo copy)* Anhaltekopie *f*, Lichtpause *f*, Blaupause *f*, Ozalidkopie *f*, Pause *f*
blue printing Lichtpauskopie *f*
blue-printing machine Lichtpausmaschine *f*
blue-printing paper Lichtpauspapier *n*
blue-printing process Lichtpausverfahren *n*
blue-sensitive film blauempfindlicher Film *m*
blue-yellow filter exposure *(reprod.)* Blau-Gelb-Filterbelichtung *f*
blunt knife stumpfes Messer *n*
blurb *(book)* Klappentext *m*, Waschzettel *m*
blurred impression verschwommener Druck *m*, verwischter Druck *m*
board Karton *m*, Pappdeckel *m*, Pappe *f*
board *v (book)* einbinden
board bending machine Pappenbiegemaschine *f*
board container Pappkarton *m*, Pappkiste *f*
board converting Kartonverarbeitung *f*, Pappebearbeitung *f*

board cutter Kartonschere *f*, Kartonschneider *m*, Pappschere *f*
board eyeletting machine Kartonösenmaschine *f*
board insert Pappeinlage *f*
board lining Kartonkaschierung *f*
board lining machine Kartonkaschiermaschine *f*
board machine *(mill)* Pappmaschine *f*
board matrix Pappmater *f*, Pappmatrize *f*
board matrix moulding Pappmatrizenprägung *f*
board mill Kartonfabrik *f*
board printing machine Pappenbedruckmaschine *f*
board processing and converting industry Kartonageindustrie *f*
board reel Kartonrolle *f*, Papprolle *f*
board slotting machine Pappenschlitzmaschine *f*
board strip Kartonstreifen *m*
board tube Kartonhülse *f*, Papphülse *f*
bodkin Ahle *f*, Einbindenadel *f*
bodkin handle Ahlenheft *n*
bodkin tip Ahlenspitze *f*
body *(brochure/book without cover)* Inhalt *m*
body matter *(type)* laufender Text *m*, glatter Satz *m*, Textsatz *m*
body of book *(without cover)* Buchinhalt *m*
body size *(type)* Schriftgrad *m*, Schriftgröße *f*, Schriftkegel *m*
body type *(as opp. to display type)* Grundschrift *f*, Laufschrift *f*, Textschrift *f*, Brotschrift *f*, normale Schrift *f*
bold condensed typeface schmalfette Schrift *f*
bold display line *(typesetting)* fette Auszeichnungszeile *f*
bold face *(type)* fette Schrift *f*
bold face capitals *pl* fette Versalien *f/pl*
bold line *(typogr.)* fette Linie *f*
bold rule Balken *m*, fette Linie *f*
bold type fetter Buchstabe *m*, fette Schrift *f*
Bologna chalk Bologneser Kreide *f*
bolt *(mech.)* Bolzen *m*
bond paper Feinpostpapier *n*
bone-dry paper knochentrockenes Papier *n*
bone folder Falzbein *n*
bone glue Knochenleim *m*
book Buch *n*
book backing Buchabpressen *n*, Hinterklebung *f*
book backing machine Buchabpreßmaschine *f*
book backing paper Hinterklebepapier *n*
bookbinder Buchbinder *m*, Buchbinderei *f*
bookbinder's blocking ink Presserfarbe *f*
bookbinder's board Buchbinderpappe *f*, Deckelpappe *f*
bookbinder's brass Buchbinderstempel *m*

bookbinder's calico - bookwork

bookbinder's calico Buchbinderleinen *n*, Einbandstoff *m*, Kaliko *n*
bookbinder's cord Heftschnur *f*
bookbinder's hammer Buchbinderhammer *m*
bookbinder's ink Buchbinderfarbe *f*
bookbinder's knife Buchbindermesser *n*
bookbinder's needle Buchbindernadel *f*, Einbindenadel *f*, Heftnadel *f*
bookbinder's saw Einschneidesäge *f*
bookbinder's type Buchbinderschrift *f*, Prägeschrift *f*
bookbinding Buchbinden *n*, Buchbinderei *f*, Bucheinband *m*, Einbinden *n*
bookbinding paper Bucheinbandpapier *n*
book block Buchblock *m*
book block feeder Buchblockanleger *m*
book bound in boards kartoniertes Buch *n*
book calico Buchleinen *n*
book case Buchdecke *f*, Decke *f*, Einbanddecke *f*
book clamp *(perfect binder)* Buchklammer *f*
book cloth Bezugsleinen *n*, Bezugsstoff *m*, Buchleinen *n*, Einbandstoff *m*
book content *(without cover)* Buchinhalt *m*
book corner Buchecke *f*
book cover Einbanddecke *f*, Buchdecke *f*, Buchdeckel *m*, Bucheinband *m*, Buchumschlag *m*, Decke *f*
book-cover design Bucheinbandentwurf *m*
book cover paper Bucheinbandpapier *n*
book decoration Buchdekoration *f*, Buchschmuck *m*
book design Buchausstattung *f*, Buchgestaltung *f*
book designer Buchgestalter *m*
book edge Buchschnitt *m*
book face *(type)* Buchschrift *f*, Werksatzschrift *f*
Book Fair Buchausstellung *f*, Buchmesse *f*
book flow line Buchfertigungsstraße *f*
book format Buchformat *n*
book forming Buchformen *n*
book forming and pressing machine Buchformpresse *f*
book fount *(type)* Buchschrift *f*, Werksatzschrift *f*
book illumination Buchmalerei *f*
book illustration Buchillustration *f*
book illustrator Buchillustrator *m*
book ink Werkdruckfarbe *f*
book in sheets ungebundenes Buch *n*
book jacket Buchumschlag *m*, Schutzumschlag *m*
book jacketing machine *(book prod.)* Schutzumschlagmaschine *f*
booklet Broschüre *f*, Heft *n*
booklet cover Broschürenumschlag *m*, Heftumschlag *m*

booklet production Broschürenherstellung *f*
booklet stitching Broschürenheftung *f*
book linen Buchleinen *n*
bookmark Blattzeichen *n*, Buchzeichen *n*, Lesezeichen *n*, Lesezeichenband *n*, Zeichenband *n*
bookmark inserting machine Zeichenbandeinlegemaschine *f*
book of fables Fabelbuch *n*
book of fairy tales Märchenbuch *n*
book of heraldry Wappenbuch *n*
book of hours Stundenbuch *n*
book ornamentation Buchschmuck *m*
book pagination *(page count)* Buchumfang *m*; *(page make-up)* Werksatzumbruch *m*
book paper Bücherpapier *n*, Werkdruckpapier *n*
bookplate Exlibris *n*
book press Werkdruckmaschine *f*
book printer Werkdruckerei *f*
book printing Bücherdruck *m*, Werkdruck *m*
book printing press Werkdruckmaschine *f*
book production Buchfertigung *f*, Buchherstellung *f*
book production line Buchfertigungsstraße *f*
book publisher(s *pl)* Buchverleger *m*
book review Buchbesprechung *f*
book rounding Buchrunden *n*
book rounding and backing machine Buchrunde- und Abpreßmaschine *f*
book rounding machine Buchrundemaschine *f*
bookseller Buchhändler *m*
book sewing Faden(buch)heftung *f*
book-sewing machine Buchheftmaschine *f*, Fadenheftmaschine *f*
book-sewing through gaze Gazeheftung *f*
bookshop Buchhandlung *f*, Buchladen *m*
book size Buchformat *n*
book spine Buchrücken *m*
book spine gluing Buchrückenbeleimung *f*
book spine gluing machine Buchrückenbeleimmaschine *f*
book spine preparation Buchrückenbearbeitung *f*
book spine shape Buchrückenform *f*
book stacker Buchstapler *m*
bookstall Kiosk *m*
bookstore Buchhandlung *f*
book thread-stitching see book sewing
book title Buchtitel *m*
book trade Buchhandel *m*
book trimmer Buchdreischneider *m*
book type Werksatzschrift *f*
bookwork *(printing)* Bücherdruck *m*, Werkdruck *m*; *(typesetting)* Werksatz *m*

bookwork composition Werksatz *m*
book wrapper Buchumschlag *m*, Schutzumschlag *m*
border *(typogr.)* Rand *m*, Umrandung *f*, Umrahmung *f*; *(printer's flower)* Leiste *f*, Zierleiste *f*
border *v* einrahmen, einfassen
bordering and backlining machine *(bookbinding)* Einfaß- und Fälzelmaschine *f*
border ornament Reihenornament *n*
border piece *(lead comp.)* Anschlußstück *n*
border rule Einfassungslinie *f*, Rahmenlinie *f*, Randlinie *f*
border with rules *v* mit Linien einrahmen
Boston press Bostonpresse *f*
botched job Pfusch *m*
botched piece of work Pfusch *m*
both-sided beidseitig
bottle label Flaschenetikett *n*
bottom knife Untermesser *n*
bottom line *(of page)* Fußzeile *f*, Schlußzeile *f*
bottom locking *(folding box)* Bodenverschluß *m*
bottom margin unterer Papierrand *m*, unterer Seitenrand *m*
bottom note Fußnote *f*
bottom of table *(tabular comp.)* Tabellenfuß *m*
bottom rule Fußlinie *f*
bottom sheet feeder *(bundle proc., mailroom)* Unterbogenanleger *m*
bottom side Unterseite *f*
bottom stitching *(folding box)* Bodenheftung *f*
bottom wire *(papermaking)* Untersieb *n*
bounce-back *(sheet)* Zurückfedern *n*
bound book gebundenes Buch *n*
bound-in insert Beihefter *m*, Einhefter *m*
box *(carton)* Schachtel *f*; *(typogr.)* Umrahmung *f*, Umrandung *f*, Rahmen *m*
box *v* *(typogr.)* mit Linien einrahmen
box aligner *(folding box prod.)* Schachtelgeradrichter *m*
boxboard Faltschachtelkarton *m*, Kartonagenkarton *m*, Kartonagenpappe *f*, Kartonpappe *f*
boxboard liner Kartonagenüberzugspapier *n*
boxboard printer Kartonagendruckerei *f*
boxboard printing Kartonagendruck *m*
box cap Schachteldeckel *m*
box corner staying machine Schachteleckenverbindemaschine *f*
box cover Schachteldeckel *m*
box covering machine Schachtelbeklebemaschine *f*, Schachtelüberziehmaschine *f*
box delivery Kastenauslage *f*

boxed ad Anzeige mit Umrandung *f*
boxed head eingerahmter Titel *m*
boxed rules *pl* Linienrahmen *m*
box erector *(folding box prod.)* Schachtelaufrichter *m*
box lid Schachteldeckel *m*
box lining machine Schachtelbeklebemaschine *f*, Schachtelüberziehmaschine *f*
box number *(advertisement)* Anzeigenchiffre *f*, Chiffre-Nummer *f*
box number advertisement Chiffreanzeige *f*, Kennziffernanzeige *f*
box rule *(typogr.)* Rahmenlinie *f*
box with rounded corners *(typogr.)* Rahmen mit runden Ecken
braces *pl* *(typesetting)* Akkoladen *f/pl*, geschweifte Klammern *f/pl*, Nasenklammer *f*
bracket *(mech.)* Halterung *f*; *(typesetting)* eckige Klammer *f*
bracket *v* *(typesetting)* einklammern, in Klammern setzen
braking roller Bremswalze *f*
brand colour Hausfarbe *f*
brass corners *pl* *(book)* Messingecken *pl*
brass die Messingstempel *m*
brass embossing plate Messingprägeplatte *f*
brass engraving Messingätzung *f*
brass etching Messingätzung *f*
brass letter Messingletter *f*
brass matrix Messingmatrize *f*
brass plate Messingplatte *f*
brass rule Messinglinie *f*
brass spaces *pl* Messingdurchschuß *m*, Messingspatien *pl*
brass type Messingschrift *f*, Messingtype *f*
bread-and-butter face *(type)* Brotschrift *f*, Textschrift *f*
break *(typesetting)* Absatz *m*, Endzeile *f*; *(reel paper)* Riß *m*
break *v* *(reel paper)* reißen
breakdown *(techn.)* Störung *f*
breakdown of machine *(techn.)* Maschinenstörung *f*
breakdown of press Druckmaschinenstörung *f*
break line *(typesetting)* Absatz *m*, Ausgangszeile *f*, Endzeile *f*
break mark *(typesetting)* Absatzzeichen *n*
break off *v* wegbrechen
break over *(overmatter)* Überhang *m*, Überlauf *m*, Übersatz *m*
break point *(text rec.)* Stoppstelle *f*, Unterbrecher *m*
brickstack *v* kreuzweise stapeln

bridge-type camera - bulk-printed matter

bridge-type camera Brückenkamera *f*
bright colours *pl* helle Farben *pl*
brighten *v (image areas, colours)* aufhellen
brighten colour *v* Farbe aufhellen
brightlight film Tageslichtfilm *m*
brightness Helligkeit *f; (lens)* Lichtstärke *f*
brightness range *(image)* Helligkeitsumfang *m*
bright room film Hellraumfilm *m*
brilliance Brillanz *f*, Glanz *m*
brilliancy see brilliance
brilliant black *(ink)* Glanzschwarz *n*
brilliant ink glänzende Farbe *f*
bring into contact *v (rollers, cylinders, doctor blade)* anstellen
bring into position *v* den Stand machen, einpassen
bring into register *v* den Stand machen, einpassen; *(colour register)* Passer einstellen; *(on press)* Register einstellen, Register machen
bring out *v* herausgeben
Bristol board Bristolkarton *m*
Bristol paper Bristolpapier *n*
brittle *(dried ink)* spröde
broadband *(telecom.)* Breitband *n*
broadband channel *(telecom.)* Breitbandkanal *m*
broadsheet Planobogen *m*
broadsheet newspaper großformatige Zeitung *f*
broadsheet size Großformat *n; (newspaper)* Broadsheet-Format *n*
broadside page Querformatseite *f*, Seite im Querformat
brochure Broschüre *f*, Prospekt *m*
brochure body *(without cover)* Broschüreninhalt *m*
brochure content *(without cover)* Broschüreninhalt *m*
brochure cover Broschürenumschlag *m*
brochure production Broschürenherstellung *f*
brochure stitching Broschürenheftung *f*
broken line *(typesetting)* see break line
broken types *pl* Fraktur *f*, Gotisch *f*, Schwabacher *f; (type classif.)* Gebrochene Schriften *pl*
bromide Papierabzug *m; (gravure)* Opal *n*
bromide drag *(photochemistry, film processor)* Bromschleppe *f*
bronze *v* bronzieren
bronze dust Bronzestaub *m*
bronze-dust *v* bronzieren
bronze ink Bronzedruckfarbe *f*, Bronzefarbe *f*
bronze letters *pl* Bronzeschrift *f*
bronze powder Bronzepulver *n*, Bronzestaub *m*

bronze printing Bronzedruck *m*, Bronzierdruck *m*
bronze printing varnish Bronzedruckfirnis *m*
bronze type Bronzeschrift *f*
bronzing *(bronze printing)* Bronzierdruck *m; (photographs)* Braunwerden *n*
bronzing machine Bronziermaschine *f*
bronzing plush Bronzierplüsch *m*
bronzing primer Bronzeunterdruckfarbe *f*
bronzing size *(primer)* Bronzeunterdruckfarbe *f*
brush Bürste *f; (artist's brush)* Pinsel *m*
brush *v* bürsten
brushed aluminium plate gebürstete Aluminiumplatte *f*
brush etching Pinselätzung *f*
brush lettering Pinselschrift *f*
brush proof Bürstenabzug *m*
brush retouching Pinselretusche *f*
brush roll *(feedboard)* Bürstenrolle *f*
brush roller Bürstenwalze *f*
brush stroke Pinselstrich *m*
brush type Pinselschrift *f*
brush-type damping system *(offset)* Bürstenfeuchtwerk *n*
bubble memory *(comp.)* Magnetblasenspeicher *m*
buckle *v* sich wölben; *(folding)* stauchen
buckled board gewölber Karton *m*
buckled paper welliges Papier *n*
buckle fold Stauchfalz *m*, Taschenfalz *m*
buckle folder Taschenfalzmaschine *f*
buckle folding Stauchfalzung *f*
buckle guide *(folding m.)* Deckrechen *m*
buckle plate *(folding m.)* Falztasche *f*
buckle-plate folding machine Taschenfalzmaschine *f*
buckling *(paper)* Welligwerden *n*
buffer Puffer *m; (comp.)* Speicher *m*
buffer agents *pl (fountain solution)* Puffersubstanzen *pl*
buffer belts *pl (mailroom)* Staubänder *pl*
buffer memory Zwischenspeicher *m*
buffer reel *(mailroom)* Pufferspule *f*
buffer section *(mailroom)* Staustrecke *f*
buffer storage Zwischenlagerung *f; (comp.)* Zwischenspeicher *m*
build-up *(deposits on blanket, rollers)* Aufbauen *n*
built-in *(machine parts)* eingebaut, integriert
bulge Wulst *m*
bulk *(paper)* Bauschigkeit *f*, Papiervolumen *n*
bulk copy *(text copy)* Mengentext *m*
bulk (factor) *(paper)* Papiervolumen *n*
bulk(ing) index *(paper)* spezifisches Volumen *n*
bulk-printed matter Massendrucksache *f*

bulk storage *(comp.)* Massenspeicher *m*
bulky folding spine auftragender Falzrücken *m*
bulky paper auftragendes Papier *n*, bauschiges Papier *n*, Dickdruckpapier *n*, voluminöses Papier *n*
bumb exposure *(camera screening)* Nachbelichtung *f*
bump turn of web *(90°)* Bahnumlenkung *f* um 90°
bundle *(mailroom)* Bündel *n*, Paket *n*, Stange *f*
bundle conveyor Paketförderer *m*
bundle conveyor system Pakettransportsystem *n*
bundle delivery Paketauslage *f*
bundle delivery by route *(mailroom)* Routenpaketauslage *f*
bundle feeder *(convert.)* Stangenanleger *m*
bundle formation Paketbildung *f*; *(convert.)* Stangenbildung *f*
bundle loading *(convert.)* Stangenbeschickung *f*
bundle processing Paketverarbeitung *f*; *(convert.)* Stangenverarbeitung *f*
bundler Paketiervorrichtung *f*
bundle stacker Paketstapler *m*
bundling machine Bündelmaschine *f*
burin Stichel *m*
burned-in printing plate eingebrannte Druckplatte *f*
burner *(ink drying)* Brenner *m*
burning-in *(offset plate)* Einbrennen *n*
burning-in of joint *(book prod.)* Falzeinbrennen *n*
burning-in oven *(offset plate)* Einbrennofen *m*
burning-in rail *(book prod.)* Falzeinbrennschiene *f*
burn into *v (film, plate)* einkopieren
burnish *v (gravure cyl.)* polieren
burn-out *(reprod.)* Ausbelichtung *f*
burn out *v (reprod., platemaking)* ausbelichten, auskopieren; *(film edges)* wegbelichten
burn-out mask *(reprod.)* Ausbelichtungsmaske *f*
burn-out of cutting edges Wegbelichten von Schnittkanten *n*
burr *(cutting)* Grat *m*
burr-free cutting gratfreies Schneiden *n*
bus *(data link)* Sammelleitung *f*
business card Empfehlungskarte *f*, Geschäftskarte *f*
business forms *pl* Geschäftsformulare *n/pl*
business forms press Formulardruckmaschine *f*
business report Geschäftsbericht *m*
business stationery Geschäftsdrucksachen *pl*
butted rules *pl (hand comp.)* zusammengestoßene Linien *pl*
butting *(pictures, web splice)* aneinanderstoßend
butt joint Stoß *m*
butt splicing *(web splice)* Stoß-an-Stoß-Bahnklebung *f*
buzzer *(warning signal)* Warnsignal *n*
by permission of the author mit Genehmigung des Verfassers
byte Byte *n*

C

cabinet *(hand comp.)* geschlossenes Regal *n*
cable connection Kabelanschluß *m*, Kabelverbindung *f*
cable link Kabelverbindung *f*
cable text Kabeltext *m*
cable TV Kabelfernsehen *n*
cache memory Hauptspeicher *m*
CAD (computer-aided design) CAD (computergestützte Entwicklung)
calcium carbonate Kalziumkarbonat *n*
calculate *v (volume, price etc.)* kalkulieren, schätzen
calculate roughly *v* überschlagen
calculate the costs *v* Kosten berechnen
calculate the volume *v (text copy)* Manuskript berechnen
calculation Kalkulation *f*
calculation disc Rechenscheibe *f*
calculation of size Formatberechnung *f*
calculation of volume *(manuscript)* Manuskriptberechnung *f*, Satzberechnung *f*, Textberechnung *f*, Umfangsberechnung *f*
calculator Kalkulator *m*; *(comp.)* Rechner *m*
calendar Kalender *m*
calendar back Kalenderrückwand *f*
calendar binding Kalenderbindung *f*
calendar block Kalenderblock *m*
calendar hanger Kalenderaufhänger *m*
calendar mount Kalenderrückwand *f*
calendar paper Kalenderpapier *n*
calendar production Kalenderfertigung *f*
calender *(papermaking)* Glättwerk *n*, Glanzkalander *m*, Kalander *m*
calender *v* kalandrieren, satinieren
calender bowl Kalanderwalze *f*
calendered paper satiniertes Papier *n*

calender embossing - carbon black

calender embossing Kalanderprägung *f*
calender graining Kalanderprägung *f*
calendering Kalandern *n*, Kalandrierung *f*, Satinage *f*
calender roller Kalanderwalze *f*
calender varnish glazing Kalanderlackierung *f*
calf binding Kalbsleder(ein)band *m*
calibrate *v (electronic systems, measuring devices)* kalibrieren, abgleichen, eichen
calibrated scale Einstellskala *f*
calibrated underlay sheets *pl (cyl. packing)* kalibrierte Unterlagebogen *m/pl*
calibration *(electronic systems, measuring devices)* Abgleich *m*, Eichung *f*, Kalibrierung *f*
calibration patch Eichfeld *n*
calibration plate Eichplatte *f*
calico Kaliko *n*
calico paper Kalikopapier *n*
calico printing Kattundruck *m*
call *(data, text)* Abruf *m*, Aufruf *m*
call *v (data, text)* abrufen, aufrufen
calligrapher Kalligraf *m*
calligraphy Kalligrafie *f*, Schreibkunst *f*
calling card Besuchskarte *f*, Visitenkarte *f*
calliper Mikrometer *f*
call on screen *v* auf Bildschirm aufrufen
cam Exzenter *m*, Exzenterkurve *f*, Kurve *f*, Nocken *m*, Steuerkurve *f*
CAM (computer-aided manufacturing) CAM (computergestützte Herstellung)
cam control Exzentersteuerung *f*, Kurvensteuerung *f*, Nockensteuerung *f*
cam disc Exzenterscheibe *f*, Kurvenscheibe *f*, Nockenscheibe *f*
cam drive Exzenterantrieb *m*
camera Kamera *f*
camera adjustment Kameraeinstellung *f*
camera back Kamerahinterkasten *f*
camera bellows *pl* Kameraauszug *m*, Kamerabalgen *m*
camera densitometer Kameradensitometer *n*, Online-Densitometer *n*
camera exposure Kameraaufnahme *f*, Kamerabelichtung *f*
camera extension Kameraauszug *m*, Kamerabalgen *m*
camera frame Kameraständer *m*
camera front box Kameravorderkasten *m*
camera lens Kameralinse *f*, Kameraobjektiv *n*
camera operator Reprofotograf *m*
camera-platemaker *(small offset)* Folienkamera *f*, Plattenautomat *m*, Plattenkamera *f*

camera-ready reprofähig, reproreif
camera scale Kameraskala *f*
camera screening Kamerarasterung *f*, Rasterfotografie *f*
camera separation *(colour sep.)* Kameraauszug *m*
camera setting Kameraeinstellung *f*
camera trolley *(horizontal camera)* Kamerawagen *m*
camera work Kameraarbeiten *pl*
cam motion Exzenterbewegung *f*
cam shaft Exzenterwelle *f*, Nockenwelle *f*
cam wheel Exzenterrad *n*
can Blechdose *f*
canard *(wrong news)* Ente *f*
cancel *v (comp.)* löschen; *(text)* durchstreichen, streichen
cancel a subscription *v* Abonnement abbestellen
cancel copy *v (text)* Text löschen
can go over druckreif, gut zum Druck, o.k. zum Druck
canned copy *(text copy)* Stehmanuskript *n*
canvas *(book cloth)* Kanvas *m*
caolin *(papermaking)* Kaolin *n*
cap see capital (letter)
capacity Kapazität *f*, Leistung *f*, Leistungsfähigkeit *f*
capacity per day *(mach.)* Tageskapazität *f*, Tagesleistung *f*
capacity utilization Kapazitätsauslastung *f*
capacity utilization rate Nutzungsgrad *m*
cap height *(typesetting)* Versalhöhe *f*
capillary film *(screen printing)* Kapillarfilm *m*
capillary tube Kapillare *f*
capital costs *pl* Kapitalkosten *pl*
capitalization *(typesetting)* Großschreibung *f*
capital (letter) Großbuchstabe *m*, Majuskel *f*, Versalbuchstabe *m*
capital letters *pl* Versalien *f/pl*
capitals *pl* Versalien *f/pl*
capitals and lowercase Groß/Kleinschreibung *f*
cap line *(typelines)* Oberlinie *f*
caps *pl* Versalien *f/pl*
caps and small caps *(typesetting)* Kapitälchen *pl* (mit großen Anfangsbuchstaben)
capsule *(summary at the beginning of a newspaper article)* Zusammenfassung *f*
caption Bildertext *m*, Bildüberschrift *f*, Bildunterschrift *f*, Legende *f*
capture *v (data, text)* erfassen
carbid-tipped knife *(cutting m.)* Hartmetallmesser *n*
carbon arc lamp *(reprod.)* Kohlebogenlampe *f*
carbon black Karbonfarbe *f*

carbon copy Kohlepapierdurchschlag *m*
carbon copy forms set Durchschreibeformularsatz *m*, Kohlepapierformularsatz *m*
carbon diapositive *(gravure)* Pigmentdiapositiv *n*
carbon film *(gravure)* Pigmentfilm *m*
carbon film copy *(gravure)* Pigmentkopie *f*
carbon gluing Kohlepapieranklebung *f*
carbon ink Pigmentfarbe *f*, Durchschreibefarbe *f*, Karbonfarbe *f*
carbonized copy paper karbonisiertes Durchschreibepapier *n*
carbonized forms set Durchschreibeformularsatz *m*, karbonisierter Formularsatz *m*
carbonizing Karbonisieren *n*
carbonizing machine Karbondruckmaschine *f*
carbonizing paper Karbonisierpapier *n*
carbonless copy paper Durchschreibepapier *n*, Farbreaktionspapier *n*, Selbstdurchschreibepapier *n*
carbonless forms set Durchschreibeformularsatz *m*, Selbstdurchschreibesatz *m*
carbon paper Karbonpapier *n*, Kohlepapier *n*
carbon printing Karbondruck *m*, Kohledruck *m*, Pigmentdruck *m*
carbon printing machine Karbondruckmaschine *f*
carbon rewind (unit) Kohlepapieraufrollung *f*
carbon rod *(arc lamp)* Kohlestift *m*
carbon tissue *(gravure)* Pigmentpapier *n*
carbon tissue dryer Pigmentpapiertrockeneinrichtung *f*
carbon tissue sensitizing Pigmentpapiersensibilisierung *f*
carbon tissue transfer Pigmentpapierübertragung *f*
carbon unwind (unit) Kohlepapierabrollung *f*
carborundum Karborund *n*
card Karte *f*
cardan shaft Kardanwelle *f*
cardboard Karton *m*, Pappdeckel *m*, Pappe *f*
cardboard box Karton *m*, Kartonage *f*, Pappkarton *m*, Pappschachtel *f*
cardboard container Kartonage *f*, Pappkiste *f*
cardboard product Kartonage *f*
card gluer *(print convert.)* Kartenkleber *m*
card index Kartei *f*
card punch Lochkartenstanzer *m*
card reader *(punched card)* Lochkartenleser *m*
card tipper *(print convert.)* Kartenkleber *m*
care *(machines)* Pflege *f*
Caroline minuscle *(type)* Karolingische Minuskel *f*
carriage Wagen *m*; *(camera)* Schlitten *m*; *(letterpress m.)* Druckkarren *m*, Karren *m*

carriage delivery Wagenauslage *f*
carriage drive *(letterpress m.)* Karrenantrieb *m*
carriage rails *pl (letterpress m.)* Karrenleisten *pl*
carriage return *(letterpress m.)* Karrenrücklauf *m*
carriage-type camera Schlittenkamera *f*
carrier *(photo, film etc.)* Trägermaterial *n*
carrier bag Tragbeutel *m*
cartographer Kartograf *m*, Kartenzeichner *m*
cartography Kartografie *f*
carton Karton *m*, Pappkarton *m*, Pappschachtel *f*, Schachtel *f*
carton blank *(box prod.)* Faltschachtelzuschnitt *m*, Kartonagenzuschnitt *m*
cartonboard Faltschachtelkarton *m*
carton insert Kartoneinlage *f*
carton printer Kartonagendrucker(ei) *m/f*
carton printing Kartonagendruck *m*
cartoon Cartoon *m*
case *(book)* see book case
casebender *(book prod.)* **automatic ~** Deckenbiegeapparat *m*
case-bound book Hartdeckelbuch *n*, hartgebundenes Buch *n*
case box *(type case)* Kastenfach *n*
cased *(noise abatement)* gekapselt
case forming station *(book prod.)* Deckenrückenformstation *f*
casein Kasein *n*
case in *v (book)* einhängen
casein resistant käseecht
case lay *(type case)* Setzkasteneinteilung *f*
case layout *(type case)* see case lay
casemaker *(book prod.)* Buchdeckenmaschine *f*
casemaking *(book prod.)* Buchdeckenfertigung *f*
casemaking machine *(book prod.)* Buchdeckenmaschine *f*, Deckenmachmaschine *f*
case rack *(for type cases)* Kastenregal *n*, Setzregal *n*, Regal ohne Setzpult
casing *(mach.)* Gehäuse *n*
casing-in machine *(book prod.)* Bucheinhängemaschine *f*
cassette Kassette *f*
cassette folder Kassettenfalzapparat *m*
cassette-type inking unit Kassettenfarbwerk *n*
cassette-type printing unit *(with printing cartridges)* Kassettendruckwerk *n*
cast *(matrix)* Abguß *m*, Form *f*; *(colour)* Stich *m*; *(type)* Guß *m*
cast *v (matrix)* abgießen; *(type)* gießen
cast alloy Gußlegierung *f*
cast-coated paper gußgestrichenes Papier *n*
caster *(mach.)* Gießapparat *m*, Gießmaschine *f*

cast in v *(matrix)* eingießen
casting *(matrix)* Abguß m; *(type)* Guß m
casting machine Gießapparat m, Gießmaschine f
casting mould *(stereotyping)* Gießform f, Gußform f
cast iron *(machine parts)* Grauguß m, Gußeisen n
cast-iron frame gußeisernes Maschinengestell n
cast-iron substructure Gußunterbau m
cast-off Manuskriptberechnung f, Satzberechnung f, Umfangsberechnung f
cast type Schriftguß m
catalog(ue) Katalog m
catalogue cover Katalogumschlag m
catchline Hauptzeile f, Schlagzeile f
catchword Stichwort n, Suchwort m, Kustode f
cathode Kathode f
cathode ray tube *(CRT, photocomp.)* Kathodenstrahlröhre f
caustic potash Ätzkali n
caustic soda Ätznatron n
caustic soda solution kaustische Sodalösung f
cavity cut *(book edge)* Hohlschnitt m
CCD camera *(charge coupled device)* CCD-Kamera f
CCD optics CCD-Optik f
CCD scanner CCD-Scanner m
cedilla *(typesetting)* Cedille f
celloglazing *(film laminating)* Cellophanierung f, Glanzfolienkaschierung f
cellophane Cellophan n, Zellglas n
cellophane window *(folding box)* Zellglasfenster n
cells pl *(gravure, anilox)* Näpfchen pl, Rasternäpfchen pl
celluloid film Cellophan n
cellulose Zellulose f
cellulose acetate Zelluloseazetat n
cellulose lacquer Zaponlack m, Zelluloselack m
cell wall *(gravure)* Rastersteg m, Steg m
center v zentrieren
center copy v *(text)* Text auf Mitte stellen
center cut Mittelschnitt m
centered dot *(typesetting)* fetter mittestehender Punkt m
center lines v *(type)* Zeilen zur Mitte stellen
center sleeve bearing *(gravure cyl.)* Pinolenlagerung f
center slitting *(web)* Mittelschnitt m
center spread Doppelseite f, durchgehende Doppelseite f, Panoramaseite f, Seitenpaar n
center type v Satz auf Mitte stellen
central control console Leitstand m
central editorial site Redaktionszentrale f

central grease lubrication Fettzentralschmierung f
centralized control zentrale Steuerung f
central lubrication Zentralschmierung f
centrally adjustable zentral verstellbar
central pressure lubrication Zentraldruckschmierung f
central processing unit *(CPU)* Hauptrechner m, Zentralrechner m
central processor *(comp.)* Zentralrechner m
central shutter *(camera)* Zentralverschluß m
central storage *(comp.)* Zentralspeicher m
central supply system Zentralversorgungssystem n
central system *(as opp. to sub-system)* Hauptsystem n
centrifugal damping system Schleuderfeuchtwerk n
centring device Zentriervorrichtung f
ceramic decal keramisches Abziehbild n
ceramic paper keramisches Papier n
ceramic printing keramischer Druck m
ceramic transfer picture keramisches Abziehbild n
cerotype Wachsradierung f
certified sale *(newspaper circulation)* kontrollierte Verkaufsauflage f
chain conveyor Kettenförderer m, Kettentransporteur m
chain delivery Kettenauslage f
chain dot Kettenpunkt m
chain drive Kettenantrieb m, Kettenzug m
chain gripper delivery Kettengreiferauslage f
chain grippers pl Kettengreifer pl
chain printer Kettendrucker m
chalcography Chalkografie f
chalk Kreide f
chalk drawing Kreidelithografie f, Kreidezeichnung f
chalking Kreiden n; *(ink)* Kalken n, Abkreiden n, Abmehlen n
chalk pencil Kreidestift m
chalk relief makeready *(letterpress printing)* Kreidereliefzurichtung f
chalky fog Kalkschleier m
chambered doctor blade *(gravure)* Kammerrakel f
change-over *(new job)* Umrüstung f, Umstellung f
change-over times pl *(new job)* Rüstzeiten f/pl, Umrüstzeiten pl, Umstellungszeiten pl, Einrichtezeiten f/pl
channel *(groove)* Rille f
channel matrix Rillmatrize f
chapter *(book)* Abschnitt m, Kapitel n

chapter heading Kapitelüberschrift *f*, Zwischentitel *m*
character Schriftzeichen *n*, Buchstabe *m*
character count *(text copy)* Manuskriptberechnung *f*, Anzahl Zeichen, Satzberechnung *f*
character definition *(photocomp.)* Randschärfe *f*, Kantenschärfe *f*, Wiedergabequalität *f*, Konturenschärfe *f*
character display *(on screen)* Zeichendarstellung *f*
character fit(ting) Buchstabenabstand *m*, Laufweite *f*, Zeichenabstand *m*
character flash *(photocomp.)* Belichtung *f*, Belichtungsgeschwindigkeit *f*
character generation Zeichengenerierung *f*
character height Schrifthöhe *f*
characteristic curve Kennlinie *f*
characteristic curve of printing Druckkennlinie *f*
character kerning *(typesetting)* Zeichenunterschneidung *f*
character memory *(text rec.)* Zeichenspeicher *m*
character outlines *pl* Schriftkontur *f*
character pair *(typesetting)* Zeichenpaar *n*
character pool *(photocomp.)* Zeichenvorrat *m*
character recognition *(optical character reading)* Zeichenerkennung *f*
character rotation Buchstabendrehung *f*
characters *pl* Schrift *f*
character set Buchstabenbreite *f*, Dickte *f*, Schriftweite *f*, Zeichenbreite *f*; *(photocomp.)* Zeichensatz *m*, Zeichenvorrat *m*
character size Schriftgrad *m*, Schriftgröße *f*
character sizing *(photocomp.)* Schriftgrößeneinstellung *f*
character sizing increments *(photocomp.)* Schriftgrößenabstufung *f*
character spacing Sperren *n*, Spationieren *n*, Buchstabenabstand *m*, Laufweite *f*, Zeichenabstand *m*
characters per second *(cps, photocomp.)* Zeichen pro Sekunde
character string Buchstabenfolge *f*, Zeichenfolge *f*
character width Buchstabenbreite *f*, Dickte *f*, Schriftdickte *f*, Schriftweite *f*, Zeichenbreite *f*
charcoal Holzkohle *f*
charcoal drawing Kohlezeichnung *f*
charge *v (costs)* berechnen, in Rechnung stellen
chart Grafik *f*, grafische Darstellung *f*, Schaubild *n*, Tafel *f*
chase *(forme chase)* Formrahmen *m*, Rahmen *m*, Schließrahmen *m*

chase holder *(platen press)* Schließrahmenhalter *m*
chase locking Formschließen *n*
chase width Rahmenweite *f*
check *v* kontrollieren, nachsehen, prüfen
check bit Prüfbit *n*
check digit *(comp.)* Prüfziffer *f*
check(ing) Kontrolle *f*, Prüfung *f*
checking copy Kontrollexemplar *n*, Prüfexemplar *n*; *(advertiser)* Belegexemplar *n*
checking sheet Kontrollbogen *m*, Probebogen *m*
check mark Kontrollzeichen *n*, Prüfzeichen *n*
check proofs with copy *v (text copy)* nach Manuskript lesen
chemical pulp *(papermaking)* Zellstoff *m*
chemical pulp digester Zellstoffauflöser *m*
chemical pulping Zellstoffherstellung *f*
chemical resistant chemikalienbeständig
chemicals *pl* Chemikalien *pl*
chemical sign *(typesetting)* chemisches Symbol *n*, chemisches Zeichen *n*
chemical woodpulp Holzzellstoff *m*
cheque book Scheckheft *n*
cheque form Scheckformular *n*, Scheckvordruck *m*
cheque ink Scheckfarbe *f*
cheque numbering Schecknumerierung *f*
cheque paper Scheckpapier *n*
cheque printing machine Scheckdruckmaschine *f*
cheques *pl (typesetting)* Assureelinie *f*, Azureelinie *f*
chiaroscuro helldunkel
chief editor Chefredakteur *m*
children's book Kinderbuch *n*
chilling machine Kältemaschine *f*
chilling tower *(web press)* Kühlwalzenstand *m*
chilling unit *(web press)* Kühlaggregat *n*
chill roll *(web press)* Kühlwalze *f*
chill roll assembly *(web press)* Kühlwalzenstand *m*
chill roll frame *(web press)* Kühlwalzenstand *m*
chill roll stand *(web press)* Kühlwalzenstand *m*
China paper Chinapapier *n*
Chinese paper Chinapapier *n*
chips *pl (book prod.)* Späne *pl*
chisel Grabstichel *m*, Stichel *m*
chock Stoß *m*
chocolate wrapper Schokoladeneinwickler *m*
choir book Gesangbuch *n*
chopper (blade) *(press folder)* Falzmesser *n*, Falzschwert *n*
chopper fold *(press folder)* Schwertfalz *m*, Messerfalz *m*

Christmas card Weihnachtskarte f
chromatic bunt, farbig
chromatic aberration Farbabweichung f; *(lens)* chromatische Farbabweichung f
chromatic colour *(reprod.)* bunte Farbe f
chromatic colour addition *(reprod.)* Buntfarbenaddition f
chromatic composition *(reprod.)* Buntaufbau m
chromatic construction *(reprod.)* Buntaufbau m
chromatic value Buntwert m, Farbwert m
chrome *(colour slide)* Colordia n, Farbdia n; *(metal)* Chrom m
chrome bath *(gravure)* Chrombad n
chrome-electrolyte *(gravure)* Chromelektrolyt n
chrome-facing *(gravure)* Verchromung f
chrome fracturing density *(gravure cyl.)* Chromrißdichte f
chrome nickel steel Chromnickelstahl m
chrome-plated cylinder verchromter Zylinder m
chrome-plating *(gravure)* Verchromung f
chrome-plating installation Verchromungsanlage f
chrome polishing *(gravure cyl.)* Chrompolieren n
chrome removal *(gravure cyl.)* Entchromen n
chrome stripping *(gravure cyl.)* Entchromen n
chromium Chrom m
chromo board Chromokarton m
chromo duplex board Chromoduplexkarton m
chromolithographer Chromolithograf m, Farblithograf m
chromolithography Chromolithografie f, Farblithografie f; *(stone printing)* Farbsteindruck m, farbiger Steindruck m
chromo paper Chromopapier n
chute delivery Rutschauslage f; *(small offset press)* Muldenauslage f
cicero *(typogr.)* Cicero n
cigarette box Zigarettenschachtel f
cigarette pack Zigarettenpackung f
cinema poster Kinoplakat n
C.I. press *(common impression cylinder press)* Druckmaschine mit gemeinsamem Gegendruckzylinder, Einzylinderdruckmaschine f
circuitry printing Schaltungsdruck m
circular board cutter Kartonkreisschere f
circular cutter Kreismesser n
circular exposure Rund(um)belichtung f
circular knife Kreismesser n, Kreisschere f
circular letter Rundschreiben f
circular saw Kreissäge f
circular screen *(camera)* Drehraster m

circulation *(newspaper, magazine)* Auflage f, Auflagenhöhe f, Verbreitung f
circulation pump Umwälzpumpe f
circulation statement *(newspaper, magazine)* Auflagenangabe f
circulation system Umwälzsystem n
circumference Umfang m
circumferential register *(web printing)* Umfangsregister n
circumferential speed Umfangsgeschwindigkeit f
circumflex accent *(typesetting)* Zirkumflexakzent m
clair-obscure helldunkel
clamp Backe f, Klemme f; *(cutting m.)* Preßbalken m; *(perfect binder)* Zange f
clamp a plate v Platte einspannen
clamp bar see clamping bar
clamping *(plate)* Aufspannen n, Einspannen n
clamping bar *(cutting m.)* Preßbalken m, Preßleiste f; *(press cyl.)* Spannschiene f, Spannleiste f, Klemmschiene f, Klemmleiste f
clamping block *(three-knife trimmer)* Preßstempel m
clamping device Einspannvorrichtung f, Klemmvorrichtung f
clamping jaw Einspannbacke f, Klemmbacke f
clamping lever Klemmhebel m
clamping pressure *(cutting m.)* Preßdruck m
clamping ring Klemmring m
clamp pressure see clamping pressure
clasp *(book)* Schließe f, Schloß n
classified ad *(as opp. to display ad)* Fließsatzanzeige f, Kleinanzeige f
classified ad matter Fließsatz m
classified pagination Fließsatzumbruch m, Kleinanzeigenumbruch m
Clean Air Act Abluftgesetz n
clean copy korrigierter Text m
cleaner *(for plates, rollers, blankets)* Reinigungsmittel n
cleaning blade *(inking unit)* Reinigungsrakel f
cleaning brush Putzbürste f, Waschbürste f
cleaning cloth Putzlappen m
cleaning rag Putzlappen m
cleaning wool Putzwolle f
clean proof *(galley proof)* korrigierter Korrekturabzug m, Revisionsbogen m, sauberer Abzug m
clean-up *(press)* Reinigung f, Reinigungsvorgang m
clean-up time Reinigungszeit f
Clean Water Act Abwassergesetz n
clear v *(comp.)* löschen

clear copy *(text copy)* leserliches Manuskript *n*
clear front cover Klarsichtdeckblatt *n*
clear text display Klartextanzeige *f*
clear type Klarschrift *f*, leserliche Schrift *f*
clear type display Klarschriftanzeige *f*
clear-write *(comp.)* Löschen/Schreiben
client Auftraggeber *m*, Kunde *m*
client's order Kundenauftrag *m*
clipping *(newspaper)* Ausschnitt *m*
clock diagram Vektorgrafik *f*
close brackets Klammer zu
closed cam guide system geschlossene Kurvenführung *f*
closed head *(folded signature)* am Kopf geschlossen, geschlossener Kopf *m*
closed loop (circuit) geschlossener Regelkreis *m*
closed sections *pl* unaufgeschnittene Bogen *pl*
closed signatures *pl* unaufgeschnittene Bogen *pl*
closed-surface substrate nichtsaugendes Druckpapier *n*
closely spaced line eng ausgeschlossene Zeile *f*, enge Zeile *f*
closely spaced matter *(type)* enger Satz *m*
close matter kompresser Satz *m*
close quote *(typesetting)* Abführungszeichen *n*, Ausführungszeichen *n*
close register genaues Register *n*; *(colour)* genauer Passer *m*
close setting *(type)* enger Satz *m*
close spacing enger Ausschluß *m*
close up *v (type matter)* zusammenrücken, Zwischenraum herausnehmen
close with quotes *v* die Anführung schließen
closing date *(news/ads)* Annahmeschluß *m*, Einsendeschluß *m*, Schlußtermin *m*
cloth *(bookbinding)* Leinen *n*
clothback *(book)* Leinenband *m*
cloth binding *(book)* Leineneinband *m*
cloth-bound in Leinen eingebunden
cloth case *(book)* Leinendecke *f*, Leineneinband *m*
cloth cover *(book)* Leinendecke *f*, Leineneinband *m*
cloth-covered plate damper stoffbezogene Feuchtauftragswalze *f*
cloth-lined leinenkaschiert
cloth lining *(book, box)* Stoffüberzug *m*
cloth printing Stoffdruck *m*, Textildruck *m*
cloud formation *(printing)* Wolkenbildung *f*
cluster (configuration) Systemgerätegruppe *f*
cluster system *(comp.)* Mehrplatzsystem *n*
clutch Kupplung *f*
clutch *v* anstellen, einkuppeln, zuschalten

coarse screen etching Grobrasterätzung *f*
coarse screen/fine screen measurement *(densitometry)* Grobraster/Feinrastermessung *f*
coarse screen halftone engraving *(letterpress)* Grobrasterautotypie *f*
coat *v* beschichten; *(emulsions)* gießen; *(paper)* streichen; *(to varnish)* lackieren
coated back (CB) *(chemically treated self-copying paper)* Rückseite beschichtet
coated front (CF) *(chemically treated self-copying paper)* Vorderseite beschichtet
coated paper gestrichenes Papier *n*
coated side beschichtete Seite *f*
coated stock gestrichenes Papier *n*
coating Auftrag *m*, Beschichtung *f*, Auftragung *f*; *(plate coating)* Schicht *f*; *(paper)* Strich *m*; *(varnishing)* Lackierung *f*
coating blade *(papermaking)* Aufstreichrakel *f*
coating engraving *(cartogr.)* Schichtgravur *f*
coating film *(varnishing)* Lackschicht *f*
coating layer *(varnishing)* Lackschicht *f*
coating machine *(papermaking)* Streichmaschine *f*; *(varnishing machine)* Lackiermaschine *f*
coating plant *(papermaking)* Streichanlage *f*
coating removal Entschichtung *f*
coating roller *(varnishing roller)* Lackierwalze *f*
coating sensitivity *(plate)* Schichtempfindlichkeit *f*
coating thickness Schichtdicke *f*
coating unit *(varnishing unit)* Lackiereinheit *f*, Lackierwerk *n*
coauthor Mitautor *m*
coaxial cable Koaxialkabel *n*
cobalt blue kobaltblau
cobalt dryer *(ink additive)* Kobalttrockner *m*
cock *v (sheets)* verkanten
cocked folding schiefwinklige Falzung *f*
cocked sheet schiefer Bogen *m*, Schrägbogen *m*
cockling *(paper)* Tellerbildung *f*, Welligwerden *n*
code Kode *m*
code *v* kodieren, verschlüsseln
code conversion Kodekonvertierung *f*, Kodeumsetzung *f*, Kodeumwandlung *f*
code converter Kodeumwandler *m*
code line imprint *(security printing)* Kodierzeileneindruck *m*
code numbering Kodenumerierung *f*
coder Kodierer *m*
code reader Kode-Leser *m*
code scanner Kode-Leser *m*
coding Kodieren *n*, Kodierung *f*
cogwheel Zahnrad *n*

coherent light - colour duplicating

coherent light *(laser)* kohärentes Licht *n*
cold air blast Kaltluftgebläse *n*
cold blocking Kaltprägung *f*
cold composition Kaltsatz *m*, nichtmetallischer Satz *m*
cold embossing Kaltprägung *f*
cold glue *(adhesive binding)* Kaltleim *m*
cold glue bound kaltleimgebunden
cold glue compound Kaltleimverbindung *f*
cold lamination Kaltkaschierung *f*
cold laminator Kaltkaschiermaschine *f*
cold sealing Kaltkaschierung *f*, Kaltsiegelung *f*
cold sealing machine Kaltkaschiermaschine *f*
cold-set web offset Coldset-Rollenoffset *m*
cold stereotyping Kaltstereotypie *f*
cold-top process *(photo-engraving)* Emailkopierverfahren *n*, Kaltemailverfahren *n*
cold type Kaltsatz *m*, nichtmetallischer Satz *m*
collapsible zusammenklappbar
collapsible carton Faltschachtel *f*
collapsible folding box Faltschachtel *f*
collate *v* zusammentragen; *(text copies)* Texte kollationieren
collating marks *pl* Flattermarken *f/pl*
collator *(forms prod.)* Kollator *m*, Zusammentragmaschine *f*
collect *v* zusammentragen; *(data, text)* erfassen
collecting basket *(film processor)* Auffangkorb *m*
collecting cylinder Sammeltrommel *f*, Sammelzylinder *m*
collecting terminal Erfassungsterminal *n*
collection *(data, text)* Erfassung *f*
collection of text copy Texterfassung *f*
collector drum Sammeltrommel *f*, Sammelzylinder *m*
collector's edition Liebhaberausgabe *f*
collect-run production *(web printing; as opp. to straight-run prod.)* Sammelproduktion *f*, gesammelte Produktion *f*
collodion Kollodium *n*
collodion cotton Kollodiumwolle *f*
collotype Lichtdruck *m*, Fototypie *f*
collotype board Lichtdruckkarton *m*
collotype gelatine Lichtdruckgelatine *f*
collotype grain Lichtdruckkorn *n*, Runzelkorn *n*
collotype paper Lichtdruckpapier *n*
collotype plate Lichtdruckplatte *f*
collotype printing Lichtdruck *m*, Fototypie *f*
collotype roller Lichtdruckwalze *f*
colon *(punctuation mark)* Doppelpunkt *m*, Kolon *n*
colorant Färbemittel *n*, Farbstoff *m*
colorimetry Farbmessung *f*

colour Farbe *f*
colour adjustment Farbeinstellung *f*
colour allocation *(electronic image proc.)* Farbzuordnung *f*
colour area Farbfläche *f*
colour balance Farbbalance *f*, Farbgleichgewicht *n*
colour balance patch *(print control bar)* Farbbalancefeld *n*
colour bar *(print control bar)* Farbkontrollstreifen *m*, Farbmeßstreifen *m*
colour boosting *(reprod.)* Farbverstärkung *f*
colour break-up Farbzerlegung *f*
colour cast Farbstich *m*
colour cast removal *(scanner)* Farbstichrücknahme *f*
colour change *(photocoating of offset plate)* Farbumschlag *m*
colour channel *(electronic reprod., densitometer)* Farbkanal *m*
colour chart Farbenkarte *f*, Farbkarte *f*, Farbtafel *f*
colour combination pattern *(newspaper printing)* Farbbelegung *f*, Farbplazierung *f*
colour component *(in the image)* Farbanteil *m*
colour computer Farbrechner *m*
colour control Farbkontrolle *f*, Farbregelung *f*, Farbsteuerung *f*
colour control bar Farbkontrollstreifen *m*, Farbmeßstreifen *m*
colour control desk Farbsteuerpult *m*
colour control patch *(print control bar)* Farbkontrollfeld *n*
colour control strip Farbkontrollstreifen *m*, Farbmeßstreifen *m*
colour control system Farbregelanlage *f*, Farbsteueranlage *f*
colour copy *(photocopy)* Farbkopie *f*
colour correction Farbkorrektur *f*
colour correction mask *(reprod.)* Farbkorrekturmaske *f*
colour deck *(newspaper press)* Eindruckwerk *n*, Farbdruckwerk *n*, Farbeindruckwerk *n*, Zusatzfarbwerk *n*
colour densitometer Farbdensitometer *n*
colour densitometry Farbdichtemessung *f*
colour density Farbdichte *f*
colour developer *(phot.)* Farbentwickler *m*
colour deviation Farbabweichung *f*, Farbtonabweichung *f*
colour duplicate *(colour reprod.)* Farbduplikat *n*, Colorduplikat *n*
colour duplicating Colorduplikatherstellung *f*

coloured - colour scale

coloured bunt, farbig
coloured book edge Farbschnitt *m*, gefärbter Buchschnitt *m*
colour editing *(electronic image proc.)* Farbkorrektur *f*
colour editing terminal *(image proc.)* Farbkorrekturterminal *m*, Farbkontrollterminal *m*
coloured paper buntes Papier *n*, Buntpapier *n*, farbiges Papier *n*
colour enlarger *(reprophotogr.)* Farbvergrößerer *m*
colour etching Farbradierung *f*
colour evaluation lamp Farbprüfleuchte *f*
colour evaluation overhead lamp Farbprüfleuchte *f* in Überkopfhöhe
colour-fast *(ink)* lichtecht
colour fastness *(ink)* Farbechtheit *f*, Lichtechtheit *f*
colour fidelity getreue Farbwiedergabe *f*
colour film Farbfilm *m*
colour filter Farbfilter *m*
colour fluctuations *pl* Farbschwankungen *pl*
colour forme *(as opp. to text or black forme)* Farb(en)form *f*, Buntdruckform
colourful farbig
colour gamut Farbfächer *m*
colour gradation Farbabstufung *f*, Farbverlauf *m*
colour guide Farbfächer *m*
colour harmony Farbharmonie *f*
colour hologramme Color-Hologramm *n*
colour image assembly Farbbildmontage *f*, Farbmontage *f*
colour image recorder Farbbildrekorder *m*
colour imposition *(newspaper printing)* Farbbelegung *f*, Farbplazierung *f*
colour information *(also digital)* Farbinformation *f*
colouring Färbung *f*, Kolorieren *n*; *(electr. image processing)* Einfärben *n*
colour intensification *(reprod.)* Farbverstärkung *f*
colour intensity Farbintensität *f*, Farbkraft *f*, Farbstärke *f*
colourist Kolorist *m*
colour key *(overlay colour film proof)* Colorkey *m*, Farbdurchsichtsproof *m*, Farbfolienproof *m*
colour lap *(colour reprod.)* Farbüberstand *m*
colourless farblos
colour linework Farbstricharbeiten *f/pl*
colour match(ing) Farbabmusterung *f*, Farbabstimmung *f*, Farbeinstellung *f*, Farbnachstellung *f*

colour matching desk Abstimmtisch *m*
colour measurement Farbmessung *f*
colour measuring system Farbmeßsystem *n*
colourmetrics Farbmetrik *f*
colour mixing chart Farbmischtafel *f*
colour monitor Farbbildschirm *m*, farbiger Monitor *m*, Farbmonitor *m*
colour negative Farbnegativ *n*
colour negative paper Farbnegativpapier *n*
colour original Farbvorlage *f*
colour page *(newspaper, magazine)* Farbseite *f*
colour page transmission *(telecom.)* Farbseitenübertragung *f*
colour photo(graph) Farbfoto *n*, Farbfotografie *f*
colour photography Farbfotografie *f*
colour pigment Farbkörper *m*, Farbpigment *n*
colour placement *(newspaper printing)* Farbbelegung *f*, Farbplazierung *f*
colour plate *(book)* Farbtafel *f*; *(letterpress)* Farbklischee *n*
colour positive paper Farbpositivpapier *n*
colour preview farbige Prüfdarstellung am Bildschirm
colour print Farbdruck *m*; *(photocopy)* Farbkopie *f*; *(photoprint)* Farbabzug *m*, Farbaufsichtsbild *n*, Farbfoto *n*
colour printing Farbdruck *m*, Buntdruck *m*, Buntfarbendruck *m*; *(multi-colour printing)* Mehrfarb(en)druck *m*
colour process etcher Farbätzer *m*
colour process etching Farbätzung *f*
colour process printing Vierfarbdruck *m*
colour process work *(colour reprod.)* Farbreproduktion *f*; *(printwork)* Vierfarbdruck *m*
colour proof Farbproof *m*, Farbprüfdruck *m*
colour proofer *(mach.)* Farbproofmaschine *f*
colour proofing Farbproofherstellung *f*
colour proofing system Farbprüfsystem *n*
colour reduction *(image proc.)* Farbrücknahme *f*
colour reflection original Farbaufsichtsvorlage *f*
colour register Farb(en)passer *m*, Farbregister *n*, Passer *m*, Einzelfarbenpasser *m*
colour rendering Farbwiedergabe *f*
colour rendition Farbwiedergabe *f*
colour reproduction Farbreproduktion *f*, Farbwiedergabe *f*; *(print)* Farbdruck *m*
colour retouching Farbretusche *f*, Farbkorrektur *f*
colour reversal paper *(colour reprod.)* Farbumkehrpapier *n*
colour sample Farbmuster *n*
colour saturation Farbsättigung *f*
colour scale Farbskala *f*

colour scanner Farbscanner *m*
colour sensitivity *(graphic arts film)* Farbempfindlichkeit *f*
colour separation *(linework)* Farbtrennung *f*; *(halftone work)* Farbauszug *m*
colour separation data *(scanner)* Farbauszugsdaten *pl*
colour separation film Farbauszugsfilm *m*
colour separation filter Farbauszugsfilter *m*
colour separation negative Farbauszugsnegativ *n*
colour separation positive Farbauszugspositiv *n*
colour separations *pl* Farbauszüge *m/pl*
colour sequence *(multi-colour printing)* Farbreihenfolge *f*, Farbfolge *f*, Druckfolge *f*
colour setting Farbeinstellung *f*
colour shade Farbnuance *f*, Farbschattierung *f*
colour shift(ing) Farbverschiebung *f*, Farbverlagerung *f*
colour signature *(as opp. to text or black signature)* Farbbogen *m*
colour slide Colordia *n*, Farbdia *n*
colour solid Farbfläche *f*
colour space *(colour theory)* Farbenraum *m*
colour specimen Farbmuster *n*
colour specimen book Farbfächer *m*
colour specimen chart Farbmusterkarte *f*
colour spectrum Farbspektrum *n*
colour stamping foil *(as opp. to gold/silver foil)* Farbprägefolie *f*
colour standard Farbnorm *f*
colour strength Farbintensität *f*, Farbkraft *f*, Farbstärke *f*
colour supplement *(newspaper)* Farbbeilage *f*, farbige Beilage *f*
colour surface Farbfläche *f*
colour synthesis Farbmischung *f*
colour temperature *(° K)* Farbtemperatur *f*
colour theory Farbenlehre *f*, Farbentheorie *f*
colour-to-colour register Farb(en)passer *m*, Einzelfarbenpasser *m*
colour tone Farbton *m*
colour transmission *(telecom.)* Farbübertragung *f*
colour transparency Colordia *n*, Farbdia *n*
colour unit *(press unit)* Farbdruckwerk *n*
colour value Farbwert *m*
colour work *(multi-colour work)* Mehrfarb(en)arbeiten *pl*
column *(newspaper, magazine)* Kolumne *f*, Rubrik *f*, Spalte *f*; *(tabular work)* Kolonne *f*
column composition *(typesetting)* Spaltensatz *m*
column cutter *(paste-up)* Spaltenschneider *m*
column depth Spaltenhöhe *f*
column galley *(lead comp.)* Spaltenschiff *n*
column gutter Raum zwischen den Spalten, Zwischenschlag *m*
column heading Rubrikkopf *m*, Rubriktitel *m*, Spaltenkopf *m*
columnist Kolumnist *m*
column matter *(typesetting)* Spaltensatz *m*
column measure *(column width)* Spaltenbreite *f*
column press Säulenpresse *f*
column rule Spaltenlinie *f*
column setting *(typesetting)* Spaltensatz *m*
column width Spaltenbreite *f*
comb binding Kammbindung *f*
combination folder *(press folder)* Kombifalzer *m*
combination folding machine *(knife fold + buckle fold)* Kombi-Falzautomat *m*
combination printing Zusammendruck *m*
combination rule *(typesetting)* Assureelinie *f*, Azureelinie *f*
combination run *(printing various jobs with one forme)* Druck mit Sammelform
combination sheet *(for multi-up processing)* Sammelbogen *m*
combined exposure *(frame exposure)* Zusammenkopieren *n*
combined forme Sammelform *f*
combined ground glass/vacuum film back *(camera)* Ansaugmattscheibe *f*
combined image and text processing integrierte Bild- und Textverarbeitung *f*
combined inking and damping system kombiniertes Farb/Feuchtwerk *n*, Hydrocolor-System *n*
combined printing Zusammendruck *m*
combined staggered stitch *(thread-stitching)* kombiniert versetzter Stich *m*
combined stencil *(screen printing)* Kombischablone *f*
combustion air *(gas dryer)* Verbrennungsluft *f*
COM (computer output on microfilm) COM (Rechnerausgabe auf Mikrofilm)
come out *v (publication)* erscheinen
comics *pl* Bilderstreifen *pl*, Comic Strips *pl*
comic strips *pl* Comic Strips *pl*, Bilderstreifen *pl*
comma Komma *n*, Beistrich *m*
command *(comp.)* Befehl *m*, Kommando *n*
command chain *(comp.)* Befehlskette *f*
command data *(comp.)* Befehlsdaten *pl*
command language *(comp.)* Befehlssprache *f*
command string *(comp.)* Befehlskette *f*
commence quote Anführung *f*
commercial artist Gebrauchsgrafiker *m*
commercial art(work) Gebrauchsgrafik *f*

commercial designer *(graphic design)* Gebrauchsgrafiker *m*
commercial forms *pl* Geschäftsformulare *n/pl*
commercial operation *(trade house)* Lohnbetrieb *m*
commercial press *(web press)* Akzidenzmaschine *f*
commercial printer *(web printer)* Akzidenzdrucker *m*, Akzidenzdruckerei *f*
commercial printing *(web printing)* Akzidenzdruck *m*
commercial (print)work *(web printing)* Akzidenzarbeiten *f/pl*, Akzidenzen *pl*
commercial stationery Geschäftsdrucksachen *pl*
commercial web offset press Akzidenzrollenoffsetmaschine *f*
commercial web press Akzidenzrollenrotation *f*
common impression cylinder press Druckmaschine mit gemeinsamem Gegendruckzylinder, Einzylinderdruckmaschine *f*
common impression flexo press Einzylinder-Flexodruckmaschine *f*
communication Kommunikation *f*
communication link Kommunikationsverbindung *f*
communications industry Kommunikationsindustrie *f*
communications network Nachrichtennetz *n*, Übertragungsnetz *n*
communication technology Kommunikationstechnik *f*
compact camera Kompaktkamera *f*
compact disc Compact Disc *f*
company brochure Firmenbroschüre *f*, Hausbroschüre *f*
company logo Firmensignet *n*, Firmenzeichen *n*
company name imprint Firmeneindruck *m*
company report Geschäftsbericht *m*
compatibility Kompatibilität *f*
compatible kompatibel
compensated delivery kreuzweise Auslage *f*, Kreuzstapelauslage *f*, Querstapelauslage *f*, Verschränktauslage *f*
compensated stack kreuzgelegter Stapel *m*, verschränkter Stapel *m*
compensating counter stacker Kreuzzählstapler *m*
compensating filter Kompensationsfilter *m*
compensating mask *(reprod.)* Kompensativmaske *f*
compensating roller see compensator roller
compensating stacker *(mailroom)* Kreuzleger *m*, Kreuzstapler *m*, Stapelkreuzleger *m*

compensator roller *(web press)* Ausgleichswalze *f*, Registerwalze *f*
compiler *(comp.)* Compiler *m*
complementary colour *(colour theory)* Ergänzungsfarbe *f*, Komplementärfarbe *f*
complete printing *v* ausdrucken, fertigdrucken
complete setting *v* aussetzen, fertigsetzen
complex matter *(typesetting)* komplizierter Satz *m*
complex work komplizierte Arbeit *f*
complimentary copy Freiexemplar *n*
compose *v (type)* setzen; *(page composition)* umbrechen
composed *(in type)* gesetzt
composer setting *(e.g. IBM composer)* Composersatz *m*, Schreibsatz *m*
composing frame *(lead comp.)* Setzpult *n*
composing rack *(lead comp.)* Setzregal *n*
composing rule Setzlinie *f*
composing stick *(hand comp.)* Winkelhaken *m*
composition *(typesetting)* Satz *m*
composition formatting Satzformatierung *f*
composition of advertising matter Anzeigensatz *m*
composition of classified ads Fließsatz *m*
composition of foreign language work Fremdsprachensatz *m*
composition of titles Titelsatz *m*
composition program Satzprogramm *n*
composition room Setzerei *f*
composition shop Setzerei *f*
composition software Satzsoftware *f*
composition system Satzsystem *n*
composition work Satz *m*, Satzarbeit *f*
compositor Schriftsetzer *m*, Setzer *m*
compositor-pressman Schweizerdegen *m*
compositor's desk *(lead comp.)* Setzpult *n*
compositor's error Satzfehler *m*, Setzfehler *m*
compound *(laminate)* Laminat *n*
compound foil Verbundfolie *f*
compound fractions *pl* Bruchziffern *pl*, gebrochene Ziffern *pl*
compounds *pl (substrates)* Verbundmaterialien *pl*
compressed air Druckluft *f*, Preßluft *f*
compressed air supply Druckluftversorgung *f*
compressed bundle *(mailroom)* gepreßter Stapel *m*
compressed signatures *pl (folded signatures)* gepreßte Falzbogen *m/pl*
compressibility *(rubber blanket)* Kompressibilität *f*
compressible rubber blanket *(as opp. to conventional)* kompressibles Gummituch *n*, Luftpolstertuch *n*

compressing Pressen *n*
computer Computer *m*, Rechner *m*
computer-aided computergestützt, EDV-gestützt, rechnergestützt
computer composition program Rechnersatzprogramm *n*
computer-controlled computergesteuert, rechnergesteuert
computer cycle Computerlauf *m*, Rechnerlauf *m*
computer exposure programmierte Belichtung *f*
computer fold Zickzackfalz *m*
computer form Computerformular *n*, EDV-Formular *n*
computer graphics Computergrafik *f*
computerized computergesteuert, EDV-gestützt, rechnergesteuert
computerized guillotine Programmschneider *m*
computer(ized) typesetting Computersatz *m*
computer language Maschinensprache *f*
computer memory Computerspeicher *m*
computer peripheral Computerperipherie *f*
computer program Computerprogramm *n*, Rechnerprogramm *n*
computer run Computerlauf *m*, Rechnerlauf *m*
computer software Computersoftware *f*, Rechnersoftware *f*
computer-to-plate exposure datengesteuerte Plattenbelichtung *f*, digitale Plattenherstellung *f*, Plattenkopie direkt aus Datenbestand
computer-to-plate system Computer-to-Plate-System *n*, datengesteuertes Plattenkopiersystem *n*
concave lens Konkavlinse *f*
concentrate *(photochem., pressroom chem.)* Konzentrat *n*
concentric line screen *(reprod.)* Zirkellinienraster *m*
concentric running *(cylinder)* Rundlauf *m*
concertina fold Leporellofalz *m*, Zickzackfalz *m*
concise dictionary Handwörterbuch *n*
condensed Grotesque schmale Grotesk *f*
condensed Roman schmale Antiqua *f*
condensed typeface schmale Schrift *f*, schmallaufende Schrift *f*
condition paper *v* Papier vorklimatisieren
configuration Anordnung *f*
connect *v* anschließen, anstellen, einkuppeln, verbinden, zuschalten
connecting points *pl (die-cut sheets)* Verbindungsstege *pl*
connecting rod Pleuelstange *f*
connection Anschluß *m*

consecutive numbering fortlaufende Numerierung *f*, vorwärtszählende Numerierung *f*
consignment Lieferung *f*
consistent quality gleichmäßige Qualität *f*
console *(system control)* Bedienungstafel *f*, Konsole *f*, Schalttafel *f*
consonant Konsonant *m*
construction Bauweise *f*
consumables *pl* Verbrauchsprodukte *pl*
consumer magazine Konsumentenzeitschrift *f*, Verbraucherzeitschrift *f*
contact *(contact copy)* Kontakt *m*, Kontaktabzug *m*
contact *v (to copy)* kopieren, kontakten, umkopieren
contact angle *(doctor blade)* Anstellwinkel *m*
contact area *(printing zone)* Drucklinie *f*, Druckzone *f*, Kontaktlinie *f*
contact box Kontaktbelichter *m*, Kontaktkopierer *m*, Kontaktkopiergerät *n*
contact control strip Kontaktkontrollstreifen *m*
contact copier Kontaktkopiergerät *n*, Kontaktkopierer *m*, Kontaktbelichter *m*
contact copy Kontaktabzug *m*, Kontaktkopie *f*, Kopie *f*
contact copying Kontakten *n*, Kontaktkopie *f*, Kopie *f*
contact exposure Kontaktbelichtung *f*, Kontaktkopie *f*, Kopie *f*
contact exposure unit see contact printer
contact film Kontaktfilm *m*
contact frame see contact printer, vacuum frame
contact-free delivery berührungslose Auslage *f*, kontaktfreie Auslage *f*
contact-free transport berührungsloser Transport *m*
contact gluing *(as opp. to nozzle gluing)* Kontaktbeleimung *f*
contacting *(reprod.)* Kontakten *n*
contact line Kontaktlinie *f*
contact negative Kontaktnegativ *n*
contact paper *(reprod.)* Kontaktpapier *n*
contact positive Kontaktpositiv *n*
contact print Kontaktabzug *m*, Kontaktkopie *f*, Kopie *f*
contact printer Kontaktkopiergerät *n*, Kontaktkopierer *m*, Kontaktbelichter *m*
contact printing Kontakten *n*, Kontaktkopie *f*, Kopie *f*
contact screen Kontaktraster *m*, Rasterfilm *m*
contact screening Kontaktrasterung *f*
contact-screen scanner *(as opp. to electronic dot generation scanner)* Kontaktrasterscanner *m*

contact work *(reprod.)* Kontaktarbeiten *pl*
container board Containerpappe *f*, Kistenpappe *f*
content *(brochure/book without cover)* Inhalt *m*
continuation *(manuscript)* Anschluß *m*
continued overleaf Fortsetzung umseitig, weiter auf der nächsten Seite
continuous copy *(unjustified text copy)* Endlostext *m*
continuous-feed damping system Filmfeuchtwerk *n*, heberloses Feuchtwerk *n*
continuous-feed inking system Filmfarbwerk *n*, heberloses Farbwerk *n*
continuous forms *pl* Endlosformulare *pl*
continuous forms press Endlosformulardruckmaschine *f*
continuous forms printing Endlosformulardruck *m*
continuous forms sets *pl* Endlosformularsätze *m/pl*
continuous gluing *(as opp. to intermittent)* kontinuierliche Leimung *f*
continuous ink duct blade formschlüssiges Farbmesser *n*
continuous load Dauerlast *f*
continuous oil lubrication Dauerölschmierung *f*
continuous operation Dauerbetrieb *m*
continuous paper Endlospapier *n*
continuous stationery Endlosdrucksachen *m/pl*, Endlosformulare *pl*, Endlospapier *n*
continuous stationery press Endlosdruckmaschine *f*, Endlosformulardruckmaschine *f*
continuous stationery printing Endlosdruck *m*, Endlosformulardruck *m*
continuous text *(non-counted)* Endlostext *m*
continuous tone Halbton *m*
continuous-tone (colour) separations *pl* Halbtonfarbauszüge *pl*
continuous-tone engraving Halbtonätzung *f*
continuous-tone etching Halbtonätzung *f*
continuous-tone exposure Halbtonaufnahme *f*
continuous-tone illustration Halbtonbild *n*
continuous-tone image Halbtonbild *n*
continuous-tone negative Halbtonnegativ *n*
continuous-tone paper Halbtonpapier *n*
continuous-tone photo(graph) Halbtonfoto *n*, Halbtonaufnahme *f*
continuous-tone picture Halbtonbild *n*
continuous-tone positive Halbtonpositiv *n*
continuous-tone printing *(gravure)* Halbtondruck *m*
continuous-tone reproduction Halbtonreproduktion *f*, Halbtonwiedergabe *f*
continuous-tone scale Halbtonskala *f*
continuous-tone wedge Halbtonkeil *m*
continuous-type damping system Filmfeuchtwerk *n*, heberloses Feuchtwerk *n*
continuous-type inking system Filmfarbwerk *n*, heberloses Farbwerk *n*
continuous type matter *(non-counted)* Endlossatz *m*
con-tone *(continuous-tone)* Halbton *m*
contour Kontur *f*
contour definition *(photocomp.)* Kantenschärfe *f*, Konturenschärfe *f*, Randschärfe *f*
contour film Konturenfilm *m*
contrast Kontrast *m*
contrast border Kontrastrand *m*
contrast compression Kontrastkompression *f*, Kontrastverringerung *f*
contrast control film Kontraststeuerfolie *f*
contrast enhancement Kontraststeigerung *f*
contrast filter Kontrastfilter *m*
contrast range Kontrastumfang *m*
contrast reducing mask Kontrastdämpfungsmaske *f*
control Kontrolle *f*, Regelung *f*, Regulierung *f*, Steuerung *f*
control *v* kontrollieren, regeln, steuern
control accuracy Steuer(ungs)genauigkeit *f*, Regelgenauigkeit *f*
control bar Kontrollstreifen *m*
control box Schaltkasten *m*, Schaltschrank *m*, Steuerkasten *m*
control button Bedienungsknopf *m*
control cabinet see control box
control character *(photocomp.)* Steuerzeichen *n*
control circuit Regelkreis *m*
control console Steuerstand *m*, Bedienungsstand *m*, Kontrollpult *n*, Schaltpult *m*
control copy Kontrollexemplar *n*, Kontrollkopie *f*, Prüfexemplar *n*
control desk Bedienungspult *n*, Kontrollpult *m*, Schaltpult *m*
control device Steuergerät *n*
control engineering Regelungstechnik *f*
controller *(computer)* Rechner *m*; *(device)* Steuergerät *n*
control lever Schalthebel *m*
control light Kontrollampe *f*
control panel Bedienungstafel *f*, Schaltbrett *n*, Schalttafel *f*
control patch *(print control bar)* Kontrollfeld *n*
control range Regelbereich *m*
control sheet Kontrollbogen *m*, Probebogen *m*
control side *(as opp. to drive side)* Bedienerseite *f*, Bedienungsseite *f*

control signal - copper type

control signal Steuersignal *n*
control strip Kontrollstreifen *m*
control technology Regelungstechnik *f*
control unit Steuereinheit *f*
control wedge *(exposure control)* Kontrollkeil *m*, Testkeil *m*
conventional doctoring *(gravure)* positive Abrakelung *f*
conventional etching *(gravure)* konventionelle Ätzung *f*
conventional gravure (process) konventioneller Tiefdruck *m*
conventional rubber blanket *(as opp. to compressible)* konventionelles Gummituch *n*
conversion *(techn.)* Umrüstung *f*, Umstellung *f*; *(data, signals)* Umwandlung *f*, Konvertierung *f*
conversion of standing matter *(type matter)* Stehsatzkonvertierung *f*
conversion plate *(offset plate)* Umkehrplatte *f*
conversion table *(typesetting)* Konvertierungstabelle *f*
conversion to lineart *(reprod.)* Strichumsetzung *f*
convert *v (techn.)* umrüsten, umstellen; *(data, signals)* konvertieren, umwandeln
converted copy *(text copy)* konvertierter Text *m*
converted text konvertierter Text *m*
converter *(device)* Konverter *m*; *(print finishing operation)* Druckverarbeiter *m*, Verarbeitungsbetrieb *m*, Veredler *m*
convertible umschaltbar, umstellbar, umsteuerbar
convertible four-colour sheet-fed offset press umstellbare Vierfarben-Bogenoffsetmaschine *f*
convertible perfector umstellbare Schön- und Widerdruckmaschine *f*
convertible to perfecting umstellbar auf Schön- und Widerdruck
converting *(data, text)* Konvertierung *f*; *(print converting)* Druckverarbeitung *f*, Druckweiterverarbeitung *f*, Veredlung *f*, Weiterverarbeitung *f*
converting line Verarbeitungslinie *f*
converting operation *(paper converting)* Verarbeitungsbetrieb *m*
convex lens Konvexlinse *f*, Sammellinse *f*
conveyor *(mailroom)* Transporteur *m*
conveyor belt Bändertransporteur *m*, Förderband *n*, Gurtförderer *m*, Transportband *n*
conveyor chain Förderkette *f*, Transportkette *f*
conveyor clamp Transportklammer *f*, Transportzange *f*
conveyor (line) Förderanlage *f*

conveyor system Fördersystem *n*, Transportsystem *n*
conveyor tape see conveyor belt
coolant Kühlmittel *n*
cooling agent Kühlmittel *n*
cooling coil Kühlschlange *f*
cooling device *(web press)* Kühlaggregat *n*
cooling machine Kältemaschine *f*
cooling water circulation *(for temperature control)* Kühlwasserumlauf *m*
coordinate-controlled page make-up koordinatengesteuerter Umbruch *m*
coordinate drawing table *(CAD)* Koordinatenzeichentisch *m*
copier *(office)* Kopierer *m*, Kopiergerät *n*
copper anode Kupferanode *f*
copper bath Kupferbad *n*
copper chips *pl* Kupferspäne *pl*
copper coating Kupferhaut *f*, Kupferschicht *f*
copper content Kupfergehalt *m*
copper deposit Kupferniederschlag *m*
coppered wire verkupferter Draht *m*
copper engraving Kupferätzung *f*, Kupfergravüre *f*
copper etching Kupferätzung *f*
copper-faced stereo verkupfertes Stereo *n*
copper-facing Verkupferung *f*
copper gravure cylinder *(as opp. to plastic-coated cyl.)* Kupfertiefdruckzylinder *m*
copper gravure process *(as opp. to gravure with plastic coated cyl.)* Kupfertiefdruck *m*
copper hardness Kupferhärte *f*
copperplate Kupferdruckplatte *f*, Kupferplatte *f*
copperplate base *(gravure cyl.)* Grundkupfer *n*
copperplate engraver Kupferstecher *m*
copperplate engraving Kupferstich *m*
copperplate for engraving Kupferstichplatte *f*
copperplate for photogravure Kupferätzplatte *f*
copperplate press Kupferdruckpresse *f*
copperplate print Kupferstich *m*
copperplate printing Kupferdruck *m*, Kupferstich-Tiefdruck *m*
copper-plating Aufkupferung *f*, Verkupferung *f*
copper-plating installation Aufkupferungsanlage *f*, Verkupferungsanlage *f*
copper recovery Kupferrückgewinnung *f*
copper removal *(gravure cyl.)* Entkupfern *n*
copper skin Kupferhaut *f*
copper stereo Kupferstereo *n*
copper stripping *(gravure cyl.)* Entkupfern *n*
copper sulfate Kupfersulfat *n*
copper type *(hand comp.)* Kupferbuchstaben *pl*

copy Kopie *f*, Abdruck *m*, Abschrift *f*, Exemplar *n*, Heft *n*, Manuskript *n*, Nutzen *m*, Satzvorlage *f*, Text *m*, Vorlage *f*
copy *v* kopieren, umkopieren
copy board Manuskripthalter *m*, Vorlagenhalter *m*
copy book *(exercise b.)* Heft *n*, Schreibheft *n*
copy book cover Schreibheftumschlag *m*
copy checking *(text copy)* Textprüfung *f*; *(web printing)* Exemplarkontrolle *f*
copy conveyor *(press delivery, mailroom)* Exemplartransporteur *m*
copy counter Exemplarzähler *m*
copy deadline *(news deadline)* Redaktionsschluß *m*
copy delivery *(web press)* Exemplarauslage *f*
copy delivery belt *(web press)* Exemplarauslageband *n*
copy design Vorlagengestaltung *f*
copy-desk work *(editorial work)* Redaktionsarbeit *f*
copy display Vorlagengestaltung *f*
copyfit calculation Manuskriptberechnung *f*, Textberechnung *f*, Umfangsberechnung *f*
copyfit software *(text proc.)* Textberechnungsprogramm *n*
copyfitting Manuskriptberechnung *f*, Satzberechnung *f*, Umfangsberechnung *f*
copy flow *(typesetting)* Zeilenfall *m*
copy holder Originalhalter *m*, Vorlagenhalter *m*; *(text copy)* Manuskripthalter *m*
copying Kopie *f*
copying frame *(platemaking)* Kopierrahmen *m*
copying ink Durchschreibefarbe *f*
copying lamp Kopierlampe *f*
copying paper Kopierpapier *n*
copying technique Kopiertechnik *f*
copy input *(text copy)* Texteingabe *f*
copy into *v* *(film, plate)* einkopieren
copy mark-up *(text copy)* Manuskriptaufbereitung *f*, Manuskriptauszeichnung *f*, Manuskriptbearbeitung *f*, Manuskriptvorbereitung *f*, Satzvorbereitung *f*
copy monitoring *(web printing)* Exemplarkontrolle *f*
copy output *(text output)* Textausgabe *f*
copy preparation *(artwork)* Druckvorlagenherstellung *f*, Originalherstellung *f*, Vorlagenherstellung *f*; *(text copy)* Manuskriptaufbereitung *f*, Manuskriptauszeichnung *f*, Manuskriptbearbeitung *f*, Manuskriptvorbereitung *f*, Satzvorbereitung *f*
copy price *(newspaper, magazine)* Einzelpreis *m*
copy processing Vorlagenverarbeitung *f*
copy production *(artwork)* Druckvorlagenherstellung *f*, Originalherstellung *f*, Vorlagenherstellung *f*
copy reader *(machine)* Belegleser *m*
copyright Copyright *n*, Autorenrecht *n*, Urheberrecht *n*, Verlagsrecht *n*, Vervielfältigungsrecht *n*
copyright imprint Copyrightvermerk *m*, Nachdruckvermerk *m*
copy scaling *(reprod.)* Formateinstellung *f*, Größeneinstellung *f*
copy size *(artwork)* Vorlagenformat *n*
copy stream *(web press delivery)* Produktstrom *m*, Schuppenstrom *m*
copy thickness Produktdicke *f*
copy-to-copy distance *(shingle stream)* Schuppenabstand *m*
copy transmission *(telecom.)* Übertragung von Druckvorlagen
copy writer *(ad writer)* Werbetexter *m*
cord *v* *(book)* kordeln
cords *pl* *(book)* Bünde *pl*, Heftbünde *pl*, Schnüre *pl*, Heftschnüre *pl*, Gebinde *n*
core chuck *(reelstand)* Spannkopf *m*
core memory *(comp.)* Kernspeicher *m*
core size *(comp.)* Speichergröße *f*
core storage *(comp.)* Kernspeicher *m*
cork blanket Korkaufzug *m*, Korktuch *n*
corner Ecke *f*
corner cutter Eckenabstoßgerät *n*, Eckenschneider *m*
corner gluing machine Eckenklebemaschine *f*, Eckenleimmaschine *f*
corner ornament Eckenverzierung *f*
corner piece *(lead comp.)* Eckstück *n*
corner punching machine Eckenausstanzmaschine *f*, Eckenstanzmaschine *f*
corner rounding Eckenrunden *n*
corner rounding machine Eckenrundstoßmaschine *f*
corner staples *pl* Eckenheftklammern *f/pl*
corner stapling Eckenheftung *f*
corner stapling machine Eckenheftmaschine *f*
corner staying machine *(folding box prod.)* Eckenverbindemaschine *f*
corona station Koronastation *f*
corona treatment Koronabehandlung *f*
corporate brochure *(company brochure)* Firmenbroschüre *f*

corporate publishing Corporate Publishing *n*, firmeneigene Drucksachenherstellung *f*, Herstellung von Firmenliteratur
corporate report Geschäftsbericht *m*
correct *v* korrigieren
corrected edition *(book)* verbesserte Ausgabe *f*
corrected line *(hot-metal comp.)* Korrekturzeile *f*
correction Korrektur *f*
correction filter Korrekturfilter *m*
correction pen *(for plates, films)* Korrekturstift *m*
correspondent *(newspaper)* Berichterstatter *m*, Korrespondent *m*
corrosion-proof korrosionsbeständig, korrosionsfest, korrosionsgeschützt
corrosion-resistant korrosionsbeständig, korrosionsfest, korrosionsgeschützt
corrugated *(board)* Wellpappe *f*; *E-flute* ~ E-Wellpappe *f*
corrugated box Wellpappkarton *m*
corrugated case Wellpappkarton *m*
corrugated container Wellpappkiste *f*
corrugated industry Wellpappenindustrie *f*
corrugated production Wellpappenherstellung *f*
cosmetic box Kosmetikpackung *f*
cost accounting Kostenrechnung *f*
cost/benefit ratio Kosten/Nutzen-Verhältnis *n*
cost calculation Kostenberechnung *f*, Kostenkalkulation *f*
cost center *(accounting)* Kostenstelle *f*
cost-effectiveness Wirtschaftlichkeit *f*
cost-efficiency Wirtschaftlichkeit *f*
cost estimating Kostenberechnung *f*, Kostenkalkulation *f*
costing Kostenberechnung *f*, Kostenkalkulation *f*
cotton(-wool) wad Wattebausch *m*
couch *v (papermaking)* gautschen
couch press Gautschpresse *f*
count Zählung *f*; *(characters, pages etc.)* Anzahl *f*
count *v* abzählen; *(characters)* auszählen
count accuracy Zählgenauigkeit *f*
counter Zähler *m*, Zählwerk *n*
counter die *(die-cutting)* Stanzgegenzurichtung *f*; *(embossing)* Patrize *f*
counter mask Gegenmaske *f*
counter plate *(die-cutting)* Stanzgegenzurichtung *f*
counter-rotating rollers *pl* gegeneinanderlaufende Walzen *pl*
counter-stacker Zählstapler *m*
counter transfer Konterumdruck *m*
counting input station *(text rec.)* rechnender Erfassungsplatz *m*

counting keyboard *(text rec.)* rechnender Erfassungsplatz *m*
couple *v* anschließen, einkuppeln, verbinden
coupling Kupplung *f*
coupling bolt Kupplungsbolzen *m*
coupling of words Wortkupplung *f*
coupon printing Kupondruck *m*
cover *(binding)* Einband *m*; *(book, magazine, brochure)* Umschlag *m*; *(machine)* Abdeckung *f*
cover *v (bookcase, box etc.)* überziehen, beziehen
coverage *(ink)* Deckung *f*
coverage properties *pl (ink)* Deckfähigkeit *f*, Deckkraft *f*
cover board Umschlagkarton *m*; *(book case)* Buchdeckel *m*, Deckelpappe *f*
covered box überzogene Schachtel *f*
covered damper roller *(offset)* bezogene Feuchtauftragswalze *f*
cover feeder Umschlaganleger *m*
cover flap Umschlagklappe *f*
cover gate *(magazine)* eingeschlagener Umschlag *m*, Umschlagklappe *f*
cover gluing Umschlaganleimung *f*
covering *(book case, box etc.)* Bezug *m*, Beklebung *f*, Überzug *m*
covering cloth *(book case)* Bezugsleinen *n*, Bezugsstoff *m*
covering paper *(book case)* Bezugspapier *n*, Deckpapier *n*, Beklebepapier *n*
cover nipping station Umschlaganpreßstation *f*
cover page Umschlagseite *f*
cover paper Umschlagpapier *n*
cover photo(graph) Umschlagfoto *n*
cover picture Titelbild *n*, Umschlagbild *n*
cover register Umschlagregister *n*
cover sheet *(binding)* Deckblatt *n*
cover story *(newspaper)* Titelstory *f*
cover title Umschlagtitel *m*
cover with flap Umschlag mit Klappe
CPU *(comp.)* Zentralrechner *m*
crack *v (dried ink)* abblättern, abplatzen
craft bookbinder Kunstbuchbinder *m*
craftman's trade Handwerksgewerbe *n*
craftman's work handwerkliche Arbeit *f*
crane *(cylinder, reel handling)* Hebekran *m*, Krananlage *f*
crank Kurbel *f*
crank handle Handkurbel *f*
crank motion Kurbelbewegung *f*
crank shaft Kurbelwelle *f*
crank wheel Kurbelrad *n*
crank wheel drive Kurbelradantrieb *m*

crash-lock bottom carton Faltbodenschachtel *f*
crash numbering *(forms set)* Durchschlagnumerierung *f*
crash perforating *(forms set)* Durchschlagperforierung *f*
crash printing *(forms set)* Durchschlagdruck *m*
crawl speed *(machine)* Schleichgang *m*
crayon Kreidestift *m*
crayon drawing Kreidelithografie *f*, Kreidezeichnung *f*
crayoning Kreideretusche *f*
crease Rille *f*; *(paper)* Falte *f*, Papierfalte *f*, Quetschfalte *f*, Runzel *f*
crease v rillen
creased *(sheet)* zerknittert
crease-free paper faltenfreies Papier *n*
creasing Rillung *f*
creasing and scoring machine Rill- und Ritzmaschine *f*
creasing knife Rillmesser *n*
creasing machine Rillmaschine *f*
creasing matrix Rillmatrize *f*
creasing roller Rillwalze *f*
creasing rule Rill-Linie *f*
creasing test *(paper)* Knitterprobe *f*
creasing wheel Rillrad *n*
create v *(image proc.)* erzeugen; *(print product)* gestalten
creative designer *(artwork prep.)* Kreativer *m*
crepe paper Kreppapier *n*
crimping *(forms set prod.)* Crimplock-Heftung *f*
crimplock device *(forms set prod.)* Crimplock-Einrichtung *f*
crimplocking *(forms set prod.)* Crimplock-Heftung *f*
crimplock set *(forms)* gecrimpter Satz *m*
crisp and clean gestochen scharf
criss-cross kreuzweise
criss-cross delivery kreuzweise Auslage *f*, Kreuzstapelauslage *f*, Querstapelauslage *f*, Verschränktauslage *f*
critic *(reviewer)* Rezensent *m*
cromalin *(hardcopy colour proof)* Cromalin *n*, Farbaufsichtsproof *m*
crop v *(image proc.)* beschneiden
crop marks *pl (image proc.)* Beschneidemarken *f/pl*, Beschnittmarken *f/pl*, Schneid(e)marken *f/pl*, Schnittmarken *f/pl*
cross bar *(mech.)* Traverse *f*
crosscheck v gegenprüfen
cross cut Querschnitt *m*
cross cutter Querschneider *m*
cross direction Querrichtung *f*

cross fold Kreuz(bruch)falz *m*, Querfalz *m*
cross gluing device Querleimeinrichtung *f*
cross gluing unit Querleimwerk *n*
cross grain *(paper)* gegen die ~/quer zur Bahnlaufrichtung *f*, gegen die ~/quer zur Laufrichtung *f*, gegen die ~/quer zur Papierlaufrichtung *f*, in Querrichtung *f*; *(short cut-off)* liegendes Format *n*
cross-grained material *(long grain instead of short grain or vice versa)* falschlaufendes Material *n*
cross-grain press *(web press)* Rollendruckmaschine *f* für liegendes Format
crosshair mark Paßkreuz *n*
cross hatching Kreuzschraffierung *f*
cross line *(typogr.)* Querlinie *f*
crossline screen Kreuzlinienraster *m*
crossover *(bastard double)* Doppelseite *f*
cross perforation Querperforierung *f*
cross reference *(text)* Querverweis *m*
cross rule Querlinie *f*
cross-ruled paper kariertes Papier *n*
cross rule under heading *(tabular matter)* Kopfabschlußlinie *f*
cross-strapping *(mailroom)* Kreuzumreifung *f*, Kreuzverschnürung *f*
cross-tying *(mailroom)* Kreuzumreifung *f*, Kreuzverschnürung *f*
cross web gegen die ~/quer zur Bahnlaufrichtung *f*, gegen die ~/quer zur Laufrichtung *f*, gegen die ~/quer zur Papierlaufrichtung *f*, in Querrichtung *f*
crosswise delivery kreuzweise Auslage *f*
crown cork printer *(tin printer)* Kronkorkendrucker *m*
CRT exposure unit *(photocomp.)* CRT-Belichter *m*
CRT photosetter *(photocomp.)* CRT-Belichter *m*
CRT photo unit *(photocomp.)* CRT-Belichter *m*
crumpled *(sheet)* zerknittert, zerknüllt
crumpled sheet Knautschbogen *m*
cryptics *pl* diakritische Zeichen *n/pl*
cumulative film Nutzensammelfilm *m*
cuneiform characters *pl* Keilschrift *f*
cupboard *(hand comp.)* geschlossenes Regal *n*
cure v *(to dry)* härten, trocknen
curling of sheet tail Einrollen der Bogenhinterkante
currency printing Banknotendruck *m*, Notendruck *m*, Papiergelddruck *m*
current density *(electropl.)* Stromdichte *f*
current intensity *(electropl.)* Stromstärke *f*

current job laufende Arbeit *f*, laufender Auftrag *m*
current production laufende Produktion *f*
current typesetting parameters *pl (for the job being handled)* aktuelle Satzparameter *pl*
cursor *(VDT)* Kursor *m*, Positionsanzeige *f*
cursor control Kursorsteuerung *f*
curved belt *(mailroom)* Kurvenband *n*
curved stereo Rundstereo *n*
curved stereo casting Rundguß *m*
cushion-shaped dot kissenförmiger Rasterpunkt *m*
customer Auftraggeber *m*, Kunde *m*
customer complaint Kundenreklamation *f*
customer file data Kundenstammsatz *m*, Kundenstammdaten *pl*
customer record *(file data)* Kundenstammsatz *m*, Kundenstammdaten *pl*
customer requirement Kundenwunsch *m*
customer service Kundenbetreuung *f*, Kundendienst *m*
customer's order Kundenauftrag *m*
customer support see customer service
customized *(modular systems)* maßgeschneidert, nach Maß, zugeschnitten
custom-made see customized
custom-tailored see customized
cut Schnitt *m*; *(letterpress plate)* Ätzung *f*, Klischee *n*
cut *v* schneiden; *(to engrave)* ätzen, gravieren
cut and leads *pl (lead comp.)* Stückdurchschuß *m*
cut away *v (with scorper)* ausstechen
cut command *(phototypesetter)* Schneidbefehl *m*
cut counter *(cutting m.)* Schnittzähler *m*
cut edge *(folded signature)* offene Seite *f*
cut edges *pl* Schnittkanten *pl*
cut film stencil *(screen printing)* Schnittschablone *f*
cut-in head eingezogener Titel *m*
cut-in initial eingezogene Initiale *f*
cut-in marginal notes *pl* eingezogene Marginalien *f/pl*
cut-off *(web printing)* Abschnitt *m*, Abschnittlänge *f*
cut off *v* abschneiden, abstellen, abschalten, ausschalten
cut-off corner schräge Ecke *f*
cut-off cylinder *(web press)* Schneidzylinder *m*
cut-off knife *(reel paster)* Abschlagmesser *n*
cut-off register *(web printing)* Abschnittregister *n*, Schnittregister *n*

cut-off register control *(web press)* Schnittregistersteuerung *f*
cut-out *(page make-up, printing, varnishing)* Aussparung *f*; *(silhouette image)* Freistellung *f*
cut out *v (a figure)* freistellen
cut-out figure freigestelltes Bild *n*, freistehendes Bild *n*
cut-out image freigestelltes Bild *n*, freistehendes Bild *n*
cut-out mask *(reprod.)* Freisteller *m*, Freistellmaske *f*
cut-out varnishing ausgesparte Lackierung *f*, Nutzenlackierung *f*
cut position *(cutting m.)* Schnittposition *f*
cut release *(cutting m.)* Schnittauslösung *f*
cutter *(cutting machine)* Schneid(e)maschine *f*
cutter-creaser Stanzpresse *f*, Stanztiegel *m*; **automatic** ~ Tiegelstanzautomat *m*
cutter operator Papierschneider *m*
cutter-sorter *(papermill)* Sortierquerschneider *m*
cutting *(newspaper)* Ausschnitt *m*
cutting accuracy Schnittgenauigkeit *f*
cutting bar *(cutting m.)* Schneidleiste *f*
cutting blade Schneidmaschinenmesser *n*, Schneidmesser *n*
cutting burr Schnittgrat *m*
cutting cylinder *(press folder)* Messerzylinder *m*, Schneidzylinder *m*
cutting die Stanzform *f*, Stanzmesser *n*, Stanzplatte *f*
cutting edges *pl* Schnittkanten *pl*
cutting film Schneidefilm *m*
cutting forme *(cutting die)* Stanzform *f*
cutting knife Schneidmaschinenmesser *n*, Schneidmesser *n*
cutting line Schnittlinie *f*
cutting line indicator *(cutting m.)* Schnittandeuter *m*
cutting machine Schneid(e)maschine *f*, Planschneider *m*
cutting marks *pl (print sheet)* Schneid(e)marken *f/pl*, Beschneidemarken *f/pl*, Beschnittmarken *f/pl*, Schnittmarken *f/pl*
cutting material Schneidgut *n*
cutting measurement *(cutting m.)* Schnittmaß *n*
cutting pile Schneid(e)stapel *m*
cutting pressure Schnittkraft *f*
cutting register Schnittregister *n*
cutting roller Schneidwalze *f*
cutting rules *pl* Schneid(e)linien *f/pl*; *(die-cutting)* Stanzlinien *pl*
cutting sequence *(cutting m.)* Schnittfolge *f*
cutting speed Schnittgeschwindigkeit *f*

cutting stick *(cutting m.)* Schneidleiste *f*
cutting stroke *(die-cutting)* Stanzhub *m*
cutting tool Schnittwerkzeug *n*
cutting waste Schneidabfall *m*, Verschnitt *m*
cutting width Schnittbreite *f*; *(cutting m.)* Schnittlänge *f*
cut to size *v* auf das Format beschneiden
cyan *(process colour)* Cyan *n*
cyan film Cyanfilm *m*
cyan forme Cyanform *f*
cyanotype see blue print, diazo print
cyan plate Cyanplatte *f*
cyan printer *(cyan plate)* Cyanplatte *f*; *(cyan sep. film)* Cyanfilm *m*
cyan separation *(reprod.)* Cyanauszug *m*
cycle *(prod. line)* Takt *m*
cycle control Taktsteuerung *f*
cycled *(prod. line)* im Takt, taktgebunden, taktgesteuert
cycled separator Taktweiche *f*
cycles/min Takte/min *m/pl*
cycle time Taktzahl *f*
cyclic storage *(comp.)* dynamischer Speicher *m*, zyklischer Speicher *m*
cylinder Zylinder *m*
cylinder arrangement Zylinderanordnung *f*
cylinder base *(gravure cyl.)* Rohling *m*, Rohzylinder *m*
cylinder bearer *(press)* Laufring *m*, Schmitzring *m*, Zylinderlaufring *m*
cylinder bearing Zylinderlager *n*, Zylinderlagerung *f*
cylinder bearing bush Zylinderlagerbüchse *f*
cylinder body Zylinderballen *m*
cylinder bushing *(gravure)* Zylinderbüchse *f*
cylinder circumference Zylinderumfang *m*
cylinder cocking *(on press)* diagonale Registerverstellung *f*, Registerdiagonalverstellung *f*
cylinder configuration Zylinderanordnung *f*
cylinder core Zylinderkern *m*
cylinder correction *(gravure)* Zylinderkorrektur *f*
cylinder dressing Zylinderaufzug *m*
cylinder face Zylinderballen *m*
cylinder flat-bed press Zylinder *m*, Zylinderflachformpresse *f*
cylinder fold *(press folder)* Zylinderfalz *m*
cylinder gap *(press cyl.)* Zylinderkanal *m*, Spannkanal *m*
cylinder gauge Zylindermarke *f*
cylinder grinding machine *(gravure)* Zylinderschleifmaschine *f*
cylinder grippers *pl* Zylindergreifer *pl*

cylinder immersion *(gravure)* Zylindereintauchung *f*
cylindering *(gravure)* Zylinderbearbeitung *f*
cylinder jacket Zylindermantel *m*
cylinder journal Zylinderzapfen *m*
cylinder lay Zylindermarke *f*
cylinder machining *(gravure)* Zylinderbearbeitung *f*
cylinder makeready Zylinderzurichtung *f*
cylinder nip Zylinderspalt *m*
cylinder nip guard Zylinderspaltschutz *m*
cylinder packing Zylinderaufzug *m*
cylinder pins *pl* Zylinderpunktur *f*
cylinder plating *(gravure)* Zylindergalvanik *f*
cylinder polishing machine Zylinderpoliermaschine *f*
cylinder preparation *(gravure)* Zylinderherstellung *f*, Tiefdruckformherstellung *f*
cylinder press *automatic* ~ Zylinderdruckautomat *m*
cylinder (printing) press Zylinder *m*, Zylinderdruckpresse *f*
cylinder proof press Zylinderabziehpresse *f*, Zylinderandruckpresse *f*
cylinder repair *(gravure)* Zylinderreparatur *f*
cylinder retouching *(gravure)* Zylinderretusche *f*
cylinder revolution Zylinderumdrehung *f*
cylinder rolling *(press)* Druckabwicklung *f*
cylinder squeeze *(impression pressure)* Überdruck *m*, zu hohe Druckbeistellung *f*
cylinder storage Zylinderlager *n*
cylinder storage rack *(gravure)* Zylinderlagergestell *n*
cylinder support *(gravure cyl.)* Zylinderauflager *n*
cylinder throw-off Zylinderabstellung *f*
cylinder transfer press Zylinderumdruckpresse *f*
cylinder turning and polishing machine *(gravure)* Zylinderdreh- und Poliermaschine *f*
cylinder undercut Einstichtiefe *f*, Schmitzringhöhe *f*, Zylindereinstich *m*, Zylinderhinterschliff *m*, Zylinderunterschliff *m*
cylinder washing machine Zylinderreinigungsanlage *f*
Cyrillic characters *pl* Kyrillische Schrift *f*

D

dabber Tupfballen *m*
dabbing Tamponieren *n*, Tupfen *n*
D/A converter (digital-analogue) D/A-Wandler (Digital-Analog) *m*
dagger *(reference mark)* Anmerkungszeichen *n*, Kreuz(zeichen) *n*
Daguerreotype Daguerreotypie *f*
daily Tageszeitung *f*
daily docket Tageszettel *m*
daily (news)paper Tageszeitung *f*
daily output *(mach.)* Tagesleistung *f*
daily press Tagespresse *f*
damp(en) *v* anfeuchten, befeuchten, feuchten
dampening see damping
damper cover Feuchtwalzenbezug *m*
damper hose Feuchtwalzenschlauch *m*
damper roller *(offset)* Feuchtauftragswalze *f*
damper washing machine Feuchtwalzenwaschmaschine *f*
damping *(offset)* Feuchtung *f*, Wasserführung *f*
damping control Feuchtmengenregulierung *f*, Feuchtmittelsteuerung *f*
damping distributor (roller) Feuchttreiber *m*, Feuchtreibzylinder *m*
damping duct roller Feuchtduktor *m*, Feuchtkastenwalze *f*, Wasserkastenwalze *f*
damping film *(offset plate)* Feuchtmittelfilm *m*
damping forme roller *(offset)* Feuchtauftragswalze *f*
damping fountain roller see damping duct roller
damping measuring system Feuchtmittelmeßgerät *n*
damping roller Feuchtwalze *f*, Wischwalze *f*
damping roller sleeve Feuchtwalzenschlauch *m*
damping roller washing machine Feuchtwalzenwaschmaschine *f*
damping solution Feuchtmittel *n*, Wischwasser *n*
damping stripe width *(damping vibrator)* Feuchtstreifenbreite *f*
damping system Feuchtsystem *n*, Feuchtwerk *n*
damping transfer roller Feuchtübertragwalze *f*
damping unit Feuchtwerk *n*
damping unit control Feuchtwerkssteuerung *f*
damping vibrator (roller) Feuchtheber *m*
damping water Feuchtwasser *n*, Wischwasser *n*
damping water fountain Feucht(wasser)kasten *m*, Wasserkasten *m*
dampstain *(paper)* Stockfleck *m*

dancer roller *(web press)* Pendelwalze *f*, Tänzerwalze *f*
dandy roll *(papermaking)* Egoutteur *m*, Wasserzeichenwalze *f*
dark colour dunkle Farbe *f*
darken *v (colour)* abdunkeln, dunklermachen
darkroom Dunkelkammer *f*
darkroom camera Zweiraumkamera *f*
darkroom door *revolving* ~ Dunkelkammerdrehtür *f*
darkroom lighting Dunkelkammerbeleuchtung *f*
darkroom safelight Dunkelkammerlampe *f*
dash *(typesetting)* Bindestrich *m*, Gedankenstrich *m*, Strich *m*
dash leaders *pl (typesetting)* Führungsstriche *m/pl*
data Daten *pl*
data back-up Datensicherung *f*
data bank Datenbank *f*
database Datenbank *f*, Datenbasis *f*, Datenbestand *m*
data carrier Datenträger *m*
data channel Datenkanal *m*
data collection Datenerfassung *f*
data communication Datenkommunikation *f*
data compression Datenkompression *f*, Datenkomprimierung *f*
data-controlled datengesteuert
data conversion Datenkonvertierung *f*, Umrechnen von Daten
data converter Datenkonverter *m*
data decompression Datendekomprimierung *f*
data entry Dateneingabe *f*
data evaluation Datenauswertung *f*
data exchange Datenaustausch *m*
data file Datei *f*, Daten *pl*, Datensatz *m*
data flow Datenfluß *m*
data format Datenformat *n*
data input Dateneingabe *f*
data line Datenleitung *f*
data link Datenverbindung *f*
data mailer *(personalized mailer)* Data-Mailer, personalisierte Werbedrucksache *f*
data management Datenverwaltung *f*
data management system Dateiverwaltungssystem *n*, Datenverwaltungssystem *n*
data network Datennetz *n*, Datenverbund *m*
data output Datenausgabe *f*
data pool Datenbestand *m*
data processing Datenverarbeitung *f*
data record *(file)* Datensatz *m*
data recording Datenerfassung *f*
data screen Datensichtgerät *n*

data securing Datensicherung *f*
data set Datenmenge *f*
data storage Datenspeicher(ung) *m/f*
data teletransmission Datenfernübertragung *f*
data terminal Datenendgerät *n*, Datensichtgerät *n*
data transfer Datenübernahme *f*, Datenübertragung *f*
data transformation Umrechnen von Daten
data transmission Datenübermittlung *f*, Datenübertragung *f*
data transmission channel Datenübertragungskanal *m*
data transmission rate Datenübertragungsrate *f*
data update Datenaktualisierung *f*
date Datum *n*, Termin *m*
date block Kalenderblock *m*
date of bookbinding Buchbindereitermin *m*
date of printing Drucktermin *m*
daylight camera Tageslichtkamera *f*
daylight cassette Tageslichtkassette *f*
daylight copying box Tageslichtkopierrahmen *m*
daylight film Tageslichtfilm *m*
daylight printing frame Tageslichtkopierrahmen *m*
daylight processing *(reprod.)* Tageslichtverarbeitung *f*
day of publication *(newspaper, magazine)* Erscheinungstag *m*
D.C. *(direct current)* Gleichstrom *m*
D.C. motor Gleichstrommotor *m*
DDCP (Direct Digital Colour Proofing) DDCP (direkt-digitale Farbproofherstellung)
DDES (Digital Data Exchange Standard) DDES (Digitaldatenaustausch-Standard)
deadline Termin *m*, Endtermin *m*; *(news/ads)* Annahmeschluß *m*, Schlußtermin *m*, Einsendeschluß *m*
deadline pressure Termindruck *m*
dead stock *(unsold copies)* unverkaufte Exemplare *n/pl*
deaths columns *pl (newspaper)* Todesanzeigen *pl*
deburr *v* abgraten, entgraten
decal *(decalcomania picture)* Abziehbild *n*
decalcomania Abziehbilderdruck *m*, Dekalkomanie *f*
decalcomania paper Abziehbilderpapier *n*
decalcomania (picture) Abziehbild *n*
decalcomania process Abziehbilderverfahren *n*
decant *v* dekantieren
dechroming *(gravure cyl.)* Entchromen *n*
dechroming salt Entchromungssalz *n*
decimal figures *pl* Dezimalzahlen *pl*

decimal point Dezimalpunkt *m*
decimal system Dezimalsystem *n*
decision-maker *(for investments)* Entscheidungsträger *m*
deck *(newspaper press)* Eindruckwerk *n*, Farbdruckwerk *n*, Farbeindruckwerk *n*, Zusatzfarbwerk *n*
deckle edge Büttenrand *m*, Papierrand des geschöpften Papiers
deckle-edged paper Büttenrandpapier *n*
declutch *v* abstellen, abkuppeln, abschalten, auskuppeln, ausschalten, entkuppeln
de-coater *(chem.)* Entschichter *m*
de-coating Entschichtung *f*
decode *v* dekodieren
decoder Dekoder *m*
decoding Dekodierung *f*
decoppering *(gravure cyl.)* Entkupfern *n*
decoration printing Dekorationsdruck *m*
decorative colour Schmuckfarbe *f*
decorative initial verzierte Initiale *f*
decorative paper Dekorationspapier *n*
decorative printing Dekorationsdruck *m*
decorative type Dekorschrift *f*, Schmuckschrift *f*
decrease contrast *v* Kontrast mindern; *(gradation)* abflachen
dedicated computer Spezialrechner *m*
dedicated system *(comp.)* Spezialsystem *n*
dedication *(book)* Widmung *f*
deep embossing Tiefprägung *f*
deepen *v (colour)* abdunkeln, dunklermachen
deep-etch *v* tiefätzen
deep-etched plate tiefgeätzte Platte *f*
deep-etching Tiefätzung *f*
deep-etch ink Tiefätzfarbe *f*
deep-etch lacquer Tiefätzlack *m*
deep freeze resistance *(ink)* Tiefkühlbeständigkeit *f*
deep inking satte Farbgebung *f*
deep page Hochformatseite *f*, Seite im Hochformat
deep tank processor *(film proc.)* Tieftankentwicklungsmaschine *f*
defective copy fehlerhaftes Exemplar *n*
define *v (comp.)* definieren, festlegen
definition *(comp.)* Definition *f*; *(image)* Details *pl*, Zeichnung *f*; *(phot.)* Schärfe *f*
definition of outlines *(photocomp.)* Konturenschärfe *f*, Kantenschärfe *f*, Randschärfe *f*
definition of reproduction Abbildungsschärfe *f*
deflecting mirror Umlenkspiegel *m*
defoaming agent Antischaumzusatz *m*

degreasing - depth of focus

degreasing Entfetten *n*
degreasing bath *(gravure cyl.)* Entfettungsbad *n*
degree of automation Automationsgrad *m*
degree sign *(typesetting)* Gradzeichen *n*
dehydration *(papermaking)* Entwässerung *f*, Wasserentzug *m*
de-inking *(paper)* Deinking *n*, Entfärben *n*
de-ionization Entionisieren *n*
de-ionizing rod Entionisierstab *m*
delay *(deadline)* Terminüberschreitung *f*
delete *v (comp.)* löschen; *(text)* ausstreichen, durchstreichen, streichen
delete character *v* Zeichen löschen
delete copy *v (text)* Text löschen
deleted matter *(type matter)* Streichsatz *m*
delete mark *(proofreading)* Deleaturzeichen *n*
deletion fluid *(for printing plates)* Korrekturmittel *n*
deletion pen *(for plates, films)* Korrekturstift *m*
deliver *v (newspaper copies)* ausliefern, austragen, liefern; *(press delivery)* auslegen
delivery Lieferung *f*, Ablieferung *f*, Auslieferung *f*; *(press)* Auslage *f*, Auslegen *n*, Ausleger *m*; *(rotary press)* Ausgang *m*
delivery belts *pl* Auslagebänder *pl*
delivery carriage Auslegerwagen *m*
delivery chain Auslagekette *f*, Auslegerkette *f*
delivery conveyor system Auslagetransportsystem *n*
delivery date Auslieferungstermin *m*, Liefertermin *m*
delivery date control Terminkontrolle *f*
delivery deadline Auslieferungstermin *m*, Liefertermin *m*
delivery fans *pl* Auslagebelüftung *f*
delivery grippers *pl* Auslagegreifer *pl*
delivery guard *(safety guard)* Auslageschutz *m*
delivery jogger Auslageschüttler *m*
delivery lighting Auslagebeleuchtung *f*
delivery of blanks *(folding box prod.)* Nutzenauslage *f*
delivery on approval *(book sales)* Ansichtssendung *f*
delivery pile Auslagestapel *m*
delivery rake Auslagerechen *m*
delivery route *(newspaper distribution)* Auslieferungsroute *f*
delivery table Auslagetisch *m*
delivery tapes *pl* Auslagebänder *pl*
delivery time Auslieferungstermin *m*
delta fold Deltafalz *m*
de luxe binding Luxuseinband *m*
de luxe edition Luxusausgabe *f*, Prachtausgabe *f*
de luxe paper Luxuspapier *n*
de luxe printed material Luxusdrucksachen *f/pl*
demand Bedarf *m*
demanding anspruchsvoll
demographic mailroom system demografisches Versandsystem *n*
demographic splitting *(mailroom)* demografisches Splitting *n*
demonstration pressroom Vorführdruckerei *f*
demonstration printshop Vorführdruckerei *f*
dense negative dichtes Negativ *n*
dense solid satte Vollfläche *f*
densitometer Densitometer *n*, Dichtemesser *m*, Dichtemeßgerät *n*
densitometer carriage *(motorized densitometric scanning)* Densitometermeßwagen *m*
densitometric measurement densitometrische Messung *f*, Dichtemessung *f*
densitometric scanning unit densitometrische Abtasteinheit *f*
densitometry Densitometrie *f*, Dichtemessung *f*
density Dichte *f*; *(film)* Deckung *f*, Schwärzung *f*
density control mark *(photocomp.)* Dichtekontrollzeichen *n*
density control wedge *(photocomp.)* Dichtekontrollzeichen *n*
density curve *(reprod.)* Schwärzungskurve *f*
density deviation Dichteabweichung *f*
density difference Dichtedifferenz *f*
density in the solids Volltondichte *f*
density measurement Dichtemessung *f*
density range Dichteumfang *m*
density range extension *(reprod.)* Dichteumfangsverlängerung *f*
density reading Dichtewert *m*
density scanning *(film processor)* Dichtemessung *f*
density value Dichtewert *m*
de-oxidize *v (gravure cyl.)* entoxidieren
departmental running costs *pl* Platzkosten *pl*
department head Abteilungsleiter *m*
department manager Abteilungsleiter *m*
department's costs *pl* Platzkosten *pl*
deposit *(blankets, rollers)* Belag *m*, Ablagerung *f*; *(electropl.)* Niederschlag *m*, Ablagerung *f*
deposit copy *(book when issued)* Pflichtexemplar *n*
depreciation *(investment goods)* Abschreibung *f*
depth gauge Tiefenmaß *n*, Tiefenmesser *m*
depth of column Kolumnenlänge *f*
depth of field *(phot.)* see depth of focus
depth of focus *(phot.)* Schärfentiefe *f*, Tiefenschärfe *f*

depth of text Texthöhe f
desaturation *(colour)* Verweißlichung f
descender *(part of the letter)* Unterlänge f
descreening Entrastern n
desensitize v desensibilisieren; *(offset plate)* entsäuern, ätzen, anätzen
de-shingling Entschuppen n
design Design n; *(construction)* Bauweise f
design v entwerfen; *(print product)* gestalten
design element Gestaltungselement n
designer Designer m, Entwerfer m
design roller *(decorative printing)* Dessinwalze f
desk calendar Tischkalender m
desk diary Tischkalender m
desktop composition Desktop-Satz m, PC-Satz m
desk-top model Tischmodell n
desktop publishing *(DTP)* Desktop Publishing n
desk-top terminal Tischterminal m
desktop type matter Desktop-Satz m, PC-Satz m
de-stacking Entstapeln n
detachable postcard *(direct mail, inline fin.)* Abtrennkarte f
detachable unit abnehmbares Aggregat n
detacking *(photopolymer plates)* Nachbehandlung f
detail enhancement *(scanner function)* Kontraststeigerung f
detail rendering *(reprod.)* Detailwiedergabe f
detail reproduction Detailwiedergabe f
details pl *(image)* Details pl, Durchzeichnung f, Zeichnung f
detail separation *(reprod.)* Detailwiedergabe f
detail zooming *(image proc.)* Hochzoomen n
detereoration in quality Qualitätsminderung f
determination of image section Bildausschnittsbestimmung f
develop v *(phot.)* entwickeln
developer *(phot.)* Entwickler m
developer bath Entwicklerbad n
developer exhaustion Entwicklererschöpfung f
developer fluctuations pl Entwicklerschwankungen pl
developer oxidation Entwickleroxidation f
developer streaks *(film)* Entwicklerstreifen m/pl
developing *(phot.)* Entwicklung f
developing agents pl Entwicklersubstanzen pl
developing bath Entwicklerbad n
developing drum Entwicklungstrommel f
developing latitude Entwicklungsspielraum m
developing pad Entwicklertampon m
developing sink Entwicklerbecken n
developing solution Entwicklerlösung f

developing table *(offset platemaking)* Entwicklungstisch m
developing tank Entwicklungstank m
developing time Entwicklungszeit f
developing tray Entwicklerschale f, Entwicklungsschale f, Entwicklungstrog m
development *(phot.)* Entwicklung f
deviation *(process)* Abweichung f
deviation from set value *(process)* Abweichung vom Sollwert
deviation station Umlenkstation f
device of a different make Fremdgerät n
dextrine glue Dextrinleim m
dextrine gum Dextrinleim m
diaeresis *(typesetting)* Diärese f, Trema n
diagonal cutter *(envelope prod.)* Schrägschneider m
diagonal register adjustment *(on press)* Registerdiagonalverstellung f
diagonal stroke Schrägstrich m
diagram Diagramm n, grafische Darstellung f, Schaubild n, Tafel f
dial handwheel Skalen-Handrad n
dial indicator Meßuhr f, Zeigerskala f
dialling line *(telecom.)* Telefonleitung f, Wählleitung f
dial-up network *(telecom.)* Telefonnetz n
diaphragm *(camera)* Blende f, Kamerablende f
diaphragm leaf Blendenlamelle f
diaphragm plane Blendenebene f
diapositive Diapositiv n
diary Kalender m, Schreibtischkalender m; *(notebook)* Notizkalender m
diary pad Kalenderblock m
diascope Diaskop n
diazo coating Diazobeschichtung f
diazo compound Diazoverbindung f
diazo copy Blaupause f, Lichtpause f, Ozalidkopie f
diazo dye Diazofarbstoff m
diazo film Diazofilm m, Diazofolie f
diazo paper Lichtpauspapier n
diazo print Blaupause f, Lichtpause f, Ozalidkopie f
diazo printing Lichtpauskopie f
diazo printing machine Lichtpausmaschine f
diazo process Lichtpausverfahren n
diazo processor *(reprod.)* Diazo-Entwicklungsmaschine f
diazo screen emulsion *(screen printing)* Diazokopierschicht f
diazotype Diazotypie f

dichromate gelatine coating - directory

dichromate gelatine coating
  Dichromat-Gelatineschicht *f*
dichromate polyvinyl alcohol coating
  PVA-Bichromat-Schicht *f*
dichromate solution *(gravure)* Bichromatlösung *f*
dictionary Lexikon *n*, Wörterbuch *n*
Didonics *pl (type classif.)* Klassizistische Antiqua *f*
Didot system *(typogr.)* Didotsches System *n*
die Matrize *f*, Stempel *m*, see also die-plate
die-board Stanzform *f*
die-cutter Stanzmaschine *f*
die-cutting Formstanzen *n*, Stanzen *n*
die-cutting forme Stanzform *f*
die-cutting machine Stanzmaschine *f*
die-cutting platen press Stanztiegel *m*,
  Stanzpresse *f*
die-cutting register Stanzregister *n*
die-maker Stanzformenmacher *m*
die-making Stanzformenbau *m*
die-plate Prägeplatte *f*, Reliefplatte *f*, Stanzform *f*, Stanzplatte *f*
die stamper Stahlstecher *m*
die-stamping Stahlstich *m*, Stahlstichdruck *m*,
  Prägedruck *m*, Prägung *f*, Reliefdruck *m*
die-stamping bronze Stahlstichbronze *f*
die-stamping hand press Stahlstichhandpresse *f*
die-stamping ink Stahlstichdruckfarbe *f*
die-stamping press Stahlstichprägepresse *f*,
  Stahlstichpresse *f*
die-transferring machine *(gravure cyl.)*
  Molettiermaschine *f*
diffusion halo Diffusionslichthof *m*
diffusion transfer *(reprod.)*
  Diffusionsübertragung *f*
diffusion transfer process *(reprod.)*
  Silberdiffusionsverfahren *n*,
  Silbersalz-Diffusionsverfahren *n*
digest *(book)* Abriß *m*
digester *(papermaking)* Kocher *m*
digital character Digitalzeichen *n*
digital colour proof digitaler Farbproof *m*
digital computer Digitalrechner *m*
digital display Digitalanzeige *f*
digital exposure unit *(photocomp.)*
  Digitalbelichter *m*
digital image Digitalbild *n*
digital image processing digitale Bildverarbeitung *f*
digital imager *(photocomp.)* Digitalbelichter *m*
digital phototypesetting digitaler Fotosatz *m*
digital proof Digitalproof *m*
digital read-out Digitalanzeige *f*

digital storage Digitalspeicher *m*
digital technology Digitaltechnik *f*
digital text processing digitale Textverarbeitung *f*
digital transmission Digitalübertragung *f*
digital typesetter *(photocomp.)* Digitalbelichter *m*
digitization Digitalisierung *f*
digitize *v* digitalisieren
digitized font *(type)* digitalisierte Schrift *f*,
  Digitalschrift *f*
digitized typeface digitalisierte Schrift *f*,
  Digitalschrift *f*
digitizer *(CAD)* Digitalisiergerät *n*
digitizing tablet Digitalisiertablett *n*
dilitho DiLitho
dim lichtschwach
dimension *(mach.)* Abmessung *f*
dimensional stability *(film)* Dimensionsstabilität *f*, Maßhaltigkeit *f*
dimensions *pl* Format *n*
diphthong Diphthong *m*, Doppellaut *m*,
  Doppelvokal *m*, Ligatur *f*, Zwielaut *m*
dipping *(electropl.)* Eintauchung *f*
dip roller Schöpfwalze *f*, Tauchwalze *f*
dip tank *(film, plate development)* Küvette *f*
direct access Direktzugriff *m*
direct access memory *(comp.)*
  Direktzugriffsspeicher (RAM) *m*, Festspeicher *m*
direct coating *(screen printing)*
  Direktbeschichtung *f*
direct copy *(gravure)* Direktkopie *f*
direct current *(D.C.)* Gleichstrom *m*
direct digital colour proofing direkt-digitale
  Farbproofherstellung *f*
direct electrostatic platemaker *(small offset)*
  elektrostatische Folienkamera *f*
direct-entry phototypesetter *(as opp. to modular system)* Fotosatzkompaktanlage *f*
direct film *(screen printing)* Direktfilm *m*
direct halftone separations *pl* Direktrasterauszüge *m/pl*
direction of web travel Bahnlaufrichtung *f*,
  Laufrichtung *f*, Papierlaufrichtung *f*
direct litho DiLitho
directly accessible fonts *(photocomp.)* Schriften im direkten Zugriff
direct mail advertising Direktwerbung *f*
direct mailings *pl* Direktmailings *pl*,
  Direktwerbedrucksachen *f/pl*
direct master camera Folienkamera *f*
directory Adreßbuch *n*, Verzeichnis *n*

directory of stored copy *(comp.)* Inhaltsverzeichnis der gespeicherten Texte
directory of suppliers *(magazine columns)* Bezugsquellenverzeichnis *n*
direct positive Direktpositiv *n*
direct-positive film Direktpositivfilm *m*, Direktumkehrfilm *m*
direct printing direktes Drucken *n*
direct screening Direktrasterung *f*
direct stencil *(screen printing)* Direktschablone *f*
dirt particles *pl* Schmutzpartikel *pl*
dirty copy unkorrigierter Korrekturabzug *m*
disassemble *v (mach.)* abbauen, demontieren
disc *(comp.)* see disk
disc feeder Scheibenanleger *m*
disc inking unit *(platen press)* Tellerfarbwerk *n*
discoloration Verblassen *n*, Verfärben *n*, Verschießen *n; (negatives)* Braunwerden *n*
disconnect *v* abstellen, abkuppeln, abschalten, auskuppeln, ausschalten, entkuppeln
disconnecting clutch Ausrückkupplung *f*
discontinued *(publication)* erscheint nicht mehr
discount Nachlaß *m*
discretionary hyphen *(text proc.)* Trennfuge *f*
disengage *v* abstellen, abkuppeln, abschalten, auskuppeln, ausschalten, entkuppeln
disk *(comp.)* Platte *f*
disk crash *(comp.)* Plattencrash *m*
disk drive *(comp.)* Plattenlaufwerk *n*, Plattenantrieb *m*
diskette *(comp.)* Diskette *f*
diskette converter Diskettenkonverter *m*
diskette drive Diskettenlaufwerk *n*
diskette format Diskettenformat *n*
diskette reader Diskettenleser *m*
disk pack *(comp.)* Plattenstapel *m*
disk storage *(comp.)* Plattenspeicher *m*
dismantle *v (mach.)* abbauen, abmontieren, demontieren
dispersing lens Zerstreuungslinse *f*
dispersion Dispersion *f*
dispersion coating *(varnish)* Dispersionslack *m*
dispersion glue *(perfect binding)* Dispersionskleber *m*
dispersion machine *(inkmaking)* Dispergiermaschine *f*
dispersion sheet Streufolie *f*
dispersion sheet exposure Streufolienbelichtung *f*
dispersion varnish Dispersionslack *m*
display Anzeige *f*, Display *n*, optische Anzeige *f*
display *v (on screen)* darstellen, anzeigen; *(in bold, italic etc.)* auszeichnen, hervorheben; *(typesetting)* ~ *in bold* mit Halbfetter auszeichnen; ~ *in italic* mit Kursiv auszeichnen; ~ *in small caps* mit Kapitälchen auszeichnen
display ad *(as opp. to classified ad)* gestaltete Anzeige *f*
display ad terminal Anzeigengestaltungsterminal *n*
display characters *pl* Auszeichnungsschrift *f*
display format *(video screen)* Darstellungsformat *n*
display line Auszeichnungszeile *f*
display matter *(type matter)* Layoutsatz *m*
display package Schaupackung *f*
display setting *(typesetting)* Layoutsatz *m*
display type Auszeichnungsschrift *f*
display type case Steckschriftkasten *m*
disposal *(waste)* Entsorgung *f*
disposal system *(waste)* Entsorgungssystem *n*
distortion *(opt.)* Verzeichnung *f*, Verzerrung *f*; *(film, rubber blanket, printed sheet etc.)* Verziehen *n*
distortion-free *(cylinders, machine parts)* biegesteif
distortion-free monitor verzerrungsfreier Bildschirm *m*
distribute *v (lead type)* ablegen
distribution *(ink)* Verteilung *f*, Verreibung *f*; *(newspaper, magazine)* Auslieferung *f*, Versand *m*
distribution area *(advertising, direct mail)* Streugebiet *n; (newspaper)* Verbreitungsgebiet *n*
distribution case *(hand comp.)* Ablegekasten *m*
distribution department *(newspaper)* Versandabteilung *f*
distribution loss *(advertising)* Streuverlust *m*
distribution network Vertriebsnetz *n*
distributor drum Reibzylinder *m*
distributor roller Reiber *m*, Reibwalze *f*, Verreibewalze *f*
diverter *(prod. line)* Verteiler *m*, Weiche *f*
divert gate *(prod. line)* Ausschleusweiche *f*
divide *v (words)* trennen
divider sheet *(binding)* Trennblatt *n*
dividing rule *(typesetting)* Trennlinie *f*
division *(words)* Trennung *f*
divisional manager Abteilungsleiter *m*
doctor blade *(gravure, anilox)* Rakel *f*, Rakelmesser *n*
doctoring Rakelung *f; (gravure, anilox)* Abrakelung *f*
documentation Dokumentation *f*

document paper - DP (data processing)

document paper Dokumentenpapier *n*, Urkundenpapier *n*
document processing Dokumentenverarbeitung *f*
document reader *(machine)* Belegleser *m*
document reading *(text proc.)* Beleglesung *f*
dog-ear Eselsohr *n*, umgeknickte Ecke *f*
dog-eared corner Eselsohr *n*, umgeknickte Ecke *f*
dome *v (box)* auswölben
dome-shaped cover *(carton box)* gewölbter Deckel *m*
domestic news Inlandsnachrichten *pl*
dot Punkt *m*; *(halftone dot, screen dot)* Rasterpunkt *m*
dot *v* punktieren
dot area Flächendeckung *f*
dot definition Punktschärfe *f*, Rasterpunktschärfe *f*
dot distortion Rasterpunktverformung *f*
dot enlargement Punktverbreiterung *f*, Punktvergrößerung *f*
dot etching *(film)* Ätzen *n*, Filmätzung *f*
dot fidelity getreue Punkt-für-Punkt-Wiedergabe *f*, punktgenaue Wiedergabe *f*
dot-for-dot reproduction getreue Punkt-für-Punkt-Wiedergabe *f*, punktgenaue Wiedergabe *f*
dot form Rasterpunktform *f*
dot formation Punktbildung *f*, Rasterpunktbildung *f*
dot fringe *(dot squeeze)* Quetschrand *m*
dot gain Punktzunahme *f*, Punktzuwachs *m*, Tonwertzunahme *f*; *(printing)* Vollerwerden *n*
dot generation Rasterpunktbildung *f*
dot halo Punkthof *m*
dot leaders *pl (typesetting)* Ausführpunkte *pl*, Führungspunkte *pl*
dot matrix *(electronic dot generation)* Punktmatrix *f*
dot percentage Rasterprozentwert *m*, Raster(ton)wert *m*
dot reduction *(film etching)* Minuskorrektur *f*, Punktverkleinerung *f*
dot reproduction Rasterpunktwiedergabe *f*
dot screen *(reprod.)* Punktraster *m*
dot shape Rasterpunktform *f*
dot sharpness Punktschärfe *f*
dot-sharp printing punktscharfer Druck *m*
dot size Rasterpunktgröße *f*
dots per inch *pl* Rasterpunkte pro Zoll
dot spread Punktverbreiterung *f*, Punktvergrößerung *f*
dot squeeze Punktquetschen *n*
dot structure *(film)* Punktaufbau *m*

dotted line *(typogr.)* punktierte Linie *f*, Punktlinie *f*
dotted rule punktierte Linie *f*, Punktlinie *f*
dotting wheel Punktierrädchen *n*
double *(lead comp.)* Hochzeit *f*
double box *(typogr.)* Doppelrahmen *m*
double-circumference cylinder Doppelumfangszylinder *m*
double-circumference web offset press Doppelumfangs-Rollenoffsetmaschine *f*
double fine rule doppelfeine Linie *f*
double forme *(two-up proc.)* Doppelform *f*
double former folder *(web press)* Doppeltrichterfalzapparat *m*
double gate fold Altarfalz *m*, Fensterfalz *m*
double hairline *(typogr.)* doppelfeine Linie *f*
double letter Doppelbuchstabe *m*
double line Doppellinie *f*, Doppelzeile *f*
double-loop binding Double-Loop-Bindung *f*
double(-page) spread Doppelseite *f*, durchgehende Doppelseite *f*, Panoramaseite *f*, Seitenpaar *n*
double parallel fold Doppelparallelfalz *m*
double printing unit Doppeldruckwerk *n*
double quotes *pl* doppelte Anführungszeichen *pl*
double reelstand *(web press)* Doppelrollenständer *m*
double reversing mirror *(camera)* Dachkantspiegel *m*
double rule Doppellinie *f*
double sheet control Doppelbogenkontrolle *f*
double sheet detector Doppelbogenkontrolle *f*
double-sided beidseitig, zweiseitig
double-sided printing plate doppelseitige Druckplatte *f*
double-size impression cylinder doppelgroßer Druckzylinder *m*
double squeegee *(screen printing)* Doppelrakel *f*
double-stream delivery *(web press)* Doppelstromauslage *f*
double wall carton Stülpdeckelschachtel *f*
double-walled cylinder doppelwandiger Zylinder *m*
double-width rotary press doppelbreite Rollendruckmaschine *f*
double-width web press doppelbreite Rollendruckmaschine *f*
down-load *v (comp.)* laden
down-stacker Abstapler *m*
downstream operations *pl (prod. line)* nachfolgende Arbeiten *pl*
down times *pl* Ausfallzeiten *pl*
DP (data processing) Datenverarbeitung *f*

d.p.i. *pl* Rasterpunkte pro Zoll
draft Entwurf *m*
drafting film Zeichenfolie *f*
drafting paper Zeichenpapier *n*
draftsman Zeichner *m*
dragon's blood Drachenblut *n*
draughtsman Zeichner *m*
draw *v* zeichnen, entwerfen
draw in *v (paper web)* einziehen
drawing Grafik *f*, Zeichnung *f*
drawing board Zeichenbrett *n*, Zeichenkarton *m*
drawing brush Zeichenpinsel *m*
drawing chalk Kreidefarbe *f*, Zeichenkreide *f*
drawing charcoal Zeichenkohle *f*
drawing copy Zeichenvorlage *f*
drawing ink Tusche *f*, Ausziehtusche *f*, Zeichentusche *f*
drawing pen Zeichenfeder *f*, Reißfeder *f*
drawing press Ziehpresse *f*
drawing table Zeichentisch *m*
drawing tool Zeichenwerkzeug *n*
drawn initial (letter) gezeichnete Initiale *f*
draw out *(printing ink)* Abstrich *m*
draw roller *(web press)* Zugwalze *f*
drawsheet *(cylinder press)* Zugbogen *m*, Straffen *m*, Deckblatt *n*
dress a plate *v* Platte unterlegen
dressing *(press cyl.)* Aufzug *m*
dress the cylinder *v* den Aufzug *m* machen
driller *(mach.)* Bohrmaschine *f*
drilling *(file holes etc.)* Bohren *n*
drilling and routing machine Bohr- und Fräsmaschine *f*
driography Driografie *f*
drip lubrication Ölberieselung *f*
drip pan *(oil)* Ölauffangblech *n*
drip tray *(oil)* Ölauffangblech *n*
drive *(comp.)* Laufwerk *n*; *(mech.)* Antrieb *m*, Getriebe *n*
drive *v (mech.)* antreiben, steuern
drive belt Treibriemen *m*
drive gears *pl* Antriebsräder *pl*
drive motor Antriebsmotor *m*
drive out *v (type matter)* ausbringen, austreiben
driver software *(imagesetter)* Treiberprogramm *n*, Treibersoftware *f*
drive shaft Antriebswelle *f*
drive side *(as opp. to operating side)* Antriebsseite *f*
driving belt Antriebsriemen *m*
driving power Antriebskraft *f*
driving shaft see drive shaft
driving wheel Treibrad *n*

drop folio Seitenzahl am Fuß
drop-in etching of text *(gravure)* Texteinätzung *f*
drop initial *(letter)* hängende Initiale *f*
drop-in of text Einfügen von Text *n*
dropline indention *(typesetting)* hängender Einzug *m*
drop-out *(book)* Buchaushänger *m*; *(printing problem)* Mönch *m*
drop shadow *(typogr.)* Schlagschatten *m*
drop shutter *(camera)* Fallverschluß *m*
drop sucker *(feeder suction head)* Fallsauger *m*
drum *(ink container)* Hobbock *m*
drum feeder Trommelanleger *m*
drum folder *(web press)* Trommelfalzwerk *n*
drum scanner *(as opp. to flat-bed scanner)* Trommelscanner *m*
dry *v* trocknen
dry-brushed aluminium plate trockengebürstete Aluminiumplatte *f*
dry dot etching *(reprod.)* Trockenätzung *f*, Trockenlithografie *f*, Trockenretusche *f*
dryer *(aggregate)* Trockner *m*
dryer conveyor Trocknerband *n*
dryer exhaust Trocknerabluft *f*
dryer glazer *(papermaking)* Hochglanzpresse *f*
dryer section *(paper machine)* Trockenpartie *f*
dry flong Trockenmater *f*
drying agent *(ink additive)* Trockenstoff *m*, Trockner *m*
drying cabinet *(film drying)* Trockenschrank *m*
drying capacity Trocknungsvermögen *n*
drying clamp Trockenklammer *f*
drying cylinder Trockentrommel *f*
drying drum Trockentrommel *f*
dry(ing) end *(paper machine)* Trockenpartie *f*
drying frame Trockenrahmen *m*
drying hood Trockenhaube *f*
drying oven Trockenofen *m*, Trocknungsofen *m*
drying properties *pl (ink)* Trocknungseigenschaft *f*
drying rack Trockengestell *n*, Trockenregal *n*
drying room Trockenraum *m*
drying time Trockenzeit *f*; *(glue)* Abbindezeit *f*
drying unit Trockenaggregat *n*
drying varnish Trockenfirnis *m*
dry lamination Trockenkaschierung *f*
dry mat Trockenmater *f*
dry needle Radiernadel *f*
dry offset Trockenoffset *m*
dry point *(engraving tool)* kalte Nadel *f*
dry point engraving *(intaglio)* Kaltnadelradierung *f*
dry printer *(foil stamping)* Trockendruckgerät *n*

dry printing - ease of servicing

dry printing *(foil stamping)* Trockendruck *m*
dry spraying Druckbestäubung *f*, Bestäubung *f*, Trockenbestäubung *f*
dry stereotyping process Trockenstereotypie *f*
dry thoroughly *v (ink, glue)* durchtrocknen
dry-to-dry processing *(film/paper proc.)* Trocken-zu-Trocken-Entwicklung *f*
dry toner *(electrophotogr.)* Trockentoner *m*
dry transfer letters *pl (e.g. Letraset)* Abreibeschrift *f*, Anreibeschrift *f*
dry transfers *pl (e.g. Letraset)* Abreibeschrift *f*, Anreibeschrift *f*
DTP composition DTP-Satz *m*
DTP (Desktop Publishing) DTP (Desktop-Publishing)
DTP type matter DTP-Satz *m*, PC-Satz *m*
dual drive *(comp.)* Doppellaufwerk *n*
dual sheet delivery Doppelbogenauslage *f*
dual sheet feeder Doppelbogenanleger *m*
dual squeegee *(screen printing)* Doppelrakel *f*
dual-stream delivery *(web press)* Doppelstromauslage *f*
duct blade *(ink duct)* Duktorlineal *n*
ductile ink *(gravure)* flüssige Farbe *f*
ductor roller *(inking unit, damping unit)* Heber *m*, Heberwalze *f*, Leckwalze *f*
ductor-type damping system Heberfeuchtwerk *n*
ductor-type inking system Heberfarbwerk *n*
duct roller Duktorwalze *f*
duct screw *(ink duct)* Farbschraube *f*, Zonenschraube *f*
dull glanzlos, matt
dull-coated paper mattgestrichenes Papier *n*
dull finish Mattglanz *m*
dull varnish Mattlack *m*
dummy Muster *n*, Skizze *f; (book)* Blindband *m*, Blindmuster *n*, Formatbuch *n*, Muster(ein)band *m*, Probeband *m*
duo-tone printing Doppeltondruck *m*, Duplexdruck *m*
dupe *(film copy)* Duplikat *n*
duplex board Duplexkarton *m*
duplex mode *(telecom.)* Duplex-Betrieb *m*
duplex paper Duplexpapier *n*
duplex printing Duplexdruck *m*
duplicate *(film copy)* Duplikat *n*
duplicate by contact *v (reprod.)* umkopieren, kontakten
duplicate print *(film copy)* Duplikat *n*
duplicating *(film contacting)* Duplikatherstellung *f; (printing)* Vervielfältigung *f*
duplicating film Duplikatfilm *m*

duplicating job *(printing)* Vervielfältigungsauftrag *m*
duplicating pad Durchschreibeblock *m*
duplication of colour transparency Colorduplikatherstellung *f*
duplicator *(office)* Bürovervielfältiger, Vervielfältigungsmaschine *f*
durability *(binding)* Haltbarkeit *f; (machine)* Lebensdauer *f*
durable binding dauerhafte Bindung *f*, haltbare Bindung *f*, strapazierfähige Bindung *f*
during machine run bei laufender Maschine *f*, während des Laufs
during press operation während des Drucks
during press run bei laufender Maschine *f*, während des Drucks
during printing operation see during press run
dust cover *(book jacket)* Schutzumschlag *m*
dust-free staubfrei
dusting *(dust removal)* Abstauben *n; (paper)* Stauben *n*
dust jacket *(book)* Schutzumschlag *m*
dust removal Abstauben *n*, Entstäubung *f; (powder removal)* Puderabsaugung *f*
dust-tight staubdicht
dusty staubig
Dvorak keyboard *(keyboard layout)* Dvorak-Tastatur *f*, fremder Tastaturplan *m*
dye Färbemittel *n*, Farbstoff *m*
dyeline *(diazo print)* Blaupause *f*, Lichtpause *f*
dyeline machine Lichtpausmaschine *f*
dyeline paper Lichtpauspapier *n*
dyeline process Lichtpausverfahren *n*
dyeline reproduction see diazo copy
dying Färbung *f*
dynamic storage *(comp.)* dynamischer Speicher *m*

E

early edition *(newspaper)* Frühausgabe *f*
early sheet *(sheet feeder)* Frühbogen *m*, Überschießbogen *m*
ease of handling see ease of operation
ease of operation Bedienerfreundlichkeit *f*, Bedienungskomfort *m*
ease of servicing Servicefreundlichkeit *f*

ease of use see ease of operation
EB curing *(ink drying)* Elektronenstrahltrocknung *f*
eccentric Exzenter *m*
eccentric drive Exzenterantrieb *m*
eccentric motion Exzenterbewegung *f*
eccentric shaft Exzenterwelle *f*
economy scanner Einstiegsscanner *m*
edge Kante *f*
edge-bend *v (newspaper offset plate)* abkanten
edge-bevelling machine *(blockmaking)* Kantenabschrägmaschine *f*
edge colouring machine *(book prod.)* Schnittfärbemaschine *f*
edge definition Kantenschärfe *f*, Randschärfe *f*; **with perfect** ~ randscharf
edge fog Randschleier *m*
edge gilder *(book)* Schnittvergolder *m*
edge gilding *(book)* Goldschnitt *m*, Schnittvergoldung *f*
edge gilding foil Goldschnittfolie *f*
edge gilding machine Goldschnittautomat *m*
edge gluing *(perfect binding)* Kantenbeleimung *f*
edge-gluing machine *(forms set prod.)* Kantenanleimmaschine *f*; **automatic** ~ Kantenverleimautomat *m*
edge gumming *(envelopes)* Randgummierung *f*
edge life *(of knife)* Messerstandzeit *f*
edge milling *(perfect binding)* Kantenfräsen *n*
edge of picture Bildrand *m*
edge planing machine *(blockmaking)* Kantenhobelmaschine *f*
edge printer *(book prod.)* Schnittbedruckautomat *m*
edge resist *(process etching)* Kantenschutzmittel *n*
edge-roll decurler *(sheet decurler)* Bogenentroller *m*, Bogenglätter *m*
edge routing *(perfect binding)* Kantenfräsen *n*
edges trimmed mit Randbeschnitt *m*
edges untrimmed ohne Randbeschnitt *m*
edge trim(ming) Kantenbeschnitt *m*, Randbeschnitt *m*
EDG scanner *(electronic dot generator scanner)* EDG-Scanner *m*, Scanner mit Rasterpunktgenerator *m*
edit *v* herausgeben, redigieren; *(text proc., image proc.)* korrigieren
edit copy *v (text)* Text bearbeiten, Text korrigieren, Text überarbeiten
editing Korrektur *f*, Redaktion *f*, Satzkorrektur *f*
editing function Korrekturfunktion *f*
editing program Korrekturprogramm *n*

editing terminal Korrekturstation *f*
edition *(book)* Auflage *f*, Ausgabe *f*, Druckausgabe *f*; *(magazine)* Ausgabe *f*
editor Schriftleiter *m*, Redakteur *m*; *(editing program)* Korrekturprogramm *n*
editorial redaktioneller Beitrag *m*, redaktioneller Bericht *m*
editorial bulletin *(news agency)* redaktionelle Meldung *f*
editorial coverage redaktionelle Berücksichtigung *f*
editorial deadline Redaktionsschluß *m*
editorial department Redaktion *f*, Redaktionsabteilung *f*
editorial features *pl* Redaktionsprogramm *n*, Redaktionsthemen *pl*
editorial office Redaktion *f*, Redaktionsbüro *n*, Redaktionsraum *m*
editorial programme Redaktionsprogramm *n*
editorial section *(as opp. to advertising section)* redaktioneller Teil *m*
editorial software Redaktionsprogramm *n*
editorial staff Redaktion *f*
editorial system Redaktionssystem *n*
editorial work Redaktion *f*, Redaktionsarbeit *f*
editor-in-chief Chefredakteur *m*, verantwortlicher Schriftleiter *m*
editors *pl (staff)* Redaktion *f*
edit station *(text proc.)* see editing terminal
EDP (electronic data processing) EDV (elektronische Datenverarb.) *f*
effect contact screen Effektkontraktraster *m*
efficiency Leistungsfähigkeit *f*, Arbeitsleistung *f*
efflux viscosimeter *(gravure)* Auslaufviskosimeter *n*
eight-page offset rotary Achtseiten-Rollenoffsetmaschine *f*
eight-page product *(web printing)* Achtseitenprodukt *n*
eight-page signature Achtseitenbogen *m*
eight-page web offset press Achtseiten-Rollenoffsetmaschine *f*
EIP (Electronic Image Processing) EBV (Elektronische Bildverarbeitung) *f*
eject *v* auswerfen
ejector Auswerfer *m*
elastic impression roller *(gravure)* Biegepresseur *m*, selbstanpressender Presseur *m*
electrical control elektrische Steuerung *f*, Steuer(ungs)elektrik *f*
electrical equipment elektrische Ausrüstung *f*
electrically operated elektromotorisch

electrochemically grained plate elektrochemisch gekörnte Platte *f*
electrode *(electropl.)* Elektrode *f*
electrode voltage *(electropl.)* Elektrodenspannung *f*
electrolysis *(electropl.)* Elektrolyse *f*
electrolyte *(electropl.)* Elektrolyt *n*
electrolytical bath elektrolytisches Bad *n*, galvanisches Bad *n*
electrolytical correction galvanische Korrektur *f*
electrolytical degreasing elektrolytisches Entfetten *n*
electromechanical engraving *(gravure cyl.)* elektromechanische Gravur *f*
electron beam Elektronenstrahl *m*
electron beam curing *(ink drying)* Elektronenstrahltrocknung *f*
electron beam engraving *(gravure cyl.)* Elektronenstrahlgravur *f*
electronic cabinet Elektronikschrank *m*
electronic character generation *(photocomp.)* elektronische Zeichengenerierung *f*
electronic control Steuerelektronik *f*, elektronische Steuerung *f*, Regelelektronik *f*
electronic data processing *(EDP)* elektronische Datenverarbeitung *f*
electronic distortion *(photocomp.)* elektronische Verzerrung *f*
electronic documentation system elektronisches Dokumentationssystem *n*
electronic dot generation *(scanner)* elektronische Rasterpunktbildung *f*, elektronischer Rasterpunktaufbau *m*
electronic dot generator *(scanner)* Raster(punkt)generator *m*
electronic dot generator scanner Scanner mit Rasterpunktgenerator *m*
electronic engraving *(gravure cyl.)* elektronische Gravur *f*
electronic image processing *(EIP)* elektronische Bildverarbeitung *f*
electronic image recording elektronische Bildaufzeichnung *f*
electronic imaging elektronische Bildaufzeichnung *f*
electronic mail *(telecom.)* elektronische Post *f*
electronic media *pl* elektronische Medien *pl*
electronic newspaper Bildschirmzeitung *f*
electronic page assembly elektronische Seitenmontage *f*, elektronischer Seitenumbruch *m*

electronic page make-up elektronischer Seitenumbruch *m*, elektronische Seitenmontage *f*
electronic pagination see electronic page make-up
electronic pre-press system elektronisches Druckvorstufensystem *n*
electronic printing system elektronisches Drucksystem *n*
electronic publishing Electronic Publishing *n*, elektronisches Publizieren *n*
electronic pulse elektronischer Impuls *m*
electronic reproduction elektronische Reproduktion *f*
electronic retouching elektronische Retusche *f*
electronics Elektronik *f*
electronic slanting *(photocomp.)* elektronisch kursivstellen
electronic type modification *(photocomp.)* elektronische Schriftmodifikation *f*
electrophotographic printer *(line printer)* elektrofotografischer Drucker *m*
electrophotographic printing plate elektrofotografische Druckplatte *f*
electrophotography Elektrofotografie *f*
electroplate *v* galvanisieren
electroplating Galvanisierung *f*
electrostatic adherence elektrostatisches Haften *n*
electrostatic charge elektrostatische Aufladung *f*
electrostatic clinging elektrostatisches Haften *n*
electrostatic colour proofing system elektrostatisches Farbprüfsystem *n*
electrostatic image transfer elektrostatische Bildübertragung *f*
electrostatic platemaking elektrostatische Plattenherstellung *f*
electrostatic powder spraying elektrostatische Druckbestäubung *f*
electrostatic print assist *(gravure)* elektrostatische Druckhilfe *f*
electrostatic printer elektrostatischer Drucker *m*
electrostatic printing master *(small offset)* elektrostatische Druckfolie *f*
electrostatic printing plate elektrostatische Druckplatte *f*
electrostatics Elektrostatik *f*
electro(type) Galvano *n*, Galvanoplastik *f*
electrotype *v* galvanisieren
electrotyping Galvanisierung *f*, Galvanoplastik *f*
elephant skin *(book case)* Elefantenhaut *f*
elevator *(paper handling)* Hebeeinrichtung *f*, Hebevorrichtung *f*

elimination of cutting edges Wegbelichten von Schnittkanten *pl*
elliptical dot Kettenpunkt *m*
em *(typogr.)* Geviert *n*
embossed box geprägte Schachtel *f*
embossed paper geprägtes Papier *n*
embossed stamping Reliefprägung *f*
embossing Prägedruck *m*, Prägung *f*, Prägen *n*
embossing and gold blocking press Präge- und Vergoldepresse *f*
embossing calender Prägekalander *m*
embossing die Prägestempel *m*, Patrize *f*
embossing felt Prägefilz *m*
embossing forme Prägeform *f*
embossing plate Prägeplatte *f*, Reliefplatte *f*, Prägeklischee *n*
embossing powder *(die-stamping)* Prägepulver *n*
embossing press Prägepresse *f*, Prägetiegel *m*; **automatic** ~ Prägeautomat *m*
embossing type Prägeschrift *f*
em-dash *(typesetting)* Geviertstrich *m*
emergency delivery *(prod. line)* Notauslage *f*
emergency gate *(prod. line)* Notweiche *f*
emergency stop Notstopp *m*
emergency stop button Notausschalter *m*, Pilztaste *f*, Schlagtaster *m*, Sicherheitsstopptaste *f*
em-quad *(lead comp.)* Quadrätchen *n*; *(typogr.)* Geviert *n*
em space *(typogr.)* Geviert *n*
emulator Emulator *m*
emulsifier *(agent)* Emulgiermittel *n*
emulsifying properties *pl* *(offset ink)* Emulgierverhalten *n*
emulsion Emulsion *f*; *(film emulsion)* Schicht *f*
emulsion adhesive Emulsionsleim *m*
emulsion against emulsion *(film contacting)* Schicht auf Schicht
emulsion fog *(film)* Grundschleier *m*
emulsion layer Emulsionsschicht *f*
emulsion sensitivity *(film)* Schichtempfindlichkeit *f*
emulsion side *(film emulsion)* Schichtseite *f*
emulsion (side) down *(film)* Schichtseite unten, seitenverkehrt
emulsion (side) up *(film)* Schichtseite oben, seitenrichtig
emulsion speed *(film)* Schichtempfindlichkeit *f*
en *(typogr.)* Halbgeviert *n*
enamelled board Emailkarton *m*, Hochglanzkarton *m*
enamelled paper Hochglanzpapier *n*

enclosure *(noise abatement)* Verschalung *f*, Einkapselung *f*
encode *v* kodieren, verschlüsseln
encoder Kodierer *m*, Kodiergerät *n*
encoding Kodieren *n*, Kodierung *f*
encyclopedia Enzyklopädie *f*, Konversationslexikon *n*, Lexikon *n*
end a full line *v* *(typesetting)* stumpf ausgehen lassen
en-dash Halbgeviertstrich *m*
end density Enddichte *f*
end even *v* *(typesetting)* stumpf ausgehen lassen
endleaf *(book)* Vorsatz *m*, Vorsatzblatt *n*, Vorsatzpapier *n*
endleaves *pl* Vorsatzblätter *n/pl*
endless punched tape Endloslochstreifen *m*
end letter *(Hebrew, Scripts etc.)* Finalbuchstabe *m*
end of line Zeilenende *n*
end-of-line instruction *(photocomp.)* Zeilenendkommando *n*
end-of-press drying Endtrocknung *f*
end on the page *v* *(type matter)* mit der Seite ausgehen
endpaper *(book)* Vorsatz *m*, Vorsatzblatt *n*, Vorsatzpapier *n*
endpapering Vorsatzklebung *f*
endpapering machine *(book prod.)* Vorsatzklebemaschine *f*
end quotation mark *(typesetting)* Abführungszeichen *n*, Ausführungszeichen *n*
endsheet *(book)* Vorsatz *m*, Vorsatzblatt *n*, Vorsatzpapier *n*
endsheet gluing Vorsatzklebung *f*
endsheet gluing machine *(book prod.)* Vorsatzklebemaschine *f*
engage *v* *(mech.)* einkuppeln, zuschalten, anstellen, einrücken
engineering works Maschinenfabrik *f*
engineer of printing Druckingenieur *m*
English Script *(type)* Englische Schreibschrift *f*
engrave *v* gravieren, stechen; *(intaglio)* radieren
engraved copperplate Kupferstichplatte *f*
engraved cylinder gravierter Zylinder *m*
engraved embossing plate Prägegravur *f*
engraved glass gravure screen Tiefdruck-Glasgravurraster *m*
engraved glass screen *(camera)* Glasgravurraster *m*
engraved plate gestochene Platte *f*, gravierte Platte *f*, Gravurplatte *f*
engraved roller Gravurwalze *f*; *(design roller)* Dessinwalze *f*

engraved rotogravure screen
  Glasgravur-Tiefdruckraster *m*
engraved screen Gravurraster *m*
engraver Graveur *m*; *(intaglio)* Radierer *m*
engrave with a chisel *v* ziselieren
engraving Gravur *f*, Stich *m*; *(intaglio)*
  Radierung *f*; *(letterpress plate)* Ätzung *f*,
  Klischee *n*
engraving film Gravierfilm *m*
engraving machine Graviermaschine *f*
engraving needle Graviernadel *f*, Ätznadel *f*
engraving roller see engraved roller
engraving stylus Graviernadel *f*, Gravierstichel
  m, Gravurstichel *m*
engraving tool Gravierinstrument *n*,
  Gravierwerkzeug *n*
enlarged edition erweiterte Ausgabe *f*
enlarged scale *(reprod.)* vergrößerter Maßstab *m*
enlargement Vergrößerung *f*
enlargement increments *pl* Vergrößerungsstufen
  pl
enlargement range *(reprod.)* Abbildungsbereich
  m, Vergrößerungsbereich *m*
enlargement ratio Vergrößerungsmaßstab *m*
enlargement scale Vergrößerungsmaßstab *m*
enlarger *(reprod.)* Vergrößerer *m*
enlarging Vergrößern *n*
en-quad *(typogr.)* Halbgeviert *n*
en space *(typogr.)* Halbgeviert *n*
enter *v (data, text)* eingeben, einlesen; *(in screen mask, business form etc.)* eintragen
enter copy *v (text)* Text eingeben
entry *(text, data)* Eingabe *f*; *(web into a unit)*
  Einlauf *m*
entry level scanner Einstiegsscanner *m*
envelope Briefhülle *f*, Briefkuvert *n*,
  Briefumschlag *m*, Kuvert *n*, Umschlag *m*
envelope flap Umschlagklappe *f*
envelope lining tissue Briefumschlagfutterseide *f*
envelope-making machine Briefumschlagmaschine
  f
envelope paper Briefumschlagpapier *n*
envelope tissue lining paper
  Kuvertfutterseidenpapier *n*
environmental control Umweltschutz *m*
environment-friendly umweltfreundlich
environment pollution Umweltverschmutzung *f*
environment protection Umweltschutz *m*
epilog(ue) *(book)* Nachwort *n*
equalization makeready *(letterpress m.)*
  Ausgleichszurichtung *f*
equalize *v (rollers)* egalisieren
equally spaced type matter ausgeglichener Satz *m*

equal sign *(typesetting)* Gleichheitszeichen *n*
equation *(maths setting)* Gleichung *f*
equip *v* ausrüsten, ausstatten
equipment Ausrüstung *f*
equivalent dot area äquivalente Flächendeckung
  f
erasable and programmable read only memory (EPROM) lösch- und programmierbarer
  Nur-Lese-Speicher (EPROM) *m*
erase *v* radieren; *(comp.)* löschen
erasing knife Radiermesser *n*
erect *v (folding box)* aufstellen; *(machine installation)* aufstellen
ergonomic design ergonomisches Design *n*
errata *pl (book)* Errata *pl*, Verzeichnis der
  Druckfehler *n*
error identification *(comp.)* Fehlererkennung *f*
error message *(comp.)* Fehlermeldung *f*,
  Störmeldung *f*
error rate *(telecom.)* Fehlerrate *f*
escape gate *(prod. line)* Notweiche *f*
escapement *(photocomp.)* horizontaler Vorschub
  m
esparto paper Espartopapier *n*
estimate Kalkulation *f*
estimate *v (volume, price etc.)* schätzen,
  kalkulieren
estimate of costs Kostenberechnung *f*
estimate of paper quantity Papierberechnung *f*
estimate of size Formatberechnung *f*
estimate of volume *(text copy)*
  Umfangsberechnung *f*, Satzberechnung *f*,
  Manuskriptberechnung *f*, Textberechnung *f*
estimate roughly *v* überschlagen
estimator Kalkulator *m*
etch *v* ätzen; *(film etching)* abschwächen;
  (intaglio) radieren; *(offset plate)* anätzen
etch away *v* abätzen
etched cylinder *(gravure)* geätzter Zylinder *m*
etched plate geätzte Platte *f*
etcher Ätzer *m*; *(intaglio)* Radierer *m*
etching *(letterpress plate)* Ätzung *f*, Klischee *n*;
  (metal plate, cylinder) Ätzen *n*; *(intaglio)*
  Radierung *f*
etching bath Ätzbad *n*
etching capability *(film)* Ätzreserve *f*
etching depth Ätztiefe *f*
etching film *(gravure)* Ätzfilm *m*
etching ink Ätzfarbe *f*
etching lye Ätzlauge *f*
etching machine Ätzmaschine *f*
etching needle Radiernadel *f*, Bolzer *m*
etching powder Ätzpulver *n*

etching resist *(gravure cyl.)* Abdecklack *m*, Ätzresist
etching solution Ätze *f*, Ätzlösung *f*, Ätzwasser *n*
etching time Ätzdauer *f*
etch in relief *v* hochätzen
European colour scale *(printing inks)* Euro(pa)skala *f*
Euroscale *(printing inks)* Euro(pa)skala *f*
evacuation of heat *(gas dryer)* Wärmeabfuhr *f*
evaluation Beurteilung *f*
evaluation of measurements meßtechnische Auswertung *f*
even distribution gleichmäßige Verteilung *f*
even folios *pl* gerade Seiten *f/pl*
evening paper Abendzeitung *f*
even inking gleichmäßige Farbführung *f*
evenly spaced type matter ausgeglichener Satz *m*
even number gerade Nummer *f*
even pages *pl* gerade Seiten *f/pl*
even spacing *(type)* gleichmäßige Raumverteilung *f*
evidence copy *(advertiser)* Belegexemplar *n*
exacting anspruchsvoll
examine *v* prüfen
exception (word) dictionary *(text proc.)* Ausnahmelexikon *n*
excess delivery *(more copies than ordered)* Überlieferung *f*, Mehrlieferung *f*
excess density *(reprod.)* Schwärzungsüberschuß *m*
excess sheets *pl* *(paper)* Überschuß *m*
exclamation mark Ausrufungszeichen *n*
exercise book Schreibheft *n*, Schulheft *n*
exercise book making machine Schulheftmaschine *f*
exhaust air Abluft *f*
exhaust air purification Abluftreinigung *f*
exhauster *(disposal)* Absaugeinrichtung *f*
exhaust fan Abluftgebläse *n*
exhaust hood Absaughaube *f*
exhaustion replenishment *(photochem.)* Erschöpfungsregenerierung *f*
exlibris Exlibris *n*, Bucheignerzeichen *n*
expand *v* *(modular system)* erweitern
expandable system ausbaufähiges System *n*
expanded type breite Schrift *f*, breitlaufende Schrift *f*
expanding shaft *(reel fixing)* Expansionswickelwelle *f*, Luftspannwelle *f*
expand in stages *v* schrittweise erweitern
expand step by step *v* schrittweise erweitern
expansion *(modular systems)* Ausbau *m*
experienced specialist erfahrener Fachmann *m*

experimental pressroom Versuchsdruckerei *f*
experimental printshop Versuchsdruckerei *f*
expert Fachmann *m*
expertise Fachwissen *n*
explosion-proof explosionsgeschützt
exponent *(typesetting)* Exponent *m*
expose *v* belichten; *(camera)* aufnehmen; *(recorder, plotter, scanner)* aufzeichnen, schreiben
expose into *v* *(film, plate)* einkopieren
expose light source *(scanner)* Aufzeichnungslichtquelle *f*, Ausgabelichtquelle *f*
expose through the lens *v* *(reprophotogr.)* im Strahlengang belichten
exposure Belichten *n*, Belichtung *f*; *(camera)* Aufnahme *f*; *(platemaking)* Kopie *f*; *(recorder, plotter)* Aufzeichnung *f*
exposure area *(camera)* Aufnahmeformat *n*
exposure calculator Belichtungscomputer *m*
exposure clock Belichtungsschaltuhr *f*
exposure computer Belichtungscomputer *m*
exposure control Belichtungssteuerung *f*
exposure control strip Kopierkontrollstreifen *m*, Kopiermeßstreifen *m*
exposure cycle Belichtungs(ab)lauf *m*
exposure cycles *pl* Belichtungstakte *pl*
exposure fan *(step exposures)* Belichtungsfächer *m*, Stufenbelichtung *f*
exposure in enlarged scale Vergrößerung *f*
exposure in reduced scale Verkleinerung *f*
exposure lamp Belichtungslampe *f*, Kopierlampe *f*
exposure latitude Belichtungsspielraum *m*
exposure light source Belichtungslampe *f*, Belichtungsquelle *f*
exposure material Aufnahmematerial *n*
exposure measuring strip Kopiermeßstreifen *m*
exposure media Aufnahmematerial *n*
exposure meter Belichtungsmesser *m*
exposure programme Belichtungsprogramm *n*
exposure routine Belichtungs(ab)lauf *m*
exposure sequence Belichtungs(ab)lauf *m*; *(step and repeat m.)* Kopierfolge *f*
exposure setting Belichtungseinstellung *f*
exposure speed Belichtungsgeschwindigkeit *f*, Belichtungsleistung *f*
exposure table Belichtungstabelle *f*
exposure time Belichtungsdauer *f*, Belichtungszeit *f*
exposure unit *(imagesetter)* Belichter *m*, Belichtungseinheit *f*
express printing Sofortdruck *m*

extend *v (modular system)* erweitern; *(gravure ink)* verschneiden
extended cover *(book)* überstehender Umschlag *m*
extender *(gravure ink)* Verschnitt *m*
extend the ink *v* Farbe verlängern
extension *(camera)* Auszug *m*; *(modular systems)* Ausbau *m*
extension phase *(modular systems)* Ausbaustufe *f*
extension step *(modular systems)* Ausbaustufe *f*
external data Fremddaten *pl*
external data acceptance Fremddatenübernahme *f*
external data conversion Fremddatenkonvertierung *f*
external data transfer Fremddatenübernahme *f*
external device Fremdgerät *n*
external storage *(comp.)* externer Speicher *m*
external system Fremdsystem *n*
extra charge Aufschlag *m*
extra charge for foreign language setting Sprachaufschlag *m*
extract *(book)* Buchauszug *m*
extraction Absaugung *f*
extra work Mehrarbeit *f*
eyelet Öse *f*, Schnürloch *n*
eyelet *v* ösen
eyelet stitching Ösenheftung *f*
eyelet stitching head Ösenheftkopf *m*
eyeletting machine Ösenmaschine *f*, Öseneinsetzmaschine *f*
eye (of type) Punze *f*

F

fabric *(screen printing)* Gewebe *n*
fabric preparation *(screen printing)* Gewebevorbehandlung *f*
fabric roughening Gewebeaufrauhung *f*
fabric stretcher Gewebespanner *m*
face *(typeface)* Schrift *f*, Schriftart *f*; *(part of the letter)* Auge *n*, Gesicht *n*
face and back printing Schön- und Widerdruck *m*
face cut Frontbeschnitt *m*, Frontschnitt *m*, Vorderbeschnitt *m*
face length *(gravure cyl.)* Ballenlänge *f*

face printing Schöndruck *m*
face-trim *v* an der Vorderseite *f* beschneiden
face trim(ming) Frontbeschnitt *m*, Vorderbeschnitt *m*
facsimile Faksimile *n*; *(telecom.)* Fax *n*, Telefax *n*
facsimile copy *(print)* Faksimiledruck *m*
facsimile link *(telecom.)* Faksimileleitung *f*
facsimile machine *(telecom.)* Telefaxgerät *n*
facsimile print Faksimiledruck *m*
facsimile printing Faksimiledruck *m*
facsimile reproduction Faksimile-Reproduktion *f*, naturgetreue Wiedergabe *f*, originalgetreue Wiedergabe *f*; *(print)* Faksimiledruck *m*
facsimile transmission *(telecom.)* Faksimile-Übertragung *f*
faded solids *pl (printing)* flaue Flächen *pl*
fade resistance *(ink)* Lichtechtheit *f*
fading *(colour)* Ausbleichen *n*, Ausbluten *n*, Auslaufen *n*, Verblassen *n*, Verfärben *n*, Verschießen *n*
fail-safe *(system)* ausfallsicher
fail-sheet stoppage Stopper *m*
faint lichtschwach
faint impression schwacher Druck *m*
fair copy *(text copy)* druckfertiges Manuskript, Reinschrift *f*
faithful rendering see faithful reproduction
faithful reproduction naturgetreue Wiedergabe *f*, originalgetreue Wiedergabe *f*
fallen type *(lead comp.)* schiefstehender Satz *m*
fall-out *(lead comp.)* Spieße *pl*
family tree *(typesetting)* Stammbaum *m*
fan *v* fächeln, wedeln; *(sheets)* auflockern, belüften, durchlüften, lüften
fan-apart blowers *pl* see fanning blowers
fan blowers *pl* see fanning blowers
fancy cord Zierschnur *f*
fancy letter verzierter Buchstabe *m*, Zierbuchstabe *m*
fancy line verzierte Linie *f*
fancy paper Dekorationspapier *n*, Fantasiepapier *n*
fancy rule verzierte Linie *f*
fancy type Dekorschrift *f*, Fantasieschrift *f*, Künstlerschrift *f*, Schmuckschrift *f*, Zierschrift *f*
fan delivery *(web press)* Schaufelradauslage *f*
fan fold Spiralfalz *m*, Zickzackfalz *m*
fan-fold *v* endlosfalzen
fan-folded pack zickzack-gefalzter Stapel *m*
fan folder Spiralfalzer *m*, Zickzackfalzapparat *m*

fanned exposures *pl (step exposures)* Stufenbelichtung *f*, Schiebekopie *f*
fanning blowers *pl (feeder)* Trennbläser *pl*, Lockerungsbläser *pl*
fan-out *(printing problem)* Breiterdrucken *n*
fan out *v (sheets)* auffächern, ausfächern, ausschuppen, fächerartig auflockern, fächern
Farmer's reducer *(film etching)* Farmer'scher Abschwächer *m*
Farmer's solution *(film etching)* Farmer'scher Abschwächer *m*
fashion magazine Modezeitschrift *f*
fast-acting plate clamps *pl (on press)* Plattenschnellspanneinrichtung *f*
fast-drying ink schnelltrocknende Farbe *f*
fasten *v* festmachen, festziehen
fastening clamp Halteklammer *f*, Klemme *f*
fast lens lichtstarkes Objektiv *n*
fastness properties *pl (ink)* Echtheiten *pl*
fatigue *(mech.)* Ermüdung *f*
fault *(techn.)* Störung *f*
fault clearance Störungsbehebung *f*
fault diagnosis *(comp.)* Fehlerdiagnose *f*
fault-finding system *(comp.)* Fehlersuchsystem *n*
faultless mängelfrei, störungsfrei
faulty cut Fehlschnitt *m*
faulty material Materialfehler *m*
fax *(telecom.)* Fax *n*, Telefax *n*
faxcopier Telefaxgerät *n*
fax message Telefax-Mitteilung *f*
feature *(article)* Artikel *m*
feed *v* anlegen, einlegen, beschicken; *(hopper loader)* auflegen
feed angle Anlagewinkel *m*
feedboard Anlagetisch *m*, Anlegertisch *m*
feeder Anlage *f*, Anleger *m*, Anlegeapparat *m*, Beschickungsgerät *n*, Beschickungsvorrichtung *f*
feeder head Anlegerkopf *m*
feeder magazine Anlegermagazin *n*
feeder on/off Anleger an/aus
feeder pile Anlegerstapel *m*
feeder timing Anlegertakt *m*
feed gauge *(sheet registration)* Anlegemarke *f*
feed grippers *pl* Zuführgreifer *pl*
feed holes Transportlochung *f*
feed in *v (data, text)* eingeben, einlesen; *(paper web)* einziehen
feed(ing) Anlage *f*, Anlegen *n*, Beschickung *f*, Zuführung *f*; *(photocomp.)* Vorschub *m*
feeding depth *(cutting m.)* Einlegetiefe *f*
feeding device Anlegevorrichtung *f*

feeding height *(cutting m.)* Einlegehöhe *f*, Einsatzhöhe *f*
feeding table Anlagetisch *m*, Anlegertisch *m*
feeding width *(cutting m.)* Einlegebreite *f*; *(flowline systems, processors)* Einlaufbreite *f*
feed ink *v* Farbe zugeben
feed in the web *v* Papierbahn einziehen
feed lay *(sheet registration)* Anlegemarke *f*
feed roller Zuführwalze *f*
feed slot *(film processor)* Einführschlitz *m*
feed tray *(film processor)* Einführtisch *m*, Eingabetisch *m*
feeler gauge Fühlerlehre *f*, Lehre *f*
felt blanket *(cyl.)* Filztuch *n*, Druckfilz *m*
felt board Filzpappe *f*
felt cover *(vacuum frame)* Filzdecke *f*
felt dressing *(cyl.)* Filzaufzug *m*
felt side *(paper)* Filzseite *f*
female die *(embossing mold)* Prägematrize *f*
female embossing Prägematrize *f*
ferric chloride *(electropl.)* Eisenchlorid *n*
ferrite core memory *(comp.)* Ferritkernspeicher *m*
festooning unit *(web press)* Bahnspeicher *m*, Papierspeicher *m*, Schlaufenspeicher *m*
festoon storage *(web press)* see festooning unit
feuilleton *(newspaper)* Feuilleton *n*
fiber puffing *(paper fiber)* Aufquellen der Papierfasern
fiber tear *(paper)* Faserriß *m*
fibre bonding *(paper)* Faserbindung *f*
fibre optic cable Glasfaserkabel *n*
fibre optics network *(telecom.)* Glasfasernetz *n*
fiction *(book; as opp. to non-fiction)* Roman *m*
field conditions *pl* Praxisbedingungen *pl*
field entry *(screen mask, form)* Feldeintrag *m*
field-tested praxiserprobt
figure Ziffer *f*; *(text figure)* Abbildung *f*, Bild *n*, Illustration *f*
figure case *(hand comp.)* Ziffernkasten *m*
file Datei *f*, Daten *pl*, Datensatz *m*
file card Karteikarte *f*
file copy Archivexemplar *n*; *(advertiser)* Belegexemplar *n*
file directory *(comp.)* Inhaltsverzeichnis *n*
file hole margin *(continuous forms)* Lochrand *m*
file hole punching Abheftlochung *f*
file holes *pl* Abheftlochung *f*
file index Ablageregister *n*; *(comp.)* Inhaltsverzeichnis *n*
file management Datenverwaltung *f*
file manager (system) Dateiverwaltungssystem *n*, Datenverwaltungssystem *n*

file name - filter 212

file name *(comp.)* Kennung *f*, Kode *m*
file storage Datenspeicher(ung) *m/f*
filing Archivierung *f*
filing cabinet Registraturschrank *m*
filing margin Heftrand *m*
filing properties *pl (repro film)* Archivfestigkeit *f*
filled-in halftones *pl (printing)* zulaufender Raster *m*
filler *(newspaper)* Füller *m*, Lückenbüßer *m*
fillers *pl (papermaking)* Füllstoffe *pl*
fill-in *(halftones)* see filling-in
fill in *v (screen mask, business form etc.)* eintragen
filling-in *(of halftones)* Zuschmieren *n*, Zulaufen *n*, Zusetzen *n*, Zugehen *n*
filling-up *(halftones)* see filling-in
film Film *m*, Folie *f; (layer)* Film *m*, Schicht *f*
film adheser Filmklebeautomat *m*
film advance *(phototypesetter)* Filmvorschub *m*
film assembly Filmmontage *f*
film base Filmträger *m*, Filmunterlage *f*
film basket *(film processor)* Filmkorb *m*
film cabinet Filmschrank *m*
film chemistry Filmchemie *f*
film cleaner Filmreiniger *m*, Folienreiniger *m*
film consumption Filmverbrauch *m*
film contact Filmkontakt *m*
film contact screen Filmkontaktraster *m*
film copy Filmnutzen *m*, Kopiervorlage *f*, Nutzenfilm *m*, Nutzenkopie *f*
film copy gravure screen Tiefdruck-Kopierraster *m*
film cutter Filmschneidegerät *n*
film cut to size Blattfilm *m*
film drying clamp Filmtrockenklammer *f*
film duplicate Filmduplikat *n*
film duplicating *(contact printing)* Kontaktkopie *f*
film edge markings *pl* Filmkanten *f/pl*, Filmränder *m/pl*, Schnittkanten *pl*
film edges *pl* Filmkanten *f/pl*, Filmränder *m/pl*, Schnittkanten *f/pl*
film etching Ätzen *n*, Filmätzung *f*, Lithografie *f*
film extrusion Folienextrusion *f*
film feed *(phototypesetter)* Filmvorschub *m*
film flat *(film montage)* Filmmontage *f*
film for aerial photography Luftaufnahmefilm *m*
film gauge Filmdicke *f*, Foliendicke *f*, Folienstärke *f*
film glue Filmkleber *m*
film grain Filmkorn *n*
film grid Standfilm *m*
film handling Filmverarbeitung *f*

film holder *(camera)* Filmbühne *f*
film-laminated board cellophanierter Karton *m*, folienkaschierter Karton *m*
film laminating Cellophanierung *f*, Folienbeschichtung *f*, Folienkaschierung *f; (acetate film)* Glanzfolienkaschierung *f*
film laminating machine Folienkaschiermaschine *f*
filmless platemaking filmlose Plattenkopie *f*
film litho Litho *n*
film lithography *(as opp. to stone lithography)* Filmlithografie *f*
film masking Abdecken *n*, Ausdecken *n*, Ausflecken *n*
film montage Filmmontage *f*
film opaque Abdeckfarbe *f*, Abdecktusche *f*
film opaquing Abdecken *n*, Ausdecken *n*, Ausflecken *n*
film overlay *(reprod.)* Filmdecker *m*
film pack Filmpackung *f*
film packaging *(mailroom)* Folienverpackung *f*
film printing Foliendruck *m*
film processing Filmverarbeitung *f*, Folienverarbeitung *f*
film processor Entwicklungsgerät *n*, Entwicklungsmaschine *f;* **automatic ~** Entwicklungsautomat *m*
film punch Filmstanze *f*, Folienstanze *f*
film recorder Filmrekorder *m*
film reel Filmrolle *f*, Filmspule *f*
film register punch Filmstanze *f*, Folienstanze *f*
film rewind Filmaufwicklung *f*, Folienaufwicklung *f*
film screen *(as opp. to glass screen)* Filmraster *m*
filmsetter *(mach.)* Fotosatzgerät *n*, Fotosatzmaschine *f*
film setting *(photocomposition)* Filmsatz *m*
film sheet Folie *f*
film size Filmformat *n*
film squeegee Filmrakel *f*, Filmabstreifrakel *f*
film stains *pl* Filmflecken *m/pl*
film stencil Filmschablone *f*
film stripping *(film assembly)* Filmmontage *f*
film tint Einkopierraster *m*, Raster *m*, Rasterfilm *m*, technischer Raster *m*
film-to-print laminating Folienkaschierung *f*
film transport Filmtransport *m*
film unwind Filmabwicklung *f*, Folienabwicklung *f*
film wrapping *(mailroom)* Folienverpackung *f*, Folieneinschlag *m*
film wrapping machine Folienpackmaschine *f*
filter Filter *m*

filter bath - flabby paper

filter bath *(phot.)* Klärbad *n*
filter factor Filterfaktor *m*
filter holder Filterhalter *m*
filtering see filtration
filtering cloth Filtrierleinen *n*
filter paper Filtrierpapier *n*
filter selection Filterwahl *f*
filter wheel Filterrad *n*
filtration Filterung *f*, Filtrieren *n*
final check Endkontrolle *f*, Nachkontrolle *f*
final costs *pl* Endkosten *pl*
final cut Endbeschnitt *m*, Fertigbeschnitt *m*
final cutting Nachschneiden *n*
final draft Reinzeichnung *f*
final drawing Reinzeichnung *f*
final drying Endtrocknung *f*
final etching Nachätzung *f*, Reinätzung *f*, Scharfätzung *f*
final film Endfilm *m*
final letter *(Hebrew, Scripts etc.)* Finalbuchstabe *m*
final output Endausgabe *f*
final page Endseite *f*
final page film Seitenendfilm *m*, seitenglatter Film *m*
final positive Endpositiv *n*
final proof Revision *f*, Revisionsabzug *m*, Revisionsbogen *m*
final quality control Ausgangskontrolle *f*, Endkontrolle *f*
final run *(printing)* Auflagendruck *m*, Fortdruck *m*
final size Endformat *n*, Endgröße *f*
final treatment Endbehandlung *f*, Nachbehandlung *f*
final trim Endbeschnitt *m*, Fertigbeschnitt *m*
fine-adjust *v* feineinstellen, feinjustieren
fine adjustment Feineinstellung *f*
fine art printers *pl* Kunstdruckerei *f*
fine board Feinkarton *m*
fine cardboard Kartonpapier *n*
fine etching Feinätzung *f*, Nachätzung *f*, Reinätzung *f*, Scharfätzung *f*
fine grain Feinkorn *n*
fine grain development *(phot.)* Feinkornentwicklung *f*
fine grain emulsion *(phot.)* Feinkornemulsion *f*
fine grain film Feinkornfilm *m*
fine line *(typogr.)* feine Linie *f*
fine line engraving Feinstrichätzung *f*
fine line etching Feinstrichätzung *f*
fineness of grain Feinkörnigkeit *f*
fine paper Feinpapier *n*

fine printing papers *pl* grafische Feinpapiere *n/pl*
fine rule feine Linie *f*
fine screen feiner Raster *m*
finger-guard Handabweiser *m*, Händeschutz *m*, Handschutz(vorrichtung) *m/f*
finger marks *pl* Fingerabdrücke *pl*
fingernail test *(paper grain)* Fingernagelprobe *f*
finger prints *pl* Fingerabdrücke *pl*
finish *(paper)* Oberfläche *f*
finished artwork Reinzeichnung *f*
finished film Endfilm *m*
finished product Fertigprodukt *n*
finishing *(print finishing)* Druckverarbeitung *f*, Buchbinderei *f*, buchbinderische Verarbeitung *f*, Druckweiterverarbeitung *f*, Weiterverarbeitung *f*, Veredlung *f*
finishing department *(binding dep.)* Buchbinderei *f*
finishing line Verarbeitungslinie *f*
first edition Erstausgabe *f*
first etching Vorätzung *f*
first forme *(for first-run printing)* Schöndruckform *f*
first line *(typesetting)* Anfangszeile *f*
first line of print Druckanfang *m*
first printable dot erster druckfähiger Punkt *m*
first proof Hauskorrektur *f*
first-run printing *(before perfecting)* Schöndruck *m*
fish glue Fischleim *m*
fit *(back-up register)* Rückseitenregister *n*, Widerdruckregister *n*
fit *v* *(mach.)* ausrüsten, ausstatten; *(typogr.)* anpassen
fit copy into a figure *v* *(text)* Text einer Figur anpassen
fit copy to layout *v* *(text)* Text einpassen
fix *v* festmachen; *(phot.)* fixieren
fix costs *pl* Fixkosten *pl*
fixed disk *(as opp. to removable disk)* Festplatte *f*
fixed disk memory Festplattenspeicher *m*
fixed head disk *(comp.)* Festkopfplatte *f*
fixed-size printing press *(as opp. to variable-size)* festformatige Druckmaschine *f*
fixed space *(typesetting)* Festausschluß *m*
fixer *(phot.)* Fixierer *m*
fixing agent Fixierer *m*
fixing bath Fixierbad *n*
fixing needle Aufstechnadel *f*
fixing salt Fixiersalz *n*
flabby paper lappiges Papier *n*

flap - floral ornament

flap Klappe *f*, Lasche *f*; *(book wrapper)* Einschlagklappe *f*; *(folding box)* Einsteckklappe *f*

flap slot *(folding box)* Einsteckschlitz *m*

flash Blitzlicht *n*

flash exposure Blitzlichtaufnahme *f*, Blitzlichtbelichtung *f*; *(camera screening)* Vorbelichtung *f*

flash lamp *(camera screening)* Vorbelichtungslampe *f*

flashlight Blitzlicht *n*

flash photo(graph) Blitzlichtaufnahme *f*

flat *(page assembly)* Montage *f*; *(position of sheets)* planliegend, plano

flat-bed die-cutter Flach(bett)stanze *f*, Hubstanze *f*

flat-bed die-cutting Flach(bett)stanzen *n*

flat-bed laser scanner Flachbett-Laserscanner *m*

flat-bed offset proofpress Flachbett-Offsetandruckmaschine *f*

flat-bed plotter *(CAD)* Flachbett-Plotter *m*

flat-bed printing Flachbettdruck *m*, Flachdruck *m*, Flachformdruck *m*

flat-bed printing press Flachbett-Druckmaschine *f*, Flachformdruckmaschine *f*

flat-bed proofing press Flachandruckpresse *f*

flat-bed scanner Flachbettscanner *m*

flat binding Einband mit geradem Rücken

flat copy flache Vorlage *f*, flaues Original *n*

flat forme Flachform *f*

flat gradation flache Gradation *f*

flat graver Flachstichel *m*

flat image *(low contrast image)* kontrastloses Bild *n*

flat negative flaches Negativ *n*, flaues Negativ *n*, weiches Negativ *n*

flatness Planlage *f*

flat original flache Vorlage *f*, flaues Original *n*, flaue Vorlage *f*

flat position Planlage *f*

flat pull *(letterpress)* Abzug ohne Zurichtung

flat reproduction flache Reproduktion *f*

flat scorper Flachstichel *m*

flat sections *pl* ungebundene Bogen *pl*

flat sheet Planobogen *m*

flat sheet delivery *(web press)* see open sheet delivery

flat spine *(book)* Flachrücken *m*, gerader Rücken *m*

flat-spine book Buch mit geradem Rücken

flat stereo Flachstereo *n*

flat stitching *(as opp. to saddle stitching)* Randheftung *f*, Seitenheftung *f*, seitliche Heftung *f*

flat tint Vollfläche *f*, Volltonfläche *f*

flat wire *(wire-stitching)* Flachdraht *m*

flesh colour *(reprod.)* Hautfarbe *f*

flesh tones *pl* *(reprod.)* Hauttöne *m/pl*

flexible binding biegsame Bindung *f*, flexible Bindung *f*; *(book)* flexibler Einband *m*

flexible cover flexibler Umschlag *m*, weicher Umschlag *m*; *(book)* flexibler Einband *m*

flexible drive shaft Kardanwelle *f*

flexible packaging flexible Packstoffe *m/pl*, flexible Verpackung *f*, Weichpackung *f*

flexible PVC Weich-PVC *f*

flexographic ink Flexodruckfarbe *f*

flexographic press Flexodruckmaschine *f*

flexographic printing Flexodruck *m*

flexography Flexodruck *m*, Flexografie *f*

flexo ink Flexodruckfarbe *f*

flexo press Flexodruckmaschine *f*

flexo printer *(person)* Flexodrucker *m*; *(mach.)* Flexodruckmaschine *f*

flexo printing Flexodruck *m*

flexo printing ink Flexodruckfarbe *f*

flexo printing press Flexodruckmaschine *f*

flexo sleeve Flexohülse *f*

flexural strength *(cylinders, machine parts)* **of high** ~ biegesteif

flicker-free monitor flimmerfreier Bildschirm *m*

flimsy paper Dünndruckpapier *n*, Florpostpapier *n*

flip image *(lateral reversal)* Bildumkehrung *f*; *(positive/negative)* Positiv/Negativumwandlung *f*

flip-top box Flip-Top-Schachtel *f*

flip-top vacuum frame *(platemaking)* schwenkbarer Kopierrahmen *m*, Wendekopierrahmen *m*

floatation dryer *(web press)* Schwebetrockner *m*

floating accents *pl* fliegende Akzente *m/pl*

floating tabs *pl* *(photocomp.)* fliegende Tabulatoren *pl*

flocking *(textile)* Beflocken *n*

flong Maternkarton *m*, Maternpappe *f*, Matrizenpappe *f*, Stereotypiepappe *f*

floor space *(machine)* Standfläche *f*

floor-type press *(newspaper rotary)* Parterredruckmaschine *f*

floppies *pl* Floppies *pl*

floppy disk Floppy-Disk *f*

floppy disk drive Floppy-Disk-Laufwerk *n*

floral ornament Verzierung *f*, Zierleiste *f*

floret Verzierung *f*, Zierleiste *f*; *(bookbinding)* Franzfilet *n*
flourish *(printer's flower)* Leiste *f*, Zierstück *n*
flow chart Fließbild *n*, Flußdiagramm *n*
flowing spray powder rieselfähiges Druckbestäubungspuder *n*
flowline Fließstrecke *f*
flowline processing Fließstreckenverarbeitung *f*
flowline system Durchlaufsystem *n*
flowline (three-knife) trimmer Fließdreischneider *m*
fluctuations *pl (process)* Schwankungen *pl*
fluff *(paper)* Flusen *pl*, Fusseln *pl*, Papierflusen *pl*, Papierfusseln *m/pl*, Papierstaub *m*
fluff-free cutting *(board)* flusenfreies Schneiden *n*
fluid grease lubrication Fließfettschmierung *f*
fluorescent light Kaltlicht *n*
fluorescent (printing) ink fluoreszierende Farbe *f*, Tagesleuchtfarbe *f*
flush bündig
flush cut Broschürenschnitt *m*
flush head bündiger Titel *m*
flushing *(ink prod.)* Flushen *n*
flush left *(type matter)* linksbündig
flush left and right Blocksatz *m*
flush matter *(type matter)* Blocksatz *m*
flush paragraph Absatz ohne Einzug
flush right *(type matter)* rechtsbündig
flush setting *(type)* Blocksatz *m*
fluttering *(paper web)* Flattern *n*
flyer *(leaflet)* Flugblatt *n*, Handzettel *m*; *(loose insert)* Beilage *f*, Einleger *m*, Einsteckbeilage *f*
flyer delivery *(press)* Rechenauslage *f*
flying imprinting unit *(web press)* fliegendes Eindruckwerk *n*
flying paster fliegender Rollenwechsler *m*
flying reelchange fliegender Rollenwechsler *m*
flying splicer fliegender Rollenwechsler *m*
flying stitching heads *pl (saddle-stitcher)* fliegende Heftköpfe *pl*
flying web-splice fliegender Rollenwechsel *m*
fly-leaf *(book)* fliegender Vorsatz *m*, Allonge *f*, Vorsatzblatt *n*
fly-title Schmutztitel *m*
fly-wheel Schwungrad *n*
foam formation Schaumbildung *f*
focal length Brennweite *f*
focal plane Brennebene *f*
focal point Brennpunkt *m*
focus Brennpunkt *m*, Fokus *m*
focus *v (camera)* scharfstellen

focusing *(camera)* Bildeinstellung *f*, Scharfstellung *f*
focusing lens *(camera)* Einstellupe *f*
focusing lens system *(camera)* Fokussierlinsensystem *n*
focusing screen *(camera)* Mattscheibe *f*
focus setting *(camera)* Bildeinstellung *f*, Scharfstellung *f*
fogging *(film)* Schleierbildung *f*
foil Folie *f*
foil blocking Folienprägung *f*
foil laminating Folienbeschichtung *f*, Folienkaschierung *f*
foil laminating machine Folienkaschiermaschine *f*
foil pouch *(heat sealing)* Folientasche *f*
foil printing Foliendruck *m*
foil processing Folienverarbeitung *f*
foil punch Folienstanze *f*
foil rewind Folienaufwicklung *f*
foil stamping Folienprägung *f*
foil thickness Foliendicke *f*, Folienstärke *f*
foil unwind Folienabwicklung *f*
fold Falz *m*, Falzbruch *m*, Falzlinie *f*
fold *v* falzen
fold control Falzkontrolle *f*
fold depth *(continuous forms printing)* Falzlänge *f*
folded brochure Faltbroschüre *f*, Faltprospekt *m*
folded edge *(as opp. to open edge)* gefalzte Seite *f*
folded-in cover *(magazine)* eingefalzter Umschlag *m*
folded-in flap *(leaflet, jacket etc.)* eingefalzte Klappe *f*
folded product Falzprodukt *n*
folded section Falzbogen *m*
folded sheet Falzbogen *m*
folded signature Falzbogen *m*
folder *(web press)* Falzapparat *m*; *(leaflet)* Broschüre *f*, Faltblatt *n*, Faltbroschüre *f*, Faltprospekt *m*, Prospekt *m*
folder cassette *(interchangeable)* Falzkassette *f*
folder feeder Falzanleger *m*
folder former *(press folder)* Falztrichter *m*
folder-gluer Faltschachtelklebemaschine *f*
folder super-structure *(web press)* Falzapparatüberbau *m*, Falzaufbau *m*
fold first *(convert.)* Falz voraus, vorne
fold-gluing Falzkleben *n*
fold in *v (flap)* einschlagen, einfalzen
folding Falzung *f*
fold(ing) accuracy Falzgenauigkeit *f*
folding and sealing machine Siegelfalzautomat *m*

folding blade - format

folding blade Falzmesser *n*, Falzschwert *n*
folding box Faltschachtel *f*
folding boxboard Faltschachtelkarton *m*
folding box gluer Faltschachtelklebemaschine *f*
folding box gluing Faltschachtelklebung *f*
folding carton Faltschachtel *f*
folding cylinder Falztrommel *f*, Falzzylinder *m*
folding drum see folding cylinder
folding jaw *(press folder)* Falzklappe *f*
folding knife Falzmesser *n*, Falzschwert *n*
folding lay *(sheet registration)* Falzanlage *f*
folding layout Falzschema *n*
folding machine Falzmaschine *f*; **automatic ~** Falzautomat *m*
fold(ing) mark Falzkreuz *n*, Falzmarke *f*
folding plow *(press folder)* Falzpflug *m*
folding register Falzregister *n*
folding resistance Falzwiderstand *m*
folding rollers *pl* Falzwalzen *pl*
folding sample Falzmuster *n*
folding spine Falzrücken *m*
folding stick Falzbein *n*
folding unit Falzwerk *n*
fold lay mark Falzanlage *f*
fold leading *(convert.)* Falz voraus, vorne
fold moistening Falzbefeuchtung *f*
fold monitoring Falzkontrolle *f*
fold-out (plate) *(book)* Ausschlagtafel *f*
fold over *v* umknicken
fold perforation Falzperforation *f*
fold pressing Falzabpressung *f*
fold softening Falzbefeuchtung *f*
fold tightening Falzverstärkung *f*
fold-to-print register Falzregister *n*
fold trailing *(convert.)* Falz hinten
fold variations *pl* Falzvariationen *pl*
folio Kolumnenziffer *f*, Pagina *f*, Seitenzahl *f*, toter Kolumnentitel *m*
folio edition *(book)* Folioausgabe *f*
folios *pl* Paginierung *f*, Seitennumerierung *f*
folio size Folioformat *n*
folio volume Foliant *m*
follow copy *(correction instruction)* nach Manuskript
follow-up control *(process control)* Nachführsteuerung *f*
follow-up display *(process control)* Nachführanzeige *f*
follow-up letter *(advertising)* Nachfaßbrief *m*
font *(typeface)* Font *m*, Fotosatzschrift *f*, Schrift *f*
font disc *(optomechanical phototypesetter)* Schriftscheibe *f*

font library Schriftenbibliothek *f*
font memory *(photocomp.)* Schriftenspeicher *m*
font selection *(phototypesetter)* Fontanwahl *f*
fonts in direct access *(photocomp.)* Schriften im direkten Zugriff
font storage *(photocomp.)* Schriftenspeicher *m*
font width *(character width)* Buchstabenbreite *f*, Dickte *f*, Schriftdickte *f*
food package Lebensmittelverpackung *f*, Nahrungsmittelpackung *f*
foot *(of the page; of the letter)* Fuß *m*
footboard *(on presses)* Laufblech *n*, Trittbrett *n*, Fußtritt *m*; *(camera)* Laufboden *m*
foot lever Fußhebel *m*
foot margin unterer Papierrand *m*, unterer Seitenrand *m*
footnote Fußnote *f*
footnote (callout) reference Fußnotenreferenz *f*
foot of page Ende der Seite
foot press Fußpresse *f*
foot rule Fußlinie *f*
foot stick Fußsteg *m*
foot trim(ming) Fußbeschnitt *m*
foot white *(make-up of lead comp.)* Unterschlag *m*
forbid hyphenation *(text proc.)* Trennverbot *n*
forced lubrication Druckschmierung *f*
foredge Vorderkante *f*; *(book)* Vorderschnitt *m*
foredge margin äußerer Papierrand *m*, äußerer Seitenrand *m*, vorderer Papierrand *m*
foredge printing *(book)* Frontdruck *m*
foreground Vordergrund *m*
foreground and background assignment *(comp.)* Vordergrund- und Hintergrundzuweisung *f*
foreground and background operation *(comp.)* Vordergrund und Hintergrundbetrieb *m*
foreground processing *(comp.)* Vordergrundverarbeitung *f*
foreign-language imprint Fremdspracheneindruck *m*
foreign language setting Fremdsprachensatz *m*
foreign news *pl* Auslandsnachrichten *pl*
foreign system Fremdsystem *n*
Foreign Types *pl* *(type classif.)* Fremde Schriften *pl*
foreman *(printing)* Druckmeister *m*
foreword *(book)* Geleitwort *n*, Vorwort *n*
forged steel Schmiedestahl *m*
forgery Fälschung *f*
forgery-proof fälschungssicher
forklift truck Gabelstapler *m*
form *(business form)* Formular *n*, Vordruck *m*
format Format *n*, Größe *f*

format adjustment Formateinstellung *f*, Größeneinstellung *f*
format change Formatänderung *f*, Formatveränderung *f*, Formatwechsel *m*
format change-over Formatumstellung *f*
formation of fungus *(fountain solution)* Pilzbildung *f*
formation of mould *(fountain solution)* Pilzbildung *f*
format range Formatbereich *m*
format setting Formateinstellung *f*, Größeneinstellung *f*
format storage *(comp.)* Formatspeicher *m*
formatted data formatierte Daten *pl*
formatted text formatierter Text *m*
formatting *(data)* Formatierung *f*
format VI printing press Druckmaschine im Format VI
forme *(print forme)* Form *f*, Druckform *f*; *(letterpress forme)* Druckstock *m*
forme assembly Formenmontage *f*
forme bed *(flat-bed press)* Druckfundament *n*, Formfundament *n*
forme carriage *(letterpress m.)* Formkarren *m*
forme chase Formrahmen *m*
forme cylinder Formzylinder *m*; *(rotary letterpress, flexography)* Klischeezylinder *m*
forme inking Einfärben der Druckform
forme positioning Formeinpassen *n*
forme positioning device Formeinpaßvorrichtung *f*
former *(press folder)* Falztrichter *m*, Trichter *m*
forme rack *(lead comp.)* Formenregal *n*
former fold *(web printing)* Längsfalz *m*, Trichterfalz *m*
former folder Trichterfalzapparat *m*
former nose *(former folder)* Trichternase *f*
forme roller Auftragswalze *f*, Formwalze *f*
former plate *(press folder)* Falztrichter *m*
former roller *(web press)* Trichterwalze *f*
former superstructure *(press folder)* Trichterüberbau *m*
forme trolley Formentransportwagen *m*
forms binding Formularheftung *f*
forms collator Formularzusammentragmaschine *f*
forms composition *(typesetting)* Formularsatz *m*
forms design Formulargestaltung *f*
forms press Formulardruckmaschine *f*
forms printer Formulardrucker *m*
forms printing Formulardruck *m*
forms production Formularherstellung *f*
forms set Formularsatz *m*
forms set gluing Formularsatzleimung *f*

forms setting *(typogr.)* Formularsatz *m*
forms stitching Formularheftung *f*
formula Formel *f*
formula setting Formelsatz *m*
fortnightly (publication) vierzehntäglich erscheinende Zeitschrift *f*
forwarding sucker *(feeder suction head)* Schleppsauger *m*
foul proof *(galley proof)* unkorrigierter Korrekturabzug *m*
found *v (type)* gießen
foundation Fundament *n*
founding *(type)* Guß *m*
foundry type Bleisatzschrift *f*, Handsatzschrift *f*, Handsatztype *f*, Schriftguß *m*
fount *(type)* Guß *m*, Schrift *f*
fountain additive Feuchtwasserzusatz *m*
fountain key *(ink duct)* Farbschraube *f*, Zonenschraube *f*
fountain roller Duktorwalze *f*, Kastenwalze *f*
fountain screw *(ink duct)* Farbschraube *f*, Zonenschraube *f*
fountain solution Feuchtmittel *n*, Wischwasser *n*
fountain solution circulator Feuchtwasserumwälzanlage *f*
fountain solution cooling Feuchtmittelkühlung *f*
fountain solution measuring system Feuchtmittelmeßgerät *n*
fountain solution mixer Feuchtwassermischgerät *n*
fountain water Feuchtwasser *n*, Wischwasser *n*
fountain water film *(offset plate)* Feuchtmittelfilm *m*
four-bath processor *(reprod.)* Vierbad-Entwicklungsgerät *n*
four-colour ad(vertisement) Vierfarbanzeige *f*
four colour both sides 4/4 farbig, vierfarbiger Schön- und Widerdruck *m*
four colour front, four reverse 4/4 farbig, vierfarbiger Schön- und Widerdruck *m*
four colour front, none reverse 4/0 farbig, vierfarbiger Schöndruck *m*
four colour front, one reverse 4/1-farbig
four-colour halftone print gerasterter Vierfarbdruck *m*
four-colour halftone set *(separations)* gerasterter Vierfarbsatz *m*
four-colour print Vierfarbdruck *m*
four-colour (printing) press Vierfarb(en)druckmaschine *f*, Vierfarbmaschine *f*
four-colour printwork Vierfarbdruck *m*

four-colour process - full-copper process

four-colour process *(printing)* Vierfarbdruck *m;* *(reprod.)* Vierfarbreproduktion *f*
four-colour proofpress Vierfarben-Andruckmaschine *f*
four-colour reproduction Vierfarbreproduktion *f*
four-colour set *(separations)* Farbsatz *m,* Vierfarbsatz *m*
four-colour sheet-fed offset press Vierfarben-Bogenoffsetmaschine *f*
four-colour subject Vierfarbsujet *n*
four colour wet-on-wet printing Vierfarben-Naß-in-Naß-Druck *m*
four-colour work Vierfarbarbeiten *f/pl*
four-column page vierspaltige Seite *f*
four-directional fold Vierbruchfalz *m*
fourdrinier machine *(papermaking)* Langsiebpapiermaschine *f*
four-em quad *(typesetting)* Konkordanz *f*
four-high unit *(newspaper offset rotary)* Achterturm *m*
four-part forms set Vierblatt-Formularsatz *m*
four-ply forms set Vierblatt-Formularsatz *m*
four-sided trimming Rundumbeschnitt *m*
fourth cover vierte Umschlagseite *f*
four-to-em space *(typesetting)* Viertelgeviert *n*
four-to-pica Viertelcicero *n*
four up *(four copies per signature)* zu vier Nutzen *m/pl*
fractional number *(typesetting)* Zahlenbruch *m*
fractional numbers *pl* Bruchziffern *pl,* gebrochene Ziffern *pl*
fraction bar *(typesetting)* Bruchstrich *m*
frame *(machine frame)* Gestell *n,* Rahmen *m;* *(typogr.)* Rahmen *m*
frame border *(typogr.)* Rahmenlinie *f*
framed ad Anzeige mit Umrandung *f*
frame drawer *(Autoplaten)* Einschieberahmen *m*
frame embossing Rahmenprägung *f*
frame exposure Rahmenkopie *f*
frame rack *(for type cases)* Kastenregal *n,* Regal mit Setzpult
frame stamping Rahmenprägung *f*
free copy Freiexemplar *n*
freely movable keyboard freibewegliche Tastatur *f*
free space *(layout, page make-up etc.)* freigeschlagener Raum *m,* Freiraum *m*
French quotes *pl* französische Anführungszeichen *pl*
French sewing *(binding)* Holländern *n*
frequency modulation *(comp.)* Frequenzmodulierung *f*
freshenup colour *v* Farbe auffrischen

freshly printed druckfrisch, frisch bedruckt
freshly printed sheet frischer Druck *m*
fresh print frischer Druck *m*
friar *(printing problem)* Mönch *m*
friction clutch Reibungskupplung *f*
friction drive Friktionsantrieb *m*
friction feeder *(folding m.)* Streichradanleger *m*
fringe *(halftone dot)* Hof *m,* Rand *m*
front and back *(pages)* Schön- und Widerdruckseite *f,* Vorder- und Rückseite *f*
front cover Titelblatt *n,* Titelseite *f*
front cover board *(book)* Vorderdeckel *m,* vorderer Buchdeckel *m*
front delivery *(press)* Frontausleger *m*
front edge Vorderkante *f*
front(-edge) margin äußerer Papierrand *m,* äußerer Seitenrand *m,* vorderer Papierrand *m*
front edge of plate Plattenvorderkante *f*
front edge of sheet Bogenvorderkante *f*
front-ends *pl* Frontend-Geräte *n/pl*
front-end system Frontend-System *n*
front-end terminal Frontend-Terminal *m,* Eingabeplatz *m,* Eingabestation *f,* Eingabeterminal *m*
front-end unit Eingabegerät *n,* Frontend-Gerät *n*
front guide *(sheet registration)* Vordermarke *f*
frontispiece Titelbild *n*
front knife Frontmesser *n*
front lay *(sheet registration)* Vordermarke *f*
front lighting *(camera)* Aufsichtsbeleuchtung *f*
front page Titelblatt *n,* Titelseite *f,* Vorderseite *f*
front side Stirnseite *f;* *(of printed sheet)* Schöndruckseite *f*
front-side printing Schöndruck *m*
front-side printing unit *(perfecting press)* Schöndruckwerk *n*
front stop *(sheet registration)* Vorderanschlag *m,* Frontanschlag *m*
front trim(ming) Frontbeschnitt *m,* Frontschnitt *m,* Vorderbeschnitt *m*
front waste *(gripper margin)* Greiferrandabfall *m*
full back *(book)* Ganzrücken *m*
full binding *(book)* Ganz(ein)band *m*
full caps *pl* große Versalien *f/pl*
full cloth binding Ganzleinenband *m*
full-colour ad(vertisement) Farbanzeige *f,* farbige Anzeige *f,* Vierfarbanzeige *f*
full-colour full-page ad Farbseite *f,* ganzseitige Vierfarbanzeige *f*
full-colour process printing Vierfarbdruck *m*
full-colour set *(separations)* Vierfarbsatz *m*
full-copper process *(full immersion of gravure cyl. into electrolyte)* Vollkupferverfahren *n*

full enclosure - gathering machine

full enclosure *(machine)* Vollkapselung *f*, Vollverschalung *f*
full face line vollfette Linie *f*
full face rule vollfette Linie *f*
full leather binding Ganzlederband *m*
full-page ad(vertisement) ganzseitige Anzeige *f*
full-page colour ad Farbseite *f*
full-page exposure Ganzseitenbelichtung *f*
full-page film Ganzseitenfilm *m*, seitenglatter Film *m*
full-page illustration ganzseitige Abbildung *f*
full-page make-up Ganzseitenumbruch *m*, Ganzseitenmontage *f*
full-page output Ganzseitenausgabe *f*; *(exposure)* Ganzseitenbelichtung *f*
full-page paste-up Ganzseitenmontage *f*
full-page recording *(exposure)* Ganzseitenbelichtung *f*
full-page text proof ganzseitiger Textkorrekturbeleg *m*
full-page transmission *(telecom.)* Ganzseitenübertragung *f*
full point *(punctuation mark)* Punkt *m*
full stop *(punctuation mark)* Punkt *m*, Schlußpunkt *m*
full-surface application *(as opp. to strip/pattern application)* Vollflächenauftrag *m*
full-surface coating *(as opp. to pattern coating)* vollflächige Lackierung *f*
full-surface varnishing *(as opp. to pattern varnishing)* vollflächige Lackierung *f*
full title Überschrift über volle Seitenbreite *f*; *(book)* Haupttitel *m*
full tone Vollton *m*
full-tone density Volltondichte *f*
full-tone patch *(print control bar)* Volltonfeld *n*
fully assembled page fertigmontierte Seite *f*
fully automatic vollautomatisch
fully utilize *v (capabilities)* ausnutzen
functional reliability Funktionssicherheit *f*
function code Funktionskode *m*
furniture *(lead comp.)* Blindmaterial *n*, Formatstege *pl*, Schließstege *pl*
furniture cabinet *(lead comp.)* Stegregal *n*
fuzz *(paper)* Flusen *pl*, Fusseln *pl*, Papierflusen *pl*, Papierfusseln *m/pl*, Papierstaub *m*

G

gallery *(web press)* Galerie *f*
gallery-type camera Brückenkamera *f*
gallery-type press *(web press)* Etagenmaschine *f*
galley *(lead comp.)* Schiff *n*, Setzschiff *n*, Zeilenschiff *n*; *(text proof)* Fahne *f*
galley exposure *(photocomp.)* Spaltenbelichtung *f*
galley output *(photocomp.)* Spaltenausgabe *f*
galley proof Fahnenabzug *m*, Satzabzug *m*, Korrekturabzug *m*, Korrekturfahne *f*, Spaltenabzug *m*
galley proof press *(letterpress)* Abziehpresse *f*, Korrekturabziehpresse *f*, Spaltenabziehpresse *f*
galley typist *(text rec.)* Texterfasser *m*
gallium iodide lamp Gallium-Jodid-Lampe *f*
Gally platen press Gallytiegel *m*
gamma *(reprod.)* Gamma *n*
gamma value Gammawert *m*
ganged separations *pl (colour sep.)* Sammelauszüge *m/pl*
gang film Nutzensammelfilm *m*
gang forme *(combined forme)* Sammelform *f*
gang printing gemischter Druck *m*
gang sheet *(for multi-up processing)* Sammelbogen *m*
gang-stitcher Sammelhefter *m*
gang stitching Sammelheftung *f*
gapping *(occurs when blankets are mounted side by side)* Auseinanderdriften *n*, Einschnüren *n*
gap sealing Spaltverschluß *m*
Garaldics *pl (type classif.)* Französische Renaissance-Antiqua *f*
gas burner *(ink drying)* Gasbrenner *m*
gas discharge lamp Gasentladungslampe *f*
gas dryer Gastrockner *m*
gas flame dryer Gasflammentrockner *m*
gas oven *(ink drying)* Gasofen *m*
gate *(prod. line)* Weiche *f*
gatefold Fensterfalz *m*
gatefolded cover *(magazine)* eingefalzter Umschlag *m*
gather *v* zusammentragen; *(data, text)* erfassen
gatherer Zusammentragmaschine *f*
gatherer-stitcher Sammelhefter *m*
gathering *(data, text)* Erfassung *f*
gathering drum Sammeltrommel *f*, Sammelzylinder *m*
gathering machine Zusammentragmaschine *f*

gathering-stitching Sammelheftung *f*
gauge *(measuring instrument)* Meßgerät *n*, Meßinstrument *n*; *(micrometer)* Mikrometer *n*
gauge loss *(rubber blanket)* Stärkeverlust *m*
gauge pin Fröschchen *n*, Kapuziner *m*
gauze *(bookbinding, screen printing)* Gaze *f*
gauze and lining station *(book prod.)* Gaze- und Fälzelstation *f*
gauze paper Gazepapier *n*
gauze stretching device *(screen preparation)* Gazeaufspannvorrichtung *f*
gauzing *(book block)* Begazen *n*
gauzing machine *(bookbinding)* Begazemaschine *f*
gear Getriebe *n*
gearbox Getriebekasten *m*
gear drive Räderantrieb *m*, Zahnradantrieb *m*
gear mark Zahnstreifen *m*
gear meshing Zahnradeingriff *m*
gear train *(drive)* Räderzug *m*
gear wheel Zahnrad *n*
gelatine Gelatine *f*
gelatine coating Gelatineschicht *f*
gelatine film Gelatinefilm *m*; *(coating)* Gelatineschicht *f*
gelatine filter Gelatinefilter *m*
gelatine hardening Gelatineschichtgerbung *f*
gelatine layer Gelatineschicht *f*
gelatine paper Gelatinepapier *n*
gelatine relief Gelatinequellrelief *n*
gelatine roller Gelatinewalze *f*
gelatine solution Gelatinelösung *f*
gelatine tracing paper Gelatinepauspapier *n*
generate *v (image proc.)* erzeugen
generation copy *(drawing)* Generationskopie *f*
generic characters *pl (VDT)* Bildschirmschrift *f*
genuine gold blocking foil Echtgoldprägefolie *f*
genuine parchment Echtpergament *n*
geometrical sign geometrisches Zeichen *n*
German accent *(typesetting)* Umlautzeichen *n*
German final s *(ß)* Schluß-s *n*
German quote marks *pl* Gänsefüßchen *pl*
get in a line *v (type)* eine Zeile einbringen
get-up of a book Buchausstattung *f*
ghost image *(printing)* Doppelbild *n*, Geisterbild *n*
ghosting *(printing problem)* Dublieren *n*, Schablonieren *n*
ghost key *(skeleton black)* Skelettschwarz *n*
giant enlargement *(reprod.)* see giant reproduction
giant poster Riesenplakat *n*

giant reproduction *(reprophotogr.)* Projektionsvergrößerung *f*
gift-wrap *(paper)* Geschenkpapier *n*
gigantography *(large-size reprod.)* Gigantografie *f*
gilding *(book edge)* Golddruck *m*, Vergoldung *f*
gilding press Vergoldepresse *f*
gilding tool Schnittwerkzeug zum Vergolden
gilt edge *(book)* Goldschnitt *m*
gilt-edged *(book)* mit Goldschnitt *m*
gilt top edge *(book)* Kopfgoldschnitt *m*
give more ink *v (press)* Farbe zugeben
glare Glanzlicht *n*
glare-free monitor blendfreier Bildschirm *m*
glass-bead blanket *(ink-repellent)* Glasperlentuch *n*
glass graining marbles *pl* Glasmärbeln *pl*
glassine paper Pergaminpapier *n*
glass measure Glasmaßstab *m*
glass mounting Glasmontage *f*
glass negative Glasnegativ *n*
glass scale Glasmaßstab *m*
glass screen *(as opp. to film screen)* Glasraster *m*
glaze Glanz *m*; *(on roller, blanket)* Glätte *f*, Glanzglätte *f*
glaze *v (paper)* kalandrieren, satinieren
glazed blanket glattes Gummituch *n*
glazed board Glacékarton *m*, Glanzkarton *m*, Glanzpappe *f*
glazed paper Glacépapier *n*, glänzendes Papier *n*, Glanzpapier *n*, satiniertes Papier *n*
glazed roller glatte Walze *f*
glazing *(paper)* Kalandern *n*, Kalandrierung *f*, Satinage *f*
glazing calender *(papermaking)* Satinierkalander *m*
glazing cylinder *(papermaking)* Glättwalze *f*, Glättzylinder *m*
glazing machine *(papermaking)* Kalander *m*, Satinierkalander *m*
glazing press *(papermaking)* Glättpresse *f*
glazing roller *(papermaking)* Glättwalze *f*, Satinierwalze *f*
global retouching *(as opp. to spot retouching)* Vollretusche *f*
gloss Glanz *m*
glossary Glossar *n*
glossiness *(paper)* Glätte *f*
glossy additive *(ink)* Glanzzusatz *m*
glossy board Glanzkarton *m*, Glanzpappe *f*
glossy coated paper glänzend gestrichenes Papier *n*, glanzgestrichenes Papier *n*
glossy gravure varnish Glanzverschnitt *m*

glossy ink glänzende Farbe *f*, Glanzfarbe *f*
glossy overprint varnish Glanzüberdrucklack *m*
glossy paper glänzendes Papier *n*, Glanzpapier *n*
glossy print *(photoprint)* Hochglanzabzug *m*
glossy varnish Glanzfirnis *m*, Glanzlack *m*
glue Kleber *m*, Leim *m*, Kleister *m*
glue *v* beleimen
glue application Beleimung *f*, Leimauftrag *m*
glue application roller *(perfect binder)* Leimauftragswalze *f*
glue applicator disc *(perfect binder)* Leimscheibe *f*
glue beads *formation of* ~ Leimwulstbildung *f*
glue brush Leimpinsel *m*
glue coating Leimschicht *f*
glued-in insert *(magazine)* eingeklebte Beilage *f*
glued-in postcard eingeklebte Postkarte *f*
glue dispersion Klebedispersion *f*
glue flap *(folding box)* Klebelasche *f*, Klebezunge *f*
glue-folding Klebefalzen *n*
glue in *v* *(inserts, reply cards)* einkleben
glue joint Klebenaht *f*
glue level control *(perfect binder)* Leimniveaukontrolle *f*
glue line Leimspur *f*
glue mill Kleistermühle *f*
glue nozzle Leimdüse *f*
glue on *v* ankleben, anleimen, aufkleben, aufleimen
glue pot Kleistertopf *m*, Leimtopf *m*; *(perfect binder)* Leimbecken *n*
glue strip Leimstreifen *m*
gluing Kleben *n*, Klebung *f*, Beleimung *f*, Leimen *n*, Leimung *f*
gluing and lining machine Klebe- und Kaschiermaschine *f*
gluing edge *(adhesive binding)* Kleberand *m*
gluing head Leimkopf *m*
gluing machine Ableimmaschine *f*, Anleimmaschine *f*, Leimmaschine *f*
gluing primer Grundierleim *m*
gluing roller Leimwalze *f*
gluing unit Leimwerk *n*
gluing(-up) Verleimen *n*
glycerine Glyzerin *n*
glycol Glykol *n*
go *in one* ~ in einem Durchgang *m*, in einem Durchlauf *m*
goffering Gaufrieren *n*
gold blocking Golddruck *m*, Goldprägung *f*, Preßvergoldung *f*, Vergoldung *f*

gold blocking and embossing press Vergolde- und Prägepresse *f*
gold-blocking ink Vergoldefarbe *f*
gold blocking press Golddruckpresse *f*, Goldprägepresse *f*, Vergoldepresse *f*
gold-blocking type Prägeschrift für Goldprägung, Vergoldeschrift *f*
gold bronze *(powder)* Goldbronze *f*
gold bronzing primer Goldunterdruckfarbe *f*
golden section *(typogr.)* Goldener Schnitt *m*
gold foil Goldfolie *f*
gold ink Golddruckfarbe *f*
gold leaf printing Blattgolddruck *m*
gold paper Goldpapier *n*
gold printing Golddruck *m*
gold rule *(bookbinding)* Goldlinie *f*
gold stamping Golddruck *m*, Goldprägung *f*, Vergoldung *f*
good and bad copy counter Getrenntzähler *m*, Gutexemplarzähler *m*
good sheet Gutbogen *m*
go on impression *v* *(rollers, cylinders)* auf Druck gehen
gossip columns *pl* *(newspaper)* Klatschspalten *f/pl*
Gothic *(type)* Gotisch *f*
Gothic face Gotisch *f*
Gothic minuscule gotische Minuskel *f*
go to press *v* in Druck gehen
govern *v* *(control)* regeln, steuern
government printer Staatsdruckerei *f*
gradation Gradation *f*, Abstufung *f*; *(vignette)* Verlauf *m*
gradation curve Gradationskurve *f*
gradation etching Verlaufätzung *f*
gradation screen Verlaufsraster *m*
gradient *(reprod.)* Gradient *m*
gradual fading *(on the printed sheet)* Farbabfall *m*
graduate *v* *(image tones)* abstufen
graduated background Hintergrundverlauf *m*
graduated scale Einstellskala *f*, Feineinstellskala *f*, Maßskala *f*
graduated tint Flächenverlauf *m*, Tonverlauf *m*
graduated tones *pl* abgestufte Tonwerte *pl*
grain *(phot.)* Korn *n*
grain *v* körnen; *(paper)* narben; *(plate, stone)* schleifen
grain *(direction)* *(paper web)* Faserrichtung *f*, Bahnlaufrichtung *f*, Laufrichtung *f*, Papierlaufrichtung *f*
grained decalcomania paper Kornpapier *n*
grained transfer paper Kornpapier *n*

graininess *(film, plate)* Körnigkeit *f*
graining *(plate, stone)* Aufrauhen *n*, Schleifen *n*
graining balls *pl (plate graining)* Märbeln *pl*, Schleifkugeln *pl*
graining marbles *pl (plate graining)* Märbeln *pl*, Schleifkugeln *pl*
graining sand *(plate, stone)* Schleifsand *m*
grain screen Kornraster *m*
grammage *(paper)* Flächengewicht *n*, Quadratmetergewicht *n*
grams per sqm *(paper)* Quadratmetergewicht *n*
graph Diagramm *n*, Grafik *f*, grafische Darstellung *f*, Schaubild *n*
graphic artist Grafiker *m*
graphic arts *pl* grafische Künste *pl*
graphic arts camera Reprokamera *f*
graphic arts consultant Druckberater *m*
graphic arts consultation Druckberatung *f*
graphic arts dealer grafischer Fachhändler *m*, grafischer Zulieferer *m*, Zulieferfirma für die Druckindustrie
graphic arts editor Fachredakteur für Druck
graphic arts exhibition Druckfachmesse *f*, grafische Fachausstellung *f*
graphic arts film Reproduktionsfilm *m*, Reprofilm *m*
graphic arts industry Druckindustrie *f*, grafische Industrie *f*, grafisches Gewerbe *n*
graphic arts journal see graphic arts magazine
graphic arts magazine Druckfachzeitschrift *f*, grafische Fachzeitschrift *f*
graphic arts photography Reprofotografie *f*
graphic arts supplier grafischer Fachhändler *m*, grafischer Zulieferer *m*, Zulieferfirma für die Druckindustrie
graphic arts trade fair grafische Fachausstellung *f*
graphic communications *pl* grafische Kommunikation *f*
graphic design grafische Gestaltung *f*
graphic designer Designer *m*, Drucksachengestalter *m*, Gestalter *m*, Grafik-Designer *m*, Grafiker *m*
graphic design studio Gestaltungsstudio *n*, Grafikatelier *n*, Grafikstudio *n*, grafisches Atelier *n*
graphic design terminal see graphic display terminal
graphic design workstation Gestaltungsarbeitsplatz *m*, grafische Arbeitsstation *f*, grafischer Arbeitsplatz *m*
graphic display grafische Gestaltung *f*

graphic display screen Gestaltungsbildschirm *m*, Grafikbildschirm *m*, grafischer Bildschirm *m*
graphic display terminal Gestaltungsterminal *n*, Grafikterminal *m*
graphic monitor see graphic display screen
graphics Bild *n*, Grafik *f*
graphic scanner Grafikscanner *m*
graphics industry Druckindustrie *f*, grafische Industrie *f*
graphics processing Bildbearbeitung *f*, Bildverarbeitung *f*, Grafikverarbeitung *f*
graphics studio Gestaltungsstudio *n*, Grafikatelier *n*, Grafikstudio *n*, grafisches Atelier *n*
graphics supply industry grafische Zulieferindustrie *f*
graphic tablet *(electronic reprod.)* Grafiktablett *n*, grafisches Tablett *n*
graphic workstation Gestaltungsarbeitsplatz *m*, grafische Arbeitsstation *f*, grafischer Arbeitsplatz *m*
graphite retouching Grafitretusche *f*
graph paper *(graded in mm)* Millimeterpapier *n*
grave accent *(typesetting)* Gravis *m*
graver *(tool)* Grabstichel *m*, Stichel *m*
gravure see gravure (printing)
gravure cylinder Tiefdruckzylinder *m*
gravure cylinder production Tiefdruckformherstellung *f*, Tiefdruckzylinderherstellung *f*
gravure etching Tiefdruckätzung *f*
gravure ink Tiefdruckfarbe *f*
gravure machine Tiefdruckmaschine *f*
gravure package printing Verpackungstiefdruck *m*
gravure paper Tiefdruckpapier *n*
gravure printer Tiefdrucker *m*
gravure (printing) Tiefdruck *m*, Kupfertiefdruck *m*, Rakeltiefdruck *m*
gravure (printing) press Tiefdruckmaschine *f*
gravure (printing) unit Tiefdruckwerk *n*
gravure (process) Tiefdruck *m*, Kupfertiefdruck *m*, Rakeltiefdruck *m*
gravure publication printing Zeitschriftentiefdruck *m*
gravure retoucher Tiefdruckretuscheur *m*
gravure screen Tiefdruckraster *m*
gravure transfer machine Tiefdruckübertragungsmaschine *f*
gravure varnish Tiefdruckfirnis *m*, Verschnitt *m*
gray see grey
grease Fett *n*, Lagerfett *n*
grease *v* einfetten, schmieren
grease cup Schmierbüchse *f*

grease gun Fettpresse *f*
grease hole see grease lubrication point
grease lubrication Fettschmierung *f*
grease lubrication point Fettschmierstelle *f*
grease nipple Schmiernippel *m*
grease-proof fettecht
grease-proof paper fettdichtes Papier *n*, Fettpapier *n*
grease-resistance Fettechtheit *f*
greasing point Fettschmierstelle *f*, Schmierstelle *f*
Greek characters *pl* griechische Schrift *f*
Greek letters *pl* griechische Schrift *f*
Greek type griechische Schrift *f*
green filter Grünfilter *m*
greenish grünlich
greetings card Glückwunschkarte *f*, Gratulationskarte *f*, Grußkarte *f*
grey addition *(reprod.)* Grauaddition *f*
grey balance Graubalance *f*
grey board Graupappe *f*
grey component replacement *(reprod.)* Unbuntaufbau *m*
grey content Grauanteil *m*
grey fog Grauschleier *m*
grey level Graustufe *f*
greyness *(colour)* Verschwärzlichung *f*
grey scale Grauskala *f*
grey scale compression Graufstufenkompression *f*
grey-scale wedge Graustufenkeil *m*
grey screen *(as opp. to magenta screen)* Grauraster *m*
grey shades *pl* Grautöne *pl*
grey step wedge Graustufenkeil *m*
grey tints *pl* Grautöne *pl*
grey tones *pl* Grautöne *pl*
grey value Grauwert *m*
grey veil Grauschleier *m*
grey-wedge Graukeil *m*
grid *(photocomp.)* Schriftscheibe *f*
grind v *(blade)* schleifen
grinding *(ink)* Anreiben *n*, Anreibung *f*
grinding and graining machine Schleif- und Körnmaschine *f*
grinding and polishing machine *(cylinder prep.)* Schleif- und Poliermaschine *f*
grinding charcoal Schleifkohle *f*
grinding disc Schleifscheibe *f*
grinding machine Schleifmaschine *f*
grinding stone Schleifstein *m*
grind off v abschleifen
grind the ink v Farbe anreiben
grip *(gripper action)* Greiferschluß *m*
gripper Greifer *m*

gripper bar Greiferbrücke *f*, Greiferleiste *f*, Greiferstange *f*
gripper bite Greiferschluß *m*
gripper cam Greiferexzenter *m*
gripper carriage Greiferwagen *m*
gripper closure Greiferschluß *m*
gripper delivery Greiferauslage *f*
gripper edge *(sheet, rubber blanket)* Greiferkante *f*
gripper fold Greiffalz *m*; *(overfold)* Überfalz *m*, Vorfalz *m*
gripper-free varnishing device greiferloses Lackierwerk *n*
gripper margin *(sheet)* Greiferrand *m*, Greifersteg *m*
gripper opening Greiferöffnung *f*
gripper opening cam Greiferöffnungskurve *f*
gripper pad Greiferauflage *f*
gripper system Greifersystem *n*
gripper transfer system Greiferüberführungssystem *n*
groove Nut *f*, Hohlkehle *f*
groove v nuten
grooved roller geriffelte Walze *f*
groove router Nutenfräser *m*
grooving Nuten *n*, Nutung *f*
grooving cylinder Nutzylinder *m*
grooving machine Nutmaschine *f*
grooving plane Nuthobel *m*
grooving rule Nutlinie *f*
grooving tool Nutkamm *m*
grotesque typefaces *pl* Groteskschriften *pl*
ground glass screen *(camera)* Mattscheibe *f*
ground hatching *(cartography)* Schummern *n*
ground-wood pulp *(papermaking)* Holzschliff *m*
gsm *(paper)* **120 ~ paper** 120 g-Papier
guard *(book)* Fälzelstreifen *m*
guard cover Schutzabdeckung *f*
guard grid Schutzgitter *n*
guard hood Schutzhaube *f*
guard plate Schutzblech *n*
guards *pl* *(safety guards)* Schutze *pl*
guide *(book)* Führer *m*
guide assembly *(process-colour stripping)* Grundmontage *f*
guide bar Führungsleiste *f*
guide cam Führungskurve *f*
guide copy *(film guide)* Anhaltekopie *f*
guide mark Führungsmarke *f*; *(sheet registration)* Ausrichtemarke *f*
guide pin Führungsstift *m*
guide rail Führungsschiene *f*
guide roller Führungswalze *f*

guilloche Guilloche *f*, Schlangenlinienverzierung *f*

guilloche *v* guillochieren, mit Schlangenlinienverzierung versehen

guilloche screen *(security printing)* Guillochenraster *m*

guillotine Schneid(e)maschine *f*; *(paper cutter)* Papierschneidemaschine *f*, Papierschneider *m*, Planschneider *m*

gum Gummi *n*, Gummierleim *m*, Kleber *m*, Konservierungsmittel *n*, Leim *m*

gum arabic *(plate conservation)* Gummiarabicum *n*

gum etch Gummiätze *f*

gummed envelope gummierter Briefumschlag *m*

gummed labels *pl* gummierte Etiketten *pl*

gummed paper gummiertes Papier *n*

gumming and labelling machine Klebe- und Etikettiermaschine *f*

gumming machine Gummiermaschine *f*

gumming roller Gummierwalze *f*

gumming station *(offset platemaking line)* Gummierungsstation *f*

gum (up) *v* gummieren, konservieren

gutta-percha Guttapercha *f*

gutter *(typogr.)* Bundsteg *m*; *(word spaces one upon the other)* Straße *f*

gutter margin Bundsteg *m*

gutterstick *(lead comp.)* Bundsteg *m*, Zwischensteg *m*

H

hairbrush Haarpinsel *m*

hair hygrometer Haarhygrometer *n*

hairline feine Linie *f*, Haarlinie *f*, Haarstrich *m*

hairline cross Fadenkreuz *n*

hairline register genaues Register *n*, haargenaues Register *n*; *(colour)* genauer Passer *m*, haarfeiner Passer *m*, haargenauer Passer *m*

hairline serifs *pl (type)* haarfeine Serifen *pl*

hairline spaces *pl (lead comp.)* Haarspatien *pl*

hair space *(lead comp.)* Haarspatium *n*, Achtelgeviert *n*

halation *(phot.)* Lichthofbildung *f*, Schleierbildung *f*

half binding *(book)* Halb(ein)band *m*

half-cloth Halbleinen *n*

half-cloth binding *(book)* Halbleinen(ein)band *m*

half cylinder segment Halbzylindersegment *n*

half-deck *(newspaper press)* Eindruckwerk *n*, Farbdruckwerk *n*, Farbeindruckwerk *n*, Zusatzfarbwerk *n*

half em-quad *(typogr.)* Halbgeviert *n*

half em space *(typogr.)* Halbgeviert *n*

half-leather binding *(book)* Halbleder(ein)band *m*

half-linen Halbleinen *n*

half-linen binding *(book)* Halbleinen(ein)band *m*

half-page ad(vertisement) halbseitige Anzeige *f*

half page spread *(ad)* halbe Seite über den Bund

half sheet Halbbogen *m*

half-size web press halbbreite Rollendruckmaschine *f*

half title Schmutztitel *m*, Vortitel *m*

halftone see halftone image, halftone reproduction

halftone areas *pl (image)* Rasterpartien *f/pl*

halftone colour separation Rasterfarbauszug *m*

halftone density *(densitometry)* Dichte Raster, D_R

halftone dot Rasterpunkt *m*

halftone engraving *(letterpress)* Autotypie *f*, Autotypieätzung *f*, Rasterätzung *f*, Rasterklischee *n*

halftone engraving on copper Kupferautotypieätzung *f*

halftone enlargement Rastervergrößerung *f*

halftone etching *(gravure cyl.)* autotypische Ätzung *f*; *(letterpress)* Autotypie *f*, Autotypieätzung *f*, Rasterätzung *f*, Rasterklischee *n*

halftone exposure Rasteraufnahme *f*, Rasterbelichtung *f*

halftone film Rasterfilm *m*

halftone gravure (process) autotypischer Tiefdruck *m*, flächenvariabler Tiefdruck *m*, Rastertiefdruck *m*

halftone image Rasterbild *n*

halftone negative Rasternegativ *n*

halftone patch *(print control bar)* Rasterfeld *n*

halftone photography Rasterfotografie *f*

halftone plate *(letterpress)* Autotypieplatte *f*

halftone positive Rasterpositiv *n*

halftone print Rasterdruck *m*

halftone printing Rasterdruck *m*

halftone process Rasterverfahren *n*; *(letterpress)* Autotypieverfahren *n*

halftone range Rasterumfang *m*

halftone reproduction - hardcover binding

halftone reproduction Rasteraufnahme *f*, Rasterbild *n*, Rasterwiedergabe *f*, Rasterreproduktion *f*
halftone screen Autotypieraster *m*, Bildraster *m*, Raster *m*
halftone separation Rasterauszug *m*
halftone separation negative Rasterauszugsnegativ *n*
halftone separation positive Rasterauszugspositiv *n*
halftone separations *pl* gerasterte Farbauszüge *m/pl*
halftone value Raster(ton)wert *m*
halftone wedge Rasterkeil *m*
half-uncial *(type)* Halbunziale *f*
half-width rotary press halbbreite Rollendruckmaschine *f*
halo *(phot.)* Hof *m*, Lichthof *m*
halo-formation *(phot.)* Lichthofbildung *f*, Schleierbildung *f*
halogen lamp Halogenlampe *f*
halogen light Halogen-Licht *n*
halogen silver Halogensilber *n*
halogen silver emulsion Halogensilberschicht *f*
hammer finished paper gehämmertes Papier *n*
hammertone finish *(machine casing)* Hammerschlaglackierung *f*
hand binding *(bookb.)* Handeinband *m*
hand blocking Handprägung *f*, Handpressung *f*
handbook Handbuch *n*
hand-bound handgebunden
hand cleaner Handreiniger *m*
hand-coloured handkoloriert
hand composition Handsatz *m*
hand composition department Handsetzerei *f*
hand compositor Handsetzer *m*
hand crank Handkurbel *f*
hand cranking Durchdrehen der Maschine von Hand
hand-cut handgeschnitten
hand-cut overlay *(makeready of letterpress forme)* Handausschnitt *m*
hand-cut plate Handschnittplatte *f*
hand-develop *v (phot.)* von Hand entwickeln
hand drive Handantrieb *m*
hand feed(ing) Handanlage *f*, Handauflage *f*, Handzuführung *f*
hand-fold *v* von Hand falzen
hand-folded sample Handfalzmuster *n*
hand gilding Handvergoldung *f*
hand guard Händeschutz *m*, Handabweiser *m*, Handschutz(vorrichtung) *m/f*
hand-held densitometer Handdensitometer *n*

handhole *(corrugated cartons)* Handgriff *m*
hand impression Handabzug *m*, Handdruck *m*
hand ink-feed roller Handauftragswalze *f*
hand inking roller Handauftragswalze *f*
H&J *(photocomp.)* Silbentrennung und Ausschließen
handle Heft *n*
hand lever Handhebel *m*
hand lever press Handhebelpresse *f*
handling Bearbeitung *f*, Verarbeitung *f*
hand-made board Büttenkarton *m*
hand-made paper Büttenpapier *n*, handgeschöpftes Papier *n*
hand-operated guillotine Handhebelschneidemaschine *f*
hand-operated letter-press Buchdruckhandpresse *f*
hand-operated numbering machine Handnumeriermaschine *f*
hand press Handpresse *f*, Stempelpresse *f*
hand press printing Handpressendruck *m*, Pressendruck *m*
hand pull *(proofpress)* Handabzug *m*
hand release *(functions)* Handauslösung *f*
hand roller Handwalze *f*
handsaw Handsäge *f*
hand stamping Handprägung *f*, Handpressung *f*
hand wheel Handrad *n*
handwriting Handschrift *f*
hanger *(wall calendar)* Aufhänger *m*
hanging figures *pl* hängende Ziffern *f/pl*
hanging indent *(typesetting)* hängender Einzug *m*
hanging type *(lead comp.)* schiefstehender Satz *m*
hang-out *(book)* Buchaushänger *m*
hang tag Anhängeetikett *n*, Anhänger *m*
hardback *(book)* Hartdeckelbuch *n*, hartgebundenes Buch *n*
hardboard Hartpappe *f*
hard-bound book Hartdeckelbuch *n*, hartgebundenes Buch *n*
hard-chromed cylinder hartverchromter Zylinder *m*
hardcopy Beleg *m*, Ausdruck *m*, Belegausdruck *m*, Hardcopy *f*, Protokoll *n*
hardcopy *v* Beleg erstellen, ausdrucken
hardcopy colour proof *(cromalin)* Cromalin *n*, Farbaufsichtsproof *m*
hardcopy output Belegausgabe *f*
hardcopy printer Belegdrucker *m*, Protokolldrucker *m*
hardcopy proof Prüfbeleg *m*
hardcover binding Harddeckelbindung *f*

hardcover book - height to paper

hardcover book Hartdeckelbuch *n*, hartgebundenes Buch *n*
hardcover brochure Hardcover-Broschüre *f*
hard disk *(comp.)* Hartplatte *f*
harden *v* härten
hardener *(chem.)* Härter *m*
hardening additive Härtezusatz *m*
hardening agent Härter *m*
hardening bath Härtebad *n*
hardening fixing bath Härtefixierbad *n*
hard fibreboard *(bookbinding)* Hartfaserpappe *f*
hard gloss Hartglanz *m*
hard negative hartes Negativ *n*
hardness meter Härteprüfgerät *n*
hard packing *(cylinder)* harter Aufzug *m*
hard paper hartes Papier *n*
hard perforation *(without groove in the impression cylinder)* Hartperforation *f*
hard print *(photo)* harter Abzug *m*
hard proof Hardproof *m*, Papierbeleg *m*
hard rubber Hartgummi *m*
hardware *(comp.)* Hardware *f*, Maschinenausrüstung *f*
harmful to health gesundheitsschädlich
harmless to health gesundheitlich unbedenklich
harmonica fold Leporellofalz *m*, Zickzackfalz *m*
hatch *v* schraffieren
hatched type schraffierte Schrift *f*
hatching *(cartogr.)* Schraffe *f*, Schraffierung *f*, Schraffur *f*
hatching apparatus Schraffierapparat *m*
hatching ruler Schraffierlineal *n*
hazardous waste gefährliche Abfallstoffe *pl*
head Kopf *m*
headband *(book)* Kapitalband *n*
headbanding *(bookb.)* Kapitalen *n*
headbanding machine Kapitalmaschine *f*
headbox *(papermaking)* Stoffauflauf(kasten) *m*
headcap *(bookb.)* Häubchen *n*
header *(editorial)* Vorspann *m*; *(typogr.)* Seitentitel *m*
heading Rubrik *f*, Titel *m*, Titelkopf *m*, Titelzeile *f*, Überschrift *f*
head letter Anfangsbuchstabe *m*, Initiale *f*
headline Hauptzeile *f*, Kopfzeile *f*, Schlagzeile *f*, Titelzeile *f*, Überschrift *f*
headline display type Titelschrift *f*
headline reversed white on black Titelzeile in negativ
headline setting Titelsatz *m*
headline typeface Titelschrift *f*
head margin oberer Papierrand *m*, oberer Seitenrand *m*

head of purchasing Einkaufsleiter *m*
head of table *(tabular matter)* Tabellenkopf *m*
head-piece *(printer's flower)* Kopfleiste *f*, Leiste *f*, Zierleiste *f*
head register Höhenregister *n*
head rule Kopflinie *f*
head stick Kopfsteg *m*
head-to-foot exposure *(step and repeat m.)* Kopf-an-Fuß-Belichtung *f*
head-to-head exposure *(step and repeat m.)* Kopf-an-Kopf-Belichtung *f*
head trim(ming) Kopfbeschnitt *m*
head white *(make-up of lead type)* Vorschlag *m*, Überschlag *m*
heated joint iron *(book prod.)* Falzeinbrennschiene *f*
heat-fused printing plate eingebrannte Druckplatte *f*
heat-fusing *(offset plate)* Einbrennen *n*
heating bar *(foil stamping)* Heizsteg *m*
heat recovery *(on press)* Wärmerückgewinnung *f*
heat-resistant hitzebeständig, wärmebeständig
heat-seal *v* heißkaschieren, heißsiegeln
heat-sealing Heißkaschierung *f*, Heißsiegeln *n*, Heißversiegelung *f*
heat-sealing foil Heißklebefolie *f*, Heißsiegelfolie *f*
heat-sealing paper Heißsiegelpapier *n*
heat-seal laminator Heißkaschiermaschine *f*
heat-set commercial press *(web press)* Illustrationsdruckmaschine *f*
heat-set ink Heatset-Farbe *f*, heißtrocknende Farbe *f*
heat-set web offset Heatset-Rollenoffset *m*
heavy and thin boxes *pl (typogr.)* dicker und dünner Rahmen ineinander
heavy-duty Hochleistungs-
heavy forme schwere Form *f*
heavy line *(typogr.)* fette Linie *f*
heavy rule fette Linie *f*
heavy solid *(printing)* schwere Fläche *f*
Hebrew characters *pl* Hebräische Schrift *f*
Hebrew type Hebräische Schrift *f*
hectograph Hektograf *m*
height adjustable höhenverstellbar
height adjustment Höheneinstellung *f*, Höhenjustierung *f*
height gauge *(cyl. packing)* Höhenmeßgerät *n*
height justification *(letterpress m.)* Höhenzurichtung *f*
heights *pl (mapmaking)* Höhenpunkte *pl*
height to paper *(lead comp.)* Schrifthöhe *f*

helical (drive) gears *pl* schrägverzahnte Antriebsräder *pl*
helically toothed schrägverzahnt
heliochrome Heliochrom *n*
heliography Heliografie *f*
heliogravure Fotogravüre *f*, Heliogravüre *f*
Helioklischograph Helioklischograph *m*
Helium-Neon laser Helium-Neon-Laser *m*
helper Hilfskraft *f*
hemp paper Hanfpapier *n*
HeNe laser *(Helium Neon)* HeNe-Laser *m*
heraldic engraver Wappengraveur *m*
hexagonal dot wabenförmiger Rasterpunkt *m*
hickey remover *(offset press)* Partisanenfänger *m*, Butzenfänger *m*
hickies *pl* Butzen *m/pl*, Partisanen *pl*, Popel *pl*
hieroglyphics *pl* Bilderschrift *f*
high-capacity Hochleistungs-
high contrast starker Kontrast *m*
high-contrast image kontrastreiches Bild *n*
high-density solid satte Vollfläche *f*
high-glaze paper hochsatiniertes Papier *n*
high gloss Hochglanz *m*
high-gloss ink Hochglanzfarbe *f*
high-gloss lamination Hochglanzkaschierung *f*
high-gloss varnish Glanzlack *m*, Hochglanzlack *m*
high-gloss varnishing Hochglanzlackierung *f*
high-grade product hochwertiges Produkt *n*
high-grammage paper schweres Papier *n*
highlight *v (typogr.)* hervorheben
highlight areas *pl (image)* Lichterpartie *f*
highlight details *pl (image)* Lichterzeichnung *f*
highlight dot *(as opp. to shadow dot)* Lichtpunkt *m*
highlight dots *pl (halftone image)* Spitzlichter *pl*, Hochlichter *pl*, Lichter *pl*
highlight exposure Hochlichtaufnahme *f*
highlight gradation Gradation in den Lichtern
highlight mask *(reprod.)* Hochlichtmaske *f*, Lichtermaske *f*
highlight patch *(print control bar)* Spitzpunktfeld *n*
highlights *pl (halftone image)* Spitzlichter *pl*, Hochlichter *pl*, Lichter *pl*
highlight separation *(image)* Lichterzeichnung *f*
highly transparent film glasklare Folie *f*
high-performance Hochleistungs-
high pile Hochstapel *m*
high-pile delivery Hochstapelauslage *f*
high-pile feeder Hochstapelanleger *m*
high polish *(gravure cyl.)* Hochglanzpolitur *f*
high-polish copper *(gravure)* Glanzkupfer *n*

high-polish coppering Glanzaufkupferung *f*
high-polish coppering bath *(gravure)* Glanzbad *n*
high-polish coppering process *(gravure)* Glanzkupferverfahren *n*
high-quality brochure anspruchsvoller Prospekt *m*
high-quality paper Qualitätspapier *n*
high-quality printing hochwertiger Druck *m*, Qualitätsdruck *m*
high-quality product Qualitätsprodukt *n*
high rack store Hochregallager *n*
high-relief embossing Hochprägung *f*, Hochreliefprägung *f*
high-relief embossing machine Hochprägemaschine *f*
high-resolution monitor hochauflösender Bildschirm *m*
high-sensitive film hochempfindlicher Film *m*
high-speed cutter Schnellschneider *m*
high-speed film hochempfindlicher Film *m*
high-speed lens lichtstarkes Objektiv *n*
high-speed press Schnelläufer *m*
high-speed printer Hochgeschwindigkeitsdrucker *m*, Schnelldrucker *m*
high-speed (printing) press Hochgeschwindigkeitsdruckmaschine *f*
high viscosity Dickflüssigkeit *f*
hinged guards *pl (safety guards)* klappbare Schutze *pl*
hinged unit abklappbares Aggregat *n*, abschwenkbares Aggregat *n*
HKS matching system *(colour matching)* HKS-Farbsystem *n*
hoax *(wrong news)* Ente *f*
hoist *(paper handling)* Aufzug *m*, Hebeeinrichtung *f*, Hebevorrichtung *f*
hoist platform Hebebühne *f*
hold-down rollers *pl* Niederhalterollen *pl*
hole perforation *(as opp. to slot perforation)* Lochperforation *f*
hollow cylinder Hohlzylinder *m*
hologram Hologramm *n*
hologram stamping Hologrammprägung *f*
holography Holografie *f*
honeycomb mount Wabenfundament *n*
honeycomb plate *(embossing/stamping)* Wabenlochplatte *f*
hood Haube *f*
hooklocking *(forms set prod.)* Crimplock-Heftung *f*
hook up *v* anschließen
hopper feeder *(gatherers, wire-stitchers etc.)* Magazinanleger *m*, Einzelanleger *m*

hopper loader Anlegermagazin *n*
horizontal camera Horizontalkamera *f*
horizontal justification *(typesetting)* Zeilenausschluß *m*
horizontal vacuum frame Horizontalkopierrahmen *m*
horizontal whirler Horizontalschleuder *f*
hose connection Schlauchverbindung *f*
host computer Hauptrechner *m*, Host-Computer *m*
host system *(as opp. to sub-system)* Hauptsystem *n*
hot-air dryer Heißlufttrockner *m*
hot-air drying Heißlufttrocknung *f*
hot-air floatation dryer Heißluftschwebetrockner *m*
hot-air jet dryer Heißluftdüsentrockner *m*
hot-calender *v* heißkalandrieren
hot embossing Heißprägen *n*, Heißprägung *f*
hot embossing types *pl* Heißprägeschriften *f/pl*
hot enamel process Heißemailverfahren *n*
hot foil stamping Heißfolienprägung *f*
hotmelt (adhesive) Heißleim *m*, Hotmelt *m*, Schmelzkleber *m*
hotmelt applicator Hotmelt-Auftragsgerät *n*
hotmelt binding Hotmelt-Bindung *f*
hotmelt bound hotmeltgebunden
hotmelt compound Heißleimverbindung *f*
hotmelt gluing Heißleimbindung *f*, Heißleimung *f*
hotmelt nozzle gluing *(as opp. to roller gluing)* Hotmelt-Düsenbeleimung *f*
hot-metal composition Bleisatz *m*, heißer Satz *m*, Maschinensatz *m*
hot-metal composition department Maschinensetzerei *f*
hot-metal compositor Maschinensetzer *m*
hot-metal typeface Bleisatzschrift *f*
hot off the press druckfrisch, frisch bedruckt, soeben erschienen
hot sealing see heat-sealing
hot (spot) carbonizing Heißkarbonisierung *f*
hot stamping Heißprägen *n*, Heißprägung *f*
hot stamping foil Heißprägefolie *f*
hot stamping press Heißprägepresse *f*
hourly cost rate Stundensatz *m*
hourly machine rate Stundensatz *m*
hourly output Stundenleistung *f*
house brochure Hausbroschüre *f*
house colour Hausfarbe *f*
house corrections *pl* Hauskorrektur *f*
house journal Hauszeitschrift *f*
house magazine Hauszeitschrift *f*

house organ Hauszeitschrift *f*
house paper Hauszeitschrift *f*
housing *(mach.)* Gehäuse *n*
hue Farbton *m*
Humanistics *pl (type classif.)* Venezianische Renaissance-Antiqua *f*
humidity Feuchtigkeit *f*, Luftfeuchtigkeit *f*
hybrid computer Hybridrechner *m*
hydraulic hydraulisch
hydraulically operated hydraulisch
hydraulic clamping *(cutting m.)* hydraulische Pressung *f*
hydraulic control hydraulische Steuerung *f*, Steuer(ungs)hydraulik *f*
hydraulics Hydraulik *f*
hydraulic system Hydraulik *f*
Hydrocolor system Hydrocolor-System *n*, kombiniertes Farb/Feuchtwerk *n*
hydrogen carbonate Hydrogenkarbonat *n*
hydrolysis Hydrolyse *f*
hydrophilic hydrophil; *(offset)* wasserfreundlich
hydrophobic hydrophob; *(offset)* wasserabstoßend
hydroquinone developer *(photochem.)* Hydrochinon-Entwickler *m*
hygrometer Feuchtigkeitsmesser *m*, Hygrometer *n*
hygroscopic feuchtigkeitsempfindlich, hygroskopisch, wasseranziehend
hygrostability Feuchtstabilität *f*
hyphen *(typesetting)* Bindestrich *m*, Divis *n*, Querstrich *m*, Trennungsstrich *m*
hyphen(ate) *v* kuppeln
hyphenation *(text proc.)* Silbentrennung *f*
hyphenation and justification *(photocomp.)* Silbentrennung und Ausschließen
hyphenation program *(text proc.)* Silbentrennprogramm *n*
hyphenation routine *(text proc.)* Silbentrennprogramm *n*
hyphenation software *(text proc.)* Silbentrennprogramm *n*
hyphened word Kuppelwort *n*

I

identify *v (to mark)* markieren

ideogram Ideogramm *n*
idiot typing *(non-counting text input)* Endloserfassung *f*
idle cut *(cutting m.)* Leerschnitt *m*
idle gear Leerlauf *m*
idle machine times *pl* Maschinenstillstandszeiten *pl*
idler roller *(web lead roller)* Leitwalze *f*, Bahnleitwalze *f*, Papierleitwalze *f*, Umlenkwalze *f*
idle running Leerlauf *m*
idling Leerlauf *m*
illegible unleserlich
illuminate *v* ausleuchten, beleuchten
illuminated area *(light table)* Leuchtfläche *f*
illumination Beleuchtung *f*; *(book)* Ausmalung *f*, Illuminierung *f*; *(camera, plate frame)* Ausleuchtung *f*
illumination angle Beleuchtungswinkel *m*
illustrate *v* abbilden, illustrieren
illustration Abbildung *f*, Bild *n*, Illustration *f*
illustration printing *(web printing)* Bilderdruck *m*, Illustrationsdruck *m*
illustration printing paper Bilderdruckpapier *n*, Illustrationsdruckpapier *n*
illustrator *(artist)* Illustrator *m*
image Bild *n*
image *v (to expose)* belichten
image and text integration integrierte Bild- und Textverarbeitung *f*
image and text processing Bild- und Textverarbeitung *f*
image area Bildfläche *f*; *(type area)* Satzspiegel *m*; *(printing)* Druckfläche *f*
image areas *pl (as opp. to non-image areas)* Bildstellen *pl*, druckende Stellen *pl*
image butting Bildstoß *m*
image carrier Bildträger *m*
image combination Bildkombination *f*
image contrast Bildkontrast *m*
image coordinate Bildkoordinate *f*
image cut-out Bildfreistellung *f*
image definition Bildschärfe *f*, Durchzeichnung *f*, Zeichnung *f*; *(photocomp.)* Kantenschärfe *f*, Konturenschärfe *f*, Randschärfe *f*
image definition in the highlights Lichterzeichnung *f*
image definition in the shadows Tiefenzeichnung *f*
image depth *(typesetting)* Satzspiegelhöhe *f*
image details *pl* see image definition
image drum *(scanner)* Bildwalze *f*

image editing Bildbearbeitung *f*, Bildkorrektur *f*, Bildverarbeitung *f*
image element Bildelement *n*
image enlargement Bildvergrößerung *f*
image-free margin *(printed sheet)* druckfreier Rand *m*
image generator Bildgenerator *m*
image handling Bildverarbeitung *f*, Bildbearbeitung *f*
image information Bildinformation *f*
image-in-image combination Bild-in-Bild-Kombination *f*
image length *(printing)* Drucklänge *f*
image manipulation Bildbearbeitung *f*, Bildmanipulation *f*, Bildverarbeitung *f*
image merging Bildmischen *n*
image modification Bildänderung *f*
image overlap Bildüberlappung *f*
image overlay Bildüberlappung *f*
image positioning Bildpositionierung *f*
image preparation Bildaufbereitung *f*
image processing Bildverarbeitung *f*, Bildbearbeitung *f*; *(EIP) electronic ~* elektronische Bildverarbeitung *f*
image quality Bildqualität *f*
imager *(photo unit)* Belichter *m*, Belichtungseinheit *f*
image receiver *(telecom.)* Bildempfänger *m*
image recorder Bildaufzeichnungsgerät *n*, Bildrekorder *m*
image recording Bildaufzeichnung *f*
image rectification Bildentzerrung *f*
image rendering Bildwiedergabe *f*
image reproduction Bildwiedergabe *f*
image resolution Bildauflösung *f*, Bildschärfe *f*; *(photocomp.)* Kantenschärfe *f*, Konturenschärfe *f*, Randschärfe *f*
image retrieval *(comp.)* Bildaufruf *m*
image reversal *(lateral reversal)* Bildumkehrung *f*
image rotation Bilddrehen *n*
image scanning Bildabtastung *f*, Bildzerlegung *f*
image section Bildausschnitt *m*
imagesetter Belichter *m*, Belichtungseinheit *f*
image shadows *pl* Bildtiefen *f/pl*
image silhouette Bildfreistellung *f*
image size Bildgröße *f*
image splitting *(on screen)* Bildteilung *f*
image transfer Bildübertragung *f*
image transmission Bildübertragung *f*
image transmitter *(telecom.)* Bildsender *m*
image width Bildbreite *f*; *(printing)* Druckbreite *f*; *(typesetting)* Satzspiegelbreite *f*

imaging Belichten *n*, Belichtung *f*, Bildaufzeichnung *f*
imaging software Belichtungsprogramm *n*
imaging unit Belichter *m*, Belichtungseinheit *f*
imitation art paper Illustrationsdruckpapier *n*
imitation chromo board Chromoersatzkarton *m*
imitation die printing see imitation die-stamping
imitation die-stamping Imitationsprägedruck *m*, Imitationsreliefdruck *m*, Stahlstichimitation *f*, unechter Stahlstich *m*
imitation grey Unechtgrau *n*
imitation leather Kunstleder *n*, Lederimitation *f*
imitation leather binding *(book)* Kunstledereinband *m*
imitation leather paper Lederimitationspapier *n*
imitation linen Kunstleinen *n*
imitation parchment Pergamentersatz *m*, Pergamin *n*, unechtes Pergament *n*
imitation relief printing see imitation die-stamping
imitation relief stamping see imitation die-stamping
immersion *(electropl.)* Eintauchung *f*
immersion colouring machine *(paper)* Tauchfärbemaschine *f*
immersion depth *(electropl.)* Eintauchtiefe *f*
immersion-type inking unit *(gravure)* Tauchfarbwerk *n*
impaling pins *pl* Punkturen *f/pl*
imperfect copy fehlerhaftes Exemplar *n*
imperfect impression Fehldruck *m*
imperfect ink coverage blaßgedruckte Stelle *f*
imperfections *pl* Mängel *m/pl*
imperfect printing mangelhafter Druck *m*
imperfect quality mangelhafte Qualität *f*
imperfect register fehlerhaftes Register *n*; *(colour register)* Fehlpasser *m*, schlechter Passer *m*
implementation *(machine parts)* Einbau *m*
impose *v* ausschießen
imposed two-up im Doppelnutzen *m*
imposer camera Imposerkamera *f*
imposing stone *(letterpress forme)* Schließplatte *f*
imposing table *(letterpress forme)* Schließplatte *f*, Schließtisch *m*
imposition Ausschließen *n*
imposition film Standfilm *m*
imposition layout Ausschießschema *n*, Standskizze *f*
imposition pattern Ausschießschema *n*
imposition scheme Ausschießschema *n*
imposition sheet Ausschießbogen *m*, Standbogen *m*
impregnated paper imprägniertes Papier *n*

impress *v (the punch to produce a matrix)* einschlagen
impression Druck *m*, Abdruck *m*
impressional strength Druckkraft *f*
impression cylinder Druckzylinder *m*, Gegendruckzylinder *m*
impression on/off Druck an/ab
impression pressure Anpreßdruck *m*, Beistelldruck *m*, Druckkraft *f*, Druckspannung *f*
impression roller *(gravure)* Presseur *m*
impressions per hour *pl (i.p.h.)* Drucke pro Stunde *m/pl*
impression throw-off *(press)* Druckabstellung *f*
impression throw-on *(press)* Druckanstellung *f*
imprimatur Imprimatur *n*, Druckerlaubnis *f*, Druckfreigabe *f*, Druckgenehmigung *f*, Druckreiferklärung *f*
imprint *(book)* Druckvermerk *m*; *(magazine, newspaper)* Impressum *n*
imprint *v* aufdrucken, eindrucken, überdrucken
imprinter *(press)* Eindruckmaschine *f*
imprinting Aufdruck *m*, Eindruck *m*, Überdruck *m*
imprinting machine Eindruckmaschine *f*
imprinting unit Eindruckwerk *n*, Zusatzfarbwerk *n*
impulse emitter Impulsgeber *m*
in A4 size im Format (DIN) A4
inactinic filter inaktinischer Filter *m*
in alphabetical order in alphabetischer Reihenfolge *f*
in ascending order in aufsteigender Reihenfolge *f*
incandescent lamp Glühlampe *f*
incentive to read Leseanreiz *m*
inching *(slow back and forth of machine)* im Tastbetrieb fahren, Vorrücken *n*, Vortippen *n*, Vor- und Zurückpunkten *n*, Vorwärts/Rückwärtstippen *n*
Inciseds *pl (type classif.)* Antiqua-Varianten *pl*
in columns spaltenweise
incomplete copy fehlerhaftes Exemplar *n*, unvollständiges Exemplar *n*
incorporated *(machine parts)* eingebaut, integriert
incorporation *(machine parts)* Einbau *m*
increase contrast *v* Kontrast steigern; *(gradation)* aufsteilen
incremental measurement *(cutting m.)* Kettenmaß *n*
incunabula *pl* Erstlingsdrucke *m/pl*, Frühdrucke *m/pl*, Inkunabeln *pl*, Wiegendruck *m*
indent *(typesetting)* Einzug *m*; *(rubber blanket)* Druckstelle *f*, Eindruckstelle *f*

indent v *(typesetting)* einziehen, einrücken; *(rubber blanket)* eindrücken
indentation see indent
indent copy v *(text)* Text einziehen
independently driven unit separat angetriebenes Aggregat n
independent of operating cycle taktfrei, taktunabhängig, taktungebunden
independent workstation Offline-Arbeitsplatz m
index *(book)* Register n
index board Karteikarton m
index card Karteikarte f
index card punching machine Karteikartenstanzmaschine f
index cutting *(thumb index)* Registerschnitt m, Registerstanzung f
index cutting and printing machine *(thumb index)* Registerschneide- und -druckmaschine f
index cutting machine *(thumb index)* Registerschneidemaschine f
index file Kartei f
index letter Indexbuchstabe m
index management *(comp.)* Indexorganisation f
index of terms Wortregister n
index organisation *(comp.)* Indexorganisation f
index perforation *(thumb index)* Registerperforation f
index register *(comp.)* Adressenregister n, Adressenverzeichnis n
index tab cut Registerschnitt m
index tabs pl Registereinschnitte m/pl
index to advertisers Verzeichnis der Inserenten
India ink *(drawing ink)* chinesische Zeichentusche f
Indian ink chinesische Tusche f
Indian red Indischrot n
India paper Bibeldruckpapier n, Chinapapier n, Dünndruckpapier n, Florpostpapier n, Indiapapier n
indirect film *(screen printing)* Indirektfilm m
indirect letterpress (printing) indirekter Buchdruck m
indirect printing process indirektes Druckverfahren n
individual addressing *(mailroom)* Einzeladressierung f
individual cut *(cutting m., as opp. to repeat cut)* Einzelschnitt m
individual drive Einzelantrieb m
individual exposure *(reprod.)* Einzelaufnahme f
individually driven unit separat angetriebenes Aggregat n
individual shot *(reprod.)* Einzelaufnahme f

indivisible line untrennbare Zeile f
industrial artist Gebrauchsgrafiker m
industrial bookbinder Großbuchbinderei f
industrial printer grafischer Großbetrieb m, Großdruckerei f
industrial printhouse grafischer Großbetrieb m, Großdruckerei f
infeed *(web into a unit)* Einlauf m
infeed belt Einführband n, Einlaufband n
infeed roller *(web press)* Einführwalze f, Einzugswalze f
infeed unit *(web press)* Einzugswerk n
inferior character *(typesetting)* tiefgestelltes Zeichen n
inferior figures pl *(typesetting)* tiefgestellte Ziffern f/pl
infinitely adjustable stufenlos verstellbar
infinitely variable stufenlos verstellbar
infinitely variable speed control stufenlose Drehzahlregelung f
infinitely variable(-speed) gear stufenloses Regelgetriebe n
infinity sign Unendlichkeitszeichen n
information Information f
information carrier Informationsträger m
information channel Informationskanal m
information processing Informationsverarbeitung f
information service Informationsdienst m, Nachrichtendienst m
information transfer Informationsübertragung f
in-house coating *(plate coating)* Selbstbeschichtung f
in-house publishing hauseigene Herstellung von Drucksachen, hausinterne Druckproduktion f
in-house sensitized printing plate selbstbeschichtete Druckplatte f
in-house sensitizing *(plate sensitizing)* Selbstbeschichtung f
in-house standard Hausstandard m, hauseigener Standard m
in-house training betriebliche Ausbildung f
initial capital großer Anfangsbuchstabe m
initial character Anfangsbuchstabe m, Initiale f
initial (letter) Anfangsbuchstabe m, Initiale f; ***two-line*** ~ zweizeiliger Anfangsbuchstabe m, zweizeilige Initiale f
initial machine settings pl Maschinengrundeinstellungen pl
initial setting *(machine)* Grundeinstellung f
initial speed *(press)* Anfangsgeschwindigkeit f
initiate an apprentice v einen Lehrling gautschen
ink *(printing)* Druckfarbe f, Farbe f

ink absorption - ink jet lettering

ink absorption Wegschlagen der Farbe *n; (paper, fountain solution)* Farbaufnahme *f*
ink absorptivity Farbaufnahmevermögen *n*
ink acceptance Farbannahme *f*
ink additive Farbzusatz *m*
ink agitator Farbrührwerk *n*, Farbverrührer *m*
ink application Farbauftrag *m*
ink ball Ballen *m*
ink blade see ink duct blade
ink brilliance Farbbrillanz *f*
ink build-up *(on rollers, blankets etc.)* Farbaufbau *m*
ink can Farbbüchse *f*, Farbdose *f*
ink cells *pl (gravure cyl.)* Farbnäpfchen *n/pl*
ink change Farbwechsel *m*
ink circulating pump Farbumwälzpumpe *f*
ink-conducting areas *pl* farbführende Stellen *f/pl*
ink consistency Farbkonsistenz *f*
ink consumption Farbverbrauch *m; calculation of* ~ Farbverbrauchsberechnung *f; measurement of* ~ Farbverbrauchsmessung *f*
ink container Farbbehälter *m*, Farbcontainer *m*, Farbtank *m*
ink control Farbkontrolle *f*, Farbregelung *f*, Farbsteuerung *f*
ink control bar Farbkontrollstreifen *m*, Farbmeßstreifen *m*
ink control strip Farbkontrollstreifen *m*, Farbmeßstreifen *m*
ink control system Farbregelanlage *f*, Farbsteueranlage *f*
ink coverage *(on print sheet)* Farbdeckung *f*
ink density Farbdichte *f*
ink density control Farbdichteregelung *f*
ink density measurement Farbdichtemessung *f*
ink density measuring and control system Farbdichtemeß- und -regelanlage *f*
ink density measuring system Farbdichtemeßanlage *f*
ink density value Farbdichtewert *m*
ink deposits *pl* Farbrückstände *pl*
ink disc *(platen press)* Farbteller *m*
ink distribution Farbverteilung *f*, Farbverreibung *f*
ink distribution roller see ink distributor (roller)
ink distribution unit Farbverreibwerk *n*, Reibfarbwerk *n*
ink distributor (roller) Farbverreiber *m*, Farbreiber *m*, Farbreibzylinder *m*, Farbverreibewalze *f*
ink drawing Tuschezeichnung *f*
ink drying Druckfarbentrocknung *f*, Farbtrocknen *n*

ink dry-up *(on rollers, blankets etc.)* Eintrocknen der Farbe, Farbtrocknen *n*
ink duct Farbkasten *m*
ink duct blade Farbmesser *n*, Duktorlineal *n*
ink (duct) knife Farbmesser *n*
ink duct profile Farbzonenprofil *n*
ink duct roller Farbduktor *m*, Farbkastenwalze *f*
ink emulsification *(offset)* Farbemulsion *f*
inker *(inking roller)* Farbwalze *f*
ink factory Druckfarbenfabrik *f*, Farbenhersteller *m*
ink feed control Farbregelung *f*, Farbsteuerung *f*
ink feed(ing) Farbführung *f*, Farbgebung *f*, Farbzufuhr *f*
ink feed system Farbfördersystem *n*
ink film Farbfilm *m*, Farbschicht *f*
ink film profile *(inking unit)* Farbschichtprofil *n*
ink flow *(through ink train)* Farbfluß *m*
ink forme roller Farbauftragswalze *f*
ink formula Farbrezept *n*
ink fountain Farbkasten *m*
ink fountain blade see ink duct blade
ink fountain key see ink key
ink fountain roller Farbduktor *m*, Farbkastenwalze *f*
ink fountain separator Farbkastenteiler *m*
ink gap *(between rollers)* Farbspalt *m*
ink glaze *(rollers)* Farbglasur *f*, Farbglätte *f*
ink gloss Farbglanz *m*
inking Auftragung der Farbe, Farbauftrag *m*, Farbführung *f*, Farbgebung *f*
ink(ing) ball Druckerballen *m*, Farbballen *m*, Tampon *m*
inking circuit *(gravure press)* Farbkreislauf *m*
inking control Farbregelung *f*, Farbsteuerung *f*
inking correction Farbkorrektur *f*
inking fluctuations *pl* Farbschwankungen *pl*
inking pad Farbkissen *n*
inking primer Unterdruckfarbe *f*
inking profile *(inking unit)* Farbschichtprofil *n*
inking reduction Farbrücknahme *f*
ink(ing) roller Farbwalze *f; (gravure)* Einfärbwalze *f*
inking system Farbwerk *n*
inking unit Farbwerk *n; (gravure)* Einfärbwerk *n*
inking-up *(ink roller, ink train)* Einfärben *n; (letterpress forme)* Einwalzen *n*
inking-up of printing forme Einfärben der Druckform
ink jet addressing Ink-Jet-Adressierung *f*, Ink-Jet-Beschriftung *f*
ink jet imprint Ink-Jet-Aufdruck *m*
ink jet lettering Ink-Jet-Beschriftung *f*

ink jet printer Inkjetdrucker *m*, Tintenstrahldrucker *m*
ink jet printing Inkjetdruck *m*, Tintenstrahldruck *m*
ink key Zonenschraube *f*, Farbschraube *f*
ink (key) adjustment Farbzoneneinstellung *f*, Farbzonenverstellung *f*, Farbeinstellung *f*, Farbstellen *n*
ink key control Farbregelung *f*, Farbsteuerung *f*
ink key motor Farbschraubenstellmotor *m*
ink key position Farbzonenstellung *f*
ink key presetting Farbvoreinstellung *f*
ink (key) setting Farbzoneneinstellung *f*, Farbeinstellung *f*, Farbstellen *n*
ink knife *(spatula)* Farbmesser *n*
ink knife gap position Farbmesserspaltstellung *f*
ink knife position Farbmesserstellung *f*
ink knife setting Farbmesserstellung *f*
ink lay-down *(on print sheet)* Farbauflage *f*, Farbdeckung *f*
ink layer Farbschicht *f*
ink level control Farbniveauregelung *f*
ink leveller Farbniveau-Konstanthalter *m*, Farbniveauregler *m*
ink level system Farbniveau-Konstanthalter *m*, Farbniveauregler *m*
inkmakers *pl* Druckfarbenfabrik *f*, Farbenhersteller *m*
inkmaking Farbenherstellung *f*
ink manufacture Farbenherstellung *f*
ink manufacturers *pl* Druckfarbenfabrik *f*, Farbenhersteller *m*
ink match(ing) Farbabmusterung *f*, Farbabstimmung *f*, Farbeinstellung *f*, Farbnachstellung *f*
ink metering *(printing press)* Farbdosierung *f*
ink metering cylinder Farbdosierzylinder *m*
ink metering duct Farbdosierkasten *m*
ink metering lever Farbdosierhebel *m*
ink metering system Farbdosiersystem *n*
ink mill Farbmühle *f*, Farbenreibmaschine *f*
ink mist *(fast running rollers)* Farbnebel *m*, Farbsprühnebel *m*
ink mixer Farbmischer *m*
ink mixing Anmachen der Farbe *n*, Farbenmischen *n*, Farbmischung *f*
ink/paper combination Farbe/Papierkombination *f*
ink production Farbenherstellung *f*
ink pump Farbpumpe *f*
ink-receptive *(offset)* farbfreundlich
ink recipe Farbrezept *n*
ink reducer Farbverdünner *m*

ink-repellent farbabstoßend, farbabweisend
ink residues *pl* Farbrückstände *pl*
ink resistance *(paper)* Tintenfestigkeit *f*
ink roller leather Reiberleder *n*
ink roller wash-up device Farbwalzenwascheinrichtung *f*
ink screw *(ink duct)* Farbschraube *f*, Zonenschraube *f*
ink setting Wegschlagen der Farbe *n*
ink shut-off *(shutting the metering elements in the ink fountain)* Farbabbau *m*
ink slice Farbspachtel *f*, Farbspatel *m*
ink slide *(metering element in the ink fountain)* Farbschieber *m*
ink slur Farbschmitz *m*
ink solvent Farblöser *m*
ink specks *pl* Farbknoten *pl*
ink splashing Farbspritzen *n*
ink splitting Farbspaltung *f*
ink stability Farbstabilität *f*
ink stone Farbtisch *m*, Farbmischstein *m*
ink stripe *(ink vibrator)* Farbstreifen *m*
ink stripe width Farbstreifenbreite *f*
ink supply Farbführung *f*, Farbgebung *f*, Farbversorgung *f*, Farbzufuhr *f*
ink supply system Farbversorgungsanlage *f*
ink table Farbtisch *m*
ink tank Farbtank *m*
ink temperature Farbtemperatur *f*
ink testing device Farbtestgerät *n*
ink thinner Farbverdünner *m*, Farbverlängerer *m*
ink tin Farbbüchse *f*, Farbdose *f*
ink train Farbwerk *n*
ink transfer Farbübertragung *f*, Farbabgabe *f*
ink trapping Farbannahme *f*
ink trough Farbwanne *f*
ink unit see inking unit
ink unit control Farbwerkssteuerung *f*
ink unit cooling Farbwerkskühlung *f*
ink unit temperature control Farbwerkstemperierung *f*
ink unit wash-up device Farbwerkswascheinrichtung *f*
ink up *v* aufwalzen; *(letterpress forme)* einschwärzen
ink vibrator *(roller)* Farbheber *m*
ink viscosity Farbviskosität *f*
ink wash-up tray Farbwaschtrog *m*
ink-water balance *(offset)* Farb-Wasser-Gleichgewicht *n*
ink-water emulsification *(offset)* Farb-Wasser-Emulsion *f*
ink zone Farbzone *f*

ink zone display - instant register system

ink zone display Farbzonenanzeige *f*
inlet *(web into a unit)* Einlauf *m*
inlet conveyor Einführband *n*, Einlaufband *n*
in-line coating *(varnishing)* Inline-Lackierung *f*, Drucklackierung *f*
in-line finishing Inline-Finishing *n*, Inline-Verarbeitung *f*
in-line operation Inline-Betrieb *m*
in-line perforation *(on press)* Druckperforation *f*
in-line processing Inline-Verarbeitung *f*
in-line varnishing Inline-Lackierung *f*; *(on press)* Drucklackierung *f*
inner diameter lichter Durchmesser *m*
inner forme *(print forme)* innere Form *f*
inner margin Bund *m*, innerer Papierrand *m*, innerer Seitenrand *m*
inner page Innenseite *f*
inner sheet *(as opp. to cover)* Innenblatt *n*
inner title *(book)* Innentitel *m*
inorganic mineral spray powder anorganisch-mineralisches Druckbestäubungspuder *n*
in-plant printer Hausdrucker(ei) *m/f*
in-plant printing department Hausdruckerei *f*
in-plant printshop Hausdruckerei *f*
in position auf Stand *m*
input *(data, text)* Eingabe *f*, Erfassung *f*
input *v (data, text)* eingeben, einlesen, erfassen
input channel Eingabekanal *m*
input coding *(comp.)* Eingangssprache *f*
input command language Eingabebefehlssprache *f*
input data Eingabedaten *pl*
input device Eingabegerät *n*
input error Eingabefehler *m*
input error checking Eingabefehlerkontrolle *f*
input keyboard Eingabetastatur *f*
input media *(scanner)* Abtastvorlage *f*
input/output *(comp.)* Eingabe/Ausgabe *f*
input scanner Eingabescanner *m*
input station Eingabeplatz *m*, Eingabestation *f*, Erfassungsplatz *m*
input terminal Eingabeterminal *m*, Eingabeplatz *m*, Eingabestation *f*, Erfassungsplatz *m*
input unit Eingabegerät *n*
in register auf Stand *m*, paßgenauer Stand *m*, registergenau, registerhaltig; *(colour register)* passergenau, passerhaltig, paßgenau
inscription Aufschrift *f*, Beschriftung *f*
insert *(bound-in)* Beihefter *m*; *(loose)* Beilage *f*, Einleger *m*
insert *v (advertisement)* einschalten; *(flyers into magazine etc.)* beilegen, einlegen, einstecken; *(text)* einrücken, einfügen

insert advertising Beilagenwerbung *f*
insert copy *v (text)* Text einfügen
inserter *(mailroom)* see inserting machine
insert folder *(in-line fin.)* Beilagenfalzeinrichtung *f*
inserting *(inserts into newspaper)* Beilegen *n*, Einlegen *n*, Einstecken *n*
inserting drum Einstecktrommel *f*
inserting machine *(mailroom)* Einsteckmaschine *f*, Beilageneinsteckmaschine *f*
inserting quoin Einlegekeil *m*
insertion *(advertisement)* Einschaltung *f*, Insertion *f*
insertion of text Einfügen von Text *n*
insert leaders Auffüllen mit Führungspunkten, Auspunkten *n*
insert sheet Einsteckbogen *m*
insert space *v (typesetting)* Zwischenraum erweitern
insert space between lines *v* Durchschuß hineinnehmen
inset *(loose insert)* Beilage *f*
inset sheet Einsteckbogen *m*
insetting *(folded sections one into another; as opp. to gathering)* Ineinanderstecken *n*, Ineinanderfalzen *n*, Einstecken *n*
inside back cover *(magazine, book)* hintere Umschlaginnenseite *f*
inside front cover vordere Umschlaginnenseite *f*
inside page Innenseite *f*
inspection Kontrolle *f*
inspection copy Kontrollexemplar *n*, Prüfexemplar *n*
inspection sheet Kontrollbogen *m*, Probebogen *m*
install *v* installieren; *(machine)* aufstellen
installation *(machine)* Aufstellung *f*, Aufbau *m*; *(machine parts)* Einbau *m*
installation and removal *(e.g. of rollers)* Ein- und Ausbau *m*
install roller *v* Walze einbauen
instant access *(data, fonts etc.)* Sofortzugriff *m*
instant lettering *pl (e.g. Letraset)* Abreibeschrift *f*, Anreibeschrift *f*
instant paper plate *(small offset)* Direktdruckplatte *f*
instant picture *(e.g. Polaroid)* Sofortbild *n*
instant picture system Sofortbildsystem *n*
instant printer Schnelldrucker *m*, Sofortdrucker *m*
instant printing Sofortdruck *m*
instant printshop Schnelldrucker *m*, Sofortdrucker *m*
instant register system Schnellpaßsystem *n*

instruct *v* instruieren, anlernen
instruction *(comp.)* Befehl *m*, Kommando *n*
instruction address *(comp.)* Befehlsadresse *f*
instruction chain *(comp.)* Befehlskette *f*
instruction code *(comp.)* Befehlskode *m*
instruction leaflet Merkblatt *n*
instruction manual Anleitungshandbuch *n*, Betriebsanleitung *f*
instructions *pl* Instruktionen *pl*
instructor Ausbilder *m*, Instruktor *m*
intaglio Tiefätzung *f*; *(copperplate engraving)* Kupferstich *m*
intaglio engraving Fotogravüre *f*
intaglio offset Offsettiefdruck *m*
intaglio photogravure Fotogravüre *f*
intaglio (printing) Tiefdruck *m*, Kupferstich-Tiefdruck *m*, Stichtiefdruck *m*
integral *(machine parts)* eingebaut, integriert
integral density integrale Dichte *f*
integral screen density *(halftone screen)* integrale Rasterdichte *f*
integral sign *(maths setting)* Integralzeichen *n*
integrated *(machine parts)* eingebaut, integriert
integrated circuit integrierte Schaltung *f*
integrated density integrale Dichte *f*
integrated image and text processing integrierte Bild- und Textverarbeitung *f*
intelligent peripherals *pl* intelligente Peripherie *f*
intelligent video terminal intelligenter Bildschirmarbeitsplatz *m*
intelligent video workstation intelligenter Bildschirmarbeitsplatz *m*
intensify colour *v* Farbe kräftiger machen
interactive dialogorientiert, interaktiv
interactive mode interaktive Arbeitsweise *f*
interactive terminal interaktiver Bildschirm *m*
interchangeable cassette Wechselkassette *f*
interchangeable ink cassette *(slide-in carriage)* Farbwechselkassette *f*
interchangeable inking unit *(cassette-type inking unit)* Wechselfarbwerk *n*
interchangeable unit austauschbares Aggregat *n*, auswechselbares Aggregat *n*
interface *(comp.)* Interface *n*, Schnittstelle *f*
interface *v* anschließen, verbinden
interference filter Interferenzfilter *m*
inter-instrument agreement *(densitometers)* Exemplarstreuung *f*
interleave *v* *(with spoil sheets)* durchschießen, einschießen
interleaved print run *(with spoil sheets)* durchschossene Auflage *f*
interleaves *pl* *(set-off sheets)* Einschießbogen *pl*

interleaving paper Durchschußpapier *n*, Einschießpapier *n*
intermediate copy Zwischenkopie *f*
intermediate cut *(cutting m.)* Zwischenschnitt *m*
intermediate etching Zwischenätzung *f*
intermediate film *(reprod.)* Zwischenfilm *m*
intermediate floor design *(web press)* Zwischendeckausführung *f*
inter(mediate) negative *(reprod.)* Zwischennegativ *n*
intermediate piling Zwischenstapeln *n*
intermediate roller Zwischenwalze *f*
intermediate storage Zwischenlagerung *f*; *(comp.)* Zwischenspeicher *m*
intermediate tones *pl* *(image)* Zwischentöne *pl*
intermittent gluing *(as opp. to continuous gluing)* intermittierende Leimung *f*
internal memory *(comp.)* interner Speicher *m*
internal storage *(comp.)* interner Speicher *m*
interspacing Buchstabenabstand *m*, Laufweite *f*, Zeichenabstand *m*
inter-unit drying *(ink drying)* Zwischendruckwerkstrocknung *f*
interword spacing Wortabstand *m*
in the back *(book, journal)* im Bund
in the press im Druck
in time for the press rechtzeitig für die Drucklegung *f*
introduce the web *v* Papierbahn einziehen
introduction *(book)* Geleitwort *n*, Vorwort *n*, Einleitung *f*
in true register see in register
inverted commas *pl* *(quote marks)* englische Anführungszeichen *pl*
investment costs *pl* Investitionskosten *pl*
invitation card Einladungskarte *f*
invoice *v* in Rechnung stellen
invoice form Rechnungsformular *n*
invoice head Rechnungskopf *m*
ion blower Ionenbläser *m*
ionizer Ionisationsstab *m*, Ionisiereinrichtung *f*
ionizing rod Ionisationsstab *m*
ionizing unit Ionisiereinrichtung *f*
I.R. dryer IR-Trockner *m*
I.R. drying IR-Trocknung *f*
I.R. emitter IR-Strahler *m*
iris diaphragm *(camera)* Irisblende *f*
I.R. radiation IR-Strahlung *f*
I.R. radiator IR-Strahler *m*
irregular shapes *pl* *(CAD)* freie Figuren *f/pl*
irrespective of machine cycle taktfrei, taktunabhängig, taktungebunden
I.R. sensitive paper IR-empfindliches Papier *n*

I.R./U.V. combination dryer
IR/UV-Kombinationstrockner *m*
ISBN number ISBN-Nummer *f*
isodensities *pl (reprod.)* Isodensiten *pl*
isodensity curves *pl (reprod.)* Isodensitenkurven *pl*
isolate *v (a figure)* freistellen
isolated figure freigestelltes Bild *n*, freistehendes Bild *n*
isopropanol Isopropanol *n*
isopropanol substitute Isopropanolersatz *m*
isopropylic alcohol Isopropylalkohol *m*
issue *(publication)* Ausgabe *f*, Heft *n*, Nummer *f*
italic *(type)* kursiv
italic capitals *pl* Kursivversalien *f/pl*
italic lower-case Kursivgemeine *pl*
italics *pl* Kursivschrift *f*
italic type Kursivschrift *f*
item *(news item)* kurze Meldung *f*, kurze Nachricht *f*
ivory board Elfenbeinkarton *m*
ivory paper Elfenbeinpapier *n*

J

jacket *(book)* Schutzumschlag *m*, Umschlag *m*
jacket flap *(book jacket)* Schutzumschlagklappe *f*
jacket wrapping *(book prod.)* Schutzumschlagumlegen *n*
jam *(in the press)* see jam-up
jam sheet Knautschbogen *m*
jam-up *(in the press)* Papierknäuel *m*, Knautscher *m*, Stopfer *m*, Wickler *m*, Papierknautscher *m*, Papierstau *m*
Japanese vellum Japanpapier *n*
Japan paper Japanpapier *n*
jaw Backe *f*
jaw cylinder *(press folder)* Falzklappenzylinder *m*
jaw fold Klappenfalz *m*
jaw folder *(web press)* Klappenfalzapparat *m*, Klappenfalzwerk *n*
jet drying Düsentrocknung *f*
jet spray damping system Düsenfeuchtwerk *n*
jig saw Dekupiersäge *f*

job Arbeit *f*, Auftrag *m*, Job *m*; *current* ~ laufender Auftrag *m*
jobbing press Akzidenzmaschine *f*; *(letterpress)* Akzidenzpresse *f*
job(bing) printer Akzidenzdrucker *m*, Akzidenzdruckerei *f*
job(bing) typesetter *(typeshop)* Akzidenzsetzerei *f*
jobbing work Akzidenzarbeiten *f/pl*, Akzidenzen *pl*; *(typesetting)* Akzidenzsatz *m*
job change(-over) Auftragswechsel *m*
job completion date Endtermin *m*
job costing Auftragskalkulation *f*
job counter *(on press)* Auflagenzähler *m*
job data Auftragsdaten *pl*
job docket Arbeitstasche *f*, Arbeitszettel *m*, Auftragsbegleitzettel *m*, Auftragstasche *f*, Auftragszettel *m*
job file Auftragsdatei *f*, Auftragsdaten *pl*
job in process laufender Auftrag *m*
job in progress laufender Auftrag *m*
job number Auftragsnummer *f*, Job-Nummer *f*
job planning Auftragsvorbereitung *f*, AV *f*
job preparation Auftragsvorbereitung *f*, AV *f*
job preparation system AV-System
job printing Akzidenzdruck *m*
job sheet Arbeitszettel *m*, Auftragszettel *m*
job ticket see job sheet
job typesetting Akzidenzsatz *m*
jog *v (sheets)* gerad(e)stoßen, aufstoßen, glattstoßen
jogger *(jogging table)* Rütteltisch *m*, Rüttler *m*, Schüttelmaschine *f*, Glattstoßmaschine *f*, Rüttelmaschine *f*; *(side jogger at delivery)* Geradstoßer *m*
jogging delivery Schüttelauslage *f*
jogging machine see jogger (sheet pile)
jogging table Rütteltisch *m*
joint Stoß *m*; *(book)* Falz *m*
joint author Co-Autor *m*, Mitautor *m*
joint forming *(book prod.)* Falzeinbrennen *n*
joint forming rail *(book prod.)* Falzeinbrennschiene *f*
joint nipping *(book prod.)* Falzeinpressen *n*
joint nipping machine *(book prod.)* Falzniederdruckpresse *f*
joint pressing *(book prod.)* Falzeinpressen *n*
journal *(of roller)* Lagerzapfen *m*; *(publication)* Zeitschrift *f*, Magazin *n*, Journal *n*
journal bearing *(roller)* Achsenlager *n*
journalist workstation Redakteursterminal *m*
jubilee publication Jubiläumsschrift *f*

justification *(type)* Ausschließen *n*, Randausgleich *m*, Ausschluß *m*; *(roller)* Justierung *f*
justification mode *(typesetting)* Ausschlußart *f*
justification range Ausschließbereich *m*
justification routine Ausschließprogramm *n*
justification zone Ausschließbereich *m*
justified copy *(text-copy)* ausgeschlossener Text *m*
justified text ausgeschlossener Text *m*
justify *v (typesetting)* ausschließen, auf Block ausschließen, auf Zeilenlänge ausschließen
justifying input station *(text rec.)* rechnender Erfassungsplatz *m*
justifying typewriter zeilenausschließende Schreibmaschine *f*
justify to full measure *v (type)* auf volle Zeilenbreite ausschließen
just published neu erschienen, soeben erschienen

K

keep baseline *v (typelines)* Schriftlinie halten
keeping colour farbehaltend
keeping properties *pl* Archivfestigkeit *f*
keep open *v (halftones, meshes)* offenhalten
keep open the image *v (printing)* Druckbild offenhalten
kern *(part of the letter)* Überhang *m*
kerned letter überhängender Buchstabe *m*, unterschnittener Buchstabe *m*
kerning *(letterspacing)* Ausgleichen *n*, Laufweite *f*; *(pair kerning)* Unterschneiden *n*, Zeichenunterschneidung *f*
kerning knife *(lead comp.)* Unterschneidemesser *n*
kettle stitch *(book)* Fitzbund *m*; *(thread-stitching)* Übernähstich *m*
key *(ink key)* Farbschraube *f*, Zonenschraube *f*; *(keyboard, keypad)* Taste *f*
key *v (data, text)* erfassen, tasten
keyboard Tastatur *f*, Klaviatur *f*
keyboard *v (data, text)* erfassen
keyboard entry *(data, text)* Erfassung *f*
keyboarding *(data, text)* Erfassung *f*
keyboarding error Satzfehler *m*, Setzfehler *m*, Tastfehler *m*

keyboarding time Erfassungsaufwand *m*, Erfassungszeit *f*
keyboard layout Tastaturplan *m*
keyboard operating speed Erfassungsgeschwindigkeit *f*, Tastgeschwindigkeit *f*
keyboard operator Erfasser *m*, Taster *m*; *(text rec.)* Texterfasser *m*
key forme *(colour registration)* Paßform *f*
key in *v (data, text)* eingeben, eintasten, erfassen
keyless inking system schraubenloses Farbwerk *n*, Kurzfarbwerk *n*
keyline drawing Konturzeichnung *f*
keypad Tastatur *f*, Tastenfeld *n*
key sequence Tastenfolge *f*
keystroke Tastenanschlag *m*
keyword Stichwort *n*, Suchwort *n*
keyword index Stichwortregister *n*, Stichwortverzeichnis *n*
kiosk Kiosk *m*
kiss printing *(light printing pressure)* leichter Beistelldruck *m*, Druck mit leichter Druckspannung
knee-joint *(mech.)* Kniegelenk *n*
knife Messer *n*
knife adjustment Messeranstellung *f*
knife block Messerblock *m*
knife change Messerwechsel *m*
knife cylinder *(press folder)* Messerzylinder *m*, Schneidzylinder *m*
knife drive Messerantrieb *m*
knife-fold *(folding machine)* Schwertfalz *m*
knife folder Schwertfalzmaschine *f*
knife folding drum Messerfalztrommel *f*
knife folding machine Schwertfalzmaschine *f*
knife grinding machine Messerschleifmaschine *f*
knife holder Messerhalter *m*
knife life Messerstandzeit *f*
knife position Messerstellung *f*
knife wear Messerabnutzung *f*, Messerverschleiß *m*
knock down *v (letterpress forme)* klopfen
knock flat *v (letterpress forme)* glattklopfen
knock up *v (sheets)* gerad(e)stoßen, aufstoßen, glattstoßen
knot-free paper knotenfreies Papier *n*
knotter *(papermaking)* Knotenfänger *m*
knurled roller geriffelte Walze *f*, Riffelwalze *f*
kraftliner Kraftliner *m*
kraft paper Kraftpapier *n*

L

label Etikett *n*
label carrier paper Etikettenträgerpapier *n*
label cutter Etikettenschneider *m*
label dispenser Etikettenspender *m*
label gluing machine Etikettenanleimmaschine *f*
labelling Etikettieren *n; (addressing)* Adressierung *f*
labelling head *(addressing head)* Adressierkopf *m*
labelling machine Etikettiermaschine *f; (addressing)* Adressiermaschine *f*
label paper Etikettenpapier *n*
label printer Etikettendrucker *m*
label printing Etikettendruck *m*
label printing press Etikettendruckmaschine *f*
label punching machine Etikettenstanzmaschine *f*
labour costs *pl* Lohnkosten *pl*
labour intensive arbeitsintensiv, personalintensiv
lack of definiton *(reprod.)* Unschärfe *f*
lag *(web tension)* Nacheilung *f*
laid lines *pl* Wasserlinien *pl*
laid paper geripptes Papier *n*, Papier mit Wasserlinien
laid tint hinterlegter Raster *m*
laminate *(compound)* Laminat *n*
laminate *v* kaschieren, laminieren
laminated board kaschierter Karton *m*
laminating Kaschierung *f*
laminating adhesive Kaschierkleber *m*
laminating film Glanzkaschierfolie *f*, Kaschierfolie *f*
laminating foil Kaschierfolie *f*
laminating machine Kaschiermaschine *f*
lamination Kaschierung *f*
lamp Lampe *f*
lamp housing Lampengehäuse *n*, Reflektor *m*
lamp trolley *(horizontal camera)* Lampenwagen *m*
LAN *(local area network)* lokales Netzwerk *n*
land line *(telecom.)* Landleitung *f*
landscape size Langformat *n*, Querformat *n*
large body size *(type)* Großkegel *m*
large circulation *(newspaper, magazine)* Großauflage *f*, hohe Auflage *f*
large-circulation newspaper große Zeitung *f*
large commercial bookbinder Großbuchbinderei *f*
large commercial printer grafischer Großbetrieb *m*, Großdruckerei *f*

large edition *(book)* Großauflage *f*, hohe Auflage *f*
large focus lens Objektiv mit großer Brennweite
large folio Großfolio *n*
large format Großformat *n*
large initial letter großer Anfangsbuchstabe *m*
large printing concern grafischer Großbetrieb *m*, Großdruckerei *f*
large-scale projection *(reprod.)* Großprojektion *f*
large-scale reproduction Großbildreproduktion *f*, Großvergrößerung *f*
large size Großformat *n*
large-size poster Großbildplakat *n*
large-size (printing) press großformatige Druckmaschine *f*
large-volume bookbinding work große Bindequote *f*
large-volume printwork Großauflage *f*, hohe Auflage *f*
laser Laser *m*
laser beam Laserstrahl *m*
laser counter *(copy counting)* Laserstrahlzählgerät *n*
laser die-board cutter Stanzform-Laserschneider *m*
laser diode Laserdiode *f*
laser diode imagesetter Laserdiodenbelichter *m*
laser dot generator *(scanner)* Laserpunktgenerator *m*
laser-engraved lasergraviert
laser engraving *(gravure cyl.)* Lasergravur *f*
laser exposure Laserbelichtung *f*
laser exposure unit Laserbelichter *m*
laser font Laserschrift *f*
laser imager Laserbelichter *m*
laser imagesetter Laserbelichter *m*
laser imaging Laserbelichtung *f*
laser output Laserausgabe *f*, Laserbelichtung *f*
laser output unit Laserausgabeeinheit *f*, Laserbelichter *m*
laser platemaking *(offset)* Laserplattenherstellung *f*
laser plotter Laserbelichter *m*, Laserplotter *m*
laser printer Laserdrucker *m*
laser recorder Laseraufzeichnungsgerät *n*, Laserbelichter *m*
laser recording Laseraufzeichnung *f*, Laserbelichtung *f*
laser scanner Laserscanner *m*
laser setter Laserbelichter *m*
lasersetting Lasersatz *m*
laser technology Lasertechnik *f*
laser typesetter Laserbelichter *m*

laser typesetting - leather-bound volume

laser typesetting Lasersatz *m*
last line *(typesetting)* Ausgangszeile *f*
late breaking news *pl* aktuelle Nachrichten *pl*, letzte Nachrichten *pl*
late issue Spätausgabe *f*
late news *pl* see late breaking news
late-night edition Nachtausgabe *f*
latent blackening latente Schwärzung *f*
latent image latentes Bild *n*
lateral alignment seitliche Ausrichtung *f*
lateral distribution *(inking unit)* seitliche Verreibung *f*
laterally adjustable seitlich verstellbar
laterally reversed seitenverkehrt
lateral movement Seitwärtsbewegung *f*
lateral register Seitenregister *n*
lateral reversal *(reprod.)* Kontern *n*, Seitenumkehr *f*
lateral shifting of web *(web printing)* seitliches Wandern der Bahn
later installation *(machine parts)* Nachrüstung *f*, späterer Einbau *m*
lathe *(cylinder machining)* Drehbank *f*
Latin characters *pl* Lateinische Schrift *f*
Latin type Lateinische Schrift *f*
lattice feed table Scherengittertisch *m*
lay a (background) tint *v* Fond einziehen
lay angle *(sheet registration)* Anlagewinkel *m*
laydown device *(book prod.)* Niederlegvorrichtung *f*, Umlegevorrichtung *f*
lay-down speed *(photocomp.)* Belichtungsgeschwindigkeit *f*
lay (edge) *(sheet registration)* Anlage *f*, Anlagekante *f*, Anlegekante *f*
layer Schicht *f*
layer thickness Schichtdicke *f*
lay flat *v (paper)* flachliegen, planliegen
lay gauge *(sheet registration)* Anlegemarke *f*
lay guide see lay mark
lay mark *(sheet registration)* Anlegemarke *f*
layout Layout *n*, Aufriß *m*, Entwurf *m*, Skizze *f*
layout design Gestaltung *f*, Layoutgestaltung *f*
layout editor Gestaltungsredakteur *m*
layout element Gestaltungselement *n*
layout film *(assembly work)* Standfilm *m*
layout instructions *pl* Layoutangaben *pl*
layout man Layouter *m*, Entwerfer *m*
layout matter *(type matter)* Layoutsatz *m*
layout pattern *(page layout)* Seitenraster *m*
layout setting *(typesetting)* Layoutsatz *m*
layout sheet Einteilungsbogen *m*
layout specifications *pl* Layoutangaben *pl*
layout terminal Gestaltungsterminal *m*

layout-true display *(video screen)* layoutgerechte Darstellung *f*
layout typesetter Layoutsetzer(ei) *m/f*
layout workstation *(layout design)* Gestaltungsarbeitsplatz *m*
lay the edge *v* Kante anlegen
lay tints *v* see to lay a tint
l. c. see lower case letter
lead *(metal)* Blei *n*; *(of the web)* Voreilung *f*
lead *v (type matter)* durchschießen
lead alloy Bleilegierung *f*
lead and slug case *(hand comp.)* Materialkasten *m*
lead anode *(electropl.)* Bleianode *f*
lead base *(blocks)* Bleiunterlage *f*
lead characters *pl* Bleibuchstaben *pl*, Bleisatzschrift *f*
lead composition Bleisatz *m*
lead cut Bleischnitt *m*
lead dust Bleistaub *m*
lead edge of plate Plattenvorderkante *f*
lead edge of print Druckanfang *m*
lead edge of sheet Bogenvorderkante *f*
leaded matter *(type matter)* durchschossener Satz *m*
lead engraving Bleischnitt *m*
leader *(leading article)* Leitartikel *m*
leadering Auffüllen mit Führungspunkten, Auspunkten *n*
leaders *pl (dot leaders)* Führungspunkte *pl*
lead furniture Bleistege *pl*
leading *(typesetting)* Durchschießen *n*, Durchschuß *m*, Zeilendurchschuß *m*; *(photocomp.)* Zeilenvorschub *m*, Vorschub *m*
leading article Leitartikel *m*
lead(ing) edge Vorderkante *f*
leading points *pl (typesetting)* see leaders
lead matrix Bleimater *f*, Bleimatrize *f*
lead mould Bleimater *f*, Bleimatrize *f*, Bleiprägung *f*
lead mount *(blocks)* Bleiunterlage *f*
lead rule Bleilinie *f*
lead stereo Bleistereo *n*
lead type Bleibuchstaben *pl*, Bleisatzschrift *f*
lead waste Bleikrätze *f*
leaflet Broschüre *f*, Flugblatt *n*, Handzettel *m*, Prospekt *m*
leased line *(comp.)* Mietleitung *f*
leather ball Buchdruckerballen *m*
leather binding *(book)* Ledereinband *m*
leather board Lederkarton *m*, Lederpappe *f*
leather-bound in Leder eingebunden
leather-bound volume *(book)* Lederband *m*

leather case *(book)* Lederdecke f, Ledereinband m
leather cover *(book)* Lederdecke f, Ledereinband m
leather(-covered) roller Lederwalze f
leather covering Lederüberzug m
leather paper Lederpapier n
leave blank v *(layout, page make-up)* freischlagen, blankschlagen, blindschlagen, freilassen
leave free space v see to leave blank
leave out v *(typesetting)* weglassen
leave white space see to leave blank
leave windows v *(layout, make-up)* see to leave blank
LED array *(photocomp.)* LED-Zeile f
LED display LED-Anzeige f, Leuchtanzeige f
LED exposure *(photocomp.)* LED-Belichtung f
ledger Geschäftsbuch n
LED (light emitting diode) LED
left(-hand) pages pl linke Seiten pl
legend *(in maps, charts etc.)* Zeichenerklärung f
legibility Lesbarkeit f
legible lesbar, leserlich
length fold Längsfalz m
length of run *(printing)* Auflagenhöhe f; *(bookbinding)* Bindequote f
length-of-run capacity *(printing plate)* Auflagenbeständigkeit f, Auflagenfestigkeit f
length register *(web printing)* Umfangsregister n
lens *(phot.)* Linse f, Objektiv n
lens adjustment Objektiveinstellung f, Objektivverstellung f
lens aperture Blendenöffnung f, Blende f, Blendenwert m, Linsenöffnung f, Objektivöffnung f
lens arrangement Linsenanordnung f
lens board *(camera)* see lens holder
lens carriage Objektivschieber m
lens defect Objektivfehler m
lens holder Optikträger m, Objektivträger m, Objektivstandarte f
lens mount Linsenfassung f, Objektivfassung f
lens opening see lens aperture
lens panel see lens holder
lens selection Objektivanwahl f, Objektivwahl f
lens shutter Objektivverschluß m
lens slide Objektivschieber m
lens system Linsensystem n
lens turret Objektivrevolver m
letter Buchstabe m, Letter f, Schriftzeichen n; *(printing letter)* Druckletter f, Type f
letter v beschriften

letter-card Briefkarte f
letter case *(hand comp.)* Schriftkasten m, Setzkasten m
letterfold Wickelfalz m
letterhead Briefkopf m
letterhead paper Briefpapier n
letterhead printing Briefbogendruck m
lettering Aufschrift f, Beschriftung f, Schriftzug m, Schriftsatz m
lettering mask see lettering overlay
lettering overlay *(reprod.)* Schriftdecker m, Textmaske f
lettering pen Schreibfeder f
lettering reversed white on black Schrift in negativ
lettermailer Briefmailer m
letter paper Briefpapier n
letter-press Buchdruckpresse f
letterpress black Buchdruckschwarz n
letterpress cartridge Buchdruck-Zylindereinschub m
letterpress imprinting unit Buchdruck-Eindruckwerk n
letterpress ink Buchdruckfarbe f
letterpress inking unit Buchdruckfarbwerk n
letterpress machine Buchdruckmaschine f
letterpress printer Buchdrucker m, Buchdruckerei f
letterpress (printing) Buchdruck m, Hochdruck m
letterpress printshop Buchdruckerei f
letterpress roller Buchdruckwalze f
letterpress rotary Buchdruck(rollen)rotation f, Rollenbuchdruckmaschine f, Hochdruck(rollen)rotation f, Rollenhochdruckmaschine f
letterpress rubber blanket Buchdruckgummituch n
letterpress varnish Buchdruckfirnis m
letterset *(printing process)* Letterset m
letterspacing Sperren n, Spationieren n, Buchstabenabstand m, Laufweite f, Zeichenabstand m
levelling *(book prod.)* Egalisierfräsen n
levelling wedge Nivellierkeil m
lever Hebel m
lever control Hebelsteuerung f
lever fastener Hebelverschluß m
lever-operated guillotine Hebelschneidemaschine f
lever-press Hebelpresse f, Stangenpresse f
lever punch Hebelstanze f

lever stick *(hand comp.)* Winkelhaken mit Keilverschluß, Winkelhaken mit Hebelverschluß
lever stop Hebelanschlag *m*
lever switch Hebelschalter *m*, Hebelumschalter *m*
library Bibliothek *f*
library routine *(photocomp.)* Schriftenprogramm *n*
libretto *(music)* Libretto *n*
lie flat *v (paper)* flachliegen, planliegen
lie in the trim *v* im Beschnitt liegen
lift Aufzug *m*
lifting and lowering Heben und Senken *n*
lifting device *(paper handling)* Hebevorrichtung *f*, Hebeeinrichtung *f*
lifting platform Hebebühne *f*
lifting sucker *(feeder suction head)* Hubsauger *m*
lift truck Hubwagen *m*
ligature *(double letter)* Ligatur *f*, Doppelbuchstabe *m*
light barrier Lichtschranke *f*
light beam receiver *(light barrier)* Reflexkopf *m*
light board Leichtpappe *f*
light box Leuchtkasten *m*
light chopper *(camera)* Verschluß *m*
light colour helle Farbe *f*, Lichtfarbe *f*
light-conducting lichtleitend
light cycles *pl (contact exposure)* Lichttakte *pl*
light desk Leuchtpult *m*
light diffusion Lichtverteilung *f*
light distribution Lichtverteilung *f*
light emission Lichtstrahlung *f*
light emitting diode *(LED)* Leuchtdiode *f*
lighten *v (image areas, colours)* aufhellen
light-fast *(ink)* lichtecht
light-fastness *(ink)* Lichtechtheit *f*
light filter Lichtfilter *m*
light gathering *(halftone dot)* Lichtfang *m*
lighting Beleuchtung *f*; *(camera, plate frame)* Ausleuchtung *f*
lighting conditions *pl* Beleuchtungsverhältnisse *pl*
light integrator *(vacuum frame)* Lichtdosiergerät *n*
light intensity Leuchtkraft *f*, Lichtintensität *f*, Lichtstärke *f*
light lock for darkroom Dunkelkammerschleuse *f*
light meter Belichtungsmesser *m*, Lichtmeßgerät *n*
light metering Lichtdosierung *f*
lightness Helligkeit *f*
light pen Lichtgriffel *m*
light-proof lichtdicht, lichtundurchlässig
light ray Lichtstrahl *m*

light-sensitive coating lichtempfindliche Schicht *f*; *(printing plate)* Kopierschicht *f*
light sensitivity Lichtempfindlichkeit *f*
light signal Lichtsignal *n*
light source Lichtquelle *f*
light table Leuchttisch *m*, Montagetisch *m*
light-tight lichtdicht
light transmission Lichtdurchlässigkeit *f*
light trap *(halftone dot)* Lichtfang *m*
light typeface leichte Schrift *f*, magere Schrift *f*
light value Lichtwert *m*
light-weight paper Dünndruckpapier *n*, Florpostpapier *n*
light-weight sheet leichter Bogen *m*
light-weight signature leichter Bogen *m*
lignin *(papermaking)* Lignin *n*
limestone powder *(anti-set-off powder)* Kalksteinpuder *n*
limewood charcoal Lindenholzkohle *f*
limited edition *(book)* begrenzte Auflage *f*, beschränkte Auflage *f*
line *(typesetting)* Zeile *f*; *(typogr.)* Linie *f*, Strich *m*
line *v (board)* kaschieren, überziehen; *(envelope, bag)* ausfüttern
lineal fold Längsfalz *m*
lineal gluing Längsleimung *f*
lineal perforation Längsperforation *f*
lineal register Längsregister *n*
Lineals *pl (type classif.)* Serifenlose Linear-Antiqua *f*
linear gradation *(reprod.)* geradlinige Gradation *f*
linearity *(densitometry)* Linearität *f*
lineart Strichgrafik *f*, Strichvorlage *f*
line by line *(type)* Zeile für Zeile
line caster *(hot-metal comp.)* Zeilengießmaschine *f*
line casting Zeilenguß *m*
line casting machine Zeilengießmaschine *f*
line composing and casting machine Zeilensetz- und -gießmaschine *f*
line composition Zeilensatz *m*
line conversion *(reprod.)* Strichumsetzung *f*
line count Zeilenzahl *f*
lined bag gefütterter Beutel *m*
lined board kaschierter Karton *m*
lined box gefütterte Schachtel *f*
lined corrugated (board) kaschierte Wellpappe *f*
line definition Strichschärfe *f*
line development *(reprod.)* Line-Entwicklung *f*
line display *(moving display)* Laufschriftanzeige *f*

line displayed in bold - list of signatures

line displayed in bold *(typesetting)* fette Auszeichnungszeile *f*
lined paper bag gefütterter Papiersack *m*
line drawing Strichzeichnung *f*
line ending Zeilenausgang *m*, Zeilenende *n*
line engraving *(letterpress plate)* Strichätzung *f*, Strichklischee *n*
line etching *(letterpress plate)* Strichätzung *f*, Strichklischee *n*
line exposure *(reprod.)* Strichaufnahme *f*
line fall *(typesetting)* Zeilenfall *m*
linefeed Zeilenvorschub *m*
linefeed inhibit *(photocomp.)* Vorschub Null *m*
line filler Zeilenfüller *m*
line film *(reprod.)* Strichfilm *m*, Line-Film *m*
line hole punching *(continuous forms)* Führungsrandlochung *f*, Randlochung *f*, Remalinerlochung *f*, Transportlochung *f*
line holes *pl (continuous forms)* Führungsrandlochung *f*, Randlochung *f*, Remalinerlochung *f*, Transportlochung *f*
line illustration Strichabbildung *f*
line justification Zeilenausschluß *m*
line length *(typesetting)* Zeilenlänge *f*, Satzbreite *f*
line length remainder *(photocomp.)* Zeilenrestlänge *f*
line mask *(reprod.)* Strichmaske *f*
line measure *(typesetting)* Zeilenbreite *f*, Zeilenlänge *f*, Satzbreite *f*
linen Leinen *n*
linen board Leinenkarton *m*
line negative *(Reprod.)* Strichnegativ *n*
linen embossed writing paper Leinenpostpapier *n*
line network *(telecom.)* Leitungsnetz *n*
linen grain screen *(reprod.)* Leinenstrukturraster *m*
linen paper Leinenpapier *n*
linen tester Fadenzähler *m*
line ornament Linienornament *n*
line perforation Strichperforation *f*
line positive *(reprod.)* Strichpositiv *n*
line powder spray device Passagepuderapparat *m*
line printer *(proof printer)* Zeilendrucker *m*
line processing *(reprod.)* Line-Entwicklung *f*
line processor *(reprod.)* Line-Entwicklungsmaschine *f*
linerboard Kaschierkarton *m*, Kaschierpappe *f*
line reproduction Strichreproduktion *f*
liner sheet Kaschierbogen *m*
line scanning Zeilenabtastung *f*
line screen *(reprod.)* Linienraster *m*
line sharpness Strichschärfe *f*

line spacing *(typesetting)* Zeilenabstand *m*, Durchschießen *n*, Durchschuß *m*, Zeilendurchschuß *m*
lines per cm *(resolution)* Linien/cm
line splitting Zeilenspaltung *f*
line spraying *(on-Press powder spraying)* Passagebestäubung *f*
line start Zeilenstart *m*
line up *v (type)* in Linie bringen
line-up sheet Standbogen *m*
line weight Linienstärke *f*, Strichstärke *f*
line width Linienbreite *f*, Zeilenbreite *f*
line work *(reprod.)* Stricharbeiten *pl*
lining *(board)* Beklebung *f*, Kaschierung *f*, Überzug *m*; *(envelope, bag)* Fütterung *f*, Futter *n*
lining adhesive Kaschierkleber *m*
lining calender Kaschierkalander *m*
lining figures *pl (as opp. to old style figures with descenders)* Antiquaziffern *pl*, liniehaltende Ziffern *pl*
lining machine Kaschiermaschine *f*
lining paper *(bookcase, box etc.)* Beklebepapier *n*, Kaschierpapier *n*, Überzugspapier *n*; *(envelope, bag)* Futterpapier *n*
lining strip *(book)* Fälzelstreifen *m*
lining tissue *(envelope, bag)* Futterseidenpapier *n*
link-up Anschluß *m*, Verbindung *f*
link (up) *v* anschließen, verbinden
lino cut Linolschnitt *m*
lino print Linoleumdruck *m*
lino printing Linoleumdruck *m*
linotype composition *(hot-metal)* Linotypesatz *m*
linotype compositor Linotypesetzer *m*
linotype machine *(slug caster)* Linotype *f*
linotype operator Linotypesetzer *m*
linotype slug Linotypezeile *f*
linseed oil Leinöl *n*
linseed oil varnish Leinölfirnis *m*
lint *(paper)* Flusen *pl*, Fusseln *pl*, Papierfusseln *m/pl*, Papierstaub *m*
linting Linting *n*, Stauben *n*
liquid carton Flüssigpackung *f*
liquid crystal display *(LCD)* Flüssigkristallanzeige *f*
liquid ink *(gravure)* flüssige Farbe *f*
liquid polymer plate Flüssigpolymerplatte *f*
liquid toner *(electrophotography)* Flüssigtoner *m*
listing paper Computer-Tabellierpapier *n*, EDV-Papier *n*, Tabellierpapier *n*
list of misprints *(errata)* Verzeichnis der Druckfehler *n*
list of signatures *(in magazine prod.)* Tapete

list of subscribers Abonnentenliste *f*, Bezieherliste *f*
literal error Setzfehler *m*
lith development *(reprod.)* Lith-Entwicklung *f*
lith film *(reprod.)* Lith-Film *m*
litho *(film litho)* Litho *n*
litho blanket Offset(druck)tuch *n*
litho board Offsetkarton *m*
litho conversion (to gravure) Offset-Tiefdruck-Konversion *f*, O-T-Konversion *f*
litho etching Lithografie *f*
litho film Litho *n*
lithograph Lithografie *f*, Steindruck *m*
lithograph *v* lithografieren
lithograph drawn on plate (or stone) Künstlerlithografie *f*
lithographer Lithograf *m*
lithographic artist Lithograf *m*
litho(graphic) chalk Fettkreide *f*, Litho(grafie)kreide *f*
litho(graphic) crayon Fettkreide *f*, Litho(grafie)kreide *f*
lithographic drawing Lithozeichnung *f*, Steinzeichnung *f*
lithographic drawing ink Lithografietusche *f*
lithographic graining stone Lithografieschleifstein *m*
lithographic hand press Steindruckhandpresse *f*
lithographic leather roller Steindruckleaderwalze *f*
lithographic pen Lithografiefeder *f*
lithographic pencil Lithografenstift *m*
lithographic press Steindruckpresse *f*, Lithografiepresse *f*
lithographic printing Lithografiedruck, Steindruck *m*
lithographic printing house Lithografieanstalt *f*
lithographic printing ink Steindruckfarbe *f*
lithographic printing paper Steindruckpapier *n*
lithographic printing press see lithographic press
lithographic rubber roller Steindruckgummiwalze *f*
lithographic stone Lithografiestein *m*
lithographic varnish Lithografenlack *m*
lithographic zinc plate Zinkoffsetplatte *f*
lithography Lithografie *f*, Steindruck *m*
litho marker Lithomarker *m*
litho offset Offset *m*
litho (offset) ink Offset(druck)farbe *f*
litho (offset) plate Flachdruckplatte *f*, Offset(druck)platte *f*
litho (offset) press Offset(druck)maschine *f*
litho (offset) printing Offsetdruck *m*

litho offset (process) Offset(druck)verfahren *n*, Offsetprozeß *m*
litho (offset) screen Offsetraster *m*
litho print Lithografie *f*
lithoprint *v* lithografieren
litho stone Lithografiestein *m*
litho stripper Offsetmontierer *m*
litho stripping *(page assembly for offset printing)* Offsetmontage *f*
lith processing *(reprod.)* Lith-Entwicklung *f*
lith processor *(reprod.)* Lith-Entwicklungsmaschine *f*
litmus paper *(chem.)* Lackmuspapier *n*, Reagenzpapier *n*
live matter *(type matter)* Stehsatz *m*
load *(mech.)* Belastung *f*, Beanspruchung *f*
load *v* beschicken; *(comp.)* laden; *(hopper loader)* einlegen, auflegen
loader Beschickungsgerät *n*, Beschickungsvorrichtung *f*
loading Beschickung *f*
loading facility Beschickungsvorrichtung *f*
loading of reelstand *(web press)* Abrollerbeschickung *f*
loading platform Laderampe *f*, Verladerampe *f*
loading ramp see loading platform
load the program *v* *(comp.)* Programm laden
local area network *(LAN)* lokales Netzwerk *n*
local authority printing plant Behördendruckerei *f*
local edition *(newspaper)* Lokalausgabe *f*
localized retouching Spotretusche *f*
local newspaper Lokalzeitung *f*
local pages *(newspaper)* Lokalseiten *pl*
local press Lokalpresse *f*
local radio Lokalradio *n*
local section *(newspaper)* Lokalteil *m*
local TV Lokalfernsehen *n*
locking *(plate)* Aufspannen *n*, Einspannen *n*
locking bar *(press cyl.)* Spannleiste *f*, Spannschiene *f*
locking lever Arretierhebel *m*
locking screw Feststellschraube *f*
lock switch Schlüsselschalter *m*
lock up *v* *(letterpress forme)* schließen
lock-up device *(letterpress forme)* Schließvorrichtung *f*
lock-up frame *(letterpress forme)* Schließrahmen *m*
lock-up gap *(press cyl.)* Spannkanal *m*
lock-up system *(press cyl.)* Spannsystem *n*
log Protokoll *n*
logo *(logotype)* Signet *n*, Logo *n*

logo scanner Logoscanner *m*
logotype Logo *n*, Logotype *f*, Mehrbuchstabenletter *f*; *(hand comp.)* Silbentype *f*
logotype matrix *(type caster)* Mehrbuchstabenmatrize *f*, Logotypenmatrize *f*
long cut-off *(web printing)* stehendes Format *n*
long-fibred paper langfaseriges Papier *n*
long grain *(paper web)* in Bahnlaufrichtung *f*, in Laufrichtung *f*, in Papierlaufrichtung *f*, Schmalbahn *f*, stehendes Format *n*
long grain paper Schmalbahnpapier *n*
long ink lange Farbe *f*
longitudinal direction Längsrichtung *f*
longitudinal fold Längsfalz *m*
longitudinal gluing Längsleimung *f*
longitudinal perforation Längsperforation *f*
longitudinal register Längsregister *n*
longitudinal shaft drive Längswellenantrieb *m*
longitudinal shifting *(web printing)* Längsverschiebung *f*
longitudinal stitching Längsheftung *f*
long-lived product *(printed product)* langlebiges Produkt *n*
long print run Großauflage *f*, hohe Auflage *f*
long run (job) Großauflage *f*, hohe Auflage *f*
long run range *in the* ~ im Hochauflagenbereich *m*
long run work see long run (job)
long-term data *(photocomp.)* Stehsatz *m*
long-term filing Langzeitarchivierung *f*, Langzeitspeicherung *f*
long-term storage *(archiving)* Langzeitarchivierung *f*, Langzeitspeicherung *f*; *(photocomp.)* Stehsatz *m*
look over *v* nachsehen
loop stitching Schlaufenheftung *f*
loose insert Beilage *f*, Einleger *m*, Einsteckbeilage *f*
loose-leaf binding Loseblattbindung *f*
loosely spaced matter splendider Satz *m*
loosen up *v (sheets)* auflockern
loose sections *pl* lose Bogen *pl*, ungebundene Bogen *pl*
loss of tone Tonverlust *m*
lottery ticket Los *n*, Lotterielos *n*
Lotto form Lottoschein *m*
low contrast geringer Kontrast *m*
low contrast image kontrastloses Bild *n*
lower-case letters *pl* Gemeine *pl*, Kleinbuchstaben *m/pl*
lowering and lifting *(cutting material)* Senken und Heben *n*

lower knife Untermesser *n*
lower margin unterer Papierrand *m*, unterer Seitenrand *m*
lower side Unterseite *f*
lower side of web Bahnunterseite *f*
lower side printing *(web printing)* Unterseitendruck *m*
lower the pile *v* Stapel senken
lower wire *(papermaking)* Untersieb *n*
low-grade paper schlechtes Papier *n*
low-grammage paper leichtes Papier *n*
low pile Kleinstapel *m*, Tiefstapel *m*
low-pile delivery Niedrigstapelauslage *f*, Tiefstapelauslage *f*
low-profile design niedrige Bauweise *f*
low-profile keyboard flache Tastatur *f*
low-quality paper schlechtes Papier *n*
low-silhouette design niedrige Bauweise *f*
low-vibration running *(machine)* vibrationsarmer Betrieb *m*, schwingungsarmer Lauf *m*
low-viscosity ink dünnflüssige Farbe *f*, lange Farbe *f*
low-volume printwork Kleinauflage *f*
lubricant Lagerfett *n*, Schmiermittel *n*
lubricate *v* ölen, schmieren
lubricating grease Schmierfett *n*
lubricating nipple Schmiernippel *m*
lubricating oil Schmieröl *n*
lubrication point Schmierstelle *f*
luminescent ink Lumineszenzdruckfarbe *f*
lump formation *(spray powder)* Klumpenbildung *f*
luxmeter *(exposure control)* Luxmeter *n*
luxury package Luxuspackung *f*
LWC paper *(light weight coated)* LWC-Papier *n*

M

machine base Maschinenfundament *n*
machine capacity Maschinenkapazität *f*, Maschinenleistung *f*
machine chest *(papermaking)* Maschinenbütte *f*
machine-coated paper maschinengestrichenes Papier *n*
machine code Maschinenkode *m*
machine composing room Maschinensetzerei *f*

machine composition - magnesium plate

machine composition *(hot-metal comp.)* Maschinensatz *m*
machine compositor Maschinensetzer *m*
machine construction Maschinenbau *m*
machine control console Maschinensteuerpult *n*
machine controls *pl* Maschinensteuerung *f*
machine design Maschinenentwicklung *f*, Maschinenkonstruktion *f*
machine development *(photochem., as opp. to tray development)* Maschinenentwicklung *f*
machine diagram Maschinenschema *n*
machine down-times *pl* Maschinenstillstandszeiten *pl*
machine enclosure Maschinenkapselung *f*
machine engineering Maschinenbau *m*
machine equipment Maschinenpark *m*
machine factory Maschinenfabrik *f*
machine-finished paper maschinenglattes Papier *n*
machine foundation Maschinenfundament *n*
machine frame Maschinengestell *n*, Maschinenrahmen *m*
machine functions *pl* Maschinenfunktionen *pl*
machine gilding Preßvergoldung *f*
machine hooding Maschinenkapselung *f*
machine language *(comp.)* Maschinensprache *f*
machine maker Maschinenhersteller *m*
machine manufacturer Maschinenhersteller *m*
machine minder Maschinenführer *m*, Maschinenmeister *m*
machine monitoring Maschinenüberwachung *f*
machine operation Maschinenbedienung *f*, Maschinenbetrieb *m*
machine output Maschinenleistung *f*
machine performance Maschinenleistung *f*
machine processing *(photochem., as opp. to tray development)* Maschinenentwicklung *f*
machine program Maschinenprogramm *n*
machine proof *(press proof)* Maschinenabzug *m*, Maschinenbogen *m*
machine-readable document maschinenlesbares Dokument *n*
machine removal Maschinendemontage *f*
machine room Maschinensaal *m*
machine ruler Liniermaschine *f*
machine ruler thread Liniermaschinenfaden *m*
machine run Maschinenlauf *m*
machinery equipment Maschinenausrüstung *f*
machinery failure Maschinendefekt *m*
machinery trouble Maschinendefekt *m*
machine-set *(type)* maschinengesetzt
machine-sized paper maschinengeleimtes Papier *n*
machine speed Maschinengeschwindigkeit *f*

machine standstill Maschinenstillstand *m*
machine start-up Maschinenstart *m*
machine start-up without jerking ruckfreier Maschinenanlauf *m*
machine start-up without jolting ruckfreier Maschinenanlauf *m*
machine stop(page) Maschinenstillstand *m*, Maschinenstopp *m*
machine supervision Maschinenüberwachung *f*
machine supervisor Maschinenführer *m*
machine tape Maschinenband *n*
machine typesetter Maschinensetzer *m*
machine wear Maschinenverschleiß *m*
mackle Schmitz *m*
mackle *v* schmitzen
macro (command) *(Comp.)* Makro *n*, Makrobefehl *m*
macroprogramming Makroprogrammierung *f*
made to measure *(modular systems)* maßgeschneidert, nach Maß, zugeschnitten
made to order see made to measure
magazine *(of feeder, line caster etc.)* Magazin *n*; *(publication)* Zeitschrift *f*, Illustrierte *f*, Magazin *n*, Journal *n*
magazine advertising Zeitschriftenwerbung *f*
magazine change *(line caster)* Magazinwechsel *m*
magazine printer and publisher Zeitschriftendruckerei und -verlag
magazine printing Zeitschriftendruck *m*
magazine printing and publishing house Zeitschriftendruckerei und -verlag
magazine shifting *(line caster)* Magazinumschaltung *f*
magazine title Zeitschriftenkopf *m*
magazine turner bars *pl (web press)* Magazinwendestangen *pl*
magazine turner-bar superstructure *(web press)* Magazinaufbau *m*
magenta *(process colour)* Magenta *n*
magenta contact screen *(reprod.)* Magentakontaktraster *m*
magenta film Magentafilm *m*
magenta forme Magentaform *f*
magenta glass screen *(camera)* Magentadistanzraster *m*
magenta plate Magentaplatte *f*
magenta printer *(magenta plate)* Magentaplatte *f*; *(magenta sep. film)* Magentafilm *m*
magenta separation *(reprod.)* Magentaauszug *m*
magnesia powder Magnesiapulver *n*
magnesium etching Magnesiumätzung *f*
magnesium plate *(letterpress plate)* Magnesiumklischee *n*, Magnesiumplatte *f*

magnetic base *(for printing plates)* Magnetunterlage *f*
magnetic card Magnetkarte *f*
magnetic cassette Magnetbandkassette *f*
magnetic cylinder *(for printing plates)* Magnetzylinder *m*
magnetic disk Magnetplatte *f*
magnetic disk store Magnetplattenspeicher *m*
magnetic document reading *(text proc.)* magnetische Beleglesung *f*
magnetic drum store *(comp.)* Magnettrommelspeicher *m*
magnetic ink Magnetfarbe *f*
magnetic ink character recognition *(MICR)* magnetische Zeichenerkennung *f*
magnetic memory Magnetspeicher *m*
magnetic saddle *(for stereotypes)* Magnetsattel *m*
magnetic store Magnetspeicher *m*
magnetic tape Magnetband *n*
magnetic tape drive Bandlaufwerk *n*
magnetic tape reader Magnetbandleser *m*
magnetic tape station Magnetbandstation *f*
magnetic tape store Magnetbandspeicher *m*
magnetography Magnetografie *f*
magnification *(reprod.)* Vergrößerung *f*
magnifier Vergrößerungsglas *n*, Fadenzähler *m*, Lupe *f*
magnifying Vergrößern *n*
magnifying glass Lupe *f*, Vergrößerungsglas *n*
magtape Magnetband *n*
mail circulation *(newspaper, magazine)* Postauflage *f*
mailer *(direct mail)* Mailer *m*, Werbedrucksache *f*
mailing *(direct mail)* Mailing *m*, Werbedrucksache *f*
mailing address Versandadresse *f*
mailing line *(mailroom)* Versandanlage *f*
mailings *pl (direct mail)* Werbeblätter *pl*
mail-order catalogue Versandhauskatalog *m*
mailroom Versandabteilung *f*, Versandraum *m*
mailroom equipment Versandraumausrüstung *f*, Versandraumeinrichtung *f*
mailroom system Versandraumanlage *f*
main bearing Hauptlager *n*
main control console *(press)* Hauptbedienungsstand *m*
main drive Hauptantrieb *m*
main exposure *(camera screening)* Hauptbelichtung *f*
mainframe computer Großrechner *m*, Hauptrechner *m*
main memory *(comp.)* Festspeicher *m*, Hauptspeicher *m*
main processor Hauptrechner *m*
main section *(print converting)* Hauptprodukt *n*
main shaft Hauptantriebswelle *f*, Hauptwelle *f*
main storage Hauptspeicher *m*
main stroke *(part of the letter)* Grundstrich *m*
main switch Hauptschalter *m*
main system *(as opp. to sub-system)* Hauptsystem *n*
maintain register within narrow limits *v* Register in engen Grenzen halten
maintenance *(mach.)* Instandhaltung *f*, Pflege *f*, Unterhalt *m*, Wartung *f*
maintenance-free wartungsfrei
maintenance requirements *pl* Wartungsbedarf *m*
main title Haupttitel *m*
majuscule Majuskel *f*
make a clean copy *v* ins Reine abschreiben
make-and-hold order Abrufauftrag *m*
make an exposure *v (camera)* aufnehmen
make colour stronger *v* Farbe kräftiger machen
make copy fit into *(text)* Text einpassen
make full use of *v (capabilities)* ausnutzen
makeready *(machine)* Einrichten *n*, Einrichtung *f*; *(letterpress)* Zurichtung *f*
make ready *v (machine)* einrichten; *(letterpress)* zurichten
makeready knife Zurichtemesser *n*
makeready of cutting-die Stanzzurichtung *f*
makeready of illustrations *(letterpress)* Bildzurichtung *f*
makeready paper *(letterpress)* Zurichtepapier *n*
makeready proof *(letterpress)* Zurichtungsabzug *m*
makeready sheet *(letterpress)* Zurichtebogen *m*
makeready times *pl* Einrichtezeiten *f/pl*, Rüstzeiten *f/pl*
makeready waste Einrichtemakulatur *f*
maker-up *(lead comp.)* Metteur *m*
make the plate ink-receptive *v* Platte farbfreundlich machen
make the plate water-receptive *v (book)* Platte wasserfreundlich machen
make-up *(page make-up)* Montage *f*, Umbruch *m*; *(lead comp.)* Mettage *f*; *(newspaper design)* Aufmachung *f*
make up *v (page make-up)* umbrechen
make-up department *(page make-up)* Montageabteilung *f*, Umbruchabteilung *f*
make-up editor Umbruchredakteur *m*
make-up galley *(lead comp.)* Umbrechschiff *n*
make-up man *(lead comp.)* Metteur *m*

make-up rules *pl* Umbruchlinien *pl*
make-up sheet Montagebogen *m*
make-up table Montagetisch *m*, Umbruchtisch *m*
male die *(embossing die)* Prägepatrize *f*
malfunction Störung *f*, Laufstörung *f*, Maschinenstörung *f*
malfunction monitoring Störungsüberwachung *f*
management information system Management-Informationssystem *n*
manganese Mangan *n*
Manilla board Manilakarton *m*
Manilla paper Manilapapier *n*, Tauenpapier *n*
manipulate *v (electronic image proc.)* manipulieren
manual Handbuch *n*, Lehrbuch *n*
manual feed(ing) Handanlage *f*, Handzuführung *f*
manual ink-feed Handeinfärbung *f*
manual inking-up Handeinfärbung *f*
manual makeready Handzurichtung *f*
manual operation Handbetrieb *m*
manual retouching *(film)* manuelle Retusche *f*
Manuals *pl (type classif.)* Handschriftliche Antiqua *f*
manual typesetting Handsatz *m*
manual waxer *(paste-up)* Handwachsgerät *n*
manuscript Manuskript *n*, Satzvorlage *f*
map Karte *f*, Landkarte *f*
mapmaker Kartenzeichner *m*, Kartograf *m*
mapmaking Kartografie *f*
map paper Atlaspapier *n*, Landkartenpapier *n*
map printing Kartendruck *m*, Landkartendruck *m*
marble *v (gravure ink)* perlen
marbled *(bood edge, endpaper)* gesprenkelt, marmoriert
marbled edge *(book)* Marmorschnitt *m*
marbled paper marmoriertes Papier *n*
marble-edged *(book)* mit Marmorschnitt
marbling Marmorierung *f*
margin Seitenrand *m*, Papierrand *m*, Rand *m*, Satzkante *f*, Steg *m*, Satzrand *m*
marginal decoration Randverzierung *f*
marginal figure Marginalziffer *f*, Randziffer *f*
marginal heading Marginaltitel *m*
marginal mark Randzeichen *n*
marginal note Randnote *f*, Marginalie *f*, Randbemerkung *f*
margin width Randbreite *f*
mark *(finger print)* Abdruck *m*; *(proofreading)* Korrektur *f*, Korrekturzeichen *n*
mark *v* markieren
market for printed matter Drucksachenmarkt *m*

marking *(mailroom)* Signieren *n*
markings *pl (on the print sheet)* Schmierstellen *pl*
mark reader Markierungsleser *m*
mark-up *(text copy)* Manuskriptaufbereitung *f*, Manuskriptauszeichnung *f*, Manuskriptbearbeitung *f*, Manuskriptvorbereitung *f*, Satzkorrektur *f*, Satzvorbereitung *f*
mark(-up) *v (proofreading)* anstreichen, anzeichnen, auszeichnen, korrigieren
mask Maske *f*; *(overlay)* Aufleger *m*, Decker *m*
mask *v* maskieren
mask cutting knife Maskenschneidmesser *n*
mask cutting system *(CAD)* Maskenschneidsystem *n*
mask entry *(video screen)* Maskeneintrag *m*
mask exposure Maskenbelichtung *f*
mask field *(video screen)* Maskenfeld *n*
mask field content *(video screen)* Maskenfeldinhalt *m*
mask generation *(video screen)* Maskenerstellung *f*
masking Maskierung *f*; *(film opaquing)* Ausdecken *n*, Abdecken *n*
masking asphalt Abdeckasphalt *m*
masking film Maskierfilm *m*, Maskierfolie *f*
masking foil Maskierfolie *f*
masking lacquer Abdecklack *m*
masking paper Abdeckpapier *n*
masking pen *(film opaquing)* Abdeckstift *m*
masking red *(film opaque)* Abdeckfarbe *f*, Abdecktusche *f*
masking tape *(red adhesive tape)* Abdeckband *n*
mask processing Maskenverarbeitung *f*
mask production Maskenherstellung *f*
mask structure *(video screen)* Maskenaufbau *m*
mass circulation Massenauflage *f*
mass-circulation magazine Massenzeitschrift *f*
mass composition *(typesetting)* Mengensatz *m*
mass edition Massenauflage *f*
mass media Massenmedien *pl*
mass printed matter Massendrucksache *f*
mass-produced magazine Massenzeitschrift *f*
mass production Massenproduktion *f*
mass storage *(comp.)* Massenspeicher *m*
master *(small offset plate)* Folie *f*
master copy Original *n*, Originalvorlage *f*
master ejector *(small offset press)* Folienauswurf *m*
master file *(comp.)* Stammdatensatz *m*
master file data Stammdaten *pl*
master file management Stammdatenverwaltung *f*

master image - mechanical paper

master image Originalbild *n*
master negative Mutternegativ *n*
master of bookbinding Buchbindermeister *m*
master of printing Druckmeister *m*
master pull unit *(small offset press)* Folieneinzug *m*
master record *(comp.)* Stammdatensatz *m*
master screen Mutterraster *m*
mast head *(magazine, newspaper)* Impressum *n*
mat Mater *f*, Matrize *f*
match *v* abgleichen; *(colour)* abstimmen, nachstellen
material costs *pl* Materialkosten *pl*
material flow Materialfluß *m*
material requirement Materialbedarf *m*
materials testing Materialprüfung *f*
material supplier Materiallieferant *m*
mathematical matter *(type)* mathematischer Satz *m*
mathematical sign mathematisches Zeichen *n*
mathematics setting see maths setting
maths setting mathematischer Satz *m*; *(formula setting)* Formelsatz *m*
matrix Mater *f*, Matrize *f*; *(for stereotyping)* Prägemater *f*
matrix board Maternkarton *m*, Maternpappe *f*, Matrizenpappe *f*
matrix calender Maternkalander *m*
matrix circulation *(type caster)* Matrizenkreislauf *m*
matrix drying press Materntrockenpresse *f*
matrix justifying machine Maternjustiermaschine *f*
matrix moulding Maternprägung *f*, Matrizenprägung *f*
matrix moulding press Maternprägepresse *f*, Matrizenprägepresse *f*
matrix powder Maternpulver *n*
matrix printer *(proof printer)* Matrixdrucker *m*
matt glanzlos, matt
matt-calendered paper mattsatiniertes Papier *n*
matt-coated paper mattgestrichenes Papier *n*
matt coating *(paper)* Mattstrich *m*
matter *(type matter)* Satz *m*
matt film Mattfilm *m*
matt finish Mattglanz *m*
matt ink Mattfarbe *f*
matt paper mattes Papier *n*
matt satin finish seidenmatter Glanz *m*
matt varnish Mattlack *m*
maximum capacity Höchstleistung *f*
maximum density *(D. max)* Maximaldichte *f*
maximum format Maximalformat *n*

maximum output Höchstleistung *f*
maximum performance Höchstleistung *f*
maximum sheet size größtes Papierformat *n*
maximum size Maximalformat *n*
maximum speed Maximalgeschwindigkeit *f*
measure *(typesetting)* Satzbreite *f*, Zeilenbreite *f*
measure *v* abmessen, messen
measured value Meßwert *m*
measurement adjustment *(cutting m.)* Maßeinstellung *f*
measurement aperture *(lens aperture)* Meßblende *f*
measurement display *(cutting m.)* Maßanzeige *f*
measurement input *(cutting m.)* Maßeingabe *f*
measurement read-out *(cutting m.)* Maßanzeige *f*
measurement setting *(cutting m.)* Maßeinstellung *f*
measurement system Maßsystem *n*
measurement techniques *pl* Meßtechniken *pl*
measuring accuracy Meßgenauigkeit *f*
measuring area Meßfeld *n*
measuring bar *(colour control console)* Meßbalken *m*
measuring carriage Meßschlitten *m*
measuring console Meßpult *n*
measuring cup Meßbecher *m*
measuring data Meßdaten *pl*
measuring field *(print control bar)* Meßfeld *n*
measuring function Meßfunktion *f*
measuring geometry Meßgeometrie *f*
measuring head Meßkopf *m*
measuring instrument Meßgerät *n*, Meßinstrument *n*
measuring lens Meßlupe *f*
measuring point Meßpunkt *m*
measuring principle Meßprinzip *n*
measuring probe Meßsonde *f*
measuring range Meßbereich *m*
measuring roller Meßwalze *f*
measuring run Meßlauf *m*
measuring scale Meßskala *f*
measuring sensor Meßfühler *m*
measuring spot Meßfleck *m*
measuring strip Meßstreifen *m*
measuring tape Maßband *n*
measuring target *(print control bar)* Meßfeld *n*
mechanical control mechanische Steuerung *f*, Steuer(ungs)mechanik *f*
mechanically grained aluminium plate mechanisch gekörnte Aluminiumplatte *f*
mechanical makeready *(letterpress)* mechanische Zurichtung *f*, Kraftzurichtung *f*
mechanical paper holzhaltiges Papier *n*

mechanical pulp *(papermaking)* Holzfaserstoff *m*, Holzschliff *m*
mechanical tint Einkopierraster *m*, Rasterfilm *m*, technischer Raster *m*
mechanical top speed mechanische Höchstgeschwindigkeit *f*
mechanical typesetting Maschinensatz *m*
Mechanistics *f (type classif.)* Serifenbetonte Linear-Antiqua *f*
media Medien *pl*, Vorlage *f*
media format *(reprod.)* Vorlagenformat *n*
media printhouse Zeitschriftendruckerei *f*
media publishing house Medienverlag *m*
medium-circulation newspaper mittlere Zeitung *f*
medium-face line stumpffeine Linie *f*
medium-face rule stumpffeine Linie *f*
medium-length run *(printing)* mittlere Auflage *f*
medium-sized printhouse mittlere Druckerei *f*
medium-size (printing) press mittelformatige Druckmaschine *f*
meet delivery date *v* Liefertermin einhalten
melting furnace Schmelzofen *m*
melting material Schmelzmetall *n*
melting pot Schmelzbecken *n*, Schmelzkessel *m*, Schmelztiegel *m*
membran switch Folientastatur *f*
memo pad Notizblock *m*
memory *(comp.)* Speicher *m*
memory access time *(comp.)* Speicherzugriffszeit *f*
memory size *(comp.)* Speichergröße *f*
menu *(comp.)* Menü *n*
menu-controlled *(comp.)* menügesteuert
menu-driven menügesteuert
menu field *(video screen)* Menüfeld *n*
mercury vapour lamp Quecksilberdampflampe *f*
merge copy *v (text)* Text mischen
mesh *(screen printing)* Gewebe *n*, Sieb *n*
mesh filling *(screen printing)* Maschenfüllung *f*
mesh opening *(screen printing)* Maschenöffnung *f*, Maschenweite *f*
message *(comp.)* Meldung *f*, Mitteilung *f*
message line *(photocomp. machine)* Infozeile *f*
metal chips *pl* Metallspäne *pl*
metal container Blechemballage *f*, Blechpackung *f*
metal corners *pl (book)* Beschlag *m*, Buchbeschlag *m*
metal cuttings *pl* Metallspäne *pl*
metal decorating Blechdruck *m*
metal decorating machine Blechdruckmaschine *f*
metal decorator Blechdrucker *m*
metal foil Metallfolie *f*

metal foil paper Metallfolienpapier *n*
metal gauze *(screen printing)* Metallgewebe *n*
metal guide *(mach.)* Führungsblech *n*
metal halide lamp *(vacuum frame)* Metall-Halogen-Lampe *f*
metallic decorative colours *pl* Metallschmuckfarben *f/pl*
metallic decorative inks *pl* Metallschmuckfarben *f/pl*
metallic edge *(book)* Metallschnitt *m*
metallic ink Metalldruckfarbe *f*, Metallikfarbe *f*
metallic paper metallisches Papier *n*
metallic stamping foil Metallprägefolie *f*
metallized paper metallisiertes Papier *n*
metallizing *(aluminium)* Aluminiumbedampfung *f*
metal mesh *(screen printing)* Metallgewebe *n*
metal packaging Blechemballage *f*, Blechpackung *f*
metal paper Metallpapier *n*
metal plate printing Metallschilderdruck *m*
metal stencil Metallschablone *f*
metal underlay *(press)* Unterlageblech *n*
metameric colours *pl* metamere Farben *pl*
meter *(measuring instrument)* Meßgerät *n*, Meßinstrument *n*
metereological sign metereologisches Zeichen *n*
metering blade Dosierrakel *f*
metering cylinder Dosierzylinder *m*
metering pump Dosierpumpe *f*
metering roller Dosierwalze *f*
methanol Methanol *n*
methyl alcohol Methylalkohol *m*
metol-hydroquinone *(photochem.)* Metol-Hydrochinon *n*
metric system metrisches System *n*; *(typogr.)* mm-System *n*
metropolitan newspaper Großstadtzeitung *f*
mezzotint Mezzotinto *n*
MICR (magnetic ink character recognition) MICR (magnetische Zeichenerkennung)
MICR numbering Magnetzeichennumerierung *f*
micro-adjust *v* feineinstellen, feinjustieren
micro adjustment Feineinstellung *f*
micro-adjustment screw Feineinstellschraube *f*
microcomputer Kleincomputer *m*, Mikrocomputer *m*
microcomputer(-based) technology Mikrocomputertechnik *f*
microcomputer control Mikrocomputersteuerung *f*
micro-corrugated board Mikrowellpappe *f*
microelectronics Mikroelektronik *f*

microfiche Mikrofiche *m*
microfilm Mikrofilm *m*
microfilming Mikroverfilmung *f*
micro-grained aluminium plate mikrogekörnte Aluminiumplatte *f*
microline Mikrolinie *f*
microline patch *(print control bar)* Mikrolinienfeld *n*
microline target *(print control bar)* Mikrolinienfeld *n*
micrometer Mikrometer *n*
micrometer screw Mikrometerschraube *f*
microphotography Mikrofotografie *f*
microprocessor Mikroprozessor *m*
microprocessor(-based) technology Mikroprozessortechnik *f*
microprocessor-controlled mikroprozessorgesteuert
microprogramming Mikroprogrammierung *f*
middle tones *pl (around 50 %)* Mitteltöne *pl*
mid-tone gradation Gradation in den Mitteltönen
mid-tones *pl (around 50 %)* Mitteltöne *pl*
mid-tone tint patch *(print control bar)* Halbtonrasterfeld *n*
millboard Karton *m*, Maschinenpappe *f*
mill converting *(paper converting)* Papierverarbeitung *f*
mill-finished paper maschinenglattes Papier *n*
mill finishing *(paper finishing)* Papierveredlung *f*
millimeter division Millimetereinteilung *f*
millimeter grid Millimetereinteilung *f; (film guide)* mm-Folie
millimeter line *(classified ad)* Millimeterzeile *f*
millimeter scale Millimeterskala *f*
milling *(book spine)* Aufrauhen *n; (ink)* Anreiben *n*, Anreibung *f*
mill roll *(paper)* Papierrolle *f*
mill the ink *v* Farbe reiben
mineral colours *pl (e.g. ochre, umbra etc.)* Erdfarben *pl*
mineral oil *(inkmaking)* Mineralöl *n*
minicomputer Kleincomputer *m*, Minicomputer *m*
minim *(music printing)* halbe Musiknote *f*
minimum density *(D. min.)* Minimaldichte *f*
minimum format Mindestformat *n*
minimum sheet size kleinstes Papierformat *n*
minimum size Mindestformat *n*
minimum weight fount *(lead comp.)* Schriftminimum *n*
minus correction *(plate, cylinder)* Minuskorrektur *f*
minuscule Minuskel *f*

minuscules *pl* Kleinbuchstaben *m/pl*
minus sign Minuszeichen *n*
minute printer Schnelldrucker *m*, Sofortdrucker *m*
mirror image seitenverkehrt
mirror type Spiegelschrift *f*
misaligned sheet *(feeding)* Schrägbogen *m*
misaligned sheet detector *(sheet feeder)* Schrägbogenkontrolle *f*
miscontact *(contact printing)* Hohlkopie *f*
mis-cut Fehlschnitt *m*
mis-cut monitoring *(cutting m.)* Fehlschnittüberwachung *f*
mis-fed sheet Fehlbogen *m*
mis-fed sheet detector Fehlbogenkontrolle *f*
misfeed *(sheet)* Fehlanlage *f*
misprint Fehldruck *m*, Druckfehler *m*
misprint *v* falschdrucken, verdrucken
misprinted sheets *pl* Makulatur *f,* Makulaturbogen *m/pl*
misprints *pl* Makulatur *f,* Makulaturbogen *m/pl*
mis-register fehlerhaftes Register *n*, Registerdifferenz *f; (colour register)* Fehlpasser *m*, Paßdifferenz *f*, Passerdifferenz *f*, Passerversatz *m*
mis-registered aus dem Register, nicht registergenau, nicht registerhaltig; *(colour)* nicht passergenau, nicht paßgenau
miss delivery date *v* Liefertermin nicht einhalten
missing dots *pl (gravure)* fehlende Rasterpunkte *m/pl*, Missing Dots *pl*
missing sheet Fehlbogen *m*
missing sheet detector Fehlbogenkontrolle *f*
missing word *(typesetting)* Fehlwort *n*
miss out *v (typesetting)* auslassen, weglassen
mitred cut *(lead comp.)* Gehrungsschnitt *m*
mitred quad *(lead comp.)* Gehrungsquadrat *n*
mitred rules *pl (lead comp.)* Gehrungslinien *pl*
mixed colours *pl (colour system)* Mischfarben *pl*
mixed forme *(for multi-up processing)* Sammelform *f*
mixed setting *(type)* gemischter Satz *m*, Mischsatz *m*
mixed sheet *(for multi-up processing)* Sammelbogen *m*
mixed starch glue Stärkemischleim *m*
mixing of typefaces Schriftmischen *n*
mix ink *v* Farbe anmachen
mobile unit fahrbares Aggregat *n*
mock title Schmutztitel *m*
mock-up Klebelayout *n*
mode *(operation)* Betriebsart *f*
modem *(telecom.)* Modem *n*

Modern Face *(type classif.)* Klassizistische Antiqua *f*
modern figures *pl (as opp. to old style figures with descenders)* Antiquaziffern *pl*, liniehaltende Ziffern *pl*
modern technology moderne Technik *f*
modern typeface moderne Schrift *f*
modular design *(system)* Modulbauweise *f*, Kastenbauweise *f*
modularity Modularität *f*
modular system Modulsystem *n*, Baukastensystem *n*
modulate *v* modulieren
modulation Modulation *f*
module Modul *n*
moiré (pattern) Moiré *n*
moisten *v* anfeuchten, befeuchten, feuchten
moisture Feuchtigkeit *f*
moisture content *(paper)* Feuchtgehalt *m*, Feuchtigkeitsgehalt *m*
moisture content of paper Papierfeuchte *f*
moisture expansion *(paper)* Feuchtdehnung *f*
moisture film *(offset plate)* Feuchtmittelfilm *m*
moisture pick-up *(paper)* Feuchtigkeitsaufnahme *f*
moisture-proof feuchtigkeitsfest
moisture-sensitive feuchtigkeitsempfindlich
moleskin *(damper cover)* Moleskin *m*, Feuchtwalzenstoff *m*
molleton *(damper cover)* Molton *m*, Feuchtwalzenstoff *m*
monitor Monitor *m*, Kontrollbildschirm *m*, Bildschirm *m*
monitor display Bildschirmanzeige *f*
monitor function Bildschirmfunktion *f*
monitoring *(process)* Kontrolle *f*, Überwachung *f*
monk *(printing problem)* Mönch *m*
monochrome einfarbig, schwarzweiß
monochrome monitor einfarbiger Bildschirm *m*
monochrome original Schwarzweißvorlage *f*
monochrome scanner Schwarzweißscanner *m*
monochrome transparency Schwarzweißdia *n*
monochrome work *(reprod.)* einfarbige Arbeiten *pl*
monocolour einfarbig, schwarzweiß
monocolour printing Einfarbendruck *m*
monocolour (printing) press Einfarbendruckmaschine *f*
monocolour printwork einfarbige Arbeiten *pl*
mono(-colour) unit *(newspaper press)* Schwarzdruckwerk *n*
monofilament polyester *(screen printing)* monofiles Polyester *n*

monogram stamping press Monogramm-Prägepresse *f*
monometal plate Einmetallplatte *f*
monotype composition *(single-type casting)* Monotypesatz *m*
monotype compositor Monotypesetzer *m*
monotype machine *(single-type caster)* Monotype *f*
monotype operator Monotypesetzer *m*
montage *(page assembly)* Montage *f*
montage colour key *(film guide)* Anhaltekopie *f*
montage film Montagefolie *f*
montage for step exposures Schiebemontage *f*
montage glue Montagekleber *m*
montage masking foil Montageabdeckfolie *f*
montage sheet Montagebogen *m*
montage wax Haftwachs *n*, Montagewachs *n*
monthly calendar Monatskalender *m*
monthly (journal) Monatszeitschrift *f*
monthly (magazine) Monatszeitschrift *f*
mordant Ätze *f*, Ätzwasser *n*
morning edition Morgenausgabe *f*
morning paper Morgenblatt *n*, Morgenzeitung *f*
morocco(-leather) binding Saffianeinband *m*
motif *(printing)* Motiv *n*
motor drive Motorantrieb *m*
motor driven elektromotorisch
motorized elektromotorisch
motorized adjusting element *(remote ink control)* Stellglied *n*
motor shaft Motorwelle *f*
mottle *v (gravure ink)* perlen
mottled *(book edge, endpaper)* gesprenkelt
mottled impression unruhiger Druck *m*, wolkiger Druck *m*
mould Mater *f*, Matrize *f*; *(fountain solution)* Algen *pl*
mould *v (a matrix)* abformen, matern
moulded board Ziehpappe *f*
moulded matrix geprägte Mater *f*
moulding *(matrix moulding)* Prägen *n*, Prägung *f*; *(fountain solution)* Pilzbildung *f*
moulding and vulcanizing press Form- und Vulkanisierpresse *f*
moulding board Prägepappe *f*
moulding press *(matrix moulding)* Schlagpresse *f*, Prägepresse *f*; **automatic** ~ Prägeautomat *m*
moulding press for electrotypes galvanoplastische Prägepresse *f*
mould-made paper handgeschöpftes Papier *n*
mould stain *(paper)* Stockfleck *m*
mount *(blockmaking)* Unterlage *f*, Fuß *m*; *(calendar)* Rückwand *f*

mount v aufstellen, montieren; *(blanket, damper sleeve, tympan sheet etc.)* aufziehen
mount a blanket v Drucktuch aufziehen
mount a plate v Platte einspannen
mounting *(plate, blanket)* Aufspannen n, Einspannen n
mounting board Aufziehkarton m
mounting film Montagefolie f
mounting glue Montagekleber m
mounting sheet Montagebogen m
mounting table Montagetisch m
mount maps v Landkarten aufziehen
mount on wood v *(blockmaking)* aufholzen, aufklotzen
mouse *(VDU control)* Maus f
movable screen beweglicher Bildschirm m
movable type bewegliche Lettern pl
move-away unit ausfahrbares Aggregat n, fahrbares Aggregat n, abklappbares Aggregat n, abschwenkbares Aggregat n
move copy v *(text)* Text rücken, Text umstellen
move matter to the left v linksbündig setzen
move matter to the right v rechtsbündig setzen
moving display *(line display)* Laufschriftanzeige f
moving head disk *(comp.)* Platte mit beweglichem Kopf
M quad *(lead comp.)* Schließgeviert n, Schließquadrat n
multi-code *(comp.)* Multi-Kode m
multi-colour(ed) mehrfarbig
multi-colour gravure (process) Mehrfarbentiefdruck m
multi-colour line engraving Mehrfarbenstrichätzung f
multi-colour offset Mehrfarbenoffset m
multi-colour printing Mehrfarb(en)druck m, Buntdruck m, Buntfarbendruck m, Farbdruck m
multi-colour (printing) press Mehrfarbendruckmaschine f
multi-colour work Mehrfarb(en)arbeiten pl
multi-column composition Mehrspaltensatz m
multi-column page make-up mehrspaltiger Umbruch m
multi-column setting *(typesetting)* Mehrspaltensatz m
multi-column work *(typesetting)* Mehrspaltensatz m
multi-component glue Mehrkomponentenkleber m
multi-computer system *(comp.)* Mehrrechnersystem n
multi-CPU system *(comp.)* Mehrrechnersystem n

multifilament polyester *(screen printing)* multifiles Polyester n
multiflash *(photocomp.)* Mehrfachbelichtung f
multi-function cable Multifunktionskabel n
multi-function key *(keyboard)* Multifunktionstaste f
multi-layer film Mehrschichtenfilm m
multi-layer montage Sandwich-Montage f
multi-metal plate *(offset)* Mehrmetallplatte f
multi-page catalogue mehrseitiger Katalog m
multi-part forms set Mehrfachformularsatz m
multiple-bath etching *(gravure cyl.)* Mehrbadätzung f
multiple copies pl *(printed copies)* Nutzen m/pl
multiple plate exposures pl *(step exposures)* Schiebekopie f
multiple run through press mehrmaliger Durchgang m, mehrmaliger Durchlauf m
multiple-up feed(ing) *(sheet feeding)* Mehrfachanlage f
multiple-ups pl *(multiple copies)* Nutzen m/pl
multiplexer *(comp.)* Multiplexer m
multiplex mode *(telecom.)* Multiplex-Betrieb m
multiplication sign *(maths setting)* Malzeichen n, Multiplikationszeichen n
multi-ply board mehrlagiger Karton m
multi-ply forms set Mehrfachformularsatz m
multiprocessor Multiprozessor m
multi-purpose machine Mehrzweckmaschine f
multi-shift operation Mehrschichtbetrieb m
multi-stage production process *(in graphic arts firms: from copy preparation through to converting)* mehrstufige Herstellung f
multi-station system *(comp.)* Mehrplatzsystem n
multitasking *(comp.)* Hintergrundverarbeitung f
multi-up jobs pl Mehrnutzenarbeiten pl
multi-up label sheet Etikettensammelbogen m
multi-up processing Mehrnutzenverarbeitung f, Nutzenverarbeitung f
multi-up production Mehrnutzenproduktion f
multi-up work Mehrnutzenarbeiten pl
multi-user system *(comp.)* Mehrbenutzersystem n
multi-web operation *(web press)* Mehrbahnbetrieb m
multi-web rotary press Mehrbahnen-Rotationsmaschine f
music book Notenbuch n
music copyist Notenschreiber m
music engraver Notenstecher m
music engraving Notenstich m, Notenstechen n
music note Musiknote f, Note f
music notebook Notenheft n
music-paper Notenpapier n

music pen Rastral *n*
music printing Musikaliendruck *m*, Musiknotendruck *m*, Notendruck *m*
music printing paper Notendruckpapier *n*
music publishers *pl* Musikverlag *m*
music sheet Notenblatt *n*
music typecase Musiknotenkasten *m*
music type composition Musiknotensatz *m*, Notensatz *m*
music typesetting Musiknotensatz *m*, Notensatz *m*

N

narrow-band filter *(densitometry)* Schmalbandfilter *m*
narrowing of ink duct width Formatbegrenzung des Farbkastens
narrow size schmales Format *n*
national newspaper überregionale Zeitung *f*
NCR forms set *(carbonless forms set)* Durchschreibeformularsatz *m*, Selbstdurchschreibesatz *m*
NCR paper Durchschreibepapier *n*, Farbreaktionspapier *n*, Selbstdurchschreibepapier *n*
NC varnish *(print finishing)* Nitrolack *m*
neck *(part of the letter)* Kopf *m*
needle bearing Nadellager *n*
needle holes *pl (sewing)* Heftlöcher *pl*
needle on *v* aufnadeln, aufstechen
needle perforation Nadelperforation *f*
needle printer *(line printer)* Nadeldrucker *m*
neg *(negative)* Negativ *n*
negative Negativ *n*
negative contact screen *(reprod.)* Negativkontaktraster *m*
negative conversion Negativumkehrung *f*
negative doctor blade gegenläufige Rakel *f*
negative doctoring *(gravure)* gegenläufige Abrakelung *f*, negative Abrakelung *f*
negative exposure Negativbelichtung *f*
negative holder *(camera)* Negativbühne *f*, Negativhalter *m*
negative plate Negativplatte *f*
negative platemaking Negativkopie *f*
negative retouching Negativretusche *f*

negative screening Negativrasterung *f*
negative storage Negativaufbewahrung *f*
negative (working) plate Negativplatte *f*
neodimium YAG laser Neodym-YAG-Laser *m*
net output Nettoausstoß *m*, Nettoleistung *f*
network *(communication)* Netz *n*, Netzwerk *n*
network *v* verbinden
network architecture Netzwerkarchitektur *f*
network system *(comp.)* Verbundsystem *n*
neutral colour neutrale Farbe *f*
neutral density filter *(reprod.)* Neutraldichtefilter *m*
neutral grey Neutralgrau *n*
neutral tone Neutralton *m*, Grauwert *m*
new edition Neuauflage *f*, Neuausgabe *f*, Neudruck *m*
new line neue Zeile *f*
new media *pl* neue Medien *pl*
new paragraph *(typesetting)* neuer Absatz *m*, neue Zeile *f*
news Zeitungsnachricht *f*
news agency *(press agency)* Nachrichtenagentur *f*, Nachrichtenbüro *n*, Zeitungsagentur *f*
news channel Nachrichtenkanal *m*
news compositor Zeitungssetzer *m*
news deadline Redaktionsschluß *m*
news headline Schlagzeile *f*, Zeitungsschlagzeile *f*
news ink Zeitungs(druck)farbe *f*
news item kurze Zeitungsmeldung *f*
news page Nachrichtenseite *f*, Zeitungsseite *f*
newspaper Zeitung *f*, Blatt *n*
newspaper ad(vertisement) Zeitungsanzeige *f*
newspaper advertising Zeitungswerbung *f*
newspaper archive Zeitungsarchiv *n*
newspaper bundle Zeitungspaket *n*
newspaper bundling press Zeitungsbündelpresse *f*
newspaper carrier Zeitungsausträger *m*, Zeitungsträger *m*
newspaper clipping Zeitungsausschnitt *m*
newspaper column Zeitungskolumne *f*
newspaper composition Zeitungssatz *m*
newspaper copy Zeitungsexemplar *n*
newspaper cutting Zeitungsausschnitt *m*
newspaper flexo(graphic) printing Zeitungsflexodruck *m*
newspaper flexography Zeitungsflexodruck *m*
newspaper flexo plate Zeitungsflexoplatte *f*
newspaper fold Zeitungsfalz *m*
newspaper format Zeitungsformat *n*
newspaper illustration Zeitungsbild *n*
newspaper imprint Zeitungsimpressum *n*
newspaper industry Zeitungsindustrie *f*
newspaper insert Zeitungsbeilage *f*

newspaper inserting machine
Zeitungseinsteckmaschine *f*
newspaper letterpress (printing)
Zeitungshochdruck *m*
newspaper maker-up *(lead comp.)*
Zeitungsmetteur *m*
newspaper offset rotary Offsetzeitungsrotation *f*
newspaper operation Zeitungsbetrieb *m*
newspaper page make-up Zeitungsumbruch *m*
newspaper pagination Zeitungsumbruch *m*
newspaper posted in wrapper *(at a reduced rate)*
Streifbandzeitung *f*
newspaper printer Zeitungsdrucker *m*,
Zeitungsdruckerei *f*
newspaper printer and publisher
Zeitungsdruckerei und -verlag
newspaper printhouse Zeitungsdruckerei *f*
news(paper) printing Zeitungsdruck *m*
newspaper printing and publishing house
Zeitungsdruckerei und -verlag
newspaper printing plant Zeitungsbetrieb *m*,
Zeitungsdruckerei *f*
newspaper (printing) press
Zeitungs(druck)maschine *f*
newspaper (processing) line Zeitungslinie *f*
newspaper production Zeitungsherstellung *f*
newspaper publisher Zeitungsverlag *m*,
Zeitungsverleger *m*, Tageszeitung *f*
newspaper publishing house Zeitungsverlag *m*
newspaper reader Zeitungsleser *m*
newspaper rotary (press)
Zeitungs(druck)maschine *f*,
Zeitungsrotation(smaschine) *f*
newspaper rotary printing Zeitungsrotationsdruck *m*
newspaper size Zeitungsformat *n*
newspaper stereotyping Zeitungsstereotypie *f*
newspaper subscription Zeitungsabonnement *n*
newspaper supplement Zeitungsbeilage *f*
newspaper technology Zeitungstechnik *f*
newspaper title Zeitungskopf *m*
newspaper typeface Zeitungsschrift *f*
newspaper wrapper Zeitungsstreifband *n*
newspaper wrapping machine
Streifbandumlegemaschine für Zeitungen
newsprint Zeitungs(druck)papier *n*,
Zeitungspapier *n*
news publishing system Zeitungssystem *n*
newsroom Redaktion *f*, Redaktionsraum *m*
news section Nachrichtenteil *m*
news service Nachrichtendienst *m*
news setting *(type)* Zeitungssatz *m*
newsstand Kiosk *m*, Zeitungsstand *m*
news transmission Nachrichtenübertragung *f*
news type Zeitungsschrift *f*
newswork *(typesetting)* Zeitungssatz *m*
Newton rings *pl* Newton-Ringe *pl*
nick *(type matrix)* Signatur *f*
nickel anode Nickelanode *f*
nickel coating Nickelüberzug *m*
nickel electrolyte Nickelelektrolyt *n*
nickel electro(type) Nickelgalvano *n*
nickel etching Nickelätzung *f*
nickel-faced stereo vernickeltes Stereo *n*
nickel-facing Vernickelung *f*
nickel-plating Vernickelung *f*
nickel(-plating) bath Nickelbad *n*
nickel-plating installation Vernickelungsanlage *f*
nickel removal *(gravure cyl.)* Entnickeln *n*
nickel stereo(type) Nickelstereo *n*
nickel stripping *(gravure cyl.)* Entnickeln *n*
night shift Nachtschicht *f*
nip *(printing nip)* Druckspalt *m*
nip guard *(cylinder system)* Spaltschutz *m*
nipping *(book block)* Abpressen *n*
nip pulleys *pl* Zugrollen *f/pl*
nip roller Preßrolle *f*, Preßwalze *f*; *(folding roller)* Falzwalze *f*
nitro(cellulose) varnish *(print finishing)* Nitrolack *m*
nitro varnishing *(print finishing)* Nitrolackierung *f*
nodular cast iron *(machine frame)* Sphäroguß *m*
noise abatement Lärmschutz *m*, Schallschutz *m*
noise-abating enclosure schalldämmende
Verkapselung *f*
noise cover Lärmkapselung *f*
noise-deadening geräuschdämpfend
noise level Lärmniveau *n*, Lärmpegel *m*
noise prevention Lärmschutz *m*
noise reduction Lärmdämpfung *f*,
Geräuschminderung *f*
noise reduction hood Lärmdämmhaube *f*,
Schallschutzabdeckung *f*
nominal and actual value comparison
Soll/Ist-Vergleich *m*
nominal depth *(typesetting)* Soll-Höhe *f*
nominal value Sollwert *m*
non-absorbent printing stock nichtsaugendes
Druckpapier *n*
non-ageing properties *pl* Alterungsbeständigkeit *f*
non-collect run *(web printing)* einfache
Produktion *f*, nichtgesammelte Produktion *f*,
ungesammelte Produktion *f*
non-counted text *(unjustified)* Endlostext *m*

non-counted type matter *(unjustified)* Endlossatz *m*
non-counting input station *(text rec.)* Endloserfassungsplatz *m*, nichtrechnender Erfassungsplatz *m*
non-counting keyboard *(text rec.)* Endloserfassungsplatz *m*, nichtrechnender Erfassungsplatz *m*
non-counting text input Endloserfassung *f*, Endlostexterfassung *f*
non-counting text recording Endlostexterfassung *f*
non-cyclical taktfrei, taktunabhängig, taktungebunden
non-fading *(ink)* lichtecht
non-image areas *pl* bildfreie Stellen *f/pl*, nichtdruckende Stellen *pl*
non-impact printer anschlagloser Drucker *m*
non-impact printing (process) berührungsloses Druckverfahren *n*
non-justifying input station *(text rec.)* Endloserfassungsplatz *m*, nichtrechnender Erfassungsplatz *m*
non-lining figures *pl* Mediävalziffern *pl*
non-neutral (tone) Buntwert *m*
non-polluting umweltfreundlich
non-printing areas *pl* bildfreie Stellen *f/pl*, nichtdruckende Stellen *pl*
non-printing gap *(cylinder gap)* druckfreier Kanalstreifen *m*, Zylinderkanal *m*
non-production times *pl* Nebenzeiten *pl*
non-stop delivery Nonstopp-Auslage *f*
non-stop feeder Nonstopp-Anleger *m*
non-stop imprinting fliegender Eindruck *m*, Nonstopp-Eindruck *m*
non-stop operation Nonstopp-Betrieb *m*
non-stop pile change Nonstopp-Stapelwechsel *m*
non-toxic gesundheitlich unbedenklich
non-toxic ink lebensmittelechte Farbe *f*
non-toxic pressroom chemicals *pl* ungiftige Druckchemikalien *pl*
non-volatile memory *(comp.)* nichtflüchtiger Speicher *m*
non-volatile store *(comp.)* nichtflüchtiger Speicher *m*
no-pack blanket No-Pack-Gummituch *n*
normal inking *(press)* Normalfärbung *f*
normal mode Normalbetrieb *m*
normal operation Normalbetrieb *m*
normal word spacing normaler Wortzwischenraum *m*
no-screen exposure *(camera screening)* Nachbelichtung *f*
no-sheet detector Fehlbogenkontrolle *f*

notch *(blade)* Scharte *f*
notched micrometer screw Mikrorastschraube *f*
note Anmerkung *f*, Note *f*
note block Notizblock *m*
notebook Notizbuch *n*; *(diary)* Notizkalender *m*
note-pad Notizblock *m*, Notizklotz *m*
note-paper Briefpapier *n*
novel Roman *m*
nozzle drying Düsentrocknung *f*
nozzle gluing *(as opp. to roller gluing)* Düsenbeleimung *f*
nuance Nuance *f*
number *(publication)* Nummer *f*, Ausgabe *f*, Heft *n*
number *v* numerieren; *(pages)* foliieren, paginieren
numbering Numerierung *f*
numbering box Numerierwerk *n*
numbering machine Numeriermaschine *f*; *automatic* ~ Numerierautomat *m*
numbering shaft Numerierwelle *f*
number of cuts Schnittanzahl *f*
number of pages Seitenanzahl *f*, Seitenumfang *m*, Seitenzahl *f*
number of revolutions Umdrehungszahl *f*, Tourenzahl *f*
number of signatures *(convert.)* Bogenzahl *f*
number pages *v* paginieren
numeral Ziffer *f*
numeric numerisch
numerical letter *(a), b) etc.)* Zahlbuchstabe *m*
nylon cloth Nylongewebe *n*
nylon gauze Nylongaze *f*
nylon plate Nylo *n*

O

obligatory field *(business form, screen mask; as opp. to optional field)* Muß-Feld *n*
oblique *(type)* kursiv
oblique edge *(book)* Schrägschnitt *m*
oblique stroke Schrägstrich *m*
oblong format Langformat *n*, Querformat *n*
oblong page Querformatseite *f*, Seite im Querformat
oblong size see oblong format
OCR (Optical Character Recognition) OCR

OCR characters *pl* OCR-Schrift *f*
OCR form OCR-Formular *n*
OCR reader OCR-Leser *m*
odd folios *pl* ungerade Seiten *f/pl*
odour extraction *(ink drying)* Geruchsabsaugung *f*
odourless ink geruchfreie Farbe *f*
OEM (Original Equipment Manufacturer) OEM (Originalgerätehersteller)
OEM product OEM-Produkt *n*
off-and-on stitch *(thread-stitching)* Wechselstich *m*
off-colour aus der Farbe *f*
office *(printshop)* Offizin *f*
office automation Büroautomation *f*
office copier Bürokopierer *m*
office documentation Bürodokumentation *f*
office duplicator Bürodruckmaschine *f*, Bürovervielfältiger *m*
office forms *pl* Büroformulare *pl*
office typesetting Bürosatz *m*
official gazette Amtsblatt *n*, Staatsanzeiger *m*
off-line machine Solo-Maschine *f*
off-line operation Offline-Betrieb *m*
off-line workstation Offline-Arbeitsplatz *m*
off-press controls *pl* Druckmaschinenfernsteuerung *f*
off-press proof Proof *m*
off-press proofing Proofherstellung *f*
off-print Abdruck *m*, Nachdruck *m*, Sonderdruck *m*; *(part of a print run)* Teilauflage *f*
offset Offset *m*
offset board Offsetkarton *m*
offset company Offsetdruckerei *f*
offset control wedge Offsettestkeil *m*
offset gravure indirekter Tiefdruck *m*
offset-gravure conversion Offset-Tiefdruck-Konversion *f*, O-T-Konversion *f*
offset-gravure conversion screen O-T-Konversionsraster *m*
offset ink Offset(druck)farbe *f*
offset litho *(film)* Litho *n*
offset lithography Offset *m*, Offsetdruck *m*
offset master *(small offset printing plate)* Offset(druck)folie *f*
offset paper Offsetpapier *n*
offset perfector Offsetperfektor *m*, Schön- und Widerdruck-Offsetmaschine *f*
offset plate correction pen Offsetplatten-Korrekturstift *m*
offset plate deletion pen Offsetplatten-Korrekturstift *m*
offset platemaking Offsetkopie *f*
offset platemaking line Offsetplattenstraße *f*
offset plate processing line Offsetplattenstraße *f*
offset pressman Offsetdrucker *m*
offset printer Offsetdrucker *m*, Offsetdruckerei *f*
offset printhouse Offsetdruckerei *f*
offset printing Offsetdruck *m*, indirekter Flachdruck *m*
offset printing forme Offset(druck)form *f*
offset printing operation Offsetdruckerei *f*
offset (printing) plate Offset(druck)platte *f*, Flachdruckplatte *f*
offset (printing) press Offset(druck)maschine *f*
offset (printing) process Offset(druck)verfahren *n*, Offsetprozeß *m*
offset printshop Offsetdruckerei *f*
offset proofing press Offsetandruckpresse *f*
offset reproduction Offsetreproduktion *f*, Wiedergabe im Offset
offset rotary (press) Offset(rollen)rotation *f*, Rollenoffsetmaschine *f*
offset sink *(plate proc.)* Offsetbecken *n*
offset spray (powder) Druckbestäubungspuder *n*
offset(ting) *(fresh ink)* Ablegen *n*, Abliegen *n*, Abschmieren *n*, Abschmutzen *n*
offset zinc Offsetzink *n*
offset zinc plate Offsetzinkplatte *f*
oil-based ink Farbe auf Ölbasis, Ölfarbe *f*
oil bath Ölbad *n*
oil bath lubrication Ölbadschmierung *f*
oil can Ölkanne *f*
oil circuit lubrication Ölumlaufschmierung *f*
oilcloth Lacktuch *n*, Wachsleinen *n*, Wachsleinwand *f*
oil drip pan *(press)* Unterlageblech *n*
oil lubrication Ölschmierung *f*
oil lubrication point Ölschmierstelle *f*
oil paper Ölpapier *n*
oilprint varnish Öldrucklack *m*
oil sprinkling Ölberieselung *f*
oilstone Ölstein *m*
oil tracing paper Ölpauspapier *n*
oil trickling Ölberieselung *f*
oil varnish Ölfirnis *m*
o.k. proof abgezeichneter Bogen *m*, Abstimmbogen *m*, Druckfreigabebogen *m*, Freigabebogen *m*, O.K.-Bogen *m*
o.k. sheet abgezeichneter Bogen *m*, Abstimmbogen *m*, Druckfreigabebogen *m*, Freigabebogen *m*, O.K.-Bogen *m*

o.k. to print druckreif, Druckerlaubnis *f*, Druckfreigabe *f*, Druckgenehmigung *f*, Druckreiferklärung *f*, gut zum Druck
old black *(type)* Fraktur *f*, Gotisch *f*, Schwabacher *f*
old face *(type)* Antiqua *f*, Mediäval *f*, Renaissance-Antiqua *f*
old German type Altdeutsch *n*
old papers *pl* Altpapier *n*
old style *(type)* Antiqua *f*, Mediäval *f*, Renaissance-Antiqua *f*
old style figures *pl* Mediävalziffern *pl*, Ziffern mit Unterlängen
oleograph Öldruck *m*
oleography Öldruck *m*
oleophilic oleophil; *(ink-receptive; offset)* farbfreundlich
oleophobic oleophob; *(ink-repellent)* farbabweisend
omit *v (typesetting)* auslassen, weglassen
omitted letter ausgelassener Buchstabe *m*
one-bath processor *(reprod.)* Einbad-Entwicklungsgerät *n*
one colour both sides 1/1-farbig, einfarbiger Schön- und Widerdruck *m*
one colour front, one reverse 1/1-farbig, einfarbiger Schön- und Widerdruck *m*
one colour front (side only) 1/0 Schöndruck *m*, einfarbiger Schöndruck *m*
one colour reverse (side) 1/0 Widerdruck *m*, einfarbiger Widerdruck *m*
one-component glue Einkomponentenkleber *m*
one-directional fold Einbruchfalz *m*
one-hand operation Einhandbedienung *f*
one-lever control Einhebelsteuerung *f*
one-part form Einblattformular *n*
one-piece page film seitenglatter Film *m*
one-sided coated paper einseitig gestrichenes Papier *n*
one-sided printing einseitiger Druck *m*, Schöndruck *m*
one-time carbon (paper) Einmalkohlepapier *n*
one-up im Einfachnutzen *m*, im Einzelnutzen *m*
one-up folded sheet Einzelnutzen-Falzbogen *m*
one-up production Einzelnutzenverarbeitung *f*
1/0 bottom *(printing)* 1/0 Widerdruck *m*, einfarbiger Widerdruck *m*
1/0 top *(printing)* 1/0 Schöndruck *m*, einfarbiger Schöndruck *m*
onion skin *(paper)* Dünndruckpapier *n*, Florpostpapier *n*
on-light Auflicht *n*
on-light measurement Auflichtmessung *f*

on-line densitometer Online-Densitometer *n*
on-line fonts *(photocomp.)* Schriften im direkten Zugriff
on-line processor *(photocomp.)* Online-Entwicklungsmaschine *f*, Online-Prozessor *m*
on-line typefaces *(photocomp.)* Schriften im direkten Zugriff
on-press web finishing *(in-line finishing)* Inline-Finishing *n*
on-screen editing Bildschirmkorrektur *f*
on the fly bei laufender Maschine *f*, im Lauf *m*
on-the-fly imprinting fliegender Eindruck *m*, Nonstopp-Eindruck *m*
on the run bei laufender Maschine *f*, im Lauf *m*
on the run adjustments *pl (machinery)* Einstellungen während des Laufs
on-the-run imprinting fliegender Eindruck *m*, Nonstopp-Eindruck *m*
on-time delivery pünktliche Lieferung *f*, termingerechte Lieferung *f*
opacity *(paper)* Opazität *f*
opal glass Opalglas *n*
opal glass plate Opalscheibe *f*
opal lamp Opallampe *f*
opaque deckend, lichtundurchlässig, opak
opaque film Opakfilm *m*
opaque ink Deckfarbe *f*
opaqueness *(ink)* Deckfähigkeit *f*, Deckkraft *f*
opaque paper nichtdurchscheinendes Papier *n*
opaque retouching *(film)* deckende Retusche *f*
opaque white Deckweiß *n*
opaquing *(film opaquing)* Abdecken *n*, Ausdecken *n*, Ausflecken *n*
opaquing pen *(film opaquing)* Abdeckstift *m*
open brackets Klammer auf
open characters *pl* see outline characters
open file *(comp.)* offener File *m*
open head *(folded signature)* am Kopf offen, offener Kopf *m*
opening column Anfangskolumne *f*
opening line *(typesetting)* Anfangszeile *f*
opening page Anfangsseite *f*
open interface *(comp.)* offene Schnittstelle *f*
open matter *(type matter)* splendider Satz *m*
open sheet Planobogen *m*, ungefalzter Bogen *m*
open sheet delivery *(on web press)* Planoauslage *f*, Planoausleger *m*, Planobogenausgang *m*
open sheet size Planoformat *n*
open side *(folded signature)* offene Seite *f*
open size *(unfolded)* offenes Format *n*
open system offenes System *n*
open time *(glue)* Öffnungszeit *f*

operate v arbeiten, bedienen, betätigen, betreiben
operating aid Bedienungshilfe f
operating comfort Bedienerfreundlichkeit f, Bedienungskomfort m
operating condition Betriebszustand m
operating console Bedienungsstand m
operating costs pl Betriebskosten pl
operating cycle Bedienungsablauf m
operating data Betriebsdaten pl
operating data logging Betriebsdatenprotokollierung f
operating desk Bedienungspult n
operating elements pl Bedienungselemente pl
operating error Bedienungsfehler m
operating fault Bedienungsfehler m
operating hours pl Betriebsstunden pl
operating instructions pl Bedienungsanleitung f
operating lever Bedienungshebel m
operating manual Bedienungshandbuch n, Betriebsanleitung f
operating mode Betriebsart f
operating panel Bedienungstafel f
operating personnel Bedienungspersonal n
operating position *(mach.)* Arbeitsstellung f
operating program *(comp.)* Betriebsprogramm n
operating side *(as opp. to drive side)* Bedienerseite f, Bedienungsseite f
operating software *(comp.)* Betriebsprogramm n
operating speed Betriebsgeschwindigkeit f
operating staff Bedienungspersonal n
operating status Betriebszustand m
operating system *(comp.)* Betriebssystem n
operation Arbeitsgang m, Bedienung f, Betrieb m, Gang m, Lauf m; **in one** ~ in einem Arbeitsgang
operational data Betriebsdaten pl
operational data recording Betriebsdatenerfassung f
operation(al) planning Betriebsplanung f
operational reliability Bedienungssicherheit f, Betriebssicherheit f
operational safety Bedienungssicherheit f, Betriebssicherheit f
operational structure Betriebsstruktur f
operation costing Betriebskalkulation f
operation sequence Bedienungsablauf m
operator Arbeitskraft f, Bediener m, Bedienungsperson f, Benutzer m
operator console Bedienerkonsole f
operator convenience Bedienerfreundlichkeit f, Bedienungskomfort m
operator-friendly bedienerfreundlich, bedienungsfreundlich, benutzerfreundlich
operator guide Bedienerführung f, Benutzerführung f
operator instructor Anwendungstechniker m
operator intervention Bedienereingriff m
operator-programmable bedienerprogrammierbar
operator surface Bedieneroberfläche f, Benutzeroberfläche f
opposite editorial *(ad position)* gegenüber Redaktion
opposite page Nebenseite f
opposite pages pl *(book, magazine)* gegenüberliegende Seiten f/pl
optical bar reader Strichkodeleser m
optical character reader *(text rec.)* Klarschriftleser m, Lesemaschine f, OCR-Leser m
optical character recognition *(OCR)* optische Zeichenerkennung f
optical density optische Dichte f
optical disk *(comp.)* optischer Plattenspeicher m, optische Speicherplatte f
optical disk drive optisches Plattenlaufwerk n
optical distortion optische Verzeichnung f
optical fibres pl Glasfasern f/pl
optically spaced *(type matter)* optisch ausgeglichen
optical mark reader optischer Markenleser m
optical reader optischer Leser m
optical scanner optischer Leser m
optical web scanner Bahnbeobachtungsgerät n, Bahnbetrachtungsgerät n
optics Optik f
optional accessories pl Sonderzubehör n
optional equipment Zusatzausrüstung f
optional field *(screen mask, form; as opp. to obligatory field)* Kann-Feld n
opto-electronic sensor opto-elektronischer Sensor m
opto-mechanical sensor opto-mechanischer Sensor m
order Auftrag m, Reihenfolge f; **rush** ~ kurzfristiger Auftrag m; **short-term** ~ kurzfristiger Auftrag m
order book Bestellbuch n
order change Auftragswechsel m
order coupon *(direct mail, in-line fin.)* Bestellcoupon m
order entry Auftragseingang m
order form Auftragsformular n, Bestellformular n
order handling Auftragsabwicklung f, Auftragsbearbeitung f
order intake Auftragseingang m

order number Auftragsnummer *f*, Bestellnummer *f*
order sheet Bestellzettel *m*
order structure Auftragsstruktur *f*
order taking Auftragsannahme *f*
organic vegetable spray powder organisch-pflanzliches Druckbestäubungspuder *n*
original Original *n*, Originalvorlage *f*
original art(work) Original *n*, Originalgrafik *f*, Originalvorlage *f*
original binding Originaleinband *m*
original copy Original *n*, Originalvorlage *f*
original edition *(book)* Erstausgabe *f*, Originalausgabe *f*
original equipment manufacturer (OEM) Originalgerätehersteller (OEM) *m*
original litho *(film)* Originallitho *n*
original (text) Urschrift *f*
origination *(art preparation)* Originalherstellung *f*, Vorlagenherstellung *f*
ornament Ornament *n*, Verzierung *f*
ornamental border Bordüre *f*, Zierrand *m*
ornamental box *(typogr.)* Schmuckrahmen *m*
ornamented initial verzierte Initiale *f*
ornamented letter verzierter Buchstabe *m*, Zierbuchstabe *m*
ornamented line verzierte Linie *f*
ornamented rule verzierte Linie *f*, Zierlinie *f*
ornamented type Schmuckschrift *f*, Zierschrift *f*
ornament piece *(lead comp.)* Anschlußstück *n*, Zierstück *n*
orphan *(typesetting)* Schusterjunge *m*
orthochromatic film *(reprod.)* Orthofilm *m*, orthochromatischer Film *m*
orthography Orthografie *f*, Rechtschreibung *f*
oscillating damping roller Feuchttreiber *m*, Feuchttreibzylinder *m*
oscillating ink roller Farbverreiber *m*, Farbreiber *m*, Farbreibzylinder *m*, Farbverreibwalze *f*
oscillating mirror *(optics)* Schwingspiegel *m*
oscillating movement Hinundherbewegung *f*
oscillating roller changierende Walze *f*, oszillierende Walze *f*, traversierende Walze *f*, Wechselreiber *m*
oscillation *(roller motion)* Changierbewegung *f*
oscillator drum Reibzylinder *m*
outdoor advertising Außenwerbung *f*
outer forme *(print forme)* äußere Form *f*
outer margin äußerer Papierrand *m*, äußerer Seitenrand *m*, vorderer Papierrand *m*
outfit *v* ausrüsten, ausstatten
outlet *(unit)* Auslauf *m*

outlet conveyor Auslaufband *n*
outline Aufriß *m*, Entwurf *m*, Skizze *f*
outline *v* entwerfen, konturieren; *(a figure)* freistellen
outline characters *pl* Konturschrift *f*, lichte Schrift *f*
outlined figure freigestelltes Bild *n*, freistehendes Bild *n*
outline form Konturform *f*
outline mask *(reprod.)* Freisteller *m*, Freistellmaske *f*
outlines *pl* Kontur *f*
outline setting *(text composition)* Konturensatz *m*
out of alignment schlecht ausgerichtet; *(type)* nicht liniehaltend
out-of-date emulsion *(film)* überalterte Emulsion *f*
out of print *(book)* vergriffen
out of register aus dem Register, nicht registergenau, nicht registerhaltig; *(colour)* nicht passergenau, nicht paßgenau
out-of-square feed(ing) schiefwinklige Anlage *f*
out-of square folding schiefwinklige Falzung *f*
out-of-square sheet *(feeding)* schiefer Bogen *m*, Schrägbogen *m*
out of stock *(book)* vergriffen
output Ausgabe *f*, Ausstoß *m*, Leistung *f*, Arbeitsleistung *f*, Leistungsfähigkeit *f*; *(imaging)* Belichten *n*, Belichtung *f*; *(line printer)* Ausdruck *m*
output *v* ausstoßen; *(line printer)* ausdrucken; *(material)* ausgeben; *(to image)* belichten
output a hardcopy *v* Beleg erstellen
output device Ausgabegerät *n*
output format Ausgabeformat *n*
output media *(scanner)* Ausgabematerial *n*
output on film Ausgabe auf Film *f*
output options *pl* Ausgabemöglichkeiten *pl*
output performance *(imagesetter)* Belichtungsgeschwindigkeit *f*, Belichtungsleistung *f*
output rate see output performance
output speed see output performance
output unit Ausgabeeinheit *f*; *(imagesetter)* Belichter *m*, Belichtungseinheit *f*
outside data Fremddaten *pl*
outside photo(graph) Außenaufnahme *f*
over *(overmatter)* Überhang *m*, Überlauf *m*, Übersatz *m*
overall retouching Vollretusche *f*
overall sensitivity *(graphic arts films/photo paper)* Allgemeinempfindlichkeit *f*

overdamping *(offset)* Überfeuchtung *f*
overdelivery *(more copies than ordered)* Überlieferung *f*
overdevelopment Überentwicklung *f*
over-etched verätzt
overexpose *v* überbelichten
overexposure Überbelichtung *f*
overflow diverter Überlaufweiche *f*
overfold Überfalz *m*, Vorfalz *m*
overhang cover board *(book case)* überhängender Buchdeckel *m*
overhaul *(mach.)* Überholung *f*
overhauled *(mach.)* überholt
overhead camera Überkopfkamera *f*, Brückenkamera *f*
overhead costs *pl* Gemeinkosten *pl*
overhead projection Tageslichtprojektion *f*
overheads *pl (overhead costs)* Gemeinkosten *pl*
overhead transparency Overhead-Folie *f*
overinking *(printing)* Überfärbung *f*
overlaid tracing *(copy prep., reprod.)* Deckertransparent *n*
overlap feeding Schuppenanlage *f*, überdeckte Anlage *f*, überlappende Anlage *f*
overlap (web) splicing überlappende Bahnklebung *f*
overlay *(makeready of cylinder)* Ausschnitt *m*, Zurichtung *f*; *(reprod.)* Aufleger *m*, Decker *m*
overlay board *(makeready of letterpress m.)* Zurichtepappe *f*
overlay colour (film) proof *(colour key)* Colorkey *m*, Farbdurchsichtsproof *m*, Farbfolienproof *m*
overlay drafting *(artwork prep.)* Schichtzeichnen *n*
overlay draughting *(artwork prep.)* Schichtzeichnen *n*
overlay exposure *(photocomp.)* Übereinanderbelichtung *f*; *(reprod.)* Einbelichtung *f*
overlay priority control *(image proc.)* Deckerprioritätssteuerung *f*
overlay rake *(folding m.)* Deckrechen *m*
overlay setting *(photocomp.)* Übereinanderbelichtung *f*
overlay sheet *(makeready of letterpress)* Zurichtebogen *m*
overleaf andere Seite *f*, nächste Seite *f*
overload Überlastung *f*
overload protection Überlastsicherung *f*
overmatter *(type)* Übersatz *m*
overpack *(impression pressure)* Überdruck *m*

overpacking *(press cylinder)* übermäßiger Aufzug *m*
overpiling Überlaufen des Stapels *n*
overpiling control Überschießkontrolle *f*
overprint *v* aufdrucken, eindrucken, überdrucken, übereinanderdrucken
overprinter *(press)* Eindruckmaschine *f*
overprint forme Eindruckform *f*
overprinting Aufdruck *m*, Aufeinanderdruck *m*, Eindruck *m*, Überdruck *m*, Übereinanderdruck *m*
overprint varnish Drucklack *m*, Überdrucklack *m*
overprint varnishing Drucklackierung *f*
overproduction Überproduktion *f*
overrun *(more copies than ordered)* Überlieferung *f*, Überproduktion *f*
overs *pl* see oversheets
oversetting *(type matter)* Übersatz *m*
oversheets *pl (allowance)* Zuschuß(bogen) *m/pl*; *(overprod.)* Überschuß *m*
overshot ink duct blade obenliegendes Farbmesser *n*
oversize Überformat *n*
oversize work Arbeiten im Überformat *n*
overstretching *(rubber blanket)* Überdehnen *n*
overstrike *(text rec.)* überschreiben, übertippen
overstrike copy *v (text)* Text überschreiben
ox gall Ochsengalle *f*
oxidation Oxidation *f*
oxidation replenishment *(photochem.)* Oxidationsregenerierung *f*
oxidative drying *(ink)* oxidative Trocknung *f*
oxide Oxid *n*
oxidize *v* oxidieren
ozalid Ozalidkopie *f*
ozalid paper Lichtpauspapier *n*, Ozalidpapier *n*

P

paced *(prod. line)* im Takt *m*, taktgebunden, taktgesteuert
paced conveyor *(mailroom)* Takttransportband *n*
paced delivery Taktauslage *f*
paced feeding Taktanlage *f*
pack Packung *f*; *(continuous stationery)* Endlosstapel *m*, Stapel *m*
package Packung *f*, Verpackung *f*

package printing Verpackungsdruck *m*
packaging Verpackung *f*, Verpacken *n*, Packung *f*, Emballage *f*
packaging design Verpackungsentwurf *m*, Verpackungsgestaltung *f*
packaging identification Packmittelkennzeichnung *f*
packaging industry Verpackungsindustrie *f*
packaging line *(mailroom)* Verpackungslinie *f*
packaging machine Verpackungsmaschine *f*
packaging manufacturer Verpackungshersteller *m*
packaging printer Verpackungsdrucker *m*
pack a plate *v* Platte unterlegen
pack collator *(continuous forms prod.)* Stapelkollator *m*
packing Verpacken *n*, Verpackung *f*; *(press cyl.)* Aufzug *m*, Unterlage *f*
packing creep *(cylinder packing)* Wandern des Zylinderaufzugs
packing foil *(press cyl.)* Unterlagefolie *f*, Unterlegfolie *f*
packing gauge *(press cyl.)* Aufzugsstärkemesser *m*
packing height *(press cyl.)* Aufzugsstärke *f*
packing latitude *(press cyl.)* Aufzugsspielraum *m*
packing (material) Packmaterial *n*
packing of platens Tiegelaufzug *m*
packing paper Packpapier *n*
packing plate *(press cyl.)* Aufzugsblech *n*
packing sheet *(press cyl.)* Aufzugsbogen *m*, Unterlagebogen *m*
packing sheets of guaranteed gauge *(cyl. packing)* kalibrierte Unterlagebogen *m/pl*
packing thickness *(press cyl.)* Aufzugsstärke *f*
pack in reams *v (paper cut to size)* einriesen
pack printer *(press)* Endlosstapeldruckmaschine *f*
pack the cylinder *v* den Aufzug *m* machen
pack-to-pack imprinter Stapel/Stapel-Eindruckmaschine *f*
pack-to-pack printer *(press)* Endlosstapeldruckmaschine *f*
pack-to-pack production *(continuous stationery)* Produktion Stapel/Stapel
pad Block *m*
pad *v* blockleimen; *(cover boards etc.)* ausstopfen, auswattieren
padded book case wattierte Buchdecke *f*
padding Leimen *n*, Blockleimung *f*, Blockverleimung *f*, Leimung *f*, Lumbecken *n*
padding press Blockleimgerät *n*
paddle wheel delivery *(web press)* Schaufelradauslage *f*
pad printer Tampondruckmaschine *f*

pad-saw Rückensäge *f*
pad stapling Blockheftung *f*
pad transfer machine Tampondruckmaschine *f*
page Seite *f*; *four-column* ~ vierspaltige Seite *f*
page *v* paginieren, foliieren
page assembly Seitenmontage *f*, Seitenumbruch *m*
page assembly system Seitenmontagesystem *n*, Seitenumbruchsystem *n*
page balance *(typogr.)* Ausgewogenheit der Seite
page combination pattern *(newspaper press)* Seitenbelegung *f*
page composition Seitenmontage *f*, Seitenumbruch *m*, Seitenaufbau *m*
page content Seitenumfang *m*, Seitenzahl *f*
page coordinates *pl (electronic page make-up)* Seitenkoordinaten *pl*
page cord *(lead comp.)* Kolumnenschnur *f*
page count Seitenanzahl *f*, Seitenumfang *m*, Seitenzahl *f*; *(book)* Buchumfang *m*
page depth Seitenhöhe *f*, Satzhöhe *f*
page description language Seitenbeschreibungssprache *f*
page dummy Seitenaufriß *m*, Seitenentwurf *m*
page format Seitenformat *n*, Seitengröße *f*
page grid Seitenraster *m*
page header *(typesetting)* Kopfzeile *f*
page imposition *(newspaper press)* Seitenbelegung *f*
page layout Seitenanordnung *f*, Seitenaufbau *m*, Seitenaufriß *m*, Seitenentwurf *m*, Seitenlayout *n*, Seitenraster *m*
page make-up Seitenmontage *f*, Seitenumbruch *m*
page make-up system Seitenmontagesystem *n*, Seitenumbruchsystem *n*
page make-up terminal Umbruchterminal *m*
page matrix Ganzseitenmater *f*, gematerte Seite *f*
page number Pagina *f*, Seitenzahl *f*, toter Kolumnentitel *m*; *(folio)* Kolumnenziffer *f*
page numbering Paginierung *f*, Seitennumerierung *f*
page orientation *(landscape/portrait)* Seitenlage *f*
page placement *(newspaper press)* Seitenbelegung *f*
page planning *(typogr.)* Seitenplanung *f*, Seitenaufbereitung *f*
page printer Seitendrucker *m*
page proof Seitenabzug *m*
page reader *(mach.)* Blattleser *m*
page size Seitenformat *n*, Seitengröße *f*
page width Seitenbreite *f*
paginate *v (page make-up)* umbrechen

paginated job *(photocomp.)* umbrochener Seitenjob *m*
pagination *(page make-up)* Seitenmontage *f*, Seitenumbruch *m*, Umbruch *m*; *(page count)* Seitenumfang *m*, Seitenanzahl *f*, Seitenzahl *f*
pagination layout Umbruchgestaltung *f*, Umbruchlayout *n*
pagination system Seitenmontagesystem *n*, Seitenumbruchsystem *n*
paging *(page numbering)* Paginierung *f*, Seitennumerierung *f*
pail *(ink container)* Hobbock *m*
pair kerning *(typesetting)* Unterschneiden *n*, Zeichenunterschneidung *f*
pale gold Bleichgold *n*
pale impression blasser Druck *m*
palette knife Farbspachtel *f*, Farbspatel *m*
pallet Palette *f*
pallet feeder Palettenanleger *m*
palletizer Palettieranlage *f*; *automatic* ~ Palettierautomat *m*
palletizing Abpalettierung *f*, Palettieren *n*
pallet loading Palettenbeschickung *f*
pallet magazine Palettenmagazin *n*
pallet removal Palettenabtransport *m*
pallet trolley Palettenwagen *m*
pallet truck Gabelhubwagen *m*
pamphlet Broschüre *f*, Prospekt *m*
pamphlet production Broschürenherstellung *f*
pamphlet stitching Broschürenheftung *f*
panchromatic film *(reprod.)* panchromatischer Film *m*, Panfilm *m*
panel *(book)* Rückenfeld *n*
pan roller Duktorwalze *f*, Kastenwalze *f*, Schöpfwalze *f*, Tauchwalze *f*
pantograph Pantograf *m*, Storchschnabel *m*
pantographic routing machine Fräspantograf *m*
Pantone ink Pantone-Farbe *f*
Pantone matching system *(colour system)* Pantone-Mischsystem *n*
paper Papier *n*; *(newspaper)* Zeitung *f*, Blatt *n*
paperback Taschenbuch *n*; *(bookb.)* Papiereinband *m*, Pappband *m*, Pappeinband *m*
paperback edition Taschenbuchausgabe *f*
paper bag Papierbeutel *m*, Papiersack *m*
paper binding Papiereinband *m*
paperboards *pl* Kartonage *f*
paperbound broschiert
paper bowl *(paper mach.)* Papierwalze *f*
paper calender *(papermaking)* Papierkalander *m*
paper calliper Papierdicke *f*, Papierstärke *f*
paper coating Papierstrich *m*

paper conditioning Papierakklimatisierung *f*, Papierkonditionierung *f*
paper consumption Papierverbrauch *m*
paper converting Papierverarbeitung *f*; *(print converting)* Druckverarbeitung *f*, Druckweiterverarbeitung *f*, Weiterverarbeitung *f*
paper converting industry papierverarbeitende Industrie *f*, Papierverarbeitungsindustrie *f*
paper copy Papierbeleg *m*
paper counter Papierzähler *m*
paper cutter Papierschneidemaschine *f*, Papierschneider *m*, Planschneider *m*
paper cutting Papierschneiden *n*
paper cutting machine Papierschneidemaschine *f*, Papierschneider *m*, Planschneider *m*
paper cut to size Bogenpapier *n*, Formatpapier *n*
paper delivery Papierlieferung *f*
paper distortion Papierverzug *m*
paper dressing *(press cyl.)* Papieraufzug *m*
paper drill Papierbohrer *m*
paper dryer Papiertrockner *m*
paper dust Papierstaub *m*
paper dust exhaust Papierstaubabsaugung *f*
paper dust extraction Papierstaubabsaugung *f*
paper edge Papierkante *f*, Papierrand *m*
paper feeding *(feeder magazine)* Papiereinstapeln *n*
paper felt Papierfilz *m*
paper fibre Papierfaser *f*
paper filling *(feeder magazine)* Papiereinstapeln *n*
paper finishing Papierverarbeitung *f*, Papierveredlung *f*
paper flong Papiermater *f*
paper format Papierformat *n*
paper gauge Papierdicke *f*, Papierstärke *f*
paper glaze Papierglätte *f*, Papierglanz *m*
paper gloss Papierglanz *m*
paper grade Papierqualität *f*, Papiersorte *f*
paper grain *(web)* Bahnlaufrichtung *f*, Laufrichtung *f*, Papierlaufrichtung *f*
paper grammage Papiergewicht *n*
paper guide Papierführung *f*
paper guiding elements *pl* Papierführungselemente *pl*
paper handling Papiertransport *m*
paper hanging device Papieraufhängevorrichtung *f*
paper hygrometer Papierfeuchtigkeitsmesser *m*
paper industry Papierindustrie *f*
paper in-feed Papiereinlauf *m*, Papiereinzug *m*
paper infeed roller Papiereinzugswalze *f*

paper introduction *(web press)* Papiereinzug *m*
paper inventory Papierbestand *m*
paper jam *(in the press)* Papierknäuel *m*, Papierknautscher *m*, Papierstau *m*, Stopfer *m*, Wickler *m*
paper knife Papiermesser *n*, Papierschneidemesser *n*
paper loading *(feeder magazine)* Papiereinstapeln *n*
papermaché Papiermaché *n*
paper machine Papiermaschine *f*
paper machine glazer Papiermaschinenglättwerk *n*
paper machine wire Papiermaschinensieb *n*
papermaker Papierhersteller *m*
paper makeready Papierzurichtung *f*
papermaking Papierherstellung *f*
paper master *(small offset paper plate)* Papierfolie *f*, Papierdruckplatte *f*, Papierplatte *f*
paper merchants *pl* Papierhändler *m*
paper mill Papierfabrik *f*, Papiermühle *f*
paper moistener Papierbefeuchter *m*
paper mould Papiermatrize *f*
paper offset plate *(small offset)* see paper plate
paper of good feel griffiges Papier *n*
paper packing Papierverpackung *f*; *(press cyl.)* Papieraufzug *m*
paper paste-up Papiermontage *f*
paper plate *(for small offset)* Papierdruckplatte *f*, Papierfolie *f*, Papierplatte *f*
paper pore Papierpore *f*
paper processing Papierverarbeitung *f*; *(print converting)* Druckweiterverarbeitung *f*, buchbinderische Verarbeitung *f*, Druckverarbeitung *f*, Weiterverarbeitung *f*
paper production Papierherstellung *f*
paper proof Papierbeleg *m*
paper quality Papierqualität *f*
paper quantity calculation Papierberechnung *f*
paper rack Papiergestell *n*
paper reel Papierrolle *f*
paper refeeding *(feeder magazine)* Papierauflegen *n*, Papiernachlegen *n*
paper refilling *(feeder magazine)* Papierauflegen *n*, Papiernachlegen *n*
paper reloading *(feeder magazine)* Papierauflegen *n*, Papiernachlegen *n*
paper replenishing *(feeder magazine)* Papierauflegen *n*, Papiernachlegen *n*
paper rewinding Papieraufrollung *f*, Papieraufwicklung *f*

paper rewind unit Papieraufrollung *f*, Papieraufwicklung *f*
paper scales *pl* Papierwaage *f*
paper scissors *pl* Papierschere *f*
paper shavings *pl* Papierschnipsel *pl*, Papierschnitzel *pl*, Papierspäne *pl*, Papierwolle *f*
paper sheet Papierbogen *m*
paper shred Papierschnipsel *pl*, Papierschnitzel *pl*, Papierspäne *pl*, Papierwolle *f*
paper shredder Papierwolf *m*, Papierzerfaserer *m*
paper shrinkage Papierschrumpfung *f*, Papierverzug *m*
paper size Papierformat *n*, Papiergröße *f*
paper sizing Papierleimung *f*
paper slipping Papierschlupf *m*
paper smoothness Papierglätte *f*
paper stock Papierlager *n*
paper stocking Papierlagerung *f*
paper storage Papierlagerung *f*; *(festoon unit in web press)* Papierspeicher *m*
paper store Papierlager *n*
paper stretch Papierdehnung *f*, Papierverzug *m*
paper strip Papierstreifen *m*
paper supplier Papierlieferant *m*
paper supply Papierversorgung *f*, Papierzufuhr *f*
paper surface Papieroberfläche *f*
paper surface structure Papieroberflächenstruktur *f*
paper surface texture Papieroberflächenstruktur *f*
paper tape Papierband *n*
paper testing Papierprüfung *f*
paper thickness Papierdicke *f*, Papierstärke *f*
paper thickness adjustment *(on press)* Druckstärkenregulierung *f*, Papierstärkenregulierung *f*
paper thickness gauge Papierlehre *f*, Papierstärkemesser *m*
paper trade Papierhandel *m*
paper transport Papiertransport *m*
paper trimmings *pl* Papierschnipsel *pl*, Papierschnitzel *pl*, Papierspäne *pl*, Papierwolle *f*
paper tube Papierhülse *f*
paper unevenness Papierunebenheiten *pl*
paper unwinding Papierabrollung *f*, Papierabwicklung *f*
paper unwind unit Papierabrollung *f*, Papierabwicklung *f*
paper volume Papiervolumen *n*
paper wastage Makulatur *f*
paper waste Makulatur *f*
paper web Papierbahn *f*

paper wetter - PE film

paper wetter Papierbefeuchter *m*
paper white Papierweiß *n*
paper width Papierbreite *f*
paper wrapping Papierverpackung *f*
paraffin Paraffin *n*
paraffin *v* paraffinieren
paraffining machine Paraffiniermaschine *f*
paraffin paper Paraffinpapier *n*
paragraph Absatz *m*
paragraph indent Absatz/Einzug *m*
paragraph mark Alineazeichen *n*
parallax *(optics)* Parallaxe *f*
parallel fold Parallelfalz *m*, Parallelbruch *m*, Wickelfalz *m*
parallel light paralleles Licht *n*
parallel processing *(comp.)* Parallelverarbeitung *f*
para rubber Paragummi *m*
parchment Pergament *n*
parchment binding Pergament(ein)band *m*
parchment board Pergamentkarton *m*
parchment paper Pergamentpapier *n*
parchment window *(envelope)* Pergaminfenster *n*
parenthesis *(typesetting)* Parenthese *f*, runde Klammer *f*
Paris white Naturkreide *f*
parity bit Prüfbit *n*
part-bound book teilgebundenes Buch *n*
part edition Teilauflage *f*
partial exposure *(reprod.)* Teilbelichtung *f*
partial occupation *(prod. line)* Teilbelegung *f*
partial run *(print run)* Teilauflage *f*
pass *(through machine)* Arbeitsgang *m*, Durchgang *m*, Durchlauf *m*; **in one ~** in einem Arbeitsgang *m*, in einem Durchgang *m*, in einem Durchlauf *m*
passage *(through machine)* see pass
pass a printed sheet *v (customer)* Druckbogen abnehmen, Druckbogen abstimmen
passed for press druckreif, gut zum Druck, o.k. zum Druck
passed proof abgezeichneter Bogen *m*, Abstimmbogen *m*, Druckfreigabebogen *m*, Freigabebogen *m*
passed sheet abgezeichneter Bogen *m*, Abstimmbogen *m*, Druckfreigabebogen *m*, Freigabebogen *m*
pass for press *v* das Imprimatur *n* geben
pasteboard geklebter Karton *m*, geleimte Pappe *f*, Karton *m*, Pappe *f*
paste dryer *(ink additive)* Trockenpaste *f*
pastel tone Pastellton *m*
pastel tone correction *(scanner function)* Pastelltonkorrektur *f*

paster *(autopaster)* Klebevorrichtung *f*, Anleimvorrichtung *f*; **automatic ~** Rollenwechsler *m*, Autopaster *m*
paster roller *(autopaster)* Klebewalze *f*
paste-up Klebemontage *f*, Klebeumbruch *m*
paste up *v (page make-up)* montieren
paste-up man Montierer *m*
paste-up of layout Klebelayout *n*
paste-up sheet Montagebogen *m*
pasting Klebung *f*
pasty ink pastöse Farbe *f*
patch *(print control bar)* Meßfeld *n*
pattern Muster *n*; *(cutting sample)* Schnittbogen *m*, Schnittmuster *n*, Schnittmusterbogen *m*
pattern coater *(varnishing unit)* Musterlackierwerk *n*
pattern coating *(varnishing)* Nutzenlackierung *f*, Musterlackierung *f*, ausgesparte Lackierung *f*, Fassonlackierung *f*
pattern gluer Musterleimwerk *n*
pattern gluing Muster(be)leimung *f*, Fassonbeleimung *f*
pattern perforation Fassonperforierung *f*, Musterperforierung *f*
pattern perforator Musterperforiereinrichtung *f*
pattern printing Dessindruck *m*
pattern roller *(design roller)* Dessinwalze *f*
pattern supplement Schnittmusterbeilage *f*
pattern varnishing see pattern coating
pay-back period Amortisationszeit *f*
PC(-based) typesetting system PC-Satzsystem *n*
PC composition PC-Satz *m*
PC composition system PC-Satzsystem *n*
PC diskette PC-Diskette *f*
PC (personal computer) PC *m*
PC typesetting PC-Satz *m*
peaking *(scanner function)* Detailkontraststeigerung *f*
peak load Spitzenbelastung *f*
peak performance Spitzenleistung *f*
peculiars *pl (pi characters)* Sonderzeichen *n/pl*
pedal operation Fußantrieb *m*
peelable layer *(masking film)* abziehbare Schicht *f*, Abziehschicht *f*
peelable masking film Maskierfilm mit abziehbarer Maskierschicht
peelable masking layer abziehbare Maskierschicht *f*
peel apart *v (sandwich material)* trennen
peel off *v (coatings)* abziehen; *(dried ink)* abblättern, abplatzen
peel off copper *v* Kupfer abschälen
PE film *(film wrapping)* PE-Folie *f*

pen Feder *f*
pen and disc ruler *(mach.)* Liniermaschine mit Feder und Rolle
pencil drawing Bleistiftzeichnung *f*
pencil layout Bleistiftentwurf *m*
pen drawing Federzeichnung *f*
penetrate *v (ink, glue etc.)* eindringen
penetration *(ink)* Wegschlagen *n*
pen plotter Penplotter *m*
pen ruling machine Liniermaschine mit Feder
pen stroke Federstrich *m*, Federzug *m*
percentage *(value)* Prozentwert *m*
percent area coverage Flächendeckungsgrad *m*, prozentuale Flächendeckung *f*, Rasterprozentwert *m*
percent dot area Flächendeckungsgrad *m*, prozentuale Flächendeckung *f*, Rasterprozentwert *m*
percent sign *(%)* Prozentzeichen *n*
perfect binder Klebebindemaschine *f*, Klebebinder *m*
perfect binding Klebebindung *f*
perfect binding machine see perfect binder
perfect-bound book klebegebundenes Buch *n*
perfecting *(back-side printing)* Widerdruck *m;* *(face and back printing)* Schön- und Widerdruck *m*
perfecting drum *(perfector press)* Wendetrommel *f*
perfecting forme Widerdruckform *f*
perfecting press Perfektor *m*, Schön- und Widerdruckmaschine *f*
perfecting register Widerdruckregister *n*
perfecting side *(back printing side)* Widerdruckseite *f*
perfecting unit *(press)* Widerdruckwerk *n*
perfector *(press)* Perfektor *m*, Schön- und Widerdruckmaschine *f*
perfector unit Schön- und Widerdruckwerk *n*, Widerdruckwerk *n*
perforate *v* perforieren, lochen
perforating Perforierung *f*
perforating bar Perforierleiste *f*
perforating comb Perforierkamm *m*
perforating cut Perforationsschnitt *m*
perforating device Perforiervorrichtung *f*
perforating disc Perforierscheibe *f*
perforating knife Perforiermesser *n*
perforating machine Perforiermaschine *f*
perforating rule Perforierlinie *f*
perforating teeth *pl* Perforierzähnchen *pl*
perforating tool Perforierwerkzeug *n*
perforating wheels *pl* Perforierrädchen *n/pl*

perforation Perforation *f*, Lochung *f*
perforation adhesive binding *(as opp. to routing adhesive binding)* Perfoklebebindung *f*
perforation fold Stanzfalz *m*
perforator Perforator *m*, Perforiermaschine *f*
performance Arbeitsleistung *f*, Leistung *f*, Leistungsfähigkeit *f*
performance limit Leistungsgrenze *f*
performance range Leistungsbereich *m*
performance targets *pl* Leistungsvorgabe *f*
perfo rule Perforierlinie *f*
perfumed ink parfümierte Druckfarbe *f*
perfumed paper parfümiertes Papier *n*
periodical Magazin *n*, Zeitschrift *f*
periodical printing Zeitschriftendruck *m*
periodicals *pl* Periodika *pl*
peripherals *pl (comp.)* Peripherie *f*, Peripheriegeräte *pl*
peripheral units *pl (comp.)* Peripherie *f*, Peripheriegeräte *pl*
periphery *(comp.)* Peripherie *f*
permanent contact hotmelt Schmelzhaftkleber *m*
permanent service Dauerbetrieb *m*
permanent stencil *(screen printing)* Permanentschablone *f*
permanent storage Langzeitarchivierung *f*, Langzeitspeicherung *f*
permission to print Druckerlaubnis *f*, Druckfreigabe *f*, Druckgenehmigung *f*, Druckreiferklärung *f*
personal computer *(PC)* Personal-Computer *m*
personalized mailer personalisierte Werbedrucksache *f*
personnel costs *pl* Personalkosten *pl*
phantom image Phantombild *n*
phone book printing Telefonbuchdruck *m*
phonetic composition phonetischer Satz *m*
phonetic lettering Lautschrift *f*
phonetic transscription phonetische Umschrift *f*
photo agency Bildagentur *f*, Bilderdienst *m*
photo album Fotoalbum *n*
photocell Fotozelle *f*
photo-chemical process fotochemischer Prozeß *m*
photochemicals *pl* Fotochemikalien *pl*
photochemistry Fotochemie *f*
photocoating *(printing plate)* Kopierschicht *f*
photocomposing Fotocomposing *n*
photocomposition Fotosatz *m*, Lichtsatz *m*
photocomposition machine Fotosatzmaschine *f*
photocomposition system Fotosatzsystem *n*
photocomposition typeface Fotosatzschrift *f*
photoconductive lichtleitend
photo-conductor Fotoleiter *m*

photocopier Fotokopiergerät *n*
photocopy Fotokopie *f*
photocopy *v* fotokopieren
photodiode Fotodiode *f*
photo-direct plate *(camera platemaker)* Fotodirektplatte *f*
photo drawing Fotozeichnung *f*
photo-electronic reproduction fotoelektronische Reproduktion *f*
photo emulsion *(graphic arts film)* Kopierschicht *f*
photo-engraver Chemigraf *m*, Fotochemigraf *m*, Klischeeätzer *m*, Klischeehersteller *m*, Klischeur *m*
photo-engravers *pl* Klischeeanstalt *f*, Reproanstalt *f*
photo-engraving Klischeeherstellung *f*, Chemigrafie *f*, Fotochemigrafie *f*, Klischeeätzung *f*
photogrammetry Fotogrammetrie *f*
photo(graph) Aufnahme *f*, Foto *n*, Fotografie *f*
photograph *v* aufnehmen, fotografieren
photographer Fotograf *m*
photographic archive Bildarchiv *n*
photographic board Fotokarton *m*
photographic falsification fotografische Verfremdung *f*
photographic gelatine fotografische Gelatine *f*
photographic grain Fotokorn *n*
photographic laboratory Fotolabor *n*
photographic material Aufnahmematerial *n*, Fotomaterial *n*
photographic media Fotomaterial *n*
photographic paper Fotopapier *n*
photographic reproduction fotografische Reproduktion *f*
photographic restoration Fotorestauration *f*
photography Fotografie *f*
photogravure (process) Tiefdruck *m*, Ätztiefdruck *m*, Rakeltiefdruck *m*
photoheadliner Titelsatzgerät *n*
photolettering Fotohandsatz *m*, Titelsatz *m*
photo lithograph Fotolithograf *m*
photo lithography Fotolithografie *f*
photo-litho retoucher Fotolithoretuscheur *m*
photolysis Fotolyse *f*
photomechanical reproduction fotomechanische Reproduktion *f*
photometer Fotometer *n*, Lichtmeßgerät *n*
photometry Lichtmessung *f*
photomontage Fotomontage *f*
photomultiplier Fotomultiplier *m*, Lichtverstärker *m*

photo paper Fotopapier *n*
photoplot *v (to image)* belichten
photoplotter *(imagesetter)* Belichter *m*, Belichtungseinheit *f*, Fotoplotter *m*
photoplotting *(imaging)* Belichten *n*, Belichtung *f*
photopolymer plate Fotopolymerplatte *f*, Kunststoffklischee *n*, Nylonklischee *n*
photoprint Fotoabzug *m*
photo report Bildbericht *m*
photoreporter Fotoreporter *m*
photoresist *(protective coating)* Abdecklack *m*, Kopierlack *m*, Schutzschicht *f*
photo semi-conductor Fotohalbleiter *m*
photosensitive coating lichtempfindliche Schicht *f*
photo sensor Fotosensor *m*
photo service house Bildagentur *f*, Bilderdienst *m*
photoset *v* belichten
photosetter Fotosatzgerät *n*, Fotosatzmaschine *f*, Belichter *m*, Belichtungseinheit *f*
photosetting Fotosatz *m*, Lichtsatz *m*, Belichten *n*, Belichtung *f*
photostat Fotokopie *f*
photo stencil *(screen printing)* Fotoschablone *f*
photo-stencil film Fotoschablonenfilm *m*
phototype Fototypie *f*, Lichtdruck *m*
phototype printing Fototypie *f*, Lichtdruck *m*
phototypesetter Fotosatzgerät *n*, Fotosatzmaschine *f*, Belichter *m*, Belichtungseinheit *f*
phototypesetting Fotosatz *m*, Lichtsatz *m*, Belichtung *f*
phototypesetting font Fotosatzschrift *f*
phototypesetting house Fotosatzbetrieb *m*
phototypesetting machine Fotosatzmaschine *f*
phototypesetting studio Fotosatzbetrieb *m*, Fotosatzstudio *n*
phototypesetting system Fotosatzsystem *n*
photo unit *(imagesetter)* Belichter *m*, Belichtungseinheit *f*
pH value pH-Wert *m*
pH (value) stabilizer *(fountain solution)* pH-Stabilisator *m*, pH-Wert-Konstanthalter *m*
pica *(typogr.)* Pica
pi-character *(typesetting)* Sonderzeichen *n*
picking Rupfen *n*
picking resistance Rupffestigkeit *f*
pick out *v (pie, lead type)* auslesen
pick-up sucker *(feeder suction head)* Trennsauger *m*
pictogram Piktogramm *n*
pictography Bilderschrift *f*
picture Bild *n*, Abbildung *f*, Illustration *f*
picture *v* abbilden

picture archive Bildarchiv *n*
picture book Bilderbuch *n*
picture copy Bildvorlage *f*
picture defect Bildfehler *m*
picture detail Bilddetail *n*, Bildausschnitt *m*
picture editor Bildredakteur *m*
picture element Bildelement *n*
picture embossing Bildprägung *f*
picture forme *(as opp. to type forme)* Bildform *f*
picture library Bildarchiv *n*
picture margin Bildrand *m*
picture matrix *(as opp. to type matrix)* Bildmater *f*
picture page Bilderseite *f*, Bildseite *f*
picture postcard Ansichtspostkarte *f*, Bildpostkarte *f*
picture quality Bildqualität *f*
picture report Bildbericht *m*
picture section *(book)* Bilderteil *m*, Bildteil *m*
picture size Bildgröße *f*
picture strips *pl* Bilderstreifen *pl*
picture supplement Bilderbeilage *f*
pie *(hand comp.)* Zwiebelfische *pl*
piece fractions *pl* Bruchziffern *pl*, gebrochene Ziffern *f*
piece-to-piece gauge tolerance *(rubber blankets)* Stärketoleranz *f*
pi-font *(photocomp.)* Sonderzeichenfont *m*
pigment Pigment *n*
pigmentation Pigmentierung *f*
pigment colour Körperfarbe *f*
pigment copy *(gravure)* Pigmentkopie *f*
pigment copying machine Pigmentkopieranlage *f*
pigment dye Körperfarbe *f*
pigmented pigmentiert
pigment film *(gravure)* Pigmentfilm *m*
pigment ink Pigmentfarbe *f*
pigment layer Pigmentschicht *f*
pigment paper *(gravure)* Pigmentpapier *n*
pigment paper dryer Pigmentpapiertrockner *m*
pigment paper transfer Pigmentpapierübertragung *f*
pigskin binding Schweinsleder(ein)band *m*
pile Stapel *m*, Stoß *m*
pile *v* abstapeln
pile board Stapelbrett *n*, Stapelplatte *f*, Stapeltisch *m*; ***descending*** ~ absenkbarer Stapeltisch *m*
pile board buffer Stapelbrettpuffer *m*
pile board shelf Stapelbrettregal *n*
pile change Stapelwechsel *m*
pile delivery Stapelauslage *f*, Stapelausleger *m*
pile descent Stapelsenkung *f*

pile drop Stapelsenkung *f*
pile elevator Stapelheber *m*
pile end board Stapelendplatte *f*
pile feeder Stapelanleger *m*
pile formation Stapelbildung *f*
pile height Stapelhöhe *f*
pile hoist Stapellift *m*
pile humidity Stapelfeuchte *f*
pile lowering Stapelsenkung *f*
pile magazine *(converting machines)* Stapelmagazin *n*
pile marking Stapelmarkierung *f*
pile reverser Stapelwender *m*
pile spraying *(powder spraying)* Stapelbestäubung *f*
pile temperature Stapeltemperatur *f*, Stapelwärme *f*
pile turner Stapelwender *m*
pile (up) *v* stapeln
pile vibrator Stapelvibrator *m*
piling Abstapeln *n*
piling properties *pl* (ink) Stapelverhalten *n*
piling(-up) *(deposits on blanket, rollers)* Aufbauen *n*; (ink) Pelzen *n*
pincer grippers *pl* Zangengreifer *pl*
pin cylinder *(web press)* Punkturzylinder *m*
pin edge *(web printing)* Punkturrand *m*
pin folder *(web press)* Punkturfalzwerk *n*
pinholes *pl* Nadelstiche *pl*, Pinholes *pl*, Punkturlöcher *n/pl*
pin on *v* aufnadeln, aufstechen
pinpointed retouching gezielte Retusche *f*
pins *pl* (pin folder) Punkturen *f/pl*, Punkturnadeln *f/pl*
pinsharp gestochen scharf
pinsharp copy spitze Kopie *f*
pinsharp dot gestochen scharfer Rasterpunkt *m*
pirate *v* nachdrucken
pirated edition unberechtigter Nachdruck *m*
pirating unberechtigter Nachdruck *m*
piston Kolben *m*
piston rod Kolbenstange *f*, Pleuelstange *f*
pixel *(picture element)* Bildelement *n*, Bildpunkt *m*, Pixel *n*
pixel art(work) Pixelgrafik *f*
pixel editing Pixelkorrektur *f*
pixel graphics Pixelgrafik *f*
pixelization Pixelauflösung *f*
pixel retouching Pixelretusche *f*
plain *(unprinted)* unbedruckt
plain initial (letter) einfache Initiale *f*
plain paper Normalpapier *n*
plain paper copier Normalpapierkopierer *m*

plain paper proof *(photocomp.)* Normalpapierabzug *m*, Korrekturbelegausdruck *m*
plain rule *(typesetting)* einfache Linie *f*
plain sheet Einfachbogen *m*
plane down *v (letterpress forme)* glattklopfen, klopfen, niederklopfen
plane mirror *(camera)* Planspiegel *m*
planer Hobel *m; (letterpress)* Klopfbrett *n*, Klopfholz *n*
planning Planung *f*
planning and assembling grid Standbogen *m*
planning board Planungstafel *f*
planning department Arbeitsvorbereitung *f*
planning film Planungsfilm *m*, Standfilm *m*
planning sheet Einteilungsbogen *m*
planographic printing *(as opp. to letterpress printing with raised and gravure printing with recessed printing elements)* Flachdruck *m*
plant director see plant manager
plant management Betriebsführung *f*, Betriebsleitung *f*
plant manager Betriebsleiter *m*, technischer Leiter *m; (printshop)* Druckereileiter *m*
plastic binding Plastikbindung *f*
plastic-coated gravure cylinder kunststoffbeschichteter Tiefdruckzylinder *m*
plastic comb *(binding)* Plastikbinderücken *m*
plastic comb binding Plastikkammbindung *f*
plastic letter *(hand comp.)* Kunststoffletter *f*
plastic master *(small offset plate)* Kunststoffdruckfolie *f*
plastic material Kunststoff *m*
plastic (printing) plate *(for small offset)* Kunststoffdruckfolie *f*
plastic roller Kunststoffwalze *f*
plastics printing Kunststoffbedruckung *f*
plate Platte *f; (printing plate)* Druckplatte *f; (book)* Bildtafel *f*, Tafel *f*
plate adjustment *(on press)* Plattenjustierung *f*
plate baking Platteneinbrennen *n*
plate bed *(flat-bed press)* Plattenbett *n*, Plattenfundament *n*
plate bender Plattenbiegegerät *n; automatic ~* Plattenabkantautomat *m*
plate cabinet Plattenschrank *m*
plate change Plattenwechsel *m*
plate clamp *(on press)* Plattenspannklemme *f*, Plattenklemme *f*
plate clamping Plattenaufspannen *n*, Platteneinspannen *n*
plate clamping bar *(press cyl.)* Plattenspannschiene *f*

plate clamping device Plattenaufspannvorrichtung *f*, Plattenklemmvorrichtung *f*
plate clamping system *(press cyl.)* Plattenspannsystem *n*
plate cleaner Plattenreiniger *m*
plate coater Plattenbeschichtungsmaschine *f*
plate coating Plattenbeschichtung *f*
plate control wedge *(exposure control)* Plattenkeil *m*
plate correction Plattenkorrektur *f*
plate correction pen Plattenkorrekturstift *m*
plate crack Plattenbruch *m*
plate cutter Plattenschere *f*, Plattenschneider *m*
plate cylinder Plattenzylinder *m; (rotary letterpress, flexography)* Klischeezylinder *m*
plate damp(en)ing Plattenfeuchtung *f*
plate damper *(roller)* Feuchtauftragswalze *f*
plate deletion pen Plattenkorrekturstift *m*
plate development Plattenentwicklung *f*
plate dispenser *(small offset)* Plattenmagazin *n*
plate dressing *(press cyl.)* Plattenunterlage *f*
plate exposure Plattenkopie *f*, Plattenbelichtung *f*
plate exposure control patch *(measuring strip)* Plattenkopiekontrollfeld *n*
plate fixing Plattenfixierung *f*
plate format Plattenformat *n*, Plattengröße *f*
plate frame operator Kopierer *m*
plate grain Plattenkorn *n*
plate graining Plattenaufrauhung *f*, Plattenkörnung *f*
plate gum Plattengummi *m*, Plattengummierung *f*, Plattengummierungsmittel *n*
plate gumming Plattengummierung *f*
plate handling Plattenbearbeitung *f*
plate height *(on cylinder)* Plattenhöhe *f*
plate inker *(inking roller)* Farbauftragswalze *f*
plate inkers on/off *(inking roller)* Farbauftragswalzen an/ab
plate inking roller Farbauftragswalze *f*
plate locking bar *(press cyl.)* Plattenspannschiene *f*
plate lock-up system *(press cyl.)* Plattenklemmvorrichtung *f*, Plattenspannsystem *n*
platemaker *(person)* Druckformhersteller *m*, Kopierer *m*
plate makeready Plattenzurichtung *f*
platemaking Plattenkopie *f*, Kopie *f*, Plattenherstellung *f*, Druckformherstellung *f*
platemaking department Kopie *f*
platemaking line Plattenstraße *f*, Plattenverarbeitungslinie *f*
platemaking room Kopie *f*

platemaking system - polishing rubber

platemaking system Plattenkopiersystem *n*
platemaking technique Kopiertechnik *f*
plate manufacture Plattenherstellung *f*
plate mount Plattenunterlage *f*
plate mounting Plattenaufspannen *n*, Platteneinspannen *n*
plate mounting device Plattenaufspannvorrichtung *f*
platen Tiegel *m*; *(platen press)* Drucktiegel *m*
platen cutter-creaser Tiegelstanzautomat *m*
platen forme Tiegeldruckform *f*
platen press Drucktiegel *m*, Tiegel *m*, Tiegeldruckpresse *f*; **automatic ~** Tiegeldruckautomat *m*
platen press die-cutting *(as opp. to flat-bed/rotary die-cutting)* Tiegelstanzen *n*
plate packing *(press cyl.)* Plattenunterlage *f*
plate positioning Standmachen der Platte *n*
plate processing Plattenbearbeitung *f*, Plattenentwicklung *f*, Plattenverarbeitung *f*
plate processing line Plattenstraße *f*, Plattenverarbeitungslinie *f*
plate processor Plattenentwicklungsmaschine *f*
plate production Plattenherstellung *f*
plate punch Plattenstanze *f*
plate rack Plattenständer *m*
plate reader *(for ink key presetting)* Plattenleser *m*
plate-ready kopierfähig
plate-ready film kopierfähiger Film *m*, plattenfertiger Film *m*
plate register Plattenregister *n*
plate registering Standmachen der Platte *n*
plate saddle *(web press)* Plattensattel *m*
plate scanner *(for ink key presetting)* Plattenscanner *m*
plate sensitivity Plattenempfindlichkeit *f*
plate size Plattenformat *n*, Plattengröße *f*
plate stacker Plattenstapler *m*
plate surface Plattenoberfläche *f*
plate thickness Plattenstärke *f*
plate wear Plattenabnutzung *f*
plate whirler *(in-house coating)* Plattenschleuder *f*
platform elevator Hebebühne *f*
plating-up Plattenaufspannen *n*, Platteneinspannen *n*
playing cardboard Spielkartenkarton *m*
playing cards *pl* Spielkarten *pl*
please turn over bitte umblättern
plot *v* aufzeichnen, schreiben; *(to image)* belichten

plotter Aufzeichnungsgerät *n*, Plotter *m*; *(imagesetter)* Belichter *m*, Belichtungseinheit *f*
plotting Aufzeichnung *f*; *(imaging)* Belichten *n*, Belichtung *f*
plow fold Pflugfalz *m*
plow folder *(web press)* Pflugfalzer *m*
plug-in circuit board *(comp.)* Steckkarte *f*
plug-in connection *(comp.)* Steckkontakt *m*, Steckverbindung *f*
plug-in module *(comp.)* Steckmodul *n*
plus correction Pluskorrektur *f*
plush cover *(damping roller)* Plüschbezug *m*
plush-covered damper roller plüschbezogene Feuchtwalze *f*
plush tampon Plüschtampon *m*
plus sheets *pl (allowance)* Zuschuß(bogen) *m/pl*
plus sign Pluszeichen *n*
plywood for blockmounting Klischeesperrholz *n*
pneumatic control pneumatische Steuerung *f*, Steuer(ungs)pneumatik *f*
pocket atlas Taschenatlas *m*
pocketbook Taschenbuch *n*
pocket diary Taschenkalender *m*
pocket dictionary Handwörterbuch *n*, Taschenwörterbuch *n*
pocket edition Taschenausgabe *f*
pocket laminating *(as opp. to roll-to-roll laminating)* Taschenkaschierung *f*
poetry setting Gedichtsatz *m*, Verssatz *m*
point *(typogr.)* Punkt *m*
point Didot *(typogr.)* Didot-Punkt *m*
point light Punktlicht *n*
point light lamp Punktlichtlampe *f*
point light source Punktlichtlampe *f*
point pica Pica-Punkt *m*
point size *(type)* Schriftgrad *m*, Schriftgröße *f*, Kegel *m*
point size range *(type)* Schriftgradbereich *m*, Schriftgrößenbereich *m*
point system *(typogr.)* Punktsystem *n*
polarize *v* polarisieren
polarized light polarisiertes Licht *n*
polarizing filter *(densitometry)* Polarisationsfilter *m*, Polarisator *m*, Polfilter *m*
polish *v* polieren, schleifen
polishing bath *(gravure cyl.)* Dekapierbad *n*
polishing brush Putzbürste *f*
polishing disc Polierscheibe *f*
polishing felt Polierfilz *m*
polishing head Polierkopf *m*, Schleifkopf *m*
polishing machine Poliermaschine *f*, Schleifmaschine *f*
polishing rubber Poliergummi *m*

polishing structure *(gravure cyl.)* Schleifbild *n*
polluting umweltschädlich
pollution control Umweltschutz *m*
polyamide Polyamid *n*
polychromatic mehrfarbig
polyester Polyester *n*
polyester film Polyesterfilm *m*, Polyesterfolie *f*
polyethylene *(PE)* Polyäthylen *n*
polyethylene coated paper
  polyäthylenbeschichtetes Papier *n*
polyethylene film *(PE film; film wrapping)*
  Polyäthylenfolie *f*
polygon mirror Polygonspiegel *m*
polymerization Polymerisation *f*
polymer plate Polymerplatte *f*
polypropylene *(PP)* Polypropylen *n*
polystyrene Polystyrol *n*
polyurethane Polyurethan *n*
polyvinyl alcohol *(PVA)* Polyvinylalkohol *m*
polyvinyl chloride *(PVC)* Polyvinylchlorid *n*
pony turner-bar *(press folder)* Pony-Wendestange *f*
poorly absorbent paper schlechtsaugendes Papier *n*
poor printing schlechter Druck *m*
popular edition Volksausgabe *f*
porcelain marbles Porzellanmärbeln *pl*
porcelain printing Porzellandruck *m*
pore-free porenfrei
porous paper durchsaugendes Papier *n*, poröses Papier *n*
port *(I/O connection)* Anschluß *m*
portrait size Hochformat *n*
position Stellung *f*, Stand *m*; *(of ad)* Plazierung *f*
position *v* positionieren, auf Stand bringen, den Stand machen, einpassen
positioning Einpassen *n*, Plazierung *f*, Positionierung *f*, Standmachen *n*
positioning accuracy Positioniergenauigkeit *f*, Standgenauigkeit *f*
positioning scale Einstellskala *f*
positive Positiv *n*
positive blue-print Positivpause *f*
positive contact screen *(reprod.)*
  Positivkontaktraster *m*
positive doctor blade mitlaufende Rakel *f*
positive doctoring *(gravure)* positive Abrakelung *f*
positive dyeline Positivpause *f*
positive/negative display *(video screen)*
  Positiv/Negativ-Darstellung *f*
positive/negative transposition *(reprod.)*
  Positiv/Negativumwandlung *f*
positive plate Positivplatte *f*
positive platemaking Positivkopie *f*
positive retoucher Positivretuscheur *m*
positive retouching Positivretusche *f*
positive screening Positivrasterung *f*
positive (working) plate Positivplatte *f*
postage rates *pl (newspaper mailing)*
  Postgebühren *f/pl*
postage stamp Briefmarke *f*, Postwertzeichen *n*
postage stamp printing Briefmarkendruck *m*
postal code PLZ *f*, Postleitzahl *f*
postal distribution Postversand *m*
postal forms *pl* Postvordrucke *pl*
postal newspaper distribution Postzeitungsdienst *m*
postal regulations *pl* Postvorschriften *pl*
postal requirements *pl* Postvorschriften *pl*
postal sorting *(mailroom)* postalische Sortierung *f*
postal wrapper Streifband *n*
postcard Postkarte *f*
postcard board Postkartenkarton *m*
postcard doubling Postkartendoppeln *n*
postcard size Postkartenformat *n*
poster Affiche *f*, Plakat *n*, Poster *n*; *multi-part ~*
  mehrteiliges Plakat *n*
poster advertising Plakatwerbung *f*
poster artist Plakatzeichner *m*
poster designer Plakatzeichner *m*
poster hanger Posteraufhänger *m*
posterizing Vergrößern *n*
poster letters *pl (hand comp.)* Plakatbuchstaben *pl*
poster mailing tube Plakatversandhülse *f*
poster paper Plakatpapier *n*
poster pillar Litfaßsäule *f*
poster printing Plakatdruck *m*
poster reproduction Großbildreproduktion *f*
poster type *(hand comp.)* Plakatbuchstaben *pl*, Plakatschrift *f*
poster work *(printing)* Plakatdruck *m*
post-exposure Nachbelichtung *f*
post-hardening Nachhärtung *f*
post-press operations *pl* Arbeiten nach dem Druck
post-press processing Druckweiterverarbeitung *f*
PostScript compatible PostScript-fähig
post-treatment Nachbehandlung *f*
potash Pottasche *f*
potassium ferricyanide rotes Blutlaugensalz *n*
potassium ferrocyanide gelbes Blutlaugensalz *n*
potentiometer Potentiometer *n*

pouch laminating *(as opp. to roll-to-roll laminating)* Taschenkaschierung *f*
pouch pocket Kaschiertasche *f*
pouring-in of metal Metalleinguß *m*
powder application Bestäubung *f*, Druckbestäubung *f*
powder consumption Puderverbrauch *m*
powder container Puderbehälter *m*
powder contamination *(press)* Verpuderung *f*
powderless etching *(blockmaking)* Einstufenätzung *f*
powder lumps *pl* Puderklumpen *pl*
powder metering Puderdosierung *f*
powder removal Abstaubung *n*, Entstäubung *f*, Puderabsaugung *f*
powder sprayer Bestäuber *m*, Bestäubungsapparat *m*, Bestäubungsgerät *n*, Druckbestäuber *m*, Puderautomat *m*, Puderbestäuber *m*, Zerstäuber *m*
powder spraying Bestäubung *f*, Druckbestäubung *f*, Trockenbestäubung *f*
power *(el.)* Leistung *f*
power consumption *(el.)* Anschlußleistung *f*, Leistungsaufnahme *f*
power requirement *(el.)* Anschlußwert *m*, Kraftbedarf *m*, Leistungsbedarf *m*
power transmission Kraftübertragung *f*
practice-oriented praxisgerecht, praxisorientiert
prayer-book Gebetbuch *n*
pre-adjustment Voreinstellung *f*
pre-alignment *(sheet feeding)* Vorausrichtung *f*
pre-angled sets of screen films vorgewinkelte Rasterfilmsätze *pl*
pre-baking solution *(offset plate)* Ein〉rennmittel *n*
pre-breaker *(folding box prod.)* Vorbrechvorrichtung *f*
preceding line *(typesetting)* vorhergehende Zeile *f*
precision engineering Präzisionstechnik *f*, Präzisionsmaschinenbau *m*
pre-defined area *(on-screen pagination)* vordefinierte Fläche *f*
preface *(book)* Vorwort *n*
pre-folder *(press folder)* Vorfalzer *m*
pre-gripper Vorgreifer *m*
preground doctor blade *(gravure)* Dünnschliffrakel *f*
prejogged stack vorgerüttelter Stapel *m*
preliminary calculation Vorkalkulation *f*
preliminary matter *(book)* Titelei *f*
preliminary pages *pl* Titelbogen *m*

prelims *pl* Titelei *f*
preloading device Vorstapeleinrichtung *f*
pre-makeready *(press cyl.)* Voreinrichten *n*, Vorzurichtung *f*
premelter *(hotmelt)* Vorschmelzgerät *n*
preparation *(makeready)* Einrichten *n*
preparation times *pl* *(makeready times)* Rüstzeiten *f/pl*, Einrichtezeiten *f/pl*
preparatory work Vorarbeiten *pl*
prepare *v (to make ready)* einrichten
prepiling device Vorstapeleinrichtung *f*
pre-press area *in the* ~ im Druckvorstufenbereich *m*
pre-press proof Proof *m*
pre-press stages *pl* Druckvorstufen *pl*
pre-press system Druckvorstufensystem *n*
pre-print *(liner sheet)* Kaschierbogen *m*
preprinted products *pl* Vorprodukte *n/pl*
preprint(ed section) feeder Vorprodukteanleger *m*
preprinted sections *pl* Vorprodukte *n/pl*, vorgedruckte Bogen *pl*
preprinted signatures *pl* vorgedruckte Bogen *pl*
preprints *pl* vorgedruckte Bogen *pl*, Vorprodukte *n/pl*
preregister system Vorregistersystem *n*
preregistration *(sheet feeding)* Vorausrichtung *f*
pre-scanning device Scannervoreinstellgerät *n*
pre-scan proof Proof *m*
prescore *v* vorrillen
pre-screened vorgerastert
preselection counter Vorwahlzähler *m*
presensitized printing plate vorbeschichtete Druckplatte *f*
presetting Voreinstellung *f*
presetting of machine Maschinenvoreinstellung *f*
presetting of press Druckmaschinenvoreinstellung *f*
presetting system Voreinstellsystem *n*
presetting value Voreinstellwert *m*
press *(hand press)* Presse *f*; *(newspapers)* Presse *f*; *(printing machine)* Druckmaschine *f*
press adjustments *pl* Druckmaschineneinstellungen *pl*
press agency Nachrichtenagentur *f*, Nachrichtenbüro *n*
press and print advertising *(as opp. to TV advertising)* gedruckte Werbung *f*
press arrangement Druckmaschinenanordnung *f*
pressboard Preßpappe *f*, Preßspan *m*
press capacity Druckmaschinenleistung *f*
press characteristics *pl* Druckkennlinie *f*, Druckmaschinenkenndaten *pl*
press configuration Druckmaschinenanordnung *f*

press construction Druckmaschinenbau *m*
press control console Druckmaschinensteuerpult *m*
press controls *pl* Druckmaschinensteuerung *f*
press cutting Zeitungsausschnitt *m*
press delivery Druckmaschinenauslage *f*; *(web press)* Rotationsausgang *m*, Rotationsmaschinenauslage *f*
press department *(journalists)* Presseabteilung *f*
press down *v* niederdrücken
press downtime Druckmaschinenstillstand *m*
press enclosure Druckmaschinenkapselung *f*
press engineering Druckmaschinenbau *m*
press equipment Druckmaschinenausrüstung *f*
press feeder Druckmaschinenanleger *m*
press-finished product Fertigprodukt *n*, Komplettdruck *m*
press folder *(web press)* Falzapparat *m*, Druckmaschinenfalzwerk *n*
press foundation Druckmaschinenfundament *n*
press frame Druckmaschinengestell *n*, Druckmaschinenrahmen *m*; *(hand press)* Pressenrahmen *m*
press functions *pl* Druckmaschinenfunktionen *pl*
press-gilding Preßvergoldung *f*
press hooding Druckmaschinenkapselung *f*
pressing Pressen *n*, Pressung *f*; *(book block)* Abpressen *n*
pressing block *(three-knife trimmer)* Preßstempel *m*
pressing device Preßvorrichtung *f*
pressing roller Preßrolle *f*, Preßwalze *f*
pressing station *(book prod.)* Anpreßstation *f*
press item *(newspaper)* Zeitungsnotiz *f*
press jack *(hand press)* Preßbengel *m*, Preßschwengel *m*
press line Drucklinie *f*
pressmakers *pl* Druckmaschinenfabrik *f*, Druckmaschinenhersteller *m*
pressman Drucker *m*
pressman's training course Druckerlehrgang *m*
press manufacture Druckmaschinenbau *m*
press manufacturers *pl* Druckmaschinenfabrik *f*, Druckmaschinenhersteller *m*
press minder Drucker *m*, Druckmaschinenführer *m*
press monitoring Druckmaschinenüberwachung *f*
press operation Druckmaschinenbedienung *f*
press operator Drucker *m*
press output Druckleistung *f*, Druckmaschinenleistung *f*; *(web press)* Rotationsausstoß *m*

press parameters *pl* Druckmaschinenkenndaten *pl*
press performance Druckmaschinenleistung *f*
pressplate Druckplatte *f*
press proof Andruck *m*, Revisionsabzug *m*, Revisionsbogen *m*
pressproof *v* andrucken
press proofing Andruck *m*
press-ready druckfertig
press removal Druckmaschinendemontage *f*
press revisor Revisor *m*
press roller Druckwalze *f*
pressroom Drucksaal *m*, Druckerei *f*, Druckmaschinensaal *m*
pressroom chemicals *pl* Druckchemikalien *pl*
pressroom chemistry Druckchemie *f*
pressroom equipment Druckereiausrüstung *f*, Druckereieinrichtung *f*, Druckmaschinenpark *m*
pressroom manager Druckereileiter *m*
pressroom supervisor Druckereileiter *m*
press run Druckmaschinenlauf *m*, Druckvorgang *m*
press section *(paper machine)* Pressenpartie *f*
press settings *pl* Druckmaschineneinstellungen *pl*
press speed Druckleistung *f*, Druckmaschinengeschwindigkeit *f*
press standstill Druckmaschinenstillstand *m*
press start-up Druckmaschinenstart *m*
press stick *(hand press)* Preßbengel *m*, Preßschwengel *m*
press stop(page) Druckmaschinenstillstand *m*, Druckunterbrechung *f*, Stopper *m*
press supervision Druckmaschinenüberwachung *f*
press supervisor Druckmaschinenführer *m*
pressure Druck *m*
pressure lubrication Druckschmierung *f*
pressure oil lubrication Druckölumlaufschmierung *f*
pressure roller Anpreßwalze *f*; *(gravure)* Presseur *m*
pressure-sensitive label Haftetikett *n*, Selbstklebeetikett *n*
pressure-sensitive paper Kontaktpapier *n*
press washer *(ink unit wash-up device)* Farbwerkswascheinrichtung *f*
press wear Druckmaschinenverschleiß *m*
prestacker Vorstapeleinrichtung *f*
pre-treatment Vorbehandlung *f*
preview *(layout-true and/or true-typographic display on screen)* Echtdarstellung (am Bildschirm) *f*, Preview-Darstellung *f*, Prüfdarstellung (am Bildschirm) *f*

preview mode *(true typographic display capability on text input terminals)* Preview-Betriebsfunktion *f*
preview terminal *(video screen separated from text input terminal for true-typographic display)* Darstellungsbildschirm *m*, Preview-Terminal *m*
previous unit *(in a line)* vorgeschaltetes Aggregat *n*
price calculation Preisberechnung *f*, Preiskalkulation *f*
price estimating Preisberechnung *f*, Preiskalkulation *f*
price imprint Preiseindruck *m*
price per 1,000 ens *(typesetting)* Tausendbuchstabenpreis *m*
price/performance ratio Preis/Leistungsverhältnis *n*
price per sheet Bogenpreis *m*
pricing Preisberechnung *f*, Preiskalkulation *f*
primary colours *pl (colour system)* Primärfarben *pl*
primer coating Grundierung *f*
primer glue Vorleim *m*
primer ink Vordruckfarbe *f*
primer printing Vordrucken *n*
primer varnish coating Vorlackierung *f*
prime the ink train *v* Farbe einlaufen lassen
priming *(e.g. for gold printing)* Vordrucken *n*
print Druck *m*, Abdruck *m*, Druckgrafik *f*, Grafik *f*; *(finger print)* Abdruck *m*; *(photoprint)* Foto *n*, Fotoabzug *m*, Papierabzug *m*
print *v* drucken; *(to copy, to contact)* kopieren
printability Bedruckbarkeit *f*
printability tester Bedruckbarkeitsprüfgerät *n*
printable bedruckbar
print advertising Drucksachenwerbung *f*, gedruckte Werbung *f*
print buyer Druckscheneinkäufer *m*
print consumer Drucksachenverbraucher *m*
print control bar Druckkontrolleiste *f*, Druckkontrollstreifen *m*
print control strip see print control bar
print converting buchbinderische Verarbeitung *f*, Druckverarbeitung *f*, Druckweiterverarbeitung *f*, Weiterverarbeitung *f*
printed gedruckt; *the book is ~ by gravure* das Buch ist im Tiefdruck gedruckt
printed circuit gedruckte Schaltung *f*
printed circuit board gedruckte Schaltung *f*, Leiterplatte *f*, Platine *f*, Printplatte *f*
printed copy *(text copy)* gedrucktes Manuskript *n*

printed fabric bedruckter Stoff *m*, bedrucktes Gewebe *n*
printed head to foot Kopf auf Fuß gedruckt
printed head to head Kopf auf Kopf gedruckt
printed image Druckbild *n*
printed matter Druckerzeugnis *n*, Druckprodukt *n*, Drucksache *f*
printed media Druckmedien *n/pl*, gedruckte Medien *pl*, Printmedien *pl*
printed (on) both sides beidseitig bedruckt, doppelseitig bedruckt, zweiseitig bedruckt
printed one side (only) einseitig bedruckt
print(ed) product Druckerzeugnis *n*, Druckprodukt *n*, Drucksache *f*
printed reproduction Druckwiedergabe *f*
printed sheet Druckbogen *m*
printed side up bedruckte Seite oben
printer *(person)* Drucker *m*; *(printshop)* Druckerei *f*; *(small press)* Druckmaschine *f*; *(line printer)* Drucker *m*
printer connection *(line printer)* Druckeranschluß *m*
printer interface *(line printer)* Druckeranschluß *m*
printer's alloy see printer's metal
printer's ball Buchdruckerballen *m*, Druckerballen *m*, Farbballen *m*
printer's blanket Drucktuch *n*
printer's error Druckfehler *m*
printer's flower Leiste *f*, Schriftornament *n*, Verzierung *f*
printer's imprint Impressum *n*
printer's ink Druckerschwärze *f*
printer-slotter Druckschlitzmaschine *f*, Druckslotter *m*
printer's metal *(type metal)* Letternmetall *n*, Schriftmetall *n*, Schriftzeug *n*
printer's ornament see printer's flower
printer's reader Hauskorrektor *m*
printer's supplier Druckbedarfsgeschäft *n*, Druckereifachgeschäft *n*, Fachgeschäft für Druckereibedarf, grafischer Fachhändler *m*, grafischer Zulieferer *m*, Zulieferfirma für die Druckindustrie
printer's supply Druckbedarfsartikel *pl*, Druckereibedarf *m*
Printers Union Gewerkschaft Druck *f*
print finishing buchbinderische Verarbeitung *f*, Druckverarbeitung *f*, Druckweiterverarbeitung *f*, Weiterverarbeitung *f*; *(surface finishing)* Druckveredlung *f*
printhouse Druckerei *f*, Druckhaus *n*
print image carrier Druckbildträger *m*

printing - printing plate conveyor

printing Druck *m*, Drucken *n*, Drucklegung *f*, Abdruck *m*
printing aids *pl* Druckhilfsmittel *pl*
printing alloy see printer's metal
printing and perfecting Schön- und Widerdruck *m*
printing and perfecting unit Schön- und Widerdruckwerk *n*
printing and publishing industry Druck- und Verlagsindustrie *f*
print(ing) area Druckfläche *f*
printing areas *pl (as opp. to non-printing areas)* Bildstellen *pl*, druckende Stellen *pl*
printing blanket Drucktuch *n*
printing block Klischee *n*
printing both sides Schön- und Widerdruck *m*
printing box see contact printer
printing capacity Druckleistung *f*
print(ing) carrier Bedruckstoff *m*
printing cartridge *(slide-in carriage)* Druckwerkseinschub *m*, Druckzylindereinschub *m*, Formateinschub *m*, herausfahrbarer Druckwerkswagen *m*, Zylindereinschub *m*
printing character Druckletter *f*, Drucktype *f*
printing characteristics *pl* Druckkennlinie *f*
printing chemicals *pl* Druckchemikalien *pl*
printing company Druckerei *f*, Druckhaus *n*, grafischer Betrieb *m*
printing conditions *pl* Druckbedingungen *pl*
print(ing) contrast Druckkontrast *m*
printing copy Druckvorlage *f*
printing costs *pl* Druckkosten *pl*
printing couple *(printing unit)* Druckwerk *n*
printing difficulties *pl* Druckschwierigkeiten *pl*
printing-down *(contact copying)* Kontaktkopie *f*
printing(-down) film Kopierfilm *m*
printing-down frame *(platemaking)* Kopierrahmen *m*
printing engineer Druckingenieur *m*
printing equipment Druckereiausrüstung *f*, Druckereieinrichtung *f*
printing estimating Druck(sachen)kalkulation *f*
printing estimator Drucksachenkalkulator *m*
print(ing) expert Druckfachmann *m*
printing firm Druckerei *f*, Druckhaus *n*, grafischer Betrieb *m*
print(ing) format Druckformat *n*
print(ing) forme Druckform *f*, Form *f*
print(ing) forme production Druckformherstellung *f*
printing frame see contact printer, vacuum frame
print(ing) gradation Druckgradation *f*

printing group *(printing unit)* Druckwerk *n*
printing house Druckerei *f*, Druckhaus *n*, grafischer Betrieb *m*
print(ing) image Druckbild *n*
printing impression Anpreßdruck *m*, Beistelldruck *m*, Druckbeistellung *f*, Druckspannung *f*
printing industry Druckindustrie *f*, grafische Industrie *f*
printing ink Druckfarbe *f*, Farbe *f*
printing ink manufacturers *pl* see inkmakers
printing instructor Druckinstrukteur *m*
print(ing) job Druckarbeit *f*, Druckauftrag *m*
print(ing) journal Druckfachzeitschrift *f*, grafische Fachzeitschrift *f*
printing lay *(sheet registration)* Druckanlage *f*
print(ing) length Drucklänge *f*
print(ing) letter Druckletter *f*, Drucktype *f*
printing machine Druckmaschine *f*
printing machine factory Druckmaschinenfabrik *f*, Druckmaschinenhersteller *m*
print(ing) magazine Druckfachzeitschrift *f*, grafische Fachzeitschrift *f*
Printing Management Association Unternehmensverband Druck *m*
print(ing) market Drucksachenmarkt *m*
printing master *(small offset plate)* Druckfolie *f*, Druckplatte *f*
printing material Bedruckstoff *m*
printing measure *(line printer)* Druckbreite *f*
printing metal see printer's metal
printing method Druckverfahren *n*
printing methods *pl* Drucktechniken *pl*
printing nip Druckspalt *m*
printing office Druckerei *f*, Offizin *f*
printing of front trim *(book)* Frontdruck *m*
printing of solids Flächendruck *m*
printing on demand Drucken nach Bedarf *n*, Printing on Demand *n*
printing operation Druckvorgang *m*, Druckereibetrieb *m*, Druckerei *f*
printing operation planning Druckereiplanung *f*
print(ing) order Druckauftrag *m*
printing-out of solids Ausdrucken von Vollflächen *n*
printing paper Druckpapier *n*
printing paste Druckpaste *f*
printing performance Druckleistung *f*
printing plant Druckanlage *f*, Druckerei *f*, Druckereibetrieb *m*
printing plate Druckplatte *f*
printing plate conveyor Druckplattenfördersystem *n*

printing plate manufacturer
   Druckplattenhersteller *m*
print(ing) preparation Druckvorbereitung *f*
printing press Druckmaschine *f*
printing press manufacturers *pl*
   Druckmaschinenfabrik *f*,
   Druckmaschinenhersteller *m*
printing pressure Anpreßdruck *m*, Beistelldruck
   m, Druckbeistellung *f*, Druckspannung *f*
printing price Druckpreis *m*
printing process Druckverfahren *n*,
   Druckvorgang *m*
print(ing) quality Druckqualität *f*, Druckausfall
   m
printing register Druckregister *n*
print(ing) result Druckausfall *m*, Druckergebnis
   n
printing sequence *(multi-colour printing)*
   Druckfolge *f*, Farbfolge *f*, Farbreihenfolge *f*
print(ing) sheet Druckbogen *m*
printing shop Druckerei *f*
printing specialist Druckfachmann *m*
print(ing) specimen Druckmuster *n*, Druckprobe
   f
printing speed Druckgeschwindigkeit *f*
printing start-up Druckanlauf *m*
print(ing) subject Druckmotiv *n*
printing substrate Bedruckstoff *m*
printing sundries *pl* Druckbedarfsartikel *pl*,
   Druckereibedarf *m*
printing techniques *pl* Drucktechniken *pl*
printing technology Drucktechnik *f*
Printing Trades Association Berufsgenossenschaft
   Druck *f*
print(ing) type Druckschrift *f*, Drucktype *f*
print(ing) unit Druckwerk *n*
print(ing) varnish Druckfirnis *m*
print(ing) width Druckbreite *f*
printing works Druckerei *f*, Druckereibetrieb *m*
printing zone Drucklinie *f*, Druckzone *f*
print in the same forme *v* mitdrucken
print into *v (film, plate)* einkopieren
print job sample Druckmuster *n*, Druckprobe *f*,
   Drucksachenmuster *n*
print lamination *(as opp. to film lamination)*
   Druckkaschierung *f*
print lay mark Druckanlage *f*
printline Druckzeile *f*
print media Druckmedien *n/pl*, gedruckte
   Medien *pl*, Printmedien *pl*
print oil *(ink additive)* Drucköl *n*
print on *v* bedrucken

print-out *(line printer)* Ausdruck *m*, Beleg *m*,
   Belegausdruck *m*, Belegausgabe *f*, Protokoll *n*
print out *v (line printer)* ausdrucken
print perforation Druckperforation *f*
print proof Andruck *m*
print proof studio Andruckstudio *n*
print run Auflage *f*, Auflagendruck *m*,
   Druckauflage *f*
print run stability *(printing plate)*
   Auflagenbeständigkeit *f*, Auflagenfestigkeit *f*
printshop Druckerei *f*, Druckmaschinensaal *m*,
   Drucksaal *m*
print start Druckanfang *m*, Druckbeginn *m*
print test Drucktest *m*
print-through Durchscheinen *n*,
   Rückseitenschwärzung *f*
print-to-cut register Schnittregister *n*;
   (die-cutting) Stanzregister *n*
print-to-embossing register Prägeregister *n*
print-to-print register Druckregister *n*
print unit Druckwerk *n*
print unit clutch Druckwerkskupplung *f*
print unit configuration Druckwerksanordnung *f*
print unit controls *pl* Druckwerkssteuerung *f*
print unit disengagement Druckwerksabkupplung
   f
print varnish Drucklack *m*
print varnishing Drucklackierung *f*
print volume *(length of run)* Auflagenhöhe *f*
print waste *v* falschdrucken, verdrucken
printwork Druck *m*, Druckarbeit *f*
prism *(lens)* Prisma *n*
private radio privater Rundfunk *m*
private television privates Fernsehen *n*
probe Meßzelle *f*
process *v (to develop)* entwickeln; *(to print)*
   drucken; *(to reproduce)* reproduzieren
process blue *(cyan)* Skalenblau *n*
process camera Reprokamera *f*; **automatic** ~
   Reproduktionsautomat *m*
process cameraman Reprofotograf *m*
process characteristics *pl* Reprokennlinie *f*
process colours *pl* Skalenfarben *pl*
process colour stripping Farbmontage *f*,
   Vierfarbmontage *f*
process-colour work Vierfarbarbeiten *f/pl*;
   (colour reprod.) Farbreproduktion *f*;
   (printwork) Vierfarbdruck *m*
process computer Prozeßrechner *m*
process control Prozeßsteuerung *f*
process department *(repro dep.)* Reproabteilung *f*
process engineer Verfahrenstechniker *m*
process engineering Verfahrenstechnik *f*

process engraver Chemigraf *m*, Fotochemigraf *m*, Klischeeätzer *m*, Klischeehersteller *m*, Klischeur *m*
process engravers *pl* chemigrafische Anstalt *f*, Klischeeanstalt *f*, Reproanstalt *f*
process engraving Chemigrafie *f*, Fotochemigrafie *f*, Klischeeätzung *f*, Klischeeherstellung *f*
process enlarger *(reprod.)* Vergrößerungskamera *f*
process film Reproduktionsfilm *m*, Reprofilm *m*
process fluctuations *pl* Prozeßschwankungen *pl*
processing Bearbeitung *f*, Verarbeitung *f*; *(phot.)* Entwicklung *f*; *(reprod.)* Reproduktion *f*
processing chemicals *pl* *(phot.)* Verarbeitungspräparate *pl*, Entwicklungschemikalien *pl*
processing instructions *pl* Verarbeitungsangaben *pl*
processing latitude *(phot.)* Entwicklungsspielraum *m*
processing techniques *pl* *(reprod.)* Reproduktionstechniken *pl*
processing time *(phot.)* Entwicklungszeit *f*
process-inherent verfahrensbedingt
process inks *pl* Skalenfarben *pl*
process instructions *pl* *(reprod.)* Reproanweisung *f*
process-integrated metallic printing Metallikbuntdruck *m*
process lens *(reprod.)* Reproobjektiv *n*
process operator *(reprod.)* Reprotechniker *m*
process photographer *(reprod.)* Reprofotograf *m*
process photography *(reprod.)* Reprofotografie *f*
process printing *(offset printing)* Offsetdruck *m*; *(process-colour work)* Vierfarbdruck *m*
process red *(magenta)* Skalenrot *n*
process specifications *pl* *(reprod.)* Reproanweisung *f*
process stability Prozeßstabilität *f*
process technician *(reprod.)* Reprotechniker *m*
process technology Verfahrenstechnik *f*
process variations *pl* Prozeßschwankungen *pl*
process yellow Skalengelb *n*
process zinc *(blockmaking)* Klischeezink *n*
producer Producer *m*
product enhancement Produktverbesserung *f*
product exposure Produktaufnahme *f*
production Produktion *f*, Fertigung *f*, Herstellung *f*
production capacity Produktionskapazität *f*
production control Produktionskontrolle *f*, Produktionssteuerung *f*

production costs *pl* Produktionskosten *pl*, Gestehungskosten *pl*, Herstellungskosten *pl*
production cycle Produktionsablauf *m*
production department costs *pl* Platzkosten *pl*
production efficiency Wirtschaftlichkeit in der Produktion
production engineer Fertigungsingenieur *m*
productioner Produktioner *m*
production facilities *pl* Produktionseinrichtungen *pl*
production film *(plate-ready film)* kopierfähiger Film *m*
production flow Produktionsfluß *m*
production in progress laufende Produktion *f*
production line Fertigungsstraße *f*
production management Produktionsleitung *f*
production manager Produktionsleiter *m*
production monitoring Produktionsüberwachung *f*
production monitoring system Produktionsüberwachungssystem *n*
production operation Produktionsbetrieb *m*
production output Produktionsgeschwindigkeit *f*; *(printing)* Fortdruckleistung *f*
production performance Produktionsgeschwindigkeit *f*
production planner Disponent *m*
production planning Arbeitsvorbereitung *f*, AV *f*, Produktionsplanung *f*
production plant Produktionsanlage *f*, Produktionsbetrieb *m*
production plate *(as opp. to proofing plate)* Fortdruckplatte *f*
production press *(as opp. to proofpress)* Fortdruckmaschine *f*
production printing *(as opp. to proofprinting)* Fortdruck *m*, Auflagendruck *m*
production printsheet Fortdruckbogen *m*
production process Produktionsprozeß *m*
production program Produktionsprogramm *n*
production rate Produktionsgeschwindigkeit *f*
production reliability Produktionssicherheit *f*
production run *(printing)* Fortdruck *m*, Auflagendruck *m*, Druckauflage *f*
production run waste *(printing)* Fortdruckmakulatur *f*
production schedule Terminplanung *f*
production sequence Produktionsablauf *m*
production site Produktionsstätte *f*
production software Produktionsprogramm *n*
production speed Produktionsgeschwindigkeit *f*
production statistics Produktionsstatistik *f*
production supervision Produktionsüberwachung *f*

production times *pl* Produktionszeiten *pl*
production totalizing system Produktionszählsystem *n*
production-true print proof fortdruckgerechter Andruck *m*
productivity control Produktivitätssteuerung *f*
product line Produktionsprogramm *n*
product range Produktionsprogramm *n*
product thickness Produktdicke *f*
professional demonstrator Anwendungstechniker *m*
profitability Rentabilität *f*, Wirtschaftlichkeit *f*
program *(comp.)* Programm *n*
program *v* programmieren
program control Programmsteuerung *f*
program cycle Programmablauf *m*
program data Programmdaten *pl*
program loading Programmeingabe *f*
programmable programmierbar
programmable keys *pl* programmierbare Tasten *f/pl*
programmable read only memory (PROM) programmierbarer Nur-Lese-Speicher (PROM) *m*
programmatic guillotine Programmschneider *m*
programmed cutting *(cutting m.)* Programmschnitt *m*
programmed in-sequence throw-on *(on press)* programmierte Folgeeinschaltung *f*
programmed printing programmiertes Drucken *n*
programmed start-up of machine programmierter Maschinenanlauf *m*
program memory Programmspeicher *m*
programmer *(mach.)* Programmiergerät *n*; *(person)* Programmierer *m*
programming Programmierung *f*
programming language Programmiersprache *f*
programming unit Programmiergerät *n*
program selection Programmwahl *f*
program sequence Programmablauf *m*, Programmfolge *f*
program step Programmierschritt *m*
program storage Programmspeicher *m*
progress chasing Terminkontrolle *f*, Terminüberwachung *f*
progressive proofs *pl* Andruckskala *f*, Farbskala *f*, Skalendrucke *pl*
progressives *pl* see progressive proofs; **set of ~** see progressive proofs
progs *pl (progressive proofs)* Andruckskala *f*, Farbskala *f*, Skalendrucke *pl*
projection Projektion *f*
projection camera Projektionskamera *f*

projection exposure *(reprophotogr.)* Projektionsbelichtung *f*
projection photography Projektionsfotografie *f*
projection plane Projektionsebene *f*
projection platemaking Projektionskopie *f*, Projektionsbelichtung *f*
promotion *(publicity)* Werbung *f*
prompt table *(video screen)* Entscheidungstabelle *f*
proof Kontrollabzug *m*, Probeabzug *m*; *(galley proof)* Korrekturabzug *m*; *(pressproof)* Andruck *m*; *(off-press proof)* Proof *m*
proof *v (off-press proof)* Proof machen; *(pressproof)* andrucken
proof copy Kontrollkopie *f*
proofer *(machine)* Proofmaschine *f*
proofing Proofherstellung *f*
proof in galley *v* abziehen in Fahnen
proofing ink Andruckfarbe *f*
proofing plate Andruckplatte *f*
proofing press see proofpress
proofing studio *(pressproofing)* Andruckstudio *n*
proofmark *(proofreading)* Korrektur *f*, Korrekturzeichen *n*
proof paper Andruckpapier *n*, Abziehpapier *n*
proofpress Andruckmaschine *f*, Andruckpresse *f*; *(galley press)* Abziehpresse *f*, Korrekturabziehpresse *f*
proof print Andruck *m*
proofprint *v* andrucken
proofprinter *(person)* Andrucker *m*
proof printing Andruck *m*
proof printing rotary Rollenandruckmaschine *f*
proof production studio Andruckstudio *n*
proofreader Hauskorrektor *m*, Korrektor *m*
proofreader's corrections *pl* Hauskorrektur *f*
proofreader's mark Korrektorenzeichen *n*, Korrekturzeichen *n*
proofreading Korrekturlesen *n*
proof sheet Kontrollbogen *m*, Korrekturabzug *m*, Korrekturbogen *m*, Probeabzug *m*, Probebogen *m*; *(proof print)* Andruckbogen *m*
proofviewing *(on screen)* Kontrolle *f*
propeller-type gripper *(Heidelberg platen press)* Propellergreifer *m*
proportional reducer proportionaler Abschwächer *m*
prospective customer potentieller Kunde *m*
prospectus Prospekt *m*
protection hood Schutzhaube *f*
protective coating Schutzlackierung *f*, Schutzschicht *f*

protective cover - put in brackets

protective cover Schutzabdeckung *f*
protective grid Schutzgitter *n*
protective layer Schutzschicht *f*
protective varnishing Schutzlackierung *f*
protocol Protokoll *n*
proven praxiserprobt
pseudo-italic *(photocomp.)* elektronisch kursiv, schräggestellt
publication Publikation *f*, Abdruck *m*, Druckerzeugnis *n*, Druckprodukt *n*, Drucksache *f*, Druckschrift *f*, Veröffentlichung *f*
publication date Erscheinungsdatum *n*
publication press *(web press)* Illustrationsdruckmaschine *f*
publication printing Zeitschriftendruck *m*; *(web printing)* Illustrationsdruck *m*
publications for young people Jugendschriften *pl*
publicity Werbung *f*
publicity matter Werbedrucksache *f*
publicity printing Werbedruck *m*
publicize *v (a product)* bewerben
public relations *pl (PR)* Öffentlichkeitsarbeit *f*
publish *v* veröffentlichen, herausgeben, verlegen; *(book also)* auflegen
published bi-monthly *(every two months)* erscheint zweimonatlich; *(semi-monthly)* erscheint zweiwöchentlich
published monthly erscheint monatlich
published semi-monthly erscheint zweiwöchentlich
published weekly erscheint wöchentlich
publisher Herausgeber *m*, Verleger *m*
publisher and bookseller Verlagsbuchhändler *m*
publishers *pl* Verlag *m*
publisher's reader Verlagslektor *m*
publishing and printing house Verlagsdruckerei *f*
publishing house Verlag *m*, Verlagshaus *n*
puck *(VDU control)* Maus *f*
pull *(lead comp.)* Abzug *m*, Probeabzug *m*
pull a proof *v (lead type)* abziehen
pull lay *(sheet feeding)* Ziehmarke *f*
pull-out *(lead comp.)* Spieße *pl*
pull roller *(web press)* Zugwalze *f*
pull sheet Zupfbogen *m*
pull strength *(rollers)* Zugkraft *f*
pull sucker *(feeder suction head)* Schleppsauger *m*
pulp *(papermaking)* Faserbrei *m*, Faserstoff *m*, Papierbrei *m*, Papierfaserstoff *m*, Papiermasse *f*, Papierstoff *m*, Stoff *m*
pulp *v (waste paper, unsaleable books)* einstampfen

pulp bleaching Faserstoffbleichung *f*
pulp box *(papermak.)* Rührbütte *f*
pulper *(papermaking)* Pulper *m*, Stoffauflöser *m*, Zerfaserer *m*
pulp mill Zellstoffabrik *f*
pulp preparation *(papermaking)* Stoffaufbereitung *f*
pulp refining *(papermaking)* Stoffmahlung *f*
pulp strainer *(papermaking)* Knotenfänger *m*
pulsed xenon lamp Xenon-Impuls-Lampe *f*
pumice powder Bimssteinmehl *n*
pumice stone Bimsstein *m*
punch *(metal type prod.)* Patrize *f*, Schriftstempel *m*, Stanzstempel *m*, Stempel *m*; *(register holes)* Lochstanze *f*, Stanze *f*
punch *v (register holes)* ausstanzen, lochen
punch cutting *(metal type prod.)* Schriftschneiden *n*, Stempelschneiden *n*
punched card Lochkarte *f*
punched tape Lochband *n*, Lochstreifen *m*
punch in *v (data, text)* eingeben, eintasten, erfassen
punching Ausstanzung *f*, Lochung *f*, Stanzen *n*
punching and eyeletting machine Loch- und Ösenmaschine *f*
punching die Stanzform *f*, Stempel *m*
punching letter Stanztype *f*
punching machine Stanzmaschine *f*
punching register Stanzregister *n*
punching stroke Stanzhub *m*
punching tool Stanzstempel *m*, Stanzwerkzeug *n*
punching type Stanztype *f*
punch perforation Stanzperforation *f*
punctuation *(typesetting)* Interpunktion *f*, Zeichensetzung *f*
punctuation marks *pl (typesetting)* Interpunktionszeichen *n/pl*, Satzzeichen *n/pl*
puncture *v* punktieren, einstechen
purchase price Anschaffungspreis *m*
purchasing department Einkaufsabteilung *f*
purchasing manager Einkaufsleiter *m*
purge and consolidate run *(comp.)* Reorganisationslauf *m*
push-button Druckknopf *m*, Drucktaste *f*
push-button control Druckknopfsteuerung *f*, Drucktastensteuerung *f*, Knopfsteuerung *f*
push guide *(sheet alignment)* Schiebemarke *f*, Stoßmarke *f*
push sidelay *(sheet alignment)* Schiebemarke *f*
put in boards *v (book)* einbinden, kartonieren
put in brackets *v (typesetting)* einklammern, in Klammern setzen

put in parenthesis *v (typesetting)* in Klammern setzen, einklammern
put in quotes *v (typesetting)* in Anführungszeichen setzen, anführen, in Gänsefüßchen setzen
put out of operation *v (unit)* stillegen
putting into operation *(machine)* Inbetriebnahme *f*, Inbetriebsetzung *f*, Ingangsetzen *n*
PVA binding *(adhesive binding)* PVA-Bindung *f*
PVC *(polyvinyl chloride)* PVC
PVC book case PVC-Bucheinband *m*
PVC coated PVC-kaschiert
PVC film PVC-Folie *f*
PVC label PVC-Etikett *n*
PVC laminated PVC-kaschiert

Q

QR effect *(rubber blanket, "quick release")* QR-Effekt *m*, schnelle Bogenfreigabe *f*
quad *(lead comp.)* Quadrat *n*
quad *v (typesetting)* ausschließen
quad case *(lead comp.)* Quadratenkasten *m*
quadding *(typesetting)* Ausschließen *n*, Ausschluß *m*
quadding mode *(typesetting)* Ausschlußart *f*
quad left linksbündig
quad middle Blocksatz *m*
quadrat *(lead comp.)* Quadrat *n*
quad right rechtsbündig
quadruple fold Vierbruchfalz *m*
qualified operator gelernte Arbeitskraft *f*, ausgebildeter Bediener *m*
qualified worker Facharbeiter *m*
quality assessment Qualitätsbeurteilung *f*
quality control Qualitätskontrolle *f*, Qualitätsüberwachung *f*
quality control strip *(printing)* Druckkontrolleiste *f*, Druckkontrollstreifen *m*
quality evaluation Qualitätsbeurteilung *f*
quality fluctuations *pl* Qualitätsschwankungen *pl*
quality impairment Qualitätsminderung *f*
quality monitoring Qualitätsüberwachung *f*
quality requirement Qualitätsanspruch *m*
quality standard Qualitätsstandard *m*, Qualitätsmaßstab *m*, Qualitätsniveau *n*
quality supervision Qualitätsüberwachung *f*

quality variations *pl* Qualitätsschwankungen *pl*
quarter binding *(book)* Halb(ein)band *m*
quarter-cloth binding *(book)* Halbleinen(ein)band *m*
quarter em space *(typesetting)* Viertelgeviert *n*
quarter fold *(web press)* Viertelfalz *m*, Dreifalz *m*, dritter Falz *m*, Magazinfalz *m*, zweiter Längsfalz *m*
quarter-leather binding *(book)* Halbleder(ein)band *m*
quarterly publication Vierteljahrsschrift *f*
quarter sheet Viertelbogen *m*
quarter tone Viertelton *m*
quarter tone tint patch *(print control bar)* Vierteltonrasterfeld *n*
quartz-iodine lamp Jod-Quarz-Lampe *f*
quaver *(music printing)* geschwänzte Musiknote *f*
question mark Fragezeichen *n*
queue processing *(comp.)* Warteschlangenverarbeitung *f*
quick-action clamping bar Schnellspannschiene *f*
quick-drying ink schnelltrocknende Farbe *f*
quick getting to print schnelles Zum-Druck-Kommen *n*
quick locking plate clamps *pl (on press)* Plattenschnellspanneinrichtung *f*
quick-print shop Schnelldrucker *m*, Sofortdrucker *m*
quick register system Schnellpaßsystem *n*
quick-set ink Quicksetfarbe *f*, schnelltrocknende Farbe *f*
quick (sheet) release schnelle Bogenfreigabe *f*
quire Falzlage *f*, Lage *f*
quire folding Lagenfalzung *f*
quire folding machine Lagenfalzmaschine *f*
quoin *(letterpress forme locking)* Keil *m*, Keilschließzeug *n*, Schließkeil *m*, Schließzeug *n*
quoin *v (letterpress forme locking)* einkeilen, keilen, schließen
quoin chase *(letterpress forme)* Keilrahmen *m*
quoining *(letterpress forme)* Formschließen *n*, Verkeilung *f*
quoin key Formenschlüssel *m*
quoin spaces *pl* Keilspatien *pl*
quotation *(typesetting)* Anführung *f*, Zitat *n*
quotation folder Angebotsmappe *f*
quotation marks *pl (typesetting)* see quote marks
quote *v (typesetting)* anführen, zitieren
quote marks *pl* Anführungszeichen *pl*; *(German quote marks)* Gänsefüßchen *pl*
quotes *pl (quote marks)* Anführungszeichen *pl*; *(German quote marks)* Gänsefüßchen *pl*

qwerty layout *(keyboard layout)* gewöhnlicher Tastaturplan *m*, üblicher Tastaturplan *m*

R

raceway *(gatherer, gatherer-stitcher)* Führungskanal *m*, Sammelkanal *m*, Transportkanal *m*
raceway (pusher) pin *(gatherer, gatherer-stitcher)* Mitnehmerfinger *m*
rack *(for standing matter, formes, type cases etc.)* Regal *n*; *(film processor)* Walzensektion *f*
radical sign Wurzelzeichen *n*
radio-frequency drying Hochfrequenztrocknung *f*
rag board Hadernpappe *f*
rag fibres *pl* Hadernstoff *m*
ragged composition *(typesetting)* Flattersatz *m*
ragged setting *(typesetting)* Flattersatz *m*
ragged type matter Flattersatz *m*
rag paper Hadernpapier *n*, Lumpenpapier *n*
rags *pl* Hadern *pl*
rainbow printing Irisdruck *m*
raised bands *pl (book)* erhabene Bünde *m/pl*
raised image *(characteristic of letterpress printing)* erhabenes Bild *n*
raise the pile *v* Stapel hochfahren
rake delivery *(press)* Rechenauslage *f*
RAM memory *(comp.)* RAM-Speicher *m*
random access Direktzugriff *m*
random access memory *(comp.)* Direktzugriffsspeicher (RAM) *m*, RAM-Speicher *m*, Schreib-Lese-Speicher (RAM) *m*
random sample *(quality control)* Stichprobe *f*
random sample reading *(quality control)* Stichprobenmessung *f*
random sampling Stichprobenentnahme *f*
random test *(quality control)* Stichprobe *f*
range *(density, screen etc.)* Umfang *m*
rapid access developer *(reprod.)* Rapid-Access-Entwickler *m*
rapid access film Rapid-Access-Film *m*
rapid access processor Rapid-Access-Entwicklungsmaschine *f*

raster image processor *(RIP)* Raster-Image-Prozessor *m*, Rasterbildprozessor *m*, Pixelflächenrechner *m*
raster image recorder *(text/image proc.)* Rasterausgabeeinheit *f*
rasterized data Rasterscandaten *pl*
raster output unit *(text/image proc.)* Rasterausgabeeinheit *f*
rating Nennwert *m*
raw data Rohdaten *pl*
raw silk gauze Naturseidengaze *f*
razor sharp gestochen scharf
RC paper *(resin coated p.)* RC-Papier *n*, kunststoffbeschichtetes Papier *n*
read *v* lesen; *(scanner)* abtasten
readability Lesbarkeit *f*
readable lesbar, leserlich
readable type leserliche Schrift *f*
read according to copy *v (text copy)* nach Manuskript lesen
reader *(mach.)* Lesegerät *n*; *(person)* Leser *m*
reader's proof *(type matter)* Hauskorrektur *f*
read for press *v* Revision lesen, Revision machen
read in *v (data, text)* einlesen
reading area *(measuring area)* Meßfeld *n*
reading head Lesekopf *m*; *(measuring head)* Meßkopf *m*
reading machine Lesegerät *n*, Lesemaschine *f*
reading probe *(measuring probe)* Meßsonde *f*
re-adjustment Nachjustierung *f*
read only memory (ROM) Festwertspeicher (ROM) *m*, Nur-Lese-Speicher (ROM) *m*
read-out Anzeige *f*, Display *n*, optische Anzeige *f*
read/write head Lese/Schreibkopf *m*
ready for contacting kopierfähig
ready for platemaking kopierfähig
ready for press see o.k. to print
ready for printing see o.k. to print
ready for printing-down kopierfähig
ready for reproduction reprofähig, reproreif
ready for typesetting satzreif
ready shortly *(book)* erscheint in Kürze
ready to go betriebsbereit
ready-to-use solution gebrauchsfertige Lösung *f*
real art paper originalgestrichenes Kunstdruckpapier *n*
real time *(comp.)* Echtzeit *f*
real time output Echtzeitausgabe *f*
real-time processing *(comp.)* Echtzeitverarbeitung *f*
real type Echtschrift *f*

real type display *(video screen)* Echtschriftdarstellung *f*, schriftgerechte Darstellung *f*
real type monitor *(photocomp.)* Echtschriftbildschirm *m*
ream *(paper)* Ries *n*
rear edge Hinterkante *f*
rear edge of plate Plattenhinterkante *f*
rear edge of sheet Bogenende *n*, Bogenhinterkante *f*
re-arrangement of text Umstellen von Text
rear side of sheet Bogenrückseite *f*
rear table *(cutting m.)* Hintertisch *m*
rebind *v (book)* aufbinden, neubinden
rebound capacity *(rubber blanket)* Rückprallelastizität *f*
re-built *(mach.)* überholt
recalculation of job costs Nachkalkulation *f*
recall *(data, text)* Abruf *m*, Aufruf *m*, Wiederaufrufen *n*
recall *v (data, text)* abrufen, aufrufen
recall copy *v (text)* Text aufrufen
re-cast *v* umschmelzen
receiver *(telecom.)* Empfangsgerät *n*
receiving device *(telecom.)* Empfangsgerät *n*
receiving end *(telecom.)* Empfangsseite *f*
receiving ramp *(mailroom)* Entladerampe *f*
receiving site *(telecom.)* Empfangsseite *f*
receiving station *(telecom.)* Empfangsstation *f*
recently published neu erschienen
receptor sheet of paper *(NCR paper)* Empfängerpapier *n*
recessed image *(gravure characteristic)* vertieftes Bild *n*
recessed printing *(gravure)* vertiefter Druck *m*
reciprocating movement Hinundherbewegung *f*
reciprocating roller changierende Walze *f*, oszillierende Walze *f*, traversierende Walze *f*
reclamation system Rückgewinnungsanlage *f*, Wiedergewinnungsanlage *f*
re-collection *(data, text)* Neuerfassung *f*
reconditioned *(mach.)* überholt
reconditioning *(mach.)* Instandsetzung *f*, Überholung *f*
record *(file)* Datensatz *m*
record *v* aufzeichnen, schreiben; *(data, text)* erfassen; *(to image)* belichten
record album Schallplattenalbum *n*
record cover Schallplattenhülle *f*
recorder Aufzeichnungsgerät *n*, Rekorder *m*
recording Aufzeichnung *f*; *(data, text)* Erfassung *f*; *(scanner)* Belichten *n*, Belichtung *f*
recording area Aufzeichnungsformat *n*

recording density Aufzeichnungsdichte *f*; *(scanner)* Schreibdichte *f*
recording head Aufzeichnungskopf *m*; *(scanner)* Schreibkopf *m*
recording media *(scanner)* Aufzeichnungsmaterial *n*
recording mode Aufzeichnungsart *f*
recording resolution Aufzeichnungsauflösung *f*, Aufzeichnungsfeinheit *f*
recording speed Aufzeichnungsgeschwindigkeit *f*; *(data, text)* Erfassungsgeschwindigkeit *f*; *(scanner)* Belichtungsleistung *f*, Belichtungsgeschwindigkeit *f*
recording unit Aufzeichnungseinheit *f*; *(data, text)* Erfassungseinheit *f*; *(scanner)* Belichter *m*, Belichtungseinheit *f*
record-keeping *(DP)* Dokumentation *f*
record lable Schallplattenetikett *n*
record sleeve Schallplattenhülle *f*
record strip *(line printer)* Protokoll *n*
recovery *(rubber blanket)* Rückfederung *f*
recovery system Rückgewinnungsanlage *f*, Wiedergewinnungsanlage *f*
rectangular rechteckig
rectangular folding winkelgenaues Falzen *n*
rectification *(phot.)* Entzerrung *f*
recto and verso (side) *(paper)* Schön- und Widerdruckseite *f*, Vorder- und Rückseite *f*
recto page Vorderseite *f*
recto side *(of printed sheet)* Schöndruckseite *f*
recto/verso printing Schön- und Widerdruck *m*
recutting Nachschneiden *n*
red adhesive tape rotes Abdeckband *n*
red chalk *(film opaque)* Rötel *m*
reddle *(film opaque)* Rötel *m*
red filter Rotfilter *m*
red opaque Rötel *m*
red-sensitive film rotempfindlicher Film *m*
reduce *v (film etching)* abschwächen
reduce colour *v* Farbe abschwächen, Farbe zurücknehmen
reduced scale *(reprod.)* verkleinerter Maßstab *m*
reduce ink *v (press)* Farbe zurücknehmen
reducer *(film etching)* Abschwächer *m*; *(ink)* Verdünner *m*, Verdünnungsmittel *n*
reduce space between lines *v* Durchschuß herausnehmen
reduce the ink *v* Farbe verdünnen
reducing *(dot etching)* Abschwächen *n*, Ätzen *n*; *(size)* Verkleinern *n*
reduction *(size)* Verkleinerung *f*
redundancy *(comp.)* Redundanz *f*
re-edition Neuauflage *f*, Neuausgabe *f*

reed paper Schilfpapier *n*
reel *(paper)* Rolle *f*; *(for the intermediate storage of preprints)* Spule *f*
reel accelerator Rollenbeschleuniger *m*
reel brake Rollenbremse *f*
reelchange Rollenwechsel *m*; **automatic** ~ Rollenwechsler *m*, Autopaster *m*
reelchange on the run fliegender Rollenwechsel *m*
reel chuck Rollenkonus *m*
reel cone Rollenkonus *m*
reel converting Rollenverarbeitung *f*
reel conveying system Rollenförderanlage *f*, Rollenfördersystem *n*
reel core Rollenhülse *f*, Rollenkern *m*
reel drive Rollenantrieb *m*
reel handling system Rollentransportsystem *n*
reel hoist Rolleneinhebevorrichtung *f*
reeling Wicklung *f*
reel lifting Rolleneinheben *n*
reel lifting device Rolleneinhebevorrichtung *f*
reel loading Rollenbeschickung *f*
reel paper Rollenpapier *n*
reel processing Rollenverarbeitung *f*
reel rewinding Rollenaufwicklung *f*
reel slitter Längsschneider *m*, Rollenschneidemaschine *f*, Rollenschneider *m*
reel splicer automatic ~ Rollenwechsler *m*, Autopaster *m*
reelstand *(web press)* Abroller *m*, Rollenstand *m*, Rollenständer *m*; **(automatic)** ~ Autopaster *m*; **three-arm** ~ dreiarmiger Rollenstand *m*
reel star Rollendrehstern *m*, Rollenstern *m*
reel storage Rollenlager *n*
reel store Rollenlager *n*
reel stub *(reelchange)* Restrolle *f*
reel supply Rollenzuführung *f*
reel-to-fold processing Rolle/Falz-Verarbeitung *f*
reel-to-fold production Produktion Rolle/Falz *f*
reel-to-pack processing Rolle/Stapel-Verarbeitung *f*
reel-to-pack production Produktion Rolle/Stapel *f*
reel-to-reel processing Rolle/Rolle-Verarbeitung *f*
reel-to-reel-production Produktion Rolle/Rolle *f*
reel-to-sheet feeder Rolle/Bogen-Anleger *m*
reel-to-sheet processing Rolle/Bogen-Verarbeitung *f*
reel-to-sheet production Produktion Rolle/Bogen *f*
reel truck Rollenwagen *m*
reel turret Rollendrehstern *m*
reel unwinding Rollenabwicklung *f*

reel width Rollenbreite *f*
re-enlargement *(reprophotogr.)* Rückvergrößerung *f*
re-entering *(data, text)* Neuerfassung *f*
re-etching Nachätzung *f*, Reinätzung *f*, Scharfätzung *f*
re-feeding *(feeder magazine)* Nachlegen *n*, Nachstapeln *n*, Wiederauflegen *n*
re-feed slot *(film processor)* Wiedereingabeschlitz *m*
reference *(typesetting)* Verweis *m*
reference book Nachschlagewerk *n*
reference call *(text proc.)* Referenzaufruf *m*
reference mark *(typesetting)* Anmerkungszeichen *n*, Hinweiszeichen *n*, Notenzeichen *n*, Verweisungszeichen *n*
reference number *(typesetting)* Notenzeichen *n*
reference sample *(book)* Vergleichsmuster *n*
reference type *(side note, footnote etc.)* Referenzart *f*
reference value Sollwert *m*
referencing *(text proc.)* Referenzierung *f*
refill *v* nachfüllen
refilling *(feeder magazine)* Nachstapeln *n*, Nachlegen *n*, Wiederauflegen *n*
refiner *(paper)* Refiner *m*
reflected light Auflicht *n*
reflected light measurement Auflichtmessung *f*
reflection artwork Aufsichtsvorlage *f*
reflection densitometer Auflichtdensitometer *n*, Aufsichtsdensitometer *n*
reflection original Aufsichtsvorlage *f*
reflective copy Aufsichtsvorlage *f*
reflector *(lamp housing)* Reflektor *m*
reflex copy Reflexkopie *f*
refrigerating machine Kältemaschine *f*
regional area network *(telecom.)* Regionalnetz *n*
regional edition *(newspaper)* Regionalausgabe *f*
regional market Regionalmarkt *m*
regional newspaper Regionalzeitung *f*
regional section *(newspaper)* Regionalteil *m*
regional supplement *(newspaper)* Regionalbeilage *f*
register Register *n*, Stand *m*; *(colour register)* Passer *m*
register *v* auf Stand bringen, ausrichten, den Stand machen, einpassen, Register einstellen, Register machen
register accuracy Registergenauigkeit *f*, Standgenauigkeit *f*; *(colour register)* Passergenauigkeit *f*
register adjustment *(on press)* Registereinstellung *f*, Registermachen *n*, Registerstellen *n*

register control Registersteuerung *f,* Registerregelung *f,* Registerkontrolle *f; (colour register)* Passerkontrolle *f,* Passerregelung *f*
register correction Registerkorrektur *f; (colour register)* Passerkorrektur *f*
register cross Paßkreuz *n*
register deviation Registerabweichung *f; (colour register)* Passerabweichung *f*
register difference Registerdifferenz *f; (colour register)* Paßdifferenz *f,* Passerdifferenz *f*
registered position paßgenauer Stand *m*
register feed drum *(press)* Registeranlegetrommel *f*
register fluctuations *pl* Registerschwankungen *pl; (colour register)* Passerschwankungen *pl*
register forme *(colour registration)* Paßform *f*
register holes *pl* Paßlochung *f,* Registerlochung *f,* Registerstanzung *f*
registering Registereinstellung *f,* Einpassen *n,* Registermachen *n,* Registerstellen *n,* Standmachen *n*
register maintenance Registerhalten *n; (colour register)* Passerhalten *n*
register mark Registermarke *f,* Passermarke *f,* Paßmarke *f,* Paßzeichen *n*
register mark recognition *(colour register)* Passermarkenerkennung *f*
register monitoring Registerkontrolle *f; (colour register)* Passerkontrolle *f*
register pin bar Paßstiftleiste *f*
register pins *pl* Paßstifte *pl,* Registerstifte *pl*
register precision Registergenauigkeit *f; (colour register)* Passergenauigkeit *f*
register punch Paßlochstanze *f,* Registerstanze *f*
register punching Registerlochung *f,* Registerstanzung *f,* Paßlochstanzung *f,* Paßlochung *f*
register (re-)adjustment *(on press)* Registerverstellung *f*
register roller *(web press)* Registerwalze *f*
register setting *(on press)* Registereinstellung *f,* Registermachen *n,* Registerstellen *n*
register shifting *(colour register)* Passerversatz *m*
register system Paßsystem *n,* Registersystem *n*
register tabs *pl* Griffregister *n,* Registereinschnitte *m/pl*
register tolerance Registertoleranz *f; (colour register)* Passertoleranz *f*
register-true registergenau, registerhaltig; *(colour register)* passergenau, passerhaltig, paßgenau
register variations *pl* Registerschwankungen *pl; (colour register)* Passerschwankungen *pl*

registration Registerstellen *n,* Registereinstellung *f,* Einpassen *n,* Ausrichtung *f,* Registermachen *n*
reglet *(lead comp.)* Reglette *f*
reglet case Reglettenkasten *m*
re-grind *v* nachschleifen
regular customer Festkunde *m,* Stammkunde *m*
regular shapes *pl (CAD)* geometrische Figuren *f/pl*
regulate *v* regeln
regulation Regelung *f,* Regulierung *f*
re-impose *v* neuausschießen, umschießen
reinforced binding verstärkter Einband *m*
re-issue *(publication)* Neuausgabe *f*
reject delivery *(prod. line)* Notauslage *f*
reject gate *(prod. line)* Notweiche *f,* Ausschleusweiche *f*
reject sheets *pl (waste sheets)* Makulatur *f,* Makulaturbogen *m/pl*
rejuvenation *(of rubber rollers, rubber blankets)* Regenerierung *f*
rejuvenator *(for rubber rollers, rubber blankets)* Regenerationsmittel *n,* Regenerat *n*
re-keying *(data, text)* Neuerfassung *f*
relative humidity relative Luftfeuchtigkeit *f*
release *v (function)* auslösen; *(sheet from blanket)* ablösen
reliable *(operation)* betriebssicher
relief embossing Reliefprägung *f*
relief embossing machine Reliefprägemaschine *f*
relief etching Hochätzung *f,* Reliefätzung *f*
relief makeready *(letterpress)* Reliefzurichtung *f*
relief map Reliefkarte *f*
relief picture Reliefbild *n*
relief printing Reliefdruck *m*
relief printing plate Reliefdruckplatte *f*
relief type Reliefschrift *f*
re-loading *(feeder magazine)* Nachlegen *n,* Nachstapeln *n,* Wiederauflegen *n*
remainders *pl (imperfect books)* Defekten *m/pl*
re-make Neuanfertigung *f*
remake a plate *v* Platte neumachen
remark Anmerkung *f*
remelting furnace *(hot metal comp.)* Umschmelzofen *m*
remission *(light)* Remission *f*
remoistenable glue *(envelopes, stamps etc.)* wiederanfeuchtbarer Leim *m,* Wiederanfeuchtgummierung *f*
remoistening *(paper web)* Wiederbefeuchtung *f*
remote adjustment Fernverstellung *f*

remote adjustment of ink keys
Farbzonenfernverstellung *f*,
Farbfernverstellung *f*

remote bureau *(newspaper)* Außenbüro *n*

remote control Fernsteuerung *f*

remote control console Fernbedienungspult *m*,
Fernsteuerpult *n*, Leitstand *m*

remote control desk see remote control console

remote control of ink keys
Farbzonenfernsteuerung *f*, Farbfernsteuerung *f*

remote control of ink zones see remote control of ink keys

remote diagnosis *(comp.)* Ferndiagnose *f*

remote editorial department Außenredaktion *f*

remote editorial site Außenredaktion *f*

remote ink control Farbfernsteuerung *f*

remote inking *(press)* Farbfernsteuerung *f*

remote inking adjustment Farbfernverstellung *f*

remote location *(publishing house)* Außenstelle *f*

remote office *(newspaper)* Außenbüro *n*

remote printing operation *(newspaper)*
Außendruckort *m*

remote printing site *(newspaper)* Außendruckort *m*

remote proofing Fernbelegausgabe *f*

remote register adjustment *(press)*
Registerfernverstellung *f*

remote register control *(press)*
Registerfernsteuerung *f*

removable hard disk *(comp.)* Wechselplatte *f*

remove air *v (from sheet pile)* Luft ausstreichen

remove by etching *v* abätzen

remove roller *v* Walze ausbauen

rendering Wiedergabe *f*

rendering of continuous tones Halbtonwiedergabe *f*

rendering of halftone dots
Rasterpunktwiedergabe *f*, Rasterwiedergabe *f*

rendering of type Schriftwiedergabe *f*

rendition see rendering

renew *v (colours)* auffrischen

re-pagination Neuumbruch *m*

repair(ing) Instandsetzung *f*, Reparatur *f*

repeat *(web printing)* Rapport *m*

repeatability Wiederholbarkeit *f*,
Reproduzierbarkeit *f*

repeatable results *pl* reproduzierbare Ergebnisse *pl*

repeat accuracy Wiederholgenauigkeit *f*

repeat ad(vertisement) Wiederholungsanzeige *f*

repeat copying Nutzenkopie *f*

repeat cut *(cutting m., as opp. to individual cut)*
Repetierschnitt *m*

repeat job Wiederholungsauftrag *m*

repeat length *(web printing)* Rapport *m*

repeat mark Dittozeichen *n*,
Wiederholungszeichen *n*

repeat order Wiederholungsauftrag *m*

repeat run *(comp.)* Neulauf *m*,
Wiederholungslauf *m*

repertoire (of characters) Zeichensatz *m*

re-piling Umstapeln *n*

replenisher *(photochem.)* Regenerationsmittel *n*,
Regenerat *n*

replenishing *(feeder magazine)* Nachlegen *n*,
Nachstapeln *n*, Wiederauflegen *n*

replenishing unit *(photochem.)* Regeneriereinheit *f*

replenishment *(photochem.)* Regenerierung *f*

replenishment against exhaustion *(photochem.)*
Regenerierung gegen Erschöpfung

replenishment against oxidation *(photochem.)*
Regenerierung gegen Oxidation

reply card *(direct mail, inline fin.)* Antwortkarte *f*

report(age) Reportage *f*

reporter Berichterstatter *m*, Reporter *m*

represent *v (on screen)* darstellen

reprint Abdruck *m*, Nachdruck *m*, Neuauflage *f*,
unveränderte Neuausgabe *f*, Neudruck *m*,
Sonderdruck *m*, Wiederabdruck *m*

reprint *v* nachdrucken, neudrucken,
wiederabdrucken

reprint copy *(text copy)* gedrucktes Manuskript *n*

repro artwork Reprovorlage *f*

repro camera Reprokamera *f*

reprocity effect *(photogr.)* Schwarzschildeffekt *m*

repro copy Reprovorlage *f*

repro department Reproabteilung *f*

repro-drafting Reprozeichnen *n*

repro draughting Reprozeichnen *n*

reproduce *v* reproduzieren, wiedergeben

reproducibility Reproduzierbarkeit *f*,
Wiederholbarkeit *f*

reproducible *(artwork)* reprofähig

reproducible results *pl* reproduzierbare Ergebnisse *pl*

reproduction Reproduktion *f*, Wiedergabe *f*,
Abdruck *m*

reproduction characteristics *pl* Reprokennlinie *f*

reproduction equipment Reprogeräte *pl*

reproduction fidelity getreue Wiedergabe *f*,
naturgetreue Wiedergabe *f*, originaltreue

Wiedergabe f, Wiedergabequalität f, Wiedergabetreue f
reproduction in actual size Reproduktion im Maßstab 1:1
reproduction in enlarged scale Vergrößerung f
reproduction in reduced scale Verkleinerung f
reproduction lens Reproobjektiv n
reproduction methods pl Reproduktionstechniken pl
reproduction photograph Reproaufnahme f
reproduction photographer Reprofotograf m
reproduction photography Reprofotografie f
reproduction process Reproduktionsverfahren n
reproduction quality Reproqualität f, Wiedergabequalität f
reproduction range Abbildungsbereich m
reproduction ratio Abbildungsmaßstab m, Reproduktionsmaßstab m
reproduction scale Abbildungsmaßstab m, Reproduktionsmaßstab m
reproduction sharpness Abbildungsschärfe f
reproduction techniques pl Reproduktionstechniken pl
reproduction technology Reproduktionstechnik f
repro film Reproduktionsfilm m, Reprofilm m
reprography Reprografie f
repro house Reproanstalt f
repro original Reprovorlage f
repro shop Reproanstalt f
repro studio Reproanstalt f
re-reeler Umroller m
re-reeling Umrollung f, Wiederaufwicklung f
re-reeling machine Umrollmaschine f
re-run (comp.) Wiederholungslauf m, Neulauf m; (repeat jot) Wiederholungsauftrag m
re-scale v (reprod.) auf ein neues Format bringen
re-scan Neuscan m
re-screening Neurasterung f
re-set v (type) neusetzen, umsetzen
re-setting (type) Neusatz m
resin (printing ink) Harz n
resin bonding (papermaking) Harzleimung f
resin-coated paper kunststoffbeschichtetes Papier n, RC-Papier n
resinification (ink) Verharzung f
resist (protective coating) Schutzschicht f
re-size v (reprod.) auf ein neues Format bringen
re-sizing (reprod.) Neuformatieren n
resolution (opt.) Auflösung f
resolving power Auflösungsvermögen n, Auflösungsfeinheit f

response card (direct mail, inline fin.) Antwortkarte f
response time (comp.) Reaktionszeit f
re-start (machine) Wiederanfahren n, Wiederanlauf m
rest position Ruhelage f, Ruhestellung f
rest roll (reelchange) Restrolle f
retail bookseller Sortimentsbuchhändler m
reticulated grain Runzelkorn n
retouch v retuschieren, überarbeiten
retoucher Retuscheur m
retouching Retusche f; (film opaquing) Abdecken n, Ausdecken n, Ausflecken n
retouching brush Retuschierpinsel m
retouching desk Retuschierpult m
retouching knife Retuschiermesser n
retouching of original Originalretusche f
retouching paint Retuschierfarbe f
retouching pen Retuschierfeder f; (film opaquing) Abdeckstift m
retouching tools pl Retuschierbesteck n
retractable keyboard versenkbare Tastatur f
retractable register pins v versenkbare Paßstifte m/pl
re-transfer (gravure cyl.) Nachübertragung f
retrieval (data, text) Abruf m, Aufruf m, Wiederaufrufen n
retrieve v (data, text) abrufen, aufrufen
retrieve copy v (text) Text aufrufen
retrofit v nachträglich anbauen, nachträglich ausrüsten
retrofit kit Einbausatz m
retrofit package Nachrüstpaket n
retrofittable nachrüstbar
return envelope (direct mail) Rückantwort-Briefumschlag m
return movement (mech.) Rücklauf m
returns pl (book sale) Remittenden pl, unverkaufte Exemplare n/pl
reversal (phot.) Umkehrung f
reversal bath Umkehrbad n
reversal exposure Umkehrkopie f
reversal film Umkehrfilm m
reversal material Umkehrmaterial n
reversal photo paper Umkehrpapier n
reversal process Umkehrprozeß m
reversal processing Umkehrentwicklung f
reverse angle doctor blade gegenläufige Rakel f
reverse (angle) doctoring (gravure) gegenläufige Abrakelung f, negative Abrakelung f
reverse characters pl Negativschrift f
reversed image umgekehrtes Bild n, Umkehrbild n; (photocomp.) Negativsatz m

reverse laterally *v (image)* kontern
reverse leading *(imagesetter)* Materialrücktransport *m*, Rücktransport *m*
reverse lettering Negativschrift *f*
reverse page Rückseite *f*
reverse side Rückseite *f*, Widerdruckseite *f*
reverse side of sheet Bogenrückseite *f*
reverse (side) printing Rückseitendruck *m*, Widerdruck *m*
reverse text *(video screen)* Negativtext *m*
reverse type Negativschrift *f*
reverse video characters *pl (video screen)* Negativschrift *f*
reverse video setting *(photocomp.)* Negativbelichtung *f*
reversible umschaltbar, umsteuerbar
reversible satellite printing unit *(web press)* umsteuerbares Satellitendruckwerk *n*
reversing drum *(perfector press)* Wendetrommel *f*
reversing mirror *(camera)* Umkehrspiegel *m*
review *(book)* Besprechung *f*, Rezension *f*; *(magazine)* Illustrierte *f*, Zeitschrift *f*, Rundschau *f*
review *v (book)* besprechen, rezensieren
review copy *(book)* Besprechungsexemplar *n*, Rezensionsexemplar *n*
reviewer *(book)* Rezensent *m*
revise *v* nachsehen, revidieren, Revision lesen, Revision machen, überarbeiten
revise copy *v (text)* Text überarbeiten
revised edition *(book)* revidierte Ausgabe *f*, verbesserte Ausgabe *f*
revised proof sheet Revisionsbogen *m*
revision Revision *f*
revolutions per hour *(r.p.h.)* Umdrehungen pro Stunde
revolving diaphragm Revolverblende *f*
rewind *v* aufwickeln
rewind development *(reprod.)* Umspulentwicklung *f*
rewinder *(rewind unit)* Aufrollung *f*, Aufwickelvorrichtung *f*, Aufwicklung *f*, Rollenaufwicklung *f*
rewinding Aufrollung *f*, Aufwicklung *f*, Wiederaufwicklung *f*
rewind unit *(web press)* Aufrollung *f*, Aufwickelvorrichtung *f*, Aufwicklung *f*, Rollenaufwicklung *f*
RGB *(Red Green Blue)* RGB
rheological properties *pl (ink)* rheologische Eigenschaften *pl*
rheology *(ink)* Rheologie *f*
rhomb shaped screen *(reprod.)* Rautenraster *m*

ribbed plate Rippenplatte *f*
ribbon *(web printing)* Papierstrang *m*, Strang *m*
ribbon gathering *(web printing)* Strangzusammenführung *f*
ribbon interleaving *(web printing)* Strangzusammenführung *f*
ribbon register *(web printing)* Strangregister *n*
ribbon stitcher Strangheftapparat *m*
ribs *pl (book)* Bünde *pl*
rice paper Reispapier *n*
rich application satter Auftrag *m*
rich gold Reichgold *n*
rich pale gold Reichbleichgold *n*
rider roller Beschwerwalze *f*, Reiterwalze *f*
right-angle conveyor *(mailroom)* Eckförderer *m*
right-angle cut rechtwinkliger Schnitt *m*
right-angle fold Kreuz(bruch)falz *m*
right-angle paper in-feed rechtwinkliger Papiereinlauf *m*
right(-hand) pages *pl* rechte Seiten *f/pl*
right-left reversed seitenverkehrt
right of publication Verlagsrecht *n*
right of reproduction Vervielfältigungsrecht *n*
right-reading seitenrichtig
rigid disk *(comp.)* Hartplatte *f*
rigid material steifes Material *n*
ring binder Ringbuch *n*, Ringordner *m*
ring binding Ringbindung *f*, Ringheftung *f*
ring coating *(gravure)* Ringbeschichtung *f*
ring lens system *(densitometer)* Ringoptik *f*
ring network connection *(comp.)* Ringleitung *f*
rinse *v* auswaschen, spülen
rinsing *(films, plates etc.)* Wässerung *f*
rinsing sink Wässerungsbecken *n*
RIP (Raster Image Prozessor) RIP (Raster-Image-Prozessor) *m*
rising of spaces *(lead type)* Spießen *n*
rising spaces *pl (lead comp.)* Spieße *pl*
rivet Niete *f*
rivet *v* nieten
riveting Nietung *f*
riveting machine Nietmaschine *f*
robust *(machine)* robust
rocking lever Kipphebel *m*
roll-away unit fahrbares Aggregat *n*
roll collator *(continuous forms prod.)* Rollenkollator *m*
roller Walze *f*
roller accumulating conveyor *(mailroom)* Stautaktförderer *m*
roller adjustment Walzeneinstellung *f*, Walzenjustierung *f*
roller bearing Rollenlager *n*, Walzenlager *n*

roller cabinet Walzenschrank *m*
roller carriage *(platen press)* Walzenwagen *m*
roller change Walzenaustausch *m*
roller chilling Walzenkühlung *f*
roller cleaning device Walzenreinigungsgerät *n*
roller coating Walzenbeschichtung *f*
roller composition Walzenmasse *f*
roller conveyor *(mailroom)* Rollenförderer *m*
roller cooling Walzenkühlung *f*
roller core Walzenkern *m*, Walzenspindel *f*
roller covering *(damping rollers)* Walzenbezug *m*
roller covering device *(damping rollers)* Walzenbezieher *m*
roller delivery Rollenauslage *f*
roller frame Walzengestell *n*, Walzenstuhl *m*
roller gauge Walzenstandprüfer *m*, Walzensteller *m*
roller glaze Walzenglätte *f*
roller handles *pl* Walzenschuhe *pl*
roller journal Walzenzapfen *m*
roller lock Walzenschloß *n*
roller marks *pl* Walzenstreifen *m/pl*
roller mill *(inkmaking)* Walzenstuhl *m*
roller nip Walzenspalt *m*
roller out of condition stumpfe Walze *f*
roller pair Walzenpaar *n*
roller rack Walzenständer *m*
roller rail Walzenlaufschiene *f*
roller re-adjustment Walzennachstellung *f*
roller reciprocation Hinundherbewegung der Walzen *f*
roller reconditioning Walzenauffrischung *f*
roller running blind blanklaufende Walze *f*
rollers *pl (trolleys)* Andrückrollen *pl*, Laufrollen *f/pl*
roller setting Walzeneinstellung *f*
roller slide *(product delivery)* Rollenrutsche *f*
roller slippage Walzenschlupf *m*
roller slur Walzenschmitz *m*
roller stripping blanklaufende Walze *f*
roller swelling Walzenquellen *n*
roller table Rollentisch *m*
roller top of former *(press folder)* Falztrichtereinzugwalze *f*, Trichtereinlaufwalze *f*
roller trolley Walzentransportwagen *m*
roller-type inking unit *(gravure)* Walzenfarbwerk *n*
roller wash Walzenwaschmittel *n*
roller washing Walzenwaschen *n*
roller washing machine Walzenwaschmaschine *f*
roller wash-up device *(inking unit)* Walzenwascheinrichtung *f*

roll film Rollfilm *m*
roll film camera Rollfilmkamera *f*
roll film cassette Rollfilmkassette *f*
roll film cutter Rollfilmschneider *m*
roll film dispenser Rollfilmspender *m*
rolling *(cylinder)* Abwicklung *f*
rolling bearing Wälzlager *n*
rolling conditions *pl (cylinder)* Abwicklungsverhältnisse *pl*
roll shutter *(camera)* Rolltuch *n*
roll(-to-roll) laminating *(as opp. to pouch laminating)* Rollenkaschierung *f*
Roman (type) römische Antiqua *f*
Roman capitals *pl (type)* römische Kapitalschrift *f*
Roman characters *pl* Lateinische Schrift *f*
Roman face *(type)* römische Antiqua *f*
Roman figures *pl* römische Ziffern *f/pl*
Roman numerals *pl* römische Ziffern *f/pl*
Roman type Lateinische Schrift *f*
roman type(face) gerad(e)stehende Schrift *f*, gewöhnliche Schrift *f*, normale Schrift *f*
Ronde Ronde *f*
room light Raumlicht *n*
room light film Raumlichtfilm *m*
room light vacuum printer Raumlichtkontaktkopiergerät *n*
rotary *(press)* see rotary press
rotary binder Karussellbinder *m*
rotary board cutter *(book prod.)* Pappenkreisschere *f*, Kreiskartonschere *f*
rotary cutter Rotationsschneider *m*
rotary cutting die Rotationsstanzform *f*
rotary cutting tool Rotationsstanzwerkzeug *n*
rotary die-cutter Rotationsstanzmaschine *f*
rotary die-cutting Rotationsstanzen *n*
rotary embossing unit Rotationsprägewerk *n*
rotary feeder Rotationsanleger *m*, Trommelanleger *m*
rotary gatherer Rotationszusammentragmaschine *f*
rotary gluer Rotationsleimwerk *n*
rotary letterpress printing Rollenbuchdruck *m*, Rollenhochdruck *m*, Rotationshochdruck *m*
rotary motion Drehbewegung *f*
rotary newspaper printing rotativer Zeitungsdruck *m*
rotary numbering box Rotationsnumeriergerät *n*
rotary offset Rollenoffset *m*
rotary offset press Offset(rollen)rotation *f*, Rollenoffsetmaschine *f*
rotary pile feeder Rundstapelanleger *m*

rotary press Rollendruckmaschine *f*, Rollenrotation *f*, Rollenrotationsmaschine *f*, Rotation *f*, Rotationsdruckmaschine *f*, Rotationsmaschine *f*
rotary press minder Rotationer *m*, Rotationsdrucker *m*
rotary press speed Rotationsgeschwindigkeit *f*
rotary printer Rotationer *m*, Rotationsdrucker *m*
rotary printing Rollendruck *m*, Rollenrotationsdruck *m*, Rotationsdruck *m*
rotary printing forme Runddruckform *f*
rotary screen printing rotativer Siebdruck *m*
rotary screen printing press Rollensiebdruckmaschine *f*
rotary sheeter Rotationsschneider *m*
rotary shell for wrap-around plates Klischeemantel für Wickelplatten
rotary stacker Drehstapler *m*
rotary stitching machine Rotationsheftmaschine *f*
rotary sucker *(feeder suction head)* Drehsauger *m*
rotary three-knife trimmer Rotationsdreischneider *m*
rotary trimmer Rotationsschneider *m*
rotated character gestürzter Buchstabe *m*
rotated page gestürzte Seite *f*
rotated type gestürzter Buchstabe *m*
rotating copying machine *(gravure)* Umlaufkopiermaschine *f*
rotogravure Rotationstiefdruck *m*, Rollentiefdruck *m*, Tiefdruck *m*
rotogravure ink Tiefdruckfarbe *f*
rotogravure paper Tiefdruckpapier *n*
rotogravure press Rollentiefdruckanlage *f*, Rollentiefdruckmaschine *f*, Rotationstiefdruckmaschine *f*, Tiefdruckmaschine *f*, Tiefdruckrollenrotation *f*, Tiefdruckrotation(smaschine) *f*
rough bending *(cardboard)* Stauchbiegen *n*
roughening *(book spine)* Aufrauhen *n*
rough milling *(gravure cyl.)* Vorfräsen *n*
roughness profile *(gravure cyl.)* Rauhheitsprofil *n*
rough proof *(galley proof)* unkorrigierter Korrekturabzug *m*
rough sketch Entwurf *m*, Rohentwurf *m*, Skizze *f*
rough surface rauhe Oberfläche *f*
round (back) binding Einband mit rundem Rücken
round-back book Buch mit rundem Rücken
round bending machine Rundbiegemaschine *f*
round chisel Boltstichel *m*
round corner cutter Rundeckenschneider *m*

round-cornering machine Eckenrundstoßmaschine *f*
round diaphragm Rundblende *f*
round(ed) back *(book)* gewölbter Rücken *m*, runder Rücken *m*
rounded corners *pl* abgerundete Ecken *pl*, Rundecken *pl*
round off *v* abrunden
round-spine book Buch mit rundem Rücken
round stereo Rundstereo *n*
round wire Runddraht *m*
route *(newspaper distribution)* Route *f*
route distribution system *(mailroom)* Routenverteilsystem *n*
routine *(comp.)* Unterprogramm *n*, Routine *f*, Software-Befehlskette *f*
routing *(perfect binding)* Aufrauhen *n*, Fräsen *n*
routing adhesive binding *(as opp. to perforation adhesive binding)* Fräsklebebindung *f*
routing edge Fräskante *f*
routing head Fräskopf *m*
routing machine Fräsapparat *m*, Fräsmaschine *f*
routing margin Fräsrand *m*
rout off *v* abfräsen
rubber Gummi *n*
rubber blanket Gummituch *n*; *(for vacuum frame)* Gummidecke *f*
rubber-covered roller gummibezogene Walze *f*
rubber design roller Gummidessinwalze *f*
rubber distributor roller Gummiverreibwalze *f*
rubber doctor blade Gummirakel *f*
rubber dressing *(cyl.)* Gummiaufzug *m*
rubber embossing blanket Prägegummituch *n*
rubber face *(of rubber blanket)* Gummideckplatte *f*
rubber gloves *pl* Gummihandschuhe *pl*
rubber offset blanket Offset(druck)tuch *n*
rubber packing *(cyl.)* Gummiaufzug *m*
rubber plate *(flexo)* Gummiklischee *n*, Gummiplatte *f*
rubber pressure roller *(gravure)* Gummipresseur *m*
rubber printing blanket Gummidrucktuch *n*
rubber roller Gummiwalze *f*
rubber squeegee Gummiquetscher *m*, Gummirakel *f*
rubber stamp Gummistempel *m*
rubber stereo Gummistereo *n*
rubber tint plate Gummitonplatte *f*
rubber type Gummibuchstaben *m/pl*
rubbing Abrieb *m*
rub off *v* abreiben
rub-off ink Rubbelfarbe *f*

rub-off lottery ticket Rubbellos *n*
rub out *v* radieren
rub-proof abriebfest, scheuerfest, wischfest
rub resistance Abriebfestigkeit *f*, Scheuerfestigkeit *f*
rub-resistant abriebfest, scheuerfest, wischfest
rule Linie *f*
rule bending machine Linienbiegemaschine *f*
rule border Linieneinfassung *f*, Linienrand *m*
rule box Linienrahmen *m*
rule box with rounded corners Linienrahmen mit runden Ecken
rule case *(lead comp.)* Linienkasten *m*
rule casting machine Liniengießmaschine *f*
rule cutter Linienschneidemaschine *f*
rule depth Linienhöhe *f*
ruled paper liniertes Papier *n*
rule grid *(tabular work)* Liniengitter *n*
rule ornament Linienornament *n*
rule perforation *(on press)* Druckperforation *f*
rule piece *(lead comp.)* Anschlußstück *n*
ruler Lineal *n*
rule(-up) *v* linieren
rule-up table Liniertisch *m*
rule weight Linienstärke *f*, Strichstärke *f*
rule width Linienbreite *f*
ruling Lineatur *f*, Linierung *f*
ruling distance *(tabular work)* Linienabstand *m*
ruling ink Linierfarbe *f*
ruling machine Liniermaschine *f*
ruling pen Ziehfeder *f*
ruling rollers *pl* Linierwalzen *f/pl*
ruling table Liniertisch *m*
ruling-up Linieren *n*
ruling work *(printing)* Liniendruck *m*; *(typesetting)* Liniensatz *m*, Liniersatz *m*
run *(print run)* Auflage *f*; *(bookbinding)* Bindequote *f*
run *v (machine)* arbeiten, laufen, bedienen; *(to print)* drucken
runability *(of the printing material)* Laufeigenschaft *f*, Verdruckbarkeit *f*
runaround *(text running around a figure)* umlaufender Text *m*
run clean *v (offset plate)* freilaufen
runner board *(on machines)* Laufblech *n*, Laufbrett *n*
runner rail Laufschiene *f*
running *(mach.)* Lauf *m*, Betrieb *m*, Gang *m*
running blind *(offset plate, roller)* Blindlaufen *n*, Blindwerden *n*
running board *(on presses)* Trittbrett *n*

running direction *(web)* Bahnlaufrichtung *f*, Laufrichtung *f*, Papierlaufrichtung *f*
running foot lebender Kolumnentitel am Fuß *m*
running head lebender Kolumnentitel *m*
running production laufende Produktion *f*
running properties *pl (printing paper)* Laufeigenschaft *f*
running speed Laufgeschwindigkeit *f*
running story *(newspaper)* Serie *f*
running text laufender Text *m*
running time totalizer *(mach.)* Betriebsstundenzähler *m*
running title see running head
run on copy *v (no new paragraph)* Text anhängen
run-ons *pl* Fortdrucke *m/pl*; **thousand** ~ (je) 1000 weitere
run-up *(mach.)* Hochlauf *m*
run up the ink *v (in inking unit)* Farbe einlaufen lassen
rush order Schnellschußauftrag *m*
rust-proofing Rostschutz *m*

S

sack Sack *m*
saddle *(plate base)* Sattel *m*; *(wire-stitcher)* Sattel *m*
saddle-stitched booklet Rückstichbroschüre *f*
saddle-stitcher Rückstichheftmaschine *f*, Sattelhefter *m*
saddle stitching Rückstichheftung *f*, Sattelheftung *f*, Falzheftung *f*, Drahtheftung durch den Rücken
saddle-stitch with thread *v* im Falz mit Faden heften
saddle-stitch with wire *v* im Falz mit Draht heften
safeguards *pl* Schutze *pl*
safety film Sicherheitsfilm *m*
safety guard Schutzvorrichtung *f*
safety guards *pl* Schutze *pl*
safety ink Sicherheitsfarbe *f*
safety lock *(cover, machine parts)* Sicherheitsverriegelung *f*
safety regulations *pl* Sicherheitsvorschriften *pl*
saffian(-leather) binding Saffianeinband *m*

sag v *(rollers, cylinders)* durchbiegen
saleable copies pl verkaufbare Exemplare pl
sales ad Verkaufsanzeige f
sales and wants pl *(classified advertising)* Verkäufe/Gesuche pl
sales folders Verkaufsprospekte pl
sales literature Verkaufsprospekte pl
sales people Verkaufspersonal n
sales rep(resentative) Außendienstmitarbeiter m
sales staff Verkaufspersonal n
sales territory Verkaufsgebiet n
same-size reproduction Reproduktion im Maßstab 1:1
sample Muster n; *(magazine insert)* Warenmuster n, Warenprobe f
sample binding *(book)* Blindband m, Blindmuster n, Formatbuch n, Muster(ein)band m, Probeband m
sample book Musterbuch n
sample copy Musterexemplar n
sample sheet Musterblatt n, Musterbogen m, Probebogen m
sample volume *(book)* Blindband m, Blindmuster n, Formatbuch n, Muster(ein)band m
sandwich foil Verbundfolie f
Sans Serif *(type classif.)* Serifenlose Linear-Antiqua f
sans serif typefaces pl serifenlose Schriften pl, Groteskschriften pl
satellite communication Nachrichtenübertragung f
satellite link Satellitenverbindung f
satellite printing unit *(web offset press)* Satellitendruckwerk n
satellite television Satellitenfernsehen n
satellite transmission *(telecom.)* Satellitenübertragung f
satin ink Satinfarbe f
save data v Daten (ab)speichern
saw-tooth effect Sägezahneffekt m
scale Skala f; *(reprod.)* Maßstab m
scale change *(reprod.)* Maßstabsveränderung f
scale grid *(e.g. on vacuum film holder)* Formatskala f
scale modification *(reprod.)* Maßstabsveränderung f
scale paper *(graded in mm)* Millimeterpapier n
scale range *(reprod.)* Maßstabsbereich m
scale setting *(reprod.)* Maßstabseinstellung f
scaling *(reprod.)* Formateinstellung f, Größeneinstellung f, Vermaßen n
scaling down Verkleinern n
scaling up Hochzoomen n, Vergrößern n

scan Scan m
scan v scannen, abtasten, aufzeichnen, schreiben
scan area Scanformat n
scan format Scanformat n
scan in v einscannen
scanline Scanlinie f, Bildlinie f
scanline beam Scanlinienstrahl m
scanline density Aufzeichnungsdichte f, Schreibdichte f
scanline signal Scanliniensignal n
scanner Scanner m, Aufzeichnungsgerät n
scanner calibration Scannereichung f, Scannerkalibrierung f
scanner contact screen Scanner-Kontaktraster m
scanner input unit Abtastscanner m, Scannereingabegerät n
scanner operator Scanner-Operator m
scanner output unit Aufzeichnungsscanner m, Scannerausgabegerät n
scanner preparation Scannervorbereitung f
scanner reader Abtastscanner m, Scannereingabegerät n
scanner-ready scannerfähig, reprofähig, reproreif
scanner recorder Aufzeichnungsscanner m, Scannerausgabegerät n, Scannerrekorder m
scanner separation *(colour sep.)* Scannerauszug m
scanner setting Scannereinstellung f
scanner set-up Scannereinstellung f, Scannervorbereitung f
scanner set-up device Scannereinstellgerät n
scanning Scannen n, Abtastung f, Aufzeichnung f
scan(ning) area Abtastbereich m, Abtastformat n, Aufzeichnungsformat n
scanning beam Abtaststrahl m
scanning copy Scanvorlage f, Abtastvorlage f
scan(ning) densitometer Scan-Densitometer m
scanning density Aufzeichnungsdichte f, Schreibdichte f
scanning device Abtastvorrichtung f
scanning drum Abtasttrommel f, Abtastwalze f, Abtastzylinder m
scanning head Abtastkopf m, Aufzeichnungskopf m, Schreibkopf m
scanning lens Abtastoptik f
scanning light source Abtastlichtquelle f
scanning line see scanline
scanning media Abtastvorlage f, Vorlagenmaterial n
scanning raster Scanraster m

scanning resolution Abtastauflösung *f*, Aufzeichnungsauflösung *f*, Aufzeichnungsfeinheit *f*
scanning size Scanformat *n*
scanning speed Abtastgeschwindigkeit *f*, Aufzeichnungsgeschwindigkeit *f*
scanning unit Abtasteinheit *f*, Aufzeichnungseinheit *f*
scattered light Streulicht *n*
scented ink Duftdruckfarbe *f*, parfümierte Druckfarbe *f*
scented paper parfümiertes Papier *n*
scentless ink geruchfreie Farbe *f*
scheduled deadline vorgesehener Termin *m*
school-book Lehrbuch *n*, Schulbuch *n*
school dictionary Schulwörterbuch *n*
school of printing Fachschule für Drucktechnik
score Ritzlinie *f*
score *v* ritzen
scoring Ritzen *n*
scoring and creasing machine Ritz- und Rillmaschine *f*
scoring knife Ritzmesser *n*
scoring machine Ritzmaschine *f*
scoring rule Ritzlinie *f*
scorper Bolzer *m*, Messerstichel *m*, Stichel *m*
scrap Schnitzel *pl*
scrape off *v* abkratzen, wegschaben
scrape out *v* ausschaben
scraper Ausschaber *m*, Schaber *m*, Schabernadel *f*, Schabmesser *m*
scraping *(film/plate)* Schaben *n*
scraping knife Schabmesser *n*
scratch Kratzer *m*
scratched negative verkratztes Negativ *n*
scratch off *v* abkratzen, wegkratzen
scratch-proof ink nagelfeste Farbe *f*
scratch resistance Kratzfestigkeit *f*
scratch test Kratzprobe *f*, Nagelprobe *f*
screen *(halftone screen)* Raster *m*; **48 l/cm ~** 48er Raster *m*; *(screen printing)* Sieb *n*; *(video screen)* Bildschirm *m*
screen *v* rastern
screen adjustment *(camera)* Rastereinstellung *f*
screen angle Rasterwinkelung *f*
screen angle indicator Rasterwinkelmesser *m*
screen aperture *(space between dots)* Rasterfenster *n*, Rasteröffnung *f*
screen buffer *(VDT)* Bildschirmspeicher *m*
screen cassette *(camera)* Rasterkassette *f*
screen code *(VDT)* Bildschirmkode *m*
screen copying frame *(gravure)* Rasterkopierrahmen *m*

screen count *(halftone screen)* Rasterfeinheit *f*, Rasterweite *f*
screen counter *(screen resolution)* Rasterlinienzähler *m*, Rasterzähler *m*
screen definition *(halftone screen)* Rasterfeinheit *f*, Rasterweite *f*
screen degreaser *(screen printing)* Siebentfetter *m*
screen density *(halftone screen)* Dichte Raster, DR, Rasterdichte *f*
screen display *(VDT)* Bildschirmanzeige *f*
screen distance *(glass screen, camera)* Rasterabstand *m*
screen dot *(halftone screen)* Rasterpunkt *m*
screened areas *pl (image)* Rasterpartien *f/pl*
screened background *(tint)* Hintergrundraster *m*
screened box *(typogr.)* gerasterter Rahmen *m*
screened colour separation Rasterfarbauszug *m*
screened film Rasterfilm *m*
screened image Rasterbild *n*
screened negative Rasternegativ *n*
screened output *(photosetter)* gerasterte Ausgabe *f*
screened positive Rasterpositiv *n*
screened reproduction Rasterreproduktion *f*
screened separation Rasterauszug *m*
screened separation negative Rasterauszugsnegativ *n*
screened separation positive Rasterauszugspositiv *n*
screened separations *pl* gerasterte Farbauszüge *m/pl*
screen emulsion *(screen printing)* Kopierschicht *f*
screen exposure *(camera)* Rasteraufnahme *f*, Rasterbelichtung *f*; *(gravure)* Rasterkopie *f*
screen fabrics *(screen printing)* Siebdruckgewebe *n*
screen filler *(screen printing)* Siebfüller *m*
screen film Rasterfilm *m*
screen frame *(screen printing)* Siebdruckrahmen *m*
screen gauze *(screen printing)* Siebdruckgaze *f*
screen holder *(camera)* Rasterhalter *m*
screen indicator *(screen definition)* Rasterlinienzähler *m*, Rasterzähler *m*
screening Aufrastern *n*, Rasterung *f*
screening of type Schriftrasterung *f*
screen line *(VDT)* Bildschirmzeile *f*
screen mask *(VDT)* Bildschirmmaske *f*
screen memory *(VDT)* Bildschirmspeicher *m*
screen patch *(print control bar)* Rasterfeld *n*
screen pattern *(moiré)* Moiré *n*
screen percentage *(screen film)* Rasterprozentwert *m*, Raster(ton)wert *m*

screen position *(camera)* Rasterstellung f
screen preparation *(screen printing)* Siebherstellung f
screen printer Siebdrucker m, Siebdruckerei f; *(small device)* Siebdruckmaschine f
screen printing Siebdruck m, Durchdruck m, Rakeldruck m, Schablonendruck m
screen printing frame Siebdruck-Kopierrahmen m
screen printing ink Siebdruckfarbe f
screen printing machine Siebdruckmaschine f
screen printshop Siebdruckerei f
screen process photo-stencil Siebdruckfotoschablone f
screen (process) printing forme Siebdruckform f
screen projection *(reprod.)* Rasterprojektion f
screen range *(halftone screen)* Rasterumfang m
screen resolution *(halftone screen)* Rasterfeinheit f, Rasterweite f
screen roller Rasterwalze f
screen rotation *(camera)* Rasterdrehung f
screen ruling *(halftone screen)* Lineatur f, Rasterfeinheit f, Rasterweite f; **48 line/cm ~** Rasterweite f von 48 L/cm
screen splitting *(VDT)* Bildschirmteilung f
screen stencil *(screen printing forme)* Siebdruckform f, Siebdruckschablone f
screen stencil film Siebdruckschablonenfilm m
screen tint Rasterton m, Rasterfond m, Rasterfläche f, Flächenton m
screen value Raster(ton)wert m
screen washer Siebwaschgerät n
screen window *(space between dots)* Rasterfenster n, Rasteröffnung f; *(VDT)* Bildschirmfenster n
screw chase Schraubenrahmen m
screw composing stick Winkelhaken mit Schraubenverschluß
screw drive *(cutting m.)* Spindelantrieb m
screw press Schraubenpresse f, Spindelpresse f, Stockpresse f
scriber cutter *(CAD)* Gravierwerkzeug n
scribe tool *(CAD)* Gravierwerkzeug n
Scripts *pl (type classif.)* Schreibschriften pl
script types *pl* Schreibschriften pl
scrolling *(video screen function)* Scrollen n
scroll saw Dekupiersäge f
scrubbing brush Waschbürste f
scuff resistance Abriebfestigkeit f, Scheuerfestigkeit f
scuff-resistant abriebfest, scheuerfest
scumming *(offset)* Tonen n; *(screen printing)* Schleierbildung f

seal gluing Verschlußklebung f
sealing *(envelopes, bags etc.)* Verschlußklebung f; *(film wrapping)* Zuschweißen n; *(plastic foil laminating)* Kaschierung f
sealing flap *(envelope)* Verschlußklappe f
sealing label Siegelmarke f
sealing machine *(mailroom)* Einschweißmaschine f
sealing station *(film wrapping)* Schweißstation f
seam gluer Nahtleimauftragsgerät n
seamless flexo roller Endlosflexodruckwalze f
search and replace routine *(text proc.)* Suche-Ersetze-Automatik f
search code *(comp.)* Suchkennung f, Suchschlüssel m
search directory *(comp.)* Suchverzeichnis n
search key *(comp.)* Suchschlüssel m
search run *(comp.)* Suchlauf m
search string *(comp.)* Suchroutine f
search term *(comp.)* Suchbegriff m
secondary colours *pl (colour system)* Sekundärfarben pl
second cover zweite Umschlagseite f
second forme *(perfecting forme)* Widerdruckform f
second(-generation) original Zweitoriginal n, Zweitvorlage f
second-hand machine Gebrauchtmaschine f
second side printing Widerdruck m
section Abschnitt m, Bogenteil m, Falzlage f, Lage f, Teilprodukt n
sectional exposure *(reprod.)* Teilbelichtung f
section for stitching Heftlage f
section mark *(§)* Paragraphenzeichen n
section stacker Lagenstapler m
secure *v (data)* sichern
security paper Sicherheitspapier n, Wertpapier n
security printer Wertpapierdruckerei f
security printing Wertpapierdruck m
see copy siehe Manuskript
segmented disk *(comp.)* segmentierte Platte f
segmented ink duct blade segmentiertes Farbmesser n
seizure of sheet *(grippers)* Bogenerfassung f
selective colour correction selektive Farbkorrektur f
selective inserting *(newspaper)* selektives Einstecken n
selector switch Wahlschalter m
self-adhesive blanket *(continuous forms presses)* Selbstklebe(druck)tuch n
self-adhesive label Selbstklebeetikett n, Haftetikett n

self-compensating impression roller *(gravure)* Biegepresseur *m*, selbstanpressender Presseur *m*
self-copying paper Selbstdurchschreibepapier *n*, Durchschreibepapier *n*, Farbreaktionspapier *n*
self-lubricating bearings *pl* selbstschmierende Lager *pl*
selfmailer Selfmailer *m*
self-sealing envelope Selbstklebeumschlag *m*
self-separating forms set gluing selbsttrennende Formularsatzleimung *f*
self-sticking label Selbstklebeetikett *n*
semi-automatic halbautomatisch
semibold typeface halbfette Schrift *f*
semibreve *(music printing)* ganze Musiknote *f*
semicolon Semikolon *n*, Strichpunkt *m*
semi-conductor Halbleiter *m*
semi-duplex mode *(telecom.)* Semiduplex-Betrieb *m*
semi-fine paper mittelfeines Papier *n*
semi-monthly (publication) vierzehntäglich erscheinende Zeitschrift *f*, zweimal monatlich erscheinende Zeitschrift *f*
semi-opaque halbdeckend
semi-satellite unit *(web offset press)* Halbsatellitendruckwerk *n*
semi-transparent halbdeckend
sender *(telecom.)* Sender *m*
sense *v* abtasten
sense of motion Bewegungsrichtung *f*
sense of rotation *(cyl.)* Drehrichtung *f*
sensing *(web control)* Abtastung *f*
sensitivity *(phot.)* Empfindlichkeit *f*
sensitize *v* *(carbon tissue)* anschleiern; *(phot.)* lichtempfindlich machen, sensibilisieren
sensitized plate lichtempfindliche Platte *f*
sensitizer Sensibilisator *m*
sensitizing Sensibilisierung *f*; *(with light-sensitive emulsion, such as plates, films)* Beschichtung mit lichtempfindlicher Emulsion *f*
sensitometry Sensitometrie *f*
sensor Sensor *m*, Fühler *m*
sensor head *(web control)* Abtastkopf *m*
sensor key Sensortaste *f*
separate *v* *(sheets in the feeder)* vereinzeln, trennen, vorlockern
separate blank delivery *(die-cutter)* Getrenntnutzenauslage *f*
separated colour Teilfarbe *f*
separating tool *(waste-stripping)* Separierwerkzeug *n*
separation *(colour)* Auszug *m*
separation film *(colour reprod.)* Auszugsfilm *m*

separation films *pl* Farbauszüge *m/pl*
separation filter Auszugsfilter *m*
separation negative Auszugsnegativ *n*, Teilfarbennegativ *n*
separation positive Auszugspositiv *n*, Teilfarbenpositiv *n*
separations *pl (colour separations)* Farbauszüge *m/pl*
separator sucker *(feeder suction head)* Trennsauger *m*
sepia Sepia *n*
sepia brown sepiabraun
sepia dye Sepiapause *f*
sequence control *(machine)* Folgeschaltung *f*, Ablaufsteuerung *f*
sequence of functions Funktionsablauf *m*
sequential access *(comp.)* sequentieller Zugriff *m*
sequential numbering fortlaufende Numerierung *f*, vorwärtszählende Numerierung *f*
serial story *(newspaper)* Fortsetzungsroman *m*
series of articles *(publication)* Artikelreihe *f*
serif *(type)* Serif *m*
serif typeface Serifenschrift *f*, serifenbetonte Schrift *f*
serrated cut Sägezahnschnitt *m*, Zackenschnitt *m*
serrated effect Sägezahneffekt *m*
serrated line Zahnlinie *f*
serrated rule Zahnlinie *f*
service engineers *pl* Monteure *pl*, Wartungspersonal *n*
service-friendly wartungsfreundlich
service house Dienstleistungsunternehmen *n*
service life *(machine)* Lebensdauer *f*
service network Servicenetz *n*
service staff Wartungspersonal *n*
servicing Instandhaltung *f*, Wartung *f*
servicing staff Monteure *pl*
servicing times *pl* Hilfszeiten *pl*
servo-component *(remote control)* Stellglied *n*
servo motor Schrittmotor *m*, Stellmotor *m*
set *(in type)* gesetzt
set *v (type)* setzen, absetzen; *(to adjust)* einstellen
set flush *v (type)* bündig setzen
set flush left *v (typesetting)* linksbündig setzen
set flush right *v (typesetting)* rechtsbündig setzen
set in columns *v (type)* spaltenweise setzen
set in figures *v* Zahl in Ziffern setzen
set in italics *v (type)* in kursiv setzen
set in motion *v* anstellen
set line by line *v (type)* Zeile auf Zeile setzen
set-off *(fresh ink)* Abliegen *n*, Abschmieren *n*, Abschmutzen *n*

set off - sharp print

set off *v (fresh ink)* ablegen, abliegen, abschmieren, abschmutzen, abziehen
set of films Filmsatz *m*
set of filters Filtersatz *m*
set-off paper *(for interleaving)* Durchschußpapier *n*, Einschießpapier *n*
set-off sheets *pl* Abschmutzbogen *m/pl*, Abschmutzmakulatur *f*, Einschießbogen *pl*, Schmutzbogen *m/pl*
set of lenses Objektivsatz *m*
set of matrices Matrizensatz *m*
set of plates Plattensatz *m*
set of progressives Andruckskala *f*, Farbskala *f*
set of progs Andruckskala *f*, Farbskala *f*
set on action *v* anstellen
set rollers *v (press)* Walzen einstellen
set (size) Buchstabenbreite *f*, Dickte *f*, Schriftweite *f*, Zeichenbreite *f*
set solid *(type)* kompreß, undurchschossen, ungesperrt
setting *(adjustment)* Einstellung *f*; *(ink)* Wegschlagen *n*; *(typesetting)* Satz *m*
setting copy Satzvorlage *f*
setting gauge Einstellehre *f*
setting of numerals Ziffernsatz *m*
setting of printing pressure Druckbeistellung *f*
setting rule Setzlinie *f*
setting scale Einstellskala *f*
setting stick *(hand comp.)* Winkelhaken *m*
setting time *(glue)* Abbindezeit *f*
setting width *(typesetting)* Satzbreite *f*
set to baseline *v* auf Schriftlinie stellen
set-up *(machine installation)* Anlage *f*, Aufstellung *f*; *(makeready)* Einrichten *n*, Einrichtung *f*
set up *v (to erect)* aufstellen; *(to adjust)* einstellen; *(to make ready)* einrichten
set-up data Einstelldaten *pl*
set-up scale Einrichteskala *f*
set-up times *pl (makeready times)* Einrichtezeiten *f/pl*, Rüstzeiten *f/pl*
set width *(type)* Dickte *f*, Schriftdickte *f*, Schriftweite *f*
set without indent *v (typesetting)* stumpf anfangen
sew *v* fadenheften
sew in *v* einheften
sewing Fadenheftung *f*, Heftung *f*, Nähen *n*
sewing gauze Heftgaze *f*
sewing machine Fadenheftmaschine *f*
sewing needle Nähnadel *f*
sewing thread Heftfaden *m*, Heftzwirn *m*
sewn geheftet

sewn book fadengeheftetes Buch *n*
sewn on bands auf Bänder genäht, auf Bünde genäht
sewn on raised cords auf echte Bünde geheftet
sewn through gauze mit Faden auf Gaze geheftet
shade Farbton *m*, Nuance *f*, Ton *m*
shade *v* abtönen
shaded box *(typogr.)* Schattenrahmen *m*
shaded colour abgetönte Farbe *f*, dunkle Farbe *f*, gedämpfte Farbe *f*
shaded line *(typogr.)* fettfeine Linie *f*
shaded rule fettfeine Linie *f*
shaded type schattierte Schrift *f*
shadow areas *pl (image)* Schattenpartien *f/pl*, Schattenstellen *f/pl*, Tiefen *pl*
shadow cast *(colour cast in shadow area)* Schattenstich *m*
shadow details *pl (image)* Tiefenzeichnung *f*
shadow dot *(halftone image)* Tiefenpunkt *m*
shadow gradation Gradation in den Tiefen
shadow mask *(reprod.)* Schattenmaske *f*, Tiefenmaske *f*
shadows *pl (image)* Schattenpartien *f/pl*, Schattenstellen *f/pl*, Tiefen *pl*
shadow separation *(image)* Tiefenzeichnung *f*
shaft *(drive)* Welle *f*
shaft bearing Wellenlager *n*
shaft cylinder *(as opp. to hollow cylinder)* Achszylinder *m*
shaft drive Wellenantrieb *m*
shaftless winding achsloses Wickeln *n*
shagreen paper Chagrinpapier *n*
shank *(part of the letter)* Schaft *m*
shape Form *f*
shaped labels *pl* formgestanzte Etiketten *n/pl*
shape of text matter Textform *f*
shape of type matter Satzform *f*
shape setting *(typogr.)* Formsatz *m*
shared logic *(comp.)* verteilte Intelligenz *f*
sharp edge scharfe Kante *f*
sharp-edged fold scharf(kantig)er Falz *m*
sharpen *v (blade)* schleifen
sharpen the dots *v* kleinerätzen, spitzerätzen, spitzermachen
sharp image scharfes Bild *n*
sharp impression scharfer Druck *m*
sharply defined edge scharfe Kante *f*
sharpness *(phot.)* Schärfe *f*
sharpness enhancement *(scanner function)* Detailkontraststeigerung *f*, Umfeldblende *f*
sharp print scharfer Druck *m*

shavings *pl (paper cutting)* Abfallstreifen *pl*, Beschnittabfall *m*, Schnitzel *pl*, Schneidabfall *m*; *(book prod.)* Späne *pl*
shavings extraction Späneabsaugung *f*
shear cut Scherschnitt *m*
sheet Blatt *n*, Bogen *m*
sheet acceleration Bogenbeschleunigung *f*
sheet aligner Bogengeradstoßer *m*
sheet alignment Bogenausrichtung *f*
sheet assembly Bogenmontage *f*, Druckformmontage *f*
sheet catcher Bogenfänger *m*
sheet cleaner Bogenreiniger *m*
sheet control Bogenkontrolle *f*
sheet correction Bogenkorrektur *f*
sheet counter Bogenzähler *m*, Bogenzählwerk *n*
sheet curling Einrollen der Bogen, Rollneigung des Bogens
sheet cutter Bogenquerschneider *m*, Bogenschneider *m*
sheet decurler Bogenentroller *m*, Bogenglätter *m*
sheet deflector Bogenweiche *f*
sheet delivery Bogenauslage *f*
sheet division Bogeneinteilung *f*
sheet dryer Bogentrockner *m*
sheet edge Bogenkante *f*
sheet entry Bogeneinlauf *m*
sheeter *(on web press)* Querschneider *m*, Planoauslage *f*, Planoausleger *m*, Planobogenausgang *m*; *(sheet cutter)* Bogenquerschneider *m*, Bogenschneider *m*
sheet fanning blowers *pl (feeder suction head)* Bogenlockerungsbläser *m/pl*
sheet-fed gravure press Bogentiefdruckmaschine *f*, Tiefdruckbogenrotation *f*
sheet-fed gravure (printing) Bogentiefdruck *m*
sheet-fed letterpress (printing) Bogenhochdruck *m*
sheet-fed letterpress rotary Buchdruckbogenrotation *f*, Hochdruckbogenrotation *f*
sheet-fed offset Bogenoffset *m*
sheet-fed offset press Bogenoffsetmaschine *f*
sheet-fed (printing) press Bogendruckmaschine *f*
sheet feeder Bogenanlage *f*, Bogenanleger *m*
sheet feeding Bogenanlage *f*, Bogenzuführung *f*
sheet film Blattfilm *m*, Planfilm *m*
sheet folder Bogenfalzmaschine *f*
sheet folding machine Bogenfalzmaschine *f*
sheet format Bogenformat *n*, Bogengröße *f*
sheet gluing machine Bogenanklebemaschine *f*
sheet gripping *(press)* Bogenerfassung *f*
sheet guide Bogenführung *f*

sheet guiding elements *pl* Bogenführungselemente *pl*
sheet hold-down device Bogenniederhalter *m*
sheet infeed Bogeneinlauf *m*
sheet interleavers *pl* Einschießbogen *pl*
sheet jogger Bogenglattstoßmaschine *f*, Bogengeradstoßer *m*
sheet layout Bogeneinteilung *f*, Standbogen *m*
sheet metal plate Blechtafel *f*
sheet outlet Bogenauslauf *m*
sheet paper Bogenpapier *n*, Formatpapier *n*
sheet pass *(through press)* Bogendurchlauf *m*, Bogendurchgang *m*; *in one* ~ in einem Bogendurchlauf *m*, in einem Druckgang
sheet perfecting drum *(perfector)* Bogenwendetrommel *f*
sheet pile Papierstapel *m*, Papierstoß *m*
sheet piling Bogenstapelung *f*, Papierstapeln *n*
sheet piling without break lines absatzfreies Papierstapeln
sheet planning Bogeneinteilung *f*
sheet prealignment Bogenvorausrichtung *f*
sheet preregistration Bogenvorausrichtung *f*
sheet pulling *(press delivery)* Bogenentnahme *f*
sheet registration Bogenausrichtung *f*
sheet release *(from grippers, cylinder nips)* Bogenfreigabe *f*
sheet removal *(press delivery)* Bogenentnahme *f*
sheet reversal Bogenwendung *f*
sheet reversing Bogenwendung *f*
sheet reversing drum *(perfector)* Bogenwendetrommel *f*
sheet revision Bogenkorrektur *f*, Bogenrevision *f*
sheet ruling machine Bogenliniermaschine *f*
sheet section Bogenteil *m*
sheet separation Bogentrennung *f*
sheet separator *(feeder suction head)* Abstreifer *m*
sheet severer Bogenabschlagvorrichtung *f*
sheet signature Bogenzeichen *n*, Bogenziffer *f*
sheet size Bogenformat *n*, Bogengröße *f*; *(paper)* Papierformat *n*, Papiergröße *f*
sheet slow-down Bogenverlangsamung *f*
sheet slow-down device Bogenbremse *f*
sheets per hour *(sph)* Bogen pro Stunde
sheet spoilage Makulatur *f*
sheet stop Bogenanschlag *m*
sheet straightening Bogenstraffung *f*
sheet stripper Bogenabstreifer *m*
sheet suction Bogenansaugung *f*
sheet tail Bogenende *n*, Bogenhinterkante *f*
sheet title Bogennorm *f*, Bogensignatur *f*
sheet transfer Bogenübergabe *f*

sheet transport - siderography

sheet transport Bogentransport *m*
sheet travel Bogendurchgang *m*, Bogendurchlauf *m*, Bogenlauf *m*
sheet travel monitoring Bogendurchlaufkontrolle *f*
sheet turning Bogenwendung *f*
sheet turning device *(screen printing)* Druckwender *m*
sheet turning drum *(perfector)* Bogenwendetrommel *f*
shelf-life *(inks, chemicals, consumables)* Lagerfähigkeit *f*, Haltbarkeit *f*
shift change Schichtwechsel *m*
shift downwards *v (subscripts)* tiefstellen
shift upwards *v (superscripts)* hochstellen
shilling stroke Schrägstrich *m*
shingle *(copy stream)* Schuppe *f*
shingle *v (sheets)* aufschuppen
shingled geschuppt
shingled copies *pl* Exemplarschuppe *f*, Produktüberlappung *f*
shingle delivery Schuppenauslage *f*
shingled sheets *pl (feeder, delivery)* Bogenschuppe *f*
shingle separator Schuppentrennung *f*
shingle spacing *(shingle stream)* Schuppenabstand *m*
shingle stream Produktstrom *m*, Schuppenstrom *m*
shingle-stream addressing Schuppenstromadressierung *f*
shingling belt Schuppenband *n*
shirting Schirting *m*
shop-window display Schaufensterdisplay *n*
shore hardness *(rubber blanket)* Shore-Härte *f*
short cut-off *(web printing)* liegendes Format *n*
short-fibred paper kurzfaseriges Papier *n*
short grain *(paper)* Breitbahn *f*; *(short cut-off)* liegendes Format *n*
short grain paper Breitbahnpapier *n*
short ink kurze Farbe *f*
short inking unit *(anilox type)* Kurzfarbwerk *n*
short leads *pl (lead comp.)* Stückdurchschuß *m*
short letters *pl (no ascender/descender; like r, n, m)* Mittellängen *pl*, kurze Buchstaben *pl*
short-lived product kurzlebiges Produkt *n*
short page Ausgangskolumne *f*, Spitzkolumne *f*
short-run and small-size printed products *pl* Kleindrucksachen *pl*
short run (job) *(printing)* Kleinauflage *f*
short story Kurzgeschichte *f*
short-term storage Zwischenlagerung *f*

short-wave I.R. radiation kurzwellige IR-Strahlung
shot *(camera)* Aufnahme *f*
shoulder *(part of the letter)* Achsel *f*, Hals *m*, Schulter *f*
show card *(shop advertising)* Aufsteller *m*
showcard board Plakatkarton *m*
show-through *(print-through)* Durchscheinen *n*
shred Schnitzel *pl*
shredder *(papermaking)* Zerfaserer *m*
shrinkage *(paper)* Eingehen *n*, Schrumpfung *f*
shrink film *(film wrapping)* Schrumpffolie *f*
shrink (film) wrapping *(mailroom)* Schrumpffolienverpackung *f*
shrink sleeving *(mailroom)* Schrumpfbanderolierung *f*
shrink tunnel *(film wrapping)* Schrumpftunnel *m*
shrink-wrap installation *(mailroom)* Schrumpfpackanlage *f*
shut-down Abstellung *f*
shut down *v (unit)* abstellen
shutter *(camera)* Verschluß *m*
shutter speed *(camera)* Verschlußgeschwindigkeit *f*
shuttle feeder Schieberanleger *m*
siccative *(ink additive)* Trockenstoff *m*, Trockner *m*, Sikkativ *n*
siccative varnish Trockenfirnis *m*
side bearings *(of the letter)* Fleisch *n*
side-effect free ink metering *(ink duct)* nebenwirkungsfreie Farbdosierung *f*
side figure *(marginal figure)* Marginalziffer *f*
side frame *(press)* Seitenwand *f*, Seitengestell *n*, Seitenrahmen *m*
side gluer Seitenbeleimungsgerät *n*
side gluing Seitenbeleimung *f*, Seitenleimung *f*
side guide *(sheet alignment)* Seitenmarke *f*, Seitenanlegemarke *f*, Seitenführung *f*
side guide aligner *(sheet alignment)* Seitenanschlag *m*
side heading *(marginal heading)* Marginaltitel *m*
side jogger *(sheet delivery)* Bündigstoßer *m*, Geradstoßer *m*
side lay *(sheet alignment)* Seitenanschlag *m*, Seitenanlegemarke *f*, Seitenmarke *f*
side(lay) register Seitenregister *f*
side lighting *(contact printing)* Hohlkopie *f*, Unterstrahlung *f*
side note Randbemerkung *f*, Marginalie *f*, Randnote *f*
side protection resist *(halftone engraving)* Flankenschutzmittel *n*
siderography *(steel etching)* Siderografie *f*

side sealing device *(film wrapping)* Seitenschweißgerät *n*
side stick Seitensteg *m*
side stitching *(as opp. to saddle stitching)* Seitenheftung *f*, seitliche Heftung *f*, Randheftung *f*
side stop *(sheet alignment)* Seitenanschlag *m*
side wall *(halftone engraving)* Flanke *f*
side welding unit *(film wrapping)* Seitenschweißgerät *n*
signature *(print sheet)* Bogen *m*, Druckbogen *m*, Signatur *f*
signature imposition Bogenausschießen *n*
signature marks *pl* Flattermarken *f/pl*
signature opening *(convert.)* Bogenöffnung *f*
signature title Bogennorm *f*, Bogensignatur *f*
silent operation *(machine)* geräuschloser Lauf *m*
silhouette *(cut-out)* Freistellung *f*, Silhouette *f*
silhouette *v (a figure)* freistellen
silhouette image freigestelltes Bild *n*, freistehendes Bild *n*
silhouette mask *(reprod.)* Freisteller *m*, Freistellmaske *f*
silicone application Silikonbeschichtung *f*
silicone applicator *(web press)* Silikonauftragsgerät *n*
silicone coating Silikonbeschichtung *f*
silicone-elastomer *(blanket gap filler)* Silikon-Elastomer *n*
silicone rubber die *(stamping)* Silikonstempel *m*
silicone spray Silikonspray *n*
silicone spray device *(web press)* Silikonsprüheinrichtung *f*
silk fabrics *(screen printing)* Seidengewebe *n*
silk printing Seidendruck *m*
silk-screen printing Siebdruck *m*
silver bath Silberbad *n*
silver bromide Silberbromid *n*
silver bronze Silberbronze *f*
silver film *(photogr.)* Silberfilm *m*
silver halide *(silver film)* Silberhalogenid *n*
silver mask *(colour reprod.)* Silbermaske *f*
silver printing ink Silberdruckfarbe *f*
silver recovery unit Silberrückgewinnungsanlage *f*
silver salt *(silver film)* Silbersalz *n*
simple stops *(camera)* Stoppblende *f*
simplex mode *(telecom.)* Simplex-Betrieb *m*
simultaneous measuring head *(scanning densitometer)* Simultanmeßkopf *m*
simultaneous operation *(comp.)* Simultanbetrieb *m*
single-colour offset press Einfarben-Offsetmaschine *f*

single-colour printing Einfarbendruck *m*
single-colour (printing) press Einfarbendruckmaschine *f*
single-colour printwork einfarbige Arbeiten *pl*
single-colour separation Einzelfarbauszug *m*
single-column headline einspaltige Überschrift *f*
single copy Einzelexemplar *n*; *(magazine)* Einzelnummer *f*
single copy sales *pl (newspaper)* Einzelverkauf *m*
single cut *(cutting m., as opp. to repeat cut)* Einzelschnitt *m*
single gate fold Deltafalz *m*
single issue *(magazine)* Einzelnummer *f*
single letter Einzelbuchstabe *m*
single number *(magazine)* Einzelnummer *f*
single quotes *pl* einfache Anführungszeichen *pl*
single reelstand *(web press)* Ein-Rollenstand *m*
single-revolution press Eintourenpresse *f*
single-roll cutter-sorter *(papermill)* Sortierquerschneider *m*
single sheet Einzelblatt *n*, Einzelbogen *m*
single-sheet feeder *(as opp. to stream feeder)* Einzelbogenanleger *m*
single-sheet processing Einzelblattverarbeitung *f*
single-sided printing einseitiger Druck *m*, Schöndruck *m*
single-station system Einzelplatzsystem *n*
single stitch *(book sewing)* einfacher Stich *m*
single strapping *(mailroom bundles)* Einmalumreifung *f*
single type *(hand comp., as opp. to block type)* Einzelbuchstabe *m*, Einzeltype *f*
single-type caster *(Monotype)* Einzelbuchstabengießapparat *m*
single-type matrix *(Monotype)* Einbuchstabenmatrize *f*
single-width web press einfachbreite Rollendruckmaschine *f*
sink *(plate processing)* Becken *n*, Spülbecken *n*, Spültrog *m*
sinking *(rubber blanket)* Einfallen *n*
situations *pl (classified advertising)* Stellenanzeigen *pl*, Arbeitsmarkt *m*
sixteen-page product *(web printing)* Sechzehnseitenprodukt *n*
sixteen page rotary press Sechzehnseiten-Rollenrotation *f*
size Format *n*, Größe *f*; *(papermaking)* Leim *m*, Leimungsmittel *n*
size adjustment Formateinstellung *f*, Größeneinstellung *f*
size change Formatänderung *f*, Formatveränderung *f*, Formatwechsel *m*

size change-over - slug caster

size change-over Formatumstellung *f*
sized board geleimte Pappe *f*
sized paper geleimtes Papier *n*
size press *(papermaking)* Leimpresse *f*
size range Formatbereich *m*
size setting Formateinstellung *f*, Größeneinstellung *f*
sizing *(paper)* Leimung *f*, Leimen *n*; *(reprod.)* Formateinstellung *f*, Größeneinstellung *f*
sizing agent *(papermaking)* Leimungsmittel *n*
sizing calender *(papermaking)* Gummierkalander *m*
sizing strength *(paper)* Oberflächenfestigkeit *f*, Rupffestigkeit *f*
skeleton black Skelettschwarz *n*
skeleton forme *(colour registration)* Paßform *f*
skeleton wheels *pl (to guide sheet over feedboard)* Bogenführungsscheiben *pl*
sketch Aufriß *m*, Entwurf *m*, Skizze *f*
skewed indent progressiver Einzug *m*
skilled operator ausgebildeter Bediener *m*, Fachkraft *f*, gelernte Arbeitskraft *f*
skilled personnel Fachkräfte *pl*
skilled staff Fachkräfte *pl*
skilled worker Facharbeiter *m*, Fachkraft *f*
skim *v* abkrätzen
skin coppering process *(gravure)* Hautaufkupferungsverfahren *n*
skin formation *(ink)* Hautbildung *f*
skinning *(ink)* Hautbildung *f*
skip numbering *(numbering box)* Wiederholnumerierung *f*, überspringende Numerierung *f*
sky-blue himmelblau
slab *(ink stone)* Farbmischstein *m*, Farbtisch *m*
Slab Serif *(type classif.)* Serifenbetonte Linear-Antiqua *f*
slack edges *pl* wellige Kanten *f/pl*
slack reel *(paper)* lose gewickelte Rolle *f*
slanted *(photocomp.)* elektronisch kursiv, kursiv, schräggestellt
slanted left or right *(photocomp.)* kursiv rechts oder links
slash Schrägstrich *m*
slate black schieferschwarz
slate paper Schieferpapier *n*
slave typesetter Hilfsbelichter *m*
sleeve *(flexo printforme)* Hülse *f*
sleeve-wrapping *(film packaging)* Banderoleneinschlag *m*, Banderolieren *n*
sleeve wrapping machine *(film packaging)* Banderoliermaschine *f*

sleeving machine *(film packaging)* Banderoliermaschine *f*
slide Schlitten *m*; *(transparency)* Dia *n*
slide *v* gleiten
slide binding *(loose leaf binding)* Klemmschienenbindung *f*
slide delivery Rutschauslage *f*
slide guide Gleitführung *f*
slide-in carriage *(interchangeable printing unit)* Formateinschub *m*, Einschubwagen *m*, Zylindereinschub *m*
slide-in cassette *(interchangeable printing unit)* Einschubkassette *f*, Formateinschub *m*
slide-in letterpress unit Buchdruck(-Zylinder)einschub *m*
slide rail Gleitschiene *f*
slide viewer Diabetrachter *m*
slide viewing box Dialeuchtplatte *f*
slide viewing wall Dialeuchtwand *f*
sliding bar *(composing stick)* Schieber *m*
sliding calliper Schieblehre *f*, Schublehre *f*
sliding diaphragm Schieberblende *f*, Steckblende *f*
slightly mechanical paper fast holzfreies Papier *n*, leicht holzhaltiges Papier *n*
slip carton *(book)* Schuber *m*, Schutzkarton *m*
slip case *(book)* Futteral *n*, Schuber *m*, Schutzkarton *m*
slip-free schlupffrei
slippage Schlupf *m*
slip(ping) Schlupf *m*
slip proof Korrekturfahne *f*, Spaltenabzug *m*
slip sheets *pl (set-off sheets)* Einschießbogen *pl*
slit diaphragm Schlitzblende *f*
slitter *(reel proc.)* Längsschneider *m*
slitter-rewinder *(reel proc.)* Längsschneider *m*, Rollenschneidemaschine *f*, Rollenschneider *m*
slitting Längsschnitt *m*
slitting and sheeting Längs- und Querschnitt *m*
slitting knife Längsschneidemesser *n*
slitting roller Schneidwalze *f*
slitting wheels *pl* Schneid(e)rädchen *pl*, Schneidrollen *pl*
slope *(densitometer)* Steilheit *f*, Steigung *f*
slot Einschnitt *m*, Schlitz *m*, Schlitzloch *n*
slot perforation Schlitzlochung *f*, Strichperforation *f*
slotting Schlitzen *n*
slotting machine Schlitzmaschine *f*
slow gear *(machine)* Schleichgang *m*
slug *(hot-metal comp.)* gegossene Schriftzeile *f*, Gußzeile *f*, Setzmaschinenzeile *f*, Zeilenguß *m*
slug caster Zeilengießmaschine *f*

slug casting Zeilenguß *m*
slug casting machine Zeilengießmaschine *f*
slug composition Maschinensatz *m*, Zeilensatz *m*
slug cutter Zeilenschneider *m*
slug saw Zeilensäge *f*
slur *(printing problem)* Dublieren *n*, Schieben *n*, Schmitz *m*
slur *v* schmitzen
slur/doubling patch *(print control bar)* Schiebe-/Dublierfeld *n*
small ad Kleinanzeige *f*
small caps *pl (typesetting)* Kapitälchen *pl*
small circulation *(newspaper, magazine)* Kleinauflage *f*
small-circulation newspaper kleine Zeitung *f*
small dot patch *(print control bar)* Spitzpunktfeld *n*
small edition Kleinauflage *f*
small-format newspaper Kleinformatzeitung *f*
small offset Kleinoffset *m*
small offset printer *(press)* Kleinoffsetmaschine *f*
small offset (printing) press Kleinoffsetmaschine *f*
small-size (printing) press kleinformatige Druckmaschine *f*
smash *(rubber blanket)* Knautscher *m*
smashing *(book block)* Abpressen *n*
smashing machine *(for book blocks)* Buchblockpresse *f*
smash-resistance *(rubber blanket)* Widerstandskraft gegen Knautscher
smeared sheet verschmierter Bogen *m*
smear-free delivery schmierfreie Auslage *f*
smearing *(printing problem)* Schmieren *n*, Abschmieren *n*, Abschmutzen *n*, Verschmieren *n*
smooth creases *v (paper)* Falten glätten
smooth machine start-up sanfter Maschinenanlauf *m*
smoothness *(paper)* Glätte *f*
smoothness tester Glätteprüfer *m*
smooth out *v (to remove air from sheet pile)* Luft ausstreichen
smooth-running *(machine)* laufruhig
smooth running of press ruhiger Maschinenlauf *m*
smooth solid glatte Volltonfläche *f*
smooth surface glatte Oberfläche *f*
smudge Schmutzfleck *m*
smudged sheet verschmierter Bogen *m*
smudge-proof wischfest
smudge-proof delivery schmierfreie Auslage *f*

smudging *(printing problem)* Schmieren *n*, Abschmieren *n*, Abschmutzen *n*, Verschmieren *n*
snap-apart set *(forms set)* Schnelltrennsatz *m*
snap-band forms set Trägerbandformularsatz *m*
snap-out perforation *(forms set prod.)* Schnelltrennperforation *f*
snap-out set *(forms set)* Schnelltrennsatz *m*
snapshot Schnappschuß *m*
soap stone Speckstein *m*
soda cellulose *(papermaking)* Natronzellstoff *m*
sodium vapour lamp Natriumdampflampe *f*
sodium woodpulp *(papermaking)* Natronzellulose *f*
softcopy *(true-typographic and/or layout-true display on screen)* Echtdarstellung (am Bildschirm) *f*, Prüfdarstellung (am Bildschirm) *f*, Softcopy *f*
soft-copy colour proof farbige Prüfdarstellung am Bildschirm
soft-copy monitor *(video screen separated from text input terminal for true-typographic display)* Darstellungsbildschirm *m*, Preview-Terminal *n*
soft cover Broschürenumschlag *m*, flexibler Umschlag *m*, weicher Umschlag *m*
soft-cover binding Broschürenbindung *f*, flexibler Einband *m*, Softcoverbindung *f*
soft dot unscharfer Punkt *m*, weicher Punkt *m*
soft-edged dot weichkantiger Rasterpunkt *m*
soft-edged dot structure *(film)* weichkantiger Punktaufbau *m*
soften *v (photogr.)* weichzeichnen
softened outline *(electronic image proc.)* Unscharfkontur *f*
soften the ink *v* Farbe geschmeidiger machen
soft focus lens Weichzeichner *m*
soft gradation flache Gradation *f*
soft image *(low contrast image)* kontrastloses Bild *n*
soft ink lange Farbe *f*
soft keys *pl (programmable keys)* programmierbare Tasten *f/pl*
soft negative weiches Negativ *n*
soft outline vignetting *(electronic image proc.)* weichverlaufende Freistellung *f*
soft pack Weichpackung *f*
soft packing *(press cylinder)* weicher Aufzug *m*
soft paper weiches Papier *n*
soft proof *(true-typographic and/or layout-true display on screen)* Echtdarstellung (am Bildschirm) *f*, Prüfdarstellung (am Bildschirm) *f*, Softproof *m*

soft proofing Prüfdarstellung (am Bildschirm) *f*
soft PVC Weich-PVC *n*
soft-sized paper halbgeleimtes Papier *n*
soft transition outline *(electronic image proc.)* weiche Kombinationsnaht *f*
soft typesetter *(video screen separated from text input terminal for true-typographic display)* Darstellungsbildschirm *m*, Preview-Terminal *m*
software Software *f*, Programm *n*
software-based softwaregestützt
software-controlled programmgesteuert
software-driven programmgesteuert
software module Programmodul *n*
software package Softwarepaket *n*, Programmpaket *n*
software routine *(comp.)* Unterprogramm *n*
software update Softwarepflege *f*
solarization Solarisation *f*
solarization effect *(photogr.)* Solarisationseffekt *m*
sold out *(book)* vergriffen
solid *(printing)* Fläche *f*, Tonfläche *f*, Vollfläche *f*, Vollton *m*, Volltonfläche *f*; *(typesetting)* kompreß, undurchschossen
solid area Tonfläche *f*, Vollfläche *f*, Volltonfläche *f*
solid board *(as opp. to corrugated)* Vollkarton *m*, Vollpappe *f*
solid colour overprint patch *(print control bar)* Übereinanderdruckfeld *n*, Vollton-Übereinanderdruckfeld *n*, Zusammendruckfeld *n*
solid cylinder Vollzylinder *m*
solid (ink) density Volltondichte *f*
solid ink patch *(print control bar)* Volltonfeld *n*
solid matter *(typesetting)* kompresser Satz *m*
solid plate *(letterpress)* Tonplatte *f*
solid polymer plate Festpolymerplatte *f*
solid set type kompresser Satz *m*
solids superimposition patch *(print control bar)* Übereinanderdruckfeld *n*, Vollton-Übereinanderdruckfeld *n*, Zusammendruckfeld *n*
solid tint Flächenton *m*, Vollton *m*
solid (tone) density Dichte Vollton, Volltondichte *f*
solidus Schrägstrich *m*
solution *(chem.)* Lösung *f*
solvent Lösemittel *n*, Lösungsmittel *n*
solvent-based ink Farbe auf Lösemittelbasis, Lösemittelfarbe *f*
solvent exhaust Lösemittelabsaugung *f*
solvent extraction Lösemittelabsaugung *f*
solvent reclamation Lösemittelrückgewinnung *f*
solvent recovery Lösemittelrückgewinnung *f*
solvent resistance Lösemittelfestigkeit *f*
solvent resistant lösemittelbeständig
solvent vapours *pl* Lösemitteldämpfe *pl*
sort *v* sortieren
sorter *(mailroom)* Sortieranlage *f*; *(small offset)* Sorter *m*
sort in alphabetical order *v* alphabetisch sortieren
sorting Sortierung *f*
sort(ing) code *(comp.)* Sortierkennung *f*
sort(ing) key *(comp.)* Sortierschlüssel *m*
sorting machine Sortiermaschine *f*
sort(ing) program *(comp.)* Sortierprogramm *n*
sort(ing) run *(comp.)* Sortierlauf *m*
sort out *v* aussortieren
sorts *pl (lead comp.)* Defekte *pl*
sound-absorbing covering schalldämmende Verkapselung
sound absorption Lärmdämpfung *f*
sound dampening Lärmdämpfung *f*
sound-deadening casing schalldämmende Verkapselung *f*
sound insulating cover Lärmdämmhaube *f*, Schallschutzabdeckung *f*
sound insulation Lärmdämpfung *f*
sound-proof enclosure Schallschutzverkleidung *f*
source language *(comp.)* Quellensprache *f*
source program *(comp.)* Quellenprogramm *n*
space *(lead comp.)* Spatium *f*
space *v (type)* durchschießen, spationieren, sperren
spaceband *(line caster)* Ausschließkeil *m*, Spatienkeil *m*
space closely *v (type)* eng ausschließen, eng halten, eng setzen
space closer *v (type)* Zwischenraum herausnehmen
space equally *v (type)* ausgleichen, gleichmäßig ausschließen
space evenly *v (type)* ausgleichen, gleichmäßig ausschließen
space left white *(layout, make-up etc.)* Aussparung *f*, freigeschlagener Raum *m*, Freiraum *m*
space line Zwischenzeile *f*; *(lead comp.)* Durchschußlinie *f*
space order *(ad space)* Anzeigenauftrag *m*
space out *v (type)* austreiben, Zwischenraum erweitern

spacer *(hand comp.)* Blindtype *f*
space requirements *pl* Platzbedarf *m*, Raumbedarf *m*
space rule *(tabular work)* Querlinie *f*
spaces *pl (lead comp.)* Spatien *pl*, Ausschluß *m*
space salesman *(advertising sales)* Anzeigenakquisiteur *m*, Anzeigenvertreter *m*
space widely *v (type)* weit ausschließen, weit setzen
space wider *v (type)* Zwischenraum erweitern
spacing *(type)* Ausschließen *n*, Raumverteilung *f*, Ausschluß *m*
spacing material *(lead comp.)* Blindmaterial *n*
spanner Schraubenschlüssel *m*
spare knife Ersatzmesser *n*
spare parts *pl* Ersatzteile *n/pl*
spare parts manual Ersatzteilkatalog *m*
spare parts service Ersatzteildienst *m*
spare parts supply Ersatzteilversorgung *f*
spare roller Ersatzwalze *f*, Reservewalze *f*
spares *pl (spare parts)* Ersatzteile *n/pl*
spares manual Ersatzteilkatalog *m*
spares stock Ersatzteillager *n*
spattle see spatula
spatula *(ink slice)* Farbmesser *n*, Farbspachtel *f*, Farbspatel *m*
special character *(typesetting)* Sonderzeichen *n*
special colour Sonderfarbe *f*
special edition Sonderausgabe *f*, Sonderheft *n*, Sondernummer *f*
special effect screen Spezialeffektraster *m*
special ink Spezialfarbe *f*
special issue Sonderausgabe *f*, Sonderheft *n*, Sondernummer *f*
specialist Fachkraft *f*, Fachmann *m*
special print Sonderdruck *m*
special production *(ink)* Anreibung *f*
special supplement Sonderbeilage *f*
specify *v (comp.)* festlegen
specimen Muster *n*
specimen book Musterbuch *n*
specimen copy Musterexemplar *n*, Probeexemplar *n*; *(magazine)* Probeheft *n*, Probenummer *f*
specimen line *(typesetting)* Musterzeile *f*, Probezeile *f*
specimen page Probeseite *f*
specimen print Probedruck *m*
specimen sheet Musterblatt *n*, Musterbogen *m*, Probebogen *m*, Probedruck *m*
specimen volume *(book)* Probeband *m*
speck *(film laminating)* Pickel *m*
speckled maserig
speckled impression fleckiger Druck *m*

spectral analysis *(colour measurement)* Spektralanalyse *f*
spectral colour Spektralfarbe *f*
spectral colour density spektrale Farbdichte *f*
spectral colour density measurement *(on press)* spektrale Farbdichtemessung *f*
spectral light distribution *(light source)* spektrale Lichtverteilung *f*
spectral range Spektralbereich *m*
spectral sensitivity *(photo-coating, photo-emulsion)* spektrale Empfindlichkeit *f*
spectrophotometer *(colour measurement)* Spektralfotometer *n*
spectrophotometric measurement *(colour measurement)* spektralfotometrische Messung *f*
speed Geschwindigkeit *f*; *(light sensitivity)* Lichtempfindlichkeit *f*, Empfindlichkeit *f*
speed-compensated drive geschwindigkeitskompensierter Antrieb *m*
speed control Drehzahlregelung *f*
speed indicator Tourenzähler *m*
speedometer Tachometer *m*
speed regulator Geschwindigkeitsregler *m*
speed up sheets *v* Bogen beschleunigen
spell *v* buchstabieren
spell check *(text proc.)* Rechtschreibprüfung *f*
spelling Orthografie *f*, Rechtschreibung *f*, Schreibung *f*, Schreibweise *f*
spelling checking *(text proc.)* Rechtschreibprüfung *f*
spelling mistake Rechtschreibfehler *m*, Schreibfehler *m*, Setzfehler *m*
spell out (in full) *v* ausschreiben, aussetzen
spherical cast iron *(machine frame)* Sphäroguß *m*
spherical nozzles *pl (air table)* Kugeldüsen *pl*
spheroid casting alloy *(machine frame)* Sphäroguß *m*
spider wheel delivery *(web press)* Schaufelradauslage *f*
spindling *(gravure cyl.)* Aufspindelung *f*
spine *(book, magazine)* Rücken *m*
spine first *(book prod.)* mit dem Rücken voran
spine fold Rückenfalz *m*
spine gluing Rückenbeleimung *f*, Rückenleimung *f*
spine leading *(book prod.)* mit dem Rücken voran
spine length Rückenlänge *f*
spine lettering Rückentitel *m*
spine preparation Rückenbearbeitung *f*
spine rounding Rückenrunden *n*

spine rounding machine Rückenrundemaschine *f*
spine router Rückenfräser *m*
spine routing Rückenfräsen *n*
spine shaping Rückenformgebung *f*
spine strip Rückenschrenz *m*
spine tape *(book)* Fälzelstreifen *m*
spine-taped *(book)* gefälzelt
spine taping *(bookb.)* Fälzelung *f*
spine-taping machine Fälzelmaschine *f*
spine thickness Rückenhöhe *f*
spine trailing *(book prod.)* mit dem Rücken hinten
spiral binding Spiralbindung *f*, Spiralheftung *f*
spiral binding machine *(bookb.)* Spiralbindemaschine *f*
spiral-bound brochure spiralgebundene Broschüre *f*, spiralisierte Broschüre *f*
spiral brush damping system Spiralbürstenfeuchtwerk *n*
spiral fold Spiralfalz *m*
spiral folder Spiralfalzer *m*
spiral wire Spiraldraht *m*
spiral wire binding Spiraldrahtbindung *f*
spirit wash Waschbenzin *n*
splice recognition *(web monitoring)* Klebstellenerkennung *f*
splicing Klebung *f*
split filter exposure *(reprod.)* Splitfilterbelichtung *f*
split fractions *pl* Bruchziffern *pl*, gebrochene Ziffern *pl*
split screen *(VDU)* geteilter Bildschirm *m*
splotchy impression klecksiger Druck *m*
spoilage *(waste sheets)* Makulatur *f*
spoils *pl* Makulatur *f*, Makulaturbogen *m/pl*
spoil sheets *pl* Makulatur *f*, Makulaturbogen *m/pl*
sponge off *v* abwischen
sponge rubber Moosgummi *n*
spool *(wire)* Spule *f*
spot colour *(second colour after black)* Schmuckfarbe *f*, Spotfarbe *f*, Zusatzfarbe *f*
spot-colour printing unit *(newspaper press)* Zusatzfarbwerk *n*
spot gluer Punktleimeinrichtung *f*
spot gluing Punktleimung *f*
spot retouching Ausschnittretusche *f*, Spotretusche *f*
spotted fleckig
spotted impression klecksiger Druck *m*
spotting-out *(film opaquing)* Ausflecken *n*
spotty impression fleckiger Druck *m*

spot varnishing ausgesparte Lackierung *f*, Nutzenlackierung *f*
spray *v (spray powder)* pudern
spray damping system *(offset)* Sprühfeuchtwerk *n*
sprayer see spray powder device
spray gluing *(as opp. to roller gluing)* Sprühbeleimung *f*
spray gun *(art prep.)* Spritzpistole *f*, Spritzapparat *m*
spraying nozzle *(powder sprayer)* Zerstäuberdüse *f*
spray powder Druckbestäubungspuder *n*
spray powder device Bestäuber *m*, Bestäubungsapparat *m*, Bestäubungsgerät *n*, Druckbestäuber *m*, Puderbestäuber *m*, Zerstäuber *m*; **automatic ~** Puderautomat *m*
spread *v (sheets, signatures)* see to shingle
spread and choke *(image proc.)* Absparen/Überfüllen *n*
spread exposure *(film contacting)* Überfüllen *n*, Überstrahlung *f*
spreading *(reprod.)* Überfüllen *n*
spring cover Klappdeckel *m*
spring-loaded pin gefederter Stift *m*
spring sucker *(feeder suction head)* Springsauger *m*
sprocket hole punching *(continuous forms)* Führungsrandlochung *f*, Randlochung *f*, Remainerlochung *f*, Transportlochung *f*
sprocket holes *pl (continuous forms)* Führungsrandlochung *f*, Randlochung *f*, Remainerlochung *f*, Transportlochung *f*
sprocket wheel Kettenrad *n*
square *(exponent figure)* Quadrat *n*
square back *(book)* Flachrücken *m*, gerader Rücken *m*
square (back) binding Einband mit geradem Rücken
square-back book Buch mit flachem Rücken
square box *(typogr.)* eckiger Rahmen *m*
square cut *(guillotine)* rechtwinkliger Schnitt *m*, Winkelschnitt *m*
square dot quadratischer Rasterpunkt *m*, Schachbrettpunkt *m*
squareness Rechtwinkligkeit *f*, Winkelmaßhaltigkeit *f*
square ruled paper kariertes Papier *n*
square scorper Vierkantstichel *m*
square trim Winkelschnitt *m*
square up *v (lead comp.)* quadratieren
squaring *(image proc.)* Auswinkelung *f*
squeegee *(screen printing)* Rakel *f*, Schleppe *f*

squeegee grinder *(screen printing)* Rakelschleifgerät *n*
squeeze *v (printing)* quetschen
squeeze roller Abquetschwalze *f*, Auspreßwalze *f*, Preßwalze *f*, Quetschwalze *f*
squeezing *(damping rollers)* Abrakeln *n*
stab *v* querheften
stabbed insert *(magazine)* Durchhefter *m*
stabbing Durchheftung *f*, Querheftung *f*
stabilization film *(reprod.)* Stabilisationsfilm *m*
stabilization paper Stabilisationspapier *n*
stabilizer *(photochem.)* Stabilisator *m*
stack Stapel *m*
stack *v* abstapeln, stapeln
stacker Abstapler *m*, Stacker *m*, Stapler *m*
stacker-bundler *(convert.)* Stangenbündler *m*
stacking Abstapeln *n*
stacking rake *(delivery)* Stapelrechen *m*
stacklift Stapellift *m*
stack of paper Papierstapel *m*, Papierstoß *m*
staff lines *pl (music printing)* Musiknotenlinien *pl*
staggered delivery versetzte Auslage *f*
staggered stitch *(thread-stitching)* versetzter Stich *m*
stained fleckig
staining *(negatives)* Braunwerden *n*
stamp Stempel *m*
stamped hologram Prägehologramm *n*
stamping *(foil stamping)* Prägedruck *m*, Prägen *n*, Prägung *f*
stamping die Prägestempel *m*
stamping foil Prägefolie *f*
stamping forme Prägeform *f*
stamping plate Prägeklischee *n*
stamping press Prägepresse *f*, Prägetiegel *m*; *automatic* ~ Prägeautomat *m*
stamp ink Stempelfarbe *f*
stamp rubber Stempelgummi *m*
stand-alone machine Solo-Maschine *f*
stand-alone system Einzelplatzsystem *n*
stand-alone unit *(as opp. to in-line unit)* unabhängige Einheit *f*
standard Norm *f*, Standard *m*, serienmäßig
standard equipment serienmäßige Ausstattung *f*
standard format Normalformat *n*, Standardformat *n*
standard height to paper *(lead type)* Normalhöhe *f*
standard illumination lamp for colour control Farbabstimmleuchte mit Normlicht
standardization Normung *f*, Standardisierung *f*
standardize *v* normen, standardisieren

standardized light Normlicht *n*
standardized lighting Normbeleuchtung *f*
standardized process-colour offset printing standardisierter Mehrfarbenoffsetdruck *m*
standard measure Normmaß *n*
standard size Normalformat *n*, Standardformat *n*
standard software *(comp.)* Standardprogramm *n*
standard stitch *(book sewing)* einfacher Stich *m*
standard type normale Schrift *f*
stand-by control Bereitschaftsschaltung *f*
standing forme *(printing forme)* Stehform *f*, Stehmontage *f*
standing matter *(type matter)* Stehsatz *m*
standing on the spine *(book prod.)* auf dem Rücken stehend
standing web *(web printing)* stehende Bahn *f*
standstill Stillstand *m*
staple Heftklammer *f*, Klammer *f*
staple *v* heften
stapling Klammerheftung *f*
starch glue Stärkekleister *m*
starch powder *(spray powder)* Stärkepuder *m*
star feeder Sternanleger *m*
star-shaped diaphragm Sternblende *f*
start *v* anstellen, einschalten
start button Startknopf *m*
starting lever Einschalthebel *m*
starting switch Einschalter *m*
start-up *(machine)* Anlauf *m*, Inbetriebnahme *f*, Inbetriebsetzung *f*, Ingangsetzen *n*
start up *v* anlaufen (lassen)
start-up register Anfangspasser *m*
start-up sequence *automatic* ~ automatische Einschaltfolge *f*
start-up time Anlaufzeit *f*
start-up waste Anfahrmakulatur *f*, Anlaufmakulatur *f*
star-type reelstand Rollenstand mit Drehstern *m*
state of the art Stand der Technik
state-of-the-art technology Stand der Technik
static charge statische Aufladung *f*
static electricity statische Elektrizität *f*
static eliminator Entelektrisator *m*
static loading statische Aufladung *f*
static memory *(comp.)* statischer Speicher *m*
static neutralizer Entelektrisator *m*
stationary backgauge *(cutting m.)* stehender Sattel *m*
stationary image *(web inspection)* stehendes Bild *n*
stationery Briefpapier *n*, Papierwaren *pl*
stationery printing Formulardruck *m*

stationery printing press - stitching

stationery printing press Formulardruckmaschine *f*
stationery production Formularherstellung *f*
statistical cost accounting Nachkalkulation *f*
statistical quality control statistische Qualitätskontrolle *f*
status line *(photocomp. machine)* Parameterzeile *f*
status message *(comp.)* Rückmeldung *f*
stearin Stearin *n*
steatite marbles *pl* Steatitkugeln *pl*
steel back-up roller *(gravure)* Stahlstützpresseur *m*
steel base Stahlunterbau *m*
steel casting Stahlguß *m*
steel die Prägeplatte aus Stahl, Stahlstempel *m*
steel distributor *(roller, cylinder)* Stahlreiber *m*
steel engraving Stahlätzung *f*
steel-face *v (electrotyping)* verstählen
steel-facing installation *(electrotyping)* Verstählungsanlage *f*
steel-plate *v (electrotyping)* verstählen
steel-plated electrotype Stahlgalvano *n*
steel(-plate) engraver Stahlstecher *m*
steel(-plate) engraving Stahlstich *m*, Stahlstichgravur *f*
steel-plating installation *(electrotyping)* Verstählungsanlage *f*
steel punch Stahlstempel *m*
steel roller Stahlwalze *f*
steel rule Stahllinie *f*
steel rule die Bandstahlform *f*, Stanzform *f*
steel rule die-cutting Bandstahlschnitt *m*
steel rules *pl* Stanzlinien *pl*
steel tape measure Stahlbandmaß *n*
steel wire brush Stahldrahtbürste *f*
steep gradation steile Gradation *f*
stem *(part of the letter)* Abstrich *m*, Grundstrich *m*, Säule *f*
stencil *(for duplicating)* Matrize *f*; *(screen printing)* Schablone *f*
stencil fabrics *pl* Schablonengewebe *n*
stencil film Schablonenfilm *m*
stencil lettering Schablonenschrift *f*
stencil making Schablonenherstellung *f*, Siebdruckformherstellung *f*
stencil mask Abdeckschablone *f*
stencil opening Schablonenöffnung *f*
stencil paper Schablonenpapier *n*
stencil removal *(screen printing)* Entschichtung *f*
stencil remover *(screen printing)* Siebentschichter *m*
step-and-repeat assembly Repetiermontage *f*

step-and-repeat copying Nutzenkopie *f*
step-and-repeat (copying) machine Repetierkopiermaschine *f*, Montagekopiermaschine *f*, Nutzenkopiermaschine *f*
step by step expansion *(modular system)* schrittweiser Ausbau *m*
step exposures *pl* Stufenbelichtung *f*, Schiebekopie *f*
stepped exposures *pl (plate exposure)* Belichtungsfächer *m*
stepping motor Schrittmotor *m*
stepping wheel delivery *(web press)* Taktradauslage *f*
step wedge *(reprod., platemaking)* Stufenkeil *m*
stereo camera Stereokamera *f*
stereo caster Gießapparat *m*
stereo mount Stereounterlage *f*
stereo rubber Klischeegummi *n*
stereoscope Stereoskop *n*
stereoscopic photograph Stereofotografie *f*
stereo(type) Stereo *n*, Stereotype *f*
stereotype *v* stereotypieren
stereotype making Stereotypie *f*
stereotype mat(rix) Stereomater *f*
stereo(type) plate Stereo(typie)platte *f*
stereotyper Stereotypeur *m*
stereotyping Stereotypie *f*
stereotyping machine Stereotypiemaschine *f*
set *(text correction not to be made)* bleibt!
stick Steg *m*
sticker Aufkleber *m*
stickiness *(ink)* Zähigkeit *f*, Zügigkeit *f*
sticking *(freshly printed sheets)* see blocking
sticky-back blanket *(continuous forms presses)* Selbstklebe(druck)tuch *n*
sticky ink klebrige Farbe *f*, zähe Farbe *f*, zügige Farbe *f*
stiff ink dickflüssige Farbe *f*, pastöse Farbe *f*, strenge Farbe *f*
stiff material steifes Material *n*
stiff paper steifes Papier *n*
stiff paper binding Steifbroschur *f*
stipple *v* punktieren
stipple-graver Punktierstichel *m*
stippler Punktiernadel *f*
stitch Stich *m*
stitch *v* heften
stitched geheftet, broschiert
stitched booklet Heft *n*
stitcher *(mach.)* Heftmaschine *f*
stitch in *v* einheften
stitching Heftung *f*

stitching head Heftkopf *m*
stitching holes *pl* Heftlöcher *pl*
stitching machine Heftapparat *m*, Heftmaschine *f*
stitching needle Heftnadel *f*
stitching saddle Heftsattel *m*
stitching unit Heftaggregat *n*
stitching wire Heftdraht *m*
stitch lap *(folding box)* Gehrungsschlitz *m*
stock *(papermaking)* Stoff *m*; *(printing material)* Bedruckstoff *m*, Druckpapier *n*, Papier *n*
stock preparation *(papermaking)* Stoffaufbereitung *f*
stock type *(paper grade)* Papierqualität *f*, Papiersorte *f*
stone carriage Steinkarren *m*
stone copying frame Steinkopierrahmen *m*
stone engraving Steingravur *f*, Steinradierung *f*
stone graining Steinschleifen *n*
stone lithography Steinlithografie *f*
stone polishing Steinschleifen *n*
stone printing Steindruck *m*
stone surface Steingrund *m*
stone transfer *(stone printing)* Steinkopie *f*
stop *(camera lens)* Blende *f*, Blendenöffnung *f*, Blendenwert *m*; *(standstill)* Stillstand *m*
stop *v* abstellen, abschalten, ausschalten
stop bath *(photochem.)* Stoppbad *n*
stop-cylinder press Stoppzylinderpresse *f*
stop diameter *(camera lens)* Blendendurchmesser *m*
stop drum *(press)* Stopptrommel *f*
stop lever Arretierhebel *m*
stop safe push button Notausschalter *m*, Pilztaste *f*, Schlagtaster *m*, Sicherheitsstopptaste *f*
stop switch Stoppschalter *m*
storage Lagerung *f*; *(comp.)* Speicher *m*, Speicherung *f*
storage capacity *(comp.)* Speichergröße *f*, Speicherkapazität *f*
storage ink *(offset plate storage)* Schutzfarbe *f*
storage medium Speichermedium *n*
store *v* *(text, data)* abspeichern, ablegen, speichern
stored data gespeicherte Daten *pl*
stored text gespeicherter Text *m*
straddle mehrspaltiger Rubrikkopf *m*, mehrspaltiger Rubriktitel *m*, mehrspaltiger Tabellenkopf *m*
straddle head mehrspaltige Überschrift *f*
straight accent Längezeichen *n*
straight colour printing *(as opp. to printing and perfecting)* Schöndruck *m*

straight-cut labels *pl* glattgeschnittene Etiketten *n/pl*
straight-edge alignment kantengenaues Ausrichten *n*
straight-edge block facettenloses Klischee *n*
straight-edge delivery kantengenaue Auslage *f*
straight-edge pile kantengenauer Stapel *m*
straighten *v* geraderichten
straight-line pen Ziehfeder *f*
straight matter *(as opp. to layout matter)* glatter Satz *m*, laufender Text *m*, Textsatz *m*
straight printing (only) press Schöndruckmaschine *f*
straight-run production *(web printing)* einfache Produktion *f*, nichtgesammelte Produktion *f*, ungesammelte Produktion *f*
straight stitching *(thread-stitching)* Heften mit unversetztem Stich
strap Umreifungsband *n*
strapping *(mailroom)* Umschnüren *n*, Umreifen *n*, Verschnüren *n*
strapping machine Umreifungsmaschine *f*, Verschnürmaschine *f*
stray light Streulicht *n*
streak-free *(printing)* streifenfrei
streaking *(printing)* Streifenbildung *f*
streaks *pl* Streifen *pl*, Schlieren *pl*
stream conveyor *(shingle stream)* Schuppenband *n*
stream delivery Schuppenauslage *f*
streamer Überschrift über volle Seitenbreite *f*
stream feeder Schuppenanleger *m*
stream feeding Schuppenanlage *f*, überlappte Anlage *f*
stream gap *(shingle stream)* Schuppenlücke *f*
stream in-feed *(shingle stream)* Schuppeneinlauf *m*
stream separator *(shingle stream)* Schuppentrennung *f*
strengthen the ink *v* Farbe strenger machen
stress *(mech.)* Belastung *f*, Beanspruchung *f*
stress *v* *(to display in bold, italic etc.)* auszeichnen, hervorheben
stressing *(typogr.)* Auszeichnung *f*, Hervorhebung *f*
stress mark Betonungszeichen *n*
stretch *(rubber blanket, fabrics)* Dehnung *f*
stretching frame *(screen printing)* Spannrahmen *m*
stretching unit *(web press)* Streckwerk *n*
stretch package Straffpackung *f*
stretch stability *(rubber blanket, fabrics)* Dehnfestigkeit *f*

strike out v *(text)* ausstreichen
strike-through *(ink)* Durchschlagen n
strike through v *(text)* durchstreichen
striking-in *(ink)* Wegschlagen n
string *(comp.)* Sequenz f
string tag Anhängeetikett n, Anhänger m
strip v strippen; *(membrane coatings)* abziehen; *(die-cut blanks)* trennen; *(page assembly)* montieren
strip coating *(varnish, glue, wax etc.)* Streifenauftrag m
strip copper v Kupfer abschälen
strip gluing Streifen(be)leimung f
strippable layer *(masking film)* abziehbare Schicht f, Abziehschicht f, Membran f
stripper *(mech.)* Abstreifer m; *(paste-up man)* Montierer m
stripper-stepper Kopiermontageautomat m
stripping *(de-coating)* Entschichtung f; *(page assembly)* Montage f; **automatic** ~ Kopiermontage f
stripping and stepping machine Kopiermontageautomat m
stripping cylinder *(waste stripping)* Ausbrechzylinder m
stripping department Montageabteilung f
stripping die *(waste stripping)* Ausbrechform f
strip(ping) film Stripfilm m
stripping forme *(waste stripping)* Ausbrechform f
stripping gelatine Abziehgelatine f
stripping-in of text Einstrippen von Text
stripping knife *(for stripping film)* Stripmesser n
stripping man *(paste-up man)* Montierer m
stripping operation *(page assembly)* Montage f
stripping pins pl *(waste stripping)* Ausbrechstifte pl
stripping table *(light table)* Montagetisch m
stripping tool *(waste-stripping)* Trennwerkzeug n, Ausbrechwerkzeug n, Separierwerkzeug n
stripping varnish *(retouching)* Abziehlack m, Retusche(abzieh)lack m
strip test *(paper)* Streifenprobe f
strip trimming *(multi-up signatures)* Streifenausschnitt m
stroke *(fractional numbers)* Querstrich m; *(mech.)* Hub m
stroke adjustment Hubverstellung f
stroke wheel *(feeder)* Ausstreichrad n
strong ink strenge Farbe f
strong light *(image)* Schlaglicht n
strong paper starkes Papier n
stub Abschnitt m
stubborn residues pl hartnäckige Rückstände pl

studio Atelier n, Studio n
sturdy *(machine)* robust
stylus Griffel m; *(gravure cyl. engraving)* Stichel m
subdued light *(reprod.)* gedämpftes Licht n
sub-heading Untertitel m, Unterrubrik f
subject *(printing)* Sujet n
subject index *(book)* Sachregister n
sub-routine *(comp.)* Unterprogramm n
subscriber Abonnent m
subscriber to the magazine XY Abonnent der Zeitschrift XY
subscribe to v abonnieren, beziehen
subscript *(typesetting)* tiefgestelltes Zeichen n
subscription Abonnement n, Bezug m, Subskription f
subscription price Abonnementpreis m
subscription to the magazine XY Abonnement der Zeitschrift XY
subsequent operations pl *(prod. line)* nachfolgende Arbeiten pl
subsequent unit *(prod. line)* nachfolgendes Aggregat n
substrate Substrat n
substratum Substrat n
substructure Unterbau m
subtitle Nebentitel m, Untertitel m, Zwischentitel m
subtractive colour synthesis subtraktive Farbmischung f
successive numbering fortlaufende Numerierung f, vorwärtszählende Numerierung f
suckers pl Vakuumsauger pl
sucker tilting *(feeder suction head)* Saugerkippung f
suction air Saugluft f
suction and air blast *(sheet separation)* Saug/Blasluft f
suction bar Saugstange f
suction/blower system *(feeder)* Blas/Saugluft f
suction board *(camera)* Saugwand f
suction brush *(feeder)* Saugbürste f
suction cups pl Vakuumsauger pl
suction device Ansaugvorrichtung f
suction feeder Sauganleger m
suction head *(feeder)* Saugkopf m
suction hood Absaughaube f
suction nozzle Saugdüse f
suction pile feeder Saugstapelanleger m
suction plate *(camera)* Saugplatte f, Saugwand f
suction removal Absaugung f
suction removal device Absaugeinrichtung f
suction roller Saugwalze f

suction tape feed table Saugbändertisch *m*
suction times *pl (contact printer, vacuum frame)* Vakuumzeiten *pl*
sulphate kraft paper Natronkraftpapier *n*
sulphate packing paper Natronpackpapier *n*
sulphate pulp *(papermaking)* Natronzellstoff *m*
sulphate sack paper Natronsackpapier *n*
sulphuric electrolyte *(electropl.)* schwefelsaures Elektrolyt *n*, Sulfatelektrolyt *n*
summary Zusammenfassung *f; (book)* Abriß *m; (of an article)* Auszug *m*
Sunday issue Sonntagsausgabe *f*
Sunday paper Sonntagsblatt *n*, Sonntagszeitung *f*
sun spots *pl (reprod.)* Sonnen *pl*
super calender *(papermaking)* Satinierkalander *m*
super-calendered paper hochsatiniertes Papier *n*
superimposed images *pl* übereinandergelegte Bilder *pl*
superimposed printing Aufeinanderdruck *m*, Übereinanderdruck *m*
superimpose images *v* Bilder übereinanderlegen
superior character *(typesetting)* hochgestelltes Zeichen *n*
superior figures *pl (typesetting)* hochgestellte Ziffern *pl*
superior fractional figures *pl* obenstehende Bruchziffern *pl*
superior letter *(music printing)* Notenbuchstabe *m*
superscript *(typesetting)* hochgestelltes Zeichen *n*
superstructure *(web press)* Überbau *m*
supervision *(process)* Kontrolle *f*, Überwachung *f*
supervisor *(comp. progr.)* Kontrollprogramm *n; (department head)* Abteilungsleiter *m*
supplement *(book)* Ergänzungsteil *m; (newspaper)* Beilage *f*
supplementary exposure *(camera screening)* Hilfsbelichtung *f*
supply Zuführung *f*, Versorgung *f*
supply cassette *(photomaterial)* Spenderkassette *f*, Vorratskassette *f*
support roller Stützwalze *f*
supra-regional newspaper überregionale Zeitung *f*
surcharge Aufschlag *m*
surface Fläche *f*, Oberfläche *f*
surface characteristics *pl* Oberflächenbeschaffenheit *f*
surface drying Oberflächentrocknung *f*
surface finishing Oberflächenveredlung *f; (of printed products)* Druckveredlung *f*
surface gloss Oberflächenglanz *m*
surface lustre Oberflächenglanz *m*
surface properties *pl* Oberflächenbeschaffenheit *f*

surface-sized paper oberflächengeleimtes Papier *n*
surface sizing *(paper)* Oberflächenleimung *f*
surface smoothness *(paper)* Oberflächenglätte *f*
surface speed Oberflächengeschwindigkeit *f*
surface stability *(paper)* Oberflächenfestigkeit *f*
surface strength *(paper)* Oberflächenfestigkeit *f*
surface tension Oberflächenspannung *f*
surface-treated oberflächenbehandelt
surround density *(reprod.)* Umgebungsdichte *f*
susceptible to picking rupfempfindlich
suspension *(papermaking)* Suspension *f*
suspension-type camera Überkopfkamera *f*
swash letter Zierbuchstabe *m*
swash type Zierschrift *f*
swelling Quellung *f*
swell resistance *(rubber blanket, roller etc.)* Quellbeständigkeit *f*, Quellfestigkeit *f*
swing-away unit abklappbares Aggregat *n*, abschwenkbares Aggregat *n*
swing gripper Schwinggreifer *m*
swinging foundation *(machine)* Schwingfundament *n*
swinging shear cut *(cutting m.)* Schwingschnitt *m*
swing-off unit abklappbares Aggregat *n*, abschwenkbares Aggregat *n*
Swiss brochure Schweizer Broschur *f*
switch Schalter *m*, Umschalter *m; (prod. line)* Weiche *f*
switchboard Schaltbrett *n*, Schalttafel *f*
switchbox Schaltkasten *m*, Schaltschrank *m*
switch button Schaltknopf *m*
switch cabinet Schaltschrank *m*
switch circuit Schaltkreis *m*
switch gear Schaltgetriebe *n*
switch-off Abschaltung *f*
switch off *v* abstellen, abschalten, ausschalten
switch on *v* anstellen, einschalten
swivel/tilting backgauge *(cutting m.)* Dreh-/Neigesattel *m*
sword opening *(folded signature)* Schwertöffnung *f*
sword-type hygrometer *(pile humidity)* Stabhygrometer *n*, Stechhygrometer *n*
sword-type thermometer *(pile temperature)* Stabthermometer *n*
swung dash *(typesetting)* Tilde *f*
syllable Silbe *f*
symbol Symbol *n*
synchronized *(prod. line)* synchronisiert, taktgenau, taktkonform
synchronous mode *(comp.)* Synchronbetrieb *m*
synthetic fibre paper Kunstfaserpapier *n*

synthetic material Kunststoff *m*
synthetic matrix Kunststoffmater *f*
synthetic paper synthetisches Papier *n*
synthetic roller Kunststoffwalze *f*
synthetic varnish Kunstfirnis *m*
system System *n*
system back-up Systemsicherung *f*
system command Systembefehl *m*, Systemkommando *n*
system computer Systemrechner *m*
system configuration Systemaufbau *m*, Systemkonfiguration *f*
system control Systemsteuerung *f*
system design Systemaufbau *m*
system-independent systemneutral, systemunabhängig
system instruction Systemanweisung *f*, Systembefehl *m*
system monitoring Systemüberwachung *f*
system network Systemverbund *m*
system of a different make Fremdsystem *n*
system operation Systembetrieb *m*
system operator Systemanwender *m*, Systembediener *m*
system printer Systemdrucker *m*
system processor Systemrechner *m*
system program Systemprogramm *n*
system software Systemprogramm *n*
system user Systemanwender *m*

T

tabbing *(tabular comp.)* Tabellensatz *m*, Tabulieren *n*
table Tabelle *f*; *(diagram)* Tafel *f*
table definition *(tabular comp.)* Tabellendefinition *f*
table head Tabellenkopf *m*
table inking unit Tischfarbwerk *n*
table line Tabellenzeile *f*
table of contents *(magazine etc.)* Inhaltsverzeichnis *n*
table row Tabellenzeile *f*
table-top model Tischmodell *n*
table-top printer Tischdrucker *m*
tabloid fold Tabloidfalz *m*
tabloid format Tabloidformat *n*
tabloid newspaper page Tabloid-Zeitungsseite *f*
tabloid signature Tabloidbogen *m*
tabloid size Tabloidformat *n*
tabs *pl (register tabs)* Griffregister *n*
tab stop *(tabular comp.)* Tabulator *m*
tabular column Tabellenspalte *f*
tabular composition Tabellensatz *m*
tabular composition software *(photocomp.)* Tabellensatzprogramm *n*
tabular field Tabellenfeld *n*
tabular form Tabellenform *f*
tabular matter tabellarischer Satz *m*, Tabellensatz *m*
tabular matter with vertical rules Tabellensatz mit Querlinien
tabular work *(typesetting)* Tabellensatz *m*
tabulated in Tabellenform *f*
tabulating machine Tabelliermaschine *f*
tab(ulator) *(tabular comp.)* Tabulator *m*
tack *(ink)* Tack *m*, Zähigkeit *f*, Zügigkeit *f*
tackmeter Farbzügigkeitsmeßgerät *n*
tacky ink dickflüssige Farbe *f*, klebrige Farbe *f*, strenge Farbe *f*, zähe Farbe *f*, zügige Farbe *f*
tag Anhängeetikett *n*, Anhänger *m*
tag knotting machine Etikettenfadenknotenmaschine *f*
tag tying machine Etikettenknüpfmaschine *f*
tailcap *(bookb.)* Häubchen *n*
tail edge *(book)* Unterschnitt *m*
tail edge of plate Plattenhinterkante *f*
tail edge of print Druckende *n*
tail margin unterer Papierrand *m*, unterer Seitenrand *m*
tailored see tailor-made
tailor-made *(modular systems)* maßgeschneidert, nach Maß, zugeschnitten
tail-piece *(printer's flower)* Endstück *n*, Fußleiste *f*, Leiste *f*, Zierleiste *f*
tail trim(ming) Fußbeschnitt *m*
take in a line *v (type)* eine Zeile einbringen
take-up cassette Aufnahmekassette *f*
talcum Talkum *n*
talk print *v* fachsimpeln
tall letter *(with ascender/descender)* langer Buchstabe *m*
tampon *(ink ball)* Ballen *m*, Tampon *m*, Buchdruckerballen *m*, Druckerballen *m*, Farbballen *m*
tan *v (phot.)* gerben
tank development Standentwicklung *f*
tannic acid Gerbsäure *f*
tannin Gerbsäure *f*
tanning Gerbung *f*

tanning developer Gerbentwickler *m*
tape Band *n*
tape cement Bänderkitt *m*
tape control *(punched tape)* Lochbandsteuerung *f*
tape delivery Bänderauslauf *m*, Bandauslage *f*
tape dispenser *(adhesive tape)* Klebebandabroller *m*
tape guide Bänderführung *f*
tape inserter *(sheet counting)* Streifeneinschießer *m*
tape measure Bandmaß *n*
tape prints *pl* Kleberänder *pl*, Klebstreifenrückstände *pl*
tape punch Lochstreifenstanzer *m*
tape reader *(punched tape)* Lochbandleser *m*, Lochstreifenleser *m*
tape streamer Bandlaufwerk *n*, Magnetbandstation *f*
tap out *v (ink)* auftupfen
target *(print control bar)* Kontrollfeld *n*, Meßfeld *n*
target value Sollwert *m*
tear Riß *m*
tear *v* reißen
tearing test *(paper)* Reißprobe *f*
tear length *(paper)* Reißlänge *f*
tear-off calendar Abreißkalender *m*
tear(-off) line *(packaging)* Aufreißlinie *f*
tear-off pad Abreißblock *m*
tear-off perforation *(packaging)* Abreißperforation *f*
tear-off tape *(packaging)* Aufreißstreifen *m*
tear resistance Einreißfestigkeit *f*, Reißfestigkeit *f*
tear strength Reißfestigkeit *f*
technical book Fachbuch *n*
technical dictionary Fachwörterbuch *n*
technical documentation technische Dokumentation *f*
technical editor Fachredakteur *m*
technical instructor Anwendungstechniker *m*
technical journal Fachzeitschrift *f*
technical knowledge Fachwissen *n*
technical literature Fachliteratur *f*
technical magazin Fachzeitschrift *f*
technical management Betriebsführung *f*, Betriebsleitung *f*
technical manager Betriebsleiter *m*, technischer Leiter *m*
technical press Fachpresse *f*
technical staff technisches Personal *n*
technical term Fachausdruck *m*

technical training Fachausbildung *f*, fachliche Schulung *f*
technician Techniker *m*
telecommunication Telekommunikation *f*
telecopier Fernkopierer *m*
telecopy Telekopie *f*
telefax Telefax *n*
telefax message Telefax-Mitteilung *f*
teleletter Telebrief *m*
telephone adtaking telefonische Anzeigenannahme *f*
telephone line *(telecom.)* Telefonleitung *f*, Wählleitung *f*
telephone network *(telecom.)* Telefonnetz *n*
telephoto(graph) Telefoto *n*
teleprinter Ferndrucker *m*
teleprocessing Fernverarbeitung *f*
telescopic sucker *(feeder suction head)* Teleskopsauger *m*
teletext Teletext *m*
teletransmission Fernübertragung *f*
teletypesetter *(TTS)* Fernsetzmaschine *f*, lochbandgesteuerte Setzmaschine *f*
teletypesetting *(hot-metal comp.)* Fernsetzen *n*
television Fernsehen *n*
tell-tale *(running head)* lebender Kolumnentitel *m*
temperature control Temperaturregelung *f*
temperature control fluid Temperiermittel *n*
temperature resistance Temperaturbeständigkeit *f*
temporary storage Zwischenlagerung *f*
tensile strain *(paper)* Zugbeanspruchung *f*
tensile strength Dehnfestigkeit *f*, Reißfestigkeit *f*, Zugfestigkeit *f*
tension stress *(rubber blanket, fabrics)* Dehnungsbeanspruchung *f*
terminal Terminal *m*, Endgerät *n*
terminal input Bildschirmerfassung *f*
terminal operator Erfasser *m*
terms of delivery Lieferungsbedingungen *pl*
terrestrial connection *(telecom.)* Landleitung *f*
test *v* prüfen
test chart *(reprod., printing)* Testtafel *f*
test device Prüfgerät *n*
test exposure Testbelichtung *f*
testing instrument Prüfgerät *n*
testing method Prüfverfahren *n*
test pull Probeabzug *m*
test run Probelauf *m*, Testlauf *m*
test wedge *(reprod.)* Prüfkeil *m*
text Text *m*
text and graphics in position Text und Bilder auf Stand *m*

text assembly Satzmontage f, Textmontage f
textbook Lehrbuch n, Textbuch n
text converter Textkonverter m
text copy Text m, Textvorlage f, Satzvorlage f; *(manuscript)* Manuskript n
text correction Textkorrektur f
text counting software *(text proc.)* Textberechnungsprogramm n
text data Textdaten pl
text editing Textbearbeitung f, Textkorrektur f
text edition (only) Textausgabe f
text entry Texteingabe f, Texterfassung f
text face *(type)* Textschrift f
text figure *(illustration)* Abbildung f, Bild n, Illustration f, Textabbildung f
text file Textdaten pl
text film Textfilm m
text formatting Textformatierung f
text handling Textverarbeitung f
textile printing Stoffdruck m, Textildruck m
textile printing machine Textildruckmaschine f
text-image integration Text/Bildintegration f
text-image merging Text/Bild-Verschmelzung f
text imprint Texteindruck m
text input Texteingabe f, Texterfassung f
text input terminal Texterfassungsterminal m
text keyboarding Texterfassung f
text line Textzeile f
text matter *(as opp. to layout matter)* glatter Satz m, Textsatz m
text module Textbaustein m
text output Textausgabe f
text overrun Textüberlauf m
text page Textseite f
text passage Textteil m
text pool stored *(text proc.)* Bestand gespeicherter Texte
text positioning Textpositionierung f
text pre-processing Satzvorverarbeitung f
text printer *(device)* Textdrucker m
text print-out Textausdruck m
text processing Textverarbeitung f
text processing system Textverarbeitungsanlage f
text proof Textabzug m, Satzabzug m
text ragged center Flattersatz Mitte
text ragged left Flattersatz linksbündig
text ragged right Flattersatz rechtsbündig
text recording Texterfassung f
text recording terminal Texterfassungsterminal m
text retrieval system Textabrufsystem n
text section *(book, as opp. to picture section)* Textteil m

text spacing *(typesetting)* Sperren n, Spationieren n
text storage Textspeicherung f
text stream laufender Text m
text string Textfolge f
text stripping *(text assembly)* Textmontage f
text system Textsystem n
text transmission Textübertragung f
the ink fills up *(halftone areas)* die Farbe setzt zu
the ink penetrates die Farbe schlägt weg
the ink picks die Farbe rupft
the ink sets off die Farbe liegt ab
the ink strikes in die Farbe schlägt weg
thermal after-burning thermische Nachverbrennung f
thermal binder Thermobindegerät n
thermal binding Thermobindung f
thermal incineration thermische Nachverbrennung f
thermal paper Thermopapier n
thermal printer Thermodrucker m
thermic after-burner (system) thermische Nachverbrennungsanlage f
thermographic printing Thermodruck m, Thermografie f, thermografischer Druck m, Reliefdruck m, unechter Stahlstich m
thermography see thermographic printing
thermoplastic binding thermoplastische Bindung f
thermosealing Heißsiegeln n; *(film wrapping)* Verschweißen n
thermostat Temperaturregler m, Thermostat m
thermotape *(backstripping)* Thermoband n
thickener *(ink)* Verdickungsmittel n
thick ink dickflüssige Farbe f
thick line *(typogr.)* Balken m
thickness gauge Dickenmesser m, Stärkemesser m
thickness loss *(rubber blanket)* Stärkeverlust m
thick printing paper Dickdruckpapier n
thin v *(gravure ink)* verschneiden
thin (card)board Halbkarton m
thin line *(typogr.)* feine Linie f
thin linen *(screen printing)* Halbgaze f
thinner *(gravure ink)* Verschnitt m; *(other inks)* Verdünner m, Verdünnungsmittel n
thin rule feine Linie f
thin space *(typesetting)* dünnes Spatium n, Viertelgeviert n
third cover dritte Umschlagseite f
35 mm camera Kleinbildkamera f
35 mm slide Kleinbilddia n
thixotropic ink thixotropische Farbe f

thorough retouching Vollretusche *f*
thousand *(print volume)* Tausend *n*; **16th to 20th** ~ 16. bis 20. Tausend *n*
thousand run-ons *pl (printing)* 1000 Fortdrucke *pl*, tausend weitere Druck
thousand-sheet price Tausendbogenpreis *m*
thread *(thread-stitching)* Faden *m*
thread break control *(thread-stitching)* Fadenbruchkontrolle *f*
thread break detector *(thread-stitching)* Fadenbruchkontrolle *f*
thread cross-over *(thread-stitching)* Kreuzfadenstich *m*
thread in *v (paper web)* einziehen
threading-in *(web press)* Bahneinzug *m*, Papiereinzug *m*
thread in the web *v* Papierbahn einziehen
thread-sealing *(bookb.)* Fadensiegeln *n*
thread-stitch *v* fadenheften, heften
thread-stitcher *(mach.)* Fadenheftmaschine *f*
thread-stitching Fadenheftung *f*
thread-stitching and knotting machine Knotenheftmaschine *f*
thread-stitching machine Fadenheftmaschine *f*
three-colour printing Dreifarbendruck *m*
three-column page dreispaltige Seite *f*
3D hologram 3D-Hologramm *n*
3D object 3D-Objekt *n*
three-directional fold Dreibruchfalz *m*
three-directional gatefold Dreibruch-Fensterfalz *m*
three-directional right-angle fold Dreibruch-Kreuzfalz *m*
three-knife trimmer Dreischneider *m*, Dreiseitenschneider *m*; **automatic** ~ Dreimesserautomat *m*
three-phase current Drehstrom *m*
three-point lay *(sheet registration)* Dreipunktanlage *f*
three-quarter tone *(around 75% area coverage)* Dreiviertelton
three-quarter tone tint patch *(print control bar)* Dreivierteltonrasterfeld *n*
three-roll mill *(inkmaking)* Dreiwalzwerk *n*
three-shift operation Dreischichtbetrieb *m*
three-sided trimming Dreiseitenbeschnitt *m*
three-to-em space *(typesetting)* Drittelgeviert *n*
threshold value *(measuring)* Schwellenwert *m*
through *(mach.)* **in one** ~ in einem Arbeitsgang *m*, in einem Durchgang *m*, in einem Durchlauf *m*
through-light Durchlicht *n*
through-light measurement Durchlichtmessung *f*

throughput Durchsatz *m*
throughput speed Durchlaufgeschwindigkeit *f*
throw-off *(mech.)* Abschaltung *f*, Ausrückung *f*
throw off impression *v* Druck abstellen
throw on *v (rollers, cylinders, docter blade)* anstellen
throw on impression *v* Druck anstellen
throw on/off impression *(press)* An/Abstellen des Drucks, Druckan- und -abstellung *f*
throw rollers on/off (impression) *v (press)* Walzen an/abstellen
thumb index Daumenregister *n*, Griffregister *n*
thumb index cutting Daumenregisterausschnitt *m*
thumb register Daumenregister *n*, Griffregister *n*
thumb test *(paper)* Daumenprobe *f*
thumb wheel Daumenrad *n*
thyristor-controlled thyristorgesteuert
ticket board Billettkarton *m*, Fahrkartenkarton *m*
ticket printing Fahrkartendruck *m*
ticket printing machine Billettdruckmaschine *f*, Fahrkartendruckmaschine *f*
tie-on label Anhängeetikett *n*, Anhänger *m*
tie up *v (book)* einschnüren
tight straff
tight deadline knapper Termin *m*
tighten *v* festziehen, straff spannen
tight fold scharf(kantig)er Falz *m*
tight justification enger Ausschluß *m*
tight line enge Zeile *f*
tight schedule knapper Termin *m*, knapper Zeitplan *m*
tilde *(typesetting)* Tilde *f*
tiltable monitor im Neigungswinkel verstellbarer Bildschirm
tilt an illustration *v* Bild kippen, Bild schrägstellen
tilt-back unit abklappbares Aggregat *n*, abschwenkbares Aggregat *n*
timed *(prod. line)* im Takt *m*, taktgebunden, taktgesteuert
timed control Taktsteuerung *f*
timed fan delivery *(web press)* Taktradauslage *f*
timed feeding Taktanlage *f*
time-proven praxiserprobt
timer Zeitgeber *m*
time sharing *(comp.)* Teilzeit *f*, Timesharing *n*
time sheet Arbeitszettel *m*, Laufzettel *m*, Tageszettel *m*
timetable setting Fahrplansatz *m*
timing switch Taktschalter *m*, Zeitschalter *m*
tin Blechdose *f*
tin alloy Legierzinn *n*
tin box Blechschachtel *f*

tin-foil printing press - top speed

tin-foil printing press Stannioldruckmaschine *f*
tinned wire verzinnter Draht *m*
tin plate Blechtafel *f*
tinplate varnishing machine Blechlackiermaschine *f*
tin printer Blechdrucker *m*
tin printing blanket Blechdrucktuch *n*
tin printing press Blechdruckmaschine *f*
tint Ton *m*, Farbton *m*; *(background tint)* Fond *m*, Rasterfond *m*
tint area Tonfläche *f*, Farbfläche *f*
tint block Tonfläche *f*, Farbfläche *f*
tinted background Fond *m*, Rasterfond *m*, farbiger Fond *m*
tinted paper buntes Papier *n*, Buntpapier *n*, farbiges Papier *n*, gefärbtes Papier *n*, Tonpapier *n*
tint engraving Tonätzung *f*
tinter *(continuous forms press)* Einfärbwerk *n*
tinting *(paper)* Einfärben *n*, Färbung *f*
tinting unit *(continuous forms press)* Einfärbwerk *n*
tint laying *(screen tint)* Rasterunterlegen *n*, Rastereinziehen *n*, Einstrippen von Tonfläche, Rasterhinterlegen *n*
tint level Raster(ton)wert *m*, Tonwert *m*
tint patch *(print control bar)* Rasterfeld *n*
tint plate *(letterpress)* Tonplatte *f*
tip *(of doctor blade)* Lamelle *f*
tip in *v (inserts, reply cards)* einkleben
tipped-in postcard eingeklebte Postkarte *f*
tissue *(screen printing)* Gewebe *n*
tissue paper Seidenpapier *n*
titanium anode *(electropl.)* Titananode *f*
title Titel *m*; *(newspaper, magazine)* Kopf *m*, Titelkopf *m*
title along the spine *(book)* Längsrückentitel *m*
title embossing Titelprägung *f*
title page Titelseite *f*, Titelblatt *n*; *(book also)* Haupttitel *m*
titling face Titelschrift *f*
toggle lever Kniehebel *m*
toggle press Kniehebelpresse *f*
tolerance Toleranz *f*
toluene *(gravure ink)* Toluol *n*
toluene recovery unit Toluol-Rückgewinnungsanlage *f*
tonal change Tonwertveränderung *f*
tonal correction Tonwertkorrektur *f*
tonal gradation Ton(wert)abstufung *f*, Ton(wert)verlauf *m*
tonal inversion *(reprod.)* Tonumkehrung *f*
tonal range Ton(wert)umfang *m*

tonal reproduction Ton(wert)wiedergabe *f*
tonal shift Ton(wert)verschiebung *f*
tonal transfer *(contact printing)* Ton(wert)übertragung *f*
tonal value Tonwert *m*
tone Ton *m*
tone balance Ton(wert)balance *f*
tone change Ton(wert)veränderung *f*
tone compression Ton(wert)kompression *f*
tone correction Ton(wert)korrektur *f*
tone data Tonwert *m*
tone down *v (colour)* abdämpfen, abdunkeln, abtönen
tone-index method *(reprod.)* Ton-Index-Methode *f*
toner *(electrophotogr.)* Toner *m*
tone range Ton(wert)umfang *m*
tone rendition Ton(wert)wiedergabe *f*
tone reproduction Ton(wert)wiedergabe *f*
tone scale Ton(wert)skala *f*
tone separation Tontrennung *f*
tone up *v (colour)* aufhellen
tone value Tonwert *m*
tone value atlas Tonwertatlas *m*
too dark copy *(as opp. to pinsharp copy)* volle Kopie *f*
tool cabinet Geräteschrank *m*, Werkzeugschrank *m*
tool cupboard Geräteschrank *m*
toothed belt Zahnriemen *m*
toothed gear(ing) Zahnradgetriebe *n*
tooth wheel Zahnrad *n*
top and under side *(paper)* Schön- und Widerdruckseite *f*
top edge Oberkante *f*
top edge gluing Kopfleimung *f*
top edge of pile Stapeloberkante *f*
top-grade paper Qualitätspapier *n*
top-grade print quality hohe Druckqualität *f*
top-grade product hochwertiges Produkt *n*, Qualitätsprodukt *n*
topicality *(news)* Aktualität *f*
topical news *pl* aktuelle Nachrichten *pl*
topographical map topografische Karte *f*
top-quality see top-grade
top sheet *(cylinder press)* Straffen *m*, Zugbogen *m*; *(mailroom)* Deckblatt *n*
top sheet feeder *(mailroom)* Deckblattanleger *m*
top side Oberseite *f*; *(of printed sheet)* Schöndruckseite *f*
top speed Höchstgeschwindigkeit *f*, Maximalgeschwindigkeit *f*, Spitzengeschwindigkeit *f*

top wire *(paper machine)* Obersieb *n*
torque wrench Drehmomentschlüssel *m*
torsion-free *(machine frame)* verwindungssteif
torsion-resistant *(machine frame)* verwindungssteif
total costs *pl* Gesamtkosten *pl*
total enclosure *(machine)* Vollkapselung *f*, Vollverschalung *f*
totalizer *(counter)* Totalisator *m*
total number of pages Gesamtseitenzahl *f*, Seitenumfang *m*
total page count Gesamtseitenzahl *f*, Seitenumfang *m*
total pagination Gesamtseitenzahl *f*, Seitenumfang *m*
total production time Gesamtfertigungszeit *f*
touch screen Berührungsbildschirm *m*
tough competition scharfer Wettbewerb *m*
touring map Reisekarte *f*
toxic gesundheitsschädlich, giftig
trace *v* pausen
tracing Durchzeichnung *f*, Pause *f*
tracing cloth Pausleinen *n*
tracing film Paushaut *f*
tracing paper Pauspapier *n*; *(for drawings, overlays etc.)* Transparentpapier *n*, Transparentzeichenpapier *n*
trade binder Lohnbuchbinderei *f*
trade binding Lohnbuchbinderei *f*
trade editor Fachredakteur *m*
trade house Lohnbetrieb *m*
trade journal Fachzeitschrift *f*
trade magazine Fachzeitschrift *f*
trade mark Warenzeichen *n*
trade paper Fachzeitschrift *f*
trade press Fachpresse *f*
trade printer Lohndruckerei *f*
trade printing Lohndruck *m*
trade setter *(typesetter)* Lohnsetzerei *f*
trade setting *(typesetting)* Lohnsatz *m*
trade typesetter Lohnsetzerei *f*
trailing edge Hinterkante *f*
trained human eye geschultes Auge *n*
trained operator ausgebildeter Bediener *m*, gelernte Arbeitskraft *f*
training Ausbildung *f*
transfer Überführung *f*, Übertragung *f*
transfer *v* übertragen; *(data, text)* übermitteln; *(transfer printing)* umdrucken
transfer characters *pl (e.g. Letraset)* Abreibeschrift *f*, Anreibeschrift *f*
transfer conveyor Überführungsband *n*

transfer cylinder Übergabezylinder *m*, Überführungstrommel *f*
transfer drum see transfer cylinder
transfer ink Umdruckfarbe *f*, Transferfarbe *f*, Fettfarbe *f*
transfer paper *(for transfer printing)* Umdruckpapier *n*
transfer picture *(decalcomania)* Abziehbild *n*
transfer press Umdruckpresse *f*
transfer printing Transferdruck *m*, Umdruck *m*; *(decalcomania)* Abziehbilderdruck *m*
transfer printing machine Umdruckmaschine *f*
transfer proof Umdruckabzug *m*
transfer roller Überführungswalze *f*, Übertragwalze *f*
transfer system Überführungssystem *n*
Transitionals *pl (type classif.)* Barock-Antiqua *f*
translucency Transparenz *f*, Lichtdurchlässigkeit *f*
translucent lichtdurchlässig, transparent
translucent paper durchscheinendes Papier *n*
transmission *(telecom.)* Übertragung *f*
transmission densitometer Durchlichtdensitometer *n*, Durchsichtsdensitometer *n*
transmission network Übertragungsnetz *n*
transmission of newspaper pages *(telecom.)* Übertragung von Zeitungsseiten
transmission rate Übertragungsrate *f*
transmission site *(telecom.)* Senderseite *f*
transmission speed Übertragungsgeschwindigkeit *f*
transmission time Übertragungszeit *f*
transmit *v* übertragen; *(data, text)* übermitteln
transmitted light Durchlicht *n*
transmitted light measurement Durchlichtmessung *f*
transmitter *(telecom.)* Sender *m*
transmitting station *(telecom.)* Sendestation *f*
transparency *(light transmission)* Lichtdurchlässigkeit *f*, Transparenz *f*; *(slide)* Dia *n*, Durchsichtsbild *n*, Durchsichtsoriginal *n*, Durchsichtsvorlage *f*
transparency facility *(camera)* Durchleuchtungseinrichtung *f*
transparency recorder Diarekorder *m*
transparency viewer Diabetrachter *m*
transparency viewing box Dialeuchtplatte *f*
transparency viewing wall Dialeuchtwand *f*
transparent lichtdurchlässig, transparent
transparent copy Durchsichtsvorlage *f*
transparent decal Glasabziehbild *n*
transparent film Transparentfolie *f*, Transparenthaut *f*

transparent inks *pl (printing inks)* lasierende Farben *f/pl*
transparent paper durchscheinendes Papier *n*
transparent picture Durchsichtsbild *n*
transparent retouching *(film)* lasierende Retusche *f*
transparent white *(ink additive)* Transparentweiß *n*, Mischweiß *n*
transport roller Transportwalze *f*
transport sucker *(feeder suction head)* Transportsauger *m*
trapping *(ink trapping)* Farbannahme *f*, Trapping *n*
travel guide Reisebuch *n*
tray development Schalenentwicklung *f*
tray etching Schalenätzung *f*
tray processing *(photochem.)* Schalenentwicklung *f*
treadle Tritthebel *m*
treadle operation Fußantrieb *m*
treadle press Tretpresse *f*, Tritthebelpresse *f*
triacetate film Triazetatfilm *m*
trial run Probelauf *m*
trial subscription Probeabonnement *n*
tricky job komplizierte Arbeit *f*
trim *v* schneiden, beschneiden
trim accuracy Schnittgenauigkeit *f*
trim area Beschnittbereich *m*
trim cut Trennschnitt *m*
trim edge Beschnittrand *m*
trimetallic plate Trimetallplatte *f*
trim exhaust Schneidabfallabsaugung *f*
trim marks *pl* Schnittmarken *f/pl*, Beschneidemarken *f/pl*, Beschnittmarken *f/pl*, Schneid(e)marken *f/pl*
trim(med) edges *pl* Schnittkanten *pl*
trimmed flush *(book)* bündig geschnitten
trimmed sheet Formatbogen *m*
trim(med) size beschnittenes Format *n*, Endformat *n*
trim(ming) Schnitt *m*, Beschnitt *m*
trim(ming) line Beschnittlinie *f*
trimmings *pl (paper)* Abfallstreifen *pl*, Beschneidemarken *f/pl*, Schnitzel *pl*, Schneidabfall *m*; *(book prod.)* Späne *pl*
trim-off Beschnitt *m*
trim off *v* abschneiden
trim (on) three sides *v* an drei Seiten beschneiden
trim removal Beschnittabsaugung *f*, Schneidabfallbeseitigung *f*
trim waste Beschnittabfall *m*, Schneidabfall *m*, Verschnitt *m*

trim waste extraction Beschnittabsaugung *f*
triplex board Triplexkarton *m*
trolley Rollwagen *m*, Transportgerät *n*, Wagen *m*:
trolleys *pl* Andrückrollen *pl*, Laufrollen *f/pl*
trouble-free störungsfrei
trouble-shooting Störungsbehebung *f*
true copy originalgetreue Kopie *f*
true grey Echtgrau *n*
true rectangular cut Winkelschnitt *m*
true rolling *(cylinder)* genaue Abwicklung *f*
true to original originalgetreu
true to register registergenau, registerhaltig; *(colour register)* passergenau, passerhaltig, paßgenau
true to scale maßstabgerecht
true-to-scale reproduction maßstabsgetreue Reproduktion *f*
true to size maßgenau
true type *(video screen display)* Echtschrift *f*; **to display in** ~ in Echtschrift *f* darstellen
true-typographic display *(video screen)* Echtschriftdarstellung *f*, schriftgerechte Darstellung *f*
T-square Reißschiene *f*
TTS machine *(hot-metal comp.)* Fernsetzmaschine *f*
tube Hülse *f*
tub-sized paper oberflächengeleimtes Papier *n*
tucker blade *(press folder)* Falzmesser *n*, Falzschwert *n*
tucker blade cylinder *(press folder)* Falzmesserzylinder *m*
tumbled sheet *(as opp. to turned steet)* umstülpter Bogen *m*
tumble forme *(print forme)* Form zum Umstülpen
tungsten film Kunstlichtfilm *m*
tungsten-halogen lamp Wolfram-Halogenlampe *f*
tungsten light Halogen-Licht *n*
tunnel dryer Trockentunnel *m*
turnbars *pl (web press)* Wendestangen *f/pl*
turnbox Stülpschachtel *f*
turncross *(web press)* Wendekreuz *n*
turned-in flap *(leaflet, jacket etc.)* eingefalzte Klappe *f*, eingeschlagene Klappe *f*
turned letter *(lead comp.)* Blockade *f*, Fliegenkopf *m*
turned sheet *(as opp. to tumbled sheet)* umschlagener Bogen *m*
turner bars *pl (web press)* Wendestangen *f/pl*
turn forme *(print forme)* Form zum Umschlagen
turn in *v (flap)* einfalzen, einschlagen

turning drum *(perfector press)* Wendetrommel *f*
turning grippers *pl* Umschlaggreifer *m/pl*
turn-key installation *(comp.)* komplettes System aus einer Hand
turn-off Abschaltung *f*
turn off *v* abstellen, abschalten, ausschalten
turn on *v* anstellen, einschalten
turnover *(article running from one page onto another)* umlaufender Text *m*
turnover reelstand *(web press)* Doppelrollenständer *m*
turntable *(mailroom)* Drehtisch *m*
turn yellow *v* vergilben
turret unwinder Drehsternwickler *m*
twin sheet delivery Doppelbogenauslage *f*
twin sheet feeder Doppelbogenanleger *m*
twin-sided beidseitig
twin-wire paper machine Doppelsiebpapiermaschine *f*
twisted sheet umdrehter Bogen *m*
twist forme *(print forme)* Form zum Umdrehen
two-arm reelstand *(web press)* Doppelrollenständer *m*
two-bath processing Zweibadentwicklung *f*
two colour front, none reverse 2/0-farbig, zweifarbiger Schöndruck *m*
two colour front, one reverse 2/1-farbig
two colour front, two reverse 2/2 farbig, zweifarbiger Schön- und Widerdruck *m*
two-colour offset press Zweifarbenoffsetmaschine *f*
two-colour overprint *(print control bar)* Zweifarbenübereinanderdruck *m*
two-colour perfecting press Zweifarben-Schön- und Widerdruckmaschine *f*
two-colour printing Zweifarbendruck *m*
two-colour (printing) press Zweifarben(druck)maschine *f*
two colours both sides 2/2 farbig, zweifarbiger Schön- und Widerdruck *m*
two-colour separation Zweifarbenauszug *m*
two-colour sheet-fed offset press Zweifarben-Bogenoffsetmaschine *f*
two-column advertisement zweispaltige Anzeige *f*
two-column page zweispaltige Seite *f*
two-directional gatefold Zweibruch-Fensterfalz *m*
two-directional right angle fold Zweibruchkreuzfalz *m*
two-em quad *(typesetting)* Doppelgeviert *n*
two-filter contrast control *(reprod.)* Zwei-Filter-Kontraststeuerung *f*
two-former folder *(web press)* Doppeltrichterfalzapparat *m*

two-layer film Zweischichtenfilm *m*
two-letter matrix Zweibuchstabenmatrize *f*
two-line initial zweizeilige Initiale *f*, zweizeiliger Anfangsbuchstabe *f*
two-on signature Bogen im Doppelnutzen
two-page spread Doppelseite *f*, durchgehende Doppelseite *f*, Panoramaseite *f*, Seitenpaar *n*
two-revolution press Zweitourenpresse *f*
two-room camera Zweiraumkamera *f*
two-sheet detector Doppelbogenkontrolle *f*
two-shift operation Zweischichtbetrieb *m*
two-sided beidseitig, zweiseitig
two-sided calendered zweiseitig kalandriert, zweiseitig satiniert
two-sided coated paper zweiseitig gestrichenes Papier *n*
two-sidedness *(paper)* Zweiseitigkeit *f*
two-sided printed sheet zweiseitig bedruckter Bogen *m*
two-sided printing zweiseitiger Druck *m*
two-sided sensitized printing plate zweiseitig vorbeschichtete Druckplatte *f*
two-up im Doppelnutzen *m*
two-up delivery Doppelbogenauslage *f*
two-up feeder Doppelbogenanleger *m*
two-up forme Doppelform *f*
two-up processing Doppelnutzenverarbeitung *f*
two-up production *in* ~ im Doppelnutzen *m*
two-web operation *(web printing)* Zwei-Bahn-Betrieb *m*
tye up *v (lead type)* ausbinden
tying *(mailroom)* Umreifen *n*, Umschnüren *n*, Verschnüren *n*
tying machine Verschnürmaschine *f*
tympan *(letterpress m.)* Aufzugsbogen *m*, Ölbogen *m*, Preßdeckel *m*, Straffen *m*, Tympan *m*, Zugbogen *m*
tympan clamp *(letterpress m.)* Aufzugsstange *f*
tympan packing *(hand press)* Deckelaufzug *m*
tympan paper see tympan
tympan sheet see tympan
type Type *f*, Schrift *f*, Buchstabe *m*, Letter *f*
type alloy Schriftlegierung *f*
type area Satzspiegel *m*, Satzfläche *f*
type bed *(flat-bed press)* Schriftfundament *n*, Druckfundament *n*
type block see type area
type board *(lead comp.)* Formbrett *n*, Satzbrett *n*
type body Schriftkegel *m*
type cabinet *(lead comp.)* Schriftkastenregal *n*, Schriftregal *n*
type carrier Schriftträger *m*, Typenträger *m*
type case Schriftkasten *m*, Setzkasten *m*

type caster see type casting machine
type casting Schriftguß *m*
type casting machine Schriftgießmaschine *f*, Typengießmaschine *f*
type cutting Schriftschneiden *n*
type design Schriftbild *n*, Schriftschnitt *m*, Schriftzeichnung *f*
type designer Schriftkünstler *m*, Schriftzeichner *m*
type director künstlerischer Leiter *m*
type embossing Schriftprägung *f*
typeface Schrift *f*, Schriftart *f*, Schriftbild *n*, Schriftschnitt *m*
typeface development Schriftentwicklung *f*
typeface drawing Schriftzeichnung *f*
typeface for jobbing work *(typesetting)* Akzidenzschrift *f*
typeface name Schriftname *m*
typeface production Schriftenfertigung *f*
type family Schriftfamilie *f*
type fit *(typogr.)* Buchstabenabstand *m*, Zwischenraum *m*
type forme *(as opp. to picture forme)* Satzform *f*, Schriftform *f*, Textform *f*
type founder Schriftgießer *m*
type founding Schriftguß *m*
type foundry Schriftgießerei *f*
type gauge typografischer Zeilenmesser *m*, Typometer *n*, Zeilenmaß *n*
type group Schriftgattung *f*
type height Schrifthöhe *f*
type-high schrifthoch
type library Schriftenbibliothek *f*
type line Schriftlinie *f*, Schriftzeile *f*
type magazine *(hot-metal comp.)* Letternmagazin *n*
type material Schriftmaterial *n*
type matrix Buchstabenmatrize *f*, Schriftmater *f*
type matter Satz *m*, Schriftsatz *m*
type metal Letternmetall *n*, Schriftmetall *n*, Schriftzeug *n*, Zeug *n*
type modification Schriftmodifikation *f*
type ornament Schriftornament *n*
type planer *(lead comp.)* Schrifthobel *m*
type quality Schriftqualität *f*
type rack *(lead comp.)* Schriftkastenregal *n*
type reproduction Schriftwiedergabe *f*
type reversed white on black Schrift in negativ
type scale see type gauge
typescript Schreibmaschinenmanuskript *n*
typeset *v* setzen; *(photocomp.)* belichten
typeset matter Satz *m*, Schriftsatz *m*

typesetter *(compositor)* Schriftsetzer *m*, Setzer *m*; *(line caster)* Setzmaschine *f*; *(photocomp.)* Belichter *m*, Belichtungseinheit *f*
typesetter interface *(photocomp.)* Belichterschnittstelle *f*
typesetting Satz *m*, Schriftsatz *m*; *(photocomp.)* Belichten *n*, Belichtung *f*
typesetting and casting machine Setz- und Gießmaschine *f*
typesetting capacity Satzkapazität *f*
typesetting code Satzkode *m*
typesetting command Satzbefehl *m*, Satzkommando *n*
typesetting computer Satzrechner *m*
typesetting correction Satzkorrektur *f*
typesetting costs *pl* Satzkosten *pl*
typesetting deadline Satztermin *m*
typesetting department Setzerei *f*
typesetting house Setzerei *f*
typesetting instruction Satzbefehl *m*
typesetting job Satzarbeit *f*
typesetting machine Setzmaschine *f*
typesetting material *(lead comp.)* Setzmaterial *n*
typesetting operation Satzbetrieb *m*
typesetting parameter Satzparameter *m*
typesetting price Satzpreis *m*
typesetting production Satzherstellung *f*
typesetting program Satzprogramm *n*
typesetting rules *pl* Satzregeln *pl*, Setzregeln *pl*
typesetting software Satzsoftware *f*
typesetting system Satzsystem *n*
typesetting work Satz *m*
typeshop Setzerei *f*
type size Schriftgrad *m*, Schriftgröße *f*
type specimen Satzmuster *n*, Schriftmuster *m*, Schriftprobe *f*
type specimen book Schriftmusterbuch *n*
type specimen collection Schriftmusterbuch *n*, Schriftmustersammlung *f*
type specimen sheet Schriftmusterblatt *n*
typestyle Schrift *f*, Schriftart *f*, Schriftbild *n*, Schriftschnitt *m*
typeview monitor *(photocomp.)* Echtschriftbildschirm *m*, WYSIWYG-Bildschirm *m*
type wear *(lead comp.)* Schriftabnutzung *f*
type wheel printer Typenraddrucker *m*
typewriter composing machine Schreibsetzmaschine *f*
typewriter composition *(e.g. IBM Composer)* Schreibsatz *m*
typewriter face Schreibmaschinenschrift *f*
typewritten copy Schreibmaschinenmanuskript *n*

typing error Satzfehler *m*, Setzfehler *m*, Tippfehler·*m*
typing paper SM-Papier *n*
typo design Typogestaltung *f*, typografische Gestaltung *f*
typographer Typograf *m*
typographical arrangement Satzanordnung *f*, Satzgestaltung *f*, Typogestaltung *f*, typografische Gestaltung *f*
typographical design see typographical arrangement
typographical instruction Satzanweisung *f*
typographical measurement typografisches Maß *n*
typographical pattern typografisches Muster *n*
typographical point typografischer Punkt *m*
typographical specification Satzanweisung *f*
typographic layout typografischer Aufbau *m*, typografisches Layout *n*
typographic scale system typografisches Maßsystem *n*
typographic unit typografische Einheit *f*
typography Typografie *f*, Typogestaltung *f*, typografische Gestaltung *f*, Satzgestaltung *f*, Schriftkunst *f*
typogravure Typogravüre *f*
typo layout typografischer Aufbau *m*, typografisches Layout *n*, Typolayout *n*

U

u.c. see uppercase letter
UCR (Under Colour Reduction/Removal) UCR (Unterfarbenreduktion)
UEF (User Exchange Format) UEF (Benutzeraustauschformat)
UF *(photocomp.; „User Format")* IWT
UF call IWT-Aufruf *m*
UF definiton IWT-Definition *f*
UF directory IWT-Verzeichnis *n*
umlaut accent *(typesetting)* Umlautzeichen *n*
unabridged ungekürzt
unbleached cardboard Naturkarton *m*
unbound copy of book ungebundenes Buch *n*
unbound sections *pl* ungebundene Bogen *pl*
uncial Unziale *f*, Unzialschrift *f*
uncial letter Unzialbuchstabe *m*, Unziale *f*
uncoated unbeschichtet

uncoated paper Naturpapier *n*, ungestrichenes Papier *n*
uncoated stock Naturpapier *n*, ungestrichenes Papier *n*
uncompensated stacks *pl* unverschränkte Stapel *pl*
uncorrected unkorrigiert
uncorrected proof *(galley proof)* unkorrigierter Korrekturabzug *m*
Under Colour Reduction *(UCR)* Unterfarbenreduktion *f*
Under Colour Removal *(UCR)* Unterfarbenbeseitigung *f*
undercutting *(contact printing)* Hohlkopie *f*, Unterstrahlung *f*
underdelivery *(less copies than ordered)* Unterlieferung *f*
under-developed unterentwickelt
underdevelopment Unterentwicklung *f*
underetching *(gravure cyl.)* Unterätzung *f*
underexposed unterbelichtet
underexposure Unterbelichtung *f*
underinking *(printing)* Unterfärbung *f*
underlapping *(shingle stream)* Unterlappung *f*
under(lay) blanket *(blanket cyl.)* Unterlagetuch *n*
underlay foil *(press cyl.)* Unterlagefolie *f*, Unterlegfolie *f*
underlay sheet *(press cyl.)* Unterlagebogen *m*
underlining *(typesetting)* Unterstreichung *f*
underpacking *(press cyl.)* Aufzug *m*
underrun *(less copies than ordered)* Unterlieferung *f*
underscoring *(typesetting)* Unterstreichung *f*
undershot ink duct blade untenliegendes Farbmesser *n*
under side *(paper)* Unterseite *f*, Widerdruckseite *f*
uneven pages *pl* ungerade Seiten *f/pl*
uneven spacing *(type)* schlechte Raumverteilung *f*
unexposed unbelichtet
unfolded ungefalzt
unformatted data unformatierte Daten *pl*
unglazed unsatiniert
uniform inking gleichmäßige Farbführung *f*
unit Aggregat *n*
unit construction (principle) *(press engineering)* Reihenbauweise *f*
unit cost Stückkosten *pl*
unit count fonts *pl* Schriften mit Einheitsabstand
unit forms sets *pl* *(as opp. to continuous forms sets)* Einzelformularsätze *m/pl*
unitized fonts *pl* Schriften mit Proportionalabstand

unit-to-unit phasing device *(printing units)* Gleichlaufsteuerung zwischen den Druckwerken
unit type press *(as opp. to five-cylinder press type)* Druckmaschine in Reihenbauweise
unjustified setting *(typesetting)* Endlossatz *m*, unausgeschlossener Satz *m*
unjustified text Endlostext *m*
unjustified type matter Endlossatz *m*
unloader Entladegerät *n*
unloading Entladen *n*
unloading platform *(mailroom)* Entladerampe *f*
unprinted unbedruckt, ungedruckt
unproductive machine times *pl* Maschinenstillstandszeiten *pl*
unpublished ungedruckt
unqualified workman ungelernte Kraft *f*
unread proof *(galley proof)* unkorrigierter Korrekturabzug *m*
unsensitized unbeschichtet
unsensitized carbon tissue *(gravure)* unsensibilisiertes Pigmentpapier *n*
unsharp contours *pl (electronic image proc.)* Unscharfkontur *f*
unsharp dot unscharfer Punkt *m*
unsharp impression unscharfer Druck *m*
unsharp masking *(scanner function)* Unscharfmaskierung *f*
unsharp printing-in *(reprod.)* Unscharfeinkopieren *n*
unsized paper ungeleimtes Papier *n*
unskilled operator ungelernte Kraft *f*
untrained operator ungelernte Kraft *f*
untrimmed sheet Rohbogen *m*
untrimmed size unbeschnittenes Format *n*
unwind *v (reel)* abwickeln, abrollen
unwind and rewind unit Ab- und Aufrollvorrichtung *f*
unwinder *(unwind unit)* Abroller *m*, Abrollung *f*, Abwicklung *f*, Rollenabwicklung *f*
unwinding Abrollung *f*, Abwicklung *f*
unwinding shaft Abrollwelle *f*
unwind unit *(web press)* Abroller *m*, Abrollung *f*, Abwicklung *f*, Rollenabwicklung *f*
up-date *v (data, text)* aktualisieren
upgradable system ausbaufähiges System *n*
upgrade *(modular systems)* Hochrüstung *f*, Ausbau *m*, Nachrüstung *f*
upgrade *v (modular systems)* erweitern, hochrüsten, nachrüsten
upgrade kit Nachrüstpaket *n*
upgrade package Nachrüstpaket *n*

uppercase letter Großbuchstabe *m*, Versalbuchstabe *m*
uppercase letters *pl* Versalien *f/pl*
uppercase R *(typesetting)* großes R
upper deck *(newspaper rotary)* Oberdeck *n*
upper knife Obermesser *n*
upper margin oberer Papierrand *m*, oberer Seitenrand *m*
upper side Oberseite *f*
upper side of web Bahnoberseite *f*
upper side printing *(web printing)* Oberseitendruck *m*
upper wire *(paper machine)* Obersieb *n*
upright format Hochformat *n*
upright page Hochformatseite *f*, Seite im Hochformat
upright sheet delivery *(convert.)* Stehendbogenauslage *f*
up to the minute *(news)* topaktuell
useful size Nutzfläche *f*, Nutzformat *n*
user Anwender *m*, Bediener *m*, Benutzer *m*
user-definable *(system functions)* benutzerdefinierbar, frei definierbar
user field *(screen mask)* Benutzerfeld *n*
user-friendly anwenderfreundlich, bedienerfreundlich, bedienungsfreundlich, benutzerfreundlich
user guide Bedienerführung *f*, Benutzerführung *f*
user interface Bedienerschnittstelle *f*
user programmable *(system functions)* benutzerprogrammierbar, frei programmierbar
user software Anwendersoftware *f*
user surface Bedieneroberfläche *f*, Benutzeroberfläche *f*
user-updateable program *(comp.)* frei pflegbares Programm
use to full potential *v* voll ausnutzen
utility *(text proc.)* Routine *f*
utility program Dienstprogramm *n*, Hilfsprogramm *n*
utilization *(machine, system)* Auslastung *f*, Ausnutzung *f*
utilize to capacity *v* voll ausnutzen
utilize to full advantage *v* voll ausnutzen
U.V. coating *(varnish)* UV-Lack *m*
U.V. curing *(ink, varnish)* UV-Härtung *f*, UV-Trocknung *f*
U.V. dryer UV-Trockner *m*
U.V. drying UV-Trocknung *f*
U.V. emitter UV-Strahler *m*
U.V. filter UV-Filter *m*
U.V. lamp UV-Lampe *f*
U.V. printing ink UV-Druckfarbe *f*

U.V. radiation UV-Strahlung f
U.V. radiator UV-Strahler m
U.V. sensitive UV-empfindlich
U.V. varnish UV-Lack m

V

vacancies pl *(classified advertising)* Stellenanzeigen pl, Arbeitsmarkt m
vacat *(unprinted)* unbedruckt
vacuum Vakuum n
vacuum build-up *(copying frame)* Vakuumaufbau m
vacuum film back *(camera)* Ansaugplatte f
vacuum film holder *(camera)* Filmsaugplatte f, Filmsaugwand f, Vakuumfilmhalter m
vacuum frame *(platemaking)* Kopierrahmen m, pneumatischer Kopierrahmen m, Vakuumkopierrahmen m
vacuum meter Vakuummeter n
vacuum printer see contact printer, vacuum frame
vacuum pump Vakuumpumpe f
vacuum-sealed can *(ink)* Vakuumdose f
vacuum times pl *(contact printer, vacuum frame)* Ansaugzeiten pl, Vakuumzeiten pl
vanishing spray powder lösliches Druckbestäubungspuder n
vapour development *(ammonia)* Dampfentwicklung f
variable-area gravure (process) autotypischer Tiefdruck m, flächenvariabler Tiefdruck m
variable area/variable depth gravure (process) halbautotypischer Tiefdruck m
variable-data imprinting Eindruck variabler Daten
variable-depth gravure (process) tiefenvariabler Tiefdruck m
variable-gamma film gammavariabler Film m
variable size veränderliches Format n
variable-size printing press formatvariable Druckmaschine f
variable(-speed) gear Regelgetriebe n, Reguliergetriebe n
variations pl *(process)* Schwankungen pl
varnish Lack m; *(ink component)* Firnis m
varnish v lackieren

varnish both sides v zweiseitig lackieren
varnish circulation Lackumlauf m
varnish coating Lackierung f, Lackschicht f, Lacküberzug m
varnish film Lackschicht f
varnishing Lackierung f
varnishing blanket Lackiertuch n
varnishing department Lackiererei f
varnishing house Lackieranstalt f, Lackiererei f
varnishing machine Lackiermaschine f
varnishing primer Grundierlack m
varnishing roller Lackierwalze f
varnishing unit Lackiereinheit f, Lackierwerk n
varnish pan Lackkasten m
varnish pan roller Lacktauchwalze f
varnish trough Lackkasten m
vat *(papermak.)* Bütte f
vat paper Büttenpapier n
vat-press Büttenpresse f
V-belt Keilriemen m
V-belt drive Keilriemenantrieb m
VDT *(video display terminal)* Bildschirm m, Bildschirmgerät n, Bildschirmterminal m, Videobildschirmgerät n
VDT workstation Bildschirmarbeitsplatz m
VDU see VDT
vector chart Vektorgrafik f
vector graph Vektorgrafik f
vector technique *(image proc.)* Vektortechnik f
vegetable oil *(inkmaking)* Pflanzenöl n
vegetable parchment Echtpergament n
vegetable size *(paper)* Harzleimung f
vehicle *(binding agent)* Bindemittel n
vellum (paper) Pergamentpapier n, Velinpapier n
velvet finished paper halbglänzendes Papier n, mattsatiniertes Papier n
velvet paper Samtpapier n, Velourspapier n
ventilate v *(sheets)* lüften, durchlüften, belüften
ventilating system Belüftungsanlage f, Lüftungsanlage f
ventilation Belüftung f
verification Kontrolle f, Prüfung f
verify v kontrollieren, prüfen
verifying keyboard Kontrolltastatur f
verso see verso side
verso blank *(unprinted)* Rückseite unbedruckt
verso page Rückseite f, Widerdruckseite f
verso printing Rückseitendruck m, Widerdruck m
verso side Rückseite f, Widerdruckseite f
vertical adjustment Höheneinstellung f, Höhenjustierung f
vertical camera Vertikalkamera f
verticale rule *(tabular work)* Vertikallinie f

vertical filing cabinet - wallpaper

vertical filing cabinet *(for archiving artwork, flats, plates etc.)* Hängeregistraturschrank *m*
vertical hatching Vertikalschraffierung *f*
vertical justification *(typesetting)* vertikaler Ausschluß *m*
vertical pile stehender Stapel *m*
vertical pile feeder Flachstapelanleger *m*
vertical spacing *(typesetting)* vertikaler Ausschluß *m*, Zeilendurchschuß *m*, Durchschießen *n*, Durchschuß *m*
vertical stack delivery *(book prod.)* Senkrechtstapelauslage *f*
vertical stamping Hubprägung *f*
vibrating damping roller Feuchtheber *m*
vibrating ink roller Farbheber *m*
vibration *(machine)* Schwingung *f*
vibration absorbent schwingungsdämpfend
vibration-free machine run schwingungsfreier Maschinenlauf *m*
vibrator *(inking, damping unit)* see vibrator roller; *(side jogger)* Geradstoßer *m*
vibrator roller *(inking, damping unit)* Heberwalze *f*, Heber *m*, Leckwalze *f*
vibrator-type damping system Heberfeuchtwerk *n*
vibrator-type inking system Heberfarbwerk *n*
video characters *pl* Bildschirmschrift *f*
videodisc Bildplatte *f*
video display *(VDT)* Bildschirmanzeige *f*
video display terminal *(VDT)* Bildschirm *m*, Bildschirmgerät *n*, Bildschirmterminal *m*, Videobildschirmgerät *n*
video display unit *(VDU)* see video display terminal
video editing Bildschirmkorrektur *f*
video editing terminal *(text proc.)* Korrekturbildschirm *m*, Korrekturterminal *m*
video grabbing Videobilderfassung *f*
video mask Bildschirmmaske *f*
video recorder Videorekorder *m*
video recording Videoaufnahme *f*
videoscan document reading *(text proc.)* optische Beleglesung *f*
video screen Bildschirm *m*
video still Videostandbild *n*
video terminal Bildschirmterminal *m*
videotext Bildschirmtext *m*, Bildschirmzeitung *f*, BTX *n*, Videotext *m*
video type Bildschirmschrift *f*
video workstation Bildschirmarbeitsplatz *m*
viewing angle Betrachtungswinkel *m*
viewing light Betrachtungsleuchte *f*
viewing screen Bildschirm *m*
viewing standard Betrachtungsnorm *f*

vignette *(ornament)* Verzierung *f*, Vignette *f*, Zierstück *n*; *(tonal gradation)* Verlauf *m*
vignetted background Hintergrundverlauf *m*
vignetted colour background Farbverlauf *m*
vignetted halftone (screen) Rasterverlauf *m*, verlaufende Rasterfläche *f*
vignetted screen tint Rasterverlauf *m*, verlaufende Rasterfläche *f*
vignetted tint Flächenverlauf *m*, Tonverlauf *m*
vignetting *(image)* Verlauf *m*
viscose sponge Viskoseschwamm *m*
visco(si)meter Viskosimeter *n*
viscosity Viskosität *f*
viscosity controller *(ink)* Viskositätsregler *m*
viscous ink dickflüssige Farbe *f*, kurze Farbe *f*, pastöse Farbe *f*, zähe Farbe *f*, zügige Farbe *f*
visiting card Besuchskarte *f*, Visitenkarte *f*
visual assessment visuelle Beurteilung *f*
visual check(ing) Sichtkontrolle *f*, visuelle Kontrolle *f*
visual communication visuelle Kommunikation *f*
visual control Sichtkontrolle *f*, visuelle Kontrolle *f*
visual evaluation visuelle Beurteilung *f*
visual judgement visuelle Beurteilung *f*
visual monitoring *(video screen)* Sichtkontrolle *f*
volatile memory *(comp.)* flüchtiger Speicher *m*
volatile store *(comp.)* flüchtiger Speicher *m*
volume *(book)* Band *m*
volume bound in cloth *(book)* Leinenband *m*
voluminous paper voluminöses Papier *n*
voluminous print run Großauflage *f*, hohe Auflage *f*
voucher copy *(advertiser)* Belegexemplar *n*
vowel Vokal *m*
vulcanization Vulkanisation *f*
vulcanize *v* vulkanisieren
vulcanizing press Vulkanisierpresse *f*

W

walkway *(on machines)* Laufblech *n*
wall calendar Wandkalender *m*
wall chart Wandkarte *f*
wall map Wandkarte *f*
wallpaper Papiertapete *f*, Tapete *f*

wallpaper embossing press Tapetenprägemaschine *f*
wallpaper printing machine Tapetendruckmaschine *f*
want ad *(as opp. to sales ad)* Suchanzeige *f*
warehousing Lagerung *f*
warm-up time *(machines)* Aufwärmzeit *f*
warped board gewölber Karton *m*, welliger Karton *m*
warped paper welliges Papier *n*
warping *(paper)* Welligwerden *n*
wash *(for plates, rollers, blankets)* Reinigungsmittel *n*, Waschmittel *n*
wash *v* waschen, spülen
wash basin *(plate processing)* Spülbecken *n*, Waschtrog *m*
washing *(films, plates etc.)* Wässerung *f*
washing solution Waschmittel *n*
washing trough Waschtrog *m*
wash off *v* abwaschen, auswaschen
wash-off film Auswaschfilm *m*
wash out *v* auswaschen, auswaschen
wash-out emulsion Auswaschemulsion *f*
wash sink Wässerungsbecken *n*
wash-up *(press)* Reinigung *f*, Reinigungsvorgang *m*
wash-up intervals *pl (press)* Reinigungsintervalle *pl*
wash-up time Reinigungszeit *f*
waste Abfälle *pl*, Makulatur *f*
waste air Abluft *f*
waste chute Abfallrutsche *f*
waste container Abfallbehälter *m*
waste deflector Makulaturweiche *f*
waste disposal Abfallentsorgung *f*
waste diverter Makulaturausschleusung *f*, Makulaturweiche *f*
waste edge cuttings *pl (web trimming)* Randstreifenabfall *m*
waste ejection Makulaturausschleusung *f*
waste ejector Makulaturweiche *f*
waste exhaustion *(trim waste)* Beschnittabsaugung *f*
waste marking *(web printing)* Makulaturmarkierung *f*
waste paper Abfallpapier *n*, Altpapier *n*, Makulatur *f*, Papierabfall *m*; *(for interleaving)* Makulaturpapier *n*
waste rate *(paper)* Makulaturanfall *m*
waste recognition *(web inspection)* Makulaturerkennung *f*
waste removal Abfallentsorgung *f*

waste re-reeling *(rotary die-cutting)* Abfallaufrollung *f*
waste run *(makeready)* Makulaturvorlauf *m*
waste sheets *pl* Ausschußbogen *m/pl*, Makulatur *f*, Makulaturbogen *m/pl*
waste shunt Makulaturweiche *f*
waste skeleton *(die-cutting)* Restgitter *n*
waste stripping *(after die-cutting)* Abfallausbrechen *n*
waste water Abwasser *n*
water-absorbing capacity *(offset ink, paper)* Wasseraufnahmevermögen *n*
water absorption *(offset ink, paper)* Wasseraufnahme *f*
water-based auf Wasserbasis, wäßrig
water-based adhesive *(perfect binding)* Dispersionskleber *m*
water-based ink Farbe auf wäßriger Basis, Wasserfarbe *f*
water-based photopolymer plate wasserauswaschbare Fotopolymerplatte *f*, wasserentwickelbare Fotopolymerplatte *f*
water-based varnish Dispersionslack *m*
water-conducting areas *pl (offset plate)* wasserführende Stellen *pl*
water-cooled wassergekühlt
water-cooling Wasserkühlung *f*
water-developed photopolymer plate wasserentwickelbare Fotopolymerplatte *f*
water distribution *(offset)* Wasserführung *f*
water fastness *(offset ink)* Wasserechtheit *f*
water fountain roller Feuchtduktor *m*, Feuchtkastenwalze *f*, Wasserkastenwalze *f*
water hardness Wasserhärte *f*
waterless offset plate wasserlose Offsetplatte *f*
waterless offset printing wasserloser Offsetdruck *m*
watermark Wasserzeichen *n*
watermark(ed) paper Wasserzeichenpapier *n*
watermark lines *pl* Wasserlinien *pl*
water marks *pl (offset)* Waschmarken *pl*, Wassermarken *pl*
water pan *(offset press)* Feucht(wasser)kasten *m*, Wasserkasten *m*
water pan roller *(damping system)* see water fountain roller
water-pan varnish *(offset)* Wasserkastenlack *m*
water pollution Wasserverschmutzung *f*
water-proof paper imprägniertes Papier *n*, wasserfestes Papier *n*
water-receptive *(offset)* wasserfreundlich
water-repellent *(offset)* wasserabstoßend

water supply *(offset)* Wasserführung *f*, Wasserzufuhr *f*
water-washed photopolymer plate wasserauswaschbare Fotopolymerplatte *f*
waved rule Wellenlinie *f*
waviness of edges *(paper)* Randwelligkeit *f*
wavy cut Wellenschnitt *m*
wavy line geschlängelte Linie *f*, Schlangenlinie *f*, Wellenlinie *f*
wavyline screen Wellenlinienraster *m*
wavy rule geschlängelte Linie *f*, Schlangenlinie *f*, Wellenlinie *f*
wax Wachs *n*
wax coater see waxer
wax engraving Wachsradierung *f*
waxer *(paste-up)* Wachsauftragsgerät *n*, Haftwachsgerät *n*, Wachsbeschichtungsgerät *n*
wax matrix Wachsmatrize *f*
wax moulding Wachsabdruck *m*, Wachsprägung *f*
wax paper Wachspapier *n*
wax size *(paper)* Wachsleim *m*
weak negative flaues Negativ *n*
wear *v (lead type)* abquetschen
wearing part Verschleißteil *n*
weatherability *(ink)* Wetterfestigkeit *f*
weather-proof ink wetterfeste Druckfarbe *f*
weather-proof poster wetterfestes Plakat *n*
weather resistance *(ink)* Wetterfestigkeit *f*
web Bahn *f*; *(paper web)* Papierbahn *f*; *(web press)* see web press
web aligner Bahnkantenregelung *f*, Bahnkantensteuerung *f*, Bahnmittenregelung *f*
webbing-up Bahneinzug *m*; *(paper web)* Papiereinzug *m*
webbing-up device *(web press)* Papiereinziehvorrichtung *f*, Bahneinzugswerk *n*
web break Bahn(ab)riß *m*, Bahnbruch *m*, Papierriß *m*
web break detector Bahnbruchmelder *m*, Bahnbruchsicherung *f*
web break recognition Bahnbrucherkennung *f*
web-butt splicing *(reelchange)* Stoß-an-Stoß-Bahnklebung *f*
web catcher Papierfangeinrichtung *f*
web center control Bahnmittenregelung *f*
web cleaner Bahnreiniger *m*
web cooling Bahnkühlung *f*
web deviation Bahnumlenkung *f*
web drying Bahntrocknung *f*
web edge control Bahnkantenregelung *f*, Bahnkantensteuerung *f*

web edge guide see web edge control
web edge sensing Bahnkantenabtastung *f*
web elongation Bahndehnung *f*
web entry Bahneinlauf *m*
web-fed flat-bed (printing) press Rollenflachformdruckmaschine *f*
web-fed gravure press Rollentiefdruckanlage *f*, Rollentiefdruckmaschine *f*, Tiefdruckrollenrotation *f*, Tiefdruckrotation(smaschine) *f*
web-fed letterpress machine Buchdruckrollenrotation *f*, Hochdruck(rollen)rotation *f*, Rollenbuchdruckmaschine *f*, Rollenhochdruckmaschine *f*
web-fed letterpress printing Rollenbuchdruck *m*, Rollenhochdruck *m*, Rotationshochdruck *m*
web-fed press see web press
web-fed proofing press Rollenandruckmaschine *f*
web fluttering Bahnflattern *n*
web guide Bahnführung *f*; *(automatic)* ~ Bahnlaufregelung *f*, Bahnlaufregler *m*
web guide roller Bahnleitwalze *f*, Papierleitwalze *f*
web guiding system Bahnlaufregelung *f*, Bahnlaufregler *m*
web infeed Bahneinlauf *m*, Bahneinzug *m*
web infeed unit Bahneinzugswerk *n*
web inlet Bahneinlauf *m*
web inspection Bahnüberwachung *f*
web inspection unit Bahnbeobachtungsgerät *n*, Bahnbetrachtungsgerät *n*
web lead Bahnführung *f*
web lead roller Bahnleitwalze *f*, Papierleitwalze *f*
web length control Bahnlängensteuerung *f*
web moistening Bahnbefeuchtung *f*
web monitoring Bahnüberwachung *f*
web offset Rollenoffset *m*
web offset newspaper press Offsetzeitungsrotation *f*
web offset press Offset(rollen)rotation *f*, Rollenoffsetmaschine *f*
web outlet Bahnauslauf *m*
web pasting *(reelchange)* Bahnklebung *f*
web path *(in the web press)* Bahndurchlauf *m*, Papierweg *m*
web press Rollendruckmaschine *f*, Rollenrotation *f*, Rollenrotationsmaschine *f*, Rotation *f*, Rotationsdruckmaschine *f*, Rotationsmaschine *f*
web press delivery Rotationsausgang *m*, Rotationsmaschinenauslage *f*
web press output Rotationsausstoß *m*

web printer Rollenrotationsdruckerei *f*, Rotationsdrucker *m*
web printing Rollendruck *m*, Rollenrotationsdruck *m*, Rotationsdruck *m*
web remoistening *(after dryer)* Bahnnachbefeuchtung *f*
web reserve *(festoon storage)* Bahnreserve *f*
web scanning *(register control)* Bahnabtastung *f*
web sensing *(register control)* Bahnabtastung *f*
web severing device Bahnkappvorrichtung *f*, Papierabschlagvorrichtung *f*
web slitter Längsschneider *m*, Bahnschneidegerät *n*
web-splice on the run fliegender Rollenwechsel *m*
web splicing *(reelchange)* Bahnklebung *f*, Bahnspleißung *f*
web splicing unit Rollenwechsler *m*, Autopaster *m*
web stretch Bahndehnung *f*
web temperature control Bahntemperaturregelung *f*
web tension Bahnspannung *f*
web tension control Bahnspannungsregelung *f*
web tension fluctuations *pl* Bahnspannungsschwankungen *pl*
web threading device *(web press)* Bahneinzugswerk *n*, Papiereinziehvorrichtung *f*
web tinting *(stationery printing)* Papierbahneinfärbung *f*
web-to-web laminating Rollenkaschierung *f*
web-to-web laminating machine Rollenkaschiermaschine *f*
web-to-web register *(multi-ribbon operation)* Schnittregister *n*
web travel Bahndurchlauf *m*, Bahnlauf *m*
web up *v (paper web)* Papierbahn einziehen
web viewer Bahnbeobachtungsgerät *n*, Bahnbetrachtungsgerät *n*
web width Bahnbreite *f*
wedding announcement Heiratsanzeige *f*, Hochzeitskarte *f*
wedge Keil *m*
wedge *v (letterpress forme)* einkeilen
wedge reader *(reprod., photochem.)* Keilleser *m*
weekend issue Wochenendausgabe *f*
weekend supplement Wochenendbeilage *f*
weekly calendar Wochenkalender *m*
weekly (magazine) Wochenzeitschrift *f*
weekly (newspaper) Wochenzeitung *f*
weekly paper Wochenzeitung *f*
weight *(type)* Schriftstärke *f*, Strichstärke *f*
welding *(film wrapping)* Zuschweißen *n*

welding machine Einschweißmaschine *f*
welding station Schweißstation *f*
well-covered solid gut gedeckte Vollfläche *f*
wet *v* anfeuchten, befeuchten, feuchten
wet-adhesive labels *pl* Naßklebeetiketten *pl*
wet-adhesive tape Naßklebeband *n*
wet-brushed aluminium plate naßgebürstete Aluminiumplatte *f*
wet end *(paper machine)* Naßpartie *f*
wet expansion *(paper)* Feuchtdehnung *f*
wet graining Naßschleifen *n*
wet grinding Naßschleifen *n*
wet offset Naßoffset *m*
wet-on-dry printing Naß-auf-Trocken-Druck *m*
wet-on-wet printing Naß-in-Naß-Druck *m*
wet picking Naßrupfen *n*
wet retouching *(film)* Naßretusche *f*
wet stamping Naßprägung *f*
wet-stretching *(paper)* Feuchtdehnung *f*
wetting Feuchtung *f*, Benetzung *f*
wetting agent *(chem.)* Netzmittel *n*
wetting box for flongs Maternfeuchtkasten *m*
wet toner *(electrophotogr.)* Naßtoner *m*
whirler *(in-house coating of plates)* Schleuder *f*
white alignment *(densitometer)* Weißabgleich *m*
white light exposure *(camera screening)* Weißbelichtung *f*
white line *(typesetting)* Blankozeile *f*, Freizeile *f*, Leerzeile *f*, Blindzeile *f*, Zwischenzeile *f*; *(lead comp.)* Quadratenzeile *f*
whitener *(paper)* Weißmacher *m*
whiteness *(paper)* Weiße *f*, Weißgrad *m*
white page Blankoseite *f*, Leerseite *f*, Vakatseite *f*
white sheet Blankobogen *m*
white space between lines Zeilenabstand *m*, Zeilendurchschuß *m*
white waste Weißmakulatur *f*
wholesale paper merchants *pl* Papiergroßhandlung *f*
wide angle lens Weitwinkelobjektiv *n*
wide-band filter *(densitometer)* Breitbandfilter *n*
widely spaced matter *(type)* splendider Satz *m*, weiter Satz *m*
wide setting *(type)* weiter Satz *m*
widow line *(typesetting)* Ausgangszeile *f*, Hurenkind *n*
width card *(photocomp.)* Dicktenkarte *f*
width of letter Buchstabenbreite *f*, Dickte *f*, Schriftdickte *f*, Schriftweite *f*
width table *(photocomp.)* Dicktentabelle *f*
Winchester disk Winchester-Platte *f*
winding Wicklung *f*
winding shaft Wickelwelle *f*

winding-up Aufrollung *f*, Aufwicklung *f*, Rollenaufwicklung *f*
window *(layout, page make-up etc.)* Aussparung *f*, freigeschlagener Raum *m*, Freiraum *m*
window card Werbeaufsteller *m*
window cutting *(envelope prod.)* Fensterstanzung *f*
window cutting and gluing machine *(envelope prod.)* Fenster-Ausstanz- und -Einklebemaschine *f*
window envelope Fensterumschlag *m*
window gluing *(envelope prod.)* Fenstereinkleben *n*
window mask *(video screen)* Fenstermaske *f*
window packaging Fensterpackung *f*
window technique *(PC)* Fenstertechnik *f*, Window-Technik *f*
wind up *v* aufwickeln
wine label Weinetikett *n*
wipe off *v* abwischen, wegwischen
wipe-on plate Wipe-on-Platte *f*
wiping cloth Wischtuch *n*
wire *(stitching)* Draht *m*
wire brush Drahtbürste *f*
wire comb binding Drahtkammbindung *f*
wire comb binding machine Drahtkammbindemaschine *f*
wire dispenser Drahtabspulvorrichtung *f*
wire gauge Drahtstärke *f*
wire gauze Drahtgaze *f*
wire head Drahtkopf *m*
wire marks *pl* *(water-marked paper)* Wasserlinien *pl*
wire message *(news agency)* Agenturmeldung *f*
wire photo agency *(telecom.)* Bildagentur *f*
wire photo(graph) *(news agency)* Agenturbild *n*, Funkbild *n*
wire photo service house *(telecom.)* Bildagentur *f*
wire ring binding Drahtringbindung *f*
wire section *(paper machine)* Siebpartie *f*
wire service *(news service)* Nachrichtendienst *m*
wire side *(paper)* Siebseite *f*
wire spool Drahtrolle *f*
wire staple Drahtheftklammer *f*, Drahtklammer *f*
wire-stapler *(mach.)* Klammerheftmaschine *f*
wire stapling Klammerheftung *f*
wire-stitch *v* drahtheften, heften
wire stitcher Drahtheftmaschine *f*
wire-stitching Drahtheftung *f*
wire stitching machine Drahtheftmaschine *f*
wire-stitching through the back *(saddle-stitching)* Rückenstichheftung *f*
wiring diagram Schaltbild *n*

with common baseline auf gleicher Schriftlinie
with correct tonal value tonwertrichtig
within easy reach in bequemer Reichweite *f*
within operator's reach in Handreichweite des Bedieners
without backgauge movement *(cutting m.)* mit stehendem Sattel *m*
without backlash *(gears)* spielfrei
with standing web bei stehender Bahn *f*
wood base *(blockmaking)* Holzfuß *m*
woodcut Holzschnitt *m*, Holzstich *m*
wood engraver Holzschneider *m*
wood engraving Holzschnitt *m*, Holzstich *m*, Xylografie *f*
wooden toggle press Holzdruckpresse *f*
wood-free paper holzfreies Papier *n*
wood letters *pl* Holzbuchstaben *pl*, Holzschrift *f*
wood mount *(blockmaking)* Holzfuß *m*
wood printing press Holzbedruckmaschine *f*
wood pulp *(papermaking)* Holzfaserstoff *m*, Holzschliff *m*
woodpulp paper holzhaltiges Papier *n*
wood type Holzbuchstaben *pl*, Holzschrift *f*
word count *(text rec.)* Wortanzahl *f*
word division Worttrennung *f*
word processing Textverarbeitung *f*
word processor Textverarbeitungsanlage *f*
wordspace Wortabstand *m*, Wortzwischenraum *m*
work Arbeit *f*
work *v* arbeiten
workability Verarbeitbarkeit *f*; *(of the printing material)* Verdruckbarkeit *f*
workable *(in the press)* verdruckbar
work and back *(printing)* Schön- und Widerdruck *m*
work and back forme Schön- und Widerdruckform *f*
work and tumble *(printing)* Umstülpen *n*
work and tumble forme *(print forme)* Form zum Umstülpen
work and turn *(printing)* Umschlagen *n*
work and turn forme *(print forme)* Form zum Umschlagen
work and twist *(printing)* Umdrehen *n*
work and twist forme *(print forme)* Form zum Umdrehen
work book Arbeitsbuch *n*
work flow Arbeitsablauf *m*, Arbeitsfluß *m*
working *(mach.)* Betrieb *m*
working area Nutzfläche *f*, Nutzformat *n*
working clothes *pl* Arbeitskleidung *f*
working conditions *pl* Arbeitsbedingungen *pl*
working environment Arbeitsumfeld *n*

working memory Arbeitsspeicher *m*
working procedures *pl* Arbeitsablauf *m*
working process Arbeitsablauf *m*
working speed Arbeitsgeschwindigkeit *f*
working storage *(comp.)* Arbeitsspeicher *m*
working surface Nutzfläche *f*, Nutzformat *n*
working temperature *(mach.)* Arbeitstemperatur *f*
working width Arbeitsbreite *f*
work in process laufende Arbeit *f*
work in progress laufende Arbeit *f*
workload Arbeitsbelastung *f*
workman Arbeitskraft *f*
work place Arbeitsplatz *m*
work plan Arbeitsplan *m*
work planning Arbeitsplanung *f*, Arbeitsvorbereitung *f*, AV *f*
work preparation Arbeitsvorbereitung *f*, AV *f*
work routine Arbeitsablauf *m*
work sample Arbeitsmuster *n*
works director see works manager
works management Betriebsleitung *f*, technische Leitung *f*
works manager Betriebsleiter *m*, technischer Leiter *m*
works paper Werkszeitung *f*
workstation Arbeitsplatz *m*; *(comp.)* Workstation *f*
workstation publishing *(as opp. to desktop publishing)* Workstation-Publishing *n*
work to schedule *v (progress chasing)* nach Plan arbeiten
worm drive *(machine)* Schleichgang *m*, Schneckenantrieb *m*
worm gear Schneckengetriebe *n*
worn type *(lead comp.)* abgenutzte Schrift *f*
wrap *v (into film, paper)* einschlagen, verpacken
wrap (angle) *(cylinder)* Umschlingungswinkel *m*
wrap-around *(web printing)* Wickler *m*
wrap-around cover *(pocket book)* durchgehender Umschlag *m*
wrap-around gravure plate Tiefdruckwickelplatte *f*
wrap-around letterpress plate Hochdruckwickelplatte *f*
wrap-around plate Wickelplatte *f*
wrapped-around signatures *pl (signatures inset one into another)* ineinandergesteckte Falzbogen *pl*
wrapper *(book)* Umschlag *m*, Schutzumschlag *m*; *(newspaper)* Banderole *f*; *(web printing)* Wickler *m*
wrappered *(paperbound)* broschiert
wrapping Verpacken *n*

wrapping machine Verpackungsmaschine *f*
wrapping paper Einschlagpapier *n*, Packpapier *n*, Verpackungspapier *n*
wrap-up *(web printing)* Wickler *m*
Wratten filter Wrattenfilter *n*
wrench Schraubenschlüssel *m*
wrinkle *(paper)* Falte *f*, Papierfalte *f*, Quetschfalte *f*, Runzel *f*
wrinkled sheet Knautschbogen *m*
wrinkle-free paper faltenfreies Papier *n*
write-off period Abschreibungsperiode *f*
writer Schriftsteller *m*
write/read head *(comp.)* Schreib/Lesekopf *m*
writing pad Schreibblock *m*
writing paper Schreibpapier *n*, Briefpapier *n*
written copy geschriebenes Manuskript *n*
written manuscript geschriebenes Manuskript *n*
wrong fount *(hand comp.)* Fisch *m*
wrong letter *(hand comp.)* Fisch *m*
wrong-reading seitenverkehrt
WYSIWYG display *("What You See Is What You Get", true typographic VDU display)* Echtschriftdarstellung *f*, schriftgerechte Darstellung *f*, WYSIWYG-Display *n*
WYSIWYG screen *(photocomp.)* Echtschriftbildschirm *m*, WYSIWYG-Bildschirm *m*

X

xenon flash Xenonblitz *m*
xenon lamp Xenonlampe *f*
xerography Xerografie *f*
x-height *(type)* Mittellänge *f*
xylograph Holzschnitt *m*
xylographer Holzschneider *m*
xylography Xylografie *f*

Y

yapp binding Holländerbindung *f*

yearbook Jahrbuch *n*
year of construction Baujahr *n*
year of publication *(newspaper, magazine)* Erscheinungsjahr *n*, Jahrgang *m*
yellow *(process colour)* Gelb *n*
yellow cast Gelbstich *m*
yellow discoloration Vergilbung *f*
yellowed copy vergilbte Vorlage *f*
yellow film Gelbfilm *m*
yellow filter Gelbfilter *m*
yellow forme Gelbform *f*
yellowing Vergilbung *f*
yellowish gelblich
yellow plate Gelbplatte *f*
yellow printer *(yellow plate)* Gelbplatte *f*; *(yellow sep. film)* Gelbfilm *m*
yellow separation *(reprod.)* Gelbauszug *m*
YMCB *(Yellow Magenta Cyan Black)* GMCS
Y-type printing unit *(newspaper offset rotary)* Y-Druckwerk *n*

zinc oxide paper Zinkoxydpapier *n*
zinc plate Zinkplatte *f*
zinc printing plate Zinkdruckplatte *f*
zinc white Deckweiß *n*, Zinkweiß *n*
zip code PLZ (Postleitzahl) *f*, Postleitzahl *f*; *(mailroom)* **to sort by** ~ nach Postleitzahlen ordnen
zip code reader *(mailroom)* Postleitzahlenleser *m*
zip code sorting Postleitzahlensortierung *f*
zonal ink metering zonale Farbdosierung *f*
zoned paper EDV-Papier *n*, Tabellierpapier *n*
zooming *(image proc.)* Hochzoomen *n*, Zoomen *n*
zoom lens Zoomobjektiv *n*

Z

zero adjustment Nullabgleich *m*, Nullstellung *f*
zero balance *(measuring devices)* Nullabgleich *m*
zeroing Nullabgleich *m*, Nullstellung *f*
zero leading *(photocomp.)* Vorschub Null *m*
zero position Nullstellung *f*
zero-speed web splicer Nullgeschwindigkeits-Rollenwechsler *m*, Speicherrollenwechsler *m*, Stillstandsrollenwechsler *m*
zero suppression *(comp.)* Nullunterdrückung *f*
z-fold Zickzackfalz *m*
zigzag fold Zickzackfalz *m*, Leporellofalz *m*
zigzag-folded brochure Leporelloprospekt *m*
zigzag folded pack zickzack-gefalzter Stapel *m*
zigzag folder Zickzackfalzapparat *m*
zigzag line Zickzacklinie *f*
zigzag perforating Zickzackperforierung *f*
zigzag rule Zickzacklinie *f*
zinc engraving *(letterpress)* Zinkklischee *n*, Zinkätzung *f*
zinc etching *(letterpress)* Zinkklischee *n*, Zinkätzung *f*
zinc-etch plate Zinkätzplatte *f*
zinc offset plate Zinkoffsetplatte *f*

Supplements

Supplements